Consumer market research handbook

CONSUMER MARKET RESEARCH HANDBOOK

Third Revised and Enlarged Edition

Editors

ROBERT M. WORCESTER

JOHN DOWNHAM

McGRAW-HILL BOOK COMPANY

London . New York . St Louis . San Francisco . Auckland
Bogotá . Guatemala . Hamburg . Lisbon . Madrid . Mexico
Montreal . New Delhi . Panama . Paris . San Juan . São Paulo
Singapore . Sydney . Tokyo . Toronto

⬜⬜⬜⬜⬜ESOMAR⬜⬜⬜⬜⬜

© E.S.O.M.A.R., 1986

European Society for Opinion and Marketing Research
Association Européenne pour les Etudes d'Opinion et de Marketing
Europäische Gesellschaft für Meinungs- und Marketingforschung

Central Secretariat:

J. J. Viottastraat 29, 1071 JP Amsterdam (The Netherlands)
Tel.: 020-642141 – Telex: 18535 esmar nl.

Founded in 1948, the European Society for Opinion and Marketing Research (E.S.O.M.A.R.) is the International body representing established marketing and market research specialists. It stands for the highest possible standards – both professionally and technically.

First published in hardback by Elsevier Science Publishers B.V. (North Holland)

British Library Cataloguing in Publication Data

Consumer Market Research Handbook – 3rd Rev. and enl. ed.
1. Marketing Research
I. Worcester, Robert M.
II. Downham, John
658.8'3
ISBN 0-07-7070755-6

PRINTED IN GREAT BRITAIN AT THE UNIVERSITY PRESS, CAMBRIDGE

Contents

PART TWO: USE OF CONSUMER MARKET RESEARCH

Preface to the third edition

The fact that a third edition of this Handbook has now been published illustrates the continuing need for a work of this kind. There have been relatively few books dealing in depth with the subject of market research which are written from a European viewpoint, and the previous editions have had a worldwide sale. The essentially practical approach adopted in 1971, and followed again in 1978 and now in 1986, is reflected in the choice of title. As a Handbook it is intended to provide a down-to-earth description of what is involved in designing, carrying out and applying market research to the kinds of problems regularly and widely encountered in business and commerce (and indeed in other fields of activity).

There is however one major and significant difference between this and the two earlier editions. When the second edition went out of print and it became clear that a third would be needed, the editors discussed with E.S.O.M.A.R. (the European Society for Opinion and Marketing Research) the possibility of publishing such a new edition under the latter's auspices. E.S.O.M.A.R. is the only large international professional body in the market research field, with members in some 50 countries worldwide. Among its other activities it has an extensive programme of conferences, seminars and publications designed to help improve professional knowledge and skills. The sponsorship of an important and widely used basic book on the subject therefore fits very naturally into these activities. The editors are extremely pleased that E.S.O.M.A.R. has agreed to this proposal, which firmly establishes the Handbook as a key international text.

The two present editors were also involved with each of the previous editions. Whereas the major responsibility for the first two was in the hands of Robert Worcester, on this third occasion the larger part of the editorial work has been handled by John Downham. The approach and format previously followed have however not been altered. As Robert wrote in his Preface to the second edition, we see the audience for the book as coming from three broad groups. First, general marketing and market research students who require a broadly based but reasonably detailed text for study and reference. Second, market research practitioners working both in research and advertising agencies and also in manufacturing and service companies. Third, executives who have the responsibility for using and applying research to the needs of their particular organizations. In trying to ensure that the book successfully caters for all these groups we have followed the policy of having a team of contributors who are all active practitioners in the field rather than academics. Between them they provide a tremendous depth of practical experience in the various aspects of research covered by the book. In addition the book contains a wide range of references, especially to articles in professional journals, where the interested reader or student can follow up in greater detail many of the issues discussed in the main text.

The last edition appeared eight years ago. The basic principles of market research and the underlying theoretical background have changed relatively little over this period. The practice of the profession has however been very strongly affected by technical developments – most obviously by the growing use of electronic technology (for data collection and transmission, as well as processing and analysis). Other trends have also had an important influence: for example, the spread of telephone ownership, the growth of cable, changes in media and distribution systems, the growing internationalization of consumers and of marketing. All this has called for more extensive amendments to the text of the book than originally seemed likely. Six chapters have in fact been completely rewritten, while many of the others have required considerable updating. The bibliography also incorporates many more recent references. An already large book has as a result become larger, but this is inevitable as the field itself develops and becomes more complex. The main structure devised for the second edition has however been retained: namely a first half dealing with the various aspects of research methodology and a second half with the different fields of application.

The focus of the book has grown more international over time. Although the authors are drawn primarily from the UK research scene – for an English-language publication this is perhaps inevitable – the thinking reflected in this volume increasingly incorporates ideas and experience from many countries. The principles and approaches applied in market research are in any case largely international in character even when the contexts in which they are used appear to differ.

Most of the authors are the same as for the second edition. In a few cases new contributions have taken over where previous authors have moved out of the field being dealt with, although in preparing the revised chapters it has still often been possible to draw upon the earlier text. Valerie Farbridge has revised John Drakeford's chapter on Interviewing and Field Control; Bryan Pymont and Gill Welch have taken over the chapter on Trade Research, and Richard Davies that on Omnibus Surveys; Peter Arnold is now a co-author of chapter 10 with Leonard England, David Seaman and Chris Blamires have joined Tony Lunn as co-authors of chapter 20; and Roger Stubbs and John Swift have jointly rewritten chapter 22. As before we are grateful to these and the other authors, who inevitably are all very busy people, for voluntarily devoting their time and effort to preparing their contributions. The final result of their work, in the form of this volume, is more-than-adequate justification for the hours involved.

My own thanks are due especially to my co-editor, Robert Worcester. We would jointly like to thank both E.S.O.M.A.R. and North-Holland, who have taken over the responsibility for publishing this third edition in hardback; McGraw-Hill for producing, for the first time, a softback version of this new edition; and also Van Nostrand Reinhold Company (the publishers of the second edition) for so readily and generously agreeing to pass over the publishing arrangements to a new set of hands. Finally, and once again, we are immensely indebted to Joann Ransdell for handling the tremendous task of preparing the index – a key element in any book of this kind.

London, 1988   John Downham busy people who voluntarily gave up their time and effort in producing their contributions to the final draft of the book. To this project this is much more than an adequate basis for a successful enterprise.

We particularly and most especially so wish to thank Robert Worcester. We would particularly wish to thank our colleagues and staff at McGraw-Hill who have, in respond, in publishing the final edition in the United States. We also wish to thank the many people who helped with earlier editions and also Van Nostrand Reinhold Company (the publishers of the second edition) for so readily and graciously agreeing to pass over their publishing arrangements to a new set of hands. Finally, once again, we are enormously indebted to John Rigdon, Jr., for that meticulous task of preparing the index, a key element in any book of this kind.

London 2005   John Billingham

PART I

Techniques of market research

PART 1

Techniques of market research

Introduction

This section, as in earlier editions, concentrates on marketing research techniques. While the section is aimed principally at practitioners and students of market research, it may also prove useful to the market research user as a guide to the methods by which the answers sought are obtained.

The section is written around the time sequence involved in carrying out a market research project. Thus, it starts with defining the problem and gaining the necessary background information before going on to techniques employed to solve marketing problems.

An attempt has been made to cover all of the major research techniques now employed perhaps at the sacrifice of depth in the analysis of the use and limitations of each technique examined. Each contributor has attempted to show the purpose of the technique covered in the chapter, its advantages and disadvantages, how it actually operates and, in each case, where to look for further information.

Definition of problems and client involvement

Marketing research is characterized by its use of orderly scientific procedure. A discussion of techniques, therefore, must begin with the first step of that procedure, i.e. define the problem. There is a saying that, 'when your marketing problems are known, they are half solved'. The role of the researcher in helping to define problems is crucial. When the researcher is properly involved, he will be able to suggest not only which technique is most applicable but what data need to be gathered. He can separate out the essential data from 'interesting information'. He can also say when market research cannot assist in the solution of the problem. Proper involvement by the researcher can overcome the common pitfall of expecting too much from research.

Marketing research data can be helpful in predicting the future, but as yet not with any degree of accuracy. Marketing research cannot yet make decisions. The marketing man must still operate in the area of uncertainty. Thus, looking ahead, market researchers will become more involved in making decisions; they will become more involved in client's problems both before research is carried out and afterwards. There will be more of a continuous relationship between researchers and marketing men. The more that the continuous relationship concept develops, the more researchers will be asked to solve problems which are not of the bushfire type. Much problem solving will then be not of the 'outright difficulty' type. Research should be involved in the recognition of hitherto unnoticed opportunities and, often, research can provide the most profitable type of problem solving.

Marketing researchers frequently employ desk research to begin to define the problem (chapter 1). Chapter 2 is concerned with qualitative and psychological techniques. Having defined the parameters of the problem from the research point of view, chapter 3 goes on to experimental design and models. Models are included in this section, but only briefly discussed, since this subject is more thoroughly treated in Part II of this book. Chapter 4 provides a 'short course' on sampling, chapter 5 covers survey questionnaire design using personal interviews. It seemed necessary to cover interviewing and field control in chapter 6 before discussing other widely used techniques, audits (chapter 7), consumer panels (chapter 8) and omnibus surveys (chapter 9). The point of view that the retailer research is closer in its techniques to consumer rather than industrial research has been taken. Thus, trade research as well as retail audits is covered in chapter 7.

The dependence on the personal interview of a decade ago has become less marked and is likely to diminish further in the future. There are postal, telephone and self-completion techniques to be considered with great strides being made in telephone research. Thus, chapter 10 deals with telephone surveys, observation and postal surveys.

Certainly, large users of research do not rely upon one technique alone. They use a combination of panels and audits, panels and surveys, audits and surveys. If any general point can be made out about choice of techniques, it is that if the client does not know much about his market or indeed much about a particular problem, he is best advised to use desk research and qualitative research and to proceed from that stage learning more and more about his market as he proceeds.

The stage has now been reached when the data have been collected by using the techniques described. What the user requires now is that the data are analysed quickly and efficiently so that the maximum amount of usable information is obtained. He also wishes to know how accurate the results are and whether the results are 'real' or can just be explained as random fluctuations. In addition, the user needs to be told of the complex inter-relationships of various parts of the data. Only when he has been given all these things is he able to use the research results with confidence, and be sure that they can profitably assist in the marketing decisions. Of course, any analysis of the data is only as good as the data that have been collected. No amount of 'playing with numbers' can get over such problems as questions asked in a biased way, questions missing from the questionnaire and incorrect measuring techniques.

In the last two decades tremendous advances have been seen in the analysis of market research surveys. Most of this has been due to the advent of the computer, which has brought speed and flexibility to the handling of data. This advance, though bringing obvious advantages, is not without its drawbacks. Previously, the researcher had, because of time and cost considerations, to limit the number of tables produced from any survey, and thus it forced him to think objectively about the analysis. It was necessary to consider only the most important hypotheses about the data, and this had the effect of disciplining the researcher in his approach to survey analysis.

Now, as the on-cost of producing a large amount of survey tabulations or extra analyses is small, there is a tendency to analyse 'everything by everything' and just 'see what comes up'. In some cases, where a new topic is being investigated, for example, this may pay dividends; but as has been pointed out, this testing of a large number of hypotheses simultaneously has to be handled carefully to avoid incorrect conclusions being drawn from the data. With this reservation, however, it must be stated that the increasing technological nature of survey analysis methods has mainly had a good influence on the analysis and interpretation of market surveys. Nowhere is this more true than in the use of advanced statistical techniques to discover important and complicated relationships in the data that have been collected (see chapter 13).

Chapter 11 describes what happens to a batch of questionnaires that have been completed. It tells how the questionnaires are checked, and how the data are transferred to a medium, such as punched cards or paper tape, which is used as input to an electronic computer. The methods of analysis given are mainly in terms of a general 'one off' quantitative survey. The temptation was resisted to include the special problems and methods of specific types of surveys such as qualitative surveys or panels and audits. Details of the analysis of the data from such sources are given in the chapters devoted to them or in the references given in those chapters.

The next chapter (12) is concerned with elementary statistics obtained from survey tabulations and the testing of statistical hypotheses using a group of testing procedures which comes under the general heading of significance tests. These are used to explain whether observed differences in the data are due to the errors of sampling. It is well known, however, that the total error in any survey result comes from non-sampling errors, e.g. non-response and measurement errors, as well as sampling errors. Market researchers have paid too little attention in the past to estimating these non-sampling errors. Attempts have been made to quantify such errors and to build them into a framework for estimating total survey error, but not much of this work has passed into current practice. The results of surveys are sometimes used as input to market forecasting exercises, especially when a survey has been repeated over a number of years. There is a body of statistical techniques subsumed under the heading of time series analysis, which can assist the researcher whose statistical analyses of surveys include future projections of market size, etc. Details are not included in this section's chapters as this would have taken too much space, and it was thought that such techniques were more often used by the statistical specialists in marketing departments than by the average market researcher. For those who wish to read about such techniques references are given at the end of the relevant chapters.

Chapter 13 deals with the more advanced statistical techniques used to analyse market research data. The techniques go under the general heading of multivariate analysis. In most cases no single thing determines what makes consumers buy the products they buy or makes them behave in a certain way. The influences on consumers are many and varied, including such things as past behaviour and attitudes to the product. It is not surprising, therefore, that multivariate statistical methods, i.e. those which examine a large number of survey characteristics simultaneously, are widely used by survey analysts. The methods used are mathematically complicated but the description of them in this chapter involves only simple algebra.

Finally, I would like again to thank Liz Nelson and Paul Harris, section editors in Part One of the First Edition, whose original thoughts and contribution were so substantial and who did the substantial and significant job of collating the chapters which for the most part still comprise Part I in this edition.

Robert M. Worcester

Chapter 1

Desk research

NIGEL NEWSON-SMITH

Desk research is not the exclusive activity of market researchers. In a monograph on desk research written for the Incorporated Society of British Advertisers, Peter Anderson remarked that 'all business executives tend to be desk researchers'. More and more, business management is concerned with sifting, absorbing, and interpreting information to aid business decisions.

However, while market researchers do not have proprietorial rights over desk research, they do reckon to have special talents in undertaking it; their skills are in collecting data, organizing it, and interpreting it against a brief; these are the primary skills required in desk research.

Desk research usually yields different data from those generated by field research, but on those occasions when it covers the same ground, desk research is very significantly cheaper. It avoids the main cost element in fieldwork, relying heavily on data other people have already collated.

Normally grouped with desk research are sales statistics, sales forecasting, and some forms of telephone surveys. For the purpose of this chapter, the first two are omitted as specialist techniques which often find their way into the market researcher's province, simply because they may suit the researcher's numerical and analytical skills. Analysis of one's own sales data, and forecasting, are, of course, relevant elements in many desk research projects. Telephone *survey* methods (as opposed to using the telephone to obtain expert assistance or factual data) are discussed in chapter 10.

Desk research is that which can be conducted from behind one's desk or by interviewing experts to obtain data; to this extent it is the antithesis of field research. The raw material for desk research is other people's data, not original data generated by a first-time survey or other original research techniques. Because of this, desk research is often referred to as the use of 'secondary data'. This is rejected here because the raw material for much desk research is *primary* in the sense that an original survey generates primary data and also because, within desk work, there are primary and secondary sources: sources which produce their own data (a survey organization, trade association, etc.) and those which quote information generated by others (typically the national and trade press).

One of the essential differences between desk research and most field research is in the prior assumptions made. Implicit at the start of a field survey is the assumption that the answer does not already exist in an available form. There is no point in indulging in relatively expensive sample survey interviewing to discover the level of tape-recorder ownership if the answer already exists somewhere other than in the secure hands of one's competitor. In contrast, a desk research project assumes at the outset that such information is available somewhere. The field researcher's skill is in knowing how to ask which sample of people the right questions. The desk researcher's skill is in knowing which information sources are likely to be the best starting points for the search. The common skills follow: that of organizing the resultant data and of interpreting them in such a way that they become useful, not just interesting, to the client.

A later section entitled 'Integration of results with field studies' raises the issue of the relative status of desk and field research in consumer – and industrial – marketing contexts. The points to be made here are:

(a) While many (rightly or wrongly) feel that industrial market research has much to learn from consumer research in the conduct of sample surveys, it is probably true that those concerned with consumer research matters have more to learn from their industrial colleagues about the use and practices of desk research.
(b) If this is so, the common practice of relying on junior researchers to 'do a quick desk study' whilst their seniors get on with the (frequently) more interesting tasks of conducting a field survey needs to be severely questioned.

Following this introduction the chapter is split into two sections: the first dealing with the uses and practices of desk research – what is desk research, what it can do, who undertakes it and in what circumstances; the second covering the all-important question of sources of information – with no sources there can be no desk research. The chapter deals with the British scene, with a small sub-section devoted to considering overseas data sources. This is because, while the practice is broadly similar the world over, the sources used vary not only in title, but in origin, from country to country.

Uses and methods of desk research

The process of desk research involves the receipt and (sometimes) translation of a question, the reference to internal or published source material and/or contact with a human source, the organization and evaluation of the resultant information, and its synthesis and interpretation. In everyday terms, you look up the answer or ask someone; the principle is simple. The practice, however, can be involved and time-consuming.

The uses of desk research

If we accept that desk research is an all-embracing information gathering and using process, then the uses are almost endless. It can be applied to any aspect of a commercial problem from the seeking of planning permissions to the examining of wage differentials.

Most lecturers and writers on the subject will point to three clear applications within the narrower aspect of consumer market research:

(a) to provide a background for a field study or other marketing activity;
(b) as a substitute for a field study;
(c) as a technique in its own right.

A fourth application is important, namely:

(d) acquisition studies.

Providing a background

Many consumer research proposals open with a statement suggesting that, prior to a field study, a search of the existing literature on the subject will be undertaken. The rationale will either be to orientate and educate the research executive or to avoid unnecessary repetition where research might have already been done. The learning application is of self-evident value: an informed executive is more likely to achieve a relevant field study than an uninformed one. In this context, desk research would take the form of checking out news reports, statistics, published surveys, etc., which together would provide a reasonably balanced picture of the market under study. This would be an informal process which would not necessarily have to be structured.

Probably the most frequent background usage of desk research is in its sampling application; the most obvious example would be the case of a field study of owners of a particular consumer durable item owned by a minority of the population. Data showing the level of ownership would be an essential prerequisite of efficient sampling which would be further helped if these data also described the characteristics and location of such owners.

The scene-setting, or background sketching, facility of the desk research function is also frequently used by New Product Development management. A manager can resort to desk research for comparative descriptions of potential markets, or for a detailed analysis of a particulair market as a first step to judge whether investment in prototype production, concept creation, field research, brainstorming, etc. (whichever is considered the right starting point) is likely to be worthwhile. Such questions as:

how big is the market?
is it expanding?
is it a concentrated or fragmented market?
is advertising heavy?

are nearly always capable of speedy answer (see also 'Acquisition studies' below).

Similarly, many an annual marketing plan is preceded by a desk research review of a market, a reappraisal of all that is known about the market situation, to judge whether assumptions and conventional wisdom still have a factual basis.

A substitute for a field study

Desk research cannot, of course, fulfil the field research role of putting supplier in direct touch with consumer. Indeed it would be as wrong to infer knowledge of consumer behaviour from a study of production statistics as it would from a single group discussion. Direct contact with the consumer, however, is not always necessary: *vide* the retail audit technique.

Where desk research can be a useful substitute is on the occasion when a serious study, or perhaps re-analysis of existing research data, can lead to perfectly valid conclusions about the market. Many a New Product Development executive has discovered that a bank of product test results will reveal fundamental truths about how the consuming public looks at a product, and their attitudes to it. The interpretation of a campaign evaluation survey can be helped by a fresh look at the results of the copy test, avoiding a further survey designed to discover why the campaign appeared to have a specific effect. Here, then, is the role of desk research as a re-user of field research data, trying to ensure that new research is not undertaken if the answer can be shown to exist already.

A technique in its own right

As distinct from occasions where desk research can adequately substitute for a field research project, there are cases where desk research is, in fact, an improvement on the field alternative. To many in the business consumer market research can be weak when it comes to an accurate description of market parameters. The first two questions potential new entrants to a market will ask are: how big is the market? and at what rate it is growing? Sampling and question technique difficulties with consumer panels and other consumer surveys can, on occasion, render them inefficient when it comes to estimating the total size of a market. Practical difficulties in the coverage of retail audits can similarly render them inefficient devices for measuring a total market. Where the market is diffused between different types of retail outlet or different types of consumer, the measurement problem intensifies. The best example of these difficulties is seen in the food market, where significant consumption occurs in the catering sector, which is notoriously difficult to measure.

In difficulties such as these, desk research frequently produces not just better data, but probably 'correct' data, lacking the disadvantage of inbuilt sampling error. Published statistics are generally freely available to describe the size of most of the markets with which industry is concerned. Data can be retrieved from the publication of statistics by a relevant government department or trade association, from trade periodicals, published market research results (these do suffer from the potential problems of sample surveys described above) and so on. From these sources it is usually possible to provide good 'hard' data about market dimensions. Market trend data can only be established from historical evidence of the kind which field research cannot gather retrospectively.

Acquisition studies
A common method of expansion is by acquisition or merger and in this area desk research is of great importance. First, most of the data required to aid a buy/no-buy decision are available from a number of printed sources. Second, the security requirements of an acquisition appraisal are extreme, and field research is incipiently less secure than desk research because more people have to be involved. In the case of an acquisition appraisal, the sort of data required are:

(a) *Company description:* company history
financial structure
financial performance
ownership and directorate
plant location
production techniques
number of employees, etc.,

and thereafter match many of the data requirements for a new product study:

(b) *Products and markets:* competitive activity
advertising and marketing, etc.

Most of the data required under (a) will be contained in: company reports, share registers, financial analysis surveys, brokers' reports, commercial directories and technical press.

In category (b) the trade press, official statistics and published survey data are all additional sources. In all cases, however, a personal contact will help add meaningful flesh to the bones; but remember, even a carefully worded question can risk security.

The scope of desk research – what sort of information?

The main-stream desk research project may well involve the description of a new consumer goods market which a manufacturer is considering entering. The sort of brief to which the researcher could be working might be as follows (FR indicates a probable requirement for field research results):

(a) *Objective:* What and who is the study for? What are the constraints? In conjunction with what should this be read?
(b) *Definition:* What is included in and excluded from the product field? (This might include a technical product specification.)
(c) *Market size:* Volume and value estimates; the importance of exports and imports.
(d) *Rate of development:* The same data over time (perhaps the last 5 to 10 years).
(e) *Competition:* A list of present producers and their brands and pack sizes. A price list. Estimates of brand share, preferably showing movement over time (FR). Launch activity.
(f) *Distribution:* Types of retail outlets involved (FR). Participation by wholesalers (FR). Retail and wholesale margins.
(g) *Advertising levels:* Volume of advertising by brand, by media.
(h) *Consumers:* Purchasing, usage, or attitude data. Product test results (FR).

Apart from relatively large-scale formal projects preceded by a written brief, much desk research activity is centred around specific questions such as:

What is the average confectionery retail margin?
How many toy shops are there in Lancashire?
Who manufactures plastic bottle closures?
What were last year's profits of my main competitors?
What is the volume of TV advertising on cosmetics?
Who are the major shareholders in XYZ Ltd?

Most frequently, however, researchers are faced with the question 'Will you tell me all you know about...?' A nonsense question. A frustrating question. A question which is not meant. What *is* meant is 'Tell me all *I* want to know about...' This requires in response a set of questions, the answers to which form the brief; and for any multi-question brief a written one is essential. The briefing process is therefore the same as for a field research project.

A note on sources

What are all these information sources, and where are they found? This chapter concludes with an abbreviated list, but in fact the sources are so many and various that an exhaustive list is just about impossible to produce. One of the first was compiled in 1975 by Elizabeth Tupper and Gordon Wills under the title 'Sources of UK Marketing Information.'[1] The book runs to 166 pages, most of which are devoted to listing and describing actual data sources. To this can be added I. Kingston and W. Benjamin, 'Directory of European Business Information Sources.[2]

Briefer lists are contained in 'Principal Sources of Marketing Information' by Christine Hull,[3] 'A Monograph on Desk Research' by Peter Anderson,[4] in various government pamphlets, and in textbooks on market research.

The desk researcher

In the case of field research, the careful user will consider the limitations of the technique before acting upon the results, or even commissioning a study. With desk research, however, one is much more in the hands of the researcher himself. The proposal is likely to include the statement: 'we will scan all relevant published materials and contact appropriate trade associations, etc.' which is vague. Unfortunately, there is little more that can be said at that stage, short of listing publications and individuals to be used as initial contacts. Desk research is rather like a treasure hunt; there might be a sense of achievement at each point on the trail, but the winner is the one who stays the course, using each clue to find the ultimate reward: it is not possible to map the entire course in advance. To this extent, the researcher is a detective; he needs qualities of nosiness, persistence, a fair degree of scepticism, even a streak of ruthlessness. Above all, he (or she, because experience suggests that women make better desk researchers than men; perhaps their patience helps) needs to keep an eye on the ball and not be diverted by tidbits of knowledge which appear on the way – collecting fascinating but irrelevant information.

First, scepticism. Early in any project, the researcher will find conflicting pieces of evidence, or at least data which are difficult to reconcile. A government might publish reports of an annual production of 400 000 tons, but the latest article by an expert in the trade magazine might suggest only 300 000 tons. A trade federation might record sales of £6 million, implying a price of £15 to £20 a ton, which the researcher recognizes as either side of the truth. These apparently conflicting pieces of evidence must be faced and subjected to several questions:

(a) Are any of the figures misprints?

(b) Have I/they got the definitions right? Are we talking of domestic consumption or is institutional usage included? Are the product definitions the same? Is the retailer's profit margin included or not?

(c) Which figure seems more *reasonable*? It is far safer to accept a sensible answer than a surprising one.

(d)· Which source is, in principle, more likely to be right? Which has an axe to grind? Which could have the wool pulled over its eyes?

(e) Where did the data come from in the first place? Have I got a primary or secondary source of information here?

(f) (In the context of a telephone or face-to-face contact) was I speaking to the expert/author or was it just the boss/assistant?

Faced with conflicting evidence, these questions spring easily to mind, but if there is only one source, or, more particularly, if all the sources agree, it requires an effort to don the mantle of scepticism. Nevertheless, an essential, if not endearing, quality required of the desk researcher is a healthy dose of scepticism (an attitude requiring proof before acceptance) if not cynicism (a predilection for fault-finding); this is where persistence comes in. Just because a fact is headlined in the press or published by the government does not *per se* make it true. The art is to discover where the press obtained the information or how the government calculated these statistics in the first place. In the latter case, the Central Statistical Office's quarterly 'Statistical News' provides a useful guide to developments in government (and some other) statistics.

Next, ruthlessness. It was Bacon who said 'knowledge itself is power' ('nam et ipsa scientia potestas est'). If this is true then there are two implications to the desk research situation. Much of the process, as we shall see, involves the use of people as sources, and to obtain information from individuals is at once difficult and easy, and for the same reason. On the one hand, people are generally much more willing to give information than one might suppose (most experienced fieldworkers confirm this), largely because communicating knowledge is an effective means of demonstrating power. On the other hand, to part with information is to an extent to part with power and it is for the this second reason that the desk researcher needs to add ruthlessness to his persistence, to make sure that he is getting the whole truth. Part information can sometimes be as dangerous as wrong information. Because many of the data used for marketing decision-making are confidential, important sources are closed to the would-be competitor, customer, or supplier researching in the same area. Commercial espionage is clearly out. The solution to the problem is in the building of a personal network of trustworthy contacts who agree to share information which, while not available to the general public but probably accessible to the professional researcher at a cost in time and/or money, can safely be shared on a reciprocal basis. It is possible to assume this information sharing role without giving away secrets or behaving in any way improperly, and many businessmen operate on this basis much of the time. An important caveat is that the desk researcher, like any other market researcher, must be relied upon to behave with propriety and rise above any suspicion of either gaining or using the information improperly; to do this and remain a good researcher, he will have to have considerable freedom to make contacts without necessarily revealing who they are. One finds that librarians and information officers frequently subscribe to a network of their opposite numbers in the government, agencies, editorial offices, manufacturing companies and so on. This is one reason why they are so frequently able to answer a variety of questions at what appears to be uncannily short notice. (Who is X Ltd's sales manager; who is the major importer of jute; what is the average summer temperature in Scotland; what directorships does Lord T...p have?)

Evaluating the results

The problems attached to the evaluation, establishing the cost effectiveness, of desk research study match those of evaluating any study. An earlier section has briefly suggested the considerations involved in trying to evaluate an individual piece of information. When looking at the results as a whole, the normal process of looking at a report from the viewpoints of understandability, believability, usability, etc. apply.

Integration of results with field studies

Desk research plays a more important part in the industrial market research scene than in consumer research. There are probably two reasons for this. Industrial market research budgets are smaller, and the comparative cheapness of desk research makes it a particularly attractive proposition; and, more importantly, desk research is frequently a more apposite technique for the solution of industrial marketing problems. Industrial marketing problems are generally less separable from technical problems, and the more esoteric aspects of consumer marketing (consumer attitudes, etc.) are absent. It is for these reasons that a typical industrial market research report will contain the results of both desk research and field research, neither taking precedence over the other. On the other hand, the typical consumer research project which sets out to describe a market scene will very rarely contain the results of a desk project. In those cases where it does, the desk results will frequently be relegated to a separate appendix volume. There are several reasons for this: primarily that desk research and field research are frequently the responsibilities of different executives and the nature of the estimates resulting from the two techniques is different.

The reliability of field research results is often expressed in terms of sampling error, whereas the reliability of desk research results cannot be quantitatively expressed. In spite of this common practice of separation, most researchers would agree that a complete marketing appreciation would be more valuable if the two sets of results were combined. That is to say, a description of consumer attitudes and consumer behaviour could be seen in its proper perspective if accompanied by an estimate of market size and rate of growth, together with a description of the distribution situation and marketing activity. Such an approach would imply the raising of a research report to the level of a marketing appreciation. Whilst this is not always desirable, it is a healthy discipline for a field research report to be introduced by an outline of what is known of the market so that the results could be viewed in perspective.

Organizing an information unit

Any sensible executive will ensure that the information which flows across his desk is categorized in such a way as to aid its future use. He will make sure that he has to hand relevant books, journals and references which will help him do his job. This library of information forms the basis of an information section, and a market research manager will add to it a number of statistical references, for example The Annual Abstract of Statistics (HMSO).

Of a different order is setting up a professional function to be the information base for a commercial or other operation. Time and money are required to achieve this: time, because each information section needs to be organized according to the requirements of its clients and only experience will show what the information demands are likely to be; money, because the purchase of printed data sources can be a costly business. An information function, while selective in its purchases and subscriptions, has to anticipate queries and briefs if it is to answer them quickly, and in order to do this must speculate – some of the speculative expenditure will inevitably prove wasted. A fully-fledged system will also need full-time staff to scan, retrieve, index, and file. Finally, and perhaps surprisingly, the capital involved in storage and retrieval equipment can amount to a considerable sum.

One further point is on the need for flexibility. A company's information needs change over time according to whether it is acting aggressively or defensively, diversifying or rationalizing, concentrating on marketing or production. Such operational or philosophical changes need to be accompanied by a change in the information base.

The contrast is therefore between the cheap and relatively easy task of maintaining an informal library of limited scope and that of building and running a professional information system.

Developments

Because the desk research process is basically a straightforward and simple one, the opportunities for *technical* development are limited. The obvious area for improvement continues, disappointingly, to be slow to develop: the opportunity for more automatic data handling. Storage and retrieval systems using micro-films, mechanical indexing, and computer technology have also been slow to develop.

In the relatively short time since the last edition of this book appeared significant changes in desk research practice have however occurred.

(a) Computerized systems of data storage and retrieval have become more common, and computerized data bases have now grown to the extent that A. Foster has published 'Which Database'[5].

(b) This in turn has facilitated the blending of external data (on market shares, competitive behaviour, the economy, etc.) with internal sales performance data in one common storage and retrieval system.

(c) The spread of agency information services, particularly press-reading services, frequently again using computer technology, has given the small user access to far more data and has speeded up the reception of foreign-based data.

(d) Many planning philosophies are becoming more 'competitive position' oriented (this natural development of planning thinking has been encouraged by the world-wide recession, driving growth markets into decline). Valuable competitive analysis material is gained from well-worn desk research sources, company reports and accounts, stockbrokers reports, the press, etc.

The other area of change has been that of data availability. Government departments, particularly since the creation of the Business Statistics Office and Central Statistical Office, are increasingly making data available outside their own departments. Further, more and more companies are prepared to exchange information and even publish it. The most noticeable change is seen overseas. Fifteen years ago, commercial information in Britain was better in quality and quantity than in most other countries of the world, with the exception of the USA, but now, although Britain is still amongst the leaders in the practice of field research, much commercial information is of a higher standard and more generally available in many European countries.

Sources

The printed word

Printed data sources are legion and most of this section is limited to a description of the type of data available from broad categories of publications. It is in no way exhaustive; it sets out to exemplify and to set the reader on the course of chasing valuable data by giving a sketch-map and some starting points. The building-up of a list of sources for just one market area is a long and painstaking business, involving careful comparison and evaluation as well as organizing and cataloguing. While there is no real alternative to building up the list on the basis of experience there are one or two short-cuts already in existence which will help; such lists as;

Daily List of Government Publications (HMSO)
Sources of UK Marketing Information (Ernest Benn)
Willing's Press Guide (Thomas Skinner Directories)
Current British Directories[6] (CBD Research Limited)
Directory of European Business Information (Ballinger)

Additionally, most trade organizations have a fund of data which they publish, for example;

Marketing Abstracts (Paper Industries Research Association)

A walk around an HMSO shop will give a good idea of the availability of official publications

The major sources are listed below under 11 headings*. Further discussion of some of these sources is to be found in T.D. Prout's 'Industrial Market Research Yearbook'.[7]

(i) *General government publications* (all available from HMSO)

Annual Abstract of Statistics
Abstract of Regional Statistics
Monthly Digest of Statistics
Regional Trends
Social Trends
Economic Trends
Statistical News
Overseas Trade Statistics
National Income and Expenditure ('Blue Book')

In varying degrees of detail, these sources give statistical data on the key demographic, social, economic, industrial, etc., areas. Perhaps more

---

* In many cases the main source of real information will be the issuing offices or actual author rather than the printed data – a later section comments on the value of personal contact.

importantly, they attribute sources and point the reader to the relevant government department for further data or expansion. For anyone likely to have a continuing interest in the business operating environment, the Annual Abstract of Statistics is essential for both its data and its list of sources; it is also a fascinating volume in its own right, covering amongst other subjects the climate, illegitimacy rates, the extent of infectious disease, air travel data, import-export statistics, educational data and so on.

The basic reference covering this section and the next is 'Guide to Official Statistics' (HMSO).

(ii) *More specialized government publications* (all available from HMSO)

Census of Population (and annual estimates)
Business Monitor series
Family Expenditure Survey
National Food Survey
Department of Employment Gazette
Financial Statistics
General Household Survey

Census data, even if they are sometimes out of date, are essential to sampling procedures. The expenditure surveys similarly provide valuable background data for those marketing consumer goods and asking the question 'what sort of people are spending how much on what goods?' One of the key sources is the Business Monitor, which describes British industry sector by sector to give, in most cases, apparent consumption (i.e. production + imports – exports) data in considerable product detail covering, for example, toys (cardboard or paper toys, table games, modelling kits, mechanical toys), leather goods (luggage and travel goods, handbags, saddlery, harness), and sports goods (gymnasium equipment, golf balls, sports gloves, fishing tackle, etc.).

(iii) *Other official publications*

British Business (from HMSO)
Inland Revenue Annual Report and Statistics (from HMSO)
Monopolies Commission Reports (from HMSO)
Economic Development Committee Reports (NEDO)

To this list one can add many other HMSO publications such as Government White Papers, old Prices and Income Board reports (a fund of quite accurate information) and many reports by the Departments of Trade, Industry, Environment, Health, Agriculture, etc., all of which impinge on many industries and marketing operations. 'British Business' is a weekly publication which reports on, amongst other matters, recently published official statistics and is probably the best source of keeping up to date with recently published official data.

(iv) *Quasi-official publications*

Trade Association Year Books
Current British Directories (CBD Research)
Directory of British Associations (CBD Research)
Councils, Committees and Boards (CBD Research)
Other Directories
Principal Companies of the European Economic Community (Graham and Trotman)
Jane's Major Companies of Europe (Macdonald and Jane's)
Who Owns Whom (Dun and Bradstreet)
Kompass Register of British Industry & Commerce (Kompass Publishers)
UK Trade Names (Kompass Publishers)

This category contains many source lists and moves from government information nearer to the commercial field. Most commercial concerns belong to the relevant trade association (Food Manufacturers' Federation, etc.) and receive their publications. There are also other trade associations and groups including.

The Advertising Association
Incorporated Society of British Advertisers
Institute of Practitioners in Advertising
Confederation of British Industry

not forgetting, of course,

Market Research Society
Industrial Marketing Research Association

Current British Directories and Directory of British Associations are self-evidently valuable elements in the library of anyone with a continuing interest in the flow of data.

(v) *Some trade research associations,* such as

Paper Industries Research Association
Fruit and Vegetable Canning Association

supplement their basic technical research function with the provision of industry statistics and the operation of information services, news bulletins, etc.

(vi) *Trade press*

The Grocer
Morning Advertiser and Licensed Restaurateur
Caterer and Hotel Keeper
Confectioner, Tobacconist, Newsagent
Chemist and Druggist
Cabinet Maker and Retail Furnisher
Packaging
Toy Trader

as well as those in industrial fields, such as

Plastics and Rubber Weekly
Paper Trade Journal
The Engineer

The list is almost endless (numbering over 2000) and is to be found in several directories, including Willing's Press Guide (Thomas Skinner Directories).

Again, most companies are aware of the various trade periodicals covering their industries; in fact, many industries are covered by more than one periodical and the art is to sort out the key publications to reduce reading time. Certainly the average trade periodical is a valuable source of data, particularly of competitors' activities.

Marketing practices and company developments can be monitored in a variety of management publications, such as:

Management Today
Advertising Weekly
Marketing
Marketing Week
Media World
Media Week

(vii) *The press*

National newspapers (probably not local newspapers)
The Economist
Investors Chronicle

The national press is an excellent medium for getting early news of, for example, market developments, and the more serious papers contain business sections, special articles and supplements and run information services which can be of particular interest. A word of caution: the press is produced at high speed and relies on people and press releases as prime information sources and, because of these factors, can make large factual errors. It is recommended to check the data before acting upon them. The author would isolate the Financial Times as by far the best source of complete continuing and reliable information for the businessman, but have a care, even these pink pages are sometimes subject to error! Press cutting services will read and abstract from the press according to a predetermined brief for a fee. Also worth examining is the Research Index (Business Surveys Ltd.) which indexes both newspaper and periodical news reports by industry and by company.

(viii) *Subscription sources*

   Retail Business (Economist Intelligence Unit)
   Marketing in Europe (Economist Intelligence Unit)
   Long Range Planning Service (Stanford Research Institute)
   Mintel (Maclaren)
   MGN Marketing Manual of the UK (Mirror Group Newspapers)

These are all additional sources of industrial or commercial information which are sold on a syndicated basis at prices ranging from less than £100 to over £2000 annually.

   They are probably of most use to those companies with a very wide range of commercial interests, and while the subjects covered do reflect to a degree the commercial interests of their clients, the publishers reserve the right to produce articles on any subject which seems to them to be appropriate. One big advantage of these services is that they structure the reports. Such reports are extremely valuable start-points for examining a new industry or market, but of comparatively little value when describing a market with which the reader is already familiar.

(ix) *Published surveys*

These range from the free to the commercially priced, from those published in the daily press to those available on request, and from the general to the particular. The British Travel Association publishes annually the findings of its travel survey which is in the form of statistics on holiday-making by British citizens. Examples of published data from syndicated research projects are the BARB television viewing data, the National Readership Survey from JICNARS and the results of the AGB Home Audit of consumer durable ownership: extracts are published and full results available to subscribers. Many market research agencies have a bank of back-data or syndicated research results which are available on subscription, the size of which is related to the contemporaneity of the data.

(x) *Financial and allied services*

Extel Services
Britain's Quoted Industrial Companies (Jordan's Surveys)
Guide to Key British Enterprises (Dun and Bradstreet)
Stock Exchange Year Book
Companies House
Stockbrokers' Reports
Bank Reviews
Times 1000 (Times Newspapers)
Directory of City Connections

The first three are specialized financial services which provide, according to different contractual arrangements, analyses of company performances, credit rating services, etc. These services would form part of any examination of acquisition candidates, of customers, or of competitors. One notable feature of the last few years is the up-grading of quality and quantity of stockbrokers' reports on industrial sectors and on companies within them. Many brokers' research departments are now sophisticated units, providing a wealth of detailed data describing market situations of use to many marketing managers, not just financial analysis. It is surprising how much businessmen still regard as confidential information about their subsidiary companies which is filed at Companies House and which is therefore available to the general public.

(xi) *Video services*

In addition to the various on-line information services or data bases (see 'Developments' above) the broadcasting companies run information and news services accessible through a television screen:

Ceefax (BBC)
Oracle (ITV)

Prestel (British Telecom) should also be included here.

Reducing the scale

A complete list of published sources would be formidable. Most information officers find it necessary to support their own information system with membership of libraries and of their own association (ASLIB). They use newspaper information services, press cutting agencies and, increasingly, information agencies and data bases. It is necessary to keep up to date with indices and bibliographies from HMSO, NEDO, CBI, ASLIB, etc. The secret is to build an internal system to cover essential and regular needs, and to support this with a network of external resources to be tapped on demand.

Internal sources

Insofar as two characteristics of desk research are its relative cheapness and the relative speed with which results can be obtained, the most effective sources of information can exist within the researcher's own office or that of his client. Internal data sources can be split into a number of categories which can be briefly described as:

Sales statistics
Field sales reports
Past market research data
The company library

The problem with these sources is that they are usually organized for specific purposes not necessarily connected with desk market research. Sales statistics are produced largely for sales and distribution control purposes; field sales reports (a valuable contribution to measuring, for example, competitors' activity) are again produced for sales management tactical purposes; market research reports are commissioned to solve either *ad hoc* problems or to undertake continuous monitoring measurement; and the information library is usually a source of scattered book shelves containing government reports, trade periodicals, etc. for general reference. As a result, although there is a wealth of information in most commercial offices, it is frequently easier to obtain the same information from outside sources, wasting both time and money. The desk researcher could profitably invest some time in trying to organize these many internal data sources in such a way that they can become a proper data base for very cheap and very quick desk research. (See also 'The Spoken Word' below.)

Overseas sources

Countries overseas have the same sort of information coverage as Britain, the coverage, completeness and contemporaneity varying proportionately with the degree of industrialization. Most industrialized countries are served by government and other official statistics, by data from trade associations and periodicals as well as from financial institutions, and by the media. The one area of difficulty is of company financial data where different local accounting obligations and procedures apply – in these cases the international banks are helpful.

Transnational or multi-national research is aided by those organizations specializing in international desk research; such as:

The Economist Intelligence Unit (London and Brussels)
Gordon International Research Associates (Geneva)
Stanford Research Institute (Menlo Park (California), London and
   Zurich)
Battelle Institute (Columbus (USA), Geneva and Frankfurt)
Business International (New York and Geneva)

It is difficult even to begin the task of listing overseas information sources. Instead it is best to suggest a few opening courses of action for those undertaking this sort of desk research for the first time.

Apart from the use of international directories and research specialists, the first step which many have found useful is contact either with their own embassy in the country of concern, or with that country's embassy in their own capital. The status and competence of commercial members of the embassy staff have risen very significantly in the last few years. Frequently, contact with our embassies is best managed by talking to the Export Services Division of the Department of Trade, which exists specifically to help British business with their export-geared information requirements. Local Chambers of Commerce operate throughout the world with varying degrees of effectiveness and helpfulness. Most sizeable companies have a continuing contact with their merchant bank which is likely to have overseas offices or associates which again can provide useful first-base information or initial contacts. On the statistical front, there are several international agencies such as:

The United Nations (and its satellites, FAO, ILO, etc.)
Organisation for Economic Co-operation and Development (OECD)
European Economic Community
International Monetary Fund

which regularly produce a mass of statistics of a commercial nature. The big problem in this area is that of time-lags, many of the data being several years out of date.

The European Society for **Market** Research (E.S.O.M.A.R.) can, through its membership in many countries, provide help by pointing the researcher in a useful direction.

There is naturally a number of generally available data sources with international or multi-national coverage. Reference works would include:

Hints to Exporters (British Overseas Trade Board)
Bibliographies of Market Surveys (UNCTAD/GATT)

World Directory of Industry & Trade Associations (UNCTAD/GATT)

Yearbook of International Associations (U.I.A. Brussels)

International Directory of Market Research Organisations (Market Research Society)

International Directory of Published Market Research (BOTB Research and Finance Management (International) Ltd.)

Business Information Sources[8] (University of California Press/Centre for Business Information, Paris)

Marketing Surveys Index (in association with the Institute of Marketing)

Europe in particular is covered by:

Directory of European Associations (CBD Research)

Europa Yearbook (Europa Publications)

European Directory of Market Research Surveys (Gower Press)

Eurofood (Agra-Canadean Publications) and AGRA Europe (Agra Europe London) covering agriculture and food

Sources of Statistics for EEC and EFTA (Dept. of Trade)

Sources of Statistics for Market Research (OECD)

Statistics Europe (CBD Research)

European Directory of Business Information Sources and Services (Centre for Business Information, Paris)

Many of the company analysis services cover several countries, for example:

Moodies Services–covering many countries throughout the world

Dun & Bradstreet–several services in USA and Europe

Kompass Registers–cover virtually all European countries

Who Owns Whom (O.W. Roskill)–volumes covering European companies and overseas subsidiaries of North American companies.

Beyond these initial contacts and international references, the process of searching for data sources and undertaking desk research is the same world-wide.

The spoken word

Most experts lay emphasis on the use of personal contact as a data source and they are right to do so. Individual people are the primary source of all information – however, people are fallible, and can be inefficient and lazy. It is wise to double check every piece of spoken evidence. Where individual personal contact is invaluable is in the ability to point to data sources. Within an information department each member leans on the experience of the other members. Probably the most overlooked source is that of personnel in one's own organization – not only do they have skills and experience, but also many have prior experience in other fields. This is where the ferreting, dogged nature of the desk researcher is so important... and so is an element of cheek – the Chairman may be the only source of information, in which case he must be asked.

This last point brings the discussion round to complete the circle. The chapter opened with the comment that businessmen are desk researchers; we close with the thought that they are data sources as well.

The involvement of specialist market researchers reflects a need for useful information, whether desk or field techniques are used. The basic skills of organizing and integrating data are common to desk and field researchers, differing only as to the data collection technique, and many commercial questions are best answered by a blend of the two techniques in the hands of one research team.

Chapter 2

Qualitative research and motivation research

PETER SAMPSON

Qualitative research is usually exploratory or diagnostic. It involves small numbers of people who are not sampled on a probabilistic basis. They may, however, be selected to represent different categories of people from a given target market or section of the community. In qualitative research no attempt is made to draw hard and fast conclusions. It is impressionistic rather than definitive. Quantitative research, on the other hand, is concerned with large numbers of people, usually members of some carefully drawn sample that is representative of a larger population. The data obtained are quantified on some basis to indicate the numbers and proportions of sample members who fall into different response categories. A degree of statistical significance is usually attributed to quantitative data and within the confines of a known margin of error, its conclusions are generalized to the population universe represented by that sample.

Motivational research

Motivation or motivational research is not synonymous with qualitative research. Very often, motives are sought and explored by qualitative techniques, but these techniques are used for a wide range of purposes other than being concerned with motives. Equally, motivations can be quantified.

The concept 'motive' is a complex one in the field of psychology. Motivation explains *why* specific behaviour takes place. Gellerman[1] has commented that 'The first and most important thing to be said about motives is that everybody has a lot of them, and that nobody has quite the same mixture as anybody else'. This observation merely points to the fact that every individual is unique, which is of little consolation to the market researcher who is concerned with identifying groups, segments, target audiences, etc., on the basis of some common characteristics. Notwithstanding, sufficient people seem to have enough in common for us to recognize fairly homogeneous groups on the basis of certain parameters that include motives, thus making the identification of these valuable.

Early psychological theories of motivation took an 'animalistic' viewpoint, with the emphasis upon biological or physiological needs such as hunger, thirst and sex. Motivation towards the satisfaction of these needs or drive states may be regarded as being universal, automatic and self-regulatory. However, they provide little explanation of social or consumer behaviour. Social or 'secondary' drives may be regarded as explaining a good deal of the variation in human behaviour. They are enduring characteristics of the individual, but vary in strength from time to time, depending upon the extent of arousal or satiation. There is general agreement among social psychologists that there are six major social drives or motives. These are the:

(a) affiliation motive (the desire to be associated with or to be in the presence of other people);
(b) acquisition motive (the desire to possess or hoard material things);
(c) prestige motive (the desire to be highly regarded by other people);
(d) power motive (the desire to control or influence other persons);
(e) altruism motive (the desire to help others);
(f) curiosity motive (the desire to explore and investigate one's surroundings).

It has been said that motives tell us why people behave as they do, but there is rarely a simple, single explanation for human behaviour. This is especially the case with the type of consumer behaviour studied by market researchers. Here, we are more likely to be concerned with discovering the reasons why people behave as they do in terms of a number of variables, some of which go to make up this complex psychological construct, 'motive'. For example, we can employ characteristics such as demographic variables (sex, age, socio-economic class, etc.) behavioural variables (e.g. heavy, medium, light consumption) and, in addition, those closer to motivation like attitudinal, personality and life-style variables. In consumer behaviour terms, there are also situational or 'market place' variables like advertising, word-of-mouth influences, in-store activity and so on. Consumer behaviour may be thought of as a function of both the person and the environment, that is personal factors like attitudes, motives and personality traits and these external situational factors.

In the market research context, motivations are important, but only in conjunction with other information. Lunn[2] distinguishes two categories of person variables:

(a) relatively specific requirements that reflect the importance given by the consumer to product attributes;
(b) more general *motives* and attitudes that are, nevertheless, close to product context, e.g. traditionalism, economy-mindedness, experimentalism, and health-consciousness. They may be regarded as 'broad consumer values' that influence and *motivate* consumers.

The uses and limitations of qualitative research

Some research problems require a more flexible approach than can be provided by the standardized interviewing techniques offered by a structured questionnaire. Under these circumstances, qualitative research may be employed. The writer[3] has listed ten common examples of the use made of qualitative research techniques:

(a) to obtain some background information where absolutely nothing is known about the problem area or product field in question;
(b) in concept identification and exploration;
(c) to identify relevant or 'salient' behaviour patterns, beliefs, opinions, attitudes, motivations, etc.;
(d) to establish priorities amongst categories of behaviour and psychological variables like beliefs, opinions, and attitudes;
(e) generally defining problem areas more fully and formulating hypotheses for further investigation and/or quantification;
(f) during a preliminary screening process in order to reduce a large number of possible contenders to a smaller number of probable ones;
(g) to obtain a large amount of data about beliefs, attitudes, etc., as data input for multivariate analysis studies;
(h) conducting post-research investigations or 'post mortems' to amplify or explain certain points emerging from some major study, without having to repeat on a large scale;
(i) in piloting questionnaires to test comprehension, word forms, the 'memory factor', etc.;
(j) where we cannot discover in a simple, straightforward way like direct questioning, why people behave as they do because the field of enquiry is personal or embarrassing in some way. In these circumstances some 'oblique' approach is called for, where projective questioning techniques may be used in a qualitative research setting.

Often qualitative research is required to stand by itself as the basis for decision making. That is, either cost or timing constraints prevent quantification or, indeed, quantification is felt unnecessary. Here, the researcher must exercise more caution and interpretative skill than is the case where more limited demands are placed upon qualitative research because subsequent quantification will take place.

One of the major drawbacks of qualitative research is its intrinsic subjectivity. After a qualitative study has been conducted and presented, often especially if the issues are subtle rather than black and white, there may exist the feeling that another researcher may have obtained a different answer. Some guard against this is to design the study to incorporate a means of cross-validation. That is, to use some form of semi-quantitative method (easily done with four–six groups upwards, where the researcher is dealing with 30+ respondents) as a check on the subjective content analysis.[4]

The techniques of qualitative research

In qualitative research, respondents are either interviewed individually or in small groups. The main interview types are the:

(a) individual 'depth', or intensive interview, lasting upwards of one hour;
(b) group interview or group discussion, lasting between one and two hours, usually, except for longer interview formats like brainstorming synectics and extended groups that may run for as long as seven hours;
(c) the semi-structured interview and shorter interviews (20–30 minutes) of the elicitation type;
(d) decision protocol interview;
(e) repertory grid interview.

In addition, there is a range of techniques that extend beyond interviewing, overlapping into areas of quantitative research. Techniques like perceptual mapping and item-by-use are borderline qualitative–quantitative approaches.

The individual 'depth' or intensive interview

Many practitioners argue that the term 'depth' interview is a misnomer in that it is too often used generically to describe a wide range of different types of interviews. (Also commonly used is the term 'mini depth', somewhat of a contradiction in terms. It usually refers to a 20–30 minute limited topic interview that is more superficial than deep.) A suggested classification of interview types that covers a range of possibilities is put forward, covering such diverse descriptions as clinical, free, focused, non-directive, extended, unstructured, semi-structured, intensive.[5]

Collectively, these interviews represent an interview type that may be described as *less-structured-more-intensive* than a standardized questionnaire-administered interview. The classification delineates three broad types:

(a) true depth or clinical interview that corresponds to the psycho-therapeutic interview and requires far longer than a single session, and is strictly speaking, outside the scope of conventional market research (Sheth[6] argues that 'the intense loyalty to Freudian psychology' which has characterized much motivation research has been largely responsible for the failure of it to contribute to consumer psychology generally);

(b) non-directive interview where, although the interviewer retains the initiative regarding the course of the interview, the respondent is given maximum freedom to respond in the manner he wishes, within reasonable bounds of relevancy;

(c) semi-structured, or focused, interview where the interviewer is required to cover a specific list of points and, although the respondent is allowed to respond freely, a much tighter control is exercised by the interviewer in order to maximize the collection of relevant data. Specific areas may be focused upon. The interviewer (or researcher) has determined *a priori* the sort of questions to which he requires answers and is merely seeking the appropriate responses from the respondent.

The group interview or group discussion

In the case of the group discussion we are concerned with a number of respondents or group 'participants' brought together under the direction of a 'group leader' or 'moderator'. There is no correct size for any group. The number of participants may vary according to the type of participant, the subject matter for discussion and the group leader's preference. For example, with highly articulate and fluent professional people, the ideal size is perhaps five or six participants. With members of the public, seven or eight would be preferred. Under certain circumstances, like conducting a group discussion among elderly people or groups of inarticulate people, and dealing with a subject not likely to be of great interest to them, the number may be increased from nine to twelve. It is important to remember, though, that the value of any particular group discussion is quite independent of its size. Another question often asked is whether participants should be seated around a table with the leader at the head, or on chairs in a circle. In the author's experience it makes no difference at all. Given the accommodation available, people should be seated as comfortably as possible in full view of each other and the moderator. If they are required to write anything down or fill in questionnaires, a table is necessary.

Whereas, in the case of the individual intensive interview, the flow of response is from the respondent to the interviewer, with the group interview the leader should play a relatively more passive role since the prime concern is group *interaction*. Each participant is encouraged to express their views, and is likewise exposed to the views of fellow group members. The leader says as little as possible and merely guides the course of discussion by, first, ensuring that participants are in fact discussing issues relevant to the problem or subject matter in question, or at least do not stray too far from this. (Often a move off at a tangent can be profitable but if in the judgement of the moderator this is not proving so, the group is refocused towards the issue under investigation.) Second, ensuring that each person participates fairly equally, which means encouraging less forthcoming members of the group, suppressing the loquacious, and seeing that no leadership force emerges from the group and takes over effective control. Goldman[7] has described five characteristics of the group discussion:

(a) the interaction among group members stimulates new ideas regarding the topic under discussion that may never be mentioned in individual interviewing;
(b) group reactions provide the opportunity to observe directly the group process;
(c) the group provides some idea of the dynamics of attitudes and opinions;
(d) discussion often provokes considerably greater spontaneity and candour than can be expected in an individual interview;
(e) the group setting is emotionally provocative in a way that an individual interview cannot be.

Brainstorming and synectics represent special examples of group interviews. In attempting to increase the involvement of individuals in the group situation, increase the amount of group interaction, reduce the inhibition of group members and encourage creative thinking, brainstorming and synectics techniques may be employed.

In the brainstorming group a heterogeneous collection of participants is selected (compared to the usually fairly homogeneous group of participants in the conventional group discussion). Typically, if the problem was one concerned with an infant food product, instead of merely talking to mothers of infants the brainstorming group would encompass men, women, young, old, married and unmarried and those with and without children. Rather than just sit down at a table or in a circle around the moderator, they may get up and walk about, break up into smaller groups, enact various role situations, etc. Whereas the average length of group discussion is 1½–1¾ hours, the brainstorming group would be likely to continue for much longer, perhaps three or four hours. The conventional group discussion would normally be a one-off affair but the brainstorming group may meet on several occasions or regularly over a period.

Synectics is a method of directing creative potential towards the solution of problems (Gordon[8]). Synectics means, literally, the joining together of different and apparently irrelevant elements. In the group interview sense this means participants. These must be drawn from a wide spectrum of educational, academic, social, and work backgrounds. They must, however, have one thing in common, the ability to think creatively. The synectics process harnesses this diverse source of creativity, directing it towards the group goal which may be the solution of a problem or generation of ideas.

Participants may be screened for high 'creativity' or 'divergent thinking' (Getzels and Jackson,[9] Hudson[10]) or 'lateral thinking' (de Bono[11]) in a number of ways. The synectics process involves a number of mechanisms, including the requirement that participants employ four different types of analogy thought process. For a detailed discussion of what is involved in synectics the reader is referred to Gordon.[8]

The synectics groups that the writer[12] describes are a very considerable modification of the Gordon approach. They involved five participants, carefully screened, and two moderators. The groups were undertaken on an *ad hoc* basis whereas the approach really required a continuous and regular operating group run over a lengthy period of time. The author concluded that in the context of generating new product ideas the synectics approach might be of value.

The extended group

A more recent innovation is the 'extended group' or the 'extended creative group' that may last for 6–7 hours. The extended group approach has been discussed by Heylen,[13] Cooper and Paule[14] and Lunn *et al.*[15] While the broad objectives remain similar, the methods of conducting such groups vary and individual practitioners tend to develop their own routines.

Essentially, extended groups provide sufficient time and opportunity, via the use of a low inhibition milieu and appropriate projective techniques, to explore beyond the superficial and the conscious rational level achieved by conventional group interviewing.

The approach adopted by the author would develop something like the following. Six respondents (that number is important since the group can be split into three pairs and two triads for specific tasks, if required) are brought together with the moderator or moderators for morning coffee (or an early evening meal). Up to an hour can be spent with participants introducing themselves, talking about their jobs, families, interests, etc., during which time they become relaxed and talkative. In the ensuing 2–3 hours session they discuss subject matter as required, 'play' with products, packs, advertisements or such stimulus material as provided, undertake projective techniques, psychodrawing, role playing and so on. An hour's break is taken for refreshments after which the group continues for a further 2–3 hours.

The programme for each session is carefully constructed to maximize the flow of relevant information, with different sections often run by different moderators.

Compared to the conventional group, the data obtained are much richer and especially so when analysed by a skilled psychologist.

The elicitation interview

For most people, many of the attitude dimensions listed in lengthy scale batteries are irrelevant or 'unimportant' because they do not enter into the purchase and brand choice decision situations. Those that really matter will be few in number. The important attributes are those that contribute to the overall determination of buying behaviour— *these are the ones that matter.*

By asking respondents open-ended questions, like 'When you actually go out to buy_____(product category) and you are in the shop, what things about_____help you to decide what type of brand to buy? (Keep on probing) — I mean, what do you take into account when buying_____?'

and

'If you had to describe_____to a friend who did not know what sort of product it was, how would you describe it? (Probe) What else would you say about it?'

'Top of the mind' or salient attributes are elicited[16] for *both products and brands,* that appear to relate to reasons for purchase and purchasing behaviour. These are examined and the key ones incorporated in an attitude battery for subsequent quantitative research.

Each respondent is able to rate about six items. On the basis of 12 items covered, with each respondent rating a selection of six, 50 observations per item will be obtained from 100 elicitation interviews.

The decision protocol interview

During the 1970s, increasing attention was directed towards the consumer decision process. That is, the series of steps leading up to the act of purchasing a particular product or brand. Traditionally, researchers had questioned consumers sometimes long after the event in an attempt to reconstruct, by inferences, these decision processes. More realistic, however, is the Decision Protocol interview[17, 18] conducted at the time of decision-making and/or actual purchase with the view to identifying the factors that led to a particular decision being taken and the linkages between those factors.

A weakness of present methods of motivational research is that they tend to be based exclusively on 'Why?' questions asked long after the event. Often, this type of data is generally inadequate. Decision Protocol Interviews are the means used in a point of purchase situation to elicit the pattern of decision making, although this will be a cognitive one.

They involve a combination of observation and in-store interviews. That is after gaining the co-operation of store-owners, interviewers are sited strategically near the display of products in question. They observe (or cameras record) purchasing behaviour. Respondents are then interviewed, the reasons for their behaviour determined and the pattern of their decision process constructed.[5,6]

About 30 decision protocol interviews using a combination of observation and questioning are usually sufficient.

The repertory or 'Kelly' grid technique

Criticism of traditional exploratory research techniques from the standpoint of their subjectivity and the occasional failure to obtain responses in the 'true language of the consumer' led to the development of the repertory grid interview in the context of market research. The repertory grid technique was felt to be a much better way of locating attitude scale items or 'constructs', from which semantic differential scales for multivariate analysis procedures could be devised.

A detailed discussion of personal construct theory is outside the scope of this chapter. The interested reader is referred to Kelly,[19] Bannister,[20,21] Frost and Braine,[22] Bannister and Mair,[23] and Riley and Palmer.[24]

In market research practice, for most exercises, the repertory grid interview varies little from the original Kelly approach in its basic form. The respondent is presented with a list of stimuli numbering from a half dozen or so to a maximum of around 30. Somewhere in the region of 16 to 20 is about optimum. A wide variety of different types of stimuli may be used. For example:

(a) products, e.g. tea, coffee, milk, drinking chocolate;
(b) brands, e.g. Typooh, Brooke Bond, Twinings;
(c) concept statements, e.g. 'slow-roasted coffee granules'.

Stimuli may be presented in the form of word labels, written statements, drawings, photographs, actual packs or products, advertisements, etc.

After removing any stimuli from the list the respondent has not heard of, or on some other grounds that require exclusion, three stimuli are presented to the respondent, who is asked to state one way in which two of them are alike and yet different from the third. The basis for similarity (the emergent pole) and the difference (the implicit pole) are recorded. The remaining stimuli are then sorted, equally between the two poles. Then another three stimuli are presented and the respondent asked to state *another* way in which two of them are alike and different from the third. The interviewer continues to present the respondent with different triads until the respondent can no longer think of any reason why two items are different from the third. When this occurs, the respondent's repertoire of constructs is said to be exhausted and the interview completed. The triads are selected according to some random procedure that ensures identical triads are never repeated.

With the repertory grid the interview situation resembles more a test than an interview. Considerable skill is required to administer such a test. A good interviewer or 'tester' is not necessarily a good 'depth interviewer' or vice versa. The information sought and collected is extremely specific. Although repertory grids may be administered in conjunction with an individual intensive interview, if the grid is executed properly, it should be exhaustive and, at the end of it, both the respondent and the interviewer will have had enough. The case for combining repertory grid interviews and individual intensive interviews is a weak one, if either is to be done properly, but there may be special circumstances where this is justified. For example, we may have a problem that can be explored initially, albeit in a somewhat speculative way, by conducting a short (perhaps highly focused) intensive interview followed by a repertory grid test using no more than half a dozen stimulus items.

A major drawback of the repertory grid interview is the tendency for some responses to be utterly valueless in terms of the type of information being sought. Two types of such responses are found. First, there are those which are too descriptive or irrelevant, and secondly, those which are too evaluative. Examples of the first type are:

(a) 'Those two come in bottles; that one comes in a cardboard packet';
(b) 'Those two are made by ABC; that one is made by XYZ'.

Typical of the second type are:

(a) 'I like those two; I don't like that one'.

Given responses like, 'My children like those two; they don't like that one' the researcher is able to transpose this into something that could form a scale such as, 'Is liked by children' – 'is not liked by children'.

This particular example shows up another problem that is faced in utilizing grid responses. According to Kelly, 'Is liked by children—is not liked by children' is not a proper construct, whereas 'Is liked by children—is liked by adults' is a construct.

Similarly, responses like 'Fizzy – not fizzy' and 'Fizzy – still' may often be obtained. A good deal of editing, rephrasing, etc., is usually required. This

Repertory Grid Sheet EMERGENT POLE ⊘	TEA	OVALTINE	COCA-COLA	COFFEE	LUCOZADE	WATER	DRINKING CHOCOLATE	MILK	RIBENA/BLACKCURRANT	SOUP	ORANGE SQUASH	MILK SHAKE	IMPLICIT POLE ⊘
Harmful to teeth	⊗	V	⊘	×	⊘	×	V	×	V	×	V	×	Not harmful to teeth
Add sugar	V	⊘	×	⊘	×	⊗	V	×	×	×	V	V	Do not add sugar
Comes in bottles	×	×	⊘	V	⊘	×	⊗	V	V	×	V	×	Comes in other containers
Not stimulant	×	V	×	⊗	V	⊘	V	⊘	V	V	V	×	Stimulant
Opaque	V	V	×	×	×	⊗	V	⊘	×	⊘	×	V	Clear
Nutritive value	×	V	×	×	V	×	⊘	V	⊘	V	⊗	×	No nutritive value
Can drink through straw	×	×	V	V	V	×	×	⊘	×	⊗	V	⊘	Cannot drink through a straw
Not addictive	×	V	⊗	×	V	⊘	V	⊘	V	V	V	V	Addictive
High caloric content	⊗	⊘	×	×	V	×	⊘	V	V	×	×	V	Low caloric content
Derived from plants	⊘	×	×	⊘	×	×	V	×	V	V	V	⊗	From other source'
Dairy product	×	⊘	×	V	×	×	⊘	V	V	⊗	×	V	Not dairy product
Fizzy	×	×	V	×	⊘	V	×	V	⊗	×	⊘	V	Still
Cannot buy frozen	Could not divide equally					×		⊘		⊘	⊗		Can buy frozen
Thirst quenching	V	⊗	V	×	×	⊘	×	×	V	×	V	⊘	Not thirst quenching

Fig. 2.1

is bound to reduce the overall objectivity of the exercise in that an element of subjective interpretation is called for. (A categorization for the different types of responses provided by repertory grids is described by the writer elsewhere. [25])

Figure 2.1 shows a typical completed grid sheet.

A single repertory grid sheet such as this will, on its own, tell the researcher very little. A series of these (any number from say, 12–40 or 50 is usual, depending on time/cost factors and the problem in hand) is content analysed by sorting, classifying, and listing the items. The collection of items obtained from the set of repertory grids would be used to form scales for subsequent attitude research. They may also be computer analysed.[24]

Descriptions of the use of the repertory grid in market research exist. Frost[26] has described an interesting use of the repertory grid technique in respect of television programs. Clemens and Thornton[27] describe the role of the repertory grid as the first stage of a 'gap analysis' approach to locate new product ideas. Sampson[3] describes how repertory grids were used to obtain pack image dimensions for male toiletries.

These examples of the use of repertory grids and, indeed, their commonest use, employ the rotated triads approach. This need not be so. A simple variation is to have one fixed element in a succession of different triads, e.g. abc, abd, abe, acd, ace, ade. Equally, although Kelly suggested that the minimum context within which a construct can be formulated comprised three elements, the grid approach can be used with just two stimuli being presented. Yet a further variation is to 'fix' one pole, and ask the respondent to supply the other, rather than supply both poles.

Completed grids may be regarded as data sheets that provide lists of actual or potential semantic differential scale items. It has been suggested that immediately after obtaining constructs, the interviewer may transform these into five, six, or seven-point scales and undertake a further scaling exercise with the same respondent. The writer[3] has argued that considerable editing and tidying up of verbalized constructs is necessary in order to produce meaningful scale items.

As far as scale item construction is concerned, the repertory grid has been criticized[28] for 'dredging up' irrelevant and non-salient dimensionality, making further refining essential. For this reason, its use has largely been superceded by the Elicitation Interview when the requirement is to find quickly and inexpensively the most salient product attributes and features.

Problems encountered during the interview situation and how they may be overcome

The writer[3] has described the various problems that may be encountered during the interview situation which serve to distort the accuracy of responses. These barriers to communication are:

(a) psychological barriers, i.e. the memory factor, emotional factors, and unconscious or repressed material;
(b) language barriers;
(c) social barriers.

Projective or 'enabling' techniques are commonly used to overcome them.

The use of projective techniques

Within the context of the individual intensive interview or conventional group discussion, use is very often made of a wide range of projective techniques.

Oppenheim[29] suggests that suitably designed projective techniques can penetrate some of the following barriers:

(a) barrier of awareness – when people are unaware of their own attitudes and motives;

(b) barrier of irrationality – to overcome the rationalizations that people make when they talk about themselves;

(c) barriers of inadmissibility and self-incrimination – when people are disinclined to admit things in a conventional interview situation;

(d) barrier of politeness – when respondents are disinclined to be critical because they are, by nature, polite and tend to behave so towards the interviewer.

By projective technique is meant the utilization of vague, ambiguous, unstructured stimulus objects or situations in order to elicit the individual's characteristic modes of perceiving his world or of behaving in it (Chaplin[30]). The underlying theory of projective questioning is that in certain circumstances it is impossible to obtain accurate information about what a person thinks and feels by asking him to explain *his* thoughts and feelings, but this information can be obtained by allowing a respondent to project these on to some other person or object. Some examples are given below.

(a) *Sentence completion tests.* The respondents are asked to complete statements like 'Women who give their families tinned vegetables are…'. 'People who don't have bank accounts are…'. 'Women who use Lux Toilet Soap…'.

(b) *Word association tests.* The respondent may be presented with a list of stimulus words and, for each one, asked to say what he thinks about when he sees the word.

(c) *Fantasy situations.* The respondents may be asked to imagine that they are motor cars, lawn mowers, or boxes of chocolates and describe their feelings.

(d) *Cartoon completion.* The respondent is shown a cartoon similar to a comic strip with 'balloons' indicating speech. Usually, two people are shown in conversation but only one balloon contains speech. The respondent's job is to fill the other balloon with his idea of what the other person is saying.

(e) *Draw a picture.* A respondent may be asked to draw or sketch a picture. Often reported studies describe how people with bank accounts, when asked to draw the interior of a bank, draw what appears to be a friendly place, whilst people without bank accounts tend to draw rather awesome and grim interiors.

(f) *Picture interpretations.* This technique is based upon the Thematic

Apperception Test (TAT) which, along with the Rorschach Ink Blot Test, must rank as the most widely known and used projective test in clinical work. Here the respondent is shown a picture – either a line drawing, illustration, or photograph – that is rather ambiguous and asked to say what is going on or tell a story about what is illustrated.

(g) *The friendly Martian.* Many research situations are concerned with low interest and low ego-involving products and subject matter. People may not perceive differences to exist, or genuinely opt for 'the most convenient' or even behave randomly. Alternatively, their comments may be expressed rationalizations rather than true reasons for underlying behaviour. Here the friendly Martian can be useful (or more recently, the character 'ET' has been used). Question forms like:

'Well suppose a Martian had landed in the middle of the High Street and wanted to open a bank account. All four major banks are there, what do you think he'd do?'
(Why? and so on) or

'Now if ET landed, went into a tobacconist and found he couldn't get King Size cigarettes (his regular brand) what would he do?' (Smoke a low tar version of that brand, another King Size brand (What?) etc.)

The depersonalization of the participant into some neutral or fantasy embodiment offers considerable scope for oblique questioning of this nature.

In projective questioning, the individual's responses are not taken at face value, i.e. with the meaning that the respondent would expect them to have, but are interpreted in terms of some pre-established psychological framework. It is here that projective tests have come in for major criticism. A considerable degree of subjectivity is exercised in the interpretation of responses to projective tests, and very often 'experts' may be in disagreement amongst themselves. For an extremely detailed review of projective techniques, the reader is referred to Murstein.[31]

Abelson's 'role rehearsal' technique

An interesting exploratory research technique is that described by Abelson.[32] In practice, role rehearsal consists of asking respondents, in a group discussion situation, to alter their behaviour pattern in some extreme way by offering an incentive for them to do so. Abelson describes a study where he asked housewives to serve chicken three times a week for a year to their family in return for $15.00 a week, and an agreement not to tell them that this arrangement had been made. According to Abelson, the approach yielded useful information on the reactions of the individuals to this offer, in terms of perceived obstacles and problems they would face, which gave some insight into their attitudes. Studies undertaken using this approach to see just how loyal consumers were to their regular brands, have brought to light some interesting information. The offer can be progressively increased in the attempt to break down strong brand loyalty. Failure to achieve this transfer at a given size of offer, and the reasons why a person will not switch brands, illustrated why brand loyalty was so strong. Furthermore, the group situation provided some interesting interaction between the 'disloyals' who caved in at the offer of a small incentive and the 'loyals' who either held out for a larger incentive or remained loyal at 'any price'.

Immediately after this section of the interview has taken place (and it is recommended that it is towards the end of a group session) respondents are told that the offer was really fictional. Participants appear to enter into the spirit of the exercise and do not mind being misled.

The selection and training of interviewers and group moderators

Many of the basic requirements for individual intensive interviewing are the same as for interviewing with a standardized, structured questionnaire (see chapter 6). However, over and above these basic skills, additional skills are required because non-standardized interviewing is a more complex task and the quality of information is to a much greater extent dependent upon the skill of the interviewer. Precisely what these are is difficult to determine and there is a distinct lack of any detailed research on this question.

There is a general agreement that 'depth' interviewers must be very carefully selected and thoroughly trained (Berent[33]). However, on the question of on what basis selection should be made and the type of person that makes a good interviewer, there is less agreement. Berent argues for selecting qualitative interviewers from amongst the 'normal quantitative field force'. He lists the necessary qualities as:

(a) the ability to relax in the interviewing situation;
(b) a friendly manner;
(c) the ability to instil confidence;
(d) to like people and be interested in them;
(e) to be broadminded.

He considers that people with strong ideas about politics, religion, or morals and people with a conventional and narrow outlook are likely to be unsuitable. Whereas the first set of qualities are obviously desirable, and narrowness and rigidity a likely disadvantage, it is difficult to imagine why the possession of strong views should be a drawback, providing the interviewer has sense enough to keep his or her views from entering into the exchange.

From the standpoint of selecting 'depth' interviewers, Berent argues in favour of having intelligent people without academic qualifications rather than psychologists. Many practioners have expressed a preference for graduates, especially in one of the social sciences and, particularly, psychologists. This preference one way or the other must be regarded as very much a personal one. There is no conclusive evidence to suggest that graduates are better than non-graduates and graduates in one discipline better than any other, except for psychologically oriented work.

As far as training is concerned, some basic instructions in interviewing methods like achieving rapport, questioning approaches, prompting and probing, is absolutely vital. The trainee interviewer should be made to listen to tape recordings of an experienced interviewer's work and to undertake a number of trial interviews on different subjects, with different respondents. These should be tape-recorded and subject to criticism by the training officer in the presence of the trainee. Even among interviewers who exhibit a flair for this sort of work, the commonest mistakes are invariably to ask leading questions and the failure to probe. These can be corrected if pointed out. Trainee interviewers should be allowed to listen to the recordings of other trainees and, through constructive criticism, improve their own performance and that of their fellow trainees. Even with experienced interviewers it is a good idea to comment constantly on their work and run refresher courses in order to develop their skills and improve their performance still further.

With group discussions, many of these considerations in respect of selection and training apply. Certainly, there is far more to conducting a group interview than merely sitting round a table with a group of people and getting them to talk. Failure to achieve interaction will result in a series of dialogues between participants and the group leader. With inexperienced group leaders this often tends to happen.

Individual group interviewing styles, even among experts, can vary. Moderating a group discussion is rather like driving a car. One can accelerate, slow down, steer the group in a different direction, change gear and arrive in the right place, go around in circles or get hopelessly lost. Just as some moderators are skilled enough to take part in a Paris Dakar Rally, others manage to reverse into their own garage doors.

There has been considerable debate about whether group discussion moderators need be psychologists. As far as conducting conventional groups are concerned there is no requirement for any particular academic background. What is important is the ability to put group participants at ease and achieve a degree of empathy with them. Equally, this is so with the interpretation function, providing no 'psychological explanations' are sought. However, with more complex interview formats like extended groups and when projective techniques are used, the non-psychologist will fail to obtain the maximum benefit from data interpretation.

Assessing performance

Apart from fairly obvious errors, like asking leading or loaded questions and the failure to probe when this was clearly called for, a skilled qualitative researcher can, by listening to the tape recording of an interview, usually make a fair assessment of the interviewer's performance from the general run of the interview and the nature of the data (notes and/or edited transcripts perhaps) provided by the interviewer. Obviously, not all interviews will be good ones. Even the most skilled interviewer can have an 'off-day' or, more commonly, a poor respondent or a poor group. Experience will help overcome these. If a respondent is very poor at communicating and verbalizing, there is a strong case for terminating the interview and finding another respondent.

The use of tape recorders and video cameras

At one time there was disagreement about the advisability of using tape recorders for individual interviews and even group discussions. Berent[33] felt the advantages (a complete record of the interview obtained without effort by the interviewer who is thus able to concentrate on the actual interview without worrying about recording information) are outweighed by the disadvantages. He described these as:

(a) the likelihood of the respondent becoming inhibited and selfconscious;
(b) tape recorders attract the interest of other members of the family;
(c) the likelihood of interruptions through tape recorder failure or having to change a tape;
(d) transcription is arduous and costly.

Wilson[34] stated that a tape recorder at an interview creates anxiety and inhibits the discussion. These are now outdated viewpoints

The writer[35] has argued that the advantages of using a tape recorder outweigh the disadvantages. A friendly relaxed approach and manner and the clear guarantee of anonymity by the interviewer can very quickly allay any suspicion and anxiety about the tape recorder on the part of the respondent. True, there are some individuals who flatly refuse to have an interview recorded but, in the author's experience, they represent less than one per cent of people approached. Moreover, it is likely that some of these people would refuse to be interviewed without a tape recorder. That tape recorders attract other members of the family does not appear to be a major disadvantage. Interviewers should be instructed always to conduct the interview with the chosen respondent *alone* and preferably in a quiet part of the house. Unfortunately, the home environment of some people does not always allow this. In some circumstances there is only one available room in the house which may have to be shared with the children and other adults. The interviewer is instructed to be as polite as possible in restraining other members of the family from joining in. Another problem in crowded homes is the television set, which the interviewer would politely ask to be turned off. If the circumstances under which the interview has to be conducted are too unfavourable, an appointment to carry this out at another time may be made or another respondent found. However, if the respondent happens to be one of an extremely small minority located only after a long and intensive search and the only time and place the interview can be obtained is a room full of children, adults, dogs, cats, and a television set, there may still be a strong case for going ahead.

In the case of individual intensive interviews, making the interviewers produce a 2000–3000 word edited transcript, including the most interesting verbatim comments, rather than produce a complete verbatim transcript, is often a satisfactory compromise.

In a study to determine the effect of accuracy of response in survey interviews by using tape recorders, Belson[36] concluded that

...the use of the machine was rarely a source of overt objection. Despite possible expectations to the contrary, this is the common experience of others reporting on the use of tape recorders in interviews.
...for the sample as a whole, the tape recording of the interview did not appear to reduce the accuracy of respondent estimates.

Nowadays, the use of tape recorders is taken for granted, although the prospective informant(s) should always be informed that a recording will be made, beforehand.

In recent years, increasing use has been made of video recorders to provide a visual as well as a sound recording, or allow several observers to watch the group or interview by a close circuit television link. Although better done (from the standpoint of lack of intrusion) through a one-way mirror, respondents seem quite happy to allow a video camera to be placed in the actual interview room. The author has encountered no evidence that this is at all off-putting, providing supplementary lighting is sensibly placed if used.

Video-taped groups have been found to be especially useful with children (playing with toys, eating sweets, etc.) and adults who are required to use their hands or undertake some other activity like eating, drinking, smoking, opening packs, etc. Filming merely to record facial expressions to supplement voice intonation and verbal responses is, in itself, likely to be of little value in cost-benefit terms.

Analysis and interpretation of data

The results of an interview or group discussion may be regarded as the results of communication between the interviewer and the respondent and, in the case of the group discussion, between respondents themselves. Communication may be analysed by a technique known as 'content analysis'. Berelson[37] defines content analysis as 'a research technique for the objective, systematic and quantitative description of the manifest content of communication'. Berelson describes 17 types of use of content analysis that in some way or another call for the quantification of content elements like words, themes, characters, items, and space-and-time measures. (It is outside the scope of this chapter to discuss approaches to content analysis in detail. The interested reader is referred to Berelson[37], and Holsti *et al.*[38])

The content analysis forms of Berelson and others have been primarily concerned with the analysis of written documents and items of communication, like newspapers. Some attempt at quantification lies behind the analysis. With the analysis of qualitative research interviews, the objective of content analysis is to abstract the relevant and important data without quantifying. Precisely how this should be done and the criteria that should be used is an area that has been neglected by market researchers until recently. Papers have appeared discussing sophisticated methods of linguistic content coding,[39,40] and the problem of interpretation generally.[41] The analysis and interpretation of qualitative data is very much an individual skill possessed more by some researchers than others.

Semiology

More recently, qualitative researchers have been looking at semiology, or semiotics, as a broad framework for the content analysis of data. Semiology is the science that studies sign systems based on both linguistic and non-linguistic communication. It studies language, non-verbal communication, signs, symbols etc., and formulates underlying rules that allow simultaneous interpretation of a multiplexity of diverse communication. Semiology extends into social communication such as art, literature, fashion and advertising and product use.

The concepts of signs and codes is an important one in semiology. Signs reflect the social mores and social order (or lack of it); codes are the systems into which signs are organized. In advertising, for example, communication takes place when the advertising message (a set of encoded signs) is decoded by recipients of the message. Thus advertising is not only about copy and visual content but the structural relationships between these and other elements of the message. The responses people make (or stimuli, in general, such as packs, products, concepts etc.) comprise a series of layers of meaning. Semiological analysis seeks to investigate these layers. (For a further discussion of semiology, see Dyer.[42])

The psychological interpretation of qualitative data

At the simplest level, analysis of overt content, 'content analysis', represents the most objective treatment. If one is looking for clues as to what behaviour is relevant to a particular problem or product field purely in a descriptive sense or what 'attitude dimensions' appear salient, this will suffice. It is when the researcher is asked to explain *why?*, why people behave as they do and so on, that the question of interpretation becomes a contentious one. The non-psychologist has his own private viewpoint, experience, perception, insight, call it what you will. The psychologist has all these things and, in addition, a familiarity with a body of theory derived from many and conflicting schools of thought. Rarely do we have, among contemporary market research psychologists, an exclusive commitment to a school of thought like Freud, Adler, Jung, Rank, etc. There may, however, be a tendency to incline slightly towards a particular viewpoint. When this occurs, the person commissioning the research must feel comfortable with the underlying psychological model as well as ensuring that the evidence upon which conclusions are based is supported by the data. This is extremely difficult for the non-psychologist to do.

Transactional analysis

The technique of Transactional Analysis ('TA') developed by Berne[43,44] has recently been used by market researchers in both a qualitative and quasi-quantitative way (Blackstone and Holmes[45]). TA can be viewed differently according to perspective. Based originally on psychoanalytic theory, when employed clinically it is a theory of personality and an approach to therapy (see Klein[46,47]). In terms of understanding consumer behaviour it offers an interesting and possibly useful model.

Any interaction between two people (in the original context) or between a consumer and a brand (in a consumer research context) can be described as a 'transaction'.

A transaction may be defined as a unit of interactive behaviour between two people, each of whom is reacting according to one of three possible ego states: Parent, Adult and Child. (These correspond, approximately, to the Freudian concepts of Super Ego, Ego and Id.)

Thus, in any transaction between two people, there are a number of combinations of the parent adult child (P A C) ego states, e.g. $P \rightleftarrows C$, $A \rightleftarrows A$ etc., and each combination will lead to differing outcomes and continued interactions.

Parent represents the state of authority, manifest as reassurance and protectiveness in a positive sense and disapproval, criticism and authoritarianism, in a negative one.

Adult represents the state of objectivity and rationality, manifest in terms of positive functional values or, negatively, as low involvement.

Child represents the state of instinct and emotion; positively, in terms of warmth, pleasure and polysensualism; and, negatively, in terms of fear, hostility and spite.

In any transaction, these ego states combine to produce outcomes P, A, C to P, A, C (Parent, Adult, Child). Blackstone and Holmes[45] describe typical consumer-brand relationships.

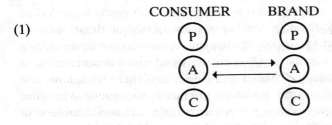

(1)

The brand is seen to deliver functional values only, such as performance, efficiency etc. In the absence of other transactions, the relationship lacks any emotional content.

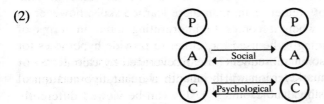

(2)

Here, there is a complementary functional and emotional attachment

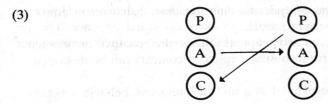

(3)

Here, the functional relationship exists, but the consumer may see the brand as, for example, 'too expensive'. This results in disapproval from the (brand) Parent to the (consumer) Child, that may give rise to feelings of guilt if the brand is used.

Data are collected, qualitatively, by conducting dialogues between the consumer and the brand. Typical dialogues may be between consumers and their 'ideal' brand and then with nominated brands and vice-versa.

Examples of dialogues are:

Smoker to ideal cigarette:

I can taste you; your tobacco is very good.....
...I like you long. Smart box.
...You taste nice...not harsh.

Cigarette's reply to smoker:

...If I can make you relaxed and happy, that's what I'm here for.
I will always try to please my customers.

It is extremely unlikely that TA represents a major new way of understanding consumer behaviour. Rather, it is a technique that provides a different viewpoint to obtain a deeper understanding of aspects such as brand choice, brand imagery, brand communication etc. Blackstone and Holmes regard it as especially useful in instances that, previously, have proved intractable to other research approaches. (For detailed discussion of the use of TA in market research, see Blackstone and Holmes[45].)

It has been argued that the psychologist or more appropriately, perhaps, the social scientist, generally can find good utilization of his skills in qualitative data collection. His discipline can also be of value in data interpretation. What is of greater value than these learned skills, however, is a sense of pragmatism when it comes to interpreting data, in terms of appreciating what it is going to be used for, either to provide hypotheses for future testing, data for some subsequent research input (i.e. scale items) or the basis upon which some decision will be made. Here an appreciation of marketing implications is invaluable.

The role of the psychologist in special interview formats, and in utilizing techniques such as projection, has already been discussed. The issues extend, obviously, to the analysis and interpretation of data also. However, not all qualitative research requires psychologically based evidence. The use of psychologists or not, must be a question for the research commissioner and research practitioner to resolve.

The choice conflicts – Which technique?
How many respondents?

There may often be a choice conflict over which to use for a given problem, between major techniques like individual intensive interviews, group discussions, the repertory grid approach, elicitation interviews etc. While certain points may be made that can guide the technique selection, the deciding factor is sometimes a personal preference, but most often a question of logistics.

As a general rule, individual intensive interviews provide more 'depth', i.e. compared to a group discussion where 'breadth' is provided. This is not implying 'depth' from the standpoint of probing the unconscious mind. It is obvious that a one-to-one interview lasting between one and two hours will generate more information appertaining to the individual than in the case where seven or eight people are interviewed collectively for the same time. If it is necessary to obtain information *in considerable detail* about people's past and current behaviour, their beliefs, opinions, and attitudes, then an individual intensive interview may be preferred. If certain broad indications are sought, a group discussion may be more appropriate. In some instances, this could mean undertaking some group discussions initially to obtain a broad understanding of the problem area and *then* undertaking individual intensive interviews either to obtain more detail, information in greater depth, or focus on specific issues.

Historically, it has often been argued that in specific instances, where the nature of the subject matter precludes the likelihood of a group of people discussing it, individual interviews would be called for. In practice, we find that there are very few subject areas where group discussion participation is found embarrassing and it is possible to conduct groups on such hitherto taboo subjects as contraception, sanitary protection and so on. The problem here is not that people refuse to discuss personal matters in the presence of others but that the amount of inhibition which does exist tends to produce a rather superficial discussion. Thus, although we are able to talk to groups of people about sanitary protection, it is likely that we could obtain much more information from an individual interview situation. The whole area of financial research presents a similar problem. Whereas people are prepared to discuss their finances in the presence of others, they are much more forthcoming when interviewed alone. The rule must be, therefore, that if detailed information on personal matters is required, individual depth interviews are to be preferred to group discussions.

The repertory grid technique has been claimed to be the most appropriate one where the problem is merely to obtain image and attitude dimensions for subsequent scaling exercises. The writer[3] has shown how, for a given problem, group discussions and repertory grids proved equally satisfactory, with neither being exhaustive in generating pack image dimensions. Current thinking suggests that, where possible, both groups and/or individual interviews should be used in conjunction with repertory grids to ensure that the total dimensionality of the product or problem field is located.[25] For locating salient attributes and product features, the elicitation interview is unquestionably the most cost-effective.

In deciding how many of what type of interview should be carried out, time and cost considerations are likely to be the determining factors. For example, in the case of group discussions there are sometimes good reasons for not mixing social classes, particularly DE and ABC_1, in which case class composition of groups may be on some basis like:

$$\textbf{AB}$$
$$\textbf{C}_1$$
$$\textbf{C}_2$$
$$\textbf{DE}$$

or $\textbf{ABC}_1$
                                   $\textbf{C}_2\textbf{DE}$

or $\textbf{AB}$
                                   $\textbf{C}_1\textbf{C}_2$
                                   $\textbf{DE}$

However, there is little evidence to support the viewpoint that men and women should not be mixed for most general discussions or that a spread of ages (excepting extremes) is disadvantageous.

If some regional split is sought (although it is unreasonable to expect the group discussion technique to do more than provide the hypothesis that 'there may be regional differences') it is unlikely that the number of groups to be carried out will allow for all possibilities. For example, a two-class, two-age split in two areas would require *eight* groups. In many instances this would be undertaken but in others compromise would be effected like:

south	ABC_1	... under 35 years
south	C_2DE	... over 35 years
north	ABC_1	... over 35 years
north	C_2DE	... under 35 years

A group discussion can cost anything between £800 to £1200 in the United Kingdom depending upon:

(a) who is being recruited, i.e. housewives are easy to find and recruit but women over 65 years with a full set of teeth are not;

(b) whether verbatim transcripts are required and whether a detailed report is to be provided;

(c) the amount of travelling time, expenses, and overnight accommodation involved;
(d) who actually conducts the group session, in terms of experience, seniority, fee commanded, etc. Generally, it can be expected that a group discussion run by a senior director of a large or specialized research agency will cost more than one undertaken by a junior executive. Experience has to be paid for;
(e) how much participants are to be paid. It is now standard practice to pay respondents as an incentive for turning up, since even if they use their own cars, respondents can be put to some personal expense. Payment varies from, say, £7–£10 for housewives coming to a morning or afternoon session, to £10–£15, for an evening group and as much as £20 for an extended group;
(f) whether a verbal debrief or full presentation is required.

Similarly, with individual intensive interviews costing between £150–£200 each, time and cost considerations will be important in determining numbers.

The writer has never found a case for conducting dozens of individual depth interviews since, after a certain point, they become extremely repetitive. Depending upon how categories are broken down, 5–6, 10–12, 20–24 seem adequate for most purposes. For example, if the subject was credit cards, something like

$$
\begin{aligned}
\text{men card owners} &= 10 \\
\text{women card owners} &= 10 \\
\text{men non-owners} &= 10 \\
\text{women non-owners} &= 10
\end{aligned}
$$

would probably be adequate. If time and money were vital considerations, a total of 24 (six in each group) may suffice. Certainly, one should not need 20-25 in each category.

With repertory grids, it has been shown by the writer[25] that high divergers produce, on average, twice as many constructs as low divergers, which could suggest that it is more worthwhile to undertake fewer repertory grid interviews than one would normally expect exclusively among respondents who are high divergers.

For deriving product attributes, the elicitation interview is extremely efficient, with samples of 100–200 being used depending on the number of stimuli and/or respondent groups being covered.

The recruitment of respondents for qualitative research

The 'explosion' of qualitative research during the past ten years has led to much debate on the question of recruiting respondents, especially for group discussions. The unscrupulous recruiter who maintains a 'panel' of 'professional group attendees' has become a source of irritation to qualitative researchers.

It is important, however, to view this problem in the correct perspective. The fact that a respondent has attended one group discussion in the recent past is unlikely to disqualify him from making a valuable contribution to another. If, however, they become frequent attendees it is difficult to imagine that some kind of learning behaviour does not start to affect their responses and they provide information they think the moderator wants to hear. This, clearly, reduces their value. The other, and perhaps more insidious, issue is the fact that these respondents may not qualify for group recruitment other than on criteria that are very loose indeed. In other words, the unscrupulous recruiter, via her own pre-selection, departs from the required qualification criteria.

The issues of respondent conditioning and misrecruitment are very different ones. Recent discussions by Schlackman[48] and Fuller[49] have dealt with special cases where 'sensitivity panels' or 'trained respondents' have been used effectively and valuably. (For detailed discussion about the use of qualitative research panels, the reader is referred to these authors.) Misrecruited respondents, on the other hand, can be of no value to anyone.

A final note

In 1978 the Qualitative Research Study Group of the MRS reviewed the practice of qualitative research[50]. It concluded:

Certainly, in practising qualitative research, the best results will only be attained when care, attention, experience and skill are brought to bear in the following ten areas:

(a) initial problem definition;
(b) research approach and methodology;
(c) sample selection;
(d) recruitment;
(e) location;
(f) skill and experience of the researcher;
(g) analysis and interpretation of results;
(h) conclusions and recommendations;
(i) verbal reporting;
(j) written reporting.

It points out, also, that the range and type of factors that affect and determine the quality and usefulness of qualitative research are, for the most part, the same as for quantitative research. It is that, simply, the relative importance of these factors differs for the two types of research.

However, the 'subjectivity' of qualitative research means that, in respect of the possible value of such work, more is vested in the particular individual carrying it out than in the case of quantitative research. This is certainly true, but also, the responsibility of the person commissioning the qualitative research is an important factor. If qualitative research is seen as a quick and inexpensive solution to a problem that is complex and subtle or an expedient alternative to more appropriate quantitative research it will be at the best disappointing and at the worse misleading. One is reminded of an ancient Chinese saying:

> *He who judges paintings by*
> *their resemblance to shapes*
> *should rightfully be considered a child.*

A postscript

During the past twelve months, and since this chapter was revised, a major debate about qualitative research has been taking place in Europe. It is between the 'cognitive' school of qualitative researchers like de Groot and the 'conative' school of people such as Fleury, Frontori, Heylen, Sampson and Bhaduri. The former believe that, due to the subjectivity of qualitative research and so-called 'lack of validity', qualitative research should not seek to go beyond a direct questioning of respondents and a strict, more literal interpretation of their responses. It is based on the premise that people do in general say what they mean and mean what they say. The opposing viewpoint, that has been dubbed "The New Qualitative Research", strongly believes in the use of 'enabling' or 'psychoscopic' techniques to identify the emotional ('conative') aspects that underlie consumer behaviour and choice and that are not easily expressed verbally, if at all. These, they believe, cannot be obtained from short interviews and group discussions that utilize detailed, highly structured interview guides. A quite different approach is recommended.

The reader may join this debate by reading references[51-53]. The first paper (de Groot[51]) expresses the view of the 'cognitivists' while the other two (Sampson[52], and Sampson and Bhaduri[53]) detail the work of the 'new' qualitative researchers.

Chapter 3

Experimental designs and models

JAMES ROTHMAN

This chapter is divided into two distinct parts: experimental design and models. The researcher must consider the question of experimental design and models before proceeding to the choice of sampling techniques, sample size or questionnaire design, hence the placing of these two subjects early on in this section.

Experimental designs

The role of experiments in marketing

According to Enis and Cox[1] experiments will be used more frequently as an aid to reaching marketing decisions. An experiment can be defined as an attempt to measure the effect of a given stimulus or to compare the effects of different stimuli. There is a sense in which, on this definition, all market research can be considered to be an experiment; since any question is a stimulus. If we believed that the questions we ask are completely understood and answered absolutely correctly by every respondent, then the sense in which market research was an experiment would be trivial. However, we know from the research carried out by Belson[2] and others that, in many cases, respondents do not understand questions or do not answer them correctly. In other words, we should try to make as few assumptions about our questions, and the answers we are likely to get from them, as possible. This means that even when preparing basic questionnaires we should bear in mind the principles of experimental design.

To take an obvious example, if we wanted to test two advertisements to find out which of them was the more persuasive, we could, if we believed that respondents always answered questions correctly, just show the two advertisements to each respondent and ask them which of the two they thought would be more likely to make them buy the product. However, life is not as easy as that and we have to find a suitable experimental procedure for testing the two advertisements, such as splitting our sample in two, exposing one advertisement to each half of the sample and then, possibly, measuring their buying behaviour after the exposure.

One point which it is convenient to make here is that in most market research we are more concerned with comparing the effects of different stimuli, rather than with making an absolute measurement of the effect of a single stimulus, and this is probably particularly true·of those areas where experimental design can be used. Thus, for example, we are more likely to be asked to say which premium offer would have the better effect on sales rather than to attempt to estimate the absolute sales increase that will be achieved by a given premium offer. Consequently, much of this chapter will be concerned with experimental designs for the purposes of making comparisons.

Definition of experimental design

If a given stimulus were always followed to exactly the same extent by exactly the same effect, and the effect of the stimulus could be measured with perfect accuracy, then experimental designs would probably not be needed. However, in most of our work, the measurements we make of the effects of stimuli are affected by many other factors. In a product test, for example, we will not find that everybody prefers one product by exactly the same amount to the other product; instead, we will find that some people like one product and some like the other and, moreover, that other factors such as the order in which the products are tried will affect our results. An experimental design, then, is a method of planning experiments in such a way that the sampling error can be measured and the results are affected as little as possible by random errors and are not confused by other factors.

Techniques for achieving good experimental designs

There are four basic ways of achieving the objectives of a good experimental design. First, we can remove or minimize these sources of error, e.g. we can reduce the effect of between-interviewer variation by ensuring that all our interviewers have been carefully trained. Again, if we are doing some type of split-sample operation we can remove the effects of between-polling district variation by ensuring that the sample is split exactly in half in each polling district. Second, if we cannot remove these random fluctuations, then we can attempt to control them, in other words, attempt to allocate them equally between the samples receiving the different stimuli. This is not always as easy as it sounds, particularly when there are many different sources of fluctuations and the number of experimental units we have is limited. One of the things we will be talking about are the types of experimental design which are useful in these circumstances. Third, besides controlling the effects of some types of fluctuation we can measure their effect and make due allowance for them, e.g. if we want to compare the effectiveness of two different forms of packaging for a product by using two samples of stores and putting the product on sale in each of the stores in one of the forms of packaging, then we have two alternative possibilities for splitting the sample and analysing the result. Firstly, we can try to match the stores by ensuring that for every store in one sample there is a store in the other sample which is identical to it in terms of turnover, type, location, etc. However, although we might be able to match our stores in terms of type or location, it is very probable that we could not match them exactly in terms of their turnover. In these circumstances, it may well be a better procedure to measure the effect of turnover on sales of the product before comparing the effects of the two different packages. Finally, if all else fails, the least we can do is to ensure the effects of these fluctuations are randomized. In other words, even if in our store test the store managers all refused to declare their turnovers, we can still assign the stores to the samples in a random fashion rather than, for example, allowing each store manager to put on sale the package he likes best. These, then, are the four procedures which we have at our command for reducing the effect of fluctuations on our measurements: we can attempt to remove or reduce these effects; attempt to control them; attempt to measure their effect separately and make allowance for them or, at the very least, ensure that there are no systematic errors and that the effects are randomized.

Conditions for good experimental designs

However, besides this there are four other requirements which we must bear in mind when we design our experiment. First, we should design our experiment in such a way that it will have adequate precision, i.e. we must employ enough experimental units on each treatment. This is the familiar problem of ensuring that our sample size is adequate so that we do not conclude that there is no significant difference between the effects of the stimuli when, in fact, the difference between them is sufficiently large to be of commercial importance. Second, the results should be applicable over a wide range, e.g. if we are comparing the effectiveness of two advertising campaigns, each of which contains a number of advertisements, then it is obviously not adequate merely to compare one advertisement from one campaign with a single advertisement from the other campaign. These two advertisements might be freaks and, whereas campaign A might in general be better than campaign B, one advertisement from campaign B might still be better than another given advertisement from campaign A. Third, as stated earlier, we must in any experiment be able at the end of all this to calculate the error in our measurements and to assess the significance of the comparisons which we make. Finally, the conditions in which the experiment is conducted must be such that the results are capable of real life application. All experiments are artificial to some extent so whether or not a particular experiment is too artificial needs to be either a matter of judgement or the subject of an empirical comparison with another experiment which, although more realistic, would be too costly for regular use.

Types of experimental design

Split runs

The simplest form of experimental design is the split run. This is the arrangement in which, say, half the sample is administered one stimulus and half the other.

In market research, split runs, in spite of their simplicity, can be extremely useful, e.g. one form of assessing the likely demand for products at different prices is to ask respondents to indicate their likelihood of buying the product if it were on sale at a given price. The price quoted can be varied between respondents and the information derived used to plot a demand curve. Again, split sample techniques can be used to test the effects of alternative question wordings and, hence, to set upper and lower bounds for the prevalence of a given opinion or attitude.

Split runs should only be used in cases such as the above where, for one reason or another, it is not advisable to administer both stimuli to the same respondent since otherwise this would be the more sensitive design.

In designing split runs, two alternatives are possible, either each interviewer can be instructed to administer all the stimuli rotating them across respondents with different starting points for different interviewers, or the different stimuli can be issued to the different interviewers for administration.

From a theoretical standpoint the former method is always preferable since it eliminates between-interviewer variance; and also if, as is usual, different interviewers operate in different sampling areas, it eliminates between-area variance. From a practical point of view, on the other hand, the former method puts a heavier strain on the interviewer and, if the sample is to be split into more than three segments, it may be necessary to adopt the second approach.

'Before and after' test

The second elementary experimental design frequently used in market research is the 'before and after' test in which a measurement is made and a stimulus is administered, either by artificial means, such as posting an advertisement to respondents, or by real life means, such as a test advertising campaign after which a measurement survey is conducted.

Two forms of 'before and after' survey are possible: that in which the second measurement survey is conducted on the same respondent as the first, and that in which it is conducted on a different sample of respondents.

Here again, the first method is theoretically preferable. However, unless the interval between the two surveys is long, there is the danger that the initial survey may itself act as a stimulus, e.g. respondents asked a brand awareness question may become conditioned and take a greater interest in brand advertising for that product group after the interview than they did before. For these reasons most 'before and after' surveys are conducted on different samples of respondents.

In this instance, as for split sample tests, there are two alternatives, the second survey can be conducted in the same sample points as the first or a fresh sample of points can be drawn. From a sampling point of view the first method is preferable. However, if the initial survey is itself likely to create so much interest that the respondents talk to their neighbours about it and so condition them it may be necessary to use the second one. A further refinement of the 'before and after' survey is to carry out an additional control survey, that is a before and after survey taking place at the same time as the test survey but in which the respondents have not received the stimulus material during the interim period. The advantage of doing this is that a correction can be made for other changes that may have been taking place during the intervening period apart from the administration of the test stimulus, e.g. there may have been competitive advertising during the interim period or, in some circumstances, changes in the weather may have affected the results of the survey. Here again, the question arises as to whether the control survey should be carried out in the same area as the test survey.

The answer this time normally depends on the way in which the stimulus has been administered. In general, the principle is to have the control sample as close to the test sample as can be achieved whilst avoiding the danger of 'carry over' effects. However, if the stimulus has been administered in a real-life situation, the control area will have to be different, say a different television area or a different newspaper circulation area to that used for the test survey.

If the control area is widely separated from the test area, the researcher must then consider carefully if it may not indeed be so widely separated that it will be unlikely to have received the same external stimuli as the test area. If this is the case, then the use of the control area will only confuse rather than assist the interpretation of the results of the experiment. Ideally, this type of problem can be overcome by the use of several test and control areas. In the UK this is possible, but expensive, for local press advertising but virtually impossible for national press or television.

At this point we need to think carefully about the role of the 'before' surveys in the test and control areas. If a number of areas are used, can we not say that if they have been properly selected the 'before' surveys are redundant since we know that the results ought to be the same for both the test and the control areas? Why not use a special case of the split runs described above – an 'after only' design?

In certain circumstances the 'after only' design will indeed be better. The use of 'before and after' designs stems from the fact that the 'before' units can often be matched more closely with the 'after' ones than the test units can be matched with the controls. Thus, if we think conditioning effects will balance out, we might even be able to use the same units for both stages of the research. The following approximate rules can be used to reach a decision on the best design:

1. Is the correlation between the before and after stages expected to be greater than 0.5?
   If 'no', use an 'after only' design.
   If 'yes',
2. Will the amount by which this correlation exceeds 0.5 be greater than half the correlation expected between the test and control units?
   If 'no', use an 'after only' design.
   If 'yes', use a 'before and after' design.

Split runs and 'before and after' studies are relatively simple experimental designs. We now proceed to the more complex designs which are occasionally used in market research.

Latin square designs
This design normally arises when the effects of a number of alternative stimuli need to be compared, and the units over which they are to be administered are known to differ along two different dimensions. One may wish, for example, to carry out a store test on an item with a very high rate

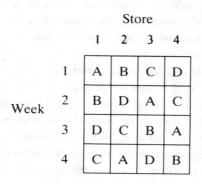

Fig. 3.1

of sale, in four stores for one week only. The sampling unit in this case is a week in a store. If we label the four different test stimuli A, B, C and D, it will be seen that if an arrangement as shown in Fig. 3.1 is employed, each test stimulus has been employed once in each week, and once in each store. Arrangements such as this, where the design can be represented by a square with the same letter appearing just once in each row and each column of the square, are known as 'Latin squares'.

More advanced versions of the same type of design known as 'Graeco-Latin squares' can be used to control the sample across three or more dimensions.

The arrangement shown in Fig. 3.2, which might be used to test a product sold at four different prices W, X, Y, Z, in four different stores, in four different weeks from four different types of display stands A, B, C, D, is an example of the 'Graeco-Latin square'.

	Store			
	1	2	3	4
Week 1	WA	XB	YC	ZD
2	YB	ZA	WD	XC
3	ZC	YD	XA	WB
4	XD	WC	ZB	YA

Fig. 3.2

As will be noted, designs of this type can be used either to control the tests across a number of different dimensions or to enable the researcher to test two or more variables such as prices, display stands or pack designs at the same time. At first glance, it may seem that testing two different variables in the same test should halve the effectiveness of the sample and consequently no advantage would be gained. In fact, whilst the accuracy of a test of several variables using the same experimental units is slightly less effective than a test across just one variable, the loss of efficiency is relatively small and more information is gained.

Factorial designs

A related type of situation which is also found in market research is that in which a product or an advertisement can be considered as being made up of a number of different factors; e.g. a food product may be considered as containing two or more flavouring ingredients in differing proportions, together with different levels of a texturizing process. Again, in an advertisement, alternative visuals may be under test, together with the inclusion or absence of some specific product claim or free offer and the use or non-use of the company logotype as well as the brand name. In these circumstances, we may wish to measure the influence of each of these factors separately – in technical language, their main effects. In addition, we may also wish to see if the presence or absence of one variable influences the effect of another, known in technical language as an 'interaction' effect.

Interaction effects can, of course, arise at several levels; e.g. in the food product sample quoted above, if both flavouring ingredients were present together, the product might receive a high appreciation score, but if either were present separately, the product might receive a lower than expected appreciation score and could even do worse than if neither were present at all. Effects of this nature are known as 'first order interactions', a 'second order interaction' being the differential effects produced by combinations of three variables taken together, and so on.

If every combination of factors is tested, we have a so-called 'complete' factorial design which enables us to measure all main effects and all interactions. If we have a large number of different factors to test, the number of combinations required can become large, especially if we need to test these at more than two basic levels, such as present and absent or high concentration and low concentration; e.g. a test of the effects of three different flavouring ingredients at three different concentration levels would require the preparation of 27 different test products.

Whilst sample sizes used in most market research studies are sufficiently large to accommodate this sort of number of test items, the cost of their production can be high. In these circumstances, an incomplete experimental design can be employed. For example, with a design such as that shown in Fig. 3.3 it will be seen that using only nine different test products we have enough information to enable us to measure main effects and first order interactions for three different ingredients A, B and C each used at three concentration levels 1, 2 and 3.

$$A_1B_1C_1 \quad A_2B_1C_2 \quad A_3B_1C_3$$
$$A_1B_2C_2 \quad A_2B_2C_3 \quad A_3B_2C_1$$
$$A_1B_3C_3 \quad A_2B_3C_1 \quad A_3B_3C_2$$

Fig. 3.3

In many tests it is reasonable to assume that higher order interactions will be small compared with the main effects and the first order interactions, and the cost savings achievable by the use of incomplete factorial designs more than offset the slight risk of making this assumption. Several works in this area such as Cox[3] contain examples of such incomplete experimental designs for various combinations of factors and levels.

Paired comparisons

An experimental design frequently found in market research is the paired comparison design in which respondents compare two different products or other stimuli. Use of these designs will also be discussed in chapter 15. A point which is worth making here, however, is that in a situation in which three or more products are to be assessed by means of a test of this nature, two alternatives are available:

(a) one product can be selected as a standard and each of the others can be tested against this;
(b) each product can be tested against every other one.

It will be seen that, in general, the second method known as the 'round robin' method involves a larger number of tests than the first. For this reason, some researchers have been tempted to use the first method. Nonetheless, it can be shown that the 'round robin' method is more efficient and can, in some circumstances, even yield information which is lost completely when the first method is used. Say, for example, we have the three products to be tested, A, B and C and the research budget permits the use of a total sample of 300 respondents. The first approach then would be to test A against C and B against C using a sample of 150 respondents for each test. On this basis, our information about the performance of A and B would be derived from 150 respondents. On the other hand, we could use the 'round robin' technique of testing A against B, B against C, and A against C, using three samples each consisting of 100 respondents. In this case, information on the performance of each of the three test samples is based on 200 respondents so that the variance is reduced by a quarter. In addition, when this is done, it may be found that product A performs better than one would expect when tested against B, but worse than one would expect when tested against C. This might arise if the different pairings encourage respondents to make comparisons along different dimensions; e.g. if A and B are similar in colour but different in flavour then when B is tested against A, respondents tend to express their flavour preference, rather than their colour preference and vice versa when B is tested against C. In these circumstances, the so-called effect of non-additivity described above can be observed. Whilst the interpretation of these non-additivity effects is often difficult, the presence of this type of effect may not be noticed and valuable information lost if the system of testing against a standard is employed.

The method for analysing 'round robin' tests is summarized in chapter 12.

Carry-over effects

These occur when the use of one stimulus affects the results obtained with another; e.g. if, in a store test, one particular stimulus administered in one week gives a high rate of sale, then this may pre-empt potential purchases that might have been made in a later week so that the effect observed for the stimulus administered in the store in the following week will be artificially depressed.

If a Latin square design is used the size of these carry-over effects can be measured if the test is continued for an additional week, without changing the stimuli between the stores. If there were no carry-over effects the sales observed in the last week should be the same as those observed in the previous week. The difference between the sales in the two periods shown represents a measure of the carry-over effects delivered by each stimulus which can be then used to correct observations made in the previous weeks[4].

Difference tests

In product tests especially, the researcher may find himself attempting to test for preference between products before it has been established whether or not the ordinary user is capable of detecting any difference between the test products. In some cases we may even be more concerned to know whether people notice a difference between the products than to know which they prefer; e.g. in existing products, the possibility of substituting a cheaper ingredient for a more expensive one can arise. However, if buyers notice the difference, the product may lose some of its franchise even if the majority of users preferred the product with the cheaper ingredient. Designs to test whether people are capable of noticing the difference between test products are known as 'difference tests'. The most common form of these is the so called 'triadic difference test' in which respondents are given three samples to try and informed that two of these are the same and one is different, and then asked to guess or state which one is the odd one out. If each of the three test products is selected by a third of the sample, the conclusion can be reached that there is no real difference between the two versions of the product. If, on the other hand, the odd one out is selected by significantly more than a third of the respondents, the opposite conclusion can be drawn. It should be noted that this type of test, since it is based on a variance of one third times two thirds, i.e. two ninths, is slightly more sensitive than a conventional product test where, if there is no preference between the two products, the variance would be one quarter.

One point to be noted in the use of this type of test is that it is important that respondents are informed that one of the three products in the triad is different from the other two. A frequent temptation is merely to ask respondents if they can notice any difference between the three and to say which one is the odd one out. This, however, means that respondents who notice a slight difference but are reluctant to commit themselves, and therefore claim that they can detect no difference, are eliminated so that the test results are distorted.

The sensitivity of difference tests can be increased by giving respondents more samples to assess; e.g. respondents may be given five samples to try and asked to sort the products into one group of three and another group of two. Analysis methods for this type of test which gives credit to respondents not only for getting a completely correct result but also a partial result such as A, B in one group and A, B, B in the other are given by Greenhalgh[5]. Another type of difference test is to ask respondents to test a number of samples and say for each one whether or not it is the same as a standard which they are given to try.

The advantage of these more elaborate techniques is that not only do they enable a greater test precision to be obtained from a given sample size but they also enable respondents to be identified as good or poor discriminators. On the other hand, in the conventional triadic difference test, since even a non-discriminator stands a one in three chance of getting the right answer it is normally not possible to identify discriminators in a situation in which, say, 30 per cent of the population can discriminate and the remainder not.

Analysis of experiments and choice of sample size

Apart from the case of the simple split run with a two-way split where a conventional student '*t*' test can be employed, the standard method of analysing the results of experiments in which experimental designs have been employed is the analysis of variance or, where the test result is known to be correlated with some characteristic of the sample unit which it is not possible to stratify out completely in the experimental design, the analysis of covariance. This last method can be reduced to an analysis of variance of deviations about a regression line.

Details of these analysis techniques are given in chapter 12. One point, however, that should be made here is that it is often mistakenly believed that the size of samples to be used in an experiment is the minimum size of sample that can be accommodated within the experimental design. Thus, if the experimental design indicated is a four-by-four Latin square, then the experiment could be conducted on a basis of sixteen sample units. This, however, is merely the minimum size of sample that can be used. The size of the sample that is necessary must still be calculated on the same basis as for any other survey (see chapter 4). Whilst experimental designs can be more efficient than conventional sampling procedures because of the way in which they stratify out the between and within unit variance, the improvement in efficiency is usually not large and it is still necessary to estimate the within unit sampling variance and, hence, derive the size of sample that is required for any given degree of accuracy. This size of sample is then achieved by means of replicating the experimental design, i.e. by repeating the experimental design for the required number of times.

Generally speaking, it is more efficient if the replications differ from each other, e.g. if it is calculated that 32 sample units are required and the sample design is to be two four-by-four Latin squares then the Latin squares employed should be different from each other.

Examples of the use of experimental designs

Voting experiment

In August 1964, when the two main political polls showed different parties in the lead, Sales Research Services Ltd. carried out an experiment to test the hypothesis that political polls had a band-wagon effect encouraging voters to vote for the party which they believed stood the greatest chance of winning. A continuous survey sample was split into three equal sub-samples and each of these sub-samples was asked a standard voting intention question together with another question designed to estimate turnout. The introduction to the questions, however, differed between the sub-samples, one being told that the latest survey showed that the Conservative party was most likely to win, the second that the Labour party was most likely to win and the third being given no information on recent survey results.

The results of the experiment showed no significant difference between the sub-samples on voting intention. On turn-out, however, the experiment showed that supporters of a particular political party showed greatest determination to vote when told that the opposing party was in the lead and least determination to vote when told that their own party was in the lead. The differences were very small; nonetheless, this example is of interest since it illustrates how a simple experiment can often throw more light on a controversy than can the most powerful argument.

NOP have used a similar experiment to show the way in which the results of the referendum on Britain joining the EEC might be affected by the wording used on the ballot paper[6].

Store front tests

The next experiment illustrates the way in which a suitable experimental design for the stimulus material under study can be used to test a general concept, i.e. to ensure that the results of the experiment are applicable over a wide range. The purpose was to determine whether the style and quality of shop-front design influenced attitudes towards stores. Each member of a panel of designers was asked independently to assign pictures of shop-fronts to one of three categories, good modern, bad modern and old-fashioned design. A check was made to ensure that designers agreed on their assignment of photographs and a few pictures where there was substantial disagreement on their category were rejected. From the remaining pictures, three examples of each design style were selected. A Latin square design was then used to assign the pictures into groups of three in such a way that each group contained one example of each design style and that each picture appeared once with each of the pictures in either of the other two categories.

An omnibus survey sample was then split into nine equivalent subsamples, each sub-sample being shown one of the groups of three pictures and asked to select the shop-front they thought best on a number of different aspects. Scores for the different shop fronts were then summed over the categories in which they appeared to yield ratings for each of the nine pictures and these ratings, in turn, were summed to yield average ratings for the design styles.

The results showed that, whilst clear differences emerged for the different design styles, it was possible for particular examples of a design style to yield inaccurate results; e.g. on drapery stores the overall preference scores were as follows:

good modern	48%
bad modern	23%
old-fashioned	29%

The average scores for three individual photographs, however, were:

good modern (photograph A)	38%
bad modern (photograph C)	27%
old-fashioned (photograph B)	43%

If these three shops only had been tested, because the good modern design was a relatively inferior member of the good modern design category whilst the old-fashioned shop was a superior member of its category, we would have reached the wrong conclusion.

An exhibition test

It was required to obtain data at low cost on the effects of different types of stimulus which can, for the purposes of this example, be considered as different prices, on the rate of sale of a product. Advantage was taken of an exhibition at which the product was placed on sale. The exhibition lasted for four weeks and the Mondays, Tuesdays, Wednesdays and Thursdays of each week were selected as test days on which sales of the product were measured. A Latin square design was used to allocate the prices to days of the week in such a way that each price was administered once on each day of the week and once in each of the four weeks that the exhibition lasted. A count was also maintained of the number of people visiting the stand on each day of the week.

From analyses of the results it was possible to produce what amounted to a demand curve for the product and also, as a by-product, to investigate the effect of day of week and week of exhibition on the sale of the product.

Store tests

Similar techniques to the above are used to assess the effects of varying stimuli on the rate of sale of the product. The use of stores rather than an exhibition enables greater flexibility and more realism to be achieved albeit at a higher research cost. Normally speaking, a period of a week or a month rather than a day is used as the test period so as to accumulate an adequate number of sales under each stimulus without the necessity of introducing too many changes into the stores. A good account of such a test is given by Woodside and Waddle[7].

Dummy stores and laboratory experiments

Another area in which test designs are frequently used is in test centre experiments in which respondents are asked to visit a centre for the purposes of research; e.g. in these centres 'find time' tests can be administered to compare the time it takes to find a brand in alternative pack designs on self-service style shelving. In these experiments the position of the test product on the shelves can be varied in accordance with the experimental design to ensure that the results are not biased by this factor.

Factorially designed product tests

An important area for the use of experimental designs is in the field of product tests. Products can be made up on the basis of a factorial design, whether complete or incomplete, with the proportions of key ingredients being varied or alternative processing systems being altered. These products can then be tested against each other using a 'round robin' design and from the results a score for each product calculated. These scores are then subjected to an analysis of variance so that the effect of each factor is tested to see whether it has a significant influence on product preference and the presence or absence of interactions are also explored. Tests of this nature are valuable not only in that they enable an optimum formulation of a product to be reached but because they can throw light on respondents' verbal statements as to their reasons for preference in a product test.

Postal surveys and mail order advertising

Here, too, experimental designs are valuable. A factorial design can be used in the pilot of a postal survey to test the effect on response rates of such factors as the wording of a covering letter, questionnaire layout, inclusion or absence of a question on a sensitive subject, etc. Many studies of this nature have been reported, e.g. Sheth and Roscoe[8]. Further details on mail surveys are given in chapter 10. A similar approach can be used in testing advertising designed to achieve a direct mail type of response.

Models in marketing research

Definition of the term model

A model is a set of assumptions about the factors which are relevant to a given situation and the relationships which exist between them. The term model is normally taken to mean one in which the assumptions are stated explicitly and relevant conclusions can be drawn by deductive (usually mathematical) methods. Hopefully, the model has also been tested in various ways by adducing evidence in favour of the initial assumptions or by testing conclusions drawn from the model. (By assumptions here we include both those in which one can be reasonably confident because they are based on repeated observation and those for which the only evidence is 'common sense' or introspection).

The role of models in research and marketing

The first way in which models are used in market research is that virtually every method of analysing research results involves a set of assumptions about the data which is equivalent to the use of, at the least, an implicit model. Usually, for example, when a scale question is employed an average score implies the assumption that the scale is of equal interval, i.e. the difference between the fourth and fifth position on the scale is assumed to be equivalent to the difference between, say, the first and second position. Methods are, of course, available for checking the equal interval assumption and experience has shown that even if a scale is not exactly of equal interval, the departures from this property are not normally sufficient to affect the conclusions one draws from the results. Nevertheless, it is important to realize that this assumption is being made.

Another example of the way in which we assume a model when analysing research results (including, of course, those from experimental designs) is the assumption of the order of interaction present in the data. As we have seen, incomplete factorial designs are frequently employed on the assumption that interactions above a certain order are unlikely to be important. Again, we normally assume that the data interrelate in a certain way, e.g. we might assume that, within a certain range, liking of a soft drink can be calculated by some equation of the type: 'appreciation score equals constant times quantity of flavour component one plus constant times quantity of flavour component two plus a small interaction effect'. We do not countenance the concept that the appreciation score might be a function of these quantities multiplied together rather than added together, i.e. we assume an additive rather than a multiplicative model. By and large, most of these assumptions are justified by the fact that, within the sort of range of variables normally found in the market research situation, it can be shown that models are reasonably robust to departures from these assumptions. Models can be used to help describe the current state of a market, to aid understanding of the reasons for the way in which it develops or as a means of predicting what will happen in the future under alternative assumptions.

Principles of behavioural models used in market research

Behavioural models in market research perform three main functions;

(a) the construction of such a model prior to the carrying out of a survey can assist in ensuring that all the relevant data are collected and, in addition, can prevent the construction of over-long questionnaires asking 'interesting' but irrelevant questions;
(b) they can simplify the analysis of the survey results by enabling the answers to several questions to be combined in a meaningful fashion and ensuring that only relevant analyses are conducted on them;
(c) they reduce the gap between the market research report and the marketing decision it is intended to assist.

One point which should be noted about models in market research is that, whereas the conventional operational research model normally has to use data which are already available and consequently is restricted by the form in which the data are produced, the market researcher building his own model can choose the method for collecting and analyzing the data to suit the requirements of the model exactly and, consequently, is not restricted in this fashion. Normally, for example, an operational researcher using data on the prevalence of a certain characteristic analysed by age and class would not be able to incorporate in his model the possibility that there is an interaction effect between age and class so that the characteristic is prevalent amongst say, young working class individuals and older middle class individuals. The researcher, on the other hand, is free to decide whether he wishes to have his analyses conducted in terms of class within age or on these characteristics taken separately. This leads to the first of our distinctions between different types of models used in market research, i.e. the distinction between global and individual models.

Global or individual models

A macro or global model is one which takes data in their conventional form for a population or a sample and attempts to relate it to other characteristics under study. An individual or micro model, on the other hand, takes each individual or unit in a sample in turn and relates the characteristics of that individual to the factor under study; it then combines the results for the individuals in the sample to produce a final result; e.g. in assessing a media schedule, a global model might simply work with conventional readership and duplication data, whereas an individual or simulation model would take each individual in the sample, calculate his expected number of exposures from the campaign, relate this to a response function and thus calculate the average response for the total sample.

The individual simulation technique has the advantage of allowing all the complexities in the data to be taken into account. On the other hand, the global model is simpler to operate; it can be more readily understood and, providing it is a correct representation of the situation, is likely to yield more accurate results than would a simulation technique. The best method is probably to work from an individual model and to attempt to build up from this an appropriate global model; e.g. the original inspiration for Ehrenberg's[9] NBD theory of consumer purchasing behaviour was that a negative binomial distribution of consumer purchases within a period would result if the assumption was made that each individual's purchases within a finite period would follow a Poisson distribution, whilst the long term frequency of individuals' purchasing behaviour followed a gamma distribution.

Similarly the later extension of this to the Dirichlet model[10] is based on the idea that consumers' purchases of the product group follow the NBD while each individual allocates purchases to brands as if at random with a set of probabilities which are distributed between consumers in accordance with another distribution – the Dirichlet.

Formal and informal models

It should be noted that not all behavioural models used in market research follow or are expressed in exact mathematical terms; e.g. many models of the way advertising works from DAGMAR[11] on have only sought to describe the process in terms of words and diagrams. Whilst pursists may wish to argue whether models of this type are, in fact, worthy of the name, such a discussion is outside the scope of this chapter. It should, however, be noted that a model is only useful in so far as it is expressed sufficiently precisely either for the model itself to be tested or for one or more of the conclusions that can be drawn from it to be verified.

Occasions or people

Many behavioural models used in market research work on the principle that people can be divided into types, e.g. buyers or not-buyers of brand A. An examination of the buying behaviour for most products, however, would indicate that truly brand-loyal buying behaviour is relatively uncommon; consequently, models which assign probabilities of buying brand A on a given occasion to individuals and, hence, work in terms of expected numbers of buying occasions rather than in terms of people, must be considered to be more realistic. Again, in interpreting test results, the conventional model is that they indicate, say, that 60% prefer brand A to brand B; unless further evidence is available a more precise model could well be that brand A is preferred to brand B on 60% of the occasions on which it is tested. This is related to the traits and types distinction between models (see below).

Whilst Lynch's[12] view may be extreme it is wise to remember his comment that samples and populations should not be construed as sets of respondents. The relevant populations in experimental consumer research consist of measures of behaviour.

Traits or types

It is often convenient to divide people up into different type groups, e.g. housewives who enjoy cooking and housewives who cook as a duty, people willing to try new things, people not willing to try new things, and so on. However, if these characteristics are studied in detail, it is likely that they will be found to be traits which people may have to a greater or lesser extent rather than type groups into which people may or may or not fall, The difference is shown in Fig. 3.4.

Frequency distribution of a trait   Frequency distribution of a type

Fig. 3.4

Segmentation and taxonomic models normally work on the type rather than the trait principle. In many instances, the type assumption is a convenient approximation and may well not distort the research results. However, if the type assumption is being made, it is important to verify either that it is valid or that the interpretation of the results is unlikely to be affected greatly if the trait principle is, in fact, more appropriate.

Static or dynamic models

Most models used in market research work on the principle of finding an explanation for behaviour in terms of attitudes or other characteristics and then assume that if an individual's characteristics or attitudes can be changed, his behaviour will alter in the direction predicted by the model. Models of this nature can be described as static since they assume that the system is not altered by its dynamic characteristics. There is, in fact, very little evidence in favour of this assumption and, indeed, the work of, for example, Hovland[13] tends to support the view that attitudes may continue to change long after the stimulus causing that change has been removed. This view is also supported by the time series models used in advertising and marketing such as adstock.[14,15] It would seem reasonable, then, to suppose that the same process of change might apply to behaviour.

The discussion whether or not changes in attitudes precede or follow changes in behaviour is related to the same question. Whilst researchers may be forced to continue to use static models and to make the static assumption until workable procedures for developing and operating a dynamic model have been discovered, it is still necessary that the nature of the static assumption should be clearly recognized.

Points in space

Congruity or dominance

Coombs[16] has pointed out that data used in the social sciences can be considered as being represented by a series of points in space. It is convenient to consider models used in market research in these terms. Thus, for example, many models work on the congruity principle, i.e. that individuals will tend to purchase products which come close to their requirements. Other models, however, work on the dominance principle, i.e. that individuals will tend to purchase the product which in their space can be represented by a point farthest along one or more evaluative axes. A congruity model can be used as an approximation to an evaluative one by placing the requirement points at the extremes of the dimensions but normally an evaluative model cannot be used to approximate a congruity one.

Measures of distance

Once the space with which we are concerned occupies more than one dimension, we have to consider the method by which distance will be measured, either for the purpose of determining relative congruity or dominance. The obvious form of measure to employ is the so-called Euclidean measure, that is to say the distance as the 'crow flies' between the two points. Those who recall Pythagoras' theorem will appreciate that this measure of distance, depending as it does on the sum of the squares of distances along each dimension, is essentially a quadratic function. Many marketing models, however, employ linear functions. The effect of using a linear instead of a quadratic function is equivalent to the use of what is called a 'city block' measure of distance, i.e. the distance between two points where one has to travel between them along a grid of roads running at right angles to each other. There is no evidence to suggest whether subjective distances are most appropriately measured by 'city block' or

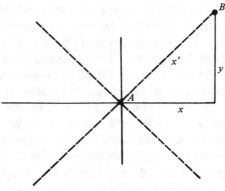

Fig. 3.5

Euclidean measures. It should, however, be noted that, whereas the Euclidean measure of distance is robust to rotations of the dimensions which constitute the space, the 'city block' measure is not. This will be seen more clearly if we consider Fig. 3.5. In this diagram, it will be seen that the Euclidean distance between the two points A and B will be the same regardless of whether the orientation of the axis is chosen to be the solid lines or the dotted lines. If a 'city block' measure of distance is employed, however, the distance between the two points in the one case will be $x + y$, whereas in the other case, it will be $\sqrt{(x^2 + y^2)}$ which will be seen to be smaller. Further transformations of the distance measure may be required to account for the relationship between behaviour or attitudes and the distance measure. A special case of such transformations are threshold models under which changes in distance below a certain level produce no effect.

Orthogonal or oblique axes
If data are be to represented by a system of points in space, it is necessary to consider whether the axes used to represent these points should be orthogonal or oblique. Using a static model it is possible to determine whether two measures are orthogonal or oblique to each other by considering whether or not they are correlated across respondents. However, the fact that two dimensions are correlated in the static case does not necessarily mean that they would also be correlated in the context of a dynamic model; again they might be orthogonal for one population and oblique for another. There is, therefore, some justification for systems of market segmentation or other types of models which use correlated measures, such as scores on different scales, as if they were, in fact, orthogonal to each other. Moreover, if a 'city block' system of measurement is employed, there is no reason for supposing that the 'streets of the city' must run at right angles to each other. So long as they run parallel to the axes of the system, whether or not the axes were orthogonal in this model

would be irrelevant. For small correlations between measures in the static case, the question of whether the distance measure employed should or should not correct for the obliqueness of the axes, is relatively unimportant. If, however, the measures do show correlations with each other which are greater than, say, 0.3 it is important, either to consider carefully whether or not a correction should be applied, or to verify that the model is robust to the alternative assumption.

The dimensional system itself

Most behavioural models used in research tend to assume that all individuals employ the same dimensional system and, frequently, it will be found that they further assume either that all individuals agree on their perception of the world but their requirements differ; or that individuals have the same requirements but differ in their perception of the world, i.e.

(a) all individuals would agree on the way in which different products rate on a particular factor, but whilst some would want a product with a high score on that factor, others would want a product with a moderate or even a low score; or

(b) all individuals are agreed that a certain factor has an evaluative content so that a high score on it is always considered to be a good thing, but the individuals differ as to which products possess this quality to the greatest extent and, thus, differ in the items they purchase.

In most instances, however, the true situation is probably that individuals differ both in their requirements and in their perceptions and models which allow both these assumptions are preferable to the more restricted type which enables only one or the other assumption to be made. Again, it is normally recognized that the weights applied to different dimensions can vary; thus, in calculating a distance measure, dimension A might be given twice the weight to that applied to dimension B. In some models the assumption is made that these weights are the same for all individuals whilst other models enable the weights to be varied between individuals so that for some, dimension A might be more important than dimension B, whereas for others the opposite would be true.

Further to these complications, however, there is also the possibility that the dimensionality of the space itself may differ between individuals. This may simply be a matter of the rotation of the dimensions differing between them. If so, correct results can still be achieved if a Euclidean space is assumed. On the other hand, it is also possible that, whereas factors A, B, and C are salient for one individual, for another three totally different factors, say D, E, and F might be salient. In theory, the question of saliency can be overcome if the importance weights can be varied between individuals. This may, however, mean that the number of dimensions that may need to be studied can become unduly large unless the system for collecting and analysing the data is modified.

Interactive or non-interactive models

In addition, to the above, a further complication is that most behavioural models will asume that there is no interaction between the scores on different dimensions. Some models of individual behaviour, however, work on a hierarchical basis such as that shown in Fig. 3.6. It will be seen that this type of model is equivalent to assuming a high degree of interaction between the dimensions.

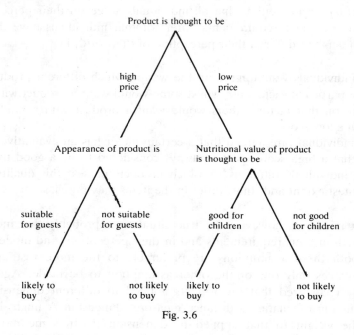

Fig. 3.6

In theory, this can be overcome by treating the interaction components as additional dimensions. In practice, however, the number of dimensions that are created becomes too great for the model to be usefully manipulated. At this point, then, it may be convenient to depart from considering data as a representation of points in space and employ other approaches. In this case, though, we need to consider whether or not the system of hierarchical needs has the same arrangement for different individuals.

General model

To sum up, the most general behavioural model would need to incorporate the following:

(a) a congruity principle instead of or as well as an evaluative one;
(b) the possibility for individuals to differ both in their perceptions and requirements;
(c) the incorporation of a dynamic element for the time that has elapsed since the change of attitude took place;
(d) the possibility for individuals to differ in the importance weight which they assign to different dimensions and even to differ in the dimensions which they select as salient;
(e) the incorporation of interaction terms whose weights differ between individuals;
(f) the interpretation of the results for each individual in a probabilistic rather than a deterministic fashion.

While programs which incorporate a number of these features are now available it is doubtful whether a completely general model would ever be a practical proposition. The researcher who selects a more restricted model must, however, be in a position to justify his choice of the factors that he considers to be relevant. It would seem that the availability of the model determines too often the selection of relevant factors rather than the reverse.

Examples of models used in market research

Finally, it may be helpful to illustrate the discussion in the preceding sections by describing some models which have been used in market research. It will be seen that many of these represent special cases of the general model outlined above. Further examples are contained in chapter 20.

Table interpretation

As we have stated earlier, even those who would deny that they are using a formal model may well be using an informal one. Conventional table interpretation is a good example of this. Table interpretation itself is discussed in chapter 12. Considered as a model, however, it should be noted that conventional systems of table interpretations assume that interaction effects, apart from those catered for in the tabulation itself, are unimportant. Furthermore, if the same variable is tabulated on a number of different factors, straightforward table interpretation tends to ignore the effects produced by correlations between these factors. Thus, a report may state that young housewives tend to buy brand A more than older ones and those with young children tend to buy brand A more than women with older children or adult families. The analysis, however, does not consider whether both of these factors influence separately the purchase of brand A or whether housewives with young children tend to have the characteristic merely because they are also younger. One way of overcoming these problems is to build and test log–linear models.[17,18]

Models of attitude change

Models of attitude change clearly have considerable relevance to advertisement planning and testing and they are frequently referred to when interpreting research results both in test situations and before and after surveys. They have, however, tended not to be used directly in market research. The reason for the lack of direct use of models of attitude change is probably twofold:

(a) the client, quite correctly, is interested in influencing behaviour and not attitudes and, consequently, models which relate attitudes or attitude change to behaviour are likely to be considered more useful;
(b) most models of attitude change normally have a qualitative rather than a quantitative format and, consequently, are not suitable for direct use.

A typical example of a model of attitude change is the Rosenberg and Abelson[19] balance model. This assumes that, if an object is associated in a positive fashion with a second object towards which the respondent already has an attitude, the attitude he will adopt towards the first object will be similar to that which the individual holds towards the second one. Conversely, if the two objects are negatively associated then the attitudes between the two objects will diverge.

The St James' model[20]

This is a model which was once widely adopted in UK market research. The model can be categorized as a 'city block' distance type of model since it states, in effect, that individuals will buy the brand of a product which comes closest to their requirements using a 'city block' distance measure. The procedure for employing the model is as follows. Respondents rate brands using say, a battery of semantic differential scales; they also rate on the same battery of scales the characteristics they would wish an ideal brand to possess. The scale scores then are factor-analysed to yield a smaller set of orthogonal or, more usually, oblique factors. For each respondent the absolute distance between his rating of each brand and of his ideal is calculated and a regression is then conducted using these distances as independent variables and the likelihood of buying the brands as the dependent ones. This likelihood is estimated either from claimed purchase data or from respondent's preference ratings. This regression is then used to derive the importance weights to be associated with the different dimensions for all respondents. Whilst the obvious measure of these importance weights might seem to be the regression coefficients themselves, the classical version of the model employs, in their place, the squared correlation coefficients between the dependent and independent variables. The results from the model are normally expressed in terms of the average distance scores for each brand from the ideal along each dimension together with the derived importance weight for that dimension and these two measures can be summarized by multiplying them together.

The Fishbein model[21]

This differs from most research models in that it concentrates on the act of purchasing the brand rather than on the brand itself and allows for the incorporation not only of beliefs about the brand but also of normative beliefs, i.e. beliefs about how the respondent himself feels he ought to behave or about how he feels others, whose opinions he considers important, would expect him to behave. Each respondent scores first his opinion of the importance of different belief statements to the decision under consideration and then of the extent to which he believes the brand under study possesses them. These two scores are multiplied together for each respondent and then summed, again for each respondent, across belief statements. A check is then made to verify that the sum of these products is correlated with the respondent's overall attitude towards the act of purchasing the product measured on a separate set of scales. A similar procedure is adopted with respect to the normative beliefs.

Finally, the relative weight to be assigned to attitudes to the purchasing act and to the normative beliefs is obtained by means of a regression between these two functions with behavioural intention as a dependent variable. It should be noted that this is the first occasion on which a regression is used in the model. The correlations between the attitudes towards the act and the beliefs/importance products are estimated separately and are not multiple correlations derived from a regression equation.

The model, then, does incorporate an internal check on its own validity which avoids the danger that, with a large number of variables, high multiple correlations can be produced merely by capitalizing on random effects.

The trade-off model (conjoint analysis)

The trade-off model[22] seeks to identify the utilities that individuals attach to different product characteristics in such a way that preferences between brands and product concepts can be explained in terms of the sum of these utilities.

This means that like the St James' model it is a 'city block' distance model but it is more realistic in that it enables individuals to differ in the relative importance that they attach to the different dimensions and does not require their utilities to be linear functions of the product characteristics. The model is, therefore, capable of meeting requirements (a), (b) and (d) of the general model which was described earlier (pp. 79 and 80).

Although certain variations in the method are possible and have been shown to produce similar results[23], the distinguishing feature of the trade-off model is that it rest on asking respondents to rank artificial products possessing different combinations of product characteristics. This illustrates the way in which the term model can be misused to describe a particular research technique rather than a view about the way people think or behave.

The NBD/LSD model of consumer purchasing behaviour

This model, which was originally developed by Ehrenberg[24], states that the number of purchasing occasions for an individual within a certain period follows a particular statistical distribution known as the negative binomial distribution. Moreover, where the penetration of the product or brand is relatively low, the distribution of purchasing occasions for buyers of the product follows an even simpler distribution known as the 'logarithmic series distribution'.

From these laws it is possible to derive a number of interesting conclusions about, for example, the number of individuals who, having purchased in one period, will cease to purchase in a following one, or the relative number of buyers to be expected in two periods of differing lengths. The occurrence of these distributions has been observed in a wide range of product fields and in overseas countries as well as in the UK and consequently it can, perhaps, claim to be the best founded of all market research models.

Sales decomposition/recomposition models

These models aim to predict the eventual 'steady state' sales level of a new product when marketed in different ways, and in the use of some of these models, the sales pattern leading up to that steady state. The prediction is derived by making separate estimates of the percentage of those who will have tried the product (i.e. its penetration) up to any given moment and of the extent to which these triers will make further purchases. Estimates of these factors are obtained from real behavioural data in a test market (e.g. Parfitt and Collins[25]), from behaviour in simulated purchase situations (e.g. Yankelovich et al.[26]), or from attitudinal questions using a double interview. A good discussion of these models, together, with an introduction which provides a useful review of 25 years of market modelling is given by Factor and Sampson.[27]

Television viewership

Another model derived by Ehrenberg and Goodhardt[28] is that for the duplication encountered between viewers of two television programs. This states that the number of individuals seeing both programs is (subject to small discrepancies, and with the exception of programs closely following each other or occuring at the same time on the same day of the week) proportional to the product of their ratings. Moreover, the constant of proportionality is dependent only upon the days of the week and channels over which the programs are broadcast. This model aids television media scheduling by enabling duplication factors to be calculated readily.

Chapter 4

Sampling

MARTIN COLLINS

Introduction

This chapter sets out to explain the concepts behind the use of sampling in market research. It outlines some of the main options available to the survey designer and discusses the way sampling is carried out in practice. More complex topics are only introduced, with recommendations for more detailed reading.

If at the end you are still not sure that you understand sampling, you are recommended to read the clear exposition by Ehrenberg[1]; if you want practical advice on how to draw a random sample, try the chapter by Hedges[2]; and if you want to follow the subject through in detail, go first to Kish.[3]

Sampling in market research

Almost all market research studies use sampling – the attempt to learn about some large group, a *population*, by looking at only a small part of it, a *sample*. Only very rarely, mostly in industrial market research, is it possible or sensible to look at the whole population.

Further, the norm in market research is a small sample, of a few hundred or perhaps a thousand. This can worry people. How can we claim to know anything about 40 million highly variable individuals from talking to only 400 or even 4000, of them? But, as will be shown, samples of this size can be surprisingly good at representing large and varied populations. Much larger samples are used in some studies – like the 30,000 interviews per year of the National Readership Survey – but this is only because we want to look separately at small sub-groups within the population. Again, these will be represented by only fairly few interviews.

However, we do need to take care in sampling because we are dealing with a population of consumers that is not just large but is highly variable. When we are dealing with a population that we are prepared to accept is homogeneous, we do not worry about the finer points of sampling. We do not expect a doctor to construct an elaborate design before taking a sample of blood for testing. We accept that whatever comes to hand will give him a good picture of the whole. Only when we are looking at a population that we know or believe to be variable do we begin to worry whether or not we have a *representative* sample.

Some basic concepts

To understand sampling and to use it well, we need to understand two basic concepts: sampling *variability* and sampling *bias*.

Sampling variability

We must lose something when we sample. We can not expect any given sample to be *exactly* representative of the population from which it was drawn. Nor can we expect two samples, independently drawn from the same population, to be exactly alike. So, each time we draw a sample in order to *estimate* a population characteristic, we must expect to get a different answer. And we must expect each of them to be 'wrong' to a degree. This is the concept of *sampling variability* or sampling *error*.

It can be seen through a simple example. Suppose we want to estimate from a sample what percentage of the houses in a particular town have garages. We list the addresses and take a sample of them, using the simplest possible method, as in drawing a lottery. Any answer is *possible*. Purely by chance, we might draw a sample – of almost any size – where *all* the houses had garages or a sample where *none* of the houses had a garage, regardless of the true ownership level in the town. But how likely is this sort of extreme outcome?

The true ownership level, unknown to us, might be 50%. Exactly half of the houses in our town have garages. When we draw one address at random, there is a probability of 1/2 that it will be a house with a garage. Then we draw a second address. Again, the probability is near enough 1/2 that it will have a garage. The probability that *both* our selected addresses have garages is $(1/2) \times (1/2)$, $(1/2)^2$ or one in four. When we draw a third address, the probability that it has a garage is still 1/2 and the probability that all three selections have garages is $(1/2)^3$ or one in eight. And so on. We might draw ten addresses all with garages: the probability of this happening is $(1/2)^{10}$ or about one in a thousand. We might draw twenty addresses all with garages, although the probability of this happening is only $(1/2)^{20}$ or about one in a million.

This shows that extreme outcomes can happen. (And, of course, the one in a million event might happen to you the first time you try it. Worse, it might happen the next time too!) But it also shows that those extreme errors are very unlikely – even with tiny samples. And they become more and more unlikely as we take larger and larger samples.

The sampling distribution

Here, where we know so much about our hypothetical town, we can assign probabilities to extreme outcomes like finding all or none with garages in a sample of ten households. We can go further and calculate the probability of finding 9 out of 10 with garages, 8 out of 10, and so on:

Number with garage	Probability of result
10 out of 10	0.001
9	0.010
8	0.044
7	0.117
6	0.205
5	0.246
4	0.205
3	0.117
2	0.044
1	0.010
0 out of 10	0.001

This is the *sampling distribution*: the pattern of all the results we could get when drawing samples of ten addresses from this particular population. It shows that we are fairly unlikely in a single sample to get the answer – which we know to be 50% – exactly right. The probability of drawing a sample where 5 out of 10 houses have a garage is 0.246 or about one in four. If we were to repeat our sampling process (i.e. picking a sample of houses) one thousand independent times, we could expect to get the answer of 50% in just 246 of these samples. But the distribution also shows that we are quite likely to get an answer close to the truth. The probability of a single sample of ten addresses including 4, 5 or 6 with garages is 0.656 (0.205 + 0.246 + 0.205), or about two in three. So, two-thirds of possible samples would yield estimates of garage-ownership between 40% and 60%. And this is with only ten addresses in a sample. We have already seen that extreme errors become less likely when we take larger samples. It follows that a larger sample is more likely to give an answer close to the truth.

So one major determinant of how accurate a sample estimate will be is the *size* of the sample on which it is based.

Variability in the population

In the example above the population of addresses is as variable as it can be – half have garages, half do not. Suppose we look at another characteristic, say ownership of double garages, which might be only 10%. Here we have far less variability. Most of the addresses are the same; they do not have double garages.

Intuitively we expect sampling in these circumstances to yield better estimates because we are dealing with a more homogeneous population. This can be shown to be the case. The probability of our drawing ten addresses all with double garages is tiny: $(1/10)^{10}$ or about one in ten billion. The probability of the other extreme, ten addresses none of which have double garages, is much higher: $(9/10)^{10}$ or about one in three. But this answer is close to the truth. The probability of our drawing ten addresses with 0, 1 or 2 double garages among them (i.e., estimating ownership at 20% or less) is as high as 0.93. That is, we have a 93% chance of drawing a sample this close to the truth.

So, the second major determinant of sample accuracy is the amount of *variability in the population*.

Estimating the likely error

These simple examples show that the likely error in a sample estimate – the probability of its being wrong by some stated amount – depends on two factors: the size of the sample and the variability of the population from which it was drawn. This confirms the intuitively obvious.

In those examples we could *calculate* the probability of an error of a given size. We could define the sampling distribution – the range of *possible* sample estimates – from which any single sample estimate would be drawn. But this depended on our knowing in advance the true incidence in the population of the attribute we were examining: ownership of garages, or of double garages. In reality we will not know the answer: why would we be doing the survey? Then we turn to the theory of sampling to help us to *estimate* the likely error in a survey result.

We conduct a single survey among, say, 100 households and find that 50% of them have a particular characteristic. We know this is only an estimate of the incidence of that characteristic in the population from which our sample was drawn. We know it is unlikely to be exactly right and we know that a different sample of 100 households would almost certainly have yielded a somewhat different estimate, perhaps 48%, 52% or even 70%.

What we have is a single example drawn from a sampling distribution. It is not likely to be exactly correct, is likely to be close to the truth, but has some chance, however small, of being wildly wrong. What we need to establish is, *which* sampling distribution is our result likely to have come from?

Theory tells us first where the sampling distribution is centred: what is its average; what is the *expected* outcome of repeated drawings from the distribution. As in the distribution calculated above for 50% garage-ownership, the likely errors in sample estimates are unsystematic. They show a pattern of scatter *around the true value*. The central point of the sampling distribution *is* the truth.

This can be checked in the tabulated example. The probabilities show that if we were to repeat the process of drawing ten addresses 1,000 different times we would expect to get one sample with 100% ownership, 10 samples with 90% ownership, 44 with 80% ownership, and so on. The average of the 1,000 different sample estimates would be 50%, the true value in the population. This average of the sampling distribution is called the *expected outcome* of the particular process.

So the sampling distribution from which our single sample of 100 has emerged is centred at – has a mean or an average equal to – the true value in the population. Theory tells us next about the *shape* of the sampling distribution. Provided we are talking about sample sizes of about 50 or more, it will be a distribution of a particular shape, called the *Normal* distribution. This will be true regardless of the distribution in the population of the variable we are investigating.

'Normal' is a name given to a distribution of a particular shape: symmetrical and bell-shaped, with more of its values close to its central point – its mean or average. This central point we know to be the truth, the population value. So this aspect of the theory (the 'Central Limit Theorem') formalises what we have already established, that we are likely to obtain an answer close to the truth.

The precise form of a Normal distribution is fully defined by just two parameters: its mean and its standard deviation (a measure of the amount of scatter in the individual values making up the distribution). Once we know these two parameters we can calculate, or look up in tables, exactly what proportion of the values in the distribution lie between any two points. For example, the tables tell us:

that 68% of the values will be within one standard deviation either side of the mean;
that 90% will be within about 1⅔ standard deviations of the mean;
that 95% will be within 2 standard deviations of the mean; and
that 99% will lie within about 2½ standard deviations of the mean.

The fact that the sampling distribution will be of this form is a very powerful finding. It will be seen to be the basis of our ability to estimate the likely error in a single sample estimate. To use the result, however, we need to know, or at least to estimate, the standard deviation of the distribution.

The standard deviation of the sampling distribution is given the special name of the *standard error*, since it says something about the likely error in a sample estimate. Where we are estimating a proportion or a percentage having a particular attribute, as in the earlier examples, the size of the standard error will depend on just two factors, our sample size and the incidence of the attribute. The latter, of course, we do not know but theory allows us to fall back on the simple expedient of using our sample value as an estimate of it.

The calculation is simple. Where p is our sample estimate of the percentage having the attribute and n is our sample size, the standard error of our estimate is

$$S.E. (p) = \sqrt{\left[\frac{p(100-p)}{n}\right]}$$

Often the value q is used to denote the completement of p – the percentage *not* having the attribute, and we have

$$S.E. (p) = \sqrt{\left(\frac{p \cdot q}{n}\right)}$$

or, in words, 'root pq over n', the familiar cry of the survey statistician.

If, then, a sample of 100 households yields an estimate that $p=50\%$ have a particular attribute, we can calculate

$$S.E. (p) = \sqrt{\left(\frac{50 \times 50}{100}\right)} = 5\%$$

This seems to complete the picture. We know that our estimate $p=50\%$ is drawn from a sampling distribution that is Normal in shape, whose mean is the true value in the population (say π) and whose standard deviation is 5%. Using the results drawn from tabulations of the Normal distribution we can say that 68% of the values in the sampling distribution, i.e. 68% of the sample estimates we might get, lie within five percentage points of the truth; or that 95% of them lie within ten percentage points (twice the standard error) of the truth. But still we do not know the truth!

Confidence limits

Our best, indeed our only, point-estimate of π, the percentage with the attribute in the population, is p, our sample estimate. But we know that π is unlikely to be *exactly* equal to p. We need to qualify our estimate by saying how far π might be from our estimate.

We know that 95% of all possible samples of 100 drawn from the sampling distribution centred on the unknown π will be within two standard errors of π (within 10 percentage points in this case). If our sample is one of those 95%, our estimate p will not differ from π by more than ten percentage points. So, at one extreme our estimate $p=50\%$ *could* have come from a sampling distribution centred on $\pi=40\%$. At the other extreme, it could have come from a sampling distribution centred on $\pi=60\%$.

Of course, our sample estimate may not come from the central 95% of an unknown sampling distribution. It might be an outlying value drawn from some other distribution where π is 30%, 70% or even 90%. The statement that π lies somewhere between 40% and 60% will only be true for 95% of all possible samples. So we call these two figures our 95% *confidence limits* and the space between them the 95% confidence *interval*.

Not only can we be 95% confident that π lies somewhere in this range, but also the 'humped' shape of the Normal distribution means that it is likely to be somewhere in the centre of the range. But the probability of this is rather less than 95%.

We can then adopt different levels of confidence. If we are prepared to accept a greater risk that our statement might be wrong we can quote a smaller range:

we can be 90% confident that π is between about 42% and 58% (i.e. within $1^2/_3$ standard errors of our estimate p);
we can be 68% (or about 70%) confident that π is between 45% and 55% (i.e. within 1 standard error of our estimate p).

These results show that when we halve the size of the confidence interval we do *not* double the risk of the population value lying outside that interval. This is because the population value is always likely to lie towards the centre of the interval. It is this result that underlies the fallacious statement we hear so often that 'samples tend to be more accurate than theory suggests'. It may also justify a less conservative approach than the norm of quoting the 95% confidence limits when qualifying a sample estimate. Most decisions are taken with less than 95% confidence and, if we can similarly accept less certainty, we can quote an appreciably smaller range.

Increasing the sample size
If we increase our sample size we expect our estimate to be more accurate. So the confidence interval, the range between our lower and upper confidence limits (say the 95% limits), will be smaller. For example, if our estimate of $p=50\%$ comes from a sample of $n=400$

$$\text{S.E. }(p) = \sqrt{\left(\frac{50 \times 50}{400}\right)} = 2\tfrac{1}{2}\%$$

95% confidence limits: $\pi: = 45\%$ to 55%

Note that to halve the 95% confidence interval we have had to *quadruple* the sample size.

The population size

The calculations above make no reference to the size of the population from which our samples are drawn. This is because, for most practical purposes, the quality of our estimates depends on the *size* of the sample, not on the proportion of the population included in it, the *sampling fraction*.

Only when our sampling fraction is large, say 1/10 or more, is it worth taking into account the size of the population. This we do by multiplying our standard error by a factor called the *finite population correction*

$$\sqrt{(1 - n/N)},$$

where n is our sample size and N is the population size.

This means that a sample of a given size will, other things being equal, perform a better job when it is drawn from a small population. But the effect is trivial in nearly all consumer market research surveys. Hence, we ignore it.

Other sample estimates

The discussion above has concentrated on the use of samples to estimate the percentage having a particular attribute because this is what most market research surveys do. This is only a particular form of the task of estimating the mean or average for any type of variable. The same theory will apply when we are trying to estimate the average value of a variable like age, height, income or the number of packets of an item bought by a householder. Only the calculations will look different.

We might, for example, estimate from a sample of 400 households that the average household bought 4.2 packets of washing powder in a three-month period. Call this estimate m. It is our estimate of the true average in the population, μ. In order to establish confidence limits for the population value μ we need to estimate the standard error of our estimate

$$\text{S.E. } (m) = \sqrt{\frac{\Sigma(x_i - m)^2}{n(n-1)}}$$

where

$$\Sigma(x_i - m)^2 = (X_1 - m)^2 + (X_2 - m)^2 + \ldots + (X_i - m)^2 + \ldots + (X_n - m)^2$$

and X_1 is the number of packets bought by household 1, X_2 the number bought by household 2, and so on.

It may be computationally easier to use an alternative form

$$\text{S.E. } (m) = \sqrt{\left\{\frac{1}{n}\Sigma x_i^2 - m^2\right\} \bigg/ n}$$

where $\Sigma x_i^2 = X_1^2 + X_2^2 + \ldots + X_i^2 + \ldots X_n^2$.

Alternatively, a computer or calculator may be used to calculate the standard deviation S of the sample values of X. Then

$$\text{S.E. } (m) = \frac{S}{\sqrt{n}}$$

Returning to our washing powder example, we might find that the standard deviation of the distribution of number of packets bought in our sample is 6 packets. The standard error of our estimate of the average number bought is (6/20), i.e. 0.3 packets. Then, using the same arguments as before:

we can be 95% confident that the average in the population μ is between $(m - 2 \text{ S.E.})$ and $(m + 2 \text{ S.E.})$, i.e. between 3.6 and 4.8;
we can be 68% confident that μ lies between 3.9 and 4.5.

(At this point, you may wish to check that the calculations given earlier for estimates of percentages are only a special case of the more general calculations given here. This you can do by assigning the value of 1 to the variable X for each of the $(n \times p)$ households with the attribute and the value of 0 to the variable X for each of the $(n \times q)$ households without the attribute.)

The theory of sampling and the setting of confidence limits extends from the estimation of averages of any kind, to estimates of totals, trends, correlation coefficients, and beyond. The only special calculation in each case is the formula needed to estimate the standard error. Such calculations are, however, beyond the scope of this chapter.

Sampling bias

We turn now to the second basic concept of sampling theory: sampling bias. This is a potential source of error in sample estimates that is *not* taken into account when we calculate confidence limits around our estimates. In many ways it is a simpler concept than that of sampling variability. But it is far more difficult to deal with. As we have seen, the problem of variability can always be reduced by increasing our sample size. The same is not true of bias. At the same time, it is potentially far more important. Almost without exception, whenever sample estimates have been shown to be wildly wrong – when a check against the true population value has become possible – the problem has been attributed to some form of bias.

Sampling bias can be defined simply in the context of what has gone before. It exists when the central point of the sampling distribution, the expected outcome of using the particular sampling process, is *not* equal to the true value in the population. Then, we can still define the likelihood of our sample estimate deviating in an unsystematic way from a central point.

But that central point is not the population value we are trying to estimate.

Any selection process that favours some members of a population at the expense of others is liable to introduce bias. If the two groups, the over-represented and the under-represented, differ in terms of the characteristic we are studying, bias will exist. Not only is a single application of the selection process likely to yield an incorrect estimate but also the *expected* outcome of using the process is an incorrect estimate.

Incomplete coverage
The problem can arise from a variety of sources. The list from which we are sampling may be incomplete. So, in the terms of one of our earlier examples, it may be that the majority of double garages in the town belong to newly built executive houses, many of which, unknown to us, have been omitted from the list (or *sampling frame*). We may be sampling from a list where only 5% of addresses have a double garage, compared with 10% in the town as a whole. Then, the expected outcome of sampling from our list – the central point around which individual sample estimates will vary – is an estimate of 5% ownership. The difference between this expected outcome and the true value is the bias arising from our use of an incomplete sampling frame. (Given our list was complete we might still, purely by chance, draw a sample that under-represented executive houses. This is not bias, although many would lazily say we have a 'biased' sample. It is just one aspect of sampling variability.)

Non-response
Perhaps the most important potential source of bias in any sample survey is the problem of non-response, where some units selected for the sample are never contacted or refuse to take part in the survey. Non-response will exist in even the best conducted surveys – no contact will be made with 10% or so of the sampled units despite all our efforts and anything from 5% to 20% will refuse to take part. If these non-responding groups differ from the respondents in terms of the characteristic we are trying to estimate our method will be biased. (In many, probably most, market research surveys, this problem is concealed through the use of sampling methods, like quota sampling, that involve no prior selection into the sample. This will be discussed later in the chapter.)

Deliberate over-representation
Sometimes sampling schemes will be designed deliberately to over-represent certain sub-groups of the population, most often to allow separate examination of those sub-groups. Subsequently, the data collected from the over-represented groups will be down-weighted in producing overall estimates. This approach, another point to be discussed further, can be highly effective. But it depends on a potentially biasing action at the stage

of sample selection being offset by an 'unbiasing' action at the stage of analysis and inference. The difficulty with *most* potential sources of bias is that we do not know what effect they have had and, therefore, we can not correct for them. (We do not, for example, have information from non-respondents that allows us to assess whether or not they are different from respondents in terms of the variables we are studying.)

This is what most clearly differentiates sampling bias from sampling variability. The latter, as we have seen, can be studied from the results of just one sample and, as we will see, can be reduced through sample design (or, in the last resort, through an increase in our sample size). A sampling bias, in contrast, can not be controlled or reduced. If we know it has been introduced and we understand its form we can take corrective action to remove it and produce unbiased estimates. Otherwise, we can only live in fear of its possible existence. For this reason, the task of designing a sample can be defined as using the available resources to minimize the *size* of unsystematic errors arising from variability and to minimize the *risk* of systematic errors arising from bias. We can not undertake to minimize the size of the latter because they are, by definition, either zero or unknown.

Sample design strategy

The theory of sampling outlined above underlies the practice of sampling in market research. But this practice often has to take into account a number of factors that lead away from the simple form of random sampling (as in a lottery) and even, in many cases, away from the whole principle of random sampling. Thus the survey designer may be concerned not only with the accuracy of his sample estimates but also with cost, speed, practicality or credibility. Often these objectives and constraints will conflict and trade-off will be needed.

Even 'accuracy' may subsume different considerations. The desire to minimize the variability of estimates (unsystematic errors) may conflict with the desire to avoid the risk of bias (systematic errors). Interest may be not only in estimates for a total population but also in estimates for sub-groups. Methods for improving sub-group estimates will often yield less good total estimates. Similarly, interest may extend beyond simple estimates of means, percentages or totals into estimates of relationships or trends.

These are highly varied requirements, to which there will rarely be an optimal solution. The survey designer will trade-off the requirements – rarely in any objective way – in deciding how to use a number of design options.

Defining the survey population

The purpose of a sample survey is to learn about a population. We have no real interest in the sample itself. The theory underlying sample-based inference assumes random (or 'probability') sampling among the whole population. This in turn requires that every member of the population has an equal chance of contributing to the sample estimate. This does not necessarily mean that every member of the population has an equal chance of selection (see the comments below on 'Weighting'). But it does demand that every member of the population has a *known* probability of selection into the sample. Otherwise, we risk bias. (As will be discussed, this is the risk involved in using non-random, e.g. quota, sampling. People have varying probabilities of entering the sample. And, because these probabilities are *unknown*, we can not apply correction factors.)

This requirement will not always be easy to meet. If we use the Registers of Electors as a sampling frame of addresses, we know that some are missing. While procedures exist for correcting these omissions, they are imperfect, expensive and time-consuming. The more usual solution is to ignore the problem. This is equivalent to redefining the coverage of a survey, the *survey population*, as being only addresses appearing in the registers. (Procedures for sampling from the Registers of Electors are given by Hedges.[2])

It is common for surveys to exclude outlying and sparsely populated parts of a country, in Britain usually the counties of Scotland north of the Caledonian Canal. Again the survey population is being redefined.

When results are needed in a hurry, we may decide to conduct a survey using telephone interviewing. Then the sample can only cover telephone-owning households and that is the population to which we can make inferences. We may use weighting or some other process to extrapolate our results to the larger population of all households. But we should be aware that we are moving out of the realms of simple inference from sample to population.

Stratification

As we have seen earlier, a single sample is unlikely to be an exact model of a population. Sampling variability will mean that some differences will exist, and they could be large. *Stratification* is a method designed to reduce this variability. It sets out to ensure that the sample matches the population in some important respects. By ensuring that different sections of the population, or strata (e.g. regions or age groups), are correctly represented in a sample, stratification aims to reduce the impact of sampling variability. If it works, it yields estimates with smaller standard errors than would emerge from an unstratified sample. (See Kish[3] for the formula.)

The success of this strategy depends upon the relevance of the stratification factor(s) employed. The object is to divide the total population into strata that differ markedly in respect of the characteristics measured in the survey. *Within* each stratum, we seek as much homogeneity as possible in terms of the same characteristics.

While the strategy appears to have great potential, its value in consumer surveys is usually small. This is because we are usually limited to area-based stratifications through our lack of prior knowledge about individuals. In the typical consumer survey we would probably like to stratify our sample in terms of age and/or social class. But the lists available to us do not label individuals in these terms. The lists usually tell us where people live. We are forced back to stratifying in terms of *area* profiles of age or social class. Unfortunately, differences between areas are usually quite small and correlations with our survey measurements rather weak. The result is that stratification will rarely improve the precision of random sample estimates by more than about 10%. Often the only advantage is cosmetic, increasing the credibility of a survey: who is going to believe the results of a sample that can be seen to be out of line with the regional distribution of the population? Fortunately, this cosmetic advantage is usually gained at virtually no cost.

The weakness of stratification in consumer surveys has led to the development of two alternatives. The first is the process of *post-stratification*. If we can not ensure that we have the correct profile when we select people into our sample we can at least correct any faults at the analysis stage by weighting our data. An example of the use of this procedure is the National Readership Survey.[4]

Post-stratification is soundly based in theory when it is applied in order to correct for chance deviations arising from sampling variability. Usually, however, it is used to correct also for the effects of varying levels of non-response between different sub-groups of the population. Then the procedure – best called in these circumstances, *cell-weighting* or *adjustment* – rests on the untested assumption that those who do respond can adequately represent those members of the same sub-group who do not respond.

A similar assumption underlies the second development, *quota-sampling*. Here there is no pre-selection of individuals. A quota of interviews is required in a particular (e.g. age × social class) cell and interviewers are left to find people who fit the specification. The assumption here is that, within a cell, all population members are fully exchangeable, that they do not differ in terms of the survey variables other than in a completely random way. We will return to discussion of quota sampling in a later section.

Multi-stage sampling (or 'Clustering')

In a personal interview survey we usually can not afford to have the interviewing spread throughout the country. In order to reduce travelling time and cost we 'cluster' our interviews into a limited number of areas: constituencies, polling districts or smaller areas. A sample of 1000 households, for example, might typically be spread over 30–40 polling districts. This procedure will usually reduce the precision of the sample estimates compared with an unclustered, 'single-stage' sample of the same size. This loss of precision will be the price to be paid for the reduction of travelling costs. (In postal or telephone surveys there is no call for interviewers to travel between addresses and the sample can, in principle, be spread throughout the population. In practice, however, multi-stage sampling is generally used for such surveys simply because it makes the task of sample *selection* easier and less costly.)

The effect of clustering the sample will depend upon two factors: the relative homogeneity of the members of each cluster and the number of interviews taken in each cluster. Homogeneity will arise when people living in a particular area are relatively similar in respect of the variable we are examining. This will be the case for many class-related variables. For example, it is known to be high in the case of home-ownership. It will not be the case for well-distributed variables (e.g. age or sex) and for most attitudinal variables. The second factor, the number of interviews taken in each cluster, is determined by the survey designer.

The relative homogeneity of the cluster members is most often summarized by a statistic called the *intra-cluster correlation coefficient* (ρ). (See the article by Harris[5] for computational details.) The value of ρ will vary from one survey question to another and, often, from one response category to another within a single question. It will usually be a very small quantity: typically 0.02 or less. But it can be much higher, around 0.2 or higher, for variables like household tenure.

Even when a variable is not *actually* distributed unevenly across the clusters it can *appear* to be so. It is normal for the workload in an area to be assigned to a single interviewer. This interviewer may introduce a degree of artificial similarity to the answers given by people in the area, through a particular way of asking the question or of interpreting the answer. (See Collins and Butcher[6] for discussion of this effect.) Because of this possibility it is unwise to assume that ρ will be less than about 0.02 for *any* survey variable.

There is so far little conclusive evidence as to what happens to the value of ρ as the clustering is 'tightened' to smaller geographical areas. It seems that a move from the Parliamentary ward to the polling district as the area of concentration has relatively little effect, but Harris[5] shows that values can be higher when clustering is very tight, as in samples where contact is attempted at every 5th or every 10th address from a random starting point.

Even quite small values of ρ – where there is little homogeneity within an area – can have a marked impact on the precision of sample estimates. This is because of the effect of the number of interviews taken in each area. The standard error of an estimate will be increased by the multiplying factor

$$\sqrt{[1+\rho(b-1)]}$$

where b is the average number of interviews conducted in each area.

So, for a quite small value of ρ of about 0.02, the standard error will be multiplied by about

1.2 if 20 interviews are taken in each area;
1.25 if 30 interviews are taken in each area;
1.33 if 40 interviews are taken in each area.

For a relatively high, but by no means exceptional, value of ρ of about 0.1, the standard error will be multiplied by about

1.7 if 20 interviews are taken in each area;
2.0 if 30 interviews are taken in each area;
2.2 if 40 interviews are taken in each area.

(A table of such effects is given by Collins and Goodhart[7] in an article that discusses the topic in more detail.)

The design factor

The multipliers of the standard error shown above are examples of *design factors*. As the name suggests they reflect the impact of introducing elements of sample design that depart from the simple random sampling format of a lottery. Such a factor can be used to summarize all the elements of sample design, both the detrimental effects of an element like clustering and the beneficial effects of an element like stratification.

Design factors, despite their potential significance, tend to be ignored in market research (and, indeed, in much academic and government research). This is because they are laborious to calculate, especially since the factor has to be calculated for every response category of every question. We can not say simply that a sample design has a design factor of a particular size; the factor will depend on the variable being considered. It is not realistic to recommend the calculation of design factors at this level, at least until adequate computer programs become widely available. The recommendation would be more reasonable in the case of a sample design and a set of questions used on a regular basis. More generally, it will be wise to make some arbitrary allowance for the effect of clustering by assuming that $\rho = 0.02$ for attitude and opinion questions or for behavioural questions where no marked social-class correlation is expected, and that $\rho = 0.1$ for questions expected to be closely correlated with social class. Then, the two sets of design factors given in the illustration above can be applied, according to the number of interviews taken in each cluster.

For example, if we have a sample of $n = 1000$ distributed over 50 areas (i.e. $b = 20$), and are looking at a response to an attitude question where 50% agreed with a statement:

$$\text{S.E. } (p) \text{ under simple random sampling} = \sqrt{\left(\frac{50 \times 50}{1000}\right)} = 1.6$$

$$\text{Design factor} = \sqrt{[1 + \rho(b-1)]} = \sqrt{1 + (0.02)(19)} = 1.2$$

$$\textit{True S.E. } (p) = 1.6 \times 1.2 = 1.9$$

$$95\% \textit{ confidence limits} = 46.2 \textit{ to } 53.8.$$

Effective sample size

When we begin to trade off cost savings against loss of accuracy, as in the case of clustering, we need a measure of cost-effectiveness. This is available in the form of a calculation of *effective sample size*.

This is the size of simple random sample that would yield the same standard error as our designed sample. It is equal to our actual sample size n, divided by the square of the design factor (usually known as the *design effect*). So, in the example just used:

$$\text{Design effect} = (\text{design factor})^2 = (1.2)^2 = 1.4$$

$$\text{Effective sample size} = n/1.4 = 700$$

We can then ask the question: which is cheaper to conduct – our clustered sample of 1,000 or an unclustered sample of 700, each of which would give us the same degree of precision? Similarly, we can compare our sample with other designs involving different degrees of clustering. A sample of 1000 spread over 100 areas, for the same variable, would have a design factor of only about 1.1, and our effective sample size would be about 850. It yields greater precision, but presumably at greater cost. If we now divide the total cost of the survey by the effective sample size for each design we have a figure for *cost per effective interview*. In this particular example, the design using 50 clusters of 20 would need to be about 20% cheaper than the 100 × 10 design for its adoption to be justified.

Again, we can only expect such calculations to be performed for survey designs and survey questions in regular use. In their absence, it is not possible to give firm rules about maximum cluster sizes. We can say, however, that it will rarely be cost-effective to conduct more than 25 to 30 interviews in each cluster (even less if very tight clustering is involved). One important exception arises when the researcher has little or no interest in total sample figures but will focus on sub-group figures only. Then the same size limit can be applied in respect of the largest sub-group.

Selection of sampling points

In the examples discussed above it was assumed that nearly equal numbers of interviews would be taken in each cluster (or at each 'sampling point'). This is usually the case, in the interests of administrative convenience and because it yields marginally better estimates. The adoption of this simplification means that we have to allow for the possibility that the areas represented by each group of interviews will vary in size. Then people living in large areas will have a lower probability of selection into our sample than people living in small areas.

This is avoided by the use, in selecting our sampling points, of sampling with *probability proportional to size*. Larger areas are given a higher probability of selection as sampling points, off-setting the lower probability of selection arising for individuals within them. (The method of achieving this is described by Hedges.[2])

Note

It is, perhaps, worthwhile here to stress the difference between stratification and multi-stage sampling. In stratification we divide the population into strata and then represent *each* of the strata in our sample. Then, homogeneity *within strata* is beneficial. In multi-stage sampling we divide the population into clusters and then represent only *some* of the clusters in our sample. Then, homogeneity *within clusters* is damaging.

Weighting

Samples are sometimes drawn in such a way that differential weights need to be applied in order to yield unbiased estimates. For example, a sub-group of special interest might be over-represented in the sample, rather than increasing the total sample size.

Except in certain cases that arise comparatively rarely in consumer research, the effect of such weighting will be to reduce the precision of the total sample estimates compared with an unweighted sample of the same size. (A formula for calculating the effect, under simple assumptions, is given in the article by Conway[8].)

The need for a design involving weighting should always be questioned closely and high relative weights should be avoided. A reasonable rule of thumb would be to avoid designs where the ratio of the largest to the smallest weighting factor exceeds 5 or 6.

Two exceptions should be noted here. For some problems it can be more efficient to over-represent parts of a population because they are more variable. This is common in industrial market research where organizations can be selected with probability proportional to some measure of their size, corrective weights being applied at the analysis stage in producing total industry statistics. This method is rarely used in consumer research. A more common exception in the latter is the survey aimed only or overwhelmingly at studying sub-groups. Then there is little or no interest in the total sample estimate and its lower precision is of little concern.

True sampling variability

The use of a design factor to inflate our estimate of the standard error of a survey measure acknowledges that we do not use simple random sampling. An approach has been suggested that will allow us to make an arbitrary allowance for this. To do any more requires that we directly estimate the *true* variability of our survey estimates. This topic is too advanced to be dealt with in detail here but an introduction may be helpful.

As described earlier, the likely error of a sample estimate depends on the scatter of the sampling distribution from which it was drawn. This distribution describes the extent to which different samples, drawn in the same way from the same population, are likely to yield different estimates. The scatter of the distribution could be established if we actually repeated the sampling process a large number of times, and plotted the results: what an experimenter would call '*replication*'.

Given that we are unwilling to do this, we may turn to simulation. One approach would be to take our sample of, say, 1,000 in 50 clusters of 20 and divide it at random into two halves, each containing 25 clusters of 20. (It is important to retain the same degree of clustering.) Then we have two sample estimates. We could then repeat the process with a different random split, yielding two more estimates. And so on. In time we will produce a picture of the amount of variability in estimates based on samples of 500 using our design. A simple adjustment for sample size will produce an estimate of the variability attached to our estimate.

This simplified description of replication is intended only to show that we can produce estimates of the likely error in *any* survey estimate. For example, we could evaluate a complex weighted estimate based on a stratified multi-stage sample, even a quota sample. Again, however, this is unlikely to be done for one-off surveys. It is laborious and anyway tells us only about the likely effects of sampling variability. We are still left with making a subjective estimate of the possible effects of bias. For more detail of the approach the reader is referred to advanced texts, e.g. Kish.[3]

Quota sampling

Thus far the discussion has been of random or probability sampling, where the final selection of sample members is deliberately handed over to chance in order to avoid subjective bias. Virtually all academic and public sector surveys, and many large commercial surveys, use such methods. The majority of commercial surveys, however, do not; instead they use quota sampling.

The method

Instead of an interviewer being issued with a pre-selected list of sample members, he or she is issued with an assignment in the form of a quota. The requirement might, for example, be to interview 40 housewives:

  20 of them aged under 45;
  20 aged 45 or over;
  15 in the ABC1 social grades;
  25 in the C2DE social grades.

In this case age and social grade are the quota controls and they are set in parallel. Alternatively, the two control variables can be interlaced or interlocked:

	ABC1	C2DE
Under 45	9	11
45 or over	6	14

In this way the structure of the sample is fixed in certain important respects but the final selection of individuals is left to the interviewer.

The underlying assumption

Quota sampling has its roots in the recognition that a sample selected at random may not match the population in some terms. Indeed, some differences are almost certain to arise from sampling variability. Stratification, the tool designed to prevent such deviations, is unable to cope because of our lack of information at the selection stage.

The assumption underlying quota sampling is that the control variables account for all the *systematic* variation in the population in terms of the survey variables. It does not require total homogeneity within each cell of the sample, but it does assume that any residual variation between people in a cell is *random*. Then, it will not matter how the individuals are chosen. (This is comparable to drawing a card from a pack 'at random'. The random element is introduced by shuffling the pack into a random order, after which any card, even the top card, will be a random selection.) The assumption is almost certainly unfounded: a very brief search will reveal, for any survey variable, a correlate (i.e. systematic variation) not included among the control variables.

Control variables

The quota control variables must be chosen to maximize the amount of variability between cells of the sample and minimize residual variability within cells. Thus, the requirements are as for effective stratification factors.

The most commonly used control variables are sex, age and social grade. Among women, it is common to control for working status and/or family size and composition. Among men, there may be controls on type of employment, e.g. on how many must work in manufacturing industry. More recent developments include the use of behavioural or attitudinal variables as controls, and a control on the number of interviews to be conducted outside working hours (i.e. evenings and weekends).

One control variable that has always caused concern is social grade. This involves asking possibly sensitive questions about the occupation of the 'head of the household' at the start of the interview. The classification is also highly error-prone, especially when shortened questioning approaches are used. A recent development has been increased use of 'random location' or 'random route' sampling in place of the control on social grade. The interviewer is given an address at which to start work, chosen at random from a heavily stratified list (e.g. using the ACORN classification). He or she is then instructed to work within a set distance from that address or to follow a random route from it, calling at, say, every fifth address. Quota controls are then set in terms of more straightforward variables like sex or age and, usually, in terms of the time of day at which interviews are to be conducted. (This method has long been popular in the USA, where quotas are filled within randomly selected city-blocks. It is sometimes misleadingly called 'quasi-random'sampling.) The method has inevitable limitations. If the interviewer works over a fairly large area, the stratifying power of the initial selection soon breaks down. If the work is highly concentrated, there will be high clustering effects.

The choice of control variables involves a compromise between the desire to minimize within-cell variation – leading to more control and more complex interlacing – and the practicability of the interviewer's task. As in stratification, the statistician's recommendation would be to increase the *number* of control variables used rather than the complexity or detail of each.

In the final analysis, it has to be admitted that quota sample designs rest in experience and inspiration rather than in prior statistical analysis of potential control variables. Above all, habit plays a major part: different survey agencies, and sometimes different researchers within them, have their own established ways of working.

Cost

The desire to use the potential of stratification, which would anyway be better met by the use of post-stratification, is not the main reason why quota sampling is so widespread. Again, habit is a major determinant, to the extent that many market researchers will never have come across a random sample. But the main arguments in favour of the approach are in terms of time and cost.

The time consideration is a simple one. A random sample requires time for sample selection. And interviewers must be given an assignment period long enough to make contact with most of the selected people. This will usually be more than a week. A quota sample, in contrast, can be set up instantly, and the interviewer's assignment period can be of only two or three days. Quota sampling is thus better placed to answer demands for quick results. This can be important, for example in studying immediate recall of, or reaction to, an event or a stimulus (such as a specific broadcast programme or commercial).

The cost consideration is rather more complex, when we begin to take into account cost-effectiveness, as discussed in the previous section. A quota sample survey will be cheaper than a similarly sized random sample. Travelling expenses and time are much lower since the interviewer does not have to search for desginated people. A typical day's work by an interviewer (currently costed at around £ 45–50) will yield 10, 12 or even 15 interviews in a quota sample survey, compared with 4,5 or at best 6 interviews in a random sample survey. Total survey costs for a quota sample will be only about 60–70% of those for a similarly sized random sample.

For some survey variables the typical quota controls of sex, age and social class are highly effective stratifiers. By the time these variables have been taken into account, most of the variation between individuals has been explained. Then a quota sample might be expected to yield estimates with lower sampling variability than those yielded by a weakly stratified random sample of the same size. Thus, the standard error and the confidence interval of the quota sample estimates will be smaller. Empirical evidence (e.g. Moser and Stuart[9]) suggests, however, that this does not happen: that the best to be expected is a quota sample estimate *equal* in precision to a random sample estimate.

This disappointing result has four explanations. Two concern the interviewer. There is a risk of systematic differences between interviewers in terms of their preferred interviewees. And there will be both systematic and haphazard errors in interpreting and applying the quota controls. The other two factors concern survey design. The interviewer is normally allowed to work within a very small area, increasing the risk of clustering effects. And her assignment is usually quite large, compounding the problem.

More generally, the quota controls do not work this well. There have been few rigorous comparisons of quota and random sampling (and even those are old results, possibly outdated by recent developments). But the evidence points to the need for careful appraisal of the value of quota sampling. The standard error of a typical quota sample estimate may well be about 1½ times as large as that of a multi-stage random sample estimate (using the same sample size), higher if the quota controls are not rigorous, lower it they are. This would imply that the total survey costs of a quota sample would need to be only about *half* those of a random sample survey of the same size.

This sort of cost differential may well apply, especially when the survey is to be conducted among a difficult-to-find minority population or when a sub-group is required to be heavily over-represented. With random sampling either of these requirements will call for an expensive screening operation, many contacts being with ineligible people. Even here, however, it should be remembered that researchers working in areas where random sampling is a requirement have developed highly efficient approaches to screening. (See Kish[3]). The cost-effectiveness of the quota sampling approach is open to considerable doubt.

The cost differential between random and quota sampling may well be even less for telephone interview surveys. The telephone is particularly suited to random sampling since repeated calls can be made at very little cost in order to contact selected respondents. In practice, however, much telephone research uses a form of quota sampling. Often this is because a very rapid turn-round is required, telephone interviewing being especially suited to fast-response research (e.g. recall of advertising the day after the transmission). Often, though, it arises simply from unfamiliarity with anything other than quota sampling.

Quota sampling is also used in telephone surveys in attempts to get round the major problem of uneven telephone penetration. Telephones are less common among some groups in the population, especially the less affluent and the elderly. So, researchers design quota samples of telephone owners to match the demographic characteristics of the total population. As with so much else in sampling practice, this tactic depends on the assumption that those people with given characteristics who *are* covered do not differ in terms of the survey topic from those with the same characteristics who are *not* covered. For some topics this assumption will be valid, for others it will not. Often, it will simply be untested. The approach can not be recommended; it will usually be wiser to acknowledge that a sample provides only coverage of the telephone-owning majority.

Sampling bias

Quota sampling and other non-random sampling methods are rejected by researchers whose findings will be the subject of open discussion (academics, government and many operators of syndicated or industry surveys). This is not because of the doubts about cost-effectiveness but because of the fear of bias.

However rigorous and well-founded the quota controls, the final selection lies with the interviewer. He or she may favour some groups of more approachable people and avoid groups who might be more difficult to interview (e.g. people who might have language difficulties) or individuals who *appear* to be unlikely to fit the quota requirements. So whole groups, and certainly some quitte large inner-city 'no go' areas, are under-represented or omitted from the quota sample.

Even in the absence of such interviewer selection biases, quota sampling will be concentrated among the more accessible members of the population. (Hence the use of quota controls on working status or time of day.) In a random sample, 10% or more of the selected individuals will not be contacted even after three or four attempts. And another 10% or more will refuse to take part in the survey. This is non-response. On the surface there is no such problem with quota sampling; at least none is, or can be, declared. But this is only because substitution is effectively allowed. People who can not be contacted at the first attempt are, by definition, excluded.

The effective rate of non-response in quota sampling – those with whom the interviewer does not come into contact and those who refuse to take part – is almost certainly huge. The average random sample survey, at the completion of all *first* calls at sampled addresses, has achieved a response rate of only about 25%. This is only boosted in subsequent calls to an 'acceptable' figure of 70–80%. The most generous claim that can be made for quota sampling is that its effective non-response rate is around 65–70%. That is, it provides coverage of only one-third or less of the population.

The significance of this depends on how much difference there is between responders and non-responders *within* a cell of the quota controls. This may be small, but we can never know. It is this uncertainty that leads to the rejection of quota sampling in surveys whose results are more open to challenge. Acceptance of the method demands faith, even if this is based on previous satisfactory experience.

It is sometimes argued that there is a difference only of degree between accepting the risks in a quota sample and accepting those arising from non-response in a random sample. This is a dangerous argument, leading inexorably towards the extreme of accepting the views of a sample of one – the Chairman or his wife. And the difference between 20–30% non-response and 65–70% non-response can hardly be called a difference of degree.

Radical approaches

The researcher who is prepared to accept the risks of non-random sampling (and almost all will accept them on some occasions, even if only for exploratory research) should sometimes consider adopting more radical approaches. These will involve *purposive* selection of sub-groups in the population for examination. This can be argued on the grounds that one has a model of the relationships between the selection and the survey variables. Or it can be argued in the context of controlled examination of the extent of a phenomenon, closer to the approaches of the physical sciences. (See Ehrenberg's discussion of 'non-sampling'.[1]) Neither group of proponents seems prepared, however, to recommend purposive or even non-random selection at the final stage of selecting *individual* respondents. And neither would suggest that the results could simply be added together to form a single sample from which inferences can be drawn to a population.

Sample size

The question most often posed to survey statisticians is how to determine sample size. This can be answered in apparently simple terms. The required sample size will depend on just three factors: the variability of the population we are examining; the sample design we are proposing to use; and the accuracy demanded of the results. In terms of a formula:

$$\text{Sample size } (n) = \frac{K^2 DF^2 p(100-p)}{L^2}$$

where:
K is the multiplier of the standard error associated with the required level of confidence that the population parameter lies within a given distance of our estimate. So, if we require 95% confidence, $K = 2$; for 90% confidence $K = 1\frac{2}{3}$; for 70% confidence $K = 1$.

DF is the design factor associated with our particular sample design in respect of the estimate p;

L is the permitted distance between p and each confidence limit. For example, we might be asked to provide an estimate accurate to within 5 percentage points; then $L = 5$.

In practice, there are many problems here that may not be obvious. Take first the term DF, the design factor. This will vary from one survey variable to another, will depend upon our chosen sample design, especially the degree of clustering employed, and will not be known! Likewise, the estimate *p* and the variability of the population will differ from one variable to another and will not be known.

In both these cases we can make some progress by concentrating on one question at a time and by making more or less informed estimates of two terms, ρ the homogeneity of the variable within the areas we choose as sampling points, and *p*. Suggestions were given earlier as to likely values of ρ. We may have some prior estimate of *p*; at worst we can set it equal to 50%, when the population variability will be at its maximum.

Suppose we are considering a variable that we expect to be quite well distributed, e.g. agreement with an attitude statement. We set $\rho = 0.02$. We have no idea how many will agree; so we set $p = 50\%$. Then we expand the term DF^2 into its full form as given earlier, giving us:

$$n = \frac{(K^2)[1 + (0.02)(b-1)](50)(50)}{L^2}$$

The user of the research now has to set accuracy requirements, which might be that we should produce an estimate that we are 95% confident lies within 5 percentage points of the truth, i.e. $K = 2$ and $L = 5$. Then:

$$n = \frac{(2^2)[1 + (0.02)(b-1)](50)(50)}{(5)^2}$$

$$= 400[1 + (0.02)(b-1)]$$

$$= 392 + 8b$$

Note that the second term here reflects the impact of multi-stage sampling. A single-stage sample of 400 would yield the required level of precision. Then $b = 1$.

We would now have a wide range of choices. We could use:

an unclustered, single-stage sample of 400;
a sample of 480 in 48 clusters of 10;
a sample of 560 in 28 clusters of 20;
a sample of 720 in 18 clusters of 40;
and so on.

This choice would be made on the basis of relative costs and practicality. Before making it, however, we would need to perform a similar calculation for each other survey variable. This process can be abbreviated by taking not more than three variables: those which yield the highest values of $(K/L)^2$, the variable where the accuracy demand is most stringent; of ρ; and of $p(100 - p)$.

All too often the result of such calculations to find the **sample size** that meets all requirements is a survey cost outside the available budget. Then, of course, the requirements must be changed. This can be done only in respect of required accuracy. The effects of such changes can be quite dramatic.

A doubling of the acceptable confidence interval e.g. from plus or minus 5% to plus or minus 10%, will reduce the required sample size by a factor of 4, e.g. from 400 to 100.

The acceptance of 90% confidence instead of 95% will reduce the required sample size by one-third. The acceptance of 70% confidence will reduce the required sample size by a factor of 4, as with the doubling of the acceptable confidence interval.

The final complication to be introduced is that we are likely to want to examine sub-group as well as total sample estimates. Then we need to concern ourselves with the sample size required in the smallest sub-group which, unless we decide to over-represent that sub-group, will determine our total sample size. This is, in fact, the way in which sample size is most often fixed. And the required sample size in the smallest sub-group is fixed not through calculation but by gut-feel. A typical researcher would probably demand a sample of 100 in the smallest sub-group.

Weighted and unweighted sample size

It is important to note that all calculations of likely error must be based on unweighted sample sizes. Clearly we should not conduct 100 interviews, weight them by a factor of 10 and pretend that we have the accuracy of a sample of 1,000.

Chapter 5

Questionnaire design

J. Marton-Williams

Every stage of a market research survey is of vital importance if valid conclusions are to be drawn from it. But the design of the questionnaire is certainly one of the most critical phases. If the required information is not covered or if the questions are posed in such a way that they make nonsense to the respondent, no amount of clever interviewing or ingenious analysis can produce useful results.

This chapter is mainly concerned with the design of structured questionnaires for use in face-to-face interviews. It does not deal with the development of guides for depth interviewing nor with the problems of questionnaires for special populations, such as retailers or professional investors, since these are covered in other chapters.

The aims of this chapter are modest; it attempts to lay down a few tentative general principles, indicate some of the hazards met in collecting information of various kinds and to describe some of the main techniques used at present, especially in the area of attitude measurement. But in the last analysis, questionnaire design cannot be learnt from books; it is a skill that has to be acquired through experience. The best method of learning the skill is to write a questionnaire, to go out and interview people with it and then to analyse it oneself.

Unfortunately, it is usually only at the trainee stage of a researcher's career that there is the opportunity to do this. Researchers are usually too busy and under too much pressure to delegate to find the time to go out into the field; the result is that they tend to become remote from the realities of the interviewing situation. A considerable amount of useful 'feedback' from the field can be obtained, however, if full use is made of that invaluable ambassador between researcher and respondent, the experienced interviewer. 'Debriefing' conferences after pilot studies can provide the opportunity for the researcher to learn how respondents reacted to the questionnaire, which questions caused difficulties and whether all sectors of the population to be covered by the survey could understand and answer validly. It is unfortunately true that a questionnaire must be designed to be comprehensible to the least able respondent.

Planning the questionnaire

The precise ground to be covered by a questionnaire arises from the brief. The first step is to decide what specific information is required in order to solve the marketing problems and to answer the questions raised in the brief.

There are often limitations of money and time which dictate the length of the questionnaire, quite apart from considerations of the amount of time that members of the public might be prepared to spend in being interviewed! Of all the information that *could* be useful, it is necessary to have some means of assessing what should be given priority. The brief obviously provides the main criteria for assessing what is most important but exploratory research can also contribute; the insight it provides into the market leads to the development of hypotheses about motivations which the survey may be required to validate. Information to test the hypotheses must be gathered in the questionnaire, e.g. depth research suggested that women who used a lot of a certain brand of disinfectant were particularly conscientious housewives who had babies or very young children. To test this hypothesis it was necessary to include a measure of the extent to which they were conscientious housewives and also to make sure that full details of household composition were collected.

Before starting to formulate actual questions, it is advisable to list in detail all the information that the questionnaire will be designed to obtain; this gives a broad indication of its length and enables a review to be made at an early stage of the degree of detail that can be covered. It is also a valuable aid to organization of the various sections and of the order in which questions will be asked. If the subject is complex and different groups within the sample need to be asked different questions, it is helpful to use a flow chart as set out in Fig. 5.1 to plan the questionnaire and to ensure that all the ground is covered with the optimum efficiency.

In planning the content, the requirements of the analysis stage must be borne in mind. If the views of the brand-loyal are to be compared with the views of those who constantly change brands, questions must be included to identify the brand-loyal and the changeable. If hypotheses are to be tested about the motivations that lead housewives to be heavy users of disinfectant, then some measure of amounts of disinfectant used must be included. It is necessary at the questionnaire design stage to formulate the broad plan for the analysis of the data, including the main variables to be used in cross tabulations and statistical techniques for testing or

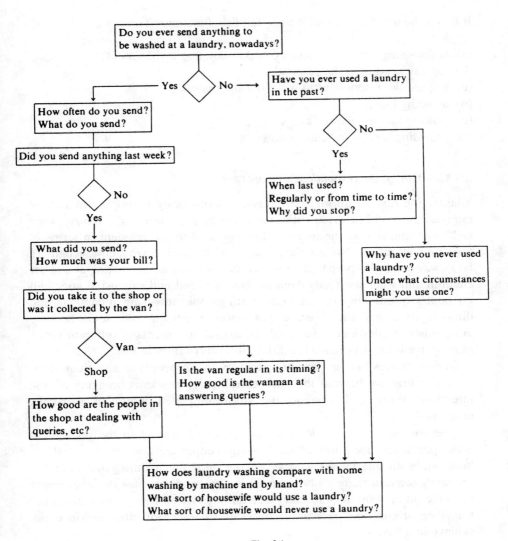

Fig. 5.1

manipulating the data, so that the information can be collected and recorded
in a way that facilitates the analysis process. All too often, consideration of
the analysis requirements is left until the questionnaire is in the field; at this
point it may be found that vital information is mising or is collected in such
a way that its use is limited.

Some general principles

A questionnaire is a tool for the collection of information from respondents.

If it is to be an efficient tool it must fulfil six functions. These are:

(a) maintaining the respondent's co-operation and involvement;
(b) communicating to the respondent;
(c) helping the respondent to work out his answers;
(d) avoiding bias;
(e) making the interviewer's task easy;
(f) providing a basis for data processing.

(a) *Maintaining the respondent's co-operation*

Maintaining *rapport* during the interview is obviously an important part of interviewing skill but the questionnaire can help or hinder the interviewer's task. The longer it is the more is demanded of the respondent in terms of time and attention. No absolute rules can be laid down about length; a housewife might be prepared to spend an hour and a half talking about her children and what she feeds them on but be bored and exhausted after half an hour's questioning on an uninteresting topic involving unfamiliar and difficult concepts; the average low income person will soon become antagonistic if questioned closely about the relative merits of different forms of investment for people paying different levels of income tax.

Questionnaires that are boring or that try to get people to give their views on topics that are beyond their scope lead to respondents breaking off the interview before it is completed. An uncompleted interview is usually unusable.

Questionnaires that are long but on topics of interest to the respondent cause problems of a different kind. Many people are able to spare half an hour when an interviewer knocks on the door, even during the day; but relatively few can spare an hour and it is often necessary for the interviewer to make an appointment to carry out the interview. This necessitates more travelling around and radically reduces the number of interviews she can achieve in a day.

Respondents sometimes become bored during an interview because they cannot perceive any overall structure or sense to the questionnaire. Having each section introduced to them gives them the feeling that they know what is going on and also usefully orientates them in relation to the subject matter; e.g. (after a series of questions about using a laundry) 'Now I'm going to ask you a few questions about doing the washing at home...'

(b) *Communication to the respondent*

The work of Payne[1] in the United States and of Belson[2] in this country have shown that respondents often fail to grasp the question that the researcher is trying to ask. Some of the most common causes of failure to communicate to the respondent are ambiguity, use of unfamiliar words, use of difficult and abstract concepts, overloading the respondent's memory and understanding with too many instructions, using vague concepts and trying to ask two questions in one.

Ambiguity

Everyone tries to avoid using ambiguous questions but, equally, everyone finds from time to time that a question is interpreted differently by different respondents. Only careful piloting can guard against this.

Use of unfamiliar words

A study by Belson and the author when in the BBC's Audience Research Department[3] indicated that many words which appear to be in quite common use are in fact not properly understood, e.g. words such as 'incentive', 'proximity' and 'discrepancy' are known by only about half the population whereas words such as 'paradox' and 'chronological' are known by only about a fifth. Although the context in which a word is used can sometimes help people to understand the word, often the effect is reversed and the unfamiliar word prevents comprehension of the whole sentence.

Use of difficult and abstract concepts

Research in the field of education has shown that both intelligence and educational level are related to the degree to which people are able to think in terms of abstract concepts. Most researchers and their clients are intelligent and highly educated and the use of abstract concepts is second nature to them. They often find it difficult to grasp that the mode of thinking of a large proportion of the population differs quite markedly from theirs.

In a pilot survey, respondents were asked to say what region of the country they felt they belonged to; they were then shown a map with a region marked on it and asked whether they agreed with this definition of their region. It was apparent that those who had not travelled about the country much, whose friends and relatives came from a small nearby area and who had not had an extensive education in geography and the reading of maps had no concept of a region as such; they were able to think only in terms of their neighbourhood or town. Their answers to the series of opinion questions which followed on how things were run in their region could have referred only to the more limited area where they lived. For the main survey it was essential to identify those who could not grasp the key concept of region or quite invalid conclusions might have been drawn.

Research has shown that questions involving abstract or generalizing concepts are more prone than other sorts of question to be affected by variations between interviewers, by the context in which they occur in the questionnaire and by minor variations in wording or presentation of response categories (Schumann and Presser[4]).

Those not used to abstract concepts tend to turn them into concrete concepts. An interviewer asked, 'How would you feel if your neighbour didn't use disinfectant?' 'Oh, I'm sure she does!' replied the respondent, 'she's ever such a clean woman!'

Overloading the respondent's memory with too many instructions

When an interviewer reads out a question, the respondent has to remember what has been said long enough to work out the answer. People's short-term memory varies considerably and some people find it quite difficult to hold even two ideas in their head at the same time.

Every time a respondent is asked to rate a brand on an attribute he has to hold two ideas in his head, the name of the brand and the scale dimension that he is to apply to it; it is common practice to help him by presenting one or other on a card. But many questions are loaded down with explanatory and conditional phrases that confuse rather than clarify; e.g. 'Do you read regularly any daily newspapers; that is, at least three out of every four issues? By "read" I mean read or look at?'

It must be stressed that it is the number of *concepts* in the question that is important – not the number of *words*. A long question can in fact aid comprehension if it is long because the concepts are repeated, perhaps in different words; Cannell[5] showed that, for example, asking about health problems with the longer of the two question versions given below obtained a greater number of reported problems:

short version: 'What health problems have you had in the past year?'

long version: 'The next question asks about health problems during the last year. This is something we are asking everyone in the survey. What health problems have you had in the past year?'

This type of question gives the respondent two chances to take in the question and also seems to remove the pressure to give hurried answers that short questions delivered fast might create. A questionnaire full of lengthy questions would be unnecessarily long and oppressive, but Cannell reports that even a few of them interspersed in the questionnaire had a general effect of obtaining fuller answers.

Using vague concepts

Vague questions tend to produce confusion in the respondent or else equally vague answers. The question 'Do you think your house is the right sort of house for your family?' was interpreted by some as meaning 'Do you like your house?' whereas others counter-questioned 'What do you mean? "Right" in what sense?'

Trying to ask two questions in one

It is often tempting to try to save time in an interview by letting one question be subsumed within another and hoping that the respondent will say if the question is inapplicable to him; e.g. 'How many hours did you spend at work last week?', instead of; 'Did you do any paid work at all last week?' and then 'How many hours did you work?' which makes quite clear that we are asking about any form of paid employment and not simply about the regular job or about unpaid work.

(c) *Working out the response*

Sometimes the mental tasks which the respondent has to perform in answering the questions put to him are quite arduous. Some of the difficulties that respondents experience are related to the problem of communicating that have already been discussed, e.g., if he is asked to hold a number of defining concepts in his head while trying to work out his answer, not only does he find it difficult to grasp the question but he may forget some of the concepts and make a mistake, a mistake which may not be apparent from his answer.

Generalizing

Survey research aims to draw a fairly broad picture of people's behaviour and attitudes; to do this, a certain amount of detail has to be ignored or glossed over. Question design often reflects this need; instead of being asked to give full and precise information about his behaviour or attitudes, the respondent is asked to generalize: 'How would you rate the performance of your car overall?' asks the interviewer. 'Well, the acceleration is very good but it doesn't pull well on the hills' replies the respondent. 'How would you rate the performance *overall*?' prompts the conscientious interviewer. But the respondent may not know how to add together 'very good' for acceleration and 'rather poor' on hills to form an overall rating.

Questions about the respondent's 'usual' behaviour also ask him to make a generalization. If his behaviour is very variable, it may not make sense to him to do so.

Research has shown that questions that are difficult for the respondent to answer because his views do not fit into the framework that the researcher is imposing may be subject to interviewer effects; he may appeal to the interviewer for help, or the interviewer may use judgement in order to arrive at a codeable answer.

Mathematical concepts

Asking the respondent to say 'on average' how many times he buys sweets in a week demands that he has a clear idea of the variability of his behaviour from week to week and then applies an arithmetical concept to the data.

Most respondents would fail on both counts. In order not to reveal their ignorance and because they want to oblige the interviewer, many would say what they 'usually' do or what they did last week, which might or might not approximate to the concept the researcher had in mind in asking the question. Requesting people to work out proportions is likely to cause similar difficulties unless kept very simple, e.g., 'Less than half, about half, more than half'.

Memory

Respondents are sometimes asked to perform prodigious feats of memory. They are asked to remember where, when and how they purchased something, how much they paid for it and where they saw it advertised. They are asked to remember what magazines they have read during the past month, when, exactly, they last decorated a room of their house, what brand of paint they used, and so on.

Trying to remember something that has been more or less forgotten or has merged into a number of other similar acts demands considerable mental effort and concentration. Respondents are not always willing or able to make this effort.

Research on this subject (Belson[6]) suggests that memory is fairly accurate where behaviour is regular, e.g., where magazines are bought on subscription, but much less accurate for the occasional departure from regularity, or for the person whose behaviour follows no regular pattern.

Pilot questioning as to how certain the respondents feels that he has remembered accurately is no proof that he has in fact done so but suggests that the relatively rare and important event is more precisely remembered than the trivial, often repeated event. The purchase of a car may be remembered in some detail for years whereas the purchase of a packet of cigarettes may be forgotten twenty-four hours later.

Steps can be taken to optimize memory accuracy by getting the respondent to recreate in his mind the total context on which the event occurred and by asking only those for whom the event occurred very recently to try to remember the details of it. Cannell[7] has shown that stressing the importance of accurate information to respondents and asking them to agree verbally or in writing to try to give accurate and complete answers results in fuller information. This makes use of the psychological mechanism of engendering a sense of commitment. Positive feedback to respondents when they take the trouble to think hard about an answer can also encourage them to make the necessary effort.

But, however skilful the questioning, it will still remain likely that many respondents will not give completely accurate information. Pilot checks can at least establish whether the respondent thinks he remembers what he actually did. Beyond this, retrospective question and answer techniques cannot go; diaries, home audits or observation techniques have to be used instead.

Indicating the answers required

An important part of helping the respondent both to understand the question and to arrive at his answer is to make sure that he knows what type of answer is required. There are basically two types of question, 'open-ended', to which the respondent replies in his own words, and 'pre-coded' where he chooses his answer from those provided. It should be clear to him which type of answer he is meant to be giving. If the question is 'pre-coded', all the alternatives should be presented to him either verbally by the interviewer or on a card. Bias can result if only the positive or only the negative answers are presented.

Another type of question that is sometimes used is one in which the question is asked in open form but the interviewer has to code the respondent's reply into a pre-coded set of answers. This procedure works well for simple factual data, e.g., 'How long have you lived in this house?' but for more complex questions, and in particular for attitude questions, it imposes a very demanding task on the interviewer who has to interpret the answer, find the appropriate code, probe for clarification if necessary and also ensure that all the respondent has to say has been extracted.

The use of cards

Cards can be a valuable aid to the respondent in helping him to work out his answer. They can be used to help him grasp and remember the concepts in the question and can indicate to him the response categories from which he is to choose his answer. Sometimes, the card bears a list of items, such as brand names, and the respondent is asked to pick items from the list in answer to the question put by the interviewer; e.g., 'Which of these brands have you ever used?' or 'Which of these brands are particularly good for colds?'. There is some evidence (Schumann and Presser[4]) that the items at the top of a list tend to be selected a little more frequently than items lower down. It is therefore a wise precaution to have more than one version of the card for each interviewer with the items in different orders.

An alternative use of cards is to present a series of response categories from which the respondent picks the one which expresses his opinion of a proposition put to him by the interviewer; e.g., 'I am going to read out some statements that people have made about doing the washing. Please tell me how much you agree or disagree with each one; pick your answer from this card'.

If items are to be put in order of preference, each item should be put on a separate card, otherwise it is difficult for the respondent to remember which items he has already selected. Separate cards are also useful if a second question is to be asked about some items; e.g., 'Please sort these cards into two piles, those brands you think you might use and those you would avoid' and 'Now from those you might use, select the three you would be most likely to use'.

'Open-ended' questions

These tax the skill of the interviewer more than most precoded questions do. She has to record the respondent's answer verbatim and simultaneously consider whether the answer makes sense in terms of the question that has been asked and whether it is likely to be fully intelligible to someone in the office who was not present at the interview. She also has to ensure that the respondent has said all he has to say on the subject.

The answers to open questions must be recorded verbatim, otherwise 'interpretation' on the part of the interviewer is likely to distort the respondent's views.

If the respondent gives an answer which does not make sense in terms of the question that was asked, the interviewer should *repeat the question as it is written on the questionnaire;* she should not re-word or explain it since this would mean that each respondent was not being asked the same question. At most, she should change the emphasis in order to stress that part of the question which the respondent seemed to misunderstand.

If an answer is vague or lacking in specific detail, the interviewer should 'probe' i.e., ask questions to obtain further information. It is in this area of interviewing skill that thorough training is most necessary since it is essential that probes should be of a very general kind; e.g., 'In what way...?' 'Can you explain about the... a little more fully?'. Even if the respondent has already talked in the course of the interview about the subject of the question, the interviewer should not assume she knows the answer and that it is safe to ask a leading question; e.g., if the respondent says, 'I wasn't satisfied with the way the machine washed my husband's shirts', the probe should be, 'Can you explain that a little more?' or 'In what way were you not satisfied?', not, 'Is that because it didn't get the collars and cuffs clean as you mentioned earlier?'

When the respondent has fully elucidated the first answer given, the interviewer should not assume that that is all he has to say on the subject but ask. 'And what else?' or, 'What other reasons?' before moving on to the next question.

If the researcher wishes to obtain reasonably full answers to open-ended questions, plenty of space must be left on the questionnaire. The interviewer will not believe that verbatim answers with careful probing are really required if there is room on the questionnaire for only about ten words.

The importance of the interviewer's role in putting over open-ended questions and probing to elucidate the answers means that the usefulness of open-ended questions in self-completion questionnaires, e.g., in postal surveys, is very limited. They can be used in telephone interviews but there are difficulties in maintaining *rapport* with the respondent while probing and writing down the answer. It would, therefore, be unwise to use a questionnaire that consisted almost entirely of open-ended questions for a telephone survey.

(d) *Avoiding bias*

The way in which a question is written can bias the answers obtained if it presents only one side of an issue to respondents. In a public opinion poll on the Common Market a question took the following form:

> Before taking their final decision about joining the Common Market, Norway, Denmark and Ireland will each have a referendum in which all the people will be able to say whether they want to join or not. Do you think that Britain should do the same?

Not surprisingly, a large majority said 'Yes'. It is pretty certain that very different results would have been obtained if the opposite position had been incorporated into the question: 'When France, Germany, Italy, Belgium, Luxembourg and Holland decided to form the Common Market, they each left the decision entirely to their Parliaments. Do you think Britain should do the same?'

In this particular case, it would have been fairly easy to construct a question that presented both sides of the issue, though it might have been necessary to have used a card to put it over in full.

Bias can also occur when examples are used to indicate to the respondent what sort of information is required. The examples are nearly always mentioned more frequently than other points in the answers.

Both of these types of biased question usually arise because the researcher has difficulty in framing a brief and comprehensible question on a rather difficult issue. The answer may be to break the question down into a number of subsidiary parts that lead up to the main point and to make full use of visual aids.

(e) *The interviewer's task*

The task that the interviewer has to perform can be made easy or difficult by the way the questionnaire is laid out. A badly laid out questionnaire leads to mistakes on the part of the interviewer: for example, it may lead her to ask wrong questions, put questions incorrectly or record the answers incorrectly.

There is a fairly widespread belief that respondents are put off by the sight of a questionnaire several pages long; efforts are made to make the questionnaire look as short as possible by using small print and cramping the questions together. But it is doubtful whether a five page questionnaire looks less intimidating to the respondent than one of ten pages and the interviewer's task is made much more difficult for no good reason. Many interviewers are in their forties and fifties and find it difficult to read very small print; lack of space between pre-coded answers (especially vertically) leads to errors in recording answers, and lack of space in which to write down the answers to open-ended questions means that the interviewer is forced to paraphrase instead of recording verbatim.

Part of the interviewer's task is to teach the respondent what is required of him. Although an interview is a dialogue between two people, it is not an ordinary conversation; the interviewer has a scripted questionnaire to follow while the respondent has to learn how he has to answer the questions. It helps both the interviewer and the respondent if a certain amount of instruction on how to answer is scripted into the early part of the questionnaire; e.g., 'For this question I have these answers listed here, so please just pick the one that fits your views most closely'.

How the question is to be asked should be indicated in the way it is laid out, including the point at which cards should be introduced. The questions should be in lower case and the instructions to the interviewer in capital letters, e.g.:

SHOW CARD. On this card are the names of some brands of toothpaste. Which ones would you say are particularly good at making your teeth white?
PROBE: Any others?
REPEAT FOR EACH ITEM IN TURN: Which ones are particularly...?

The instructions to the interviewer to omit certain questions on the basis of the respondent's responses to other questions are usually called 'skip instructions'. A good method, and one that minimizes error, is to indicate which question should be asked next against each set of response categories. It is then a simple matter to indicate that different response categories lead on to different questions (see questionnaire example at end of chapter). This method obviates the necessity for lengthy verbal instructions ('IF YES ASK Q.2, IF NO GO TO Q.30'), or arrows, which can be confusing.

(f) *Providing a basis for data processing*

A great deal of time and money can be saved if the questionnaire is laid out in such a way that the data can be punched on to cards straight from the questionnaire without being transferred to another sheet. Open-ended questions obviously have to be coded at a later stage but for all those questions to which answer categories are given, code numbers can be provided and the interviewers asked to ring the relevant number to indicate the respondent's answer during the course of the interview. The questionnaire example at the end of this chapter indicates how this can be done so that it is easy for the interviewer to see which code she should ring and also easy for the card puncher to read. (In this example, the numbers in brackets indicate on to which punch card column the answers to each question are punched.)

The use of piloting

There are two main types of piloting, methodological pilots which are specifically designed to provide data for the development of measuring tools such as attitude scales, and questionnaire pilots designed to ensure the efficiency of the questions. Methodological piloting is discussed in the section on measuring attitude and beliefs. This section deals only with questionnaire piloting.

Piloting plays a vital part in questionnaire development but it too often consists only of getting some interviewers to conduct a few interviews 'to see if the questionnaire works'. Simply using a questionnaire will reveal the most obvious faults and ambiguities because the respondent will ask questions or give answers which clearly indicate incomprehension; but questionnaires can apparently work quite well in that respondents give what appear to be reasonable answers while, in fact, there are wide variations in interpretation or even complete misunderstandings hidden below the surface.

Interviewers should be specially trained in the requirements of piloting. It is useful, however, to use some relatively inexperienced interviewers on pilots, as well as highly skilled and experienced ones, because they throw more light on the sorts of problems which the less experienced interviewer is likely to come across in the field.

Pilot questionnaires should be laid out with plenty of space so that interviewers have room to record any spontaneous comments or explanations that respondents give while working out their answers. Interviewers should be instructed to write in all comments made by the respondents and any alterations made to the wording of the question or additional explanations that they gave in order to help the respondent understand. (This often reveals that the purpose and meaning of the question was not clear to the interviewer.) The interviewer should also follow up some of the questions by asking, 'Can you tell me what you understand by this question (or statement)?' and, 'Can you tell me what you had in mind when you answered...?' This probing reveals the hidden ambiguities and misunderstandings. Questions involving memory can be followed up by, 'How clearly can you remember this particular purchase? What fixed it in your mind?'

To go back over the whole questionnaire in this manner can be very time-consuming, it is sometimes carried out as a separate operation, a different interviewer calling back on the respondent later on in the day. Often, however, just key questions are picked out for this treatment and they are followed up during the course of the interview or, if this disrupts the flow too much, at the end. The interviewer might say, 'We are trying out this questionnaire and want to make sure that the questions make sense, so can I go back quickly over some of the answers you gave?' This positions the process as a trial of the questionnaire and not an examination of the respondent's ability to understand. The amount of time taken can be reduced by dividing the questions to be examined in detail among the interviewers so that each deals with only three or four.

It is also extremely useful to ask interviewers to tape record some of their pilot interviews so that the researcher can listen to the interview and hear for himself what difficulties came up. Simply listening to the tape recordings can be very informative but the evaluation of the questions can be improved if the interaction between interviewer and respondent is coded (Cannell,[8] Morton-Williams[9]). A very simple coding frame to be applied to each question might be:

Question asking and first response:
Interviewer: 1.1 asked question as worded
             1.2 changed wording of question
             1.3 failed to read whole question/all precodes
             1.4 failed to follow skip instruction correctly

Respondent: 2.1 answered adequately for recording
            2.2 failed to answer adequately
            2.3 asked for repeat of question
            2.4 asked for explanation/interpretation
            2.5 other indication of misunderstanding or possible invalid answer

Secondary behaviour:
Interviewer: 3.1 repeated question
             3.2 correct use of probes
             3.3 incorrect use of probes
             3.4 gave interpretation of question
             3.5 failed to probe when should have

Respondent: 4.1 answered adequately for recording
            4.2 failed to answer adequately
            4.3 other indication of misunderstanding or possible invalid response.

The value of coding the tape recorded pilot interviews in this way (even if there are only a few of them) is that it forces the researcher to make a systematic and objective appraisal of each question; for example, if there are several occasions of misreading a question, then the wording or the layout of the question may need improvement; similarly, if respondents fail to give answers that fit the precoded categories or to answer the question in the way intended, it might indicate that the question is unclear or is not couched in terms that fit the respondent's frame of reference, or that the precoded categories are inappropriate or ill defined.

Apart from studying the pilot questionnaires and listening to tape recorded interviews, it is useful to have reports from the interviewers working on the pilot in which they summarize their findings under a number of headings provided by the researcher. These might be:

'selling' the survey and persuading the respondent to take part;
the opening questions;
the length of interview;
the flow of the interview;
any particularly difficult questions;
any problems of interviewers' instructions;
any layout problems.

Questions for behavioural information

Information on consumer behaviour is usually required in order to give a picture of where and when the product is being bought, how it is used and into what context of more general behaviour its usage fits. It is also needed in order to provide a basis for discovering what sorts of people (in terms of characteristics and attitudes) use the product. For this latter purpose, it is usually necessary to identify particular 'behaviour groups' for use in tabulation such as present and past users, heavy and light users, and so on. These groups must be precisely defined and questions asked to identify them.

The main difficulties in designing questions to collect behavioural information concern the problem of getting respondents to remember accurately and trying to get them to distinguish between what they 'usually' do and what, precisely, they did last time. There can also sometimes be difficulties in getting respondents to generalize about their behaviour. Techniques other than question-and-answer surveys have to be used when accuracy is essential. The information collected from surveys can be only an approximation. The researcher's job is not only to make the approximation as close as possible but also to have some idea from piloting as to what kind of errors are likely to occur.

Some of the most common types of behavioural questions and their problems can be discussed separately.

Product group definition

Before asking people whether they have ever used a product, make sure they know what is included; e.g., in asking housewives whether they have ever used a laundry, it may be necessary to ensure that they understand that this does not include launderettes or dry cleaning. In asking people whether they have ever taken a tonic, indicate whether tonic wines, doctors' prescribed tonics or vitamin pills etc. are included or not. Make sure that they understand that by 'ever used' you mean tried once and gave up as well as used regularly.

Frequency questions

When a respondent is asked to say 'how often' he does something or 'how many times' he does it within a particular time period, he is usually being asked to generalize about his behaviour since there is almost certain to be some irregularity. The tendency is for him to give his *ideal* behaviour, from which he may frequently deviate; e.g., a person may think that the proper number of baths he ought to take in a week is four, though more often than not he may only get around to taking two, but may quite honestly believe that he usually takes four baths a week. Furthermore, he may be reluctant to admit that he only took two last week. To obtain accurate information it may be necessary to ask a series of questions e.g., 'Quite a lot of people find it difficult to take as many baths as they wish because of shortage of time or because they're tired, or for other reasons; do you ever find you miss baths for this sort of reason?'. This can then be followed up with questions about the number of baths taken last week, preferably by getting him to recreate the week in his mind rather than by just asking him to give the number of baths taken; e.g., 'Now would you think back over last week, and tell me on which days you happened to take a bath?'.

Questions which proceed from what the respondent 'usually' does to what he 'happened to do last week' assist accuracy because he is less tempted to falsify his account of what he did last week on the grounds that it is atypical. It must be remembered, however, that what the respondent claims he 'usually' does is likely to represent his ideal rather than his average behaviour.

'Where?' and 'when?' questions

Questions which ask where a product was purchased or where advertising for the product was seen are particularly subject to memory failure unless the event was a particularly important one for the respondent or clearly linked to a date. Because it is difficult to remember precisely, the respondent tends to say what he thinks was most likely to be the case.

Time tends to contract in memory with the result that people tend to remember events as having happened more recently than they really did. Difficulties of remembering lead respondents to substitute what they think they *usually* do for what they actually did. In answer to questions such as 'When did you last buy a bottle of disinfectant?' respondents are likely to claim that they bought one within the last seven days because they feel that it ought to be part of their once a week grocery purchasing and they know that they bought some not very long ago. Yet estimates of the total disinfectant market based on those claiming to buy within the past seven days are usually of the order of four times the most conservative estimate of the market based on sales information.

'How much?' questions

Respondents can sometimes remember how much of a product they bought or used on a recent occasion as long as the units are clear cut, but they frequently cannot remember how much they paid for it (especially if the item was part of a larger bill) and are usually unaware of bottle or can sizes, especially when a number of size variations are available. Metrication has further confused this issue.

Brand names

In some product fields where brand attachment is not strong, respondents sometimes cannot remember accurately which brand they last purchased or have in the house at present. Brands of stockings or tights are rapidly forgotten and a kitchen check might reveal confusion between brands of soft drink or brands of detergent.

Measuring attitudes and beliefs

The measurement of attitudes is a vast subject that can only be touched on in this chapter. For a more comprehensive review of measuring techniques and also for papers on the main theories of attitude, the reader is referred to Fishbein.[10]

It is useful to distinguish between the more general 'life-style' attitudes, such as attitudes towards the job of being a housewife or towards saving, and the more specific attitudes to brands or products. The term 'image' is reserved for these more specific brand evaluations.

The relationship between attitudes and beliefs

Attitudes can be defined as emotionally toned evaluations about events, object or activities. They are evaluations because they assess things as good or bad, desirable or undesirable. They are emotionally toned in that the events, objects or activities with which the attitudes are connected arouse pleasure, joy, pain, anger, fear, anxiety, etc; e.g., people who hold the attitude that saving money is a very good thing are likely to feel happy when they have a lot of money deposited in a Building Society and very anxious when they have no money saved.

The direction that the evaluation of the object or event takes, however, and the type of emotion felt is likely to be affected by a person's *beliefs* about the object, event or activity. If he believes that having money saved gives security, he is likely to feel anxious if he has no savings. If, on the other hand, he believes that one can only save by stinting one's family, he may feel guilty of meanness if any money accumulates in the bank. This last example demonstrates that beliefs can also carry evaluations.

Fishbein[11] has pointed out that it is important in attitude research to distinguish between evaluations of the subject that is being investigated, beliefs about it and evaluations of these beliefs. All three may be included implicitly within one measuring technique. Sometimes, this results in a valid measure of attitude because everyone agrees with the evaluation placed on the belief. The statement, 'Potatoes are nutritious' for example, is a statement of belief. Everyone may agree, however, that nutritiousness is a desirable attribute: therefore anyone who disagrees with the statement is giving a low evaluation to potatoes. The belief statement 'potatoes are fattening' may not carry the same evaluation for everyone (thin people may want to get fatter); and those who agree with it are not necessarily giving a low evaluation to potatoes. The evaluation attached to the belief would, in this case, have to be measured separately in order to know whether it was contributing positively, negatively or neutrally to the overall evaluation of the subject being studied.

Saliency of attitude

One of the problems of investigating attitudes with structured questionnaires is that it is difficult to avoid putting words into people's mouths. It is impossible to ask someone whether he agrees or disagrees with a proposition without putting the subject of the proposition into his mind. He may agree strongly with the proposition, yet he may never have given the matter any thought before. The term 'saliency' is used to describe the extent to which a particular attitude is actively in people's minds before the interviewer asks specific questions about it.

The saliency of an attitude is usually measured by a series of open-ended questions which progressively 'home in' on the target attitude. In a study of attitudes to the noise of aircraft around Heathrow,[12] for instance, respondents were asked a series of questions designed to discover whether aircraft noise was sufficiently annoying for it consciously to affect their pleasure in living in their home; e.g., 'What do you dislike about living around here?'; 'If you could change just one thing about living round here, what would it be?'; 'Have you ever thought of moving away from here? Why?' and, 'What are the main kinds of noise you hear round here?' No mention of aircraft or aircraft noise was made in the interview until all these questions had been asked. The answers to these questions indicated the extent to which people were consciously aware of aircraft noise as a source of disturbance.

Dimensionality of attitudes

Open-ended questions can indicate whether a particular subject is uppermost in people's minds and what the main opinions are that people hold about the subject; but they can, at best, be only crude indications of how people feel. In particular, open questions cannot assess how strongly people feel about a subject.

The main purpose of measuring attitudes in market research is usually to be able to make comparisons between the attitudes of different groups of consumers, e.g., users and non-users of the product or brand. To make valid comparisons between groups, it is essential to be able to measure the the position of all the people in the groups on the attitude and how strongly they feel about it. This implies that attitudes are dimensions along which people can be positioned. This concept of the dimensionality of attitudes underlies all of the main techniques of attitude measurement.

Attitudes and opinions that are simple, clear-cut and readily accessible to conscious introspection can be measured by single questions, e.g., people's optimism about their future financial prospects was measured by a simple self-rating scale, 'Over the next five years or so, do you expect your financial situation to:

improve a lot;
improve a little;
stay about the same;
get a bit worse;
get a lot worse?'

The more complex and fundamental attitudes which underlie specific opinions cannot be so easily measured, however. It is unlikely, for instance, that people would give a valid answer if asked to rate themselves on the extent to which they were conscientious housewives or concerned with maintaining their financial independence. This is partly because people are not usually aware of these broader attitudes and therefore cannot introspect accurately about them, and partly because these broad attitudes are *generalizations* about the people and, as already discussed, people find it very difficult to generalize.

The broad underlying dimensions of attitude are usually measured by batteries of questions which measure different aspects of the attitude and are then combined in some way to give an overall measure of the underlying attitude. The main methods of forming attitude batteries are discussed later in this chapter, but first it is necessary to consider the basic ingredients of attitude measurement, the questioning methods used in the interview situation.

Questioning techniques

The most common basic tool of attitude measurement is the *rating scale,* by which the respondent is asked to indicate his position on a dimension of opinion. Other techniques involve the ascription of adjectives to concepts, or vice versa, or a choice between alternative attitudinal positions. Rating scales can be verbal, numerical or diagrammatic. Verbal rating scales may take the form of the 'financial optimism' scale given above in which a single clear-cut concept may be presented which embodies the attitude or belief. The respondent is then asked to say whether he agrees or disagrees and how strongly (or whether he believes it to be true or untrue). Several concepts may be presented one after the other and the respondent may be asked to use the same response framework for replying to each; e.g., 'Tell me how much you agree or disagree with each of these statements:

(a) everyone should disinfect their drains everyday;
(b) only those in old houses need use disinfectant;
(c) those who use a lot of disinfectant must be dirty people.

On the whole, research[4,13] indicates that a five point scale with a mid-position (e.g. 'neither agree nor disagree') is most readily comprehensible to respondents and enables them to express their views. Longer scales tend to provide too fine a gradation and it is difficult to find unambiguous non-overlapping descriptions for them. Some researchers prefer to use four point scales and to do away with the middle position on the grounds that everyone has a view, even though it may not be strongly held, and can be usefully pushed to express it. (Sometimes a mid-point is provided on the questionnaire for the interviewer to use but is not presented to the respondent.)

The evidence indicates that whether or not a mid-point is presented to respondents does not affect the distribution of answers (when the mid-point answers are ignored), though $10 - 20\%$ more endorse the mid-point when it is presented than do so when it is hidden. Including or omitting the mid-point in a scale can therefore be a matter of personal judgement within the context of the requirements of a particular question.

A 'no opinion' or 'don't know' category should usually be provided for the interviewer to use if the respondent is unable to give an answer though it need not necessarily be offered to the respondent. If the 'No opinion/don't know' category is offered to respondents, there is usually an increase in its use of about 20%. Some researchers argue that they are only interested in informed opinion and that it should therefore be offered; others are of the opinion that it presents respondents with too easy an option. Studies[4] have shown that about 30% of respondents will give an opinion on a completely fictious issue, if no 'No opinion' category is given. These answers are not randomly distributed but indicate that respondents apply some broad attitudinal position to interpreting the question. It therefore seems that researchers should present a 'no opinion' category if they are interested in informed opinion but should not do so if they are interested in respondents' general disposition towards the subject. They should also take into account how knowledgeable people are likely to be on the subject and how broad or specific the subject covered by the question is.

Belson[14] has investigated the effects of the order in which the categories are presented in verbal rating scales on the distribution of answers along the scale. He found that the positive answers were more frequently endorsed when they were presented at the top of the scale than when the scale was reversed and the positive answer appeared at the bottom. Putting the negative response categories at the top of the scale tended to give a better distribution of answers across the categories. There are, therefore, advantages in presenting the negative categories first, provided that it does not lead to confusion for the respondent.

There is no case for varying the order of presentation of rating scales from one interview to another, since this could lead to a situation where apparent differences in attitude between sub-groups of the sample were due to there being more people in one group than in the other having the scales presented in a particular way.

Numerical rating scales take several forms. Respondents may be asked to give scores out of ten, out of five or some other number. They might be asked, for instance, to score a cake mix that they have just tested on a number of attributes such as ease of making, lightness, tastiness and so on. Alternatively, they might be asked to score different brands according to their suitability for some purpose.

In using scoring systems the evaluation to be placed on the top score must be indisputable. (A product could not be scored for 'sweetness' for instance, because respondents cannot be certain whether the top point of the scale means 'too sweet' or 'just right'.)

Numerical scales are often favoured because they enable the researcher to use a longer scale without the problem of having to find descriptive phrases; it is also assumed that there are equal intervals between each step of the scale (which cannot always be assumed with verbal scales). It is doubtful, however, whether there are any real advantages in using numerical scales as respondents do not always grasp readily what they mean or use them properly. Scores out of ten tend to carry particular connotations from school marking systems in that a score of five is often regarded as a low score rather than a mid-point; the respondent thus may in effect use only the top part of the scale. A study[15] involving a seven-point numerical 'ladder' scale in which verbal descriptions were given against the mid-point and both extremes, was found to get a disproportionate number of answers at the point carrying the verbal descriptions. Follow up interviews with respondents revealed that many did not understand the numerical aspect of the scale and simply used the points with the verbal description. It was also found that interviewers varied considerably in the ways in which they instructed respondents in the use of the scale and that there was a certain amount of variability in the answers obtained that was simply due to the interviewers. If numerical scales are used, they should therefore be carefully piloted to ensure that respondents really understand what is required of them and the instructions on how to use them should be scripted into the questionnaire and not simply left to the interviewer.

Diagrammatic rating scales are as varied as the imaginations of the research people who invent them. They may be representational or abstract. The example in Fig. 5.2 below is a simple way of measuring pure evaluation independently of descriptive content by a representational scale; 'Which of these faces best expresses how you felt about the sweetness of the product?'. In this example, the most favourable response means 'just right' while the least favourable response might mean 'too sweet' or 'not sweet enough'. It would clearly be necessary to ask those who gave a poor rating what was wrong with the sweetness of the product.

Fig. 5.2

Diagrammatic scales can present the dimension as a set of categories:

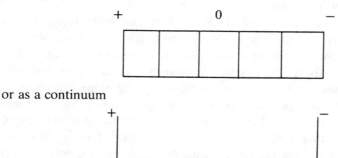

The respondent is simply asked to indicate his position on the scale. Numerical values can easily be assigned to respondents' positions on the scales which are presented with categories but continuous scales present more of a problem. It is usually necessary to impose categories on the continuum for scoring purposes. The argument in favour of continuous diagrammatic scales is that they do not impose a set of categories of a pre-defined size and number. On the other hand, in common with all diagrammatic scales, they tend to involve the respondent in abstract thinking and to present ideas in a way that is unfamiliar.

Semantic differential scales are very popular in measuring brand, product or company images. These combine elements of both verbal and diagrammatic scales.

The technique was developed by Osgood[16] to investigate the meaning which concepts had for people. He presented concepts e.g., 'the American nation' or 'coloured people' and asked respondents to rate them on seven-point scales, the end points of which were defined by pairs of adjectives:

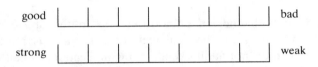

Market researchers have adapted the technique by using a brand, product, or company name as the concept and often using quite complex descriptive and evaluative phrases to define the ends of the scale. The advantage of the technique is that several brands can be quite rapidly rated on several different scales (say four brands on fifteen scales or six brands on ten scales) and comparisons made between them. Often, the respondent is shown how the scales are to be used and is then asked to fill them in himself. Numerical values can be assigned to the scale positions and comparisons made between the various brands (or between users and non-users of a brand) in terms of mean scores.

The pairs of adjectives or phrases used to define the ends of the scale should, of course, be very carefully selected to be relevant to the market being investigated. The Kelly Repertory Grid technique, described by Sampson in chapter 2 on Qualitative and Motivation Research, is often used to throw up attributes and to define the scale ends.

Some people prefer to use only 'monopolar' scales, such as 'sweet – not sweet' while others may use 'bipolar' scales, such as 'sweet – sour' where appropriate. The mid-point of the scale has different meanings for these two types of scale. On monopolar scales, the mid-point is simply a step on the scale from 'not sweet' to 'sweet' whereas on a bipolar scale the mid-point is a neutral point meaning 'neither sweet nor sour'. It can also be used to represent a 'no opinion' point on bipolar scales while a separate 'no opinion' category is necessary for monopolar scales.

Five-point rather than seven-point semantic scales are usually used in market research on the grounds that five points are easier for the interviewer to explain and for the respondent to grasp. Inspection of respondents' answer patterns on seven-point scales certainly seems to suggest that many fail to use all the positions but confine their answers to the extreme position and one other on each side of the mid-point. The meaning of the scale positions on five-point scales can easily be described by turning it into a verbal rating scale.

Interviewers need a script in the questionnaire on how to explain semantic differential scales to respondents. A few trial examples should always be provided to make sure that the respondent has understood.

Ascription of adjectives to brands is another questioning technique for measuring brand images. The respondent is handed a list of brands and asked to say which of them fit a particular adjective well; e.g., 'Which of the brands on this list are particularly sweet?' or 'And which are not at all sweet?'.

By presenting both ends of an attribute, as in the above example, a simplified brand rating can be achieved; i.e., a brand is rated either as 'particularly sweet' or 'not at all sweet' or, by implication, as neither one nor the other.

Two measures for each brand on each attribute can be derived from this: 'image strength', which is the proportion of the sample mentioning the brand as being either sweet or not sweet and 'image direction', which is the proportion of those mentioning it as sweet or not sweet who assign it to each side of the dichotomy.

Joyce[17] has indicated that this simple technique is quicker and easier to administer in the field than semantic scales, that it provides sharper discrimination between brands and that it is more sensitive in pinpointing changes in brand images over time. It is not suitable, however, for making comparisons between brands which differ markedly in share of the market and familiarity, since the unfamiliar brands tend to be swamped by the familiar brands and thus are not mentioned.

Presenting alternative attitude positions is a useful technique for explaining the relative importance of conflicting values. Most people would agree, for instance, with the proposition that they ought to save when the country is in financial difficulties yet many people do not do so because they feel that inflation makes saving pointless. If two propositions are presented as equally sensible alternatives, the tendency to agree glibly is reduced and the respondent is forced to think out his position;

e.g., 'Which of these two statements do you agree with most?' (SHOW CARD AND READ)

'People should save money when the country is in financial difficulties', or 'It's better to spend your money when the country is in financial difficulties because prices keep going up'.

Similarly, most people would like to consider themselves to be safe and careful drivers and also to be skilful and confident drivers, but the relative degree of importance which an individual motorist attaches to these adjectives could indicate differences in driving attitudes and values. Motorists were, therefore, asked to choose between a number of opposing adjectives, as follows:

As a motorist, would you rather be described as:

considerate or quick-witted;
confident or safe;
careful or skilful?

Which of these descriptions would you object to more:

timid or foolhardy;
aggressive or hesitant;
impatient or slow?

One of each pair of words described a more introvert type of motorist while the other described a more extrovert type. Each word was paired with another which, in the opinion of a panel of judges, was equally favourable or unfavourable.

The use of projective techniques in attitude measurement

Most projective techniques are not suitable for use in attitude measurement in structured questionnaires. The majority require open-ended answers, which cannot be used as efficient means of measurement, and often require a high degree of subjective interpretation. (See chapter 2 for a description of the use of projective techniques in qualitative research.)

Indirect questioning techniques can, of course, be used in structured questionnaires, such as asking the respondent to say what sort of person would or would not use a particular product or brand. Most of the different measurement techniques described above could be applied within this framework; semantic differential scales, for instance:

Such questions as 'If your car were to become a person, what sort of person would it be?' can also be structured in the same way.

Sentence completion can be used in a structured form in which the respondent is asked to select one of several alternative ways of finishing a sentence, but this moves away from the truly projective nature of the technique and it becomes simply another method of presenting a scale or a series of propositions.

Attitude batteries

The development of attitude batteries that combine the answers to several questions so as to measure a general underlying attitude usually requires special preparatory work. To ensure that the items that go into the battery all contribute efficiently to the measurement of the attitude, it is usually necessary to try out a large number of items in a methodological pilot study of 100 to 200 respondents and then to apply various criteria for selecting those items which are the most appropriate. This procedure is commonly called 'attitude scaling'.

There are four main types of attitude scaling techniques:

(a) the Thurstone method of 'equal-appearing intervals';
(b) the Likert method of summated ratings;
(c) Guttman cumulative scales;
(d) scales based on item intercorrelations.

The last is the most commonly used in market research nowadays.

Each will be described briefly in turn but the reader is referred to the relevant literature for a fuller exposition.

Thurstone scaling[18] involves devising (or collecting from free interviewing) a large number of opinion statements on the attitude subject. Preferably about 100 statements are collected. The attitude dimension to be measured is broadly, but clearly, defined. A panel of at least 100 people is then asked to rate the opinion statements on an 11-point scale according to how favourable or unfavourable each one is in terms of the attitude to be measured.

Those items are selected from each of the eleven scale positions about which there is most agreement from the judges. Each item is given a weight according to its median scale position. It is called the method of 'equal appearing intervals' because the eleven groups into which the judges divide the statements are meant to be equally spaced along the favourable/ unfavourable continuum. The scale, now reduced to about twenty items, is then ready for use. Respondents are asked simply to endorse all the statements with which they agree. They are given a score on the attitude dimension by averaging the scale weights of all the items they have endorsed. This method of scaling is very laborious and its validity depends on the judges being drawn from the same population as that on which it is intended to use the scale. The average member of the public is likely to have some difficulty in acting as a judge without his agreement or disagreement with the statement influencing or confusing his judgement.

Likert scaling[19] also starts with a large number of opinion statements but, instead of a panel of judges, a sample of respondents is asked to rate each statement on a verbal scale from 'agree strongly' through a 'no opinion' mid-point to 'disagree strongly'. The answer categories are given weights from 1 to 5 or 5 to 1 depending on whether the statement is positive or negative in relation to the underlying attitude. Each respondent is then given a score by summing the weights attached to each of his answers. Items are then selected for inclusion in the final scale by applying a criterion of internal consistency; a group of respondents with high scores and a group with low scores (say the top and bottom 10%) are selected and their answers to each item are compared. The means for each item for each of the two groups are computed and the items which show the biggest difference between the means are retained.

Guttman cumulative scales[20] utilize the hierarchical property of questions that lie at different points along the same attitude dimension. A simple example illustrates the principle: if we ask people to say whether they are (a) over 20 years of age, (b) over 40 years of age, or (c) over 60 years of age, their answers will form a 'scalogram' pattern in that all those over 40 would also endorse that they are over 20, and those who are over 60 would endorse that they are over both the lesser ages. If the answers are hierarchic, a person's answer pattern can be deduced from his overall score.

To discover whether the scalogram pattern exists, the items are placed in order of the number of people endorsing each along one dimension and the individuals are placed in order of number of items they have endorsed along the other dimension and their answer patterns entered in the matrix.

'Scalogram analysis' is then carried out (for which computer programs are available); this allows individual items or people to be shifted about slightly in order to optimize the scalogram pattern. The closeness with which a series of questions approaches perfect scalability is measured by the coefficient of reproducibility which is assessed by the following formula;

$$\frac{\text{number of deviations from the 'perfect' scale pattern}}{\text{number of questions} \times \text{number of respondents}}$$

A value of about 0.90 for the coefficient of reproducibility is usually taken as the lower acceptable limit for inferring scalability.

Guttman scales have the property of being strictly 'unidimensional', i.e., of measuring one, and only one, underlying dimension of attitude. In practice, it is extremely difficult to develop a satisfactory Guttman scale to measure attitudes unless the attitudes to be measured have a logical hierarchical foundation, as attitudes to aircraft noise do. In the study of the effects of aircraft noise round Heathrow already quoted[12], a Guttman scale of annoyance was used. This took the form of a series of questions about the effects of aircraft noise, e.g., 'Does the noise of aircraft ever wake you up? Interfere with conversation? Make your television flicker?' etc., followed by, 'When this happens, how annoyed does it make you feel?' It can be argued that the louder the aircraft passing overhead, the wider the range of disturbances caused and the more annoyed people are likely to be; the scale is thus in a sense based on the hierarchic nature of noise measurements.

The 'unidimensionality' of Guttman scaling is an attractive concept to many people but, except in rare cases, it is extremely difficult if not impossible to develop a Guttman scale that both scales well according to his criterion and ends up containing items that have a high degree of face validity.

Scales based on item intercorrelations are more generally used nowadays in survey research. The Thurstone, Likert and Guttman scaling techniques all depend on the subjective definition by the researcher of an attitude dimension and then set out to develop a scale for measuring it. But, however thorough the initial exploratory research, it is not easy for a researcher to obtain a completely clear understanding of the structure of attitudes; what he identifies as a single broad attitude dimension may in fact consist of two separate dimensions which have little relationship to each other. Conversely, what he thought to be two distinct dimensions may turn out to be so closely related that they can be combined for all practical purposes.

Scaling techniques based on the intercorrelations between attitude items enable the researcher to test out and refine his hypotheses about the structure of attitudes in the particular field being investigated; they also give him the opportunity of identifying attitudes at different levels ranging from very specific opinions to very broad general 'life-style' attitudes.

Factor analysis is the statistical method most widely used in the development of attitude scales; its application in the field of market research has grown rapidly with the availability of well-tried computer programs for the technique which has brought the cost down within the reach of most attitude survey budgets.

There are different types of factor analysis of which the one most appropriate to attitude scaling problems is that known as 'principal component analysis'.(Experts might argue that this is not really a form of factor analysis at all but a separate technique. Colloquial usage has led, however, to principal component analysis being called 'factor analysis'). The basic function of principal component analysis is quite easy to grasp without there being any necessity to understand the mathematics underlying it. Its use, therefore, need not be confined to statisticians. It can be applied when there are a lot of different measurements for the same sample of people. In attitude research it can, for instance, be applied to semantic differential scales, to ratings applied to opinion statements or any other measurements provided the total sample is rated on each item.

The first step is to calculate the correlation between each and every other item. The matrix of correlations provides the input for the principal component analysis. (A program for calculating the intercorrelations is usually an integral part of any factor analysis program.)

Principal component analysis sorts all the measurements into a number of groups or 'factors' on the basis of the extent to which they are measuring common ground. This is assessed by examining within the computer each person's pattern of answers for all the items and identifying the items which tend to have common patterns. The assumption is made that items which are shown to belong to the same factor are measuring something in common, e.g., an underlying attitude dimension. Examination of the content of the items usually indicates fairly clearly what the underlying dimension is.

In addition to grouping attitude items into factors and indicating any which do not fit the factors, a 'factor loading' is given to each item. This is a figure from -1.0 to $+1.0$ which indicates the extent to which each item is associated with the dimension underlying the factor. The factor loading is therefore an indication of the efficiency with which each item measures the underlying factor. Another measure given by most programs of factor analysis indicates how much of the total variance of all the items is accounted for by each of the factors.

Principal component analysis can be used to help identify the relevant attitude dimensions and to examine the efficiency of specific items in measuring the attitude dimensions.

In a study of attitudes to savings[21], a number of hypotheses about the attitudes that led people to save were developed on the basis of a qualitative study. A list of about 25 statements of opinion were derived from the depth interviews and administered to a sample of 130 members of the public as a methodological pilot. The results were subjected to principal component analysis. A 'four factor' solution grouped the statements broadly as had been expected from the qualitative study but indicated which statements were the most efficient at measuring each factor. The four factors are listed below together with names which were given them after the content of the main items had been examined to identify the common element underlying them.

FACTOR I   Temperamental difficulty in saving

Loading

- 0.75   I have never been able to save.
- 0.74   Unless you have some specific reason to save, it's better to spend and enjoy it.
- 0.69   I believe in enjoying my money now and letting the future take care of itself.
- 0.63   I don't feel it's necessary to save just now.
- 0.55   I can't help spending all I earn.

FACTOR II   Sense of solidity

Loading

- 0.81   If you've got a bit of money saved you are not so likely to be pushed around.
- 0.72   Your opinions carry more weight if you've got money saved.
- 0.68   You don't feel successful until you've got money saved.
- 0.54   I'd like to feel I was worth something.

FACTOR III   Concern with independence

Loading

- 0.85   I hate to feel I might have to ask someone for financial help.
- 0.80   I hate to feel that a minor emergency could cause me financial embarrassment.
- 0.54   Money not needed should be saved rather than spent on luxuries.
- 0.43   It would worry me if I had no savings at all.

FACTOR IV   Feelings of financial security

Loading

- 0.65   I feel it's unlikely I shall have any financial emergencies in the near future.
- 0.54   I always feel there might be a financial emergency at any time.
- 0.45   I can't help spending all I earn.

Items can be selected from each factor to use in the main survey to measure the attitudes which have been identified. The number of items selected depends on the degree of reliability desired (the more items, the more reliable the measure) and the amount of space available in the questionnaire. Each respondent can be given a score for each attitude by using the Likert method of weighting each response category and summing the weights. A further refinement is to weight each item by its factor loading so that the more important items in measuring the attitude play a bigger part in the overall score.

Principal component analysis is often applied to measures of brand image using semantic differential scales. It is usually used in a methodological pilot to identify the main dimensions and to provide a basis for reducing the number of scales to be included in the main survey.

Although factor analysis methods add a number of refinements to attitude scaling, some would argue that some of these (e.g. using factor loadings to weight the items) are unnecessary. McKennell[22,] for instance, points out that, except where the structure of attitudes is particularly complex, a study of a correlation matrix of all the attitude items, perhaps aided by relatively simple techniques such as McQuitty's Hierarchical Linkage or Coefficient Alpha, can identify the main dimensions of attitude measured by the items as effectively as factor analysis without imposing a particular mathematical model on the data (as is implicit in the choice of a method of factor analysis). Both McQuitty and Coefficient Alpha work with average correlations; the reader is referred to the literature for details[23,24].

The 'priority evaluator' approach

A study of attitudes, especially if related to other information about people and to their behaviour, can provide a considerable degree of understanding as to why people behave as they do and buy the products they buy. But some purchasing decisions are very complex because the object being purchased has several aspects which are important to the purchaser. A holiday, a car or a new house must meet the purchaser's requirements in several respects. Often, however, the purchaser's choice is limited by what is available and by considerations of price. A broad understanding of his attitudes and motivations may therefore not give a very good indication of what his purchasing behaviour is likely to be. In addition we need to know to which attributes he gives priority and how he trades off one against the other to arrive at his choice. The Priority Evaluator approach has been developed to cope with this complex kind of decision.[25]

The first step is to identify the four to six main features that people take into account in making their choice; in choosing a package holiday, the main aspects to be considered might be the crowdedness of the resort, type of hotel, nearness to the sea and the sort of food served. For each of these aspects, a scale could be devised to indicate the various possibilities available to purchasers. For example, the following types of hotel might be listed:

Round-the-clock room service, several bars and lounges, swimming pool, variable meal times;
Day time room service, one bar and lounge, small swimming pool, fixed meal times;

Breakfast time room service, bar lounge, no pool, fixed meal times:
Pension-type hotel, fixed meal times.

It is apparent that each of these categories will have different implications
for the price of the holiday: the next step is therefore to attach a value to
each category in each scale which represents the contribution that choosing
that category would make to the total cost of the holiday. When this
procedure has been followed for each set of categories, it can readily be
seen that selecting one category from each set will indicate a particular type
of holiday against which a price can be set. The values allocated can vary
from scale to scale; for instance, type of hotel might be more important than
the other three scales in determining price of holiday, and this would be
reflected by higher values being attached to it.

This set of four scales could then be used in a number of ways: first,
respondents might be asked to rate their last holiday on each scale. By
adding the numerical values assigned to each category indicated, the number
of 'points' that that holiday was worth can be arrived at. Respondents might
then be asked to indicate what changes, if any, they would have liked to
have made to their holiday without altering its overall price, in other words,
they are given the chance to alter the categories chosen by 'trading-off' one
against the other; e.g., someone might decide that he would prefer a less
crowded resort and that to obtain it he was prepared to accept a lower
standard of amenity in the hotel.

Respondents might then be asked how much they were prepared to spend
on their next holiday and be given a number of points to represent this; they
would then be asked to allocate the points across the four scales to indicate
again what mix of categories they would like to buy.

To help respondents in the task they are asked to do, the different scale
categories are often illustrated with line drawings to put them over
realistically. In addition, the respondent is given a set of counters which
represent the points he has to allocate.

Careful preliminary work has to go into devising and testing out the scales
and their categories; interviewers need full briefing and training in how to
administer the scales; respondents need to be allowed time to learn what
they have to do and to consider their choices carefully; it is therefore
apparent that this technique cannot simply be grafted on to an attitude
survey. But it does provide a useful method for more focused studies of the
ways in which consumers make complex choices.

Classification of respondents

It is usual practice to collect personal details about the respondent and his
household at the end of the interview, such as age, occupation, socio-

economic class, household composition, etc. The purpose of this information is to provide:

(a) control over the sample;
(b) a check on the sample;
(c) profile descriptions of sub-groups of the sample;
(d) breakdown groups for analysis.

Control over the sample

Many market research surveys are based on quota sampling in which the interviewer is asked to find so many men and so many women, so many in each age group, so many in each socio-economic group, and so on. To check that the sample has been correctly constituted, it is necessary to record on the questionnaire the details of the variables used in controlling the selection of respondents. Region, town size and urban/rural classification is usually controlled by the allocation of interviewing areas and is not left to the discretion of the interviewer; these data are often identified on the questionnaire by a quota number. The interviewer, however, has to select respondents from within her area to fit the quota she has been given using, perhaps, three or four variables, some of which may be 'interlocking', e.g., the age and social class quota may be specified separately for men and women, thus making them interlock with sex.

A check on the sample

It is practical to use only a small number of variables in selecting a quota sample. The variables chosen are obviously those which are considered to be most relevant to the particular survey; there may, however, be others which have some relevance but which could not be used as controls without making sample selection extremely difficult and expensive; for example, housewives might be selected using age, socio-economic class and working status as controls; in such a case, it would be likely that a cross-section of mothers with children in different age groups would also be obtained because this is related to age and working status. The socio-economic class control should also ensure a correct proportion with the use of a car, but both these variables could usefully be checked against published statistics based on large random samples to ensure that no bias has crept in.

When random sampling methods are used, it is also useful to check the distributions of the classification variables against those collected from other large-scale random sample surveys or against census data to ensure that sampling error, refusals, or problems in contacting people have not resulted in bias.

Profile description of sub-groups of the sample

Much of the value of survey research comes from making comparisons between sub-groups of the sample that show different purchasing, usage or attitude patterns. An important use of classification data is to provide profile descriptions of these different sub-groups in the market.

Breakdown groups for use in analysis

In examining survey results, it is also often relevant to compare the purchasing, usage, and attitude patterns of different segments of the population; analysis may therefore be carried out using classification variables to define breakdown groups. This underlines again the point made earlier that it is essential to consider the requirements of analysis in some detail when the questionnaire is being designed.

Classification variables for inclusion

The classification variables that should be included in the questionnaire will depend on the particular requirements of the survey for controlling and checking the sample and for providing profile descriptions and breakdown groups. The following variables are ones for each of which there is (in the UK at least) an established system of classification and published population statistics:

Area variables:
geographical region;
type of area;
density of population;
socio-economic index;
person per room index.

Accommodation variables:
type of accommodation;
type of tenure;
length of residence;
age of building;
number of rooms;
accommodation amenities;
garage facilities.

Household variables:
household size;
household structure;
gross household income;

socio-economic group of head of household (as shown in The Classification of Occupation[26]);

socio-economic grade of household, (used in National Readership Surveys[27]);

types of vehicle owned;

household vehicle ownership;

household possessions;

telephone ownership.

Individual variables:
age of individual;

sex of individual;

status in the household;

marital status;

activity status, e.g., working full/part-time, retired, studying, etc;

socio-economic group;

personal income (gross or net);

terminal education age;

educational qualifications;

type of school attended;

driving characteristics.

There may be others, not included in this list, which are important in a particular case. The UK National Readership Survey[27] provides information on a number of variables of interest to specific markets, e.g., pet ownership, possession of gardens.

There are several arguments in favour of using standard methods of classification wherever possible[28]; apart from enabling proper sample control and checking to be maintained, it ensures at least some comparability between surveys taken at different times and on different subjects. The National Readership Survey[27] is the most widely-used source of information in the UK for setting quota controls in the market research field and, because it is the main source of media information, is also a standard to which other survey data are often compared; for this reason the conventions set up by it for defining classification variables are generally established in market research.

As the typical 'classification page' of a questionnaire (see Appendix) indicates, the question which the interviewer should ask in order to collect the classification information are not always specified. This is a practice which can be carried too far since it relies overmuch on the assumption that all interviewers have received the same type and amount of training. It also depends heavily on interviewers remembering definitions accurately while trying to conduct the interview. Collection of enough detail on occupation of the head of household to classify his socio-economic group accurately is probably the item that suffers most from this practice.

Appendix: Excerpt from National Savings Survey Questionnaire

No.	Question	Answer	Code	Skip to
36.	SHOW CARD 5 Can you tell me, very roughly, how much money you have saved or invested altogether in these forms of saving?	£50 or less £51–£200 £201–£500 £501–£1000 £1001–£3000 More Don't know	(69) 1 2 3 4 5 6 7	37
37.	In which form of saving do you have *most* money?	Only one form held Premium Bonds National Savings Certificates Building Society P.O.S.B. Ordinary Account P.O.S.B. Investment Account Bank Deposit Account National Development Bonds Defence Bonds Unit Trusts Stocks and Shares Trustee S.B. Ordinary Account Trustee S.B. Special Investment A/c Local Authorities Other	(70) 1 2 3 4 5 6 7 8 9 0 X V (71) 1 2 3	38
38.	SHOW CARD 6 What is this saving for? For any of these purposes (CARD) or for other purposes?	For emergencies For meeting large household bills For holidays, Christmas, etc. For security in later life To provide an income Other _____	(72) 1 2 3 4 5 6	39
39.	Why did you choose that particular form of saving? PROBE		(73) (74)	40
	IF ONLY ONE FORM OF SAVING, GO TO Q.41. IF MORE THAN ONE, ASK FOR EACH REMAINING IN ORDER OF SIZE: ASK SEPARATELY FOR ALL OTHER TYPES OF SAVING HELD	(WRITE IN TYPE) Type of saving	(10)	
40.a	SHOW CARD 6 What are the savings in .... for?	For emergencies For meeting large household bills For holidays, Christmas, etc. For security in later life To provide an income Others	(11) 1 2 3 4 5 6	

No.	Question	Answer	Code	Skip to
b	SHOW CARD 5 What are the savings .... for?	(WRITE IN TYPE) Type of saving	(12)	
		For emergencies for meeting large household bills For holidays, Christmas, etc.. For security in later life To provide an income Others	(13) 1 2 3 4 5 6	
c	SHOW CARD 6 What are the savings in .... for?	(WRITE IN TYPE) Type of saving	(14)	
		For emergencies for meeting large household bills For holidays, Christmas, etc. For security in later life To provide an income Others	(15) 1 2 3 4 5 6	

No.	Question	Answer	Held (16)	0-2 (17)	3-5 (18)	6-10 (19)	11 + (20)	CR (21)	Skip to
41.a	SHOW CARD 7 Are there any types of saving on this list which you held in the past but no larger hold?	None	1	1	1	1	1	1	
		Premium Bonds	2	2	2	2	2	2	
b	IF YES: ASK FOR EACH HELD	Nat. Sav. Certs.	3	3	3	3	3	3	
	How long ago did you cash the last	Building Society	4	4	4	4	4	4	
	of them?	P.O.S.B. (O)	5	5	5	5	5	5	
	Within the last 2 years	P.O.S.B. (I)	6	6	6	6	6	6	
	3-5 years ago	Bank Deposit A/c	7	7	7	7	7	7	42
	6-10 years ago	Nat. Devel. Bonds	8	8	8	8	8	8	
	or longer	Defence Bonds	9	9	9	9	9	9	
		Unit Trusts	0	0	0	0	0	0	
		Stocks and Shares	X	X	X	X	X	X	
		Trustee (O)	V	V	V	V	V	V	
			(22)	(23)	(24)	(25)	(26)	(27)	
	(CR = Can't remember)	Trustee (I)	1	1	1	1	1	1	
		Local Authority	2	2	2	2	2	2	
		Other	3	3	3	3	3	3	

No.	Question	Answer	Code	Skip to
42.	Do you yourself pay any life insurance premiums?	Yes	(28) 1	43
		No	2	45
43.	Can you tell me about how much you pay per month in premiums?	£1 or less £2 to £5 £6 to £10 £11 to £20 More Don't know	3 4 5 6 7 8	44
44.	In general, do you think of your life insurance as a method of saving or just as insurance?	A method of saving just insurance Don't know	9 0 ×	45
45.	Do you have a current bank account at present?	Yes No	(29) 1 2	46

No.	Question	Answer	(a) Most	(b) Very	Skip to
46.a	SHOW CARD 8 Which of these is *most* important to you in choosing a form of saving or investment?		(30)		
b	Which others would you also consider to be *very* important?	A chance for the capital to grow	1	7	
		Complete security of the capital	2	8	
		A high interest rate	3	9	47
		Tax concessions on the interest	4	0	
		Quick and easy to get your money out	5	X	
		(Don't know)	6	V	

No.	Question	Answer	Code	Skip to
47.	Do you think of yourself as being	READ: Well off Fairly well of Neither well off nor hard up A little bit hard up Very hard up (Don't know)	(31) 1 2 3 4 5 6	48
48.	Over the next couple of years, do you think your income/your family income will:	READ: Increase a lot Increase a little Decrease or Stay about the same (Don't know)	7 8 9 0 X	49
49.	Do you feel that your future financially is:	READ: Completely secure Very secure Fairly secure Rather insecure (Don't know)	(32) 1 2 3 4 5	50
50. a	I am going to read a pair of statements. Will you tell me which you feel is closest to your opinion: When the country is in difficulties: 　　　People should save all they can OR　　People would be wiser to spend before inflation makes prices rise 　　　　　　　　　　　　　　　　(Don't know) CONTINUE WITH REMAINING PAIRS		(33) 1 2 3	
b	When the country is in difficulties: 　　　People should buy government sponsored savings OR　　You should still buy the type of saving which suits you best 　　　　　　　　　　　　　　　　(Don't know)		4 5 6	
c	I prefer not to buy Government savings when the wrong Party is in power OR　　The Party in power does not affect my choice of savings at all 　　　　　　　　　　　　　　　　(Don't know)		7 8 9	51
d	I never consider how the money I save is being used OR　　I would only choose savings methods which I felt would make good use of my money 　　　　　　　　　　　　　　　　(Don't know)		0 X V	
e	Your savings are put to best use by the Government OR　　Your savings are put to best use by private enterprise 　　　　　　　　　　　　　　　　(Don't know)		(34) 1 2 3	
51.a	It is best to spread your savings OR　　It's best to put all your savings in one good form 　　　　　　　　　　　　　　　　(Don't know)		4 5 6	(b) 52
b	Can you tell me why you think that it's best to .... ?		(35) 52 (36)	

Typical questionnaire classification page

Name _____

Address _____

_____

Position in family:	(19)
head of household	1
housewife	2
other adult	3

Occupation of head of household

_____

	(20)
Informant: not working	1
┌──── working	2
Is there a pension scheme with Yes	3
your job? No	4
IF YES: are deductions made Yes	5
from your pay for it or not? No	6
Do you have an income of your Yes	7
own? ┌── No	8

(Skip to age)

IF YES: Which of these income
groups do you come in?

(CARD 9) (Gross income)	
(Yearly) *(Weekly)*	(21)
– £1500 (under £30)	1
£1500 - £1749 (£30 - £34.95)	2
£1750 - £1999 (£35 - £39.95)	3
£2000 - £2249 (£40 - £44.95)	4
£2250 - £2749 (£45 - £49.95)	5
£2750 - £3249 (£50 - £62.95)	6
£3250 - £3750 (£63 - £71.95)	7
£3750 + (£72 +)	8

	(22)
Do you pay tax at the standard	
rate on any of your Yes	1
income? No	2
Don't know	3

	(23)
Do you pay higher rate Yes	1
tax? No	2
Don't know	3

---

	(10) - (12)
Quota District Number	
Quota District Name	

Age:		(13)
	16-24	1
	25-34	2
	35-44	3
	45-64	4
	65+	5

Class:		
	A	6
	B	7
	C1	8
	C2	9
	D	0
	E	X

Sex:		(14)
	male	1
	female	2
Status: married		3
┌──── single/widowed/divorced		4
Are you engaged or Yes		5
planning to get married? No		6

		(15)
IF MARRIED 0-2 years		1
How long have you 3-5 years		2
been married? 6-10 years		3
Longer		4

		Total	Earns
		(16)	(17)
(a) *Total in household* One		1	1
Two		2	2
(b) *How many of* Three		3	3
them are wage Four		4	4
earners? Five		5	5
Six +		6	6

Is your home: (READ OUT)	(18)
rented furnished	1
rented unfurnished	2
being bought on mortgage	3
fully paid for and owned	4
or rent free with the job?	5

Interviewers name: _____

Date of interview: / / _____

Length of interview: mins. _____

Chapter 6

Interviewing and field control

JOHN F. DRAKEFORD and VALERIE FARBRIDGE[*]

The role of the interview in survey research

Most survey research requires the collection of information or observations from representative samples of particular populations. These samples can comprise individual members of the public where information, when aggregated, aims to reflect the behaviour or opinions of the *total* population or *sub-samples* of it (e.g. housewives, AB class male householders, single working women). Alternatively, these samples can comprise individuals within specialist groups, such as manufacturers, retailers, businessmen, where information may be needed either about the behaviour and opinions of these respondents as individuals, or about the establishments (e.g. companies, shops, etc.) that they represent.

Irrespective of the *type* of information to be collected, virtually all of this work, if postal surveys are excluded, demands *personal* contact of some kind between an interviewer and a respondent. The fundamental importance of this requirement can not be overstated; as far as the sponsor of a particular survey is concerned, this personal contact between an interviewer and a respondent is nearly always the only direct link he has with the user or potential user of his products or services. In certain circumstances, particularly in small (usually industrial) markets or where the identity of customers or potential customers is already known, it may be possible for a manufacturer to establish this direct personal contact himself or through his representatives; indeed in some specialist fields a complete census of customers or potential customers may be possible, and there is no need to use sample survey methods. In situations like these, it is not uncommon for salesmen to be used to report back to management with information

[*] The original chapter by John Drakeford has been updated for this edition by Valerie Farbridge.

collected by them from customers or potential customers. There are a number of serious dangers in this approach, principally that representatives or salesmen are almost certainly not able to collect relevant information, nor trained to collect it in a systematic and controlled way. They will often have a vested interest in the survey results and bias the results accordingly.

The special relationship between salesmen and customers or potential customers is almost certain to introduce bias in the way questions are asked, the way they are answered, the way they are recorded and the way the aggregated results are interpreted. Where a research sponsor seeks information from a 'mass market', it is of course, impossible for him to have direct contact in this way. Nevertheless, the dangers of ever using 'committed' or involved people as interviewers, without adequate training and control in the special kind of personal content required in survey research, can not be overemphasized.

It must be stressed that, in this chapter, we are concerned with the role of *professionally trained research interviewers* who alone should be responsible for this vital phase in any project.

Putting the interview in context

The need for information in survey research to be collected most often by personal contact of this kind must be seen against the background of how particular surveys are structured and planned. The complex nature of survey research nowadays, and the need to employ specialists at various phases in a project, means that the questionnaire, recording form, diary, or inventory designed for use by the interviewer can not be planned solely with him or her, or indeed the respondent, in mind. Of particular importance here is the need to appreciate that:

(a) the survey sponsor will have his own special requirements in terms of the information or observations he needs to collect;
(b) the researcher in control of the project who is translating these requirements into practical survey methodology will have open to him a wide range of techniques and procedures;
(c) the questionnaire, recording form, diary or inventory incorporating these must be usable by the interviewer in a face-to-face situation, and comprehensible to the respondent;
(d) completed documents must be capable of processing through a number of different routines – *manual* checking and editing, listing open-ended responses, preparing a code frame, coding itself, and *mechanical* transfer to punched cards, computer tapes and data analysis.
(e) the resultant findings must be capable of interpretation in depth, and of *real use* to the survey sponsor.

Any project, therefore, will pass through a number of phases, and no one phase can be allowed to dominate; even the best questionnaire must be something of a compromise, in needing to take account of these various requirements.

In the recent past, a great deal of attention has been paid to new techniques and procedures in questionnaire design, and to ways of assembling and analysing the data collected in the most meaningful (albeit often highly complex) way, with all the refinements in, for instance, multivariate analysis that the widespread use of computers and computer software can bring. Less attention than it deserves has perhaps been paid to the vital interviewing phase in survey research; the actual eliciting and recording of information and the clear need to impose on this standards of the highest quality.

Field organizations

The most important types of field organization in countries with well developed research facilities are as follows:

(a) Those integrated totally into large independent research practitioner companies. There is a central Field Management Organization (usually at head office), and a structure of field supervisors and interviewers on a national basis.

(b) Similar field 'structures' belonging to large research companies but where these are 'hived' off as separate independent companies. Such field organizations are of course used on a day-to-day basis by the 'parent' research company, but this structure provides the opprtunity to present 'fieldwork only ' as a speciality to those buyers wishing only to make use of the fieldwork element outside their own company, or to subcontract fieldwork to one specialist, data processing to another, and so on.

(c) 'Specialist' field forces of a totally independent kind, not linked to any research company offering a full range of services, and not usually offering anything other than fieldwork, with the appropriate administrative back up.

(d) The field forces built up and employed privately and regularly by manufacturing companies or advertising agencies.

(e) Finally, there are the 'private lists' of supervisors and interwiewers held by many research buyers and practitioners. These lists have been built up over time, and constructed to fit a user's particular needs (e.g. a team of properly trained group discussion recruiters; teams of interviewers in selected towns capable of administering hall tests; interviewers specializing in unstructured interviewing work with businessmen, doctors, etc.).

In buying fieldwork as a part of a complete project 'package' or if buying fieldwork only, a researcher will have to satisfy himself as to the standards of that organization or individual interviewer (see later check list for buyers). Many interviewers (who are, after all, almost all freelance) work for several field forces and are therefore exposed to and controlled by different field organizations with different standards, different procedures. Sometimes this can cause problems, especially if an interviewer is on the books of several field forces and works fairly regularly for them. As an insurance policy, therefore, the research buyer needs to know that interviewers have been trained for a particular field force (as opposed to just names on a list). Very few research organizations of any kind can these days afford an exclusive field force, or one where interviewers are on a permanent salaried basis, but all should provide training and supervision.

The need for training and control

If the need for professionally trained interviewers in survey research is accepted, it follows that detailed attention has to be paid to the ways in which these interviewers are selected, trained and subsequently controlled in their day-to-day work. This is necessary especially because:

(a) the range of problems that survey research is called upon to solve is extensive and varied;

(b) to the researcher planning a project, a wide variety of sampling procedures, of survey techniques, interviewing methods, and analysis procedures is available. These can be used in various combinations with equal effectiveness to solve a particular problem; in other words, the ways in which different research organizations will use the techniques available in attempting to solve similar or even identical problems will vary; indeed it is unreasonable to suggest that there should always be a single, standard method of approach;

(c) the characteristics of respondents from whom information is to be collected, or about whom observations are to be made, will vary widely within a particular survey, and even more *between* surveys;

(d) whatever standards are imposed on the interviewers by selection, training and quality-control, interviewers will themselves vary in being members of field forces with different structures, in their own personal characteristics and backgrounds, in the depth and variation of initial training and subsequent retraining, in the types of survey in which they may specialize, and in the frequency with which they are engaged.

These variations in types of research, characteristics of respondents, and structure and methods of field forces, can only emphasize further need for a high degree of overall efficiency in day-to-day fieldwork and, wherever possible, the aim of standardizing and further improving basic procedures.

For the interested student, there is available a range of data on the importance of maintaining very rigorous basic procedures, particularly the valuable experimental work conducted and reported on by W. A. Belson (see the Bibliography).

Types of interviewer and interviewing

The wide-ranging nature of survey research includes many projects where it may be inappropriate to use part time interviewers in a field force, however well trained and controlled they may be, for 'conventional' face-to-face interviewing.

Such projects will need information collected by:

(a) Structured or unstructured interviews, especially in *industrial and commercial companies*, with top level management or employees who need to be approached because of the specialist (often highly technical) nature of the information they can provide. In industrial research surveys, for instance, it is often desirable to employ specially selected and trained interviewers of a rather higher calibre than those used on research surveys of a fairly standardized and conventional kind. These interviewers may also need to have some technical knowledge of the particular survey topics being investigated.

(b) Group interviewing, or single interviews of an extended and unstructured kind, most often described as 'group discussions' or 'depth interviews'. Work of this type is usually of an exploratory nature where attitudes and beliefs are examined and collated, but in an unquantified way, in order to elicit hypotheses for further study, or to ensure that the full range of attitudes, beliefs and vocabulary are extracted early enough to ensure inclusion in a subsequent quantified stage of research. Here, ideally, psychologists or sociologists specially trained in this type of work should be used, particularly where the topics to be explored are of a particularly personal, delicate or intimate nature. It is, of course, not uncommon for researchers without special psychological or sociological training to be used for work of this kind and, indeed, this has some value if the main purpose is to inform the researcher planning and controlling a survey about the way in which people behave and think about the particular topic. There are, however, great dangers in relegating this type of interviewing to inexperienced researchers, who will fail to appreciate often enough the subtleties of approach required and the all important and difficult task of extracting the appropriate data, and putting the right emphasis on it in subsequent stages of research.

(c) Telephone interviewing: with telephone ownership amongst the general public at about 80%, certain sub-sections of the population and the business sector being virtually 100%, this is a very fast growing area of data collection. In addition, the creation of 'central location' interviewing with batteries of 'phone booths equipped with listening-in devices ensures that supervision is very effective and the interviewers' work is controlled to a very high degree. Computer Assisted Telephone Interviewing (CATI) or 'direct entry' interviewing is another telephone development which, while requiring a very disciplined approach in questionnaire design, reduces wrong filtering totally. The basic training given to interviewers has to be supplemented with practice in telephone usage, keybord and visual display units. The voice of the interviewer becomes a very important element.

The task of a conventional field force

Having said this, it is nevertheless true that the great majority of survey research projects are likely to use interviewers who belong to field forces of the kinds described earlier. Before dealing with how these field forces operate, it is worthwhile reviewing the range of tasks which such interviewers can be called upon to carry out. Major areas of activity include:

(a) conventional face-to-face interviews where usage, attitude, behavioural and opinion information is being collected, either in home or in the street;
(b) carrying out sampling procedures either quota or preselected names or addresses;
(c) recruiting members of the public to take part in product testing where existing or new products are placed in homes and/or used over a controlled period;
(d) selection and recruitment of members of the public to take part in research sessions at groups, hall tests, ad testing etc.;
(e) selection and recruitment of individuals to be members of a panel to report over a lengthy period, on purchasing behaviour etc.;
(f) courtesy calls, made from time to time on individuals reporting as panel members, to check on performance, answer queries, and possibly to reactivate disinterested panel members;
(g) exploratory interviewing, often of a fairly unstructured nature, sometimes at the pilot stage of a project, where experiments are being conducted on the design and content of a questionnaire or recording form, whose final version will subsequently be used in a major survey;
(h) telephone interviewing to collect information on the spot using either a structured or unstructured questionnaire or to arrange an appointment for a subsequent face-to-face interview;
(i) certain industrial or commercial interviewing;

(j) observing, counting and classifying individuals, and/or vehicles, in traffic studies, parking studies, shop research etc.

(k) shop audits and domestic pantry checks, where interviewers are required to inspect and check ranges of products held and to calculate from invoices, or other records, sales volume, purchasing rates etc.

The varying nature of the types of task interviewers are called upon to perform further emphasises the need to maximize efficiency of field force operations and to impose stringent interviewer control.

Field management organization

Head office organization

The administration of a field force engaged on this varied work requires a carefully structured central organization from which field work can be planned, and to which individual interviewers and supervisors must report. The complexity of this central organization will, of course, vary with the size of the field force and the nature of its work.

In a small field force, perhaps operated by a manufacturer solely for his own research purposes, full-time salaried or part-time interviewers may work only in a particular town or region of the country. Such a force will require only a small head office team to control adequately the comparatively few interviewers involved; indeed, these interviewers will be seen personally by head office staff fairly frequently. It is worth noting here that there are in fact very few exclusive field forces operated by manufacturers or advertising agencies. In larger, mostly nationally spread, field forces of the type operated by many independent research organisations, teams of several hundred interviewers will be employed, often regularly for several days of the week, on repeat surveys, panels, omnibus surveys and so on, but nevertheless usually on a part-time rather than a full-time basis. Field organization here must be on much larger scale, and there will often be separate field managers at head office looking after separate teams of interviewers, some of whom will operate 'across the board' on a wide variety of projects, and some of whom will be confined to continuous audit and panel work for which they will be specially trained.

The work of head office field staff in larger organizations is likely to be sectionalized, different staff members having different responsibilities. These separate sections of responsibility will include:

(a) the selection, training and retraining of interviewers;
(b) costing surveys, negotiating rates of pay with interviewers, and ensuring prompt payment on delivery of completed work of an acceptable standard;

(c) booking interviewers for survey work or arranging for them to be booked through supervisors;

(d) despatching work material;

(e) day-to-day supervision and control of interviewers in the field;

(f) the receipt and checking of completed work;

(g) following up substandard work, arranging for reinterviewing or substitute interviewing, checking on suspect interviewers, etc.;

(h) administrative matters concerned with quality control, training sessions, briefing conferences, etc.;

(i) the continual updating of the *interviewer manual* on basic procedures and the *supervisor's manual* on any new instructions.

Supervisors

The volume and complexity of this work in large field forces will also almost certainly necessitate a supervisory level, interposed *between* head office staff and individual interviewers. Supervisors of this type will usually have had considerable depth of interviewing experience previously, and will often be employed in their supervisory role on a full-time salaried basis. They will be in frequent contact with head office staff and responsible, usually on a regional basis, for controlling a team of interviewers in their areas on the basis of 10–30 interviewers per supervisor. The interviewer to supervisor ratio is crucial. This control will include the allocation of work to individuals in an area, attending briefing conferences, dealing with queries arising from interviewers about research projects or from head office about interviewers, maintaining supervision in the field and assisting in interviewer training. In a large field force, a supervisor has a very real part to play in maintaining interviewer efficiency and morale, and it should be emphasized that supervisors' allegiance *must* be firmly to the head office and not to individual interviewers for whom they are responsible. Supervisors should come to head office on a regular basis for conferences or workshops in addition to attending briefing sessions.

Maintaining sufficiently frequent personal contact with interviewers working relatively infrequently, or with those in remote areas, can be a real problem. Maintaining interviewer efficiency and morale is considerably helped by the existence of a supervisory force, and by the attendance of interviewers at briefing conferences and training sessions. Nevertheless there is *no substitute* for head office contact with individual interviewers as often as practicable. Personal briefings held at head office or regionally on major *ad hoc* surveys or at suitable intervals on audit and panel work, with attendance by head office field force and research executives handling projects, have a most important role to play here.

The selection and training of interviewers

Selection

National and local press advertising, spontaneous application and 'word of mouth' recommendation are the main ways in which prospective interviewers can be contacted initially. If selection is to be effective, at least one personal interview with each candidate, certainly at the supervisory level, will be required. The qualities and basic characteristics that go to make up a succesful interviewer, notwithstanding the necessary training to follow initial selection, are such that it is extremely dangerous to engage new interviewers (even if they claim extensive past experience) by correspondence, without this important face-to-face contact.

At this exploratory stage it is important to compile key information about a prospective candidate. If the candidate is later selected, trained and used as a member of the field force, this information should be stored in an interviewer 'data bank' or 'card index' system, and these aggregated records *must* be updated constantly.

The key information to be sought from a prospect should include at least the following:

a photograph;
full name and address;
sex and age;
social grade;
marital status;
family composition;
car ownership/usage;
telephone details;
educational attainments;
previous business experience, if any;
previous (general) research experience;
previous interviewing experience;
number of field forces worked for (past and current);
types of survey experience;
suitability if appropriate for specialist work (e.g. shop audits, telephone interviewing, group discussion, recruitment and hostessing);
voice (type, accent, etc.);
dress and manner.

In compiling this information – obviously only at a personal interview – the candidate's general attitude to market research and interviewing can be explored. The first interview will lead to a decision on whether or not the candidate is suitable for training, and remember here that irrespective of past experience some retraining is essential.

Formal training

Formal 'in office' training is advisable as a first stage. Whether this is undertaken at supervisory level in the regions or at head office will depend on the size and structure of the field force, and the number of candidates coming forward at a particular time. The duration of such a formal training session will vary from one field force to another, but there will be general agreement that such training shall occupy not less than two, preferably up to five, days.

The formal training course, after a suitable introduction to the nature and purpose of survey research and the way in which interviewing is integrated with the other phases of the project, will include:

(a) instruction on the basic *sampling procedures* to be followed, use of maps to determine boundaries and grid references, sampling at preselected addresses, the concept and implementation of random walk sampling and quota sampling methods;

(b) *questionnaire design* with particular emphasis on how to ask questions, strict adherence to the written content, prompting and probing, questionnaire routing, skips and recording demographic and other classification.data;

(c) *methods of introduction* to a potential respondent, how to deal with queries about survey sponsorship, keeping respondents to the point, clarifying vague replies, dealing with unsuitable respondents, possible refusals, and with queries as to why respondent was chosen for interview;

(d) *methods of quality control* used by the field force (supervisor checks, postal checks, office check, editing, etc.), and steps that are taken on queries or suspect work;

(e) *administrative details about procedures* for interviewer booking; briefing methods, allocation of work, receiving return of completed work, methods of payment and the relationships and the method of contact between the interviewer, supervisor, and head office staff.

As part of this formal training, interviewers should be encouraged to conduct 'in office' interviews with dummy questionnaires; demonstration interviews will be given by head office staff and supervisors and, ideally, some system of rating interviewer performance even at this early stage should be devised. It is helpful to tape record demonstration and test interviews and to play these back during the training sessions. If training is on a large enough scale, initial criticism of performance should be actively encouraged. It is well worth while at the close of such formal training sessions also to administer short written tests to interviewers, which will further assist in decisions about potential for further training.

Training in the field

Formal first-stage training of the kind described above will eliminate applicants who for one reason or another are below standard or, less dramatically, felt to be suitable only for certain types of survey work.

There is, however, no substitute for training in the field and prospective interviewers passing successfully through formal training need to move on rapidly to this phase before final decisions are taken about their acceptability for future work.

Most often, training in the field will be conducted by a supervisor (who will of course have been similarly trained in the past) in which she herself will demonstrate various interviewing techniques in the field with the trainee observing; this will be followed by test interviews by the trainee in the presence of the supervisor and, finally, if at all possible, the assessment by the supervisor of a batch of interviews completed by the trainee on her own. This assessment can be achieved by a detailed examination of completed questionnaires, a full discussion with the applicant of any problems encountered, or by supervisor call-backs on the respondent interviewed during this test phase. The stark reality of this training in the field will almost certainly show which trainees may have mastered the theory adequately enough but are unlikely in practice to be of a sufficiently high standard.

Formal and field training of the kind described above should be regarded as the least that should be done to ensure competent performance, once successful candidates have been enlisted for future work. Obviously, during the first few weeks in the field, a new interviewer will have to be supervised and controlled very closely, to ensure that standards are being maintained. In addition it is advisable to accompany an interviewer whenever they are given a task for the first time, e.g. a product test or recruiting for a hall etc.

Both the formal and field training described are essential for new interviewers: they are also advisable as a method of retraining and bringing up to date older established members of a field force.

All supervisors and interviewers working in the field must be supplied with identity cards indicating details about themselves and the organization for whom they are working. Apart from a need from time to time to convince doubtful respondents about the authenticity of a particular study, the use of such cards is invaluable in demonstrating that interviewers are *not* 'saleswomen in disguise'. Examples of (non-research) organizations masquerading as interviewers conducting a survey, where the real purpose (either immediate or in a later follow-up) is selling, are unfortunately not infrequent. Any way therefore which helps to make this important distinction between survey research and selling must be encouraged, since our industry depends very heavily on the voluntary (and usually free) co-operation of members of the public, and we all have responsibilities to them.

In Britain the MRS Code of Conduct sets out these responsibilities to the general public in detail and all supervisors and interviewers need to be made aware of what they are, by being given a copy of the relevant sections.

The interviewing manual

To complement training, all interviewers need to be supplied with a manual which sets out in detail general procedural rules and methods to be followed on the various types of project that the interviewer is likely to encounter. Basically, these rules will comprise those dealt with fully at the initial training session, but, of course, they will need to be amended frequently and brought up to date by head office staff as new procedures and new techniques are developed.

Every interviewer must be encouraged to master the contents of the manual and to use it for day-to-day reference in the field, prior to attempting to contact their supervisor or head office to resolve queries. In addition to the manual carried, an interviewer is, of course, supplied with further instructions in writing, specific to each project, even with an additional personal briefing. Any interviewers engaged on repeat surveys or on audit and panel work will need to be supplied with detailed instructions about checking methods to be used, products, prices and pack sizes to be checked, and so on.

Briefing interviewers

As we have said, contact between interviewers and head office staff or supervisors needs to be maintained as frequently as possible. Formal training or retraining sessions held periodically, however, will tend to deal mostly with basic issues of a general nature. On each specific survey special briefing procedures need to be adopted to deal with problems and procedures peculiar to that survey. This briefing can take one of a number of forms depending on the complexity of the project, the extent to which it introduces new requirements, the number of interviewers required to work on the project, and the time available for pre-field work instruction.

Briefings on panel and audits work

Where interviewers are in contact regularly with panel members, reporting weekly, monthly or quarterly on individual shops or homes, basic interviewing and checking procedures are unlikely to vary substantially from period to period. Keeping the instruction manual on a project of this kind up to date should allow these procedures to be followed satisfactorily each time a contact is made. This does not mean, of course, that an interviewer may not receive additional instructions for each new visit or that the normal quality control checks in the field will not be imposed.

There will be a need to call together interviewers working on such projects for refresher briefings from time to time, in order to discuss problems which arise, the implementation of new checking techniques, and so on. In continuous audit or panel work it is essential for slackness and boredom to be avoided. Here, either random or specially timed supervisor checks on interviewers will prove invaluable in ensuring the maintenance of accuracy.

Survey briefings

Where special *ad hoc* surveys are concerned, briefing practices will vary more widely. On major surveys, particularly those involving fresh interviewers or new survey techniques, it is certainly of considerable value to brief all interviewers personally, either at head office or regionally, with research staff and head office field staff and area supervisors in attendance. Such briefings, however, are costly and the time required for them may not always be available.

Personal briefings

Where they take place, these personal briefings will comprise:

(a) a detailed description by the appropriate member of head office staff of the background to, and the nature and purpose of, the survey. If the content of the survey is of a technical nature it is sometimes useful to have the client himself present to answer questions;
(b) instructions about how respondents are to be selected for an interview with particular emphasis on any changes in standard procedures for pre-selected address sampling, random routes, or quota controls;
(c) an exposition of the questionnaire to be used, to ensure that interviewers fully understand the nature of the questions, how they are to be asked, question routing, skips, etc.;
(d) general discussion with interviewers of any problem arising;
(e) test interviews, either between pairs of interviewers chosen at random on the spot or by interviewers with a member of head office staff;
(f) further discussion of any additional problems arising;
(g) the allocation of work material and discussion of any administrative problems relating to field work dates and deadlines, methods of payment, and so on.

Ideally, personal briefing of this kind should be attended by head office representatives; where this is impracticable, similar personal briefings can be run at supervisor level on a regional basis. Ideally, personal briefings can only really be considered unnecessary where *all* interviewers concerned have fairly recently worked on an identical or very similar project.

Postal and telephone briefings

These are necessary substitutes for personal briefings in many cases, and in certain circumstances can be regarded as adequate, provided interviewers so briefed are encouraged to raise any queries immediately with their supervisors or with head office, so that these can be dealt with before field work commences. In all cases like this it is essential that the interviewer *thoroughly reads and completely understands* the written instructions that will have been supplied with the work material. It is worthwhile also building in the additional safeguard of inspecting the first day's work of each interviewer to decide whether any interviewers should be rebriefed before continuing.

Pilot briefing

A special comment about briefings on pilot research is worthwhile, because here both the requirements and the procedures tend to be different. At the planning stage on major projects, it is a widespread practice for a research organization to test and develop a number of versions of a questionnaire in draft, prior to agreeing the version to be used in the main survey.

Pilot interviewing may be needed at various stages, with a highly structured and almost final draft which has been worked on for some time by head office staff who may also have, themselves, tested earlier versions by pilot interviews in the field or with a much more flexible document which now needs further refinement with the guidance of interviewers who have used it in the field. On normal survey work, the very fact that interviewers are required to adopt a consistent approach, and not to deviate from written instructions and the printed questionnaire, makes some interviewers unsuitable for use in exploratory pilot work. What is required here is a much more flexible approach, where interviewers are actively encouraged to use their initiative, and to report back to head office staff about the best way in which questions can be phrased or ordered in a questionnaire and whether there are any significant errors or omissions. It follows that supervisors themselves or interviewers of the highest calibre are likely to be best suited for this pilot work. After pilot briefing and pilot field work, debriefing sessions where each interviewer is invited to contribute to further improvements in questionnaire design prior to the main survey, can be invaluable.

If the pilot is required to check the length of the questionnaire or the 'number per day', clearly it is more sensible to use 'average' interviewers.

Quality control

A rigorous and planned approach to selecting and training interviewers, and the implementation wherever possible of briefing sessions prior to field work, will do much to ensure that high standards in the field are maintained. However, there are great differences between theory and practice in interviewing, not least because of the very real stresses that are imposed on interviewers in the course of their work. Interviewing with the very best type of questionnaire is not easy, and having also to combat such factors as bad weather, complex instructions, difficult quotas, difficult respondents, tiredness, etc., adds to the stress in the field – something which it is all too easy to forget as an office-based researcher. Indeed, in setting up quality control systems there is no substitute for field experience, and all those concerned with research planning or head office field organization need to spend occasional days in the field; this is always valuable, even if not always enjoyable!

No matter how carefully a project is planned, the nature of the project itself, the characteristics of the respondents and the differences between interviewers or, indeed, variation in performance of a single interviewer from day to day can and often do give rise to problems in interviewing that could not have been foreseen. It is necessary, therefore, to impose additional checks against these eventualities, with the aim of maintaining overall performance in the field at the highest possible level.

Control by supervisors

The ratio of supervisors to interviewers will, of couse, vary from one field force to another, and, indeed, with variations in project nature and interviewers there can be no correct level of supervision. The ratio must be such that no single interviewer goes too long without contact with and checks by the supervisor on projects, quite apart from additional contct through briefings and training sessions. A considerable amount of time here will be devoted by supervisors to the control of new interviewers or interviewers whose performance is poor or even suspect.

Control imposed by supervisors will usually take the form either of accompanying interviewers on an assignment, or conducting spot checks on respondents and re-interviewing them as soon as possible after their first interview, or else of scrutiny of completed work before it is passed back to head office for subsequent processing. Accompanying interviewers in their work has some advantages, particularly in terms of ensuring that no deviations are occurring in the basic methods laid down, and is useful on the one hand for keeping interviewer morale high, and on the other for making it clear that field force management are concerned on a continuing basis with maintaining the standards of performance of individual interviewers.

However, the advantages of this type of control are limited; any interviewer can have an 'off day', or be at a stage in a project where unusual difficulties appear to be arising, atypical of a more normal situation. A more useful form of control is the regular checking of interviewers' work by recalling on respondents, to establish first whether the interview took place, and second how it was conducted in broad terms, how long it took, and so on. Such spot checks will need to be conducted rapidly after the first interview, otherwise a respondent may reflect changes in behaviour or opinion of a real nature which give the false impression that a first interview was inaccurate in some way. There is some merit in having completed work routed through supervisors before transmission to head office. This will ensure that genuine problems can be dealt with quickly and suitable corrective action taken. Checking of this type should be organized on a rota system so that all interviewers are checked in their turn.

Postal checks

It is a widespread practice to send prepaid postcards or letters to respondents to enquire whether an interview was carried out and the opportunity is often taken to ask additional questions. Such a postal check, however, can only be a partial check, and extreme care has to be taken in the selection of any check questions to be asked, otherwise differences in response will be apparent which are quite unrelated to interviewer performance. In theory, it is possible to conduct 100% postal checks on all work of all interviewers all the time, but this is extremely costly, cumbersome and probably unnecessary, because the very nature of postal checks means that replies from respondents themselves will never be at the 100% level. A more common approach is to:

(a) select batches of interviewers in rotation over time, and submit all their work on one survey to postal checks at the 100% level; or
(b) check a randomly selected proportion of all interviewers' work on all surveys, but at a much lower level, say 10–20%.

Both of these approaches have advantages and disadvantages; actual practice will depend on the nature of the surveys being conducted by a particular field force, the number of interviewers involved, and background knowledge at head office of individual interviewer performance over time.

Check editing

Even if some scrutiny of completed work is undertaken at the supervisor level, it will be essential to impose further check editing procedures on work that has reached head office for subsequent processing. This check editing can again be operated in various ways, by sampling either proportions of interviewers or of their work; it will concern itself principally with sources of error such as:

(a) failure to adhere to sampling instructions – the failure to select appropriate individuals at preselected addresses or failure to complete set quotas of work;
(b) the omission of vital demographic data such as age, occupation, income level, socio-economic class, family size, etc.;
(c) the omission of specific questions, or failure to follow correctly routing instructions through a questionnaire;
(d) a tendency, most often apparent on open-ended responses, to generate inadequate or vague replies.

Apart from the additional measure of control this check editing imposes on a day to day basis, it is of considerable importance as a basis for head office to build up a backlog of performance data about each interviewer. These data will come from a number of sources, and need to be compiled into readily available records which show, for each interviewer, such aspects of performance as:

(a) levels of response rate by respondents to postal checks carried out;
(b) any evidence from these of possible falsification of interviews (e.g. interviewing someone other than the alleged respondent recorded) or of 'making-up' replies for interviews which never took place;
(c) the number of errors found in recording classification data;
(d) the levels at which omission or misrouting occur;
(e) rates per day achieved in initial contacts and in successfully completed interviews.

Ideally a data bank of information of this kind should be compiled to enable performance of individual interviewers to be compared with average performance. The aspects of performance listed above can be built into this system, as also can analyses on particular projects of the kinds of responses different interviewers are obtaining to questions. Obviously if suspicion is aroused at any stage about an interviewer's performance, through supervisor checks, postal checks, check editing, or cumulative evidence from the data bank, immediate follow-up action will need to be taken.

The aim of quality control of this kind must be to minimize errors and maintain individual interviewer standards at the highest possible level. Deliberate cheating, despite all the precautions taken, is extremely difficult to detect. In general, the evidence is that such cheating is at a low level, not least because of the very rigorous approach to quality control that most research organizations adopt.

In order to be effective, of course, it is absolutely *vital* that *all* interviewers are fully aware that these various checks are made and they should be equally aware of the penalties which can follow from substandard performance; in particular, that information about individual performance is exchanged among research organizations.

A check list for buyers

Some readers, as members of independent research organizations or specialist field companies, will be actively engaged with the problems of interviewing and field control on a day-to-day basis, especially if their responsibilities include operating and controlling a field force. Most of these will already be well aware of the problems in interviewing that can arise, and will be implementing the quality control procedures described here. Other readers, however, as sponsors of survey research, will be buying expertise from independent research organizations or specialist field forces. They will, no doubt, be equally concerned about the problem in research of maintaining high interviewing standards, and will wish to satisfy themselves that the organizations from whom they buy research are, in fact, adopting acceptable control procedures where appropriate. Perhaps a useful way to summarize what has been said is to present, particularly for the benefit of these readers, a check list of points which need to be borne in mind when checking upon the credentials of a particular research organization. Such a check list would certainly include the following:

Research planning and design:
(a) Is the right degree of emphasis placed upon the interviewing phase of a project, compared with the other phases through which the project has to go?
(b) How are the questionnaires, recording forms, diaries or inventories laid out, and by whom are they designed?
(c) Has the designer any interviewing experience, and has he or she at any stage piloted the questionnaire?
(d) Are instructions to interviewers comprehensive; and who drafted them?
(e) Are the sampling procedures to be used in the project feasible in the field?
(f) How are the interviewers instructed on these sampling procedures and under what circumstances, if any, are they allowed to deviate from instructions?
(g) What checks are imposed to ensure that a sampling plan is followed?

Field control
(a) How is the field management at head office organized in general and in relation to the implementation of a particular project?
(b) How much contact is there between head office staff and the supervisors and interviewers?
(c) What documentation exists as a control on contact rates, interviewing rates, etc.?
(d) How is supervision in the field organized and how are queries that arise in the field dealt with?
(e) What is the ratio between supervisors and interviewers and what responsibilities have the supervisors for maintaining adequate interviewer standards?
(f) What procedures are followed in briefing interviewers, either personally by post or telephone?
(g) How well are these procedures supported by written material of a general kind (e.g. interviewer manual) or of a kind specific to the survey (e.g. instructions, call-sheets, etc.)?

The interviewers:
(a) What is the composition of the field force and how has it been built up?
(b) How are the interviewers initially selected?
(c) How are they trained, either at formal training sessions or in the field?
(d) How frequently are the interviewers seen by head office staff and supervisors?
(e) Are they aware of the nature and depth of the quality control procedures conducted?
(f) What are their terms of employment and how are they paid?
(g) How regularly do the interviewers work for the organization?
(h) To what extent do they work also for other field forces?
(i) What methods of identification are carried?

Quality control:
(a) What checks are imposed on interviewers while work is in the field and how are the problems and queries resolved?
(b) How often and at what level are supervisor spot checks, postal checks, revisits to respondents conducted as further control measures?
(c) What are the check-editing procedures once work has been returned to head office and how are queries and suspect interviewing dealt with?
(d) Has the organization been able to build up a data bank on individual interviewer performance; if so, what does this data bank comprise?

While the vital importance of controls on interviewing will be recognized, the way these are imposed will vary from one organization to another. Clearly, no perfect system of control can exist, in a situation where survey research deals with such a wide variety of projects and where the composition and structure of field forces necessarily differs. The aim, however, must be to achieve the best possible combination of controls, consistent with the nature of the field force, the money available, and the time span (often relatively short) over which particular projects are conducted.

Chapter 7

Trade research

BRIAN PYMONT and GILL WELCH

Trade research is a collective term for a series of specially developed techniques serving the needs and objectives of marketing management at the various stages of the distribution network. Just as the elementary methods of consumer research have been adapted and improved to gear them more specifically to particular problems, so the basic techniques of research among the distributive trades have been refined from the original to meet current demands. This chapter deals with the basic techniques and illustrates a few of the applications and developments that have occurred. It makes no attempt to be comprehensive.

Of all the expenditure on trade research, by far the most is spent on retail and wholesale audits; the remainder is probably divided evenly between distribution checks and *ad hoc* research at the point of sale, in particular surveys among the retail trade. Almost inevitably, therefore, the emphasis in this chapter will be upon trade audits. Those readers who wish to pursue their interest in audits are referred to Melhuish, Nowik and Yates.[1-3]

Trade audits

Most manufacturers requiring national retail audit data subscribe to the syndicated services offered by the specialist agencies in the field. Historically some manufacturers have conducted their own audits, largely for reasons of frequency of reporting, speed of preparation, the need for product panels rather than shop indices or the volume of information required. Most notable among the national syndicated services in the UK have been

---

* The section on Trade Audits has been prepared by Brian Pymont and that on *Ad Hoc* Trade Studies by Gill Welch. Both draw on the chapter by Brian Hughes in the previous edition.

Nielsen, Stats MR and Retail Audits whilst the Mars group has conducted the largest and most comprehensive manufacturer-operated audit. Even the Mars group, however, has yielded to the huge cost pressures of an in-house audit and now, through Mars Group Services, offers its audit for third-party sale on non-competitive product fields.

In test markets, that is in TV regions or test towns, perhaps a few more manufacturers venture to carry out audit measurements independently, even though there are adequate facilities available from the specialist agencies who almost invariably have active (sometimes dormant) panels of shops available in the appropriate areas. Some agencies actually specialize in these smaller-scale, localized audits.

The use of retail audits to management

Information from retail audits is important to marketing management in the areas of both strategic and tactical decision making.

Information leading to strategic decision making can frequently be obtained by simple observation of long-term trends indicated by this source. These trends enable management to predict with some accuracy the size of the market in which the company is operating currently and in the future. It can tell management how the company is performing relative to its competitiors in terms of market share and, within the overall picture of market share, it can pick out dramatic movements by individual brands, brands of a certain type, formulation, or price range, perhaps indicate a need for the company to review its product mix, its pricing policy, where it should concentrate its promotional expenditure, etc.

Provided the company possesses the other information necessary to assess which brands are likely to be profitable and which relatively unprofitable in the long term, retail audit can contribute to a large extent in succesful long-term profit planning. To put it another way, retail audit data can provide a framework of basic knowledge of market movements to which may be linked a myriad of other marketing factors–such as raw material prices and availability, machinery and labour requirements, competitive strengths and weaknesses–and, equally important, movements in consumer behaviour and retail attitudes to equip a company with signposts to find the direction in which profitability is most likely to lie in the long term.

The use of audit data in a tactical role is also important, although this use tends to be evaluative of what has happened in the past as much as predictive as to what is to happen in the future, e.g. management will look back on recent promotional campaigns to assess their effectiveness and, by building up a picture composed of evaluations of several such recent performances, be better able to select those courses of short term activity which are effective. Likewise, this study of past action can help management avoid the more obvious pitfalls, e.g. the repetition of clearly disastrous sales promotions. Perhaps the major short term value is the ability to read quickly and to act upon competitive successes and failures.

In summary, audit data, imperfect though it may be in part, is one of the best aids at the disposal of marketing management for keeping informed about the market place in a quantitative, relatively unbiased way, month by month and year by year.

Collecting the information

The technique of auditing is simple and straightforward. Auditors visit the sample shops at predetermined intervals and at each visit they count stock and record deliveries. Sales during the interval between visits is simply calculated thus:

OPENING STOCK + DELIVERIES − CLOSING STOCK = SALES

It should not be inferred from this bald statement that auditing is easy; considerable discipline and an organized approach are essential to obtain accurate estimates. Auditors must be trained to examine each stock location searching for the brands that make up the product class. As these are observed and counted they must be recorded separately against the location in which they are found so that stock in dump bins, shelves, or self service stands, i.e. in the selling area, can be distinguished from that held in the stockroom, the yard, or elsewhere, i.e. out of the selling area. The same care and attention is necessary in annotating delivery information. Each invoice, delivery note, or daybook entry must be scrutinized to be certain that all relevant delivery information is collected. Each delivery must be recorded against the source of purchase to distinguish between the conventional wholesaler, cash and carry, head office, or direct from the manufacturer. The whole operation must be systematic, deliberate, and rigorous for errors in stock counts, or missed invoices will give false sales readings, possibly leading to a misinterpretation of the expanded results. Additional data are also collected by the auditors, selling price, promotional packs, special offers and any other information that could be of value. Thus, for each sample shop, a pattern of trading in the period is prepared; when added to the data collected from other sample shops a comprehensive picture of the market as a whole is constructed.

An example of an audit form is given in Fig. 7.1.

In the case of the major multiple grocery groups, Sainsbury, Tesco, Asda, Fine Fare, Safeway and Argyll, delivery data is nowadays provided by the groups themselves in the form of computer tapes. Data for sample stores is then extracted by the research suppliers. The physical stock count in sample stores is still carried out by the research suppliers, however, except in the case of Sainsbury who do not permit auditors to enter their stores and therefore provide stock data from their own procedures.

Shop name
address

1.	BRAND:	NAME SIZE VARIATION		A Lge	A Hdv	B Lge	B Lge 2p off
2.	Sales last audit			224	82	43	12
3.	Brand code		6·11	010.121	010.141	010.221	010.324
4.	Price information		12·14	7p	4p	10½p	10½p
5.	Delivery details since last audit	Wholesale	15·19				
		Cash and carry	20·24				
		Direct and head office	25·29	96 / 9+ / 18 / 18 288	36 36		13 / 18 / 18 144
6.	Opening stock		30·34	71	73	89	132
7.	Opening stock plus deliveries		(5 + 6)	359	109	89	276
8.	Stock this audit and use of display material	a. Counter		Forward Reserve D	Forward Reserve D	Forward Reserve D	Forward Reserve D
		b. Shelf		9	7	12	27
		c. Window					
		d. Floor					
		e. S/S Stand					
		f. Dumper					
		g. Storeroom		144		40	30
9.	Total stock a..g incl.		35·45	9 144	7	12 40	27 30
10.	Closing stock		46·50	153	7	52	57
11.	Sales this audit (7 minus 10)		51·55	206	102	'37	219
12.	Special information						
13.	Comments						

Fig.7.1 An example of an audit form.

In the future there is no doubt that audit data, at the top end of the trade at any rate, will be provided from the data captured by electronic scanning. Sales out of the store will thus be measured directly by Electronic Point of Sale registers, rather than indirectly from stocks and deliveries as at present. Progress in this direction is, however, slow and it may well be the 1990s before EPOS becomes a major input to retail audit data.

Preparing the data

Each entry and calculation made by the auditors in the shops must be subject to rigorous examination at the processing centre, each notation of stocks and deliveries, addition and calculation of sales for each brand size and type, must be physically checked. The most recent sales must be compared with the previous sales history of that brand and size in that shop and only if it is 'reasonable' or anomalies explained by known activity such as promotions or price changes should it be used in the preparation of the report. The auditor's notes are of great importance here to help account for changes or unusual levels of sales, deliveries or stocks following marketing activity. The emphasis at the processing centre, as in the field work, must be upon accuracy and thorough checking.

Once this scrutiny is completed, totals are made up of the stocks, the deliveries, and the sales for all the shops for each of the 'itemized' brands and sizes separately (collectively for that group of less important brands that are to be shown in the report as 'all others'). For small audits, such as those in test towns, the bulk of the processing is then complete except for the totalling of the shops found to be either in stock or to have made sales during the period of the various brands. These small audits are the exception, however. Most audit data need to be grossed up or expanded to universe levels. The process of totalling is common to both small and large 'national' audits, except that in the latter case the shops are first sorted into cells (shop type within area) and then totalled. For each cell the value of the universe is known and the expansion is simply:

$$\frac{\text{UNIVERSE}}{\text{SAMPLE}} \times \text{SALES (OR STOCK OR DELIVERIES)}$$

By adding the expanded cell data, area totals and shop type totals are obtained and, thus, a representation of the national market is constructed.

The bulk of national audits today, of course, are processed by computer and the methods vary in detail from the one described. But whatever facility is used it is essential that the most stringent checks are applied at every stage.

The data provided

Though each of the service companies, and those manufacturers who conduct their own audits, have developed their own distinctive style of table presentation, the same basic data are common to them all. A description of these essential tables is followed by a brief outline of some of the additional analyses that are possible.

Consumer sales are sales made over the counter to customers during the audit period and shown both on a sterling or cash paid basis and as volume when the expression is package or weight. These tables normally also feature the share of the market accounted for by each itemized brand.

Retailer deliveries or purchases from wholesalers and manufacturers made by the shop during the audit period and normally expressed as volume on a package or weight basis.

Retail stock, the stock of the product encountered at the last shop check, expressed in packages or weight.

Stock cover, a tabulation of the length of time stocks will last, based upon current rates of sale. With seasonal products, this table is more meaningfully presented in terms of anticipated future sales which is not difficult to calculate once sufficient back data are available.

Average stocks and average sales per shop handling, literally averaging the total stocks and sales by the number of shops in current distribution in order to present the true-life situation of the stockist.

Average prices paid by consumers, as the heading implies, a simple average of all items and brands based upon prices encountered at closing stock.

Distribution, which takes two forms, the first, 'numerical', is based upon the proportion of shops handling the product at some time during the audit period (maximum), and subsequently the proportion actually in stock (effective) at the end of the period, the difference between the two figures being the shops 'out of stock'. The same basic information, but calculated upon the proportions of total annual grocery turnover represented by the shops handling it and 'in stock' at the end of the period, is termed 'sterling distribution'.

Showings, or information about the display material encountered in the shops at the last check. This is usually divided into groups, e.g. advertising material, which would include showcards or mobiles, self-selection, incorporating dispensers, outers from which customers make their own selection and dump bins and, lastly, stock presentations, pyramids, or features.

These basic tables represent the bulk of the tables provided as standard in most audit reports both from research agencies and by those manufacturers conducting their own audit. Each of these is analysed or broken down by region, either television area, the Registrar General's standard regions, or into individual or combinations of the manufacturer's sales divisions. Further analysis by shop type or form of organization, multiple, co-operative and independent, the latter divided by size, or membership of voluntary group, is also normal. By this means, a total and composite picture of the retail trade is obtained.

There are several other useful tabulations which can be prepared from the basic data, some examples of these follow.

Forward and reserve stocks, which is a simple division of the stock levels already annotated but divided between that which is in the forward selling area, the shop itself and, thus, available to the consumer, and that which is in the stock or storeroom.

Source of delivery, a broad division of the volume of retail deliveries from the three main sources, wholesaler, manufacturers, and the multiple head office.

Frequency distribution of shops selling at individual prices, literally an annotation of the proportions of stockists selling each brand size at given prices and most useful when contrasted with frequency distribution of prices paid.

Frequency distribution of prices paid, when the volume sold at each price can be compared with the proportion of stockists selling at these prices so that the extent and impact of price cuts, promotions, and dealing can be better assessed.

Frequency distribution of stock, which either shows the proportion of stockists holding given levels of stock, or is expressed as stockists holding levels equal to given week's sales (stock cover). From this, an analysis can be made of marginal stockists.

Marginal stockists, which identifies the areas and shop types holding minimal stock levels, either in absolute or relative stock cover terms.

Marginal purchases analysis, another frequency distribution analysis of the amounts delivered to retailers during the audit period.

Analyses of combination of brands stocked puts into real terms the extent to which individual brands are competing together in stores.

Cumulative distribution, a useful measure to check on the developments in distribution of new brands and the extent to which new stockists are being attracted and old stockists failing to re-order. It is particularly appropriate in test market evaluations.

There are many other forms of special analyses, each designed to answer a specific problem. No useful purpose will be served in making an exhaustive list in this chapter; a little thought and some ingenuity is all that is required to conceive yet another presentation, more meaningful or pertinent to the matter in hand. For those who buy a syndicated service, the client executive allocated to the account is the most useful source for discussion, consultation, and general advice in the matter of special analyses. He can warn of the problems and difficulties and he understands the extent to which the audit information can be reliably adapted.

Omitted from the list of basic and supplementary tables is 'back data'. For manufacturers entering a new product field much useful background can be obtained from past history; all retail audit companies will sell back data at a discount, obviously at a greater discount if a forward contract is entered into. Special analyses of back data, however, are not generally available and the cost of re-analyses is normally prohibitive.

The sample

The types of sample used in retail audits fall into two distinct types, those that mirror a particular trade or type of shop, e.g. grocers, chemists, or hardware, and the, at present, relatively specialized which attempt to reflect the characteristic distribution of a product class, e.g. confectionery, or tobacco. In the latter, a combination of store types is used in the panel of shops, grocers, confectionery/tobacco/newsagents, cinemas, public houses, canteens in factories and offices, restaurants, garages, etc., all linked in such proportions that the data represent the totality of outlets selling the product.

When investigating the sample of outlets covered by A. C. Nielsen, Retail Audits, Stats MR, and any other audit firm, it is advisable to check the representativeness of the sample. It has been impossble for audit firms to gain the co-operation of *all* large multiple grocery groups, large chemists such as Boots and important food outlets such as Marks & Spencer. Obviously, the lack of representativeness can affect estimates of turnover by units and volume. Therefore, when assessing the validity of the estimates, the user is well advised to look for minimum/maximum estimates with some indication of 'best guess'.

More and more interest is being shown by manufacturers in a 'product class' index. A manufacturer of aerosol air fresheners, for example, can buy an audit sample which reflects the distribution of the product, adequate numbers of grocers, chemists, and hardware stores all linked by the research agency, audited at the same time and processed and presented to the client as fully representative of the product class distribution and, thus, a market totality.

While this development of product sample as opposed to shop type sample continues, there are several basic rules followed by all the agencies and those few manufacturers who conduct their own audits, in constructing their samples. Figure 7.2 depicts more than adequately the problem that faces the sample designer. From it can be seen the problem posed by attempting to reflect just one type of shop. Later, the application of this same principle is used with modifications when a product class sample is drawn but the same basic principles must be enforced.

The fundamental rule in retail audit sampling is to sample volume of sales rather than the number of stores – provided that such a procedure yields an adequate number of stores in each sample cell. Thus in the grocery trade for example, sampling in the early to mid 1970s was pro rata to sales volume. Such has been the developing dominance of the multiple groups, however, that to sample on volume alone in the 1980s would mean a shop sample base in the independent sector which was too small in the context of regional data. Figure 7.2 describes the pragmatic adaptation of the rules

GROCERS

	Number of stores	Total sales volume	Audit sample
	(%)	(%)	(%)
Co-operatives	7	13	14
Multiples	8	67	44
Independents	85	20	42

Fig. 7.2 The relationship of number of stores, sales volume and audit sample.

followed by most shop audit suppliers in the grocery trade. Such has been the growth of the large selling units operated by the Co-ops and major multiples that an audit sample of 700 stores will today cover 9% of all grocery volume.

Taking the concept of auditing volume rather than stores a stage further, where the sample attempts to reflect the whole spectrum of sales of the product class, a sample could be constructed in the following manner (see Fig. 7.3). Here, the considerations of adequate sample cell size and the need to expand the data to national estimates force the designer to reflect the total sales volume of the product only in each shop type, and within each to contain sufficient of the various organizations to give approximately equal cell bases in order to provide the most reliable estimates consistent with the economies of a modest sample.

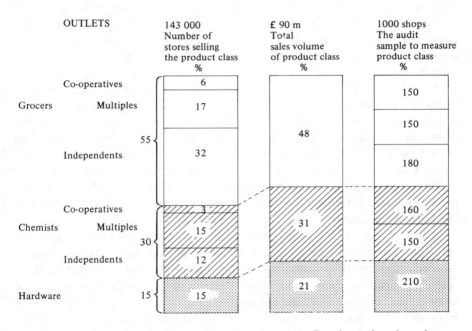

Fig. 7.3   An example where the audit sample attempts to reflect the product class sales.

Whatever type of sample is favoured (product class or shop type index) it is clearly important that the sample itself should be, as far as possible, stable; inevitably with rebuilding, reorganization, sickness, and expiry of leases, there will be sample losses from time to time and these are unavoidable, but positive steps must be taken to keep refusals to co-operate further to a minimum. Some companies operating audits make a point of providing panel retailers with information, all make payments for the facility, make appointments for the following visit, are courteous and take care to trouble the retailer as little as possible consistent, that is, with collecting the correct information. Recruitment of replacement shops must be carefully policed to ensure that the refusal rate is not so large as to warp the results. Regular sample censuses or large distribution checks are essential periodically to check that the sample shops continue to reflect the universe.

All companies who operate audits guarantee that the identity of organizations and the individual shops who co-operate with them will be preserved and under no circumstances revealed to anyone without permission. This is an assurance which all research agencies involved in this type of work respect most thoroughly.

Frequency of reporting

Most of the national syndicated audit services are geared to preparing reports every two months, although Nielsen and Stats MR offer a monthly option. The Mars Group Services audit, now on third-party sale in non-competitive markets, operates on a four-weekly audit cycle. In spite of the bi-monthly norm, there are, however, several product classes for which more frequent reports are desirable, particularly seasonal ones where a 'burst' pattern of reports is more appropriate. Examples of these would include soups in winter, salad cream and mayonnaise in summer, paints and decorating materials in spring and autumn, and so on. Often, the level of stock held in the retail trade at the end of the season is the most important item of data to manufacturers. Increased frequency of reporting is more expensive, however, and unless the time required by the agency to prepare the reports is considerably shortened, a more frequent service is difficult to use fully and properly.

In test market audits where the sample of shops is comparatively small and the processing simple, audits are generally available at four-weekly intervals. Indeed, this is usually demanded since the object of test audits is often to measure short term activity or to obtain quick assessments of competitive tactics. An audit can be prepared to report even more frequently, but this is inevitably by special arrangement, and one example occurred some years ago when a national audit of approximately two hundred grocers was set up to audit daily, though reports were prepared only each week. The project ran successfully but once the pattern of sales by day of week was established and the seasonal differences observed, the auditing frequency dropped to weekly for reasons of cost. In national audits a bi-monthly report is more normal; more frequent reports can be arranged, at a price.

Client service

One of the attractions of buying from a syndicated service is that most companies that provide audits to manufacturers and distributors feature, as part of their service, the availability of a client service executive. It is his duty to maintain regular and frequent contact with clients in order to ensure that the data obtained from the audit are related to current problems and presented in the most easily understood way.

In contrast, the client service executive can never know more about the client's business than the client himself. Although he can only advise the client he can compare current market situations with what has occurred in others, since one of the duties of a client service executive is that he serves a number of non-competitive accounts and that he has a wide experience of the problems that face manufacturers, gained from practical experience. The experienced client service executive is not concerned with theories but with the practical, profitable, successful selling of his client's product. His purpose in life can be summarized as the responsibility to provide his client with the precise marketing intelligence necessary to aid the taking of sound marketing decisions. The value of his service, however, is directly correlated to the degree to which he enjoys his client's confidence and all who consider subscribing to a retail audit service need to be satisfied that the client service executive allocated to their account is a person with whom they feel they can discuss fully the problems of the company, in order to profit from that person's experience.

Validation

This is a necessary exercise to gauge the extent to which ex-factory shipment is being recorded by the audit. It forms the basis of the level of confidence that can be put upon the results, it indicates the adjustment necessary to account for differences and, of prime importance, the interpretation and use that can be made of the information about the market as a whole and competition, both strategically and tactically.

The calculation should be made at least half-yearly, more frequently for seasonal products, but always using moving annual totals of consumer sales and factory shipments in order to smooth the figures and avoid freak results caused by the inevitable varying time lapse between shipment and delivery to the store. Basically the formula is:

$$\frac{\text{Changes in stocks} + \text{Consumer Sales}}{\text{Factory Shipment}}$$

In Table 7.1 it can be seen that in the ideal situation, using audit information from a sample designed to reflect the full spectrum of outlets (a product class audit rather than a type of shop index, e.g. grocers), the changes in stock retail, wholesale, and multiple head office levels are all taken into account. Individual companies will need to make other

Table 7.1

| Product | Change in stocks | | | | Over-counter sales (5) | Total (4) + (5) (6) | Factory despatches (7) | per cent (6) to (7) (8) | 1967/68 per cent | 1966/67 per cent | 1965/66 per cent | 1964/65 per cent |
	Retail (1)	W/S (2)	H.O. (3)	Total (4)								
Brand A	+ 28.4	+ 21.4	+ 0.3	+ 50.1	1693.4	1743.5	1752.0	100	100	98	96	101
Brand B	+ 1.6	− 6.2	− 2.2	− 6.8	891.7	884.9	998.6	89	89	88	91	77
Brand C	− 0.1	− 7.6	+ 4.7	− 3.0	1398.9	1395.9	1341.5	104	100	97	98	100
Brand D	− 10.8	− 10.20	− 4.5	− 25.5	354.0	328.5	333.7	98	99	129	—	—
Total all brands	+ 19.1	− 2.6	− 1.7	+ 14.8	4338.0	4352.8	4425.8	98	98	96	96	99

adjustments. If the audit information available relates to only one type of shop, say grocers, and significant company sales are made through other outlet types, some allowance for the unaudited sales volume must be made. Other adjustments not featured in Table 7.1 should be made for sales through particular important retailers known not to co-operate with the audit.

As a general rule the higher the distribution and the greater the sales volume, the better the validation is likely to be.

Costs

It is most important to realize that the nature of an audit is its measurement of changes in the market over time, and that its value, therefore, is long term. Though it can, no doubt, help to resolve immediate problems, its real worth is the facility it gives management to observe, understand, and profit from changes both in the market as a whole and the individual parts of the market, pointing out areas of opportunity and weakness. It is essentially a continuous research vehicle and becomes integrated in company marketing thought. Once available as an aid to planning and market assesment, it is insidious in that it becomes difficult to conceive of ever having been without it.

The cost of an audit, whether as part of a syndicated service, a specially set up 'exclusive' panel or a test market, naturally reflects the complexity and amount of work involved. The number of shops, the frequency of visits, literally the volume of individual brands to be itemized and their incidence or distribution, the size of the market under study, the degree of breakdown required, the extra analyses, the interpretative function provided as part of the service and the length of contract, are all components of the cost. Some economies can be made by asking competing agencies for quotations and making use of the slightly different specifications, the different sample sizes providing the greatest opportunity for economy.

Case histories

Such is the confidential nature of the relationship between the research agency providing retail audit facilities and their clients (and the jealously guarded examples held by the manufacturers who conduct their own audits) that the illustrations of the practical use of audit information are limited to the few that follow. Nonetheless, they serve adequately to show the practical use of the data.

Case history 1
Quite apart from the special analyses of audit information carried out by the service company for a particular manufacturer, there are obvious gains in

information and a fresh understanding of changing market characteristics to
be made by reassembly of the standard data. In the following example the
grouping of individual brands with an empirical but meaningful (to the
manufacturer) reassembly of the data revealed to him the growth in a
particular sector of the trade. A number of individual minor brands had
been seen to be enlarging but the full significance of this growth was only
demonstrated when the data were re-presented (see Fig. 7.4). Re-analysis of
audit information by pack size, price, product type, company, or other
meaningful grouping should be carried out as a matter of course, in order to
get the most from the data and to determine the early indications of change.

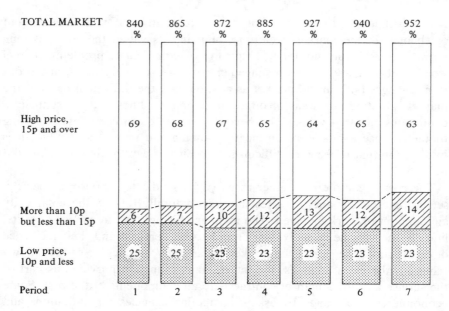

Fig. 7.4   Case history 1.

Case history 2
Confident of success following pre-tests of his commercial, the manufacturer
required reassurance so tested the sales effectiveness of the advertising for
his new product by buying time in all television areas except the Midlands.
Linked with the television campaign was a heavy sales drive to obtain
distribution. The data in Table 7.2 show that, although there was apparent
increase in distribution for the brand in the Midlands, the consumer reaction
was much less marked than in the areas where television had been used.

Case history 3
This example features the use of audit data to assist management in forward
planning. The figures shown in Table 7.3 are indices on a bi-monthly moving
annual total basis, in sterling turnover, for the total market.

Table 7.2   Case history 2

	London	South	West	Lancs	Yorks	Tyne	Scotland	Midlands
Brand A								
Sales share								
Pd1	23	25	10	8	16	23	27	25
Pd2	27	23	20	14	24	14	23	14
Pd3	54	53	62	69	48	44	42	23
Sterling distribution								
Pd1	81	82	60	79	61	53	55	56
Pd2	85	86	61	80	69	58	70	53
Pd3	92	94	84	90	75	79	82	69

(Courtesy A. C. Nielsen)

In making the first forward projection, management took simply the average of the growth for the first seven periods, 10.6%. At that time, distribution was already high at 85% numerical, 94% by value and it was assumed that advertising expenditure, as a percentage of sales, would remain constant at 22% as it had been in the two earlier years. With the benefit of hindsight, the final projected figure of 447 was remarkably close to the actual market size reached of 451, although there were signs in the periods immediately following the projection that the market had begun to slow down indicating that the projection would overstate. Management thus elected to make a second projection once again based on the average growth, this time for the preceding twelve months, which was 9.6%. There had been a marked increase in advertising expenditure, however, which, as a proportion of sales, now stood at 33%. Further, distribution had improved and for the last four periods of the projection stood at 88% numerical and 97% sterling (by value). Both these factors contributed towards the substantial difference between the two estimates and also from the actual market levels achieved.

Table 7.3   Case history 3

Moving annual totals																
Actual	100	110	123	134	147	163	182	198	212	230	255	284	319	361	411	451
First projection								↓	201	222	245	261	300	332	367	405	447
difference									+3	+10	+15	+6	+16	+13	+6	−6	−4
Second projection											↓	279	306	336	368	405
difference												−5	−13	−25	−43	−46

(Courtesy A. C. Nielsen)

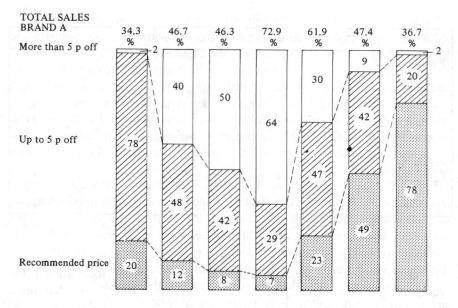

Fig. 7.5   Case history 4.

Case history 4

Sales of a recent nationally launched brand were seen to develop at a very fast rate (see Fig. 7.5). It was known from salesmen's reports that the brand was being dealt in heavily with selected retailers and was also being supported by a national 'money-off' offer. The intention was clearly to encourage trial. Analysis by price noted by the auditor at closing stock enabled sales to be analysed in detail, which revealed the very extensive below-the-line activity and entirely explained the rise in sales. Though backing at these levels could clearly not be maintained, the brand leader countered by more modest retail dealing and consumer offers, reducing the impact of the new brand and, as support was withdrawn, the brand reverted to its pre-promoted level.

Invoice analysis

As the name suggests, these are analyses of the delivery notes and invoices of goods bought by the retailers or wholesalers. No attempt is made to count stock, unlike the full retail audit and, consequently, tabulations are limited. This is adequate, however, for some product classes, the notable example being the full range of ethical pharmaceuticals. To all intents and purposes the retail stock level of the bulk of ethicals is constant, the retailer either ordering specifically for each prescription or replenishing his limited stock promptly. Obviously, the vast range of items prohibits any but the largest chemists carrying adequate stocks and one consequence of this is the remarkable wholesale service provided to chemists, twice daily. In this trade, then, stocks are constant and thus deliveries to the retailer are equivalent to over-the-counter sales to the customer.

The technique offers several advantages in that retailer co-operation is not strained, it is cheaper since the auditor does not need to spend time stock counting, and it should be faster since fewer analyses or tabulations are necessary. Where it is reasonable to assume that stocks are either constant or immaterial since their sale is imminent because of their nature, such as when shelf life is short, an invoice analysis is a useful and cheap alternative to the retail audit.

The next logical stage in the development of general invoice analysis has taken place in America. The research agency involved in pioneering the method is taking advantage of the (relatively) high degree of stock control exercised by distributors, to sell the concept of invoice analysis to manufacturers. The service is not confined to samples of retailers but reflects the whole structure of the distributive chain—wholesalers, head offices, and individual shops. It is fast, less expensive, and highly succesful.

This application in the UK is likely to be slower, the less 'organized' end of the trade is larger and it could be some time before the process of rationalization makes this technique more obvious. However, there are various products that could be adequately measured by invoice analysis such as cigarettes, perishables such as sausages, whole cheeses, fresh and chilled meat, bacon, fish, fresh fruit, and vegetables, and other merchandise which should only be handled by the shop staff. Currently the sales or deliveries of most of these products are not recorded or available to management even though organizations for their promotion and marketing exist.

Distribution checks

The battle for distribution and shelf space continues. The manufacturer wants high distribution, more shelf space, prime positioning and point of sale activity in store to increase sales and strengthen his brands. The retailer wants the best balance of product range, brand representation and pricing within his chosen marketing policy to attract and retain shoppers. Both are striving for brand share in their markets and the resultant highly competitive interface creates a vital need for detailed and continuous information on the in-store situation – mainly for the manufacturer but, increasingly, for the retailer as well.

Apart from the general need to monitor distribution levels and pricing for good housekeeping reasons, a manufacturer needs reliable information to assess the efficiency of his own distribution policies and networks, strategies and tactics. Many manufacturers experiment with varying cover and call rates; salesmen are concentrated in some areas and thinned out in others;

free mail-outs for immediate initial distribution are increasingly used as are commando sales forces. The effect on distribution of bonusing and dealings needs to be offset against the cost and the sales achieved. The measurement of exposure to new brands and line extensions is clearly dependent upon in-store checks as are checks on competitive pricing and point-of-sale activity. The rapid dissemination of distribution check data to sales regions is one of numerous tools the manufacturer uses to police the efficiency of his own sales force.

Whilst a retail audit also generates information on distribution, the high cost of auditing usually limits the sample size too much for it to provide the extent of diagnostic detail that is required by the manufacturer. To deal effectively with the distribution problems of today, the manufacturer needs information not only in broad terms, such as performance in multiple grocers in Scotland, Co-operatives in the Midlands, but more importantly, in terms of distribution by *name* of multiple chain, Co-op, symbol group, and so on.

As such large samples of outlets are required, the numbers are dependent on the extent to which the data needs to be interrogated. For example, to adequately represent the grocery trade in the UK a sample in excess of 2000 outlets would be required, divided into the main categories of multiple chains, Co-operatives, symbol groups (franchised) and independents and then further divided into adequate and representative sub-samples of named chains.

By equal cell sampling adequate coverage of both large and small multiple chains can be achieved with the proviso that the more homogenous the outlets belonging to a particular chain are, the smaller the sample that need be drawn to represent that chain. Chains that operate stores with differing price strategies (generally known as price bands) need to be represented adequately in each price band and this will dictate a greater number of such stores being monitored compared to a chain with a single strategy across all its outlets. Imbalance in the sample created by equal cell sampling or over-representation of particular chains is restored at the expansion stage by weighting data according to each cell's presence in the universe so as to provide correct national and area totals and within these, the shop type and named chain totals.

With the ever changing retail scene, take-overs, mergers and store expansions/closures have to be constantly monitored in order that representation can be kept up to date.

The basic data obtained from a distribution check is generally shown in two complementary forms:

(a) *Numerical distribution* – simply the proportion of shops of a particular type or name in a particular area found to be in stock at the time of fieldwork (after weighting to correct sample imbalances).

(b) *Sterling distribution* – this reflects the *quality* of distribution i.e. the volume of sales accounted for by the numerical levels of distribution established. Ideally this would be weighted in accordance with the turnover for each outlet visited but, because retailers are reluctant to release such information, the more common form of weighting is based on the number of full and part-time staff working in each outlet visited. Thus the level of distribution observed in a store staffed by 100 people would be worth ten times the distribution found in a store staffed by ten people.

Apart from the basic data described above a range of additional measurements can be offered by distribution checks. These include:

– average mean price for a brand and range of prices observed;
– degree of overlap in stocking of various brands;
– physical measurement of shelf space devoted to a brand;
– a count of 'facings' per brand i.e. the number of pack fronts/pack sides visible on a shelf;
– presence of promoted packs (banded packs, special offer packs etc.);
– the incidence of different types of point of sale material, special displays, dump bins, demonstrations.

All of the above types of information can be established by observation, permitting the 'investigator' to operate independently of shop management. By questioning store staff it is possible to establish the source of supply, i.e. the use of cash-and-carry wholesalers by the smaller retailers. Likewise, a measure of 'temporary-out-of-stock' can be established by enquiring whether a brand that is not visible in the store is usually stocked.

By analysis the data can be refined further to reflect manufacturer sales regions where they differ from the standard regional divisions, or to reflect direct and indirect trading between a manufacturer and a retail chain.

A number of research agencies specialize in syndicated distribution checks. These are carried out periodically across a wide range of retail sectors, usually monthly or bi-monthly in the fmcg markets and quarterly or less frequently in other markets. Most feature calls on a continuous sample, a form of panel operation.

Syndication enables the cost to an individual subscriber to be kept to a minimum, a matter of a few pence per item checked per outlet in many cases. Syndication requires compliance with pre-determined fieldwork dates and sample demographics although timings to suit, or sample extensions, can be arranged at higher cost.

Information needs to be processed very quickly, within a few days for sample bases up to the 1000 outlet mark and 2–3 weeks for the larger comprehensive services.

Price checks

In most respects the procedures for operating distribution checks apply equally to price checks. However, several important differences related to the use of price data sets them apart from distribution checks.

Most retail chains operate two and four-weekly cycles whereby all stores or bands of stores in the chain should carry the same price 'promotions'. Hence a manufacturer needs fast feedback on price information, not only to monitor own versus competitor's prices but to observe the effect of bonusing and other price incentives offered to the retailer (e.g. to what extent are trade bonuses passed on to the customer). A fast feedback of such data permits the manufacturer to negotiate with the trade on topical features rather than historic ones.

Price checks therefore need to be carried out more frequently than distribution checks per se (i.e. from weekly to four-weekly depending on the coverage required) with smaller samples of stores usually restricted to the main multiple groups. At the weekly price check level it is relevant to speak in terms of a one day fieldwork period (i.e. the same day each week) with data being issued two to three days later. The larger four-weekly checks may have up to a three day fieldwork period with data issue following after five to six working days.

Feature checks

Whilst not a generic term of reference in the market place, a feature check is a measure of price-promoted brands and other point of sale activity carried on in-store. A feature check represents a logical extension to distribution/price checks and links in with the entire area of point of sale activity.

As a marketing tool, a regular, frequent and composite measure of standard retailer price features, actual price, other point of sale activity and facings or shelf measurement (i.e. a comprehensive account of most in-store variables) can be compared to ex-factory account sales or retail audit data to gauge the effect of point of sale activity.

The general uniformity of trade 'promotions' across all stores in a multiple chain per trading cycle (or across a recognizable band of stores within a multiple chain) means that the quality of in-store activity rather than the extent is being measured. Therefore, relatively small but well structured samples can be monitored, facilitating fast data turn round and relatively low cost. The use of models at the data analysis stage permits rapid interpretation of the data and subsequent action.

Ad hoc trade studies

In the last 10–20 years the retail trade has undergone a major shift towards increasing concentration of volume and buying power among large multiple and voluntary group organizations. Similarly the number of products available has dramatically increased, and manufacturers are facing competition between themselves for distribution and shelf space. As a result, manufacturers and other suppliers of product or services to the retail trade have become aware of the need for more information about the needs and attitudes of the retail trade than can be provided solely by feedback from the sales force.

Selecting and obtaining trade channels and the motivation and performance of retailers are key influences on the effectiveness of every other marketing decision of the manufacturer or supplier. The co-operation and support of the retailer is obviously crucial for obtaining distribution for a new product and for such activities as special point of sale displays and certain types of consumer promotion. Trade studies are therefore carried out to examine attitudes in connection with the image of the company and its competitors, its products or services, pricing policies, selling methods, distribution policies, advertising and promotional policies, trade incentives, new product history, etc. Trade studies are also conducted to evaluate reaction to new product concepts, suitability of packaging, and so on.

In other words the range of topics covered in trade studies can be as broad as that covered in consumer research. Similarly, the techniques of trade studies differ little in principle from those of consumer research. It is important, however, to draw out the distinction between trade and consumer research arising out of the different characteristics of the two universes. A fundamental distinction lies in sampling procedures.

Sampling in trade studies

Samples of retailers have to be taken from a heterogeneous universe with a high degree of concentration in size, type and geographic location. These characteristics suggest the more frequent use of stratified probability sampling methods in trade research in order to achieve adequate representation of all types. This involves dividing or stratifying the universe into more homogeneous groups and then selecting a random sample from within each. An example of such a sampling frame would be type of trade × form of organization × turnover size within region.

Two main problems arise in this type of sampling exercise. First, precise definition of the characteristics or types can be difficult. Errors can easily occur: for example, the distinction between a department store and a furniture store, wholesalers that are both cash-and-carry and conventional. Second, it is necessary to have information on the sampling frames, ideally a complete list with details of all significant characteristics. Only in this way can the results be aggregated to give estimates of the whole population. Unfortunately, this is difficult with the current paucity of relevant census data in countries such as the UK, particularly with the constantly changing characteristics of the retail and wholesale trade. Steps have been taken by the Department of Trade, largely at the instigation of the Market Research Society, to meet the need for information in these areas. In addition, the television contractors conduct their own censuses and re-analyse and update Department of Trade estimates. Often the most useful sources for filling sample frames are directories and trade registers such as Benn's Hardware Directory, the Chemists Register, the Grocer's Supermarket Directory, Classified Telephone Directories while curiously, but not ominously, fairly exhaustive listings can be obtained through the Inland Revenue and local authority rating lists. Directory lists can be easily obtained from many sources (e.g. Current British Directories: C.B.D. Research), but care must be exercised in using directories as most are bound to be out of date before they are in print and some, particularly trade association membership lists, contain many serious omissions.

It is difficult to generalize about the appropriate sizes of samples in trade research. However, sample sizes smaller than those generally used in consumer surveys usually suffice. Care must be taken in choosing a sample size to avoid attempting a census rather than a sample. The important determinants of sample size are obviously the objectives of the study and accuracy required, the nature of the universe, the number of categories or sub-samples to be analysed and the type or level of respondent to be interviewed.

Interviewing in trade studies

Apart from the difficulties of sampling set out above, another major problem in conducting trade surveys is the correct identification of a respondent, particularly in studies of buying procedures. In multiple or co-operative retail outlets buying decisions are rarely taken at the retail manager level. Moreover, buying decisions taken at the head offices of multiples or co-operatives may not be the responsibility of a single individual. In these situations several interviews may be undertaken within a single organization. More generally, the scope of trade research can be usefully extended by questioning not only the retailer but also his staff and his customers as they make their purchases, go through checkouts or emerge from the store. A recent study of trade incentives by an oil company included interviews with forecourt attendants and workshop staff as well as garage proprietors. It is obviously vital in such studies that the permission and co-operation of the manager (both local and head office, as appropriate) is obtained.

Contacting the appropriate respondents and arranging appointments for interviews is crucial to secure a high rate of successful interviews. Generally speaking, a higher interview success rate is achieved when interviews are pre-arranged as opposed to 'cold calls'. The quickest and most efficient way of arranging interviews is by telephone, especially for identifying the correct respondent. The retailer is a busy man and his time is limited. While it follows that a short interview will have a lower rate of failure-to-complete, successful interviews extending well over an hour are frequently achieved. Peripheral questions should be edited out of the questionnaire and as much information as possible obtained by observation rather than questioning. The brands stocked, the numbers of fixtures, floor displays, product locations and space, the use of particular forms of promotion material can all be observed or noted and need not require questions to be put to the retailer. Where possible, however, observations should be cross-checked with the retailer and vice versa.

Interviewing in trade surveys is often structured but semi-structured or non-directive interviewing can be more productive. While the last is not structured in the sense that precise questions are formulated in advance and asked in a given sequence, non-directive interviews are not casual discussions; there is usually a high degree of precision in both the questioning and classification of results. There can be problems of communication in trade survey interviewing. It is obviously important to use the language and idiom of the section of the retail trade under study. Expressions which are familiar to managers of multiples are not necessarily as well known to the independent. Grocery terms are not those in common use among the hardware trade. Considering the grocery trade only, the following terms have been found to be confusing even within that trade and serve to illustrate the very real need for preparation and care in this area:

allocation	in-store promotion	return
backing card	lines	run
bonus	long runs	shelftalker
broken bulk	marketed	shrink wrap
cover	merchandise	spectacular
direct	movement	splits
expanded	offer	stack
fixture	operator	stand
flash pack	pack	stand strips
floor display	period	stock loading
group	promotion	units
indirect	quote	volume

The above discussion has implicitly been concerned with face-to-face interviewing. The techniques of postal questionnaires and telephone interviewing can be used to advantage in trade surveys, perhaps to a greater extent than in consumer research. The use of postal questionnaires is covered in chapter 10, and it is sufficient to say that the same rules and pitfalls of using postal questionnaires in consumer research apply in trade surveys.

On the other hand, use of the telephone in trade surveys does not suffer some of the problems apparent in consumer research. Telephone ownership is not a source of sampling bias since every retailer, virtually without exception, is on the telephone. Telephone interviewing enjoys the obvious benefits of time and cost savings, and because the telephone is so much a part of business life interviews are conducted under familiar and almost normal circumstances. There are however two main disadvantages of using the telephone in trade surveys. First, there are the obvious limitations on certain types of questioning, especially those where visual aids are usually necessary, e.g. image rating scales. Second, it is not possible to assess the physical environment of the respondent that in personal interviewing provides valuable classification data and illuminates the answers of respondents.

Trade surveys confront the researcher with certain additional problems not generally encountered in consumer research. Some of these problems require imagination and creativity while others can only be resolved in a pragmatic way. Above all, however, the advice and recommendations applying to research elsewhere in in this volume should be employed with the utmost rigour in trade surveys. A clear understanding of the problem, care in constructing the questionnaire, pilot interviews to check interpretation and flow, the relevance of questions, the ability of the respondent to answer the questions and the adequacy of the sample must all be thoroughly checked out before the main fieldwork starts.

Point-of-sale studies

Manufacturers, in response to the growing power and sophistication of the retail trade's strategies for space utilization, have increasingly been directing effort and expenditure towards activities at the point of sale. Merchandizing support, pricing and consumer promotional schemes can all be readily monitored using a store-related check. However, this by itself will not provide an adequate quantification of the return on investment. In the not-too-distant future retailers will themselves be able to obtain this data via scanning checkouts at the point of sale. Recognizing this, manufacturers are demanding research services enabling them to monitor more closely the in-store situation and in particular the *effect* their activities have.

The manufacturer needs to know not only how much additional volume any particular point-of-sale activity generates but also whether that activity reinforces brand strengths, stimulates trial, encourages repeat purchase, increases quantity bought, or, on the negative side, whether it merely encourages temporary 'stocking up' among existing buyers or even discourages purchase.

Trade research of this type can thus operate at two levels. The first is primarily descriptive: *what* are the effects of the activity in question? The second deals more with the dynamics: *how and why* are these effects achieved?

Measuring the effect

One method of measuring the effect of point-of-sale is by special analysis of available *continuous data*, such as shop audits, consumer panels and price/feature checks. This is, of course, a relatively long-term method and involves collection of data prior to the point-of-sale activity being measured.

Special analyses may be conducted on *retail audits* such as those provided by Nielsen and (in the UK) Stats MR. These would provide an indication of the 'first level' effects such as out-of-stocks and price reductions. However, the need to preserve the confidentiality of the retailer's data means that effects on sales can only be presented in terms of groupings of outlets which can span a variety of retail accounts.

Consumer panels can take the account marketeer one step closer to understanding in depth the effect of point of sale. However, because of problems of sample size, regional structure of existing consumer panels which can affect shop data, and lack of information on exposure to point of sale activity, the application tends again to be limited to 'first level' effects.

Adhoc experiments are quite commonly used to evaluate effects of point-of-sale activity. These may be done by using one outlet over a long period, or a panel of outlets over a rather shorter time-scale. With a panel of stores, bias due to between-store differences and between-period effects can be neutralized by use of a Latin square experimental design.

To utilize this type of research to the fullest a simple audit of sales is insufficient, albeit necessary. Further insight into the way in which the point-of-sale activity works can be gained by supplementing the sales audit with *observation* of customers at the point of sale, and by *interviewing* them once a choice has been made. Such research takes us into the area of 'second-level' effects.

The dynamics of point of sale

While all the above methods provide an assessment of the effect of point of sale activity on sales levels and the last goes some way to providing data on *how* the activity is working, none of them allow the manufacturer an understanding of the full dynamics of point of sale. For instance: is there variation by product field; what is the influence of the chain and its style of trading; is there variation at individual outlet level; is the type of shopping trip important. Only with an appreciation of these effects will the manufacturer be able to decide on more effective point of sale strategies.

An approach to understanding the dynamics of point of sale involves marrying several of the techniques described above and elsewhere in this book. The first element in the research is to ascertain whether, and to what extent, point of sale activity has affected the purchase decision. In order to do this one needs to know not only what was purchased, but also whether that was different from what was *intended* as a purchase. It is clearly important that intentions and actual purchases must be measured on the *same* people. (A major basic research project has demonstrated that prior questioning need not affect purchasing behaviour if the experiment is appropriately designed.) Obviously the questionnaire would establish the reasons, as the consumer relates them, for discrepancies between intentions and actual purchases.

This questionnaire is augmented by a complete log of in-store activity on the same day, including range, space allocation, prices, promotions, special offers, special features and displays, etc. Further questioning, usually by means of a self-completion postal questionnaire, can establish general behavioural information, on general shopping habits for example. Integration of all three sets of data provides a valuable insight into the dynamics of point of sale.

Chapter 8

Panel research

JOHN PARFITT

This chapter is concerned with panels. Like so many common English words placed in a market research context, its special research meaning is entirely familiar to the practitioners and confusing to the layman. Its nearest common meaning is a list of names (doctors, jurors, etc.), but in its research meaning this list of names has to be performing certain functions for certain desired objectives before it takes the form of a panel.

There are a wide variety of panel techniques available in Great Britain and some are permanent and some short term. Their functions and characteristics are described later in this chapter. All these panels have two common distinguishing characteristics with regard to the type of data they are designed to obtain and the method of obtaining it:

(a) Panels are based on a representative sample of individuals or households from the universe being studied (e.g. all private households, all households with TV sets, all cigarette smokers, etc.). Each individual or household panel member records (or permits the recording of) their complete activity in some factual aspect of consumer behaviour, such as their purchases in a defined range of consumer products or their television viewing.

(b) This measurement is ideally a continuous process over time, by virtue of retaining the same sample of respondents over the full period of measurement and obtaining from them a continuous and complete record of the required data. The collection of these data has, therefore, to be at regular and frequent intervals.

There are two basic objectives of panels, whatever specific data they are designed to collect. These are to:

(a) collect detailed and accurate information of the anatomy of consumer behaviour and the characteristics of the consumers; in other words, to obtain such precise information about the behaviour of each consumer or group of consumers that the differences in behaviour can be clearly recognized and the relevant characteristics recorded. This refers, of course, to basically factual data about behaviour and not attitudinal data and in this respect panels offer the possibility of much greater accuracy and detail than is normally possible from single call interviewing techniques;

(b) obtain information on the dynamics of consumer behaviour over time. The continuous study of the behaviour of individual consumers over time, made possible by the panel techniques, enables measurements to be made of the consistencies and inconsistencies of consumer behaviour, exact measurements of the frequency and volume of purchases/viewing/reading (whatever is being measured) and the response to given stimuli – advertising, brand launches, program changes, or whatever.

Why use panels?

It requires little knowledge of research to see that these can be difficult objectives to attain in full. The problem of respondent co-operation alone is a formidable one. Panels require a lot of 'know-how' to be run efficiently and, above all, they are expensive to operate. It is relevant to ask, therefore, why bother to set up panels anyway, what use do they have and in what sense do they have advantages over research techniques that may be cheaper and easier to operate? After all, sample size for sample size it will be far cheaper to call on a sample of respondents only once and interview them on, say, their purchasing behaviour for the last three months than to set up a panel that records these data for three months, so what advantages do panels offer for the extra money and time?

The answer to this question is in two parts:

(a) Panels have marked advantages in the amount and accuracy of the data that can be obtained from one source, compared with the normal alternative of single call interview techniques (see 'Technical considerations in panels').

(b) The depth of analysis of the dynamics of consumer behaviour possible from the continuous nature of panel measurements offers unique opportunities to understand the ways in which the consumer behaves under given stimuli (see 'Analysis of panel data').

The marketing need for panel data

The wide range of panel and repetitive survey services currently available in Great Britain has grown not out of the steady widening of technical research knowledge as to how to operate them, since this was known substantially long before the majority of the services began (even if it has been polished en route), but out of the marketing need and, therefore, demand for the data they provide. The first of these services to be launched in Great Britain was the household consumer panel technique (the Attwood panel started in 1948). In the years since 1955 and, particularly, in the six years from 1964 to 1970, many other panel services have been set up to meet specific marketing requirements for data. What were the marketing requirements which caused the development of the consumer panels?

A leaflet published by Arthur D. Little Inc. makes the challenging statement: 'Marketing managers are being inundated with data but starved of information'. The distinction drawn by the writer is between data (facts about the world) and information (answers to specific questions). In measuring consumer purchasing and attitudes, one is gathering 'data' (as defined) but one is also gathering them selectively with a view to transmuting them into 'information' (as defined). There are certain recurrent questions in marketing which the manufacturer's research department knows to be of perennial interest and, therefore, facilities have been created to provide the 'data' which will yield the necessary 'information'. The questions are of the type:

How many people buy my product?
How much do they buy?
Who are my competitors?
How strong are they?
Are we/they gaining or losing?
What sort of people buy our/their products?
Is any brand responsive to promotion?
Has it regional/shop-type strengths and weaknesses? etc.

Marketing people are very interested in the detailed anatomy of the market and also in its dynamic characteristics. Monitoring services of various sorts have grown up to satisfy this need and among these the consumer panel technique.

The type of service which has evolved reflects the nature of the need. A mail order house, for instance, obtains a great deal of information from its own internally collected statistics. The exact response to any advertisement may be determined right down to the last unit sold and the name and address of each customer. A seller of expensive consumer durables such as Rolls-Royce may go even further and seek to maintain a 'cradle to grave' record of each vehicle that leaves the factory. A soap powder manufacturer, on the other hand, may sell 5 million units per week of a big brand and, without some fairly elaborate system of data collection, he will have little idea of the final destination of these packets after his own transport and distribution organization has offloaded them at the delivery point. Similarly, apart from a few rather barren industry statistics, supplied by his trade association, he will have little knowledge of what his competitors are doing. It is with the information needs of manufacturers at this 'low cost/repeat purchase' end of the spectrum rather that at the 'high cost/consumer durable' end that consumer panels are mainly concerned.

The manufacturer who is interested in the market standing of low-cost repeat purchase items is faced with two main choices of data source. He may choose a method which takes a measurement at some point in the chain of wholesale and retail distribution. Commercial services are available which measure such things as warehouse withdrawal (mainly in the US), retail sales, retail distribution (retail audits and distribution checks). Such techniques are described elsewhere in this volume. His alternative is to pick a method which goes directly to the final link in the chain, the consumer, and again there are many commercial services which take measurements at this point. They fall into two broad categories – interview survey techniques, and continuous consumer panels. Some of the relative merits of interview surveys and panels with regard to the accuracy and detail of the data that can be obtained from respondents are discussed in a later section. For the time being it is sufficient to mention that it is the continuity of the data supplied by consumer panels that gives them particular value in providing marketing information.

People's actions are often a better guide to their character than their expressed opinions. Consumer panels are concerned mainly with consumer *behaviour*, i.e. actions not opinions. Again, a motion picture conveys more information than a snapshot. A snapshot of a hundred housewives might reveal that thirty of them were wearing hats. A second picture of another hundred might turn up the same proportion of hat-wearers. What does one conclude? – that 30 % of housewives wear hats? A continuous film record of the behaviour of one of these groups might show that all its members wear hats, but that they do so only 30 % of the time. Such a finding would be entirely consistent with the snapshot evidence, but might well lead to different conclusions, particularly if one happened to be a hatter. Consumer panels are *continuous:* they aim to cover *all* the purchases of each panel member over time in the field under study.

Thus, the consumer panel technique operates by confining itself to the collection of basically factual data about consumer purchasing behaviour, containing the minimum of respondent bias or conditioning resulting from seeking opinions or searching the respondents' memories about purchasing behaviour, and transmuting it by analysis into marketing 'information' for the study, not only of the detailed anatomy of the market but also of the dynamics of consumer behaviour over time.

The types of panel services available

Continuous consumer purchasing panels

The majority of permanent panel services are purchasing panels, based either on samples of households or individuals. The principles of some key ones operating in Great Britain in 1984 were:

Panel service	Date of formation	Reporting sample size	Data collection method	Type of data collected	Standard reporting periods
Attwood Consumer Panel/Individuals Panel	1948/1970	4000 households 10.000 individuals	Postal diary	Purchases of household consumer goods/personal consumer goods	4-weekly and/or quarterly
AGB Television Consumer Audit	1964	6600 households	Home audit	Purchases of household consumer goods	4-weekly
TCPI (Individuals Panel)	1973	10.000 adults 1500 children	Postal diary	Purchases of personal consumer goods	One or two-monthly
RSGB Baby Panel	1967	1650 mothers with babies	Diary and interviewers	Purchases of consumer goods for use by babies	4-weekly and/or quarterly
RBL Motorists Panel	1964	4000 individual motorists	Postal diary	Purchases of petrol, oil and car accessories	4-weekly
Agridata Farming Panels	1971	Two Panels of Farmers arable and livestock 3000 total	Personal interview	Purchases of sprays, fertilizers, feeds etc.	Quarterly
AGB Index	1978	10.000 individuals	Personal	Spending habits, savings, insurance	Monthly

There are two basic alternatives for collecting data in consumer purchasing panels. There are the home audit and the diary method.

The home audit

A panel is recruited and agrees to one main condition, i.e. that once a week (or at some other agreed interval) the panel member will admit an auditor into her home and will permit her to check household stocks of any product field in which she may be interested. Secondary conditions are that the panel member will save up used cartons, wrappers, etc., in a special receptacle provided by the auditor and that she will also answer a short questionnaire when the auditor calls (since some required information about the purchase will not be obtainable from the package alone). The auditor then checks all household stocks and *marks* the packets that have not been marked in previous weeks. She then checks the receptacle for used packs, ignores anything that has been marked at a previous call, and adds to the total any used pack which has not been marked. Thus, the purchases for the week are counted as all packets found in stock, in use or in the empty packet receptacle, that had not been marked at previous calls.

The diary method

A panel member is recruited and undertakes to record in a preprinted diary all purchases, made either by herself or by other members of the family, in certain nominated product fields. Every week (or at some agreed interval) she returns the diary to the research company. She may or may not be provided with a receptacle for used packets (as an aid to memory). If she normally receives and returns diaries by post, she will be visited periodically by a representative of the research company so that the contact is kept 'alive' and is not allowed to grow stale, and to provide an 'educational' function where necessary. Some diary panels rely on interviewer collection of the diaries anyway – this is more expensive but it does combine some advantages of both systems. Successful experimental work has been conducted in which the respondent passes the purchasing data by telephone. In this instance the diary performs the function of an aide-mémoire.

All operators of consumer purchasing panels use one or other of these methods of data collection but predominantly it is the diary method that is used. A great deal has been said about the advantages of the one method or the other in the collection of panel data and remarkably little has been written for publication. The home audit method appeals to the imagination more as an objective method putting less burden on the panel members than the diary method, which may be subject to problems of understanding, memory, and fatigue. In practice, the differences between the two methods appear to be much less marked that they appear to be in theory, i.e. judging from parallel data from the Attwood panel (postal diary) and the TCA panel (home audit). Nevertheless, there are differences and the principal advantages and disadvantages of the two data collection methods appear to be as follows:

(a) Postal diary collection methods are cheaper to operate than home audits and, as the method is not dependent on regular personal calls, the sample does not need to be so closely clustered as for home audits. A part of these two advantages disappears when interviewers are used for diary collection.

(b) The initial panel recruitment rate is probably higher for the home audit method than for the diary method. In both cases recruitment is by personal interview. How important this factor is is a moot point bearing in mind that in the USA national diary panels are usually recruited by mail and produce a 10–15% recruitment rate, compared with, say, 50% for diary panels in Great Britain and higher for home audit panels; and yet the American panels are reported to produce very reliable purchasing data.

(c) The continuity of panel membership is probably higher for the home audit method than for the postal diary method. A 'drop out' rate of 25–30% per annum can be expected from a postal diary panel and 10% has been quoted for home audit panels, although this latter figure sounds low allowing for the normal rates of death and home removal in this country. The use of interviewers to collect diaries almost certainly reduces the 'drop out' rate below the level quoted above for diary panels, since it is known that regular calling has a beneficial effect on continuity of panel membership.

(d) Home audits are entirely dependent on getting regular access to the home for the collection of data, which postal diary panels are not. On the other hand the non-receipt of a diary for a particular week calls for very quick action from the research company to collect the diary if the record is not to be lost.

(e) The two methods have different advantages and disadvantages in the collection of certain types of data. Thus, home audits record very accurately any promotions, special offers, etc., marked on the pack. Pick-up of other promotions is adequate but probably no better than diary records. Foodstuffs which are bought loose and consumed quickly are hard to check in home audits, and wrappers which may start to smell after a brief storage may be missing from the audit bin and missed from the audit. These present no particular problem in a diary record. Diaries are probably better than audits at picking up the purchases of 'other family members', e.g. the teenage daughter's personal bottle of shampoo or father's extra tube of toothpaste packed in the overnight bag may well be missed even in a conscientious audit.

(f) The diary method can cover a wider range of goods and services than the home audit method as such, since it is not dependent on physical evidence of purchases for its data collection. Thus, it can collect data on products with important unbranded sectors, like eggs, sausages and cheese, or products difficult to audit in the home, like paint or garden products, or services like hairdressing, cinema visits, or dry cleaning. Naturally, these data can be collected on home audits also but only by the introduction of diaries or by interviewer-administered questionnaires.

Although both audit and diary panels have their imperfections, both methods have over long periods been shown in Great Britain to provide accurate market share and trend data over a wide range of product fields. The technical weaknesses do not manifest themselves to any very great extent if the aim is simply to produce aggregate market share data by weekly or quarterly periods; and this was the type of service which the panel companies were originally set up to supply. Indeed, the bulk of their income is still derived from the sale of such standard reports.

Of the continuous consumer purchasing panels operating in Great Britain in 1984 one, the TCA panel, relies on the home audit method and the remainder on the diary method, with or without interviewer collection of diaries. Two are household panels (the Attwood Consumer Panel and the AGB home audit panel) set up for the collection of purchasing data on products which are basically for household use. In these panels it is the housewife who is recruited for co-operation in the collection of the data, both because she is usually the most readily available of the household members and also because she will normally be the main agent of purchase for products of this kind. The Attwood consumer panel did for some years rely on supplementary data from diaries issued to other household members for recording purchases of a more personal kind, e.g. shampoos, toilet soaps, records, etc. This was done on the grounds that these are purchases which the housewife might not otherwise be aware of and therefore would not record in her household diary. The logical consequence of this technique is the more recent development in continuous panel services – personal panels.

Two personal panels have been set up on a national basis – the AGB TCPI and the Attwood AMSAC panel, although the latter was drawn from the same households as the Household Panel. The method of operation of these is basically similar to that of household diary panels except that the data are collected from individuals rather than households and the range of products on which data can be collected goes far beyond what is considered to be feasible from a household panel, e.g. it includes make-up, confectionery, etc., which are essentially personal purchases for personal consumption often beyond the home. The principal problem in collection of these types of data is to ensure that the panel members record their purchases as soon after making them as possible, since the frequency of purchase is often far higher than for products normally recorded in household panels; and the evidence of purchase, i.e. packaging, often disappears quickly after purchase as does the memory of the purchase. Experimental work has suggested that a more portable form of diary than is necessary for a household panel is a valuable aid to complete an accurate recording of personal purchases of this kind.

Two other continuous consumer purchasing panels mentioned in the summary – the RSGB Baby Panel and RBL Motorist Panel – are essentially aimed at special interest groups (mothers with babies, and motorists) but otherwise work on normal diary panel lines. The motorist panel comes closer to a personal panel than the others and relies on a small-size diary which can be kept in the car to ensure that petrol and oil purchases are recorded as soon as possible after they are made. The baby panel has particularly acute recruitment problems, compared with the normal run of panels, since only mothers with young babies are of interest and they need to be recruited as soon after the birth of the child as possible. And once the baby is over two years of age panel membership is no longer required.

The Agridata Farming Panels are a very special form of panel and come near the boundaries of the techniques covered in this chapter. Quarterly personal interviews with the farmers establish purchases of products necessary for farming – chemicals, sprays, animal health products, feedstuffs, etc. Both diaries and invoice auditing had been used to collect the data before the personal interview was adopted.

Short-term consumer purchasing panels [1]

Unlike the continuous panels, the short-term consumer purchasing panels do not usually operate on a syndicated service basis. They are designed for a specific purpose, usually only for one client, and their duration is determined by the measurements necessary to answer the marketing problems for which they were set up. A minimum of twelve weeks and a maximum of a year are the usual limits of these short-term panels. The objectives of these are numerous but the most important of them are:

(a) To measure test marketing activity, particularly in terms of product penetration and repeat purchasing, in test towns or in small areas where the continuous panel services do not yield samples of a sufficient size.

(b) To test out alternative marketing choices, e.g. alternative promotional activities, in controlled conditions in order to determine which is likely to be the most efficient in general use, or to discover whether existing policies could be modified without detriment to the product's sales. To do this, different matched panels are subjected to the different marketing pressures under observation and the purchasing behaviour of the samples are compared, usually in penetration and repeat purchasing terms. There are sometimes as many as half a dozen matched panels under observation at the same time, although the number is usually only two or three. They may all be located in the same district or town, or sometimes they are located in different areas depending on how closely the stimuli being applied can be confined to the households under observation. Thus, a test of different advertising campaigns usually has to take place in several areas, as the advertising cannot be confined to small districts; whereas a comparison of different promotional activities can often be carried out within the same district or town.

(c) A third use of short-term consumer panels is where information is required from the panel households or where they are subjected to special marketing pressures which would be considered conditioning and detrimental to the future buying behaviour of permanent panel members. Thus, purchasing behaviour collected from the panel may need to be related to information on their attitudes to the product or awareness of its advertising, etc. This is perfectly feasible with a short-term panel. Indeed the application of awareness and attitude questions at the end of the panel's life is a standard feature of the technique, whereas such information obtained from a permanent panel might be considered harmful to the representativeness of the panel's future buying behaviour.

The data collection methods employed in short-term panels are much the same as those described earlier for the continuous panel services. The principal difference is that the recruitment rate for short-term panels is usually higher than for permanent panels since more respondents are prepared to participate in panels when they know exactly how long it is for, and when the burden of data required from them is relatively small.

Consumer product consumption panels

In the same way that consumer purchasing behaviour is complex and liable to exaggeration and over-simplification in single call interview situations so, too, is consumer consumption behaviour of the products they buy or make. The pattern of product consumption, the uses to which products are put, the occasions of consumption, who consumes them, in what quantities and with what other products, etc., can be measured most accurately over time by means of a panel. These are normally very short-term panels set up long enough to allow for running-in and the normal cycle of consumption behaviour, for which an average period may be eight weeks duration, dependent on the average frequency of consumption and purchase of the product under observation.

Like short-term purchasing panels, the panels to measure product consumption are usually set up for one specific purpose and for one client. The purpose normally requires some disguise as far as the respondent is concerned to avoid over-reporting of consumption behaviour, and this is usually achieved by measuring a wider range of product consumption than is required for the study. The scope of product consumption panels is wide. In the experience of the author examples of them give some illustrations of the size, subject, and duration of panels of this kind. Panels set up to measure the preparation and consumption in the home of soups and canned puddings had a sample of 1000 housewives and lasted for eight weeks. During this time, housewives recorded the occasions of serving the products, details of other foods eaten with them, who ate them, full details of the product served, etc. An edible fats consumption panel consisted of 1000 housewives and lasted for three weeks (some in winter, spring, and summer) and obtained full details and the quantities of each purpose for which butter, margarine, etc., was used. A clothes washing habits panel of 300 housewives ran for six weeks and obtained full details of the washes carried out, the main clothes categories washed and of the washing products used.

It is normal at the finish of the panel operation to interview the respondent in order to obtain attitude and awareness data and to relate these to consumption habits.

Shopping panels for pre-launch prediction measurements [2]

This research technique is really a variant of the consumer purchasing panel and is designed to measure the repeat purchase potential for a new product without having to launch it first. There are two main variants, permanent syndicated panels like the Mini-Test Service, and short-term tailor-made panels like the MPL Brandshare Service. Both provide means of bringing the housewife's shopping to her and thus exposing her to test products not yet on the market.

The Forecast Mini-Test Panel consists of a demographically controlled sample of housewives in a town (Forecast have a 600 housewife panel in both Southampton and Manchester) who have expressed their willingness to purchase products from a travelling shop. The travelling shop is, in fact, run by the research company and calls on each housewife once a week. Each housewife is regularly supplied with a brochure containing illustrations of all the products and brands she can purchase and an order form (which, in effect, is the equivalent of a panel diary). The operation carries the usual range of brands in each product field it covers, and these are at carefully controlled but competitive prices. In addition, however, it introduces new brands or varieties which are not available on the general market and using the brochure as an advertising medium and applying normal promotion schemes where necessary it promotes these products to the panel.

The MPL Brandshare example recruits an *ad hoc* panel for each test, tailored by region and respondent characteristics to the potential market of the product under test, e.g. heavy buyers of key competitive products, buyers of a house brand in the same market (to measure cannibalization) etc. Panel members are exposed to the new product and its advertising at a pre-panel briefing. The panel normally lasts for 10 calls (weekly or fortnightly) to establish the repeat purchase rate, and then members are interviewed about the product at the end.

Both types of panel tend to achieve an abnormally high penetration for the new brand, compared with what would probably happen in a real test market situation. They provide, however, a realistic impression of the likely repeat purchasing rate the brand would achieve in the market. It is on this latter measurement that the panel largely depends for its assessment of whether the brand would be successful or not if it were launched.

Television-viewing panels

The television-viewing panel technique was developed by Nielsen in the USA and, at the time of the start of commercial television in Great Britain, by TAM. This service is now operated by AGB on behalf of BARB.

The panel is recruited from households with television sets and the primary measurement is achieved by means of a meter attached to the set which records the time when the set is turned on or off and the station it is tuned to and, aided by push button recording, who is in the room with the set. From these data are estimated the total household viewing audiences to each channel in each ITV area and also the demographic composition of these audiences.

By consumer purchasing panel standards panel sizes in each area are comparatively small, as is shown below, and this can be attributed to the comparative simplicity and stability of television viewing behaviour compared with the complexities of consumer purchasing behaviour.

BARB panel sample sizes in each ITV area:
Television meter households in each area

London	350	Central Scotland	200	Ulster	100
Central	300	North East England	200	Border	100
North West	300	Wales and the West	300	South West England	150
Yorkshire	250	East of England	300	North Scotland	100
		South	350		
		Total in Great Britain 3000 households			

The recruitment rate for television viewing panels and the continuity of panel membership is traditionally higher than for consumer purchasing panels (particularly of the diary panels). This can be attributed to the smaller burden on the respondents, the relatively greater attractiveness of television panel membership and to the higher rewards offered. This subject of television viewing panels is covered in greater depth in chapter 25.

Product testing panels

Product testing panels are more in use in the USA than in this country. Their title is slightly inaccurate since they are usually used for collecting data quite as much as for testing products. They lack many of the common characteristics of the panels so far described since there is seldom any continuity in the data collection or product testing functions; their continuity is solely in the fact that a particular sample of respondents of known characteristics is retained for a semi-continuous miscellany of research enquiries. They are at their optimum use when the cost of interviewer field work for national enquiries is at its maximum in relation to postal costs (as in the USA or France) and for this reason have made rather less headway in Great Britain where travelling distances and field work costs are comparatively low. Their principal use in

Britain has been by manufacturers running their own panels, and this has been primarily to retain the maximum control and secrecy in their product development.

Technical considerations in panels

Sample selection

As panels are usually intended to operate for a considerable length of time, if not indefinitely, considerable care is applied in sample selection at recruitment. The Attwood consumer panel, for example, was based on 250 local government sample district clusters of 16 households in each. These were selected in a four-stage stratified random sample, the last stage of which was the selection of addresses at a fixed interval from the electoral registers of wards selected at the third stage. The resulting sample was proportionately correct by four town size groups within 15 control areas in the country and demographically balanced within each of the 15 areas.

It is not sufficient, however, just to exercise this care at the initial recruitment stage. Similar controls have to be applied in two other panel-sampling procedures. The first of these relates to panel maintenance, i.e. the replacement of households which are removed or remove themselves from the panel. This is a continuous process and each removed household has to be replaced by another with similar demographic and area characteristics. To provide these 'quotas' a large number of households selected by the methods described above have to be surveyed and held in readiness for the occasion when they need to be used as panel replacements.

The second sampling procedure relates to actual reporting periods. Any panel has a reserve over and above its basic reporting number to allow for slow or non-return of purchasing records in any one period. This reserve (usually about 10%) has to be large enough so that in any period a fully balanced area and demographic sample of reporting households can be drawn within a minimum waiting period, otherwise panel reporting would be delayed whilst the returns from demographically deficient groups were awaited.

The validity of panel data

The fact that panel recruitment rates may vary from as little as 10 to 15% of initial contacts in postal recruitment in the USA to around 50% for diary panels in Great Britain and higher for home audit and *ad hoc* panels has already been discussed. Thus, there are a lot of people who refuse to join panels, and this sometimes raises doubts about the representativeness of those who do. A source of evidence which suggests that panels are representative comes from some experimental work to create psychological or attitude grouping scales with which to classify panel housewives. An initial set of attitude scales designed ultimately to be related to consumer purchasing behaviour on the panel were applied initially to a random sample of 3600 non-panel housewives. The results obtained from the random sample and later from the panel housewives show a close similarity in attitude groupings, as may be seen in Table 8.1.

The extremes of each scale are composed largely of different housewives. It is not unreasonable to assume that if the consumer panel sample was fundamentally unrepresentative of the domestic household population then significant differences would appear in these attitude scales and, in its turn, in purchasing behaviour.

In theory, the simplest way to test the validity of purchasing data obtained from panels is to compare them with data obtained from other sources. In practice this is difficult, partly because very little other reliable information is available and, where it is available, it is often hard to make direct comparisons with panel results. This is because household consumer panels measure only purchases taken into the home and, in some fields, this excludes important areas of consumption beyond the home. Where such information does exist, and it is usually in the form of total production figures for the retail market, then the panel results (grossed-up) normally range from about two-thirds to 100 % of these tonnages, depending on how much purchasing occurs beyond the home. In the case of flour, for instance, where there is little non-domestic consumption of retail packs the panel pick-up is virtually 100 %. In the case of toilet soaps, where there is much more consumption of the retail pack beyond home, then the panel pick-up is about 90 %, and so on. In general, with one or two notable exceptions, consumer panels reflect total domestic purchasing of products with accuracy, where valid comparisons can be made.

The question of whether panel housewives get conditioned in their purchasing behaviour by long membership of the panel is one on which some direct evidence can be produced. Two separate studies are shown which, while not being fully conclusive, do at least provide no evidence of this type of conditioning. The first example is taken from the STAFCO consumer panel in France and it compares two demographically matched samples of panel households; the first long-serving panel members (five years or more) and the second more recently recruited members. Two potential types of conditioning are studied; the first that panel membership tends to induce greater brand loyalty, and the second that it tends to produce greater price consciousness and, therefore, more attention is paid to obtaining price advantages (see Tables 8.2 and 8.3).

This study at least shows that there is no progressive conditioning of panel housewives. The behaviour of the longer serving panel members is virtually identical with that of shorter service members. A similar study carried out in the Attwood panel in Germany showed similar results. It does not, however, preclude the possibility that all the conditioning occurs in the first few months

Table 8.1 *A comparison of attitude groupings in a random sample of the total housewife population and among Attwood Consumer Panel members*

Attitude scale:	Rigidity in housework		Traditionalism in housework		Economy consciousness		Conservatism in shopping	
	Random sample	Consumer panel	Random sample	Consumer panel	Random sample	Consumer panel	Random sample	Consumer panel
Total housewives	100 %	100 %	100 %	100 %	100 %	100 %	100 %	100 %
No. of housewives falling into each group on the scale								
1. Very rigid/traditional/ economy conscious/ conservative	9 %	7 %	13 %	12 %	10 %	10 %	10 %	10 %
2.	13 %	12 %	21 %	24 %	38 %	35 %	13 %	13 %
3.	22 %	24 %	29 %	29 %	24 %	31 %	44 %	48 %
4.	35 %	35 %	25 %	24 %	16 %	16 %		
5. Flexible/modern minded/not economy conscious/not conservative	21 %	22 %	11 %	11 %	11 %	8 %	33 %	29 %

Source: Attwood Consumer Panel, Great Britain.

Table 8.2 *Average number of brands purchased – by length of panel membership*

	(Brands purchased in a 12-week period)			
	Dentifrice	Margarine	Toilet soap	Washing powder
Long service panel members (recruited 1955–1960)	1.23	1.29	1.45	1.98
Shorter service members (recruited 1961–1964)	1.22	1.31	1.42	1.98

Table 8.3 *Average price paid per 100 g – by length of panel membership*

	Average price paid in a 12-week period (francs per 100 gs)			
	Dentifrice	Margarine	Toilet soap	Washing powder
Long service panel members (recruited 1955–1960)	2.05	N.A.	0.77	N.A.
Shorter service members (recruited 1961–1964)	2.09	N.A.	0.77	N.A.

Source: STAFCO Consumer Panel 12 weeks ending 27 December, 1964.

of panel membership and thereafter ceases. The second analysis is taken from the Attwood Consumer Panel in Great Britain at the time when the basic sample size was increased from 2000 households to 4000. The purchasing levels in 25 product fields were compared between the old 2000 panel (containing a high proportion of long service members) and the newly recruited 2000 panel (who by definition were all short-service members) to see whether any variations which occurred were beyond those which would be attributed to chance after allowing for the variations in the range of chance differences which would occur for fields of different size and frequency of purchase. In fact, 13 of the fields showed some upward movement in total purchases and 12 showed some downward movement, but in only two cases were these movements statistically significant. These results suggest that even during the first year of panel membership there are no basic differences in product purchasing levels from those obtaining after longer services (Table 8.4).

If conditioning does not seem to occur to any great extent in practice – and in general terms the evidence suggests that a continuous consumer panel is a

Table 8.4 Normalized deviates of percentage differences between purchasing levels of old and new panels

Normalized deviate	over -2	-2 to -1	-1 to 0	0 to 1	1 to 2	over 2	Total fields
Actual	0	3	9	7	4	2	25
Expected	0.6	3.4	8.5	8.5	3.4	0.6	25

representative measuring instrument – there still remains the fact that consumer panels do tend to have minority areas of unrepresentativeness. There are at least three known minorities of the domestic population that consumer panels tend to under-represent. These are the two extremes of the population, the very prosperous and the very poor (particularly the very poor and old). The third group are the fluctuating and transitory households composed mainly of young single men (or women) living particularly in the centres of the larger cities. It is likely that these groups tend to be underrepresented to some extent in most market research samples.

Continuity of reporting

As one of the principal advantages of panels is the continuity of the data, clearly continuity of reporting by panel members is of paramount importance. This is particularly true of the more sophisticated analyses of panel data, which rely heavily on complete continuity of reporting by the panel members included.

Continuity is directly influenced by three factors: the rewards offered for panel membership, the degree of interest the panel members have in participation, and the ease with which they can supply the data required. Probably all panel operations offer some reward for the services of the members; these range from direct money payments, through stamp schemes in exchange for gifts, to free television set maintenance in the case of television-viewing panel members who own their own sets. Clearly, there are limits set by the commercial viability of the panel operation itself to the size of the payments to its members. Suffice it to say that the payments themselves can hardly be regarded as the 'rate for the job' and therefore continuity is very much dependent on the interest of the panel member.

The degree of interest the panel members have is a very important factor. There is little doubt that frequent visits by friendly auditors/interviewers has an important effect, as does the exchange of chatty notes between a *nom de plume* at head office and the panel members (the Americans are so much better at this than researchers in Great Britain). A cordial relationship between the panel member and the panel company is at least as important as the payments.

The interest of the panel members is very much influenced by the ease with which they can supply the data required of them. Confusion about what they are supposed to do, even on small points, is a great destroyer of interest. People essentially like to co-operate and do not like to be made to feel inadequate to what has been set them, by a failure to understand what they are supposed to do. Clarity, particularly in diary layout, is vital. One special feature of this factor is the problem that respondents usually do not understand that to report a non-purchase is as important as reporting a purchase, i.e. a genuinely empty audit bin is as important as a full one. There is a danger, particularly in the early stages of panel membership, that respondents will create purchases or find packages rather than report nothing. Thus, in short-term panels in particular it is necessary to cover a wide enough range of products for most of the sample to have purchased at least one item per diary-reporting period (usually weekly); for the rest it is a matter of respondent education that a non-purchase is as interesting as a purchase.

The volume and accuracy of panel data, compared with interview surveys

Panels are used to measure aspects of consumer behaviour which are complex and variable, e.g. purchasing or viewing behaviour over time and where a relatively high degree of accuracy in the measurement is required. This second point is important because, for instance in the measurement of purchasing behaviour, for many purposes the high degree of accuracy and detail offered by a panel may not be necessary to obtain the information required for a particular marketing decision. In such cases, and there are many, using a panel might prove to be an expensive luxury and a cheaper single interview survey would suffice adequately.

How complex and subtle purchasing behaviour can be is often not fully appreciated. This is illustrated in Fig. 8.1 and 8.2. In Fig. 8.1 the purchases of 350 households in seven product fields (of high purchase frequency) over two consecutive eight-week periods is studied by individual households, showing the amount of variation in total purchases between the first and second periods. The average change for the total sample over these two periods was negligible – from 21.3 to 21.5 packages per household, or an increase of less than 1%. However, in 49% of the households studied purchases changed by more than 20%, thus illustrating that even in the most apparently stable market situations there is considerable and diverse movement below the surface.

Figure 8.2 illustrates the purchases of a brand of washing powder over the period of a year and the proportion of these purchases that were made with promotions. The complexity of this situation speaks for itself, and it is only part of the picture since the problem of purchases of competitive brands is ignored in this illustration.

It is generally accepted among researchers that if you interview a respondent

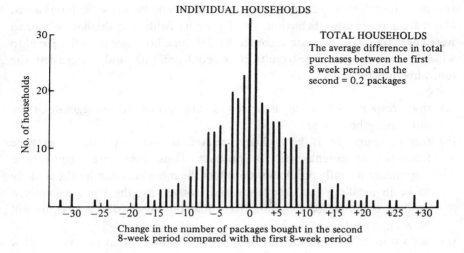

Fig. 8.1. Individual household variations in purchasing levels in the total of seven product fields between one 8-week period and the next. Source: Attwood Consumer Panel.

asking him (or, more likely, her) to recall purchasing behaviour in a consumer product field, there is a strong likelihood that the frequency and quantity of purchases will tend to be exaggerated and the complexity of purchasing behaviour over-simplified. This hypothesis was tested in an experimental

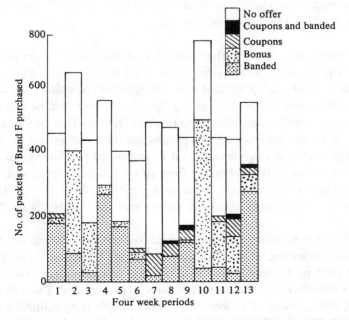

Fig. 8.2 Proportion of purchases of a washing powder brand made on promotions.
Source: Attwood Consumer Panel.

research study [3] in which 1000 consumer panel housewives were interviewed about their purchasing behaviour in 12 product fields and the data obtained were compared with the data recorded by the same housewives in the panel to which they belonged. The results obtained from this study suggested the following conclusions:

(a) that respondents when interviewed are prone to exaggerate their purchasing behaviour;

(b) this exaggeration is very closely related to the respondent's average frequency of purchase of the product. Thus, the more frequently a respondent actually purchases a product the more accurate he/she is likely to be in recalling that frequency and, conversely, the less frequently a product is purchased the more likely that the purchasing behaviour will be exaggerated;

(c) in its turn this conclusion has two effects. The first is that products with a high average frequency of purchase tend to be exaggerated least in interview surveys. Table 8.5 summarizes these findings from the experimental study. The second effect is that within any product field the gap between the volume of purchases of high- and low-frequency buyers is artificially narrowed in an interview situation because the latter tend to exaggerate their purchases more than the former;

(d) there is dramatic over-simplification of brand switching behaviour over time in an interview situation. Broadly, respondents tend to equate their most recent brand buying behaviour to their 'normal' behaviour over time, whether this is accurate or not.

Broadbent and Mooney in their follow-on to this study [4] point out that for certain purposes (in this case selection of print media against light, medium, and heavy buyers of products) the exaggeration obtained at single-call interviews does not distort the rank order of purchase volume too seriously and does not, therefore, invalidate the results obtained. This may be so, but as this is a relatively insensitive use of purchasing data it does not alter the fact that a high degree of exaggeration and distortion of purchasing behaviour is present in purchasing data obtained from single call interviews; and for many of the studies of purchasing behaviour required from panel data such distortion would seriously affect the accuracy of the results obtained.

As well as the accuracy possible in panel techniques in obtaining the sheer volume of purchasing, or consumption habits, or television viewing data or whatever over time, there is also an advantage in comparison with interview surveys in the volume of ancillary data that can be obtained. This advantage is, as yet, relatively unexploited. Because a panel sample is by definition available over a long period these ancillary data can be collected, and perfected, at intervals and not cause respondent fatigue which might result from their

Table 8.5 The relationship between average frequency of purchase and interview exaggeration of total purchase volume

Product field	Average frequency of purchase		Interview exaggeration factor – volume of purchases (panel diary returns = 100)			
	Average interval between purchases– weeks	Rank order	Panel housewives when interviewed		Matched non-panel housewives*	
			Exaggeration factor	Rank order	Exaggeration factor	Rank order
Tea	1 week or less	(1)	116	(1)	136	(2)
Margarine	1.1	(2)	128	(3)	123	(1)
Washing powders	3.0	(3)	124	(2)	143	(4)
Washing-up liquids	3.5	(4)	178	(5)	210	(5)
Baked beans	4.5	(5)	152	(4)	140	(3)
Toilet soap	4.9	(6)	208	(9)	261	(8)
Canned soups (summer)	5.3	(7)	200	(8)	298	(10)
Instant coffee	6.2	(8)	179	(6)	245	(7)
Jam	9.4	(9)	194	(7)	235	(6)
Dentifrice	9.7	(10)	217	(10)	282	(9)
Floor and furniture polish	15.9	(11)	292	(11)	396	(11)

* A matched sample of 1000 housewives who were not members of the Attwood panel were also interviewed, using the same questionnaire as for the panel housewives. In general they exaggerated their purchasing behaviour more than panel housewives and this is attributed to the fact that the latter had a better idea of their purchasing behaviour from their habit of recording it in the panel diaries. The rank order of exaggeration is, however, similar.

collection at one-point in time as would be necessary in single call interview surveys. These ancillary data fall into two distinct categories:

(a) consumer classfication data for the better identification of types of consumer behaviour. Into this category fall all the normal demographic characteristics of the consumer which would be collected as a matter of course in the recruitment of a panel. In addition there is a vast range of classification characteristics which might prove relevant to the purposes of the panel, the ownership of goods and services, leisure time activities, shopping habits, consumption habits, income and occupational categories, etc. It has also proved possible to obtain psychological or attitude classifications of panel members. The advantage of the panel technique is that classification data can be collected and tried by analysis for its relevance and usefulness in isolating consumer behaviour characteristics and, if found wanting, can be rejected or modified. It is a continuous process;

(b) ancillary data which are known, or suspected, to have an influence on consumer behaviour and therefore can be collected alongside the main data of the panel and applied to get a better understanding of processes of consumer activity. Into this category comes the collection of readership and television-viewing data for application to consumer purchase panels, and holiday and other travel activities in relation to motorist panels.

As far as the collection of ancillary data from the single source of the panel is concerned, there is still a considerable potential to be tapped. This should be one of the major areas of development of panel techniques.

The analysis of panel data

Panels, whether they are short-term or continuous, provide an almost indigestible mass of data which have to be translated into a limited amount of information which can be absorbed and acted upon. This is, of course, true of almost all research work but it is a particularly acute problem for panels simply because of the sheer volume of data flowing in as a continuous process. The efficient use of panels, therefore, lies in the standard and relevance of the analyses obtained from the data.

The analyses derived from the data of consumer purchasing panels can be conveniently divided into three groups:

(a) standard trend analyses produced at regular intervals, usually four-weekly, which show the progress of the market and of its principal brands;

(b) 'simple' special analyses designed to show the anatomy of the characteristics of purchasing behaviour and of the consumers. These are not usually produced on a continuous basis but rather as and when required, usually when some significant change is thought to have occurred in the market which requires further study;

(c) 'complex' special analyses designed to examine the fundamental patterns of consumer behaviour, particularly in relation to specific bursts of major marketing activity.

The remainder of this section illustrates examples of analyses in the three groups.

Standard trend analyses

These differ in detail from one purchasing panel operation to another but are similar in purpose and provide the content of the basic reports. The normal reporting period is four weeks, long enough to provide enough data of significance to analyse and short enough to show trends while there is still time to take action. In special and urgent cases data may be produced on a weekly basis, but this is rare.

The analysis tables in the four-weekly report shows the number of buyers in the total product field in the period and the buyers of each of the brands and subsections (if any) of the field. A similar table shows the total quantities purchased (again by brands) expressed in whatever quantity measure is most appropriate to the field – expenditure, weight, packets, standard units, etc. The current four-weekly period is usually shown alongside similar data from previous periods, going back for perhaps as long as a year, and this provides a ready reading of trends. Other data may also be shown in the report where this is relevant to the interpretation of the trends, such as the proportion of purchases made in different types of consumer promotions, etc.

The trend analyses of purchasing panel data are the essential preliminaries to all other panel analysis work. They provide the broad picture of the market but they are not the *raison d'être* of panels since similar information could be obtained from other research techniques, e.g. shop audits, regular *ad hoc* surveys, and they make no use of the real advantage of panels, their continuity of reporting.

'Simple' special analyses

The term 'simple' is derived not from the ease with which the analysis is provided (it may in fact be relatively difficult to provide) but from the nature of the information it supplies. The examples given here are not meant to provide a comprehensive list of the analyses that are possible but are meant to be illustrative of the range of analyses.

The first example, in Fig. 8.3, relates consumer demographic characteristics to purchasing behaviour. In this particular example it relates the weight of total self-raising flour purchases in 13 weeks to the age of housewife purchasers for the total market and one particular brand. The brand in question shows a higher average age of purchaster than the total market. This is a particularly simple example of the great range of consumer classification analyses possible from panel data. A second example is shown in Fig. 8.4, which relates the quantity of purchases of baby products in a 12-week period to whether the baby is the first, second, third, etc., in that family. Clearly, experience in bringing up babies influences purchasing behaviour.

Panels habitually collect a lot of associated data about the item purchased – for example, the price paid, the day of the purchase, and the type of shop from which it was made and whether any promotions were involved. These data provide useful information.

In Fig. 8.5 a series of analyses have been summarized to show the trend in

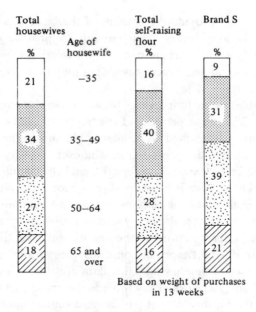

Based on weight of purchases
in 13 weeks

Fig. 8.3 Self-raising flour purchases, by age of housewife.

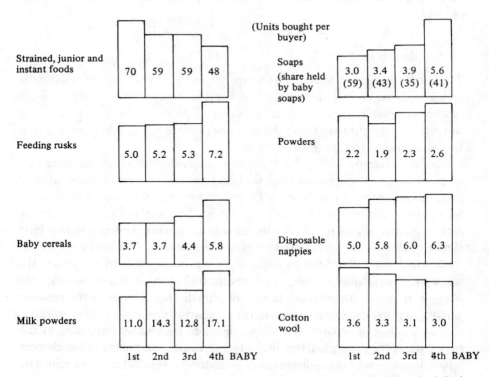

Fig. 8.4 The volume of purchases of a range of baby products related to whether the baby is
the first child or not. Source: RSGB Baby Panel.

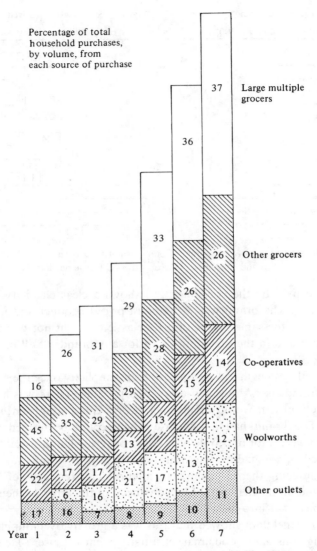

Percentage of total
household purchases,
by volume, from
each source of purchase

Large multiple grocers

Other grocers

Co-operatives

Woolworths

Other outlets

Year 1   2   3   4   5   6   7

Fig. 8.5 Consumer purchases by type of outlet in a rapidly expanding food field.
Source: Attwood Consumer Panel.

importance of the different types of outlets in the growth of a fast-moving food product. It shows clearly that the rate of growth of purchases of the product differs markedly from one type of outlet to another and gives a clear warning light to any brand which is not keeping pace in the outlets expanding at the fastest rate. It does, incidentally, give strength to the point made in the chapter on trade research of the importance of measuring a product in more than one type of outlet.

Another example, shown in Fig. 8.6, relates purchases of a food brand to the

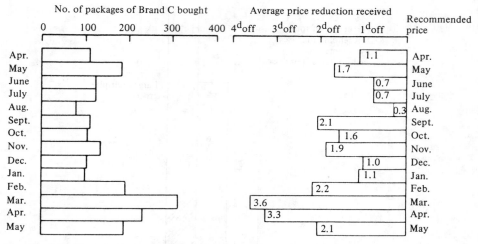

Fig. 8.6   The relationship of the volume of purchases of food Brand C to the average price
paid by the consumer. Source: Attwood Consumer Panel.

average price paid by the consumer and shows a clear elasticity of demand related to price. The brand was a premium priced product and it should be emphasized that the same degree of price elasticity might not be present for a lower priced brand in the same market or for any brands at all in some other product field.

'Simple' analyses begin to lose some of their simplicity once they get into the realm of defining 'users' and 'non-users' of a product. There was a time when many marketing men would divide their world quite simply into these two categories. The brand had a franchise which could be termed 'users' and beyond them were a lot of people who could be termed 'non-users'. Marketing skill consisted of persuading the 'non-users' that your brand was really very good, then inducing them to sample it, after which experience of the sterling qualities of the brand they would be convinced of the error of their ways and would be converted into 'users'.

Analysis of panel data showed that this was a grossly oversimplified view of a fast-moving consumer goods market. Firstly, what is a user? Does she have to buy once only to qualify or does she have to buy twenty times? Does she have to take all her purchases in the product field in your brand or only part of them – if part, then what proportion would you settle for? Secondly, how much substance is there in the belief that persuasion will induce trial, which will in turn induce loyalty to the brand? Experience shows that the trial/conversion process can happen when a significant innovation hits the market place, but that more often than not there is a constant battle for position going on between closely matched brands, with smallish strongholds being held on a long-term basis and much of the territory in a more or less fluid state, being held sometimes by one brand and at other times by another, and with no brand making permanent gain.

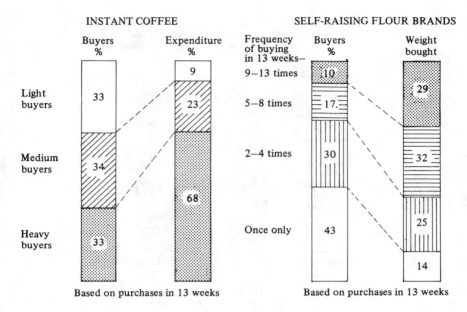

Fig. 8.7 Analyses of frequency of purchase examples from instant coffee and self-raising flour: Brand S. Source: Attwood Consumer Panel.

The following analysis examples illustrate some of the purchasing behaviour characteristics described above.

Figure 8.7 shows the frequency of purchase of buyers of instant coffee and the buyers of a brand of self-raising flour. In both case it is a relatively small minority of buyers who account for a majority of total purchases of the product.

Figure 8.8 shows a measure of continuity of purchasing, i.e. a form of loyalty measurement, for a leading brand of toothpaste in which it will be seen that nearly half the quantity of the brand purchased in a six-month period was accounted for by less than 20% of the buyers who were 'loyal' to the brand, and that 46% of the buyers were moving in or out of the market for the brand and accounted for only a small proportion of the total purchases.

The user/non-user concept of a market is replaced, therefore, in analysis terms by the two concepts of 'market penetration' i.e. those who buy the brand at least once in a given time period, and 'brand loyalty'. Brand loyalty is subject to a number of interpretations depending upon the analyses used. The analysis of continuity of purchasing in Fig. 8.8 is a relatively crude definition, and the type of analysis which examines total purchases in a product field for each individual panel member in a given period of time and then expresses purchases of a given brand as a proportion of the total comes closer to an exact definition. This has its problems, however, since very light buyers tend to show brand loyalty merely because they have less opportunity to switch brands, and in this type of analysis need to be isolated from the heavier buyers.

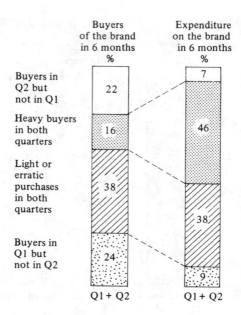

Fig. 8.8   Continuity of purchasing over a 6-month period: example of a brand leader in the
toothpaste market. Source: Attwood Consumer Panel.

Figure 8.9, which shows the extent to which buyers of toilet soap are loyal to one brand, illustrates both the relatively limited extent of 100% loyalty to a brand in a highly competitive market and, what we have already seen, that a high proportion of the buyers in any field accounts for only a small part of total purchases.

There are many other forms of special analyses, each designed to answer specific problems, and the illustrations here are meant only to indicate a little of the possibilities of 'simple' analyses from panel data. Nothing has been said at all of many of the analysis types regularly produced from panel data of which the following is a list of examples:

(a)   purchases by size of pack;
(b)   quantity of the product bought on each purchase occasion;
(c)   day of the week on which purchases are made;
(d)   extent to which different individual consumers purchase products with the same 'family' brand name, e.g. Colmans, Ajax, Heinz, etc.;
(e)   the limits of duplication between brands by which consumers confine their purchases to a limited group of the total brands available;
(f)   the extent of purchasing 'own label' brands compared with nationally advertised brands, among consumers who shop at supermarkets;
(g)   loyalty to flavours rather than brands in certain food fields;
(h)   price consciousness by demographic groups;
(i)   the relationship of quantity of purchases to size of household.

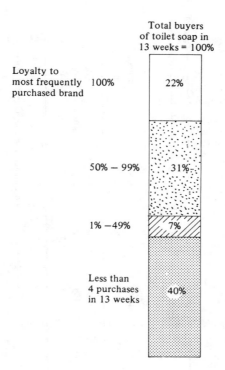

Fig. 8.9 The extent to which buyers of toilet soap are completely loyal to one brand in a 13-week period. Source: Attwood Consumer Panel.

'Complex' special analyses

The dividing line between 'simple' and 'complex' analyses of panel data is not an easy one to define and there is probably little to be gained from pursuing the definition to the bitter end anyway. Included in the latter category are the analyses which call for the collection of special ancillary data from panels, e.g. media exposure data, attitude grouping data, etc., or which examine the fundamental characteristics of consumer behaviour for the purpose of a more complete understanding of the complex processes by which marketing stimuli influence purchases.

The first example of this type of analysis is of the use of readership and television viewing data collected from panel housewives to measure the influence of advertising on purchasing behaviour. The principle employed in this analysis is to isolate the purchasing behaviour of housewives exposed to a particular advertising campaign from those who were not.

In this particular example, involving a food product brand, a press advertising campaign spread over a two-year period has been superimposed on the normal television advertising support for the brand. A common sample of panel housewives who were reporting their purchases over the full two years

Table 8.6 The sales effect of a press campaign for brand X, by readership categories

	Total housewives		Heavy readers		Medium readers		Light readers		Non-readers	
	Volume of purchases	Brand share index	Volume	Brand share	Volume	Brand share	Volume	Brand share	Volume	Brand share
Q4 1964*	100	100	100	100	100	100	100	100	100	100
Q4 1965	106	105	115	116	112	109	104	106	96	95
Q4 1966	91	97	107	112	102	111	75	84	90	91

* Before press campaign began.

Source: Attwood Consumer Panel, Great Britain.

has been selected and these have been classified according to their likely exposure to the advertising (based on their readership of the publications used in the campaign) into heavy, medium, light, and non-reader categories.

The purchases of the brand (in volume and market share) were measured in the quarter year prior to the start of the press campaign and in the same period in the two succeeding years, as shown in Table 8.6.

After the first year of the advertising campaign the volume of purchases and share indices have a consistent relationship with the amount of exposure to the press advertising – those not exposed showing a decline in purchases, those most exposed showing the greatest increase in purchases. By the end of the second year there had been an absolute decline in purchases of the brand for reasons beyond the control of this particular press campaign. The only groups whose purchases have not fallen below the 1964 level are the heavy and medium reader groups. It would seem that in the second year light readership was not sufficient to counteract the tendency for purchases of the brand to decline.

There is a further analysis which has been extracted for this study and this relates to the relative effectiveness of the press advertising on housewives who have (or have not) been exposed heavily to the television advertising for the same brand. The television advertising is a relatively common element running through the whole period of the study, including the period before the press campaign began (Q4, 1964). Table 8.7 illustrates this analysis. The readership groups have been split into two (rather than four) in the interests of sample size.

Table 8.7 The trend of purchasers of brand X by the volume of exposure to the TV and press advertising

Readership:	Heavy and medium readers				Light and non-readers			
Television:	Heavy and medium viewers		Light and non-viewers		Heavy and medium viewers		Light and non-viewers	
	Volume	Share	Volume	Share	Volume	Share	Volume	Share
Q4 1964 *	100	100	100	100	100	100	100	100
Q4 1965	105	105	123	119	97	99	105	103
Q4 1966	96	104	113	119	83	91	80	83

* Before the press campaign began.

Source: *Attwood Consumer Panel, Great Britain.*

Almost all the increase in purchases among the heavy and medium reading groups is confined to those who had *not* already been exposed heavily to the television advertising. The implication of this is that the television advertising had already raised the level of purchasing of its heavy viewers as far as it was likely to go before the press campaign began. Certainly, the general level of purchases of the heavy and medium ITV viewers was some 10 % higher than that for the light and non-ITV viewers before the press campaign began.

The second analysis example is drawn from relating an attitudinal classification of panel housewives to their purchasing behaviour. The principle adopted in this approach is that housewives with identical demographic characteristics show considerable differences in purchasing behaviour and it is possible and, indeed, likely that these relate to differences in fundamental attitudes to activities like shopping, housework, cooking, trying new products, etc., which in their turn reflect in their purchasing behaviour. If this hypothesis is correct, and the attitudes which relate to the differences in the purchasing behaviour can be measured, this will have an important bearing not only in understanding the marketing approach to be made to purchasers of a particular product but also in identifying where potential purchasers are most likely to be found. Table 8.8 shows an analysis based on experimental work on the Attwood Consumer Panel where two types of floor and furniture polish (wax and aerosol) show similar demographic profiles among purchasers but strongly contrasting attitude profiles. This type of analysis is represented in the continuous consumer panel services at the present time mainly by experimental work; it is not offered as a regular service but it is an important indicator of the direction in which these services can develop in the future. There are, of course, limits to the extent to which attitude data can be collected in the permanent panels without conditioning future purchasing behaviour; but general attitude data not related directly to questions on brand or product purchasing are certainly well within these limits. Such limitations do not apply to short-term panels, where the attitude questioning is confined to interviewing immediately after the end of the panel operation, and this service is regularly applied in short-term panels to provide an additional dimension in the interpretation of the purchasing data [1].

The remaining examples of 'complex' analysis of panel data are derived from

Table 8.8 *Social class and attitude to housework profiles of purchasers of two types of polish*

	Social class				Attitude to housework scale				
	AB	C	D1	D2E	1 Very traditional	2	3	4	5 Modern- minded
Proportion of housewives buying:					100 = Average level of buying of the polish types				
Wax polish	134	111	94	93	110	110	105	84	68
Aerosol polish	170	110	98	85	45	91	100	109	146

Source: *Attwood Consumer Panel, Great Britain*

the study of the underlying patterns of consumer purchasing behaviour using a model which predicts future market share by measuring the likely penetration and the likely repeat purchasing rate for the brand under study. The analysis was originally devised to predict the share of newly launched brands but has since been developed to study the longer term effects of promotions, or advertising campaigns, or other marketing activity for established brands.

The launch of 'Signal' toothpaste is shown in the next example. Figure 8.10 shows the penetration and repeat purchasing rate achieved by the brand in the weeks following the launch of the brand. They show two characteristics which

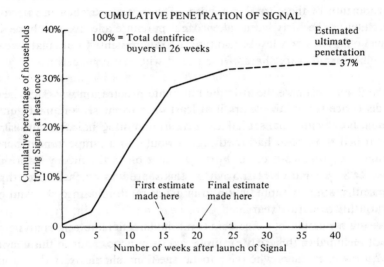

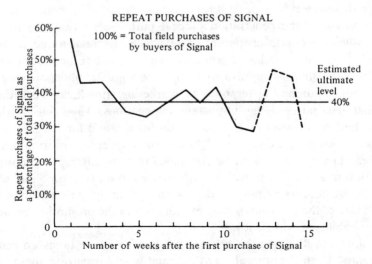

Fig. 8.10 The cumulative penetration and repeat-purchasing rate for Signal in the period immediately after its launch.

are common to virtually all analyses of this kind:

(a) After a time the cumulative penetration of the brand, i.e. the number of people buying the brand for the first time, shows a declining rate of increase. Once the shape of the curve is determined and a declining rate of increase is observed, it is possible to make a reasonable estimate of the ultimate likely penetration.

(b) The repeat purchasing rate is calculated by taking the total volume of purchases in the product field made by people who have tried the brand under study and expressing the repeat purchases of that brand as a proportion of these total purchases. This repeat purchasing rate usually declines in the early weeks after a first purchase and eventually begins to level off. When this levelling-off occurs it is possible to calculate what the equilibrium market share of the brand will be.

In the Signal example the estimated ultimate penetration was 37 %, i.e. 37 % of all dentifrice buyers would try it at least once in the reasonable future, and the repeat purchasing rate settled down at around 40 %, i.e. after curiosity had been satisfied those who had tried Signal would, on average, repeat purchase the brand four times out of 10. Forty per cent of 37 % would yield a market share of 14.8 %. Figure 8.11 shows that this share was reached some three or four months after the prediction was made and remained a valid share prediction for over two years.

There are a number of refinements and qualifications to this analysis which were not included in this early example and there is no space in this chapter to deal with them. Readers who wish to pursue them should read the published work on this subject [5].

The product of the penetration × repeat purchase analysis has proved to give a forward estimate of market share which has been found to be very reliable in frequently purchased product categories. The accumulation of many examples of the analysis has also contributed to a greater understanding of the way consumer purchasing responds to marketing stimuli. In particular, one 'rule' that has emerged has important implications. This 'rule' is that on average the later a buyer enters the market for a brand for the first time the lower her repeat purchasing rate will be and the smaller the contribution to the future brand share. Thus, it can be concluded that any attempt to improve the penetration of a brand, e.g. with a particularly attractive promotion, will not yield a repeat purchasing rate for buyers brought in by the promotion higher than the rate of the marginal buyers existing before the promotion began; and in all probability it will be lower.

An example to illustrate this concept is taken from an established detergent brand, brand L. In the normal way the brand would penetrate about 20 % of the buyers in the market in, say, a six-month period and achieve an average repeat purchasing rate of 25 % (which would be normal in a highly competitive

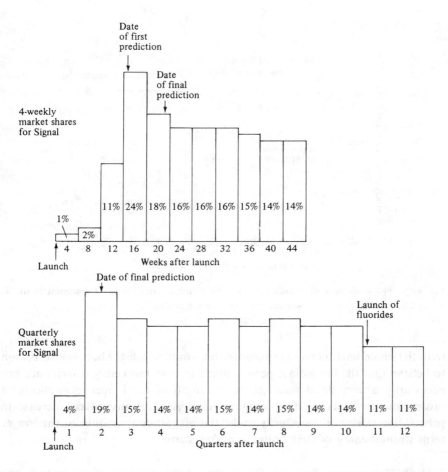

Fig. 8.11   The extent of validity of the brand share prediction made for Signal.
Source: Attwood Consumer Panel.

relatively disloyal market with five or six major brands to choose from), thus indicating that its market share is around 5 %. In this example a 50 % price-cut promotion was introduced and Fig. 8.12 illustrates the effect of this on the cumulative penetration of the brand, with an increase from 20 to 31 %.

It will be seen from Table 8.9, however, that the repeat purchasing rate of the 11 % additional buyers brought in by the offer was only 4 % after the offer had finished, compared with an average of 25 % for those buyers who had been purchasing brand L before the offer began.

Thus, the offer produced a 55 % increase in penetration (which would have produced a large temporary increase in brand share at the time of the offer) and only 8.5 % increase in brand share after the offer. This is not to say that that was an unsatisfactory result for the offer but purely that the long-term effects, measured in terms of repeat purchasing, are very much more subdued

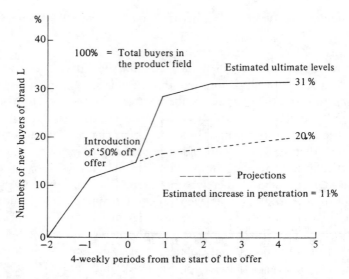

Fig. 8.12   The effect of a 50 % price cut on the cumulative penetration of detergent Brand L.
Source: Attwood Consumer Panel.

than the immediate increase in penetration would suggest. There is also reason to believe that the immediate penetration effects of marketing activity are not necessarily a very good guide to the strength of the longer-term effects; a promotion, for instance, that yields a relatively high immediate increase in penetration does not necessarily make the biggest contribution to the longer term strengthening of that brand's market share.

Table 8.9 *The contribution made to the ultimate share of brand L by buyers introduced by the offer*

Brand L (50 % price cut offer)	Ultimate penetration	×	Repeat purchasing rate	×	Buying rate index	=	Ultimate brand share
Before introduction of the offer	20 %	×	25 %	×	1.03	=	5.15 %
After introduction of the offer							
buyers before offer	20 %	×	25 %	×	1.03	=	5.15 %
buyers after offer	11 %	×	4 %	×	1.01	=	0.45 %
							5.60 %

The continuous study of the underlying patterns of consumer purchasing behaviour

Somewhere locked in the panel data accumulated over the years lie the answers to a range of marketing questions. Some important work has been carried out to extract the essence of these data and find marketing 'laws', e.g. Ehrenberg,[6] but for the most part the more sophisticated analysis of panel data has been carried out primarily to pursue specific and 'limited' objectives, such as to predict the future share of a new brand or to measure the sales effect of a particular advertising campaign. The analyses have been relatively expensive to carry out and, therefore, no attempt has been made to introduce them as a matter of course at each point of major change in advertising, promotion, etc. A data bank of case histories in a particular market would reveal far more of the fundamental factors influencing purchasing behaviour in that market than the occasional isolated analysis, however sophisticated. The increasing use of panel raw data for computer analysis by client companies must eventually lead to this situation and, assuming that the appropriate ancillary data mentioned in this chapter are also by then regularly available, panels will at long last be used to their full advantage. Panel analysis will then fully serve its dual purpose, to provide:

(a) immediate data on the development of trends and consumer characteristics in the market – the traditional rôle of panels;
(b) the more fundamental data on how consumers react to given marketing activity to determine how they are likely to react to future marketing activity.

Modern technology and panel data collection

So far in this country only the TV viewing panels have really reflected the advances in technology as far as data collection is concerned. However, the time is not far away when electronic developments will bring about revolutionary changes in the way consumer panel data are collected also. This has already begun, primarily in the USA. The three principal agents of this change are:

(a) laser scanners for reading bar codes on product packs;
(b) split-cable techniques for measuring subtle controlled changes in media exposure; and
(c) TV-telephone linked communication systems which will link panel members with the research agency and its computer.

Already in the USA the use of the bar scanners in shops linked to identification tags of panel shoppers have transformed the method, speed, and accuracy with which purchasing information is collected – and at the same time brought the shop audit and the consumer panel into the same method of measurement. Linked with split-cable TV, it has also been able to relate purchasing directly with TV advertising exposure.

Laser scanners have been used for some time in Europe experimentally. In January 1986 the first fully operational service was introduced in Europe – the Scan 5000 Service run by Nielsen in France. This uses 10 Consumer Panels each of 500 households who are regular shoppers in 10 selected super-markets and whose purchases are measured by laser scanning at these outlets. Whether the split-cable techniques follow so readily depends on more uncertain issues, not least the legislation to permit changes in the advertising signal.

Chapter 9

Omnibus surveys

RICHARD DAVIES

Introduction

Omnibus surveys are in very widespread use within the market research industry and have become a well-established, valuable and cost-effective means of conducting market research surveys. This chapter explains briefly what omnibus surveys are and how they operate, and then goes on to examine the specific strengths and weaknesses of this particular research methodology. Though there are many market research problems which can be very adequately solved using the omnibus technique, equally there are some situations where they are inappropriate. Thus it is very important for the research practitioner to be aware of the advantages and the limitations that omnibus surveys offer in order to make the most effective use of them.

Definition

An omnibus survey is very similar to an *ad hoc* survey except that the questionnaire, instead of being entirely devoted to one project, is shared by a number of projects each with their own separate sub-questionnaire. These separate questionnaires are usually on entirely different subjects and are linked together to form one composite questionnaire for the purposes of administering the survey. The reason that omnibus surveys of this type are so popular is that they enable the research practitioner to save costs by sharing the expenditure for conducting the survey across a number of interested parties.

The cost benefits of omnibus surveys arise from the fact that fieldwork forms the major cost component of most market research surveys, and these fieldwork costs are relatively insensitive to the length of the questionnaire. This is not to say that questionnaire length does not have an influence on fieldwork costs, but this influence is small relative to the cost of contacting the required sample. For example, a survey amongst 2000 housewives asking 15 questions will cost little more in fieldwork time and expenses than an identical survey asking two questions. This situation arises because the majority of the interviewer's time is taken up by making successful contact with each eligible respondent, and in relation to this the amount of time actually questioning the respondent is not large in most cases.

The principle of sharing or syndicating costs in this way is not unique to omnibus surveys. A number of syndicated surveys exist where the results of a survey are sold either in part or in their entirety to a number of different clients. (Examples of this would be the Taylor Nelson Monitor or the Target Group Index run by BMRB.) These surveys are sometimes classed as omnibus surveys. However, for the purposes of this chapter omnibus surveys are defined in the strict sense as syndicated surveys where the questionnaire is a combination of smaller questionnaires each of which is unique to a particular project and where the client has control over the questions to be asked in his particular section.

Basic method of operation

In principle it would be perfectly possible for research buyers to get together to share fieldwork costs and set up their own omnibus survey. All that would be required would be to find a number of other researchers concurrently planning a survey with similar sample designs and to create one master questionnaire from the individual questionnaires. In practice, however, the difficulty of finding other buyers with similar requirements in terms of sample size, type and timing would be extremely difficult and time-consuming to organize. The field is therefore very much left to market research agencies, who by weighing up the likely demand for omnibus type surveys and offering space on a master questionnaire carry out the planning, fieldwork and analysis of such surveys. A very wide range of services are now available on this basis (further details can be found later in this chapter) and they vary widely in terms of sample size, sample composition, timing and frequency. The research buyer is therefore in a position to select the service which offers him the most appropriate facilities for his requirements.

Omnibus services are usually operated on the basis of a fixed rate card. Typically this follows the following format:

a fixed entry fee;
a fixed cost per precoded question (usually with a restriction on the number of codes);
a fixed cost for open-ended questions (higher than for precoded questions and again usually with a restriction on the number of codes);
usually, extra costs for show cards.

Most omnibus surveys operate to a fixed time schedule and the client is provided with a deadline for receipt of the questionnaire by the research agency. Thus if the research agency does not receive the questionnaire by the deadline date then it cannot be included on the omnibus for that period. This is an important point to bear in mind as usually the questionnaire deadline is about one week before the start of fieldwork. The results from omnibus surveys are usually presented in tabular print-out form to a set analysis format which normally includes a demographic and area breakdown as part of the standard cost. Further analysis beyond standard breakdowns is usually available at extra cost. Additionally some research companies will provide an interpretative summary for an additional cost.

Design considerations

Before it is possible to embark on an omnibus survey there are a number of design issues which need to be considered in order to determine the most appropriate approach, or indeed to determine whether an omnibus survey is appropriate at all.

Sampling method

A number of different sampling methods are adopted in omnibus surveys. Most of these are variations on the basic random (probability) and quota sampling methods, and the reader is referred to chapter 4 of this volume for a discussion of the merits of each particular type. The sampling method is obviously fixed by the research agency offering the service, and in this sense cannot be influenced by the research buyer. However, there is a wide variation of sampling methods available in omnibus surveys, some companies even offering a choice between both random and quota sampling methods.

Another important consideration is the number of sampling points and interviewers being used, as this has an important influence on the design effect of the survey – the more interviewers the lower the design effect (again reference should be made to chapter 4 for a discussion of this issue). Although in the end the research practitioner is buying · from what is available in terms of sampling method it is important with omnibus surveys not to lose sight of the particular method employed. The final choice will be based on considerations of cost versus efficiency but it is important that the same consideration be given to omnibus surveys in this respect as is given to conventional *ad hoc* surveys.

Questionnaire

As a rule the same principles apply to omnibus questionnaires as apply to questionnaires in general, and the reader is referred to chapter 5 for a discussion of the issues. However, there are some factors which are particularly relevant to omnibus questionnaires and where special considerations apply.

The first point to remember when designing a questionnaire for an omnibus survey is that the questions will be appearing with many others, often in completely different product fields. Unless the questions happen to be first in the master questionnaire, a questionnaire on one subject will always be preceded by another on a totally unrelated topic. It is therefore advisable to begin the questions for any given subject area with a short introduction to indicate to the respondent that a change in subject is about to occur. Failure to appreciate this point can result in the following sequence of questions occurring:

Q. Which of the following brands of toothpaste have you heard of?
   (SHOW CARD)

Q. And which brand of toothpaste did you last purchase?

Q. And could you tell me the names of the brands of toothpaste that you have in the house at present?

Q. Have you flown in an aircraft in the last 12 months?

Each separate sequence of questions would have appeared very reasonable to the toothpaste client and the client interested in air travel. However, to the respondent, the switch without warning from toothpaste to air travel could become confusing, especially when you consider that any omnibus survey could be composed of a large number of different subject areas. This could quite easily affect the accuracy and quality of the response to a given set of questions. Each new subject area should be prefaced by a sentence to introduce the subject to the respondent. In the case of the air travel example, this could be accomplished by inserting 'I would now like to change the subject and talk to you about something completely different' before the air travel question.

This raises a general point about omnibus questionnaires which will be discussed in more detail later. This is the fact that the individual buyer usually has no control over the position of his questions in the master questionnaire, or on the overall length of the master questionnaire itself, or on the subject areas that precede his particular questions. All three factors have a very important influence on the response to a given set of questions, and are factors which need to be borne in mind. In practice, a large measure of responsibility rests with the research agency providing the service to bring particular problems to the attention of clients. This may at times involve refusal by the agency to accept an individual client's questionnaire because the subject clashes with another subject on the questionnaire or because the space available on the master questionnaire has been fully taken up. In general the research agencies have been found to operate these principles fairly sensibly.

A further point which is relevant to questionnaire design for omnibus surveys is that complex questions and question-routing should be avoided. Given that respondents are being questioned about a number of unrelated subject areas, it becomes difficult in the space and time available on most omnibus surveys to do more than ask fairly simple straightforward questions. Complex questions or detailed probing are really beyond the scope of the technique. Similarly, complicated routing instructions between questions should be avoided. Interviewers are unlikely to be personally briefed on particular subject areas and thus any complex filtering system by which respondents are routed to different parts of the questionnaire could give rise to problems. Again, however, most research agencies should be responsible enough to point this out if complexity becomes sufficient to jeopardize the accuracy of the responses.

Omnibus questionnaires are often agreed at short notice and under tight time constraints. This can lead to errors if the questionnaire is communicated to the research agency over the telephone. For this reason it is strongly recommended that omnibus questionnaires are communicated from the buyer to the research agency *in writing*, and where possible the research agency should confirm by sending the client a copy of the proposed questionnaire in its final form. Many omnibus suppliers do in fact adopt this rule as part of their standard practice.

Interviewing method

Although the door-to-door interviewer-administered questionnaire is by far the most common method of conducting omnibus surveys, it is by no means the only one. Telephone omnibuses are rapidly establishing themselves and are now offered by a number of companies. Although these might not necessarily be suitable for all requirements (e.g. where visual stimuli are required to be shown) they do have the advantage of being very quick. This makes the 24-hour turnaround from submitting questions to getting results a practical reality and can be very useful when time is of the essence. Telphone omnibuses can have other advantages over door-to-door interviews and reference should be made to chapter 10 for a more detailed discussion of the advantages and disadvantages.

Besides telephone omnibuses a number of other specialist services are offered. Omnibus hall-testing facilities are available which enable researchers to syndicate hall-testing costs. The advantage of these services is that they enable more complex stimuli to be used than in the conventional omnibus (e.g. advertising, concept, product etc.). Costs are usually calculated not on a per-question basis but on a time basis, so that participating clients would buy a fixed amount of interviewing time on the survey. A further extension of this concept is the Qualitative Omnibus in which clients can buy a fixed amount of time in a group discussion. This can be useful where an in-depth probing into a particular issue is felt to be necessary but where the project cannot justify a full length qualitative investigation in its own right.

Sample size and composition

Most conventional omnibus surveys operate on the basis of a fixed representative sample of adults (usually aged 15+) which is then split into smaller samples of men, women and housewives.

For example, a typical omnibus survey might interview 2000 adults each week – covering 1000 men, 1000 women and including 800 housewives. The service normally allows the target sample to be selected from within these components, the cost usually being structured on the basis of the particular sample required (i.e. a discount would be offered if it were required to question only the 800 housewives in the sample and not the whole sample of 2000 adults).

Often it is a requirement to interview a more specialized sample (e.g. frozen food buyers). In this case a screening question could be added to the omnibus to identify the particular group required and all subsequent questions would be asked only of this group. Again cost discounts would usually be available in this situation depending on the size of the sub-sample interviewed. Ideally of course it is important to have some idea of the incidence of the target sample in the population at large so that an appropriate 'effective' sample size can be estimated.

Fairly specialized samples are a common requirement with omnibus surveys and have given rise to a number of surveys which specialize in particular target groups. the following list gives some idea of the services available in a country such as the UK but is not intended to be exhaustive:

Motorists
Teenagers
Bank account holders
Mothers with babies
Children
Heads of households
Parents
Pet owners
Small business owners
Catering establishments

Ethnic groups
Doctors
Regional samples – Scotland, Northern Ireland

These operate in very much the same way as all-adult omnibus surveys but are usually based on smaller samples and are conducted less frequently than the former.

Experimental design

To the extent that most omnibus surveys are conducted to collect information and not for conducting experiments, considerations of experimental design are less applicable to omnibus surveys than to *ad hoc* research. There are obvious limitations placed on omnibus surveys in terms of what can be achieved as regards experimental designs, and research suppliers differ in the extent to which flexibility is permissible. There are two experimental designs which are, however, in very common use with omnibus studies:

Pre and post studies

These are usually conducted to measure the effect of some stimulus by taking a measure of consumer reaction before the event and after the event. Typical examples of this might be assessing reaction to a TV campaign, or monitoring the performance of a new brand or the relaunch of an existing brand. Clearly this design involves the use of more than one omnibus. Careful consideration should be given to the selection of the omnibus used to ensure that the timing of both the pre and post surveys are appropriate for the stimuli being measured. It is also important to ensure that the same supplier is used for both pre and post survey so that any 'contractor' effect can be eliminated.

Split runs

Research suppliers differ in the extent to which split runs are available on omnibus surveys. It is usual for a split run to be conducted so that the two halves of the sample can be exposed to different stimuli of some sort and the differences noted. The obvious problem here with omnibus surveys is that there is a limitation in the type of stimuli that can be dealt with. For example, a split run involving the testing of two concepts is usually feasible but it would not be feasible to test two TV advertisements in the same way. Similarly some companies place restrictions on the use of packs or products in this context. One further point worth bearing in mind is the method the research supplier uses to split the sample. It is preferable from the sampling viewpoint to do this on the basis of each interviewer alternating interviews between the two stimuli. In practice this can be a source of confusion, particularly when more than two stimuli are involved, and the more practical approach of distributing the stimuli to different interviewers is usually adopted.

Fieldwork, coding and analysis

Much the same considerations apply to omnibus surveys as apply to ordinary *ad hoc* research projects as far as these aspects are concerned. Fieldwork quality is a consideration which always has to be borne in mind in all research and it is as important to maintain standards in omnibus surveys as in any other.

Coding problems are also similar to those found in ordinary *ad hoc* projects, and there are of course a number of different ways of coding the information obtained. In omnibus surveys, use is frequently made of the open-ended question which has precodes on the questionnaire enabling the interviewer to categorize the respondents' comments. Most research suppliers put a restriction on the standard number of coding positions available for open-ended questions. Above this limit additional extra costs are incurred, but these are not normally large and it would usually be unwise to limit the codes for open-ended questions merely on the basis of cost. Unlike *ad hoc* surveys where the client can often leave much of the coding decisions to the research agency, in an omnibus survey the client should be prepared to specify more closely the coding positions he requires wherever this is possible.

Most research agencies provide demographic and regional breakdowns as standard. It is important to check, however, that the demographic breaks offered are appropriate for the particular project in hand, as for example age breaks are not always defined in the same way. More detailed analysis of omnibus surveys above and beyond the standard analysis provided by the research supplier is normally available at extra cost. It is usually better, however, to keep any such more detailed extra analyses separate from the basic analysis in order to avoid any time delays. The exception here would be where a specific sub-sample has been identified on the questionnaire or where a split run is being carried out, in which case it is important to build the appropriate analysis requirements into the main body of the report.

Applications

It will be clear from the preceding sections that omnibus surveys can be used in a large variety of applications. There are certain areas, however, where omnibus surveys have particular suitability and this section examines some of these in more detail.

Minority samples

Omnibus surveys can be particularly useful when the researcher is seeking to question a sub-group within the population at large. Clearly if the sub-group is a small proportion of the total population, it can be very expensive to find them by means of conventional *ad hoc* research. The use of omnibus surveys in this context thus becomes extremely cost-effective, for example when trying to find users of a minority brand. Once the target respondents have been identified the omnibus survey itself may then be used to ask more detailed questions. Alternatively, by establishing a respondent's willingness to participate in further research a more comprehensive follow-up survey can then be organized. The follow-up survey might, for example, involve testing products or advertising. Usually such a follow-up survey would involve a postal or telephone contact with the respondent, because the geographical distribution of the selected target group is likely to be widespread and this could make a personal call-back prohibitively expensive. One point to bear in mind here is that the response rate to such a follow-up survey conducted by post will vary but is unlikely to exceed 65–70%. This obviously needs to be taken in account in determining sample sizes.

Sequential or cumulative sampling

This takes advantage of the fact that omnibus surveys are carried out at regular intervals. Thus it becomes possible to build up a sample through time. This can be useful in two principal ways:

(a) When looking for a minority sample as detailed in the previous section, if the incidence of the minority group is very low then a single omnibus survey might not generate a large enough sample to investigate further. Subsequent omnibus surveys can be used to boost this number by repeating the recruitment question. When sufficient target group respondents have been identified, the follow-up survey can be initiated. Caution is needed, however, to the extent that the sample will have been recruited at different times. The researcher will need to satisfy himself that the elapsed time between recruiting the various components of the sample will not have an influence on the particular variable being researched. Many general omnibus surveys are repeated at frequent intervals (often weekly or fortnightly) so that this time interval can be quite small if required.

(b) A further application of the cumulative sampling approach on omnibus surveys is the flexibility they offer in generating information to a specified level of accuracy. Most surveys are carried out to estimate the proportion of the population, or a sub-group of the population, which has a particular attribute or makes a particular comment. This estimate is, of course, subject to sampling error which is related to the sample size and the actual population proportion being estimated. Where it is required to measure this proportion (unknown in advance) to a required degree of accuracy, it is necessary to have flexibility in terms of sample size. Omnibus surveys can provide this flexibility by use of the cumulative sampling approach. In this way, a series of omnibus surveys can be planned and results are accumulated as each one is conducted until a sufficiently large sample is achieved to give the required degree of statistical accuracy. As soon as this is achieved no further omnibus surveys are conducted. The risk of having a sample that is too small or unnecessarily large (thereby incurring considerable cost) is therefore avoided. Again, however, the time interval between the omnibus surveys needs to be given careful thought in terms of any potential influence on the statistic being measured. A further consideration is that the use of successive omnibus surveys inevitably delays getting the results. (This approach is however rarely used in practice, and to some extent has been superseded by telephone interviewing which offers an even greater degree of sample size flexibility.)

Split runs

A general discussion of the use of split runs in omnibus surveys has already been covered, under design considerations. However, one specific application of the split run technique is in piloting questionnaires. An omnibus survey using the split run technique can, for example, be used to test two alternative forms of a question prior to the commissioning of the main fieldwork stage for a conventional *ad hoc* project.

Time series (tracking)

The fact that omnibus surveys are conducted at regular intervals enables trends through time to be measured. This can vary from the simple repetition of a survey once a year (at the same time period each year) through to more frequent checks at regular intervals through the year. In this way it is possible to conduct 'tracking' type studies using omnibus surveys. Typical applications for this might be brand image monitors or advertising monitors.

There are, however, some limitations to using omnibus surveys in this way and these should be given careful consideration before adopting the omnibus approach. Apart from considerations of questionnaire length, complexity, position in the master questionnaire and of course cost comparison with *ad hoc* surveys, there is also the limitation that interviewing is not absolutely continuous using this method. Omnibus surveys operate with discrete fieldwork periods (typically spread over 3–4 days). When used to track measurements through time, this can make them over-sensitive to the influence of events occurring just prior to fieldwork. The obvious example of this might be measuring advertising awareness through time where competitive advertising activity occurs during the week of fieldwork thereby distorting the data. If continuous interviewing is an essential requirement, then omnibus surveys should usually be avoided.

Most research agencies offer discounts for the regular use of omnibus surveys and this can lead to substantial cost advantages over the *ad hoc* equivalent.

International research

A number of research agencies offer an international omnibus service in which omnibus facilities are available in a large number of countries around the world. These offer a number of advantages to the international researcher:

(a) Where they have already been examined critically and used by a number of clients they should be reasonably reliable. This is very useful for the researcher who from a distance does not have time to go into the facilities and reliability of a particular supplier in detail.

(b) Where multi-national studies are required, it is usually possible to use the omnibus approach to conduct research simultaneously in a number of different countries. Because it is relatively easy for a research company to transfer its omnibus survey design across countries, it is usually easier to obtain comparable results using omnibus surveys than it is by designing separate *ad hoc* studies in each country.

Benefits and limitations

Summary of benefits

A number of benefits of omnibus surveys have already been referred to and it should have become fairly clear by now that the principal advantages are cost and time, although others will be important in particular circumstances.

Cost

Cost savings as compared to *ad hoc* surveys are achieved by syndication. However, the cost structure of omnibus surveys works on the basis of a fixed cost per question, so that the cost saving over an equivalent *ad hoc* survey diminishes as the number of questions increases. Eventually a breakeven point will be reached where the cost of the two approaches will be identical and beyond this *ad hoc* surveys become cheaper. It is impossible to define this breakeven point in general terms as it depends on a number of factors.

However, it is important to recognize that it does exist and is often a good idea, particularly where large studies are being considered, to cost both methods.

The cost advantages of omnibus surveys when a particular sub-group of the population is required do not always apply where there may be alternative *ad hoc* methods which compare favourably in cost terms. For instance, where a sample characteristic can be identified *before interview* an *ad hoc* survey might well be cheaper than omnibus surveys as it is then only necessary to contact those respondents with the required characteristic. Examples of this might be a regional sample, people living in a particular housing type or people who shop in a specific retail outlet. In this latter case respondents might well be recruited in an *ad hoc* survey outside the particular store in question. This might be more efficient in cost terms than interviewing a representative sample of all adults on an omnibus and filtering out the required respondents.

Time

There are a number of ways in which omnibus surveys can shorten the time between deciding to conduct some research and receiving the results:

(a) The work of preparation before undertaking fieldwork can be considerably reduced on an omnibus survey since the sampling and fieldwork will have already been organized.
(b) Omnibus surveys usually use a larger number of interviewers than an equivalent *ad hoc* survey and this can reduce the fieldwork time necessary. This is particularly true when large samples are involved.
(c) Analysis of the results is usually quicker on an omnibus survey because the analysis routines and procedures are standardized.
(d) It can happen that because of crowded schedules the availability of interviewers for an *ad hoc* project may be limited and time may be lost waiting for the appropriate interviewers to be available.

Other benefits

Reference has already been made to some of the applications where omnibus surveys have particular benefits (e.g. in searching for minority samples). In addition it is worth remembering that omnibus surveys may often offer significant benefits over *ad hoc* surveys in terms of sampling accuracy. This stems from the fact that typically for a given sampling method and sample size an omnibus survey is likely to utilize more interviewers and more sampling points. It may also be possible to complete the fieldwork in a shorter time period than an equivalent *ad hoc* survey.

Summary of limitations

There are, of course, also certain disadvantages associated with omnibus surveys, and these do need to be carefully considered. Principal amongst the disadvantages are the constraints that are imposed by the nature of the survey itself:

(a) questionnaire length may be constrained;
(b) complex questions or detailed probing can be a problem;
(c) there are limitations on the type of experimental design that can be carried out, so that not all research problems are appropriate for omnibus surveys;
(d) there are limitations on the type and number of stimuli that can be used (e.g. testing television commercials is not practicable with an omnibus survey);
(e) timing is not flexible in the sense that fieldwork for a given survey is fixed and the timing of fieldwork cannot be altered to suit the requirements of a particular client. (However, in practice, because of the large number of competing services available, it is usually possible to select an omnibus survey whose timing fits very closely with requirements).

Beyond these practical constraints some thought needs to be given to the issues of questionnaire order effects, and the effect that other subject areas included in the omnibus might have on a particular set of questions. These factors are frequently ignored but can have an important influence on responses. There are two situations in particular where the influence of these factors should be of particular concern:

(a) where the information being collected is of an attitudinal rather than a factual (behavioural) nature.
(b) where time series data is being collected so that comparisons are being made between successive omnibus surveys. In this case the extreme would be where the questions appear first in the master questionnaire on one survey and last in the master questionnaire on another survey. Order effects in this case might be large enough to affect the comparability of the data.

To some extent these factors can be controlled by discussion with the research supplier (for example by standardizing the question positioning in the master questionnaire for repeat surveys), and certainly where repeat surveys are planned the research practitioner must be prepared to raise these issues with the supplier.

Services available

It is impossible to provide a comprehensive list of available omnibus services because of the quantity and variety offered in terms of:

sampling method
sample size
sample composition
timing.

Some idea of the range of services has been given in the previous sections. Most of the larger UK research agencies offer omnibus facilities, many providing a wide range of different services, as do those in other countries. The reader is referred to the Market Research Society Year Book and other directories which indicate those companies offering omnibus surveys. In the UK further reference should be made to the Market Research Society Monthly Newsletter where most of the major omnibus services are advertised, including several of the international services.

Chapter 10

Telephone, mail and other techniques

LEONARD ENGLAND and PETER ARNOLD*

Of the chapters in this section of the book the majority are basically concerned with forms of market research which imply personal confrontation of interviewer and respondent. Yet it seems inevitable that in volume terms at least (if not in importance) the share of such direct interviewing is steadily declining.

To some extent this is due to the greater use of electronic equipment which is now being employed not merely for television measurement and for audits but also experimentally for various *ad hoc* approaches with question-and-answer channelled through the television screen. But far more important, in the context of this chapter at least, is the major growth of telephone interviewing.[1]

In the 1970 edition of this work, a whole chapter was devoted to postal surveys while telephone interviewing was dismissed in a few lines. By the second edition of 1978, mail had been absorbed into the present chapter while telephone interviewing was expanded from a few lines to a few pages. Nevertheless the original author, while fully acknowledging the emergence of a new and growing technique, felt that for a long time its limitations would continue to outweigh its advantages. He was wrong; and six years further on he welcomes a co-author whose demonstration of the range and quality of telephone research indicates the developments taking place. Here is an admirable illustration of how fast, and often how unexpectedly, changes in market research techniques can occur.

Nevertheless, whatever the speed with which telephone interviewing is becoming one of the major resources – as a latersection shows, it is estimated that over a quarter of all interviews in the United Kingdom are now being carried out in this way – the ground rules remain much the same.

---

* For this edition Peter Arnold has contributed the section on Telephone Research while Leonard England has revised the remaining sections of the chapter.

This chapter is still concerned with occasions when the 'standard' forms of interviewing are inappropriate, though before a fourth edition of this work appears it seems likely that such a definition will need revision.

In general terms three situations call for the use of techniques other than 'standard' interviewing. The *first* of these is when those to be interviewed are widely scattered or otherwise difficult (and expensive) to contact, or when a large number of interviews are required in a very short space of time. It involves the use of:

(a) telephone surveys; or
(b) mail surveys.

These approaches have increasing and more general advantages as greater interviewing skill in general survey work brings with it increases in the interviewer's reward and therefore higher costs per interview. But other advantages also operate when the universes concerned are ideally suited to this form of approach: e.g. surveys on current subscribers for telephone companies or surveys on known users of direct mail.

The *second* situation occurs when surveys involve the co-operation of respondents over a long time or when the interviewer is unable to be present for the whole of the time with which the interview should be involved. The need here is for:

(c) self-completion questionnaires.

The *third* area operates when it is thought likely that standard techniques will fail to uncover the basic reasons involved in decision-making. In many cases qualitative work (see chapter 2) will mean that any questionnaire developed will allow useful and relevant answers to emerge rather than those which are superficial and 'unexpected'. There are, however, occasions when respondents themselves have, perhaps, no idea of what they do let alone why they do it: or where they are unable to report accurately how they order a pint of beer, or how long it takes them to cross a road. For these occasions the following techniques might need to be considered:

(d) use of 'ironmongery';
(e) counts;
(f) observation;
(g) anthropological participation.

These seven techniques each call for a sub-section to themselves but at greatly differing lengths, with by far the greatest attention being paid to telephone interviewing. Postal surveys – always of greater importance in the technical literature than in the market place because of the ease with which simple response rate experiments can be carried out! – are now clearly past their peak and it is difficult to see that there are many fields where for long they will hold an advantage over the telephone. All other techniques considered remain peripheral, often serving a vital purpose, sometimes benefiting from the new technology, but likely to be called on only when somewhat extraordinary problems are involved.

Table 10.1 summarizes very briefly the advantages and disadvantages for all the techniques considered in this chapter, together with the main uses to which each can be put. In a final section some general comments are made on the value of, and the problems involved in, techniques other than direct interviewer–respondent confrontation.

Telephone research

When the last edition of this book was published only 40% of UK households had a telephone. The use of the telephone as a research tool was consequently restricted primarily to interviewing executives and professional people; groups of consumers who were most likely to be on the telephone – primarily owners of expensive durables, readers of the upmarket press, users of credit cards, etc.; and samples of 'consumers' derived from lists of addresses with telephone numbers extracted from manufacturers' records. The telephone was primarily an industrial research tool, and interviewing was in the main carried out by interviewers from their own homes, by interviewers who spent most of their time conducting personal interviews.

Marginally more than 80% of UK households now have access to a telephone in their home (if one includes business phones that are effectively in private households). Industrial interviewing continues to rely heavily on the telephone. The principal change, however, is in the growing use of the telephone as a method of carrying out general consumer interviews.

Although opinions vary, it has been suggested that at the time of writing, telephone interviewing could account for 10% or more of all UK market research revenue and for something of the order of 30% of all interviews.

The history of telephone interviewing in America has much to do with the current growth of telephone research in the UK and Europe. In overall terms, the use of the phone for interviewing 'took off' in the USA when:

(a) the domestic penetration of the telephone had risen to 7 in every 10 households;
(b) 'Central Telephone Interviewing' (CTI) was invented;
(c) personal interviewing was proven to be increasingly expensive and difficult;
(d) speed of turnround started to become all important;
(e) it was realized that modern computer technology offered methodological and cost advantages.

Table 10.1

Method	Some uses	Some advantages	Some disadvantages
(a) Telephone	(i) When simultaneous interviews needed	Cost	Lack of rapport
		Speed	Interviews must often be shorter
	(ii) When individual calls are very far apart		Less easy to use show cards, pictures
			Uneven incidence of telephone ownership
(b) Mail	When respondents are difficult to contact	Cost	Unrepresentative sample
		No interviewer 'interference'	Lack of control of questionnaire completion
(c) Self-completion	When interview should be completed but interviewer cannot be present	Cost	As with mail surveys (e.g. misunderstanding bias; only short questionnaire possible)
		Accuracy of reporting close to action involved	
(d)(i) Psycho-galvanometer	When respondent unlikely to be aware of own responses	Prestige and similar answers need not be considered	Unreal surroundings
			Little data about why
			Cost of large samples
(ii) Tachisto-scope etc.	To test detailed physical behaviour, particularly of eye reaction	Ability to measure action in a detail not available by other methods	Unreal surroundings
			Little data about why
			Cost of large samples
(e) Count	When requirement implies only total numbers of people involved in certain actions	Cost	Little data about 'why'
		Speed	No analysis possible by profile of individual
		Large samples	
(f) Observation	When the concern is more with *how* people act than *why*	Direct observation of what people do rather than what they *say* they do	Cost
			Sample structure
(g) Participant observation	When only information at a very detailed level is of value	Depth of response	Very high cost and very long time taken
			Problems of representative sa

This is very much the current position in countries such as the UK.

There are significant differences between the rules for personal interviewing and the rules for telephone interviewing. The modes of questioning, the introduction, the wording of individual questions etc., must often be different if for no other reason than that those questioned react differently to any given stimulus depending on whether they are being asked questions by a visible person sitting in their front room or by an impersonal 'voice' over the telephone. There are obviously also sampling issues to be considered.

Those with experience of interviewing by telephone would be the first to point out that:

(a) because of the still biased ownership of telephones, the approach must for certain purposes be queried on sampling grounds. Much sterling work has been done and continues to be done in this area in the UK by the Market Research Development Fund of the Market Research Society (the MRDF);

(b) the data collected by telephone are different from those collected in face-to-face interviews. One cannot conclude, however, that simply because the data are different those collected by telephone are 'wrong'. Although there is little real experimental evidence to be found in the literature, some evidence suggest that respondents are more likely to respond honestly to sensitive questions over the phone. This is mainly due to the fact that interviews over the phone are more remote and consequently, in a sense, more confidential and less threatening. Experimental research carried out in the US tends to show that one gets more accurate answers to questions about income, investment, illness and 'sexual matters' over the phone. (The MRDF has just commissioned experimental research to investigate the differences in answers given to the same questions asked in face-to-face and telephone interviews.);

(c) questionnaires written for administration over the phone need to be written differently. This is in part because one needs to be more chatty to hold the respondent's attention, and in part because one cannot generally use visual stimulus material unless one goes to the trouble of sending material through the post prior to conducting the main telephone interview. (As we will see later, the 'power' and applicability of the telephone interview can be greatly enhanced if one combines telephone interviewing with other data collection techniques.)

The principal attractions of telephone interviewing relate to speed, control and cost-effectiveness. The centralized approach maximizes these attributes. In Telephone Centres one has total control over the interviewing process. Given 100% supervision it is obviously possible to ensure that questionnaires are administered exactly as intended to the correct respondents. One can also reduce fieldwork periods to the minimum as the time required for the despatch and return of documents is reduced to zero. The combination of Central Telephone Interviewing (CTI) with direct data entry (DDE) methods, or the wholesale computerization of the total telephone interviewing process – Computer Assisted Telephone Interviewing (CATI) –

has meant that through 'mechanization' telephone surveys can be conducted in very short periods.

Before one can make a judgement of the appropriateness of the telephone for any given survey, one needs to be able to answer a number of key questions:

(a) Would a sample drawn entirely from those on the phone be biased? IF YES: Can the bias be removed quite simply by demographic weighting or is it something more fundamental? (For example there is evidence to suggest that the telephone is a durable and is consequently a discriminator as far as the purchase of durables is concerned. Special analysis of a variety of data sources shows that telephone owners, even when matched demographically to non-owners, are more likely to be owners of other durables.)

(b) Does one need to ask any questions that cannot realistically be covered over the phone? In particular, does one need to show any stimulus material? IF YES: Can one get round this either by using an adapted questioning approach or by using a combination method of data collection – personal + phone, or phone + post?

(c) Ultimately, is phone the best approach? It is not always.

Each of these principal questions are considered in further detail below.

Telephone sampling

There are basically six methods of sampling for telephone surveys:

(a) Randomly from telephone directories (most typically, fixed interval stratified by region or unstratified).

(b) Randomly using directory-assisted methods (the Directory-Assisted Plus-One method being most commonly used).

(c) Random digit dialling.

(d) From lists supplied by clients.

(e) From lists derived from 'Trade Directories' (more commonly used for 'industrial' interviewing).

(f) From other surveys. (The telephone is particularly useful for following up those previously interviewed, either to collect further information that has been proven to be important as a result of analysis, or because 'time has passed' and attitudes or behaviour may have been modified by events.)

Random fixed interval sampling

Given that one has a full set of reasonably up-to-date telephone directories, and given that one knows the number of entries in each directory, one can draw a fixed interval random sample – stratified or unstratified – by taking every *x*th number from each selected directory, either on a clustered or unclustered basis.

Telephone exchange areas can be used to define standard regions, TV areas, client's regional sales areas, etc. One can therefore stratify one's sample according to any of the usual regional parameters. Samples can be as clustered or as unclustered as desired. One of the principal benefits of telephone research is that one can produce totally unclustered samples, and hence interviews, at no cost penalty. Theoretically at least, one can reduce design factors to almost unity. By using unclustered samples, one can therefore reduce sample sizes to the minimum.

Directory-assisted methods

A random sample drawn from directories will always exclude those who prefer to remain ex-directory. Although this is still a minor problem in the UK, there is a small percentage of telephone owners – predominantly ABs – who are excluded from randomly selected directory-based samples. This obviously varies from area to area.

Directory-assisted sampling methods are based on the premise that telephone numbers in the UK are allocated in blocks. If one selects a number from the directory one is safe in assuming that that particular number exists. If 1 is added to that number it is highly probable that the new number generated also exists. The new number generated by adding 1

i.e. 01-643-2111

would become 01-643-2112

has the characteristic of being either a listed *or* an unlisted number.

On the disadvantage side, it means that one samples a very small proportion of non-existing numbers, a larger proportion of defunct numbers and an even larger proportion of business numbers – numbers that can be avoided by sampling directly from directories. The approach does however have two key advantages. It samples unlisted numbers and consequently gives a better sample of all phone-owning households. It is also a very neat approach for producing matched samples – perfectly matched samples, for tracking exercises. If one draws an initial start sample from directories and then adds 1 to produce a DA + 1 sample for interviewing, one can create a series of matched samples for tracking by adding a further two digits to the DA + 1 listing. One adds 2 rather than 1 to create each subsequent sample because there are a few domestic households that have 2 consecutive phone numbers, but there are very few indeed that have 3. One can produce a fairly large number of samples by this method before sampling efficiency is significantly reduced.

Random digit dialling

It is not necessary to draw samples or start-numbers from directories. As an alternative one can ring random numbers within specified exchange codes. In practice one cannot leave it to interviewers to generate these random numbers. They can best be generated by one of two methods – either manually within exchange codes using random number tables, or (when using CATI) by computer random number generators. Although this method of sampling is attractive as it requires little organized sampling, it is less efficient and hence less cost-effective as a significant proportion of the numbers generated are non-existent.

The technique thus generates a much higher percentage of non-effective numbers than the sampling methods described earlier. This sampling method becomes more attractive if one has a computer system designed to maximize one's chances of selecting existing numbers. This can be done by using a combination of directory-assisted and true random digit dialling sampling methods.

Sampling from lists

This approach is obvious. Provided one is happy that the source list is representative of the universe to be sampled, sampling can be carried out using any systematic method.

Sampling from previous surveys

This method of sampling requires no explanation. One mentions it, not because it illustrates any novel sampling method, but because this approach demonstrates an important use of telephone interviewing. It is sometimes impossible to predetermine all the relevant questions to be asked in an initial interviewed survey; follow-up interviews carried out in the light of the preliminary findings can therefore often add a further dimension.

Recall interviews are frequently easier by phone, either as the principal method of interviewing or in those cases where interviewers have failed to make personal contact.

Questionnaire construction for the telephone

As telephone interviewing relies totally on remote verbal communication, it is that much more important to ensure that 'the script' flows and keeps the respondent's interest.

The introduction

The first 30 seconds are all-important. If one is going to build up a 'relationship' with one's respondent one has to do it in the first few seconds.

Experience shows that if one gets off on the wrong footing one can never regain the ground lost. The cardinal points – the 'musts' – are:

(a) Be relaxed. You have to sound friendly if you want to forge a relationship.
(b) Give your name. Be sure to mention your Christian name. You will never break the ice if you insist on formality.
(c) Answer the obvious questions...
   ...why *you* are ringing
   ...what you want
   ...how long it will take
   ...why *this interview* is important
   ...who are you working for
   before the respondent has a chance to ask.

The interviewer's manner is as important as the wording of the questionnaire.

Question types
The basic rule must be that there is little that you can't ask over the phone if you 'ask it right'. Basic precoded questions are no problem and open-ended questions are straightforward if you probe properly. Answers tend to be curtailed in telephone interviews quite simply because there is no opportunity for non-verbal prompts. If you want full answers you have to work harder. The administration of scales is straightforward providing one realizes that the approaches developed over the years for other modes of interviewing are not necessarily suitable for telephone interviewing.

There are basically two modes most suitable for administering scales over the phone:

(a) *Marks out of 10* (because of schooling, the concept of marks-out-of-10 is well understood). One can also use the telephone dial to demonstrate the scoring system.
(b) *Unfolding*. 4-point scales are easy to handle if one offers the scale in two parts. To administer a 4-point scale over the phone one first asks whether the respondent agrees or disagrees with the dimension to be rated. One then asks... 'by a lot or a little?' Respondents learn this game very quickly.

Provided one can settle for 4- or 10-point scales there is no problem administering scales over the phone. The administration of 5- and 7-point scales is somewhat more problematic. There is however a way:

(c) *'Write your own'*. The vast majority of those interviewed are willing and able to find a pencil and paper and write lists. If absolutely necessary, scales can be created this way. (However, see the comments below.)

Batteries of scales can also be administered. The natural assumption is that show-cards cannot be used in telephone interviews. 'Write your own' is a way round the more general visual-prompt problem. The example given below can be adapted to work for both batteries of scales and prompted awareness questions.

'Q. I am now going to ask you about your views of a number of different companies. Could you find something to write with and scrap of paper. OK? I am going to give you a number of company names... can you please write them down.
READ OUT NAMES ON THE LIST. THEN ASK THE RESPONDENT TO READ BACK THE LIST. ONLY CONTINUE WHEN YOU ARE SURE THAT THE LIST WRITTEN DOWN IS COMPLETE AND CORRECT.
Which of the companies shown on your list...
are the best at...?
...have you seen advertising for in the last few months?
...are most likely to think that...?'

Using Ehrenberg couplets one can effectively use this approach to administer 3-point scales simultaneously across a number of companies/brands.

Surprisingly perhaps, respondents *are* willing to write their own lists, even quite long ones. The key to using this approach is to get them to read back what they have written before using the list, just to check that the list is correct. One can obviously get them to write other things – concept statements, unfamiliar and unpronounceable names which can be spelled out, etc.

The examples given above illustrate a few of the ways in which lateral thinking can be used to solve telephone questionnaire administration problems. Hopefully, the examples quoted also serve to illustrate the fact that 'there isn't much that can't be asked over the phone' – at least technically.

The use of the telephone – solus, or in combination with other methods of data collection

As is often the case, any mode of interviewing often becomes more attractive when it is used in connection with other alternate modes of data collection. Having said that, the telephone can be used for many jobs for which it would not immediately seem to be appropriate. To illustrate the flexibility of the telephone as a mode of data collection, often used in combination with other methods of data capture, a number of examples are given below.

Product placement and recall

Traditionally product placement studies are carried out personally. This can become very expensive when multiple recalls are required as interviewing expenses escalate rapidly. Given that one is dealing with light-weight products that can be sent by post, one can recruit and recall by telephone. This becomes a particularly cost-effective approach when multiple recalls are required. As is the general case with telephone interviewing, one can also reap the benefits of unclustered sampling. When interviewing by phone from central facilities there is no cost benefit to be derived from clustering.

As mentioned earlier, top-up recalls can be carried out by phone on projects that rely principally on face-to-face interviewing. Multiple personal recalls are very expensive, multiple recalls by phone are not.

Placement and recall studies are really short-term panels. This example illustrates the general point that the telephone is a very cost-effective method of collecting information from all manner of panels.

Pre-testing radio commercials

Although there are obvious limitations to the use of visual stimulus material in telephone interviewing, there are no limitations to the use of audio-stimuli.

There is a great variety of hardware available that can be used to play audio tapes over the phone. The telephone consequently affords a most effective method of pre-testing radio commercials.

Again, there is a general lesson in this example: Audio prompts of all kinds are appropriate.

Advertising tracking studies

Random sampling methods such as Directory-Assisted Plus One enable one to produce multiple perfectly matched samples inexpensively – a pre-requisite for effective tracking studies. Speed and control are the other advantages offered by the telephone. Should it be required, fieldwork periods can be timed to the hour. Given the size of central telephone interviewing facilities nowadays it is perfectly feasible to carry out 500 or 1000 interviews in a single evening. Such control is often essential in tracking studies.

Tactical market evaluation

The modern marketeer is growingly demanding answers to tactical issues on a 'zero leadtime' basis. Central telephone interviewing is the one method of collecting *ad hoc* data that makes this all possible. Given the current state of the art, it is becoming commonplace to set-up and report on surveys within

24 hours. The telephone has permitted the commissioning of many valuable tactical research projects that would never have been considered in the past.

The speed and control afforded by the telephone approach thus often makes the difference between a viable and a non-viable survey.

International projects

Interviewing from a central location need not be restricted by national borders. Provided one has interviewers with the relevant language capabilities one can interview anywhere in the world. Why would one want to do this? Although it is unlikely to be a cost-effective way of carrying out very large quantitative exercises, it can be especially useful for:

(a) investigatory exercises/feasibility studies;
(b) piloting;
(c) group recruitment.

Intrigue and flattery lead to very high response rates on internationally dialled telephone surveys. It may sound slightly improbable, but there are many more difficult ways of recruiting a group of doctors in Germany!

If one thinks laterally, one will find that there are very few real restrictions to the use of the telephone as a method of data collection. There obviously are restrictions, but they are far fewer than one might first expect.

Final comments

There is still much to be learned about telephone interviewing. Logic points to certain universes where the method is inappropriate simply because of *sample biases*. There are other cases where the *interview content* mitigates against the use of the phone. *Interview length* can also be a block to the use of this method of data collection. There is a myth that telephone interviews cannot last for more than about 15 minutes. This is untrue: it is perfectly possible to carry out very long interviews over the phone, but only if the subject matter is interesting. Long boring questionnaires cannot be administered; and complex tasks cannot generally be performed.

Even given these restrictions, there are a multitude of cases where the telephone is appropriate. As knowledge increases and telephone penetration climbs, the applicability of the telephone approach will continue to broaden.

Mail surveys

It has already been noted that mail surveys generate a disproportionate amount of technical comment, at least in part because they are easy and cheap to use as the basis of experiment. For the same reason they seem always to be the amateur's first do-it-yourself approach to market research. 'Let's do our own survey' almost always develops into home-made questions circulated for postal reply. Inevitably such an approach usually produces results that are not merely irrelevant but also dangerous; for postal surveys very easily provide misleading results if the questions are ambiguous or if those who reply are not a true cross-section of the target market.

There remain, of course, many right reasons for carrying out mail surveys. The *first* of these is the simple one that there may be no other method of carrying out a survey economically. To contact *personally* all those who have bought waste-disposal units or invalid chairs in the last month would imply a survey of a cost which no manufacturer is likely to be able to contemplate. But a properly organized, professionally controlled *mail* survey can provide a good deal of relevant data at a reasonable price. To take a quite different example, to interview people leaving a theatre is a very complex problem, for all interviewing has to be jammed into 10 or 15 minutes: to leave questionnaires in programmes ensures a larger, if not disinterested, sample.

An outstanding example of the success of a survey carried out by post which would be too expensive by other means is the regular 'Target Group Index' run by the British Market Research Bureau[2]. Technically, perhaps, this can be counted as a self-completion questionnaire (considered in the next sub-section) since the postal questionnaire is prefaced by a personal visit from an interviewer. But when the 'briefing' is completed, respondents are asked to provide broad details of their buying habits of some 350 different products. And they do. Personal interviewing time is, in consequence, cut to a fraction.

The second instance when it is right to use mail occurs when the sample is, by its nature, involved in using mail; in consequence, a postal questionnaire is the natural means to carry out a survey. A study, for example, amongst members of a book club, used to filling in a monthly questionnaire to state which books they required, or among those who have recently completed a quiz-type competition, would best be done by post, for people would answer in their own time and in their own way. Were interviewers to call, their sample might not even be as good because these people could well contain a disproportionate number of those acutely difficult to contact by normal means, living neither in accessible points nor in communities.

The third reason for using mail is related to the questionnaire itself. Most questions asked in interviews expect an off-the-cuff reply: detail is usually obtained by means of a whole series of subsidiary questions rather than by obtaining a more lengthy considered reply. But there are studies better done if the respondent has plenty of time either to think out the answers he intends to give (If you had £100 to spend on your garden, how would you spend it?) or to work out detailed answers (Where did you go on holiday in each of the last ten years?; or buying habits in the TGI detail referred to above).

General approach

The whole approach to mail surveys must, of course, be as closely geared to the potential respondent as is the case with any other type of survey: at its crudest, either with post or personal interviews, the busy housewife must somehow be pushed to answer even a small number of questions, although the enthusiast talking about his hobby may, with great pleasure, answer a 20-page questionnaire. But just as the financial advantage of a postal survey is the absence of the face-to-face interview, so its technical disadvantage is that the respondent is faced not with somebody helping, cajoling, co-operating in interview completion but with a questionnaire which can be filled in tomorrow just as well as today. The art of a good postal survey is to humanize it as much as possible to show that even if real people are not delivering it they have at least written it and are concerned whether you reply or not.

Wherever possible, therefore, postal questionnaires should be accompanied by a personal indication of concern – ideally personally addressed to an individual, certainly signed by an individual from the company concerned. Follow-up reminder letters, probably becoming more and more personal and friendly, also serve this purpose.

So, of course, do incentives, the area covered by so much experimentation. What happens if one sends personally stamped envelopes instead of reply paid? if one adds a ballpoint or a postal order? if one offers a small lottery prize? or a large one? All extras are effective, providing higher response rates, though final effectiveness is likely to be governed more by other factors such as general interest in the subject of the study or length and comprehensibility of the questionnaire. But all incentives are, in any case, a reflection of care and concern: anything which shows that the agency sending the questionnaire realizes that it is going to a human being is likely to increase the likelihood of reply.

It is clearly impossible in a few pages to describe the techniques involved in coping with mail surveys – indeed, one of the standard books on mail surveys is almost as long as the present volume[3]. What is vital, at all stages of administration, is to keep a tight control on speed and nature of return, methods of sending reminder letters while continuing to show concern for the confidentiality of reply (if this is necessary), checking whether the 'right' person is replying – often within the household an unexpected or irrelevant member may reply.

The sample

The greater the care the greater the likely response rate. Clearly this is vital for reasons already mentioned, the permanent worry that those who do not answer are different in kind from those who do. And while a *prima facie* case may be made out for assuming a representative sample has been obtained when those returned reflect those despatched on known data (e.g. ratio of men to women) this does not alter the basic worry that they may not do so on the essentials of the survey – usually that of interest in the subject covered.

Very high success rates can be obtained either when one is dealing with enthusiasts (such as owners of new cars) or when all the processes concerning control of the survey are applied very rigorously – the Government Social Survey have many examples of such successes[4]. Given that these *are* achieved, then a major advantage of postal interviewing – selective sampling – can be fully utilized. In most personal interviews a *representative* sample of the population is selected either because the geographical scatter of specialist groups makes interviewing only such people prohibitively expensive, or because at the beginning of the survey there is no means of defining use or interest. Postal surveys are more likely to begin with lists, the very existence of which define respondents. And it is, of course, just as cheap to send out 1000 questionnaires to 1000 towns as it is to send them out all to one square mile.

It is possible, in consequence, to concentrate on sections of the potential which would repay special study. A survey on mail order buying, for example, might involve 500 customers: a random selection would, perhaps, provide 300 buying once every year, 150 buying once every three months and 50 buying every month – in other words, most replies would be from irregular buyers, whereas clearly the views of the heavy spenders are of greatest interest. A postal survey can 'over-weight' the heavy spender by making sure that half the interviews are sent out to monthly spenders, a quarter each to less relevant, less frequent groups. Computer weighting can bring figures back to a representative sample but the most vital group is no longer based on very small numbers.

This is a technique which is of particular relevance in follow-up surveys where postal questionnaires are used either in series on the same people or to gain further data from those already personally interviewed once. Here a very full office study can be made to decide on those people of particular interest and the right people can be selected rather than those financially most convenient.

The questionnaire

But with postal surveys–indeed, as with any survey–value ultimately depends on the extent to which questions asked can provide the data required. And there are in postal surveys a whole series of problems not shared by personal interviewing. In particular, these are:

length
intelligibility
bias

It is probably true that most personal interviews are longer than they should be, but whether or not this is the case there is little difficulty, with a well laid out questionnaire and a well trained interviewer, of going through 15–20 pages of questions. It *is* possible too with postal surveys, especially with specialized interested groups (such as readers, of 'Which?' or people discussing their main hobby). But the problem becomes a far more complex one to persuade the respondent to go on and on.

Much can be done to this end by making the pages interesting and the completion of questions more of a game. Cartoons and drawings can help, as can changes of typeface. But probably more important than any of this is the need for an *obvious* sense of purpose. Why am I being asked this question? What is the point of all these stupid additions?

One aspect of 'intelligibility' – the second important consideration in a postal questionnaire – is precisely to explain why questions are being asked and why answers are important. Lay-out again can help greatly but cannot get rid of the problem.

Perhaps even more important within the framework of intelligibility is the question of semantics. Probing cannot be done in a postal questionnaire and therefore piloting becomes increasingly important – and yet, because the questionnaire must *look* simple, many, both clients and practitioners, assume that it *is* simple and do not bother.

A covering letter explaining the reasons and purposes of the questionnaire is usually a very great help, and can indeed explain certain inherent problems within the main document. But this too, of course, must not merely be human (never 'Dear Sir or Madam') but must also be intelligible.

To explain is in itself sometimes to create bias – the third, and perhaps the most intractable of the problems of postal questionnaires. The essential difficulty here is caused by the fact that with a postal questionnaire the respondent may answer questions in any order he cares to, and certainly is likely to have read the whole of the questionnaire before he begins to answer it at all. Now it is often vital in a personal questionnaire that the respondent begins by answering in generals terms – which is your favourite washing powder? – before the main concern of the survey becomes obvious – what do you think of Persil? Once she knows of the interest in Persil, the housewife's objections and biases could well overload all parts of the survey. In personal interviews this can be avoided: in postal surveys it cannot.

For precisely the same reason it is impossible to ask – at least in this simple form – any questions such as 'What brands of paint have you ever heard of?' Between reading the questionnaire and answering it, a period of anything from a few hours to a few weeks, the respondent will be conscious of brands of paint, will be more aware (but to an unknown degree) of commercials, press advertisements, posters, even shop displays: even brands *used* are likely to be increased as memory is jarred–or simply as other members of the family are asked to add their memories to make the questionnaire a joint effort.

The essentials in mail surveys

Maximum involvement and maximum value from a postal questionnaire can probably be gained by use of these principles:

rouse curiosity;
make importance clear;
make relevance *to the respondent* clear;
be easy to understand;
be interesting;
be easy to complete;
be easy to return.

But with all this it must be clearly understood that answers from a postal questionnaire are different in kind from those of a personal interview – less spontaneous, more considered, less affected by the involvement of a third person, more likely (however high the response rate) to over-emphasize the interested. None of these points necessarily vitiates or even devalues answers given – indeed, it has been shown above that while, for example, time taken to think can vitiate replies to some types of questions (Name as many brands as you can think of) it adds value to others (How would you spend £100 on ...?). But they do make it important to realize that the variations which do exist imply that the answers given are not always measuring the same thing in postal surveys as in personal ones.

Self-completion questionnaires

All mail surveys are, of course, self completion questionnaires. Reference should also be made, however, to other forms, particularly to the fact that self-completion questionnaires can be of considerable value *in conjunction with* standard interviewer studies as part of what is, in effect, one questionnaire. In these circumstances they are not usually sent by post but left by the interviewer.

This is particularly the case in product tests. In some cases, the test can be

made on the spot; in others it does not matter a great deal if comments are
not collected until the interviewer returns to obtain views on the product.
There is an intermediate group of cases, however, when the *immediate*
reaction of the housewife, and perhaps also of her family, is of considerable
importance. As examples of this we may cite:

(a) A cough mixture left with people to take when they got a cough.
    Although those taking part were asked to contact the market research
    company as soon as the cough developed, to arrange a personal
    interview, some report on the immediate interchange of cough and
    remedy seemed essential and this was done by means of a form left with
    the respondent.
(b) A new product which involved unfamiliar cooking patterns. When the
    housewife was in the process of making it, it was essential that she
    should also make a note of snags which she encountered, the immediate
    results and the immediate comments of the family.
(c) A paired comparison test of two cigarettes. To do the test while the
    interviewer waited would make it most unreal. To leave it to the
    respondent in his own time was far more realistic provided that he was
    sure to record what his feelings were at the time rather than recalling
    them at a later stage.

An alternative approach involves the self-completion questionnaire as a
form of *aide-mémoire*. Development of new products may be assisted by
knowledge of how current products are used in a detail for which memory
may be dangerous except over very short periods. A new form of instant
coffee, for example, may depend for its success on how many cups are made
at any one time, or a new baby food on whether the mother usually
prepares food for the baby at the same time as food for adult members of
the household. Recording of this kind is, of course, close to the diary panels
considered in chapter 8, but there is no need for a panel to be involved, the
respondent being asked to co-operate only in a single study.

This approach is also of value on occasions where respondents would be
able to tell the interviewer their answers but might be somewhat
embarrassed to do so. Probably this is less important today than it was even
ten years ago, e.g. on a recent survey a few sudden questions on brands of
contraceptives used appeared to cause very little problem even though both
interviewers and respondents were specifically told to omit these if they
wished. On the other hand, answers thought to be *socially unacceptable*, e.g.
strong approval of South African apartheid policies, could well be expressed
by some people more forcibly on a piece of paper than to a total stranger.

Self-completion interviews of the kinds so far considered assume
completion in the home. A separate use of the same technique is involved
when self-completion means mass-completion. The most obvious instance of

this is that of theatre tests when a representative sample is invited to see a series of films interspersed by commercials. At various stages in the performance the audience is invited to answer questions usually about the products concerned in the advertisements. Which would they buy? What do they see as particular advantages and disadvantages of each?

Questionnaires are distributed for self-completion primarily because of the expense and time involved in the simultaneous personal interviewing of all people in a theatre, but in consequence the approach suffers from most of the same limitations as any other form of self-completion and mail questionnaire. It does, however, have one major advantage over other forms. In the course of an evening, respondents may well fill in half a dozen *separate* simple questionnaires. However, they have filled in the first ones unaware of what is to follow. This removes the bias which sometimes can exist in any form of self-completion survey caused by respondents knowing in advance what further questions he is likely to be asked.

The whole technique of using in-home self-completion questionnaires, however, could be dramatically affected by their translation into terms of video or of 'interactive' terminals linked to the research agency's offices.

Ironmongery

In the techniques so far considered, the main variations from the standard interview approach are in the *method* of data collection rather than in what is collected. Whether the interview is asked personally, or left for the respondent to fill in, or posted, or asked over the telephone, the question-and-answer approach applies, and the information collected is recorded and coded in a standard form. For the techniques now to be discussed in this chapter, this no longer applies; the interviewer is no longer a recorder of what is said, the respondent is no longer necessarily expected to provide in words or writing what she is doing and saying and thinking. Actions are now speaking rather than words. Hardware and counts and observation imply the use of an interviewer to report what is happening; they watch, they do not ask.

In operations of this kind, much help can be given by the use of mechanical equipment; indeed, in some instances such equipment can, in fact, provide data which could not be obtained in any other way. Almost without exception, however, apart from the use of television meters*, such 'hardware' has been found to have only limited use in market research and

---

* Although audience measurement devices are of the same kind as those considered in this section, they are the subject of separate discussion in chapter 25. It is perhaps relevant to point out, however, that metering devices need to measure not only 'sets tuned in' but also 'people present' – and even then do not measure the degree of attention (if any) being paid to the set.

the last five years have probably witnessed no new gadgetry of even passing importance. A description of how some current machinery works may in itself indicate the reason for the limitations.

We must include in this category the *camera*. On occasions this may be used only to provide still photographs, e.g. for use in a survey covering a representative sample of kitchens to discover the extent to which there was room in them (if necessary after rearrangement) to add extra durable goods. It is more likely, however, to be a moving record. One case using this technique was carried out by the London Transport Executive[5]. The object of the study was to assess the proportion of the population given the opportunity to view posters on bus sides. On special buses following randomly selected standard routes, cameras were placed above the advertisement used as a test. By replaying the film thus made available it was possible to analyse in part the nature of the potential audience (defined as those passing the bus and at least part facing it) and from this to make deductions as to the total audience.

Such a survey naturally cannot be concerned in any way with whether respondents did see the advertisements concerned, only with whether they had the *opportunity*. Much of the equipment devised is more specifically concerned with what the eye does, in fact, see and what it passes to the brain. For a year or so in the early 1960s work with special equipment was carried out on subliminal advertising and the effect of messages displayed too fast for the eye apparently to see but yet probably absorbed; and at a later stage there was a belief that data as to the state of mind of a purchaser in a supermarket could be disclosed by recording the 'blink rate'. A concealed special camera recorded the speed at which the shopper blinked; the slower the blink rate the more 'hypnotized' by choice she was said to be, the more open to suggestion. A separate technique widely discussed a few years ago involved pupil dilation, the average percentage change in this being assumed to measure the degree of interest in the advertisement or display being studied[6]. On another study – this time not involving a camera – fingerprints were recorded to test page traffic on a magazine. All these 'machines' are now generally discredited.

The *psychogalvanometer* remains with us and has been used far more[7]. The respondent watches television or reads copy, 'wired' by means of small suction cap electrodes fitted to the back of his hand. These are connected to a machine recording sweat variations. Precise nervous reactions are thus recorded to what he is seeing. As with many other techniques considered in this chapter, the main objection is the question of what any reaction means. In certain cases, it must be admitted, tape recording provides *in parallel* what the respondent is saying as his reactions are being recorded on the psychogalvanometer, but this again does not necessarily mean that the respondent will behave in a predictable way in a subsequent behavioural situation.

The *tachisotoscope*[7] is far more widely accepted although it is probably far less used than five or ten years ago. This machine tests to calibrations of one hundredth of a second the reaction of a respondent to what he sees though a shutter; it may be a test of the comparative legibility of pack or label design or the extent to which one pack stands out against all its competitors, or the *part* of the advertisement which is most likely to be seen first. A simple tachistoscope measures a single stimulus at a time, but further developments with stereoscope or binocular models allow the exposure of two stimuli simultaneously with independent and variable light densities and, at the same time, allow tests to be made on eye dominance. Other things being equal, it is assumed that the name or the display which is recognized in the fastest time is the most likely to be successful. However, other things rarely are equal, of course, and there is a good deal of evidence that the most effective advertisement is the one which is less likely to be seen immediately but is studied in detail when it is. Used side by side with other techniques, however, the tachistoscope can be of considerable importance.

All these techniques are, in fact, best used in conjunction with direct interviewing. A rather newer form of eye camera can *only* be used in such conjunction by a procedure known as DEMOS.[8] This springs from the need to be able to relate what is remembered in advertisements to what has definitely been seen. Is complete lack of recall of an advertisement due to the fact that the respondent has not, in fact, seen it all, her eye having completely overlooked the page; or has she seen it and found it so totally uninteresting that she has no recollection of having seen it? By means of an ingenious lay-out of mirrors and camera the respondent is watched unobserved as she turns the pages of a magazine, and a record is made of the time she has taken page by page, and area by area. A later questionnaire considers her recall of advertisements and relates this to what she has seen and how long she has spent reading it. This is a case where mechanical aids are used to assist the interviewing technique rather than to replace it. There are other forms of hardware with much the same purpose, and in the foreseeable future portable video machines or cassettes may be attached to television sets to allow this kind of advertising testing to be carried out in the more realistic surroundings of the respondent's own home.

Counts

Between the use of mechanical equipment and of observation lies the simple count. 'Simple' is, perhaps, a misnomer if the count technique is assumed (as is technically possible) to embrace almost all forms of audience meter recording and retail audits. Occasions exist, however, when a count carried out by interviewers can provide more useful data than an actual interview.

At the beginning of the Second World War civilians were supposed to carry their gas-masks wherever they went[9]. These were, however, cumbersome and most people chose to forget them. On certain occasions it was noticed that the proportions carrying them seemed to rise sharply, and a study of the news on the progress of the war revealed what appeared to be a consistent relationship between the proportions carrying gas-masks and the state of general morale. Counts were consistently carried out to assess morale until such time as the fear of gas attack so abated that few people carried masks on any occasions at all. This technique could not be validated since direct questioning (at a time when it might have been thought unpatriotic to be depressed) revealed that the stated comments of the general public showed a far closer relationship to the official attitude of 'do or die'. In more recent applications, however, the same technique has been used in a number of projects to provide data difficult to collect in other ways; to take one example, operational research has apparently established that pedestrian subways will not generally be used when the time taken to travel through the subway is markedly longer than that taken above ground. It is highly doubtful, however, if people consciously realize this fact, and certainly they would not have been able to answer with any precision before a particular subway was built. Simple timings of road-crossing under laboratory conditions were meaningless when little was known about traffic flows or the difference in speed of crossing at different times of day.

An unpublished survey of this kind was conducted with the traffic entering and leaving one of London's main railway stations. Brief interviews first established the proportions likely to be crossing given roads where subways were planned, and preliminary counts checked the numbers crossing such roads at various times of the day. Then, using a random selection technique and stopwatch, interviewers timed pedestrians from the moment they reached the curb they planned to step off to the moment they were able to step on to the opposite one. Average times were calculated and it became apparent that subways costing many thousands of pounds would be unlikely to be used at least for some years to come; for the most part people did not have to wait long enough to make them likely to go down one flight of steps and up the other.

Counts can also establish data which would, again, not be forthcoming from direct questioning because of difficulties of obtaining either correct samples or answers unaffected by memory or fear of consequences of reply. The 'dustbin audit' of AGB described in chapter 8 is one such example. In similar vein, however, it is possible to estimate the extent of all-day parking in meter areas by checking registration numbers of cars either remaining on one meter (with the meter being fed) or moving very short distances. It is a simple matter on the computer if regular counts are held through the day to record the time at which a car enters the area and the time at which it leaves it, and by so doing to calculate the extent to which meters are used by all-day parkers. Direct questioning presents major problems.

Counts suffer from the same problems as many other techniques described in this chapter: they record but they do not explain. There are many cases, however, where accurate reporting is all that is, in fact, required and where direct interviewing will not provide such clear data.

Observation

The research use of investigator observation was made widely known in this country as a result of work before the war by Mass-Observation: basically its founders, Tom Harrisson and Charles Madge[9] argued that there were very many areas of knowledge in which people would not answer correctly, either because they did not know the correct reply or because they would be unwilling to tell from embarrassment or from various reasons of prestige.

In the 50 or so years since the founding of Mass-Observation many arguments have weakened the original thesis. Their early work was epitomized by vivid descriptions of public events such as wrestling matches and election meetings or of private and family matters, but these are now covered more simply, if not more efficiently, by the use of documentary film, particularly in television. Techniques of asking questions have improved and extended, and in parallel with this the principle of the question-and-answer survey has become more widely accepted; respondents are thus less reticent in revealing intimate information or that which is difficult to collect, and motivation research has helped to define in what areas questions are appropriate. A recent study by an anthropologist, for example, provided vivid and important data on class variations in food habits, including the significance of liquid content and of the shape of the foods most often served. The technique used to obtain this material involved observation over a period of months at all meals within individual families. Before the last 20 years or so such an elaborate research procedure would almost certainly have been necessary: but is very difficult to believe that in the 1970s a carefully constructed questionnaire would not have provided the same data at one tenth of the cost. Nevertheless, the need for observation remains. Observation has been described [10] as a primary tool of social enquiry which becomes a scientific technique when it:

(a) serves a formulated research purpose;
(b) is planned systematically;
(c) is recorded systematically and related to general propositions;
(d) is subject to checks and controls on validity and reliability.

In the intense forms of the technique, which are mainly anthropologically inspired, there are a separate set of problems discussed later. Simpler techniques, however, are now gaining wide favour again. Many recent developments, for example, involve a skilled investigator watching some simple household process to find areas for new product development. At what stage, for example, in her cleaning routine does the housewife find something difficult to clean with which a new gadget might help[11]? Are there new products which the housewife could use as instant or convenience foods which would help her with regular meals? This can be expanded widely in many areas. No housewife could probably tell exactly how much salt or cornflour she uses in simple recipes and she would be unlikely even to admit that she often guessed; certainly, for whatever reasons, estimates from direct questionnaires are almost always very inflated. Observation, however, particularly when its main purpose is masked, can provide better data on how the housewife acts.

Few beer drinkers would know in exactly what terms they asked for their beer – they would *think* or *report* that they said 'Half of lager, please', when what they probably said was 'The same again, Fred'. Nor would they always know the extent to which what they had ordered was, in fact, supplied. Do they get the same in all pubs, for example, when they ask for a 'pint of the best' or 'half of keg'? To brewers this is vital in terms of advertising copy and in the extent to which criticism of their product perhaps springs from the wrong product being provided by the barman.

Observation techniques are also of use in studying more detailed behaviourist patterns. One study[12], for example, related the actual driving of motorists to their driving personalities assessed by a series of psychological questions. The driving assessment involved three observers taking drivers on a standard test route, one in the front giving instructions as to where the driver was to go, two in the back recording handling of gears and clutch, use of side mirrors, number of times the car concerned overtook or was overtaken and so on. The driver knew that he was being studied but the system was so simple and the observers so well concealed that it seemed almost certain that after the first few minutes driving behaviour became normal.

It is of course possible for an observer to infiltrate a group solely to observe anonymously. Tom Harrisson and many of his colleagues may well have been known to have had special interests in their membership of groups, but Mass-Observation also used Celia Fremlin to work for a time in a wartime factory with nobody at all aware of her daily write-ups of the situation or of the sociological content of some of her 'innocent' questions. But there can be very few market research problems which will justify such an elaborate set-up.

There remain two basic problems about all observation work. The first is that the cost involved, not only in observation but in writing up and training, usually implies limited regional areas or small sample bases, and the critics can, in consequence, always fault it on the grounds that what has been found out would not apply elsewhere. Most of the early work done by Mass-

Observation, for example, concentrated on studying one Lancashire town in great detail, and even though a few further towns were studied with less concentration there is little evidence available to indicate that what emerged from one town was true even for another ten miles away, let alone for another part of the country – though, to be fair, those involved never stressed typicality.

It is also true (although not for participant observation) that studies can only report on what happens and draw conclusions from this, excluding the 'why's' of what is done. Sometimes these speak for themselves, like the elaborate treating rituals found in many pubs whereby all those involved in groups find themselves, at the end of the evening, having paid out the same sums; but others are open to a series of different interpretations. Work was carried out, for example, on the selection of books from public libraries. People were observed at a distance; details including the extent to which they read titles, looked at books, the parts of the book which they looked at and so on were noted. But what did it mean if a person picked up a book, looked at the cover, read the last page and put it down again? That he had read it already? That it had an unhappy ending? That there were too many long words or too many pages? All these interpretations were possible, none could be accepted as definitive; and probably the reader, even if he had been asked, would not have been able to unscramble his motives.

One must also stress that these forms of observation require training and that few interviewers, however skilled at questionnaire techniques, are able to carry out this sort of work. It is necessary to spot and record the relevant detail and to report it in quite objective terms. An interviewer may well be used to writing down precisely what has been said; it is quite a different thing to decide herself what should be recorded about actions rather than words. (Theoretically she does not decide but records everything, but in practice she has to be selective.)

In a quite different category to the use of video or television teams, the instant camera now holds a place among observation techniques. Suppose a survey is required on the extent to which telephone boxes are vandalized: it is very easy to be aware of whether or not a box has been so treated, but very difficult to write down a clear list of instructions which define for the benefit of interviewers what counts as vandalization. An instant camera, however, solves the problem in that the interviewer simply *records* the state of the kiosk without comment, and leaves the office to make the definition.

Participation

In the observation techniques so far described the interviewer has served in the function of an impartial observer – almost an automaton – and an essential of the observer's function has sometimes been that those observed do not know that they are being observed. We have seen that one of the serious limitations of such techniques lies in the fact that little or no information is obtained for the reasons behind the actions observed.

It does not follow, however, that the observer *has* to be anonymous. There is a sense in which any group discussion involves an observer playing a role in the exploration of the subject of the study and certainly in synectic groups this aspect becomes increasingly important (see chapter 2). Even if we may exclude this field, however, this section must include reference to what may be called participant observation. This technique owes much to the early work of the anthropologists and ethnologists and, again, was introduced into the market research field by Tom Harrisson (who would probably not have drawn the division made here between participant and non-participant observation[13]). It is now widely accepted by journalists and users of the documentary (witness the television film on the Royal Family where journalists and cameramen accompanied the Queen through private and public engagements over a long period) but its research uses are even more strictly limited than those of simpler forms of observation, almost entirely because of the length of time involved in laying the groundwork.

Many sociological studies make great use of the continuous observation of a single family to reveal, for example, kinship patterns or socialization of children, but it is not often that market research needs to explore issues at such depth. An observer using this approach must first find a family he thinks will be likely to illustrate the problems with which he is concerned: he has then to persuade them to accept him into the family circle for all events, weddings, funerals, quarrels and so on, and he must then continuously ask his questions slowly and carefully so as not to destroy any mutual trust or create suspicion. And when results are written up he is open to constant criticism, which is extremely difficult to answer, that had he taken a family in a different road, let alone in a different town, the conclusion which he had drawn would not have been the same. He must prove too that his presence has not affected the situation.

There is little doubt of the value of these techniques at the academic level and it is probable that the method has considerable uses in market research not so far really exploited; for example, for studies of shops and their customers or reactions to given events taking place over a short period. It seems unlikely, however, that it will ever be of great importance in the market research armoury.

The above, of course, assumes that the researcher must be 'injected' into a group and must make himself accepted by it; but what if a series of observers all report on their own family circle in which they are already accepted? This again was a technique developed by Mass-Observation in the years before the Second World War and used fairly widely until the end of that war. Some hundreds of people reported monthly on what they themselves were doing, and how those with whom they were directly concerned were reacting to events.

Changes in social climate and in sociology itself tended to make this work increasingly less useful and it is doubtful if there could be a revival in this approach except in specialized areas such as the recording of dreams or fears. Reports were inevitably subjective, to a degree which made it difficult to know what weight to put on individual comments, however graphically expressed; but perhaps more important was the fact that in the mid-thirties there were many working class people anxious to express themselves in this way but unable to get a job which allowed them to do so; today the increasing influence of higher education has meant that panels of observers of the kind considered here become more and more composed of teachers and civil servants, precisely those groups most likely to be willing to answer mail and other forms of questionnaire when the need arises.

Some general comments

Much of this chapter has been devoted to stressing the drawbacks of techniques described, most of which are, in fact, attempts to cope with some of the more complex problems facing the researcher: sometimes, how can I get the answer at a cost which is reasonable–sometimes, how can I get the answer when the respondent himself does not know it?

Telephone and mail surveys are 'cheap' in that they make feasible surveys which could not be considered by personal contact: but this does not alter the fact that they may sometimes retain the snags (of being unrepresentative, of presenting problems of answer interpretation) which make many hesitate to use them. And at the other end of the scale, use of hardware or participant observation produces costs per 'interview' which are so high as to preclude uses of samples of more than 50 or 60, too small to satisfy any statistician.

It is probable that the researcher will always have to live with these problems, and the only practical solution is the compromise of the largest and 'best' sample which is feasible within the prescribed budget. Certainly, if the techniques employed seem to be producing results not obtainable by other methods but appearing to be of real use, the argument for using them in whatever detail possible seems a strong one.

A second point is, perhaps, more fundamental although not often discussed. A convention of market research (although it is obviously open to much argument, especially from the psychologists) is that the nature of the direct interview is such that it provides information only at *one* level of consciousness or communication and that this is a useful level. There are many others which could be used from the subconscious world of dreams to the purely formal one of polite and meaningless conversation. In another dimension, the interview usually (though by no means always) involves an immediate answer to an immediate question while, to take an extreme, the anthropological approach to a subject may be discussed intensively over weeks. A 'deeper' answer is not necessarily a 'better' one or, in more practical terms, one of which greater use can be made, but is not measuring the same thing. Private opinion is not always a different level of public opinion.

Similarly, while interviewer personality probably makes less difference to the nature of answers provided than was at one time assumed, the degree and nature of the rapport must in some way show through the answers to any study. This rapport must be different if, on the one hand, the 'interviewer' is a person who lives as part of the family circle for months, if on the other he is seen as the hand on the switch of the psychogalvanometer. Again, the 'best' approach must, to some extent, be recommended on pragmatic grounds.

For all their weaknesses and unsolved difficulties of comparison, do the special techniques considered here offer something not otherwise able to be provided? If they do, then there is reason for using them. If they do not, there is none.

Chapter 11

Editing, coding and processing of market research data

G. W. ROUGHTON

In earlier chapters techniques have been described for obtaining market research data. These techniques provide raw disaggregated data. Before this can be used it must be converted from its raw state into finished tabulations. These show the findings of the survey, and will allow statistical and other appropriate tests to be applied. To do this will involve editing, coding and processing. Editing is carried out to correct or remove obvious logical or factual errors; coding to classify informant responses in terms of a predetermined coding frame; and processing to produce summaries of the results. These are often in the form of cross tabulations to show the presence or absence of relevant relationships.

Forms of data

Data for market research purposes can originate in several ways. A common one is from interviewer-administered questionnaires. These consist of lists of precoded and open-ended questions. In precoded questions, interviewers mark or 'code' the appropriate pre-printed answer to show into which category (printed on the questionnaire as a 'precode') the informant's reply falls. To a question such as 'Have you purchased a washing machine in the past twelve months?', an obvious set of precoded answers would be 'Yes', 'No' and, for the sake of completeness, 'Don't know'. It is important to include categories such as 'don't know' so as to leave as little doubt as possible as to the precode into which a particular answer should be placed. Badly conceived precodes will mean that the interviewer has some difficulty in fitting answers into the precoded list. As a result, errors may be introduced by inadvertently forcing answers into precodes to which they do not belong. It is unwise to use precodes where an interviewer, unless specially trained, is required to exercise any degree of judgement in determining into which category the answers should fall.

In open-ended questions, informants' replies are written out by the interviewer. There may be some probing with answers of several sentences. In other cases, where a question is purely a factual one, an open-ended answer may consist of only one or two words. For example, a question about consumption could elicit a number as an answer.

Precoding of questionnaires can greatly reduce processing time and the cost of coding. It also tells the interviewer the kind and detail of answers expected. From these points of view precoded questions should, therefore, be used in preference to purely open-ended questions.

There are many other types of document that can form input for market research purposes. In certain kinds of study, e.g. postal surveys, a self-completion questionnaire is used. They are largely precoded and extremely simple. Although they are different in certain respects from interviewer questionnaires, the steps through which they subsequently pass are exactly the same. Also, instead of or in conjunction with carrying out interviews using a questionnaire, interviewers may record the activities or behaviour of informants on specially designed transfer sheets or other forms of document which may be designed for automatic reading. The speed, reliability and flexibility of automatic questionnaire reading is continuing to develop with the availability of various new technologies, and is likely to increase in the future.

Editing

Whatever the type of document or other source of the data, the first stage through which it must pass is editing. It is a truism to say that not every interviewer will ask and correctly record answers to every question that should have been asked of every informant. Nor, indeed, will every informant necessarily be so obliging as to answer every appropriate question. The result is that survey data is normally less than perfect. Although one could reject data which contained any errors at all, this could mean that a considerable amount of useful information was being thrown away simply because of one or two trivial errors at some stage in its collection. The purpose of editing is to reduce or remove the effects of these minor errors. The two major sources of error data arise from:

(a) *Poorly designed questionnaires and/or instructions:* Errors arising from this source are intractable. There is usually little, if anything, that can be done at the editing stage to retrieve fundamental survey design errors. There is little remedy for missing questions, or incorrect instructions. The best thing to do is to try to make as much use as possible of the data which have been correctly obtained (see chapter 5).

(b) *Poor quality interviewing:* Interviewer errors and poor quality interviewing are likely to lead to poor quality responses. This is a serious source of error. It invokes the GIGO principle familiar to all in the computer world (Garbage In = Garbage Out). Although adequate correction of errors of this kind is difficult at the editing stage, an experienced editor can frequently retrieve useful data even if only ameliorating the poor-quality interviewing. The justification for editing in these circumstances is that it is wasteful to reject a questionnaire which contains some usable data even though there may be parts that are unusable.

Types of error

Missing data

For a variety of reasons, it frequently occurs that an interviewer omits to ask a question which she should have asked or alternatively omits to record the answer. In these circumstances, one might begin by attempting to infer the answer from other data on the questionnaire. In some cases this is possible. For example, possession of a driving licence might be inferred from other behavioural data that had been collected on driving even though an actual question on possession had not been coded. Conversely there are other occasions when the only solution is to raise a specific 'not answered' code. This latter type of code demonstrates that the absence of answers has been positively checked by the editor(s) concerned. The objective is to allow the questionnaire to be used even though less than 100% perfect. Revisiting informants to obtain missing data is often not feasible due to timing or other administrative considerations.

Incorrect logic

This occurs when a question or group of questions are answered which should not have been answered or are not answered when they should have been. This latter is a form of missing data. In the former case, a decision has to be made whether to use the information which should not have been collected; is there a way in which the 'bonus' data can be used? The alternative is to delete the redundant answers, maintaining the original logic of the questionnaire. It is difficult to give a general ruling on which procedure to adopt as it would depend upon the objects of the survey, the size of the sub-base required for meaningful analyses, and what sort of logical errors are occurring. Generally, however, greater homogeneity in the data will result if the original logic is followed and the 'bonus' data is deleted.

Informant misunderstanding

It is sometimes clear to an experienced editor that an informant has misunderstood a question or questions. This can result from poor questionnaire design, or poor interviewing, or from the informants themselves. Sometimes it is possible to infer the correct answer from the data recorded, or at least to distinguish between those informants who have understood the question correctly and those who have not. If an appropriate code or codes are raised to indicate this, then answers can be based only upon those informants who have understood the question correctly. The resultant data is likely to be more robust than combining answers of those who have understood with answers of those who have misunderstood.

Inconsistent or erroneous answers

Informants will sometimes change their mind during the progress of an interview. As a result, it becomes clear that answers given at one point in an interview may be inconsistent with those given later on. It is a matter of judgement as to what whould be done in these circumstances. Informants do change their minds, particularly as a result of intense questioning, which can condition them on a subject, if not actually educate them. One can remove these inconsistencies, but this may force an unreal pattern on the answers. In other cases erroneous factual answers may be recorded. One needs to determine whether these are due to incorrect recording by the interviewer or arise from the answers to the questions themselves. In the latter case, the fact that the informant has given an erroneous answer may itself be an important item of data. In certain other cases, however, the recording of obviously erroneous data does cause trouble; e.g. in computations of consumption it is important that pack sizes, prices, etc., are correctly recorded – the inclusion of an additional zero multiplies by 10 with potentially spectacular effects on, for example, market size estimates.

Frivolous data

Occasionally it is obvious to an editor that an informant has been insincere in the conduct of the interview. Questionnaires of this kind would not normally be submitted by competent interviewers, but should be withdrawn if they are. Questionnaires in which the informant has obviously lost interest and has given up half-way should similarly be withdrawn.

Editing may be carried out as a separate operation or in conjunction with coding. It may be carried out manually or with the help of computers. The latter is increasingly common. It is rare for survey data to be usable without some form of editing. The aim is to do whatever is legitimately possible to reduce errors in prior stages. In general it is better to correct by reference back to the original documents, and then to modify the individual input records, the raw data, on an informant-by-informant basis. Computer programs do often allow global editing of an automatic or semi-automatic kind. This should be used with care. There are aggregate forms of editing that some computer programs can apply at the output stage of tables – in effect table editing e.g. forcing responses to 100%, etc. Editing the input data is more thorough, and will ensure that the results of the survey are more consistent. However, editing of the output can be quicker and less costly. It is necessary to make early decisions as to which errors are to be dealt with by input correction and which dealt with at the output stage. At the moment, we are concerned with the raw data at the input stage. The principal reasons for editing should now be clear but it may be useful to review them briefly.

Editing can help improve the data itself. Second, the effect of unedited data upon the inexperienced can be disturbing. Many laymen studying survey data have doubts about the legitimacy of taking samples of a population rather than carrying out a census. They are not aware of the various stages through which the data have gone and they may, indeed, find the results highly distasteful. It is not uncommon, therefore, for considerable importance to be attached in these circumstances to minor obvious faults in the data. It is important to establish the proper level of confidence. Trivial errors, e.g. resulting in percentages adding to less than 100, e.g. 96, 97, etc. will rarely affect any conclusion likely to be drawn from the data. However, if trivial errors are obvious in the final tabulations which in the view of the reader could be put right with only five minutes effort, then it obviously conveys a slipshod and unsatisfactory impression.

On the other hand, 100% consistency gives a delusion of accuracy that is not real and is fairly time-consuming to achieve. It is important that users of data should be aware that it has limitations, but at the same time have complete confidence in what they see before them. Editing has to draw a happy medium between pressing a completely unreal rigidity upon data and at the same time preventing the more obvious idiocies appearing in the final output.

Editing methods

Editing can be carried out manually, manually under computer control, or solely by computer. There were mechanical methods of editing involving punch card sorting machines. These are now largely obsolete. Current methods are described more fully below. Before discussing editing more fully, it should again be said that some editing may involve attempting to replace missing data. A fairly rigorous attitude must be taken over this. Legitimate inference is generally acceptable but, at a certain point, inspired guesswork can begin to add information to the data not inherent in its original collection. At a certain point, this would clearly become unethical. Although a correction rate of 1 % may seem quite acceptable, many tabulations are often based upon sub-samples where the proportion of 'corrected' data can translate to a substantially higher figure. So care needs to be taken to ensure that editing does not become 'creative'.

Manual editing

In manual editing each survey document is thoroughly examined by an editor who is fully conversant with the conditions the document should meet. This is done before the documents are transferred to punched cards or otherwise entered into a computer file. The editor must have a written set of instructions specifying the conditions the questionnaire or other document must satisfy, and what action is to be taken if an error is found. As little as possible should be left to judgement. Different individuals will, without rigid control, edit differently, and this will introduce differences which arise from differences between editors rather than in the data itself. Hence the need for comprehensive written instructions. The operation itself involves making appropriate corrections, and raising or deleting specific codes on the original survey document. It is essential that this should be carried out in a distinctive colour, e.g. green, which the interviewers have been specifically told not to use. It is then clear exactly what editing has been done. In this way it is also possible for a supervisor to examine the work done by any particular editor.

Editing instructions should take the editor systematically through the questionnaire or other document showing for each question in the order on the questionnaire what should have happened. The editing instructions will, therefore, follow the logic of the questionnaire. It is customary to lay them out in a stylized format and for these to include coding instructions for the open-ended questions as and when they come up. Written instructions are also important to users of the data, so they know what editing has been done. The format of instructions varies from one organization to the other. However, an example of some typical editing instructions are given below in Table 11.1.

Instructions such as these may not mean a great deal in the absence of the questionnaire to which they apply. They perhaps do indicate, however, the minutiae of detail that good editing instructions must follow. (NB: The references to 'V', 'X', etc. and to 'C.10', 'C.11', etc. are ways that codes are often defined when data is being transferred to punch cards.)

Editing, say, 1000 twenty-minute interview questionnaires might typically require 80–100 manhours to complete by an experienced person. It is perhaps important to say that editing is something that requires experience to be done effectively and accurately. Although it is simple in concept, it can prove tedious and demanding to inexperienced people. The use of unskilled students

Table 11.1. *Some typical editing instructions*

Question	Editing/coding instructions	Code category	Code	Col
	Classification. *Occupational grouping.* Check group ringed against Occupation of Head of Household *Age.* One precode to be ringed between V–2 in C.10 *Children.* Code V or X to be ringed in C.11 *Product tried first.* Code V or X to be ringed in C.12 *Area.* One precode to be ringed in C.13			
1	At least one precode to be ringed in C.14			
2 (a)	Code V or X to be ringed in C.18 *All coded X in C.18* Code V or X to be ringed in C.19			
3	Check that following sections are asked of correct members of the household by checking with Q.I. as to the composition of the household. At least one precode to be ringed in relevant columns. If N/A leave blank Columns 21, 23, 25 and 27 will not be used.	Milk . . . . 8 All other foods 9		20 and 22 and 24 and 26

or temporary office staff for this function can sometimes result in more errors being introduced than are removed.

The editing process requires some manual component where any element of judgement has to be exercised by the editor; in other words, where it is not possible by means of a precise set of logical rules to say what should happen in a given set of circumstances. This will occur whenever an editing instruction lays down that the editor should try to infer the answer to the question from elsewhere in the questionnaire without specifying where. Manual editing has the advantage that it can be started during the course of the fieldwork, often in sufficient time for interviewers to be informed of the more obvious errors which are occurring. The editor can exercise judgement as to whether or not to accept a questionnaire in total, and is in a better position than any computer-based method to assess the overall plausibility of a survey document. In consequence it is easier for an editor to write appropriate reports to interviewers on the quality of the work that has been done.

The principal drawback with manual editing is that it is usually more costly than computer methods and, though it is rarely critical in the timing of a survey, it does require greater elapsed time from start to finish. Editors also make errors and it sometimes happens that errors are still found in data that has been 100% manually edited.

Manual and computer editing

Any form of editing involving computers (or any other machine) means that the data needs to be available in a computer or machine-readable form, normally as 'file' on a computer. The setting-up of such a file can be done in several different ways. A set of specifications are prepared that define the range and form of codes that may appear, together with relevant logic instructions. These drive an edit program which lists the observations or interviews that contain errors together with details of what the errors are. The questionnaires are then examined with the error listing for each informant, and editing is carried out on the magnetic data file. After correction the edit program is run again. It usually requires more than one attempt to get all the data clean. Correction of some errors will sometimes uncover others. This procedure involves close interaction between the editor and the appropriate computer runs. It enables thorough and exhaustive logical checks to be carried out.

Computer editing

A number of computer editing packages not only enable errors to be identified, but also enable appropriate action to be specified as to what changes should be made to the file to correct it. This approach is global in its operation, and takes no account of special conditions that may apply to a particular informant. It has the advantage of being quick and inexpensive. It does, however, have its dangers. Writing specifications is a form of programming that requires some training. It is a task often left to specialist bureaux.

Interviewer assessment

The editing stage of a survey may also be one at which assessments of fieldwork are made and interviewer performance is judged. In many organizations, editors will compile reports on interviewers' work which can be forwarded to fieldstaff who can take appropriate remedial action. Computerized methods enable analyses by interviewer to be carried out automatically. The advantages of this latter form of quality control are obvious but are beyond the scope of organizations without the appropriate data processing facilities. Editors can often provide useful information on the quality of questionnaire design and layout and if their advice, though from a lowly source, is heeded some useful minor improvements to questionnaires may result.

Coding

In open-ended questions it is common to obtain a wide variety of answers. It is usually necessary to group these answers together in some way. This is the first function of coding. The second function is to assign numeric or other codes to each category of answer so as to allow subsequent computer processing of the results. Grouping of answers is required because one cannot cope with responses to a question where there are dozens of different answers. The proportion of informants giving each answer is often extremely small and many of the answers are either very similar or convey exactly the same sense. Grouping greatly eases drawing general conclusions.

Coding begins with the preparation of coding instructions on both the groupings of answers and on the codes to be assigned to each group. A coder (who may also be the editor) then compares the actual answers on each questionnaire with the various categories given on the coding frame. The coder then decides into which category or categories the informant's answer falls and then assigns the appropriate code or codes. The codes are usually written on the questionnaire and, as with editing, a distinctive colour should be used for this purpose. Part of a typical coding frame might look as follows:

Table 11.2   Some typical coding instructions for open-enden responses to what informants disliked a food product.

4(b) and 5(b)	Code for R.24 in cols. 21 and 22 Code for M.51 in Cols. 25 and 26	Not enough taste/flavour	V	
		Powdery taste/uncooked taste	X	
		Disliked oatmeal taste/like porridge	0	
		Too dry	1	21
		Too mushy/soggy	2	
		Dislike appearance/looked horrible	3	and
		Disliked fruit/raisins hard	4	25
		too bitty/lumpy	5	
		too much fruit/raisins	6	
		Not enough fruit/raisins	7	
		Not a good texture/coarse/ not smooth	8	
		Takes too long to eat	9	
		Disliked the nuts	V	
		Disliked flakes of oatmeal	X	
		Stuck in teeth	0	22
		Too heavy/stodgy	1	
		Too sweet	2	and
			3	
			4	26
			5	
			6	
		Just disliked it (unspec.)	7	
		Other dislikes	8	
		DK/NA/nothing disliked	9	

To prepare coding instructions involves taking a sub-sample of the data and producing an exhaustive listing of all the answers obtained from each question to be coded. No attempt is made to group the answers although it will rapidly become clear that there is a considerable overlap both in words and sense between some of the separate answers which are listed. Each time a 'new' answer is found to a particular question it is entered on the listing sheet, and each time an answer is repeated the closest previous answer on the listing sheet is marked. This will give a rough count of the number of times each particular answer has occurred. This extended listing is then inspected and similar answers grouped together.

In producing the preliminary listings an attempt should be made to ensure that it is based on a reasonable sample of the data. This should consist of at least 100 questionnaires. If the first 100 questionnaires recieved are taken, these may not be representative of the total number. It may over-represent the work of certain interviewers, certain areas or certain time periods. Although timing considerations often press for coding to be carried out simultaneously with fieldwork, a poorly designed coding frame can result if the preliminary listings are based on a poor subset of the total data. Answers may then occur in subsequent questionnaires for which no code was assigned when the coding frame was devised. Although coding frames should always provide for the addition of some extra codes, it will quite frequently happen that coders will put answers for which there is no code into an 'others' category. Tabulations based on poor coding frames may end up with a high proportion of replies coded as 'other'.

Codes may be based on the data itself and are thus oriented round the replies which informants give; or they may be based on the objectives of the survey. A question on informants' comprehension of an advertisement, for example, can be coded on the replies they gave or in terms of whether, from their reply, they appeared to understand a specified message in the advertisement. The fact that a particular part of the message was not noticed or understood can be an important conclusion. In certain cases, therefore, a combination of the two is required. In these circumstances two separate sets of codes may be used for the question(s) concerned, with double coding in each case. Whatever form of coding is adopted, however, it is important that the coding frame takes cognizance of the survey objectives. Without bearing these in mind there is a danger that parts of the analysis will be irrelevant.

The designer of a coding frame should avoid having too many codes in order to provide sensitive discrimination between different answers, and too few codes, which result in coders tending to lump answers together in the same categories even though there may be important, though subtle, differences between them. The likelihood of this can be reduced by examining the preliminary listing in terms of the survey objectives, and the proposed coding frame. At the same time the proposed codes should be examined to ensure that they are not ambiguous as this also reduces the efficiency of the coding.

In recent years some attention has been given to the use of computers for performing textual analysis of informant responses. Given that responses are entered as text, there is the possibility of some degree of automatic coding, but perhaps of greater importance is the possibility of establishing the vocabularies and patterns of words that consumers use. This has a particular relevance in measuring comprehension and recall in advertising. An important additional advantage of entering open-ended reponses into a computer is that listing of these can provide a much greater depth of understanding and give a more personal dimension to the data.

When organizing coding operations, it is important that careful control is kept of the code sheets, so that if additional codes are added after coding has started, this is transcribed on to all the coding sheets in use. It is not an uncommon practice for the supervisor responsible to keep all coding sheets and to hand these out on a daily basis to the coders concerned. In addition, the supervisor must ensure that coding is carried out consistently: that each coder will code a particular response in the same way(s). This requires thorough checking of each coder's work at the beginning of the coding operation. Consistency grows over time within a particular team of coders. Another method of ensuring consistency is for a particular question or set of questions to be entirely coded by one coder or team of coders, another question or set of questions by a different coder/team, and so on. Though greater consistency is achieved, more time may be involved in the coding operation. In some cases, a mixture of both methods is used. This is applicable where the majority of questions are straightforward but where there are perhaps one or two questions requiring a very high degree of consistency or special technical knowledge. In these cases, the latter questions may be reserved for one specially appointed coder.

Like editing, coding may in concept seem a comparatively simple operation. However, unless it is carefully organized and appropriately skilled staff used, the quality will be poor. It is not particularly easy to find staff with the intellectual ability to carry out interpretive work of this kind who are also willing to accept its tedious nature.

Data preparation

We have referred to punch cards and to other forms of 'data transport', i.e. the means of translating questionnaires or other documents into a form that enables processing by computers. Although this is not necessary for projects analysed by hand, a valid method still widely used for small surveys, it is essential for surveys of size, complexity, or continuity. The conversion from documents to, say, cards is carried out on punch or other machines, which may be manually operated. Whatever the medium into which the data is transferred, the objective is to achieve a format that is compatible with computer input devices and can be analysed by the software. The form of input needs to be taken into account in the design of the original questionnaire or other survey document. Failing this, it may be necessary for the data to be manually transferred to a special transfer sheet from which the subsequent transformation takes place. This introduces an additional stage with consequences on time and cost. The principal methods of data input are discussed below. Some years ago these included paper tape, but this method is now little used.

Punch cards

Although newer methods of data transport are developing, punch cards are still widely used, and it is useful to understand them. The standard form of punch card is a small light card measuring approximately 7 3/8in. × 3 1/4in. (the size of an 1890 dollar bill, and invented by Dr Hollerith) and is notionally divided into 80 columns. On each column a rectangular hole or set of holes may be punched in any of 12 positions. Cards may be singly punched, in which case there will be a maximum of one hole per column, or multi-punched where there may be any number of holes punched in up to all 12 positions. The latter case is rare, and should be avoided as some card reading devices (principally the mechanical ones) cannot read columns with more than a specified number of positions punched. The bottom ten positions on any column are referred to by the numbers 0 to 9 respectively. The top two positions are referred to variously as V and X, A and B, Y and X and 12 and 11, etc. Columns are referred to by the numbers 1 to 80. Any position on a card can, therefore, be defined by its column number and hole code, e.g. column 13, code 1, or C13/1; column 61, code 2 or C61/2, etc. Thus, analysis can specified in a form such as: give a count of the number of times each position on, say, column 48, contains a hole (a hole corresponds to a particular answer either already printed on the questionnaire, or subsequently assigned when the coding frame is prepared). Such counts may be based on all the cards for the survey or only on a sub-group, e.g. those with, say, 2 punched on column 14. This enables extremely complex logical filtering to be carried out. The assignment of columns and codes on a questionnaire is an integral part of its design. Table 11.2 gave some examples of codes. When the codes ('V' ... '3', etc.) are printed directly on the questionnaire, interviewers ring them to indicate the informant's response, and operators can punch the cards directly from the questionnaire itself. Card column numbers are often identified by small numbers printed above columns of codes on the left hand side of questionnaires. Longer questionnaires are likely to require several cards for all information. Those relating to a particular informant or household will be linked by a common serial number punched on, say, the first four columns of every card together with a card number on, say, the fifth column.

There are many bureaux who can carry out card punching on a subcontract basis. It is wiser to use those who have had specialist experience in market research work which has its own peculiarities. Virtually all the major software packages for survey analysis can operate on punch card data.

Direct data entry

These systems have developed rapidly in recent years with the advent of the micro computer. They enable the survey data to be 'punched' in a very similar way to that for punch cards, but the output is a magnetic file instead of physical packs of cards. This file may be created on a small diskette or tape. The more sophisticated systems may include simultaneous editing, checking against lists, output measurement, merging to larger files, and numerous other features. They may operate under the control of a master computer, or through separate micro processors. This is an increasingly used form of data entry. There is much more flexibility in defining the data than with punch cards. The notion of columns and codes is not an imposed requirement. However, it is not unusual to have 'columns' but they can run up to any number desired. One is not restricted to 12 codes: all the letters in the alphabet may be used, or there may be multi-digit codes.

Both methods above involve data being read by an operator who then enters it on whatever type of machine is being used. Experienced operators can expect to achieve punching speeds of 6 to 7000 key depressions per hour on market research questionnaires, although for short periods or on simple work, e.g. transfer sheets, speeds may be very much higher. Alternatively, for badly structured questionnaires or where the operator is asked to check data as it is entered, the rate may fall, sometimes considerably. After entry, it is customary as a quality-control measure for all or part of it to be re-entered as a verification check. The re-entered data is electronically compared with the original. If the two 'images' are the same, the record is accepted. If there are differences, the operator can establish which was correct and ensure that the right image is the one permanently stored. A typical survey involving, say, 1000 punch cards may involve some 100,000 key depressions requiring perhaps 20 to 30 hours for punching and verification.

Document reading

There are now relatively inexpensive machines which can read documents directly. This is certainly worth considering for certain types of questionnaires, but usually requires a good deal of pre-planning. Instead of the documents being read by human operators they are read by a machine which creates a computer file of the data. This procedure cuts out the need for verification, and enables data to be transcribed very much more quickly. However, considerable care must be taken in the design and printing of the document to be read. Interviewers must take greater care in marking questionnaires. In certain, but not all, cases an error in marking may mean filling in a fresh questionnaire. The quality of printing required, particularly in the registration of the answer spaces with respect to the top and side of the paper, is beyond the scope of most organizations with only the normal stencil or small offset printing facilities. This method will provide a substantial increase in speed at the processing stage but takes slightly longer to set up at the design stage. Recent technical development in readers and the development of standardized answer sheets are making this technique much easier to use. It is probable, therefore, that this form of transfer will become much more important in the future.

Analysis

Once the editing, coding and entry (if machine processing is envisaged) stages are completed the data is ready for analysis. The object at this stage is to summarize individual items of data, questionnaires or whatever, so that one can readily know how many informants in the sample gave each of the possible replies to each question. This summary data is presented as tables which show the results for the whole sample and for sub-groups of it, e.g. for males and females separately, young people/old people, etc. This kind of cross-tabulation is extremely important in discovering relevant relationships within the data, and is a standard form of market research analysis. A typical example is as follows:

TABLE	DISTRIBUTION OF PRODUCT X AND PRODUCT Y						
ANALYSED BY	FORM OF ORGANISATION – SELF SERVICE –						
	ESTIMATED SALES PER WEEK						
BASE	ALL GROCERS INTERVIEWED IN GREAT BRITAIN						

					Column percentages		
RESPONSES		FORM OF ORGANISATION				SELF SERVICE	
		Total	Co-oper-ative	Multi-ple	Volunt. Chain	Inde-pendent	+2000 Sq ft	−2000 Sq. ft	Count Serve
		2724	409	511	632	1072	436	700	1588
PRODUCT X	IS	14	9	23	18	12	24	16	12
	TOS	3	3	3	3	2	3	5	2
PRODUCT Y	IS	29	38	33	34	24	43	35	25
	TOS	5	5	4	5	6	5	4	5

PROJECT NO 2839

Fig. 11.1 Example of a table showing distribution of products X and Y in grocers.

TABLE NO 2
QUESTION 7

ESTIMATED SALES PER WEEK				
£100	−£200	−£500	+£500	Not Given
223	531	811	1068	91
4	7	16	24	14
1	2	4	3	4
15	23	30	40	20
5	6	6	4	1

REF 1/61/70   1485

Fig. 11.1   (continued)

Analysis may be carried out by hand, or by computer. Mechanical methods have now been largely superseded. Computers are the principal method, but hand methods are certainly useful for smaller surveys and can be done with only minimal use of external facilities.

Hand analysis

Hand analysis involves the preparation of outline tables or hand summary sheets. One or more of these sheets is prepared for each question. The replies to questions are written down the left-hand side of the sheet, with appropriate columns across the sheet for any cross-tabulations that may be required. This latter point is explained more fully later on.

Analysis is carried out one question at a time. Using the appropriate hand summary sheet, every questionnaire is examined and an entry made on the appropriate line of the hand summary sheet corresponding to the answer(s) given to that question. It is customary in many organisations for the marking of the summary sheet to take the form of five-bar gate scores – four upright marks, with the fifth marked across, e.g. JHT JHT II, etc. Each complete 'gate' represents five responses. This simplifies subsequent counting-up. Where more than one answer is possible to a question the sum of scores against each response will add to more than the total number of questionnaires involved. In order to ensure that this is not due to errors in summating, it is normal to provide at the bottom of the sheet concerned appropriate 'overlap' categories. Thus, when the two entries to the sheet are made for one question, an additional entry is also made to a category called 'Overlap 1'. Where three entries are made, the additional entry would be made to a category called 'Overlap 2'; etc. In this way, a record is kept of the extent of multi-coding of replies. On completion of the summarizing the replies and overlap scores are added up. The overlap scores are further weighted by 1, 2, 3, etc. according to the number of overlaps they represent to give the number of replies which were second (or more) replies. This figure is subtracted from the total replies. The result should be equal to the number of questionnaires which have been summarized. This kind of checking is essential in hand analysis. It is extremely easy for errors to creep in, particularly when this kind of work is done quickly or by inexperienced staff.

Questionnaires are first bundled into groups or batches. Each bundle is counted and the total number of questionnaires written on each bundle. Each person summarizing then deals with one particular question, i.e. summary sheet, going through one bundle at a time. On completion of each bundle the cumulative scores including overlaps can be counted and checked. Not only does this emphasize the need for accuracy all the time, but if the recording of replies for each bundle is kept separate on the summary sheet then it is an extremely easy matter to put any errors right by only going through the bundle in error. Not to follow this kind of procedure means that if checking is left to the end, and errors are found, it is necessary to resummarize every bundle for the question(s) in error.

When it is desired to carry out cross-tabulations in which replies to one question are analysed either by classification information or replies to other questions, it is essential to sort the questionnaires into bundles corresponding to the breakdowns involved. This must be done one break within the other. This ensures that the figures within each breakdown add back to the same total figure as well as keeping the actual summarizing to a minimum. As an example, let us suppose it was desired to analyse some data by two area codes, three age groups and two social classes, the questionnaires would be sorted into twelve bundles of the following composition:

Bundle	Area code	Age group	Social class
1	1	16 to 34	ABC1
2	1		C2DE
3	1	35 to 54	ABC1
4	1		C2DE
5	1	55+	ABC1
6	1		C2DE
7	2	16 to 34	ABC1
etc.			

Results for each bundle would be summarized within separate columns on summary sheets. The replies would then be added up within each column. From these subtotals the breakdown total is obtained. Thus results for areas 1 and 2 are obtained by adding the subtotals for columns 1 to 6 and 7 to 12 respectively on the summary sheets; for the 16–34 age groups by adding columns 1, 2, 7 and 8, etc. This method obviously ensures that inconsistencies across breakdowns are removed. Where these procedures cannot be followed, only relatively small samples should be analysed by hand.

If additional tables are needed, the above operations are repeated, perhaps with the questionnaires bundled in a different way or ways. Rigorous control is essential if errors are to be avoided. The process lacks flexibility and requires tight quality controls. However, it does have some advantages. It can be extremely quick in producing 'top line' results to key questions during, for example, a hall test to show by the end of field work which product was preferred in a product test, or by summarizing simultaneously with booking-in from the field. Because of higher fixed costs associated with other forms of analysis, including the possible need for special equipment, or the need to deal with outside suppliers, hand analysis can be extremely economic for carrying out occasional surveys on limited samples.

Computer analysis

Computers have not only revolutionalized the way in which analysis is done but have had an equally major effect on the form and value of analysis. Mechanical and hand methods confined results to producing raw numbers and simple percentages. Computers enable a very wide variety of other kinds of statistics to be produced. This includes a whole range of multivariate methods (see chapter 13). Statistical tests of various kinds can be carried out on a exhaustive scale. Computers allow rigorous checking and manipulation of the data. At the same time, they have reduced the absolute cost of analysing data. Weighting of data to correct for biases in samples can be carried out with more precision. Grossed-up population estimates can be output automatically. There are numerous other advantages which is why virtually all survey analysis is now done by computers. This has been given a significant boost by the increasing availability of small machines including micro computers such as the IBM PC/AT and others.

One should distinguish between micro computers and mini or main frame machines. These latter types of machine are the ones on which most analysis is done. Micro computers are not as well suited to continuous running of long queues of jobs. Both types of machine contain a number of common devices such as: input facilities from keyboard, magnetic files, tape, punch cards or other equipment; a central processing unit (CPU); and one or more output devices or printers on which results are produced. Larger machines are likely to have several magnetic disks and also magnetic tape systems. These are linked to the CPU and may be used for the storage of data and results. The actual devices vary from one installation to another. Larger installations usually have a greater number of peripheral units as well as bigger and more powerful CPU's.

In brief, for a computer to analyse data the following is necessary. The data must exist in a form that can be read into the computer. A set of specifications must be prepared which will tell the computer what to do, and one or more computer programs must be available which are capable of accepting the specification statements, interpreting them, reading and processing the data in whatever form it is provided, and outputting the desired results in some sort of permanent form. Usually, several programs are required which are linked together to form a comprehensive analysis system, referred to in jargon terms as a 'software package'.

The principal limitations of computers now lie in the power of the software packages available. Although programming these packages was at one time a protracted activity, the increasing availability and sophistication of high-level programming languages has made the task more manageable. This has been matched by the substantial improvements in hardware performance inherent in the newer machines. As a result most of the early difficulties have been overcome. Computers can carry out virtually any analysis which the user can conceive.

The actual writing of an appropriate software package is not something with which a survey practitioner need be concerned. This can only be done by experienced computer programmers. Such teams are normally found in computer bureaux or software organizations. Once the package has been written it remains fixed for some time. One does not need to concern oneself with the actual mechanics of the programs but rather with how to use them. It is important to distinguish between the writing of a program or package and the writing of a set of specifications to be read by a program or package in processing a particular survey. The latter operation, 'spec writing', is something with which the practitioner may well be concerned.

Most bureaux and other organizations offering market research analysis offer specification writing and job set-up as part of their service. Skills in spec writing are analogous to those of programming, but in addition require an understanding of the nature of survey data, and, most important, a clear understanding of the user's analysis requirements. Specification writing can be learnt and as a result it is possible to undertake analysis on a 'DIY' basis with possible savings in time and cost. Whereas one should not underestimate the effort required to make cost-effective use of major packages, a number of new 'user-friendly' packages are beginning to appear which enable the relatively inexperienced to become proficient in a matter of days.

Specifications are used to define things such as labels for tables, rows, and columns, the filter base for each table, the definition in logical terms and in terms of the format of the data for the rows and columns of each table, the form of output, any editing or rearrangement of the data, etc. Analysis packages have numerous options which provide considerable flexibility to the user. Thus tables or other output can be produced in many different forms to meet the precise needs of individual users.

Although one can contract processing to whichever computer bureaux submits the lowest quotation for carrying out the work involved, it pays to have some knowledge of the characteristics of the software packages being used. There are a number of reasons for this. First, some packages are particularly appropriate for some forms of analysis whereas others are not. Computer organizations sometimes quote for jobs for which their software is either inappropriate or can only be made appropriate with a greater or lesser amount of reprogramming. Although the job may be done at the original budget (there are many cases where this has involved the computer organization in substantial losses), the execution is likely to be more difficult, and may involve substantial additional time in dealing with queries and problems. A knowledge of the characteristics of different packages enables inappropriate ones to be avoided. Second, where a practitioner is able to match the way he specifies his analysis to the input requirements of a particular package, there will be a considerable saving in time and costs. Most of the cost savings will come from the improvement in communication. The awareness of the range and capability of particular packages enables their potential to be much more fully exploited.

Specifications are commonly prepared as a computer file of statements. This may be done through a proprietary word processing package; by a special editor that is supplied as part of the package and has some built in checking; or by a 'menu' driven procedure in which the user is prompted as to requirements. The result file is then passed through a 'compiler' which checks it and prepares it for running the job concerned. A 'driver' or command file may then be used to combine a particular specification file with the required data file, and process these as a job to produce an output file containing the tabulations required. On larger machines these processes will be occurring simultaneously for several jobs at once. On micro machines with lesser computing power, it is probable that only one job at a time will be carried out. The specification languages vary as does the amount of skill in using them. A general trend is towards simplification and the use of 'natural' language: here the aim is to enable the specifications to be given in a form very close to the way the user thinks of his analysis requirements. A number of developments in this respect have been paralleled in other computing fields in which user-friendliness has been of major importance. Perhaps the best known examples of this are in spread sheets such as Lotus 1-2-3 and Visicalc.

Most software packages are a compromise between a number of desirable objects which may to some extent be incompatible. Efficiency in execution, for example, may be sacrificed to some extent for ease of specification. The software package that is best for everything is more or less an impossible dream. It is very much a case of horses for courses. Simple software packages are right for simple surveys. Small computers are cheaper for small surveys; and so on. Clearly, some judicious shopping enables one to gauge which packages to use for different kinds of project.

Some of the factors which a user might consider in deciding whether a particular package is suitable for particular job are the following:

(a) How easy is it to specify the analysis requirments to the specifications writer(s)?
(b) Are table, column, and row labels adequate without further annotation?
(c) Does the package have sufficient editing and recoding features to ensure that 'clean' data is produced?
(d) Can multi-card surveys or special data formats present problems?
(e) Is the layout of the tables sufficiently clear that secondary transcription by typing, etc., is unnecessary?
(f) Are the output options sufficiently flexible to produce data in the form appropriate to the practitioner's need?
(g) Can tables be formed with sufficient flexibility to allow virtually any code or set of codes on any card or other data input to appear in a single table?
(h) Can weighting be carried out easily without, for example, having to create factors for each informant?
(i) Is the package able to cope with the size of the job without numerous reruns or very long runs?
(j) Do your requirements mean changes to the package, or can they be handled easily within the existing capabilities?

These are some of the main questions on which one needs to be satisfied. There are others, of course, particularly when the processing is atypical in any way.

It is beyond the scope of this chapter to make more than a passing reference to specific software packages, although a smaller number are briefly mentioned below. For fuller information it is really necessary to study the user manuals produced by the proprietors of the packages concerned. This is also necessary because the packages themselves undergo continuous development and upgrading. From time to time various organizations publish directories of packages suitable for survey processing. In Britain the best known such list is published by the Study Group on Computers in Survey Analysis (SGCSA). They do not have offices, but either the British Computer Society or the Market Research Society can advise as to who is the current secretary of SGCSA. A recent copy of this directory (1983) gave brief details of 119 items of software of which 68 were new. The scope of these packages is extremely varied. Each program is classified as to which of the following functions it can fulfil: Editing, Data management, Tabulation, Descriptive statistics and Statistical analysis together with a brief description by the authors.

A number of market research companies have their own computers, and many of them carry out a considerable amount of work for other agencies or practitioners who require cross-tabulation. Names of such companies in the UK may be obtained by reference to AMSO (The Association of Market Survey Organizations) or to the Market Research Society. In addition there are several computer bureaux who specialize in market research processing. These include: Demotab, Quantime, The Tab Shop, and Digitab. There are many others offering very personalized services such as 'Numbers', Weeks/Inglis, and several freelancers who use other people's facilities. For multivariate work, SIA is an important bureau; and for transportation surveys, Pinpoint and Systematica can offer specialist assistance – particularly on large scale projects.

Some of the major packages are very briefly commented upon below. Fuller details can be obtained from the relevant manuals. In each case, some guidance is given as to where the package may be used. It is probable that around two thirds of the survey processing in Great Britain uses one or other of these packages.

STAR: This package was originally designed for the PDP/11 range of computers, but has now migrated upwards into the VAX range. It is compiler based, and there is little that it cannot do. The STAR specification language has to be learnt, but once mastered the package is extremely powerful. It is well supported having been in progressive development since 1976. It also has multivariate capabilities, and several other features. This package may be purchased, leased, or used on a bureau basis. A number of market research companies have installed it as their inhouse package.

TWINKLE: This is a 'user-friendly' version of STAR which is menu driven, making it possible for inexperienced specification writers to produce useful work with only a few hours learning. It may be leased or used on a bureau basis.

QUANTUM: This package has a long pedigree, and was originally designed to run on a Prime computer, but is now available on a wider range of machines. Several market research companies have installed it 'in-house', and it has proved itself a solid work horse over the years.

MERLIN: Produced in its first version in the early 1970s, it has developed through three major upgrades, and has most of the features of a high level processing language similar to STAR and QUANTUM. Its specification language is particularly powerful, and offers great flexibility in the type of tables that can be produced – going well beyond conventional cross-tabulation capabilities.

SPSS: Originally developed for certain kinds of academic work, this package has now become more available in the commercial area, particularly as a result of its low-priced implementation on the IBM PC/XT. It has powerful capabilities for secondary (multivariate) analysis, graphics, communications and data management. Perhaps a significant additional advantage is that there are now several published texts documenting the package in full.

SAS: A long-established package that became prominent on the IBM/360 series of computers, it has now been implemented on several mainframe machines. Supporting packages provide integrated graphics, report writing, and econometric capabilities.

The above packages are all mini or mainframe based, and are relatively costly to purchase or lease. There are a multitude of other packages designed for micro computers. In this field there has been substantial development in recent years. Because they are relatively inexpensive (often under £ 1000), it is possible for smaller departments to justify them. Some of the recent offerings include: Marquis, Microquest and Snap. These packages all run on the better known micro computers, are demonstrated at appropriate exhibitions, and are installed in 10 or more sites. Whilst these packages are less costly they tend to be much slower, and are not really suitable for 'bulk' processing where output running to several hundred tables may be required.

Some of the micro packages support additional features that enable graphical output to be produced directly on to graph plotters or slides. In some cases tables can be 'exported' into spread sheet type programs, such as Lotus 1-2-3, which can provide very powerful capabilities for further table manipulation. With tables stored on disk, they can be imported directly into the text of typed reports. This provides the convenient possibility of merging tables and text without secondary re-typing.

Computer input

Although we have already discussed data input, computers have certain particular requirements. First, they can be more sensitive to faults in data. At the same time they can be more accurate in tabulating precisely what is there. Thus, the GIGO ('Garbage in = Garbage out') principle applies. Data records with errors must be 'cleaned' or the tables may also contain errors. This is particularly important when the computer output will be sent directly to the final user. The cleaning-up operation is likely to involve, among other things, the removal of redundant, erroneous or rogue codes; logic checking with resultant amendments to the data; and general sense checking. To ensure 'perfect' output these operations themselves must be carried out by computer. Manual or mechanical editing is seldom good enough. Although this takes extra time at the preparation stage, it can often save time at the output stage.

Some packages contain comprehensive editing features. However, it is quite frequent for this to be carried out at a prior stage by special programs. The data are then checked on the computer to ensure that they are 100 % correct before the tabulation runs are carried out. For example in multi-card surveys it is necessary to check that the correct number of cards are present for each informant. Most packages which accept multi-card data will reject invalid or mismatched sets. This can result in a substantial loss of data. Many bureaux have special programs for checking matching and identifying which serial numbers or cards are invalid. Corrections of this kind are usually done manually, and sometimes involve referring back to original questionnaires. The pack may then be checked again on the computer.

Although many bureaux will accept data on punch cards, these are usually converted to magnetic tape form. This is relatively inexpensive and provides a much easier access method than reverting back to cards each time a run is required. It is important to establish clearly whether one's data is being 'saved' by a bureaux or alternatively it is necessary to make one's own arrangement for archival storage. However, in some cases it is stored on card only. In these latter cases great care must be taken to avoid degradation of the card pack through wrecking, mishandling or other causes. In these circumstances it is possible that tables run on separate occasions may well contain differences when they should, in fact, be the same.

Computer weighting

It is frequently necessary to weight data to correct for differences between the composition of the sample achieved and known characteristics of the universe from which it was drawn. If, for example, one found that a sample contained too many men, most cross-tabulation packages can correct this by assigning separate weights to male and female informants such that the sample which is used for the analysis has the correct (mathematical) composition. Many computer packages now have features that enable weights to be calculated automatically given target sample composition characteristics. Some packages can do this in a way that minimizes the spread of weights applied and thus ameliorates the effect of weighting on the sample design factor. Common characteristics for which targets are set for weighting include demographics: age, class, sex, area, etc.

Checking computer output

Occasionally computers themselves make mistakes. When they do so, more often than not the result is obvious and spectacular. However, most errors in computer output arise either because the input data contain errors (referred to above) or because errors have been made in the specifications of the table concerned. It is rare, especially on a survey of any size, for there to be no errors at all on any of the output. For these reasons checking should be carried out. How this is done will vary from one organization to another. A good starting point is often through a 'hole count'. This gives a simple addition of the number of times each code has appeared, with percentages on the total sample and perhaps a frequency distribution showing the number of codes on each column. These counts may be in a raw form that corresponds directly to the number of questionnaires that are being analysed. The advantage of hole counts is that they can be produced with little or no specification, and are carried out quickly by most tabulation systems. A hole count is particularly useful in identifying specification errors. However the final checking must be on the finished tables themselves. How this is done varies. The procedure outlined below is less than perfect, but rigorous checking procedures may not be worth the delay they will cause in relation to the increased accuracy which may result. Here are some simple steps;

(a) If any weighting was carried out, calculate manually what the weighted sample base size should have been. If the computer gives you another result, there may be something wrong with the weighting. If so, all the tables may be wrong.

(b) Similarly, if the unweighted sample size is markedly different to what you expect, a serious fault may have occurred.

(c) The base figures should then be checked for each of the different base filters for each analysis breakdown. These should add back, where appropriate, to the total sample. It is probable that, if they are correct for one table with a particular base and breakdown, they will be correct for all other similar tables.

(d) Tables now need to be examined individually for the presence of correct labelling.

(e) The total column should be examined for sense and its addition to 100% (this may be slightly different due to rounding off), although this latter check may be done by the computer in some cases.

(f) The number of rejects should be examined. Rejects are informants who qualified for inclusion in the table but for whom no information was found in the data to the question being tabulated. If this number is high it is indicative of an error.

It will be noticed that checking of the data within the table has not been suggested. If the margins, i.e. the base figures and the total column, are checked and correct, then the data within the table will also normally be correct. The elimination of this part of the checking greatly reduces the time involved.

Conclusion

Editing, coding, and data processing are obviously an important part of producing any market research survey. They are largely clerical operations which to a greater or lesser extent make use of modern data processing techniques. The general principles are much the same as those applying to other forms of paper processing. The disciplines necessary in an automated accounting system have much in common with those necessary in market research. Although there is considerable literature on market research or statistical techniques, and also on data processing in general, there is comparatively little literature available on this latter area which is applicable to market research. It is an area which tends to be taken for granted. There are textbooks on some packages (e.g. SPSS, BMD, etc.), particularly those that originated at a university. There have been some important papers on the subject which are certainly worth further study. A list of some of these is given in the Bibliography. In the absence of further reading, however, attention to detail and common sense will enable the conscientious practitioner to handle the editing, coding and processing of most kinds of survey.

Chapter 12

Statistics and significance testing

PAUL HARRIS

Statistics may be defined as 'the collection, analysis and interpretation of numerical data'. As market research is concerned mostly with counting and measuring, it is not surprising that the theory of statistics can play an important part in assisting researchers to collect valid samples of data, and in helping them to draw correct conclusions from those data. The 'collection' aspect of statistics has already been covered in chapters 3 and 4 on experimental design and sampling. In this chapter, the emphasis will be on the 'analysis and interpretation' aspects of statistics dealing mainly with simple descriptive measures calculated from survey data and the testing of hypotheses about those data. The more advanced statistical techniques used for interpreting market research data will be covered in chapter 13. The techniques and significance tests described below are those which have been found most useful in interpreting survey tabulations. This is not an exhaustive list, by any means, and the reader who wishes to know more about statistical analysis in market research may consult the texts given in the references at the end of the book.

Types of market research data

Classified data

This is defined as data which have been collected using only different classifications or categories as the measuring scale. Much of the demographic data collected on market research questionnaires, for example, is of this type, consisting of groups of respondents who fall into one of a number of classifications. Two obvious examples are sex and marital status, where the categories would be:

Sex	Marital status
Male	Single
Female	Married
	Widowed
	Divorced

The numerical data are simply obtained by counting the frequency of occurrence of respondents in each classification. The various classifications used form a type of measurement scale known as a *nominal* scale. The basic property of this weakest form of measurement scale is that items or people that fall into one classification are different in some way from those falling in the other classifications. When the frequency counts for each classification are each divided by a base figure, such as the total number of respondents in the survey, and are multiplied by 100, a percentage is obtained for each classification. A frequency count and a percentage for a number of classifications is one of the most commonly occurring formats of market survey tabulations. The statistical treatment of these counts and percentages will form a large part of this chapter.

Ranked data

Data are often collected by classifications which are not only different, but where some classifications are 'higher' or 'lower' than other classifications in some sense. A common example in market research is where purchasers of various amounts of a product are classified as:

(a) heavy buyers (e.g. over ten packets);
(b) medium buyers (e.g. five to nine packets);
(c) light buyers (e.g. one to four packets).

Another example is where respondents are asked about their attitudes towards a product on semantic scales such as:

(a) very sweet;
(b) sweet;
(c) neither sweet nor bitter;
(d) bitter;
(e) very bitter.

A third example is when respondents are asked to rank a number of products in order of preference, giving classifications of 1st, 2nd, 3rd ... etc. When the number of products is two this is the often-used 'paired-comparison design'. In all these examples the classifications on the scales have a natural ordering, which distinguishes them from the previously defined classified data.

Numerical data are obtained from the count of respondents for each classification and its associated percentage. The natural order of classifications for ranked data gives the researcher more scope in analysing data of this type, which are often referred to as *ordinal* scale data.

Measured data

Under this heading are included all data where the scale of measurement consists not of labelled classifications, but real numerical values. Obvious examples are height (in metres), age (in years), and number of packets of 'brand B' bought last week. Measured data include the two types of measurement which are known as *interval* scales and *ratio* scales. In the former, the distance between two positions on the numerical scale is known and is interpretable numerically, and in the latter the ratio of two positions on the scale is independent of the unit of measurement. The ratio scale has the further property that its zero point is known and meaningful. An example of interval measurement is temperature which can be measured on Fahrenheit or centigrade scales. Height is a good example of the use of ratio measurement, where the ratio of two heights is the same, irrespective of whether they are measured in feet and inches or in metres.

A further distinction between types of measured data is that of *discrete* (or *discontinuous*) data and *continuous* data. Discrete data occur when the measurement scale consists of a number of distinct numerical values such as 'the number of times a certain advertisement has been seen in the last month'. The values on the scale must be 0, 1, 2, 3, ... etc., with intermediate values such as 1.5 being impossible. No such restriction is applicable to continuous data where the measurements may be taken to any number of decimal places, depending only on the accuracy of the measuring instruments being used. In practice, continuous data such as height are usually collected to distinct values such as two decimal places of metres.

Under the heading of measured data are included data obtained from semantic rating scales, to which simple discrete numerical scores have been attached. An example of two such scoring systems commonly used is given below:

	Score	Score
A preferred to B very much	5	+2
A preferred to B a little	4	+1
No preference	3	0
B preferred to A a little	2	−1
B preferred to A very much	1	−2

This practice of taking an ordinal or ranked measuring scale and giving the various classifications a numerical score is widespread in market research. By doing so the researcher is assuming that underlying the semantic scale is a continuous numerical scale which it is not possible to measure accurately, and that the numerical values given correspond approximately to positions on that scale. If such assumptions can be validly made, then a lot more can be done with the data statistically.

Simple descriptive statistics

In this section a number of summarizing features of measured data will be given.

Frequency distributions

If data have been collected on the number of 1 kg bags of flour bought by 200 housewives each month, it would be confusing to list all 200 values obtained. It is much better to display the data in the form of a *frequency distribution* as below:

Number of 1 kg bags bought	Frequency of occurrence = no. of housewives buying
0	12
1	15
2	20
3	40
4	60
5	30
6	15
7	5
8	3
	―
	200
	―

In this form, the data can be more easily understood and interpreted, especially as this frequency distribution (or 'distribution' as it is often simply called) may be represented pictorially as in Fig. 12.1. This graphical representation of a frequency distribution is known as a *histogram*. In the above example the data are given for a discrete distribution, but these two ways of displaying data are equally useful for continuous data. All one has to do is group the continuous data values into convenient groupings or class intervals and count the number of observations in each class. A number of classes between 8 and 15 is usually adequate. If data on height were collected

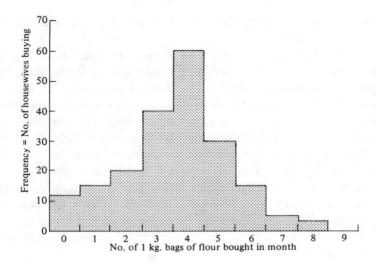

Fig. 12.1 Histogram of frequency distribution of flour purchases.

in metres, part of the frequency distribution might be as follows:

Height (m)	Frequency = no. of people
1.51–1.55	20
1.56–1.60	27
1.61–1.65	34
1.66–1.70	46
⋮	⋮

Continuous data that have been grouped into class intervals may also be represented by a *frequency curve*, which is obtained by drawing a smooth curve through the mid-points of the top of each bar on the histogram. An example of a frequency curve derived from a histogram is shown below in Fig. 12.2.

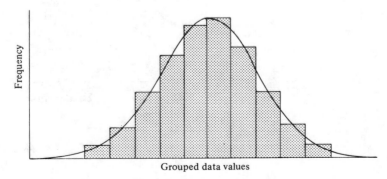

Fig. 12.2 Frequency curve.

The mean, variance, standard deviation and standard error of a distribution

Although the frequency distribution and histogram describe a set of data in simple terms, an even more valuable condensation of the data may be obtained by calculating a single value which summarizes the distribution. Such a value is the *arithmetic mean* or just simply the *mean* of the distribution. It is often referred to as the *average*, but this is not strictly correct as the mean is only one of a number of averages that may be calculated from a distribution. Other averages are the *mode* defined as the data value with the highest frequency, and the *median* defined as the middle value when all the data values are arranged in order of magnitude. To show how to calculate the mean of a distribution the previous data on bags of flour will be used. It is customary to denote the data values by 'x' and the frequency of occurrence by those values by 'f'. The mean, which is usually denoted by $\bar{x}$ (x – bar), is calculated by using the formula

$$\bar{x} = \frac{\Sigma f x}{\Sigma f} \quad \text{where } \Sigma = \text{ the sum of}$$

Putting the formula into words we have – multiply each data value (x) by its associated frequency (f), add up these multiplications and divide their total by sum of the frequencies. This has been done below for the data on flour.

Number of 1 kg bags bought	Frequency	
x	f	fx
0	12	0
1	15	15
2	20	40
3	40	120
4	60	240
5	30	150
6	15	90
7	5	35
8	3	24
	$\Sigma f = 200$	$\Sigma f x = 714$

$$\bar{x} = \frac{\Sigma f x}{\Sigma f} = \frac{714}{200} = 3.57$$

Reference to Fig. 12.1 shows that the value of the mean of the distribution lies near the middle of the data values. Both the median and the mode of this distribution are equal to 4. To calculate the mean of a continuous distribution it is necessary to take the midpoints of the class intervals as the data values (x). In the height example given above the values would be:

Height (m)	Midpoint	Frequency
	x	f
1.51–1.55	1.53	20
1.56–1.60	1.58	27
1.61–1.65	1.63	34
1.66–1.70	1.68	46
.	.	.
.	.	.
.	.	.

Not only it is useful to have a summarizing value such as a mean for a distribution but it is also of interest to have another value which indicates how much the individual data values are spread around the mean. Such a value is given by a quantity called the *variance* of the distribution, or by the square root of the variance, known as the *standard deviation*. In terms of the data values (x), the frequencies (f) and the mean ($\bar{x}$) they are defined as:

$$\text{Variance} = s^2 = \frac{\Sigma f (x - \bar{x})^2}{\Sigma f - 1}$$

$$\text{Standard deviation} = s = \sqrt{\frac{\Sigma f (x - \bar{x})^2}{\Sigma f - 1}}$$

The calculation of these two quantities, using the data on bags of flour, is demonstrated below.

Number of 1 kg bags bought	Frequency	$x - \bar{x}$	$(x - \bar{x})^2$	$f(x - \bar{x})^2$
x	f			
0	12	−3.57	12.74	152.88
1	15	−2.57	6.60	99.00
2	20	−1.57	2.46	49.20
3	40	−0.57	0.32	12.80
4	60	0.43	0.18	10.80
5	30	1.43	2.04	61.20
6	15	2.43	5.90	88.50
7	5	3.43	11.76	58.80
8	3	4.43	19.62	58.86
	$\Sigma f = 200$			$\Sigma f (x - \bar{x})^2 = 592.04$

$$\text{Variance} = s^2 = \frac{\Sigma f(x - \bar{x})^2}{\Sigma f - 1} = \frac{592.04}{199} = 2.98$$

$$\text{Standard deviation} = s = \sqrt{\frac{\Sigma f(x - \bar{x})^2}{\Sigma f - 1}} = \sqrt{2.98} = 1.73$$

It is quite usual to replace Σf by the symbol n, i.e. $n = \Sigma f$. Figure 12.3 below shows two hypothetical distributions, each with the same mean of $\bar{x} = 5$ units. For distribution A, which has data values ranging from 3 to 7 units, the variance and standard deviation would both be smaller than that for distribution B, where the data values range more widely from zero to 10.

There is a further important statistic that can be calculated from a distribution, namely, the *standard error of the mean*. To explain this term it is necessary to refer back to the theory of random sampling given in chapter 4. Suppose it is known that in a certain town the true average number of persons per household (based on *all* households) is $\bar{X} = 3.12$ with a standard deviation of $S = 1.00$. The values are denoted by capital X and S as they are population values and not sample values. If a random sample of 250 households is selected from the town it would be possible to calculate the mean number of persons per household for this sample. Let the mean of this sample be denoted by $\bar{x}_1$. Putting this value to one side, a second random sample of 250 households is selected and the mean ($\bar{x}_2$) is calculated. Similarly,

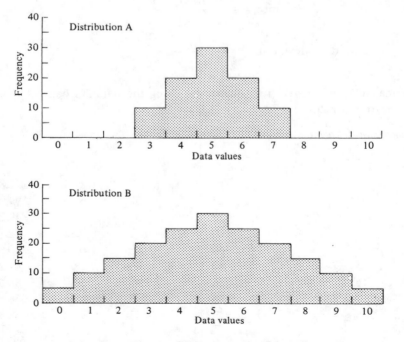

Fig. 12.3   Frequency distributions of hypothetical data.

a third sample of 250 is selected, giving $\bar{x}_3$, and so on, until 100 samples have been collected. The resulting 100 values of $\bar{x}$ may then be grouped into a frequency distribution. In general the 100 values of $\bar{x}$ will all be fairly close to the population mean, $\bar{X} = 3.12$. In fact, their distribution should have a mean, i.e. the mean of all the 100 means, which is indistinguishable or nearly indistinguishable from the value 3.12. Certainly, if all possible samples of 250 households were selected from the town, then the mean of the frequency distribution of all possible sample means would be exactly 3.12 (see page 90 of chapter 4). The distribution of sample means will have a bell-shape distribution, which is known as the *normal distribution*. The standard deviation of the distribution of 100 means may be calculated and it is usually called the *standard error of the mean*. Fortunately, it is not necessary to draw a large number of samples to estimate the standard error, as its value may be calculated from the single sample that is normally selected. If a sample of n members is selected and the standard deviation (s) calculated for some data values (x) then the standard error of the mean ($\bar{x}$) is given by:

$$\text{Standard error } (\bar{x}) = \frac{s}{\sqrt{n}}$$

If the data collected consists of percentages (p) then the statistics defined above take a simple form

		Values for percentages data
mean	$\bar{x}$	p
variance	s^2	$pq, \quad \text{where } q = 100 - p$
standard deviation	s	$\sqrt{pq}$
standard error	$\dfrac{s}{\sqrt{n}}$	$\sqrt{\dfrac{pq}{n}}$

Principles of significance testing

The market researcher, when interpreting the results of a market survey, has a large number of tables of frequencies and percentages to examine. These results, being based on a sample, will be subject to sampling errors. When the researcher selects two figures for comparison he has to assure himself that any difference between the two figures cannot be explained solely by sampling error. Only then may he validly draw attention to the difference in figures. The *significance test* is a device which enables the researcher to reach a decision objectively in such matters. In this section, the general principles of significance testing will be described. In later sections significance tests for use with various types of market research data will be given.

The null hypothesis and the alternative hypothesis

A significance test is used to decide whether to accept or reject hypotheses concerning the sample data that have been collected. The first step in a significance test is to set up a special hypothesis known as a *null hypothesis* (usually denoted by H_0). It is so called because it is quite often expressed in null or negative terms. A typical one in market research, not in negative terms, would be 'The percentage of men in the population who smoke is $P = 50\%$'. Next, the researcher must define an *alternative hypothesis* (H_1) which may be accepted if the null hypothesis is rejected. The corresponding alternative hypothesis to the null hypothesis stated above might be, 'Percentage P is not equal to 50%'. A significance test based on this alternative hypothesis would be of the type known as a *two-tailed test*, as it states that P may be either higher or lower than 50%. Two examples of alternative hypotheses each of which lead to a separate *one-tailed test* are given below.

(a) P is greater than 50%;
(b) P is less than 50%.

Both of these predict a difference in *one* direction only.

Testing the null hypothesis

The steps employed in conducting a significance test are best explained in the context of an example. In this section the hypothesis concerning the percentage of men who smoke will be tested using the two-tailed alternative hypothesis. To test the validity of the null hypothesis a random sample of n men, e.g. $n = 250$, is selected from the population of all men, and from the data values the statistic to be tested (p_1) is calculated, p_1 being the proportion of men who smoke. This is the result from just one sample. It would be possible in theory, as described in the previous section on the standard error of the mean, to draw all possible samples of size $n = 250$ from the population to produce a large number of estimates $p_1, p_2, p_3, \ldots$, etc. If these estimates were formed into a frequency distribution it would be a normal distribution. If the null hypothesis is true, this distribution, which is called the *sampling distribution of the test statistic*, will have a mean of $P = 50\%$ and a standard error of:

$$\sqrt{\frac{PQ}{n}} = \sqrt{\frac{50(100 - 50)}{250}} = \sqrt{10} = 3.16\%$$

Figure 12.4 shows this particular distribution, from which it can be seen that, if the null hypothesis is true, then a sample value of p_1 lower than 40% or higher than 60% is very unlikely. Of course, it is possible that a sample of

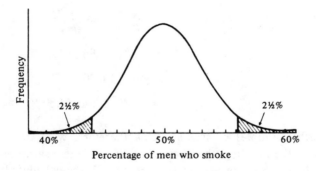

Fig. 12.4 Sampling distribution of a test statistic.

$n = 250$ will give $p_1 = 40\%$ even when the null hypothesis of $P = 50\%$ is true; but this would probably not occur. What the researcher has to decide now is where to place cut-off points on this distribution beyond which he is not prepared to accept that the null hypothesis is true but that an alternative hypothesis is true. These cut-off points are normally referred to as critical values in the statistical literature. To assist in this decision a valuable property of the normal distribution may be used. In any normal distribution the area of the distribution outside the limits, arithmetic mean $\pm z$ standard deviations (where z is any number), can be calculated.

Three examples are given below:

(a) only 5% of the area is outside the limits, mean ± 1.96 standard deviations;
(b) only 1% of the area is outside the limits, mean ± 2.58 standard deviations;
(c) only 0.1% of the area is outside the limits, mean ± 3.29 standard deviations.

Tables of the areas of the normal distribution have been calculated and one version is given in Table 12.1. It gives the area of the distribution beyond certain multiples of the standard deviation for one tail of the distribution only. The value corresponding to $z = 1.96$, for example, is 0.025 on one tail and, therefore, as stated above, 0.05 or 5% of the area of the curve is outside 1.96 standard deviations.

Figure 12.4 shows the critical values for the men smokers example, giving the limits outside which 5% of the area of the distribution lies ($2\frac{1}{2}\%$ on each tail). As this is a distribution of a mean, the standard error of the mean must be used in place of the standard deviation to calculate the critical values. These are given by:

$$\text{mean} \pm 1.96 \text{ standard errors} = P\% \pm 1.96 \sqrt{\frac{PQ}{n}}$$

$$= 50\% \pm 1.96 \,(3.16)$$

$$= 50\% \pm 6.20\%$$

$$= 43.80\% \text{ and } 56.20\%$$

If all possible samples of size $n = 250$, therefore, were drawn from the population and the null hypothesis were true, 5% of these samples would give a value less than 43.80% or greater than 56.20%. If the calculated value of p_1 from the one sample actually selected is outside these two limits, then the null hypothesis is rejected and the alternative hypothesis is accepted. Alternatively, if p_1 is within the limits, then the null hypothesis is accepted. When such a decision is made in practice there is a chance that an error will be made. There is a 5% chance that the null hypothesis may be rejected when, in fact, it is true because the sample just happened to be one of the five per cent of all possible samples that will always fall outside the specified limits. This chosen value of 5% is known as the *significance level* of the test and is often stated in the form $\alpha = 0.05$. In other words, it is often stated as a probability of 5 in 100, i.e. a 1 in 20 chance, that an error will be made. The significance level is often referred to as the *type I error*. Of course, there is nothing to stop the researcher using the 10% or 1%, or any other significance level; it depends on the error he is prepared to accept when making the decision. If the calculated value of the test statistic p_1 obtained from the sample is found to be outside the calculated limits it is said to be *significant* at the chosen level of significance. If it was found from the sample, for example, that 42% of men smoke, this result would be significant as the difference 50 to 42% is greater than 1.96 standard errors, and the null hypothesis that the population percentage is 50% would be rejected.

It is important to note that, although $P = 50\%$ has been rejected, nothing has been said in this significance test as to the true value of P, except that it is different from 50%. In this case the best estimate of P is given by the sample estimate $p_1 = 42\%$. This estimate will be subject to sampling error and it is not possible to state categorically that $P = 42\%$. All that can be done is to give limits known as *confidence limits* within which the true value of P will lie. These limits are based on the areas of the normal distribution and are given by:

$$p_1\% \pm Z \sqrt{\frac{p_1\%(100 - p_1)\%}{n}}$$

When $Z = 1.96$ standard errors, then 95% of the area of the normal distribution is covered by these limits which would then be known as 95% confidence limits. In the present example for sample size $n = 250$ and

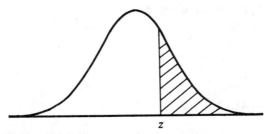

Table 12.1 *Table of probabilities associated with values as extreme as observed values of z in the normal distribution*

The body of the table gives one-tailed probabilities under H_0 of z. The left-hand marginal column gives various values of z to one decimal place. The top row gives various values to the second decimal place. Thus, for example, the one-tailed p of $z \geq 0.11$ or $z \leq -0.11$ is $p = 0.4562$.

z	0.00	0.01	0.02	0.03	0.04	0.05	0.06	0.07	0.08	0.09
0.0	0.5000	0.4960	0.4920	0.4880	0.4840	0.4801	0.4761	0.4721	0.4681	0.4641
0.1	0.4602	0.4562	0.4522	0.4483	0.4443	0.4404	0.4364	0.4325	0.4286	0.4247
0.2	0.4207	0.4168	0.4129	0.4090	0.4052	0.4013	0.3974	0.3936	0.3897	0.3859
0.3	0.3821	0.3783	0.3745	0.3707	0.3669	0.3632	0.3594	0.3557	0.3520	0.3483
0.4	0.3446	0.3409	0.3372	0.3336	0.3300	0.3264	0.3228	0.3192	0.3156	0.3121
0.5	0.3085	0.3050	0.3015	0.2981	0.2946	0.2912	0.2877	0.2843	0.2810	0.2776
0.6	0.2743	0.2709	0.2676	0.2643	0.2611	0.2578	0.2546	0.2514	0.2483	0.2451
0.7	0.2420	0.2389	0.2358	0.2327	0.2296	0.2266	0.2236	0.2206	0.2177	0.2148
0.8	0.2119	0.2090	0.2061	0.2033	0.2005	0.1977	0.1949	0.1922	0.1894	0.1867
0.9	0.1841	0.1814	0.1788	0.1762	0.1736	0.1711	0.1685	0.1660	0.1635	0.1611
1.0	0.1587	0.1562	0.1539	0.1515	0.1492	0.1469	0.1446	0.1423	0.1401	0.1379
1.1	0.1357	0.1335	0.1314	0.1292	0.1271	0.1251	0.1230	0.1210	0.1190	0.1170
1.2	0.1151	0.1131	0.1112	0.1093	0.1075	0.1056	0.1038	0.1020	0.1003	0.0985
1.3	0.0968	0.0951	0.0934	0.0918	0.0901	0.0885	0.0869	0.0853	0.0838	0.0823
1.4	0.0808	0.0793	0.0778	0.0764	0.0749	0.0735	0.0721	0.0708	0.0694	0.0681
1.5	0.0668	0.0655	0.0643	0.0630	0.0618	0.0606	0.0594	0.0582	0.0571	0.0559
1.6	0.0548	0.0537	0.0526	0.0516	0.0505	0.0495	0.0485	0.0475	0.0465	0.0455
1.7	0.0446	0.0436	0.0427	0.0418	0.0409	0.0401	0.0392	0.0384	0.0375	0.0367
1.8	0.0359	0.0351	0.0344	0.0336	0.0329	0.0322	0.0314	0.0307	0.0301	0.0294
1.9	0.0287	0.0281	0.0274	0.0268	0.0262	0.0256	0.0250	0.0244	0.0239	0.0233
2.0	0.0228	0.0222	0.0217	0.0212	0.0207	0.0202	0.0197	0.0192	0.0188	0.0183
2.1	0.0179	0.0174	0.0170	0.0166	0.0162	0.0158	0.0154	0.0150	0.0146	0.0143
2.2	0.0139	0.0136	0.0132	0.0129	0.0125	0.0122	0.0119	0.0116	0.0113	0.0110
2.3	0.0107	0.0104	0.0102	0.0099	0.0096	0.0094	0.0091	0.0089	0.0087	0.0084
2.4	0.0082	0.0080	0.0078	0.0075	0.0073	0.0071	0.0069	0.0068	0.0066	0.0064
2.5	0.0062	0.0060	0.0059	0.0057	0.0055	0.0054	0.0052	0.0051	0.0049	0.0048
2.6	0.0047	0.0045	0.0044	0.0043	0.0041	0.0040	0.0039	0.0038	0.0037	0.0036
2.7	0.0035	0.0034	0.0033	0.0032	0.0031	0.0030	0.0029	0.0028	0.0027	0.0026
2.8	0.0026	0.0025	0.0024	0.0023	0.0023	0.0022	0.0021	0.0021	0.0020	0.0019
2.9	0.0019	0.0018	0.0018	0.0017	0.0016	0.0016	0.0015	0.0015	0.0014	0.0014
3.0	0.0013	0.0013	0.0013	0.0012	0.0012	0.0011	0.0011	0.0011	0.0010	0.0010
3.1	0.0010	0.0009	0.0009	0.0009	0.00C8	0.0008	0.0008	0.0008	0.0007	0.0007
3.2	0.0007									
3.3	0.0005									
3.4	0.0003									
3.5	0.00023									
3.6	0.00016									
3.7	0.00011									
3.8	0.00007									
3.9	0.00005									
4.0	0.00003									

The above table is reproduced from *Non-Parametric Statistics for The Behavioural Sciences* by Sidney Siegel by permission of the McGraw-Hill Publishing Co. Ltd, the publishers.
Note: The blanks in the lower part of the table indicate that the values do not differ appreciably from those in the column headed '0.00'.

$p_1 = 42\%$, the 95% limits are given by:

$$42\% \pm 1.96 \sqrt{\frac{42 \times 58}{250}}$$

$$42\% \pm 6.12\%$$

$$35.88\% \text{ to } 48.12\%$$

Appendix A gives 95% confidence limits for various sample sizes and a selection of observed percentages. It may be used to give approximate answers to confidence limit problems.

   The type I error (or significance level) is not the only error that can be made when doing a significance test. Whereas the type I error is the error of saying a result is significant when it is not, the *type II error* is the error of saying a result is not significant when it is. To explain this new concept the previous null hypothesis H_0 will be tested against the one-tailed alternative hypothesis (H_1) that 'P is greater than 50%'. The assumption will now be made that, unknown to the researcher, in fact the alternative hypothesis is true and that $P = 54\%$ in the population of all men. Just as it is possible to have the sampling distribution for the null hypothesis, so it is also possible to construct a theoretical sampling distribution for when the alternative hypothesis is true. This distribution will also be a normal distribution based on the principle of selecting all possible samples from a population where $P = 54\%$ and its standard error will be given by:

$$\sqrt{\frac{54\%(100 - 54)\%}{250}} = \sqrt{9.94} = 3.15 \text{ per cent}$$

The sample size is assumed to be $n = 250$ as before and a 5% significance level will be used. Figure 12.5 shows the sampling distribution of samples of $n = 250$ when the null hypothesis (H_0) is true and beneath it is the sampling distribution for samples $n = 250$ when the alternative hypothesis (H_1) is true, and in particular when $P = 54\%$. As the alternative hypothesis only specifies values of P greater than 50%, only the right-hand tail of the null hypothesis sampling distribution is used in the significance test. Table 12.1 of the area of the normal distribution can be used to find the cut-off point, beyond which 5% of this distribution will lie. This value is given by:

$$\text{mean} + 1.645 \text{ standard errors} = 50\% + 1.645 \,(3.16\%)$$

$$= 50\% + 5.20\%$$

$$= 55.2 \text{ per cent}$$

If, in the one sample actually selected, it is found that the proportion of men who smoke is $p_1 = 55.2\%$ or greater, then the null hypothesis that $P = 50\%$

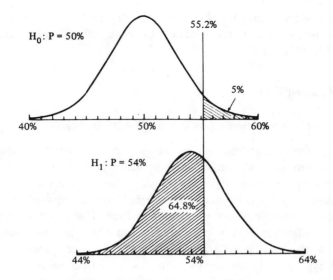

Fig. 12.5   Sampling distributions of the null and alternative hypotheses.

in the population is rejected. If p_1 is any value less than 55.2% then there is no reason to doubt the null hypothesis, as 95% of all possible samples will give a result less than 55.2% when the null hypothesis is true. However, if the latter decision is made in the present example where, unknown to the researcher, P is actually equal to 54%, there is a 64.8% chance that the decision will be wrong. This can be seen by referring to the bottom distribution of $P = 54\%$ in Fig. 12.5. The area of the distribution to the left of the significance criterion (55.2%) may be calculated using Table 12.1 of the normal distribution. It is the area shown shaded, and is found to be 64.8%. This chance of error is known as the type II error. It is quite often denoted by β and is sometimes expressed, like the significance level, as a probability. The present example would give $\beta = 0.648$.

If the chances of reaching a correct decision in a significance test are to be high, then both the significance level and the type II error ought to be kept to a minimum. This can be done by increasing the sample size, as this reduces the standard error and the spread of the sampling distributions of the null and alternative hypothesis. To make $\alpha = \beta = 0.05$ in the present example, when testing H_0 against the specific alternative hypothesis that $P = 54\%$, would require a sample size of approximately $n = 1680$.

Some useful significance tests in market research

This section will be concerned with giving examples of a number of the most frequently used significance tests in market research. Some tests are more suitable for use on certain types of data than others. For this reason the tests most suited to the three types of data previously defined will be given under those three headings below.

Tests on classified data

Testing the difference between two independent percentages

Very often, the researcher wishes to judge whether two independent percentages from different samples are significantly different. He may wish, for example, to know whether a percentage $p_1 \%$, based on a random sample of size n_1 selected in 1970, is significantly different from an equivalent percentage $p_2 \%$ based on a sample of size n_2 selected in 1968. The null hypothesis is that there is no difference in the percentages and that the two samples were selected from the same population in which the true percentage is $P \%$. The alternative hypothesis is that the two samples come from different populations in which the two percentages P_1 and P_2 are different, giving a two-tailed test. If the null hypothesis is true, then $p_1 \%$ and $p_2 \%$ are both estimates of $P \%$. To find out whether the difference $p_1 \% - p_2 \%$ is significant, the standard error of $p_1 \% - p_2 \%$, when the null hypothesis is true, is needed. This is given by the formula:

$$\text{Standard error } (p_1 - p_2) = \sqrt{p(100 - p)\left[\frac{1}{n_1} + \frac{1}{n_2}\right]}$$

where

$$p = \frac{n_1 p_1 + n_2 p_2}{n_1 + n_2}$$

is the best estimate of the unknown population percentage $P \%$. Tables giving the value of this standard error for various values of n_1, n_2, and p are available[1]. If the difference $p_1 - p_2$ is greater than 1.96 times its standard error then this observed difference can be declared significant at the 5% level. Appendix B may be used to give approximate answers to this problem. It shows for various value of n_1, n_2, and p the differences needed between p_1 and p_2 to be significant at the 5% level.

Example. In 1968 a random sample of $n_1 = 400$ men showed that $p_1 = 42.5\%$ of them regularly read a certain newspaper. Two years later, in a random sample of $n_2 = 200$ men, it was found that $p_2 = 35.0\%$ of them read that newspaper. Is the difference significant or can it be explained as the random fluctuations of sampling? The first step in this test is to calculate:

$$p = \frac{(400 \times 42.5) + (200 \times 35.0)}{400 + 200} = 40.0 \text{ per cent}$$

The standard error of $(p_1 - p_2)$ is then:

$$\text{Standard error } (p_1 - p_2) = \sqrt{40 \times 60\left[\tfrac{1}{400} + \tfrac{1}{200}\right]} = 4.24 \text{ per cent}$$

Dividing $p_1 - p_2$ by its standard error gives:

$$\frac{p_1 - p_2}{\text{standard error } (p_1 - p_2)} = \frac{42.5\% - 35.0\%}{4.24\%} = \frac{7.5\%}{4.24\%} = 1.77$$

The observed difference is less than 1.96 times its standard error and, therefore, it is not an unusual value to obtain from the sampling distribution when the null hypothesis is true. Accordingly, the conclusion is reached that these data do not give any reason to reject the null hypothesis that there has been no change in the percentage of men reading the newspaper.

Testing the difference between two correlated percentages

(a) Mutually exclusive classifications

Questions to which the respondent may give only *one* of a number of answers occur frequently on market research questionnaires. The analysis of such questions results in a series of percentages adding up to 100% based on a sample of size n. The testing of the difference between two such percentages is complicated by the fact that if one of the percentages goes up, then one or more of the other percentages must go down, as they all must add to 100%. The test differs from the previous one on independent percentages by having a different formula for the standard error:

$$\text{Standard error } (p_1 - p_2) = \sqrt{\frac{1}{n}(p_1 q_1 + p_2 q_2 + 2 p_1 p_2)}$$

where

$$q_1 = 100 - p_1$$
$$q_2 = 100 - p_2$$

Example. From a random sample of $n = 400$ housewives the following results were obtained in answer to the question 'Which brand of coffee do you buy most often?':

brand A	$p_1 = 40\%$
brand B	$p_2 = 30\%$
brand C	$p_3 = 12\%$
brand D	$p_4 = 11\%$
no regular brand	$p_5 = 7\%$
	100%

The null hypothesis to be tested is that there is no difference between brand A and brand B and that the observed difference in percentages can be explained as sampling variations. The alternative hypothesis is that there is a difference in the percentage share held by these two brands. The standard error of the difference is given by

$$\text{Standard error } (p_1 - p_2) = \sqrt{\tfrac{1}{400}[(40 \times 60) + (30 \times 70) + 2(40 \times 30)]}$$

$$= 4.15 \text{ per cent}$$

The observed difference $p_1 - p_2 = 10\%$ is 2.41 times this standard error and is significant at the 5% level. The data, therefore, suggest that there is a real difference between these two brands.

A quick alternative approximate way of calculating the significance criterion value z is to use the actual numbers of housewives choosing brand A and brand B. Denote these by n_A and n_B and the criterion is

$$z = \frac{n_A - n_B}{\sqrt{n_A + n_B}}$$

In the above example, $n_A = 160$ and $n_B = 120$, giving

$$z = \frac{160 - 120}{\sqrt{160 + 120}} = 2.39$$

(b) Overlapping classifications

With some market research questions the respondent may give more than one answer. The result of analysing such a question will be in the form of a number of percentages adding up to more than 100%, being based on the sample size n. As an example consider the question, 'Which brands of soap did you buy in the last seven days?' The housewives asked this question could possibly have bought more than one brand. To test the difference between two brand percentages a different standard error formula is needed to account for the overlap between brands.

$$\text{Standard error } (p_1 - p_2) = \sqrt{\frac{1}{n}[p_1 q_1 + p_2 q_2 + 2(p_1 p_2 - p_{12})]}$$

where $p_{12} = $ the overlap proportion, i.e. the proportion buying both brands.

For arithmetical reasons it is best to convert all the percentages in the above standard error formula to proportions when doing the calculation and multiply the answer at the end by 100 to give the standard error as a percentage.

Example. The following data were obtained from a sample of $n = 2000$ men who were asked which brands of petrol they had used in the previous three months:

brand 1	$p_1 = 25\%$
brand 2	$p_2 = 20\%$
brand 3	$p_3 = 18\%$
brand 4	$p_4 = 18\%$
brand 5	$p_5 = 11\%$
brand 6	$p_6 = 13\%$
brand 7	$p_7 = 12\%$

$$117\%$$

The difference between brands 1 and 2 is to be tested for significance, the null hypothesis being that there is no difference between the two percentages p_1 and p_2 in the population from which the sample was drawn. The alternative hypothesis is that the two brands have different shares of the market. The survey results also show that $p_{12} = 8\%$ of men had bought both brands 1 and 2 in the previous three months. To calculate the standard error the three relevant percentages, $p_1 = 25\%$, $p_2 = 20\%$ and $p_{12} = 8\%$, are converted to the three proportions 0.25, 0.20, and 0.08 respectively.

Standard error $(p_1 - p_2)$

$$= \sqrt{\tfrac{1}{2000}[(0.25 \times 0.75) + (0.2 \times 0.8) + 2(\{0.25 \times 0.2\} - 0.08)]}$$

$$= 0.0120 = 1.20\%$$

The actual difference $p_1 - p_2 = 25\% - 20\% = 5\%$ is 4.17 times its standard error. The ratio is higher than the value 3.29 needed to be significant at the 0.1% level, and it can be concluded that a real difference exists in the population from which the sample of $n = 2000$ men was selected.

As before with mutually exclusive classification there is a quick approximate way to arrive at the significance test criterion value z. This is calculated using the number of men using Brand 1 and not Brand 2 and the number of men using Brand 2 but not Brand 1. Denoting these by n_1 and n_2 repectively, the z value is given by:

$$z = \frac{n_1 - n_2}{\sqrt{n_1 + n_2}}$$

In the above example the proportion using both brands is 8% and the following two-way table may be formed:

		Brand 1		
		Used	Not used	Total
Brand 2	Used	160	**240**	400
	Not used	**340**	1.260	1.600
	Total	500	1.500	2.000

Thus $n_1 = 340$; $n_2 = 240$

and $z = \dfrac{340 - 240}{\sqrt{340 + 240}} = 4.15$

The chi-square Test.   Two-way classification tables usually form a prominent part of the results from a market survey. A typical example is given below, based on $n = 650$ housewives.

	Social class			
Purchasing habits	*AB*	*C1*	*C2DE*	*Total*
Brand A bought most often	35	72	172	279
Brand B bought most often	21	62	164	247
Brand C bought most often	14	26	84	124
Total	70	160	420	650

When both the row classifications and the column classifications are independent, i.e. a respondent can be in only one cell of the table, the differences in the cell frequencies may be tested for significance by using the chi-square test. This test enables one to say whether the observed cell frequencies are in agreement with the frequencies expected when the null hypothesis is true. The formula for computing the test criterion is best explained in terms of an example.

Example.   The above data on 650 housewives will be used in this example. The null hypothesis to be tested is that the brand shares are all equal for the three social classes and that differences observed in the above sample data reflect only sampling variation. This unknown distribution of brand shares is best estimated by pooling the data for the three social classes. This is given by the total column in the above table. If the null hypothesis is true then each column (social class grouping) will have its row (brand) frequencies in the same ratio as the total column's row frequencies. It is thus possible to work out an expected frequency for each cell of the table. This may be most easily done by using the following rule. The expected frequency for a given cell is obtained by multiplying its row total by its column total and dividing the result by the grand total. Thus for the cell 'brand A/social class AB' the expected frequency is:

$$E = \frac{279 \times 70}{650} = 30.0$$

The data are reproduced below with each expected frequency (E) being given in brackets next to its observed frequency (O).

	Social class			
	AB	*C1*	*C2DE*	Total
Brand A	35(30.0)	72(68.7)	172(180.3)	279
Brand B	21(26.6)	62(60.8)	164(159.6)	247
Brand C	14(13.4)	26(30.5)	84(80.1)	124
	70	160	420	650

It will be noted that the expected frequencies add down and across to the column and row totals respectively. The next step in the test is to calculate the test criterion:

$$\chi^2 = \Sigma \frac{(O-E)^2}{E}$$

where O denotes observed frequency and E denotes expected frequency and the summation is over all cells of the data. This quantity χ^2 will not have a normally distributed sampling distribution like previously-discussed test statistics. It will be distributed, when the null hypothesis is true, like another well known statistical distribution, the χ-square distribution. The calculation of χ^2 for this example is given below.

O	E	$(O-E)$	$(O-E)^2$	$\dfrac{(O-E)^2}{E}$
35	30.0	5.0	25.00	1.83
21	26.6	−5.6	31.36	1.18
14	13.4	0.6	0.36	0.03
72	68.7	3.3	10.89	0.16
62	60.8	1.2	1.44	0.02
26	30.5	−4.5	20.25	0.66
172	180.3	−8.3	68.89	0.38
164	159.6	4.4	19.36	0.12
84	80.1	3.9	15.21	0.19

$$\chi^2 = \Sigma \frac{(O-E)^2}{E} = 3.57$$

The chi-square distribution does not have a fixed shape like the normal distribution but takes many forms dependent on a quantity known as its *degrees of freedom*. In the context of a multi-cell table, or contingency table as it is often called, the degrees of freedom are calculated as $df = (r-1)(c-1)$ where r is the number of rows and c is the number of columns. In this case $df = (3-1)(3-1) = 4$. Table 12.2 gives, for various degrees of freedom, the values that χ^2 must attain to be significant at certain levels. For $df =$ four degrees of freedom χ^2 must be 9.49 or greater to be significant at the 5% level. The observed value of $\chi^2 = 3.57$ falls well short of this value, so these data give no evidence to doubt the null hypothesis that purchasing habits are the same for all three social class groupings.

The quantity χ^2 has a distribution like the chi-square distribution only when the expected frequencies (E) are large. How large is a matter of opinion and conflicting advice is often given in statistical texts. For tables with more than one degree of freedom, Cochran[2] suggests that less than 20% of the cells in the table should have expected frequencies less than five and that no cells in the table should have E less than one. If the data do not meet these restrictions, then row and/or column classifications may be combined until the expected frequencies are of sufficient size. The merging of rows or columns must only be done, however, if the resulting classifications are meaningful. The calculation of χ^2 is done using discrete numbers whereas the chi-square distribution is a continuous distribution. If the calculation of χ^2 includes what is known as *Yates' correction for continuity*, then it approximates much better to the chi-square distribution, especially with small expected frequencies. The correction consists of adding a half to each negative value of $(O-E)$ and subtracting a half from each positive value of $(O-E)$.

In the case of 2×2 two-way classification tables the formula for χ^2 takes a special form. Denoting the four cells of a 2×2 table by the letters a, b, c, d, we have

		Total
a	b	$a+b$
c	d	$c+d$
$a+c$	$b+d$	$n = a+b+c+d$

The formula for χ^2, including the correction for continuity, then becomes:

$$\chi^2 = \frac{n(|ad-bc|-n/2)^2}{(a+b)(c+d)(a+c)(b+d)} \quad \text{with one degree of freedom.}$$

The vertical lines enclosing the expression $ad-bc$ mean that the positive value of the expression must be taken, irrespective of whether it turns out to be positive or negative.

Example. The following data were collected from a random sample of $n = 100$ women.

	Social class		
	*ABC*1	*C2DE*	*Total*
Owners of sewing machines	23	13	36
Non-owners	12	52	64
	35	65	100

The null hypothesis to be tested is that the ownership of sewing machines is at the same level for both social class groupings. The alternative hypothesis is that he ownership levels are different:

$$\chi^2 = \frac{100[|(23)(52) - (13)(12)| - \frac{100}{2}]^2}{(36)(64)(35)(65)} = 18.7$$

Table 12.2 shows that for one degree of freedom the value $\chi^2 = 18.7$ is significant at the 0.1 % level, and on the evidence of these data it must be concluded that the ownership levels are different for the two social class groupings. The ownership levels are for *ABC*1 equal to $p_1 = \frac{23}{35} = 65.7\%$ and for *C2DE* equal to $p_2 = \frac{13}{65} = 20.0\%$. They have been put in percentage form to indicate that the chi-square test for 2×2 tables is equivalent to the test of two independent percentages given above.

McNemar's Test. This test is useful for 2×2 tables where the data have come from matched samples. The term matched samples includes those cases where each respondent in one sample is matched, on a number of criteria, to a respondent in a second sample, and also the case where the same sample of respondents is interviewed twice. The data from such 2×2 tables may often be presented, as below, in a form which might suggest that the ordinary chi-square test is applicable. This example shows the results of interviewing the same sample of respondents twelve months after a previous interview, about ownership of refrigerators.

	Interview 1	*Interview 2*
Refrigerator owners	a	b
Non-owners	c	d
	$a+c$	$b+d$

It is incorrect to treat the two interviews as two independent samples and do a chi-square test to see whether the proportion of owners has increased or decreased. It is necessary to examine the changes from the first interview to the second.

Table 12.2 Table of significant values of chi-square *

df	Probability under H_0 that $X^2 \geq$ chi-square													
	0.99	0.98	0.95	0.90	0.80	0.70	0.50	0.30	0.20	0.10	0.05	0.02	0.01	0.001
1	0.00016	0.00063	0.0039	0.016	0.064	0.15	0.46	1.07	1.64	2.71	3.84	5.41	6.64	10.83
2	0.02	0.04	0.10	0.21	0.45	0.71	1.39	2.41	3.22	4.60	5.99	7.82	9.21	13.82
3	0.12	0.18	0.35	0.58	1.00	1.42	2.37	3.66	4.64	6.25	7.82	9.84	11.34	16.27
4	0.30	0.43	0.71	1.06	1.65	2.20	3.36	4.88	5.99	7.78	9.49	11.67	13.28	18.46
5	0.55	0.75	1.14	1.61	2.34	3.00	4.35	6.06	7.29	9.24	11.07	13.39	15.09	20.52
6	0.87	1.13	1.64	2.20	3.07	3.83	5.35	7.23	8.56	10.64	12.59	15.03	16.81	22.46
7	1.24	1.56	2.17	2.83	3.82	4.67	6.35	8.38	9.80	12.02	14.07	16.62	18.48	24.32
8	1.65	2.03	2.73	3.49	4.59	5.53	7.34	9.52	11.03	13.36	15.51	18.17	20.09	26.12
9	2.09	2.53	3.32	4.17	5.38	6.39	8.34	10.66	12.24	14.68	16.92	19.68	21.67	27.88
10	2.56	3.06	3.94	4.86	6.18	7.27	9.34	11.78	13.44	15.99	18.31	21.16	23.21	29.59
11	3.05	3.61	4.58	5.58	6.99	8.15	10.34	12.90	14.63	17.28	19.68	22.62	24.72	31.26
12	3.57	4.18	5.23	6.30	7.81	9.03	11.34	14.01	15.81	18.55	21.03	24.05	26.22	32.91
13	4.11	4.76	5.89	7.04	8.63	9.93	12.34	15.12	16.98	19.81	22.36	25.47	27.69	34.53
14	4.66	5.37	6.57	7.79	9.47	10.82	13.34	16.22	18.15	21.06	23.68	26.87	29.14	36.12
15	5.23	5.98	7.26	8.55	10.31	11.72	14.34	17.32	19.31	22.31	25.00	28.26	30.58	37.70

16	5.81	6.61	7.96	9.31	11.15	12.62	15.34	18.42	20.46	23.54	26.30	29.63	32.00	39.29
17	6.41	7.26	8.67	10.08	12.00	13.53	16.34	19.51	21.62	24.77	27.59	31.00	33.41	40.75
18	7.02	7.91	9.39	10.86	12.86	14.44	17.34	20.60	22.76	25.99	28.87	32.35	34.80	42.31
19	7.63	8.57	10.12	11.65	13.72	15.35	18.34	21.69	23.90	27.20	30.14	33.69	36.19	43.82
20	8.26	9.24	10.85	12.44	14.58	16.27	19.34	22.78	25.04	28.41	31.41	35.02	37.57	45.32
21	8.90	9.92	11.59	13.24	15.44	17.18	20.34	23.86	26.17	29.62	32.67	36.34	38.93	46.80
22	9.54	10.60	12.34	14.04	16.31	18.10	21.34	24.94	27.30	30.81	33.92	37.66	40.29	48.27
23	10.20	11.29	13.09	14.85	17.19	19.02	22.34	26.02	28.43	32.01	35.17	38.97	41.64	49.73
24	10.86	11.99	13.85	15.66	18.06	19.94	23.34	27.10	29.55	33.20	36.42	40.27	42.98	51.18
25	11.52	12.70	14.61	16.47	18.94	20.87	24.34	28.17	30.68	34.38	37.65	41.57	44.31	52.62
26	12.20	13.41	15.38	17.29	19.82	21.79	25.34	29.25	31.80	35.56	38.88	42.86	45.64	54.05
27	12.88	14.12	16.15	18.11	20.70	22.72	26.34	30.32	32.91	36.74	40.11	44.14	46.96	55.48
28	13.56	14.85	16.93	18.94	21.59	23.65	27.34	31.39	34.03	37.92	41.34	45.42	48.28	56.89
29	14.26	15.57	17.71	19.77	22.48	24.58	28.34	32.46	35.14	39.09	42.56	46.69	49.59	58.30
30	14.95	16.31	18.49	20.60	23.36	25.51	29.34	33.53	36.25	40.26	43.77	47.96	50.89	59.70

* Table 12.2 is abridged from Table IV of Fisher and Yates: *Statistical tables for biological, agricultural and medical research*, published by Oliver and Boyd Ltd., Edinburgh by permission of the authors and publishers.

First interview

		Owner	Non-owner	Total
Second	Owner	e	f	b
interview	Non-owner	g	h	d
	Total	a	c	$n = a+c = b+d$

It is important to notice that all that has been done is recast the data in a different form. The marginal totals $(a, b, c\ d)$ of the 'changes' table correspond to the same values $a, b, c,$ and d in the previous table. To test the null hypothesis that the proportion of owners has neither increased nor decreased it is only necessary to consider the cell values f and g, as these are the only two cells that contribute to any change. If the null hypothesis is true the total number of respondents who change their ownership status will be evenly divided between these two cells. Thus, the expected value E for both these two cells is $(f+g)/2$. Having obtained observed and expected frequencies for these two cells, as given below, the usual formula for χ^2 may now be applied to these data.

	Observed (O)	Expected (E)
Non-owner to owner	f	$\dfrac{f+g}{2}$
Owner to non-owner	g	$\dfrac{f+g}{2}$
Total	$f+g$	

$$\chi^2 = \Sigma \frac{(O-E)^2}{E}$$

$$\chi^2 = \frac{[f-(f+g)/2]^2}{(f+g)/2} + \frac{[g-(f+g)/2]^2}{(f+g)/2}$$

$$\chi^2 = \frac{(f-g)^2}{f+g} \quad \text{with one degree of freedom.}$$

With a correction for continuity, the formula becomes:

$$\chi^2 = \frac{(|f-g|-1)^2}{f+g}$$

Table 12.2 of significant values of χ^2 may, therefore, be used to test the validity of the null hypothesis.

Example. A random sample of $n = 500$ motorists are interviewed, before a new advertising campaign for motoring magazine A, to estimate the proportion who regularly read the magazine. The same 500 motorists are reinterviewed some time after the campaign is finished and the following data are obtained.

		First interview		
		Readers	*Non-readers*	Total
Second	Readers	203	66	269
interview	Non-readers	41	190	231
	Total	244	256	500

The null hypothesis is that there has been no change in the readership level, this being tested against the alternative hypothesis that some change has taken place. The test criterion is calculated as:

$$\chi^2 = \frac{(|66-41|-1)^2}{66+41} = \frac{(24)^2}{107} = 5.38$$

Reference to Table 12.2 shows that, for one degree of freedom, $\chi^2 = 5.38$ is significant at the 5% level. The data suggest that there has been a real change in the readership for magazine A.

Tests on ranked data

Testing rating scales

(a) *The Kolmogorov-Smirnov test for two independent samples*
Semantic rating scales are extensively used by market researchers. An example of such a scale would be:

(a) very good quality;
(b) good quality;
(c) neither good nor bad quality;
(d) bad quality;
(e) very bad quality.

This scale represents a non-numerical ranking of the attribute 'quality'. The Kolmogorov-Smirnov test assumes that underlying this scale is a hypothetical numerical measuring scale, to which the five statements approximate. In a later section actual numbers will be attached to each position on such scales, and more powerful statistical tests will be carried out, involving assumptions about the underlying numerical scale.

The Kolmogorov-Smirnov test may be used to compare two sets of percentages on the same rating scale obtained from two independent samples. The test consists of cumulating the percentages for each sample separately, and finding the maximum difference between any two cumulative percentages at any of the positions on the scale. This maximum difference may be compared against known theoretical values to judge its significance.

Example. A random sample of $n_1 = 200$ men and an independent random sample of $n_2 = 200$ women were asked to assess a new brand of sherry in terms of its sweetness/dryness. The results of the test were as follows.

	Men (per cent)	Women (per cent)
Very sweet	18.5	15.0
Sweet	22.5	17.5
Neither sweet nor dry	29.0	25.0
Dry	20.0	22.5
Very dry	10.0	20.0

The null hypothesis to be tested is that there is no difference in assessment by men and women, against the alternative hypothesis that there are some differences. This gives a two-tailed test. Denoting the percentages for men by p_1 and for women by p_2 the calculation of the maximum difference D between the cumulated percentages proceeds as below.

p_1	p_2	Cumulative $p_1 = A$	Cumulative $p_2 = B$	$D = \|A - B\|$
18.5	15.0	18.5	15.0	3.5
22.5	17.5	41.0	32.5	8.5
29.0	25.0	70.0	57.5	12.5
20.0	22.5	90.0	80.0	10.0
10.0	20.0	100.0	100.0	—

In a two-tailed test the maximum *positive* difference $D = |A - B|$ is taken as the test criterion irrespective of whether the difference is positive or negative. In this example, $D = 12.5$. The significant values of D for two samples of size n_1 and n_2 are shown below. The sample value of D must equal or exceed these values to be significant at a given level.

Significance level (per cent)	Significant value of D $\sqrt{\dfrac{n_1 + n_2}{n_1 n_2}}$ times:
10	122
5	136
1	163
0.1	195

Using the 5% significance level it is calculated that D must equal or exceed the value,

$$D = 136 \sqrt{\frac{200 + 200}{200 \times 200}} = 13.6$$

The sample value of $D = 12.5$ is less than this, and therefore these data lead to the conclusion that there is no difference in the assessment of the new sherry by men and women.

For this particular significance test a one-tailed test will also be given, as the significance testing procedure differs from that of a two-tailed test. The null hypothesis will now be tested against the alternative hypothesis that men rate the product sweeter than do women. The calculation of the test statistic D is the same as for the two-tailed test, except that the sign of D in the last column of the above calculation is retained. If A is greater than B, then D is positive, and if B is greater than A then D is negative. The maximum value of D, in the direction predicted by the alternative hypothesis, is taken as the test statistic. In the present example this means considering only *positive* values of D, which would indicate men rating the product sweeter. In the one-tailed test the calculated value of D must be equal to or greater than:

$$\chi^2 = 4D^2 \left[\frac{n_1 n_2}{n_1 + n_2} \right]$$

a quantity which has the chi-square distribution with two degrees of freedom, when D is expressed as a proportion and not as a percentage. In the example $D = 12.5\%$ or 0.125 as a proportion and χ^2 is found to be equal to:

$$\chi^2 = 4(0.125)^2 \left[\frac{200 \times 200}{200 + 200} \right] = 6.25$$

Table 12.2 of the significance points of the chi-square distribution shows that for two degrees of freedom $\chi^2 = 5.99$ would be significant at the 5% level. The calculated value of $\chi^2 = 6.25$ is greater than this and it may be argued that the data support the alternative hypothesis that men judge the new sherry to be sweeter than do women. This result is different from that obtained previously by using a two-tailed test, and illustrates the point that a one-tailed test is always better at rejecting the null hypothesis than a two-tailed test.

(b) *The Sign Test for two matched samples*

The 'sign test' may be used in a number of market research contexts, but here it is demonstrated in the situation where two matched samples of respondents rate two items, or where the same sample of respondents rates both items. The results are often presented in survey reports in a form which gives the impression that the Kolmogorov-Smirnov test for two independent samples is appropriate. An example of this would be where $n = 200$ men were asked to rate two improved versions, X and Y, of an existing after-shave lotion. The data would probably be presented as below, in terms of frequencies and percentages.

	Version X	per cent	*Version Y*	per cent
Like very much	82	(41.0)	50	(25.0)
Like	57	(28.5)	70	(35.0)
Neither like nor dislike	29	(14.5)	40	(20.0)
Dislike	18	(9.0)	30	(15.0)
Dislike very much	14	(7.0)	10	(5.0)
	200	(100.0)	200	(100.0)

As the samples are matched a different approach is needed, which involves presenting one rating analysed by the other in the form of a two-way table. The sign test is then applied to some of the cells of this two-way table.

Example. The data below show the results obtained by analysing version X ratings against version Y ratings in the example on after-shave lotion.

		Rating on version X					
		Like very much	*Like*	*Neither like nor dislike*	*Dislike*	*Dislike very much*	*Total*
	Like very much	20	20	4	4	2	50
Rating	Like	30	20	10	5	5	70
on	Neither	18	10	8	3	1	40
version Y	Dislike	10	7	5	4	4	30
	Dislike very much	4	0	2	2	2	10
	Total	82	57	29	18	14	200

The null hypothesis is that there is no difference in the ratings for the two versions, and this will be tested against the alternative hypothesis that one or other of the two new versions is better liked. If the null hypothesis is true then the number of men rating X more favourable than Y on the scale ought to be the same as the number of men rating Y more favourably than X. Usually those rating X above Y are denoted by a $+$ sign and those rating Y above X by a $-$ sign, and this is how the sign test gets its name. The test consists of comparing the observed numbers rating X above and below Y with their expected frequencies. The test criterion turn out to be identical to the criterion of McNemars test.

	Observed	Expected
Number rating X above $Y(+)$	f	$\dfrac{f+g}{2}$
Number rating X below $Y(-)$	g	$\dfrac{f+g}{2}$
	$\overline{f+g}$	

$$\chi^2 = \frac{(|f-g|-1)^2}{f+g} \quad \text{with one degree of freedom}$$

In the example the number rating X above Y is obtained by summing the frequencies in the lower triangle of the above two-way table and the number rating Y above X is obtained from the sum of the frequencies in the upper triangle. Those men giving equal ratings are not used in the test, but the size of this group should be taken into account when interpreting the result of the significance test. Two summations give $f = 88$ and $g = 58$.

$$\chi^2 = \frac{(|88-58|-1)^2}{88+58} = 5.76$$

From Table 12.2 of the chi-square distribution with one degree of freedom it can be seen that a value of 5.76 is significant at the 2% level. The observed differences in the two ratings do not appear to be due to sampling fluctuations, and the data suggest that version X is the better product.

Testing numerical rankings

A technique that is often used in market research, especially in product tests, is for respondents to be shown a number of objects and asked to rank them (1st, 2nd, 3rd, ... etc.) in order of preference or acceptability. Special methods have been developed to test the significance of the results from data ranked in this way.

(a) *Ranking of two objects – paired comparisons*
In paired comparison tests objects are presented in pairs to respondents. The respondent is asked to state which object he prefers, i.e. he ranks them first and second. If more than two objects are to be tested it is possible to arrange that every respondent makes a judgement on all possible pairs. This situation is known as a 'balanced paired comparison experiment' or 'round robin'. In practice, respondents do not always consider all possible pairs of objects but only compare some pairs. Even so, it is possible to arrange that each pair of

objects is judged by the same number of respondents. If the number of objects being tested is denoted by t, and n measurements are made on each possible pair, then the total number of possible pairs is given by:

$$\frac{t(t-1)}{2}$$

and the total judgements or rankings will be:

$$\frac{nt(t-1)}{2}$$

When comparing two objects, say A_1 and A_2, a score of one will be given to the preferred object and a score of zero to the object not preferred.

	Object		
	A_1	A_2	
Respondent 1	1	0	A_1 preferred to A_2
Respondent 2	0	1	A_2 preferred to A_1
Respondent 3	1	0	A_1 preferred to A_2
Respondent 4	1	0	A_1 preferred to A_2
	$a_1 = 3$	$a_2 = 1$	

The total score a_1 for each of the t objects is used for testing the significance of paired comparison data.

Usually, this type of test is run to determine which objects are preferred overall, and in particular to find the 'best' object. This aim may be accomplished by comparing pairs of scores a_i and a_j on objects A_i and A_j for significant differences. Unfortunately, if the number of objects in the test is large, so is the number of possible pairs and therefore if a large number of significance tests are carried out on the data the probability of obtaining an apparently significant difference just by chance will be quite high. To guard against this the data are examined by an *overall test of significance* to see whether the scores $a_1 a_2 a_3 \ldots$ etc. as a set are significantly different. The test criterion is given by the expression:

$$D = \frac{4\left[\Sigma a_i^2 - \dfrac{tn^2(t-1)^2}{4}\right]}{nt}$$

This quantity has the chi-square distribution with $(t-1)$ degree of freedom. If this test gives a significant result at the chosen significance level, it indicates that some significant differences between scores exist. Individual pairs of scores may then be tested for significant differences by using the so-called *least significant difference* criterion defined by:

$$m = 1.96 \sqrt{\frac{nt}{2} + \frac{1}{2}}$$

Any pair of scores whose difference is equal to or greater than m may be declared significant at the 5% level. Replacing 1.96 by 2.58 or 3.29 gives equivalent criteria at the 1% and 0.1% levels respectively.

Example. $n = 60$ respondents were asked to do paired comparisons on all possible pairs of $t = 5$ types of biscuit, each respondent making $t(t-1)/2 = 10$ judgements. The total scores for each biscuit were:

$$a_1 = 132 \qquad a_2 = 102 \qquad a_3 = 178 \qquad a_4 = 48 \qquad a_5 = 140$$

Squaring the scores for each biscuit gives:

$$a_1{}^2 = 17\,424; \; a_2{}^2 = 10\,404; \; a_3{}^2 = 31\,684; \; a_4{}^2 = 2304; \; a_5{}^2 = 19\,600$$

Summing these squared scores $\Sigma a_i{}^2 = 81\,416$

$$D = \frac{4\left[81\,416 - \dfrac{5(60)^2(4)^2}{4}\right]}{(60)(5)} = 125.55$$

With $t-1 = 4$ degrees of freedom, Table 12.2 of percentage points of the chi-square distribution shows that at the 0.1% level D has to be 18.46 or greater to be significant. The computed value of $D = 125.55$ is therefore very highly significant and indicates that real differences between biscuits' scores do exist. Using the least significance difference criterion at the 5% significance level the critical value is:

$$m = 1.96 \sqrt{\frac{60 \times 5}{2} + \frac{1}{2}} = 24.51$$

Any difference in scores equal to or greater than 24.51 may be declared significantly different at the 5% level. However, it must be remembered that not too many significance tests should be carried out on the same set of data. Strictly speaking, one ought to test for significance only those pairs which are thought, before the experiment is carried out, to be a comparison of interest and not on pairs of scores which, when inspecting the data, just happen to look as if they might be significant. It is quite likely that the object with the highest score will be significantly different from the one with the lowest score even when the null hypothesis of no differences between any scores is true. Further analyses on paired comparison data are given by David.[3] Among these is a special version for paired comparisons of a technique known as *analysis of variance*, which will be described later in this chapter. It uses a seven-point rating scale of preferences scored from $+3$ to -3 and allows for the effect of order of presentation of objects to respondents. This special version of the technique is due to Scheffé and the interested reader may consult his original article[4] for details.

In some market research applications it is not feasible for respondents to try more than one pair. In this case the total possible pairs are formed and an equal number of respondent try each pair but nobody tests more than one pair. The judgements on the various pairs are therefore independent and a different analysis is required.

For each pair of products the Net Preference is calculated. For the pair A and B, for example, it is defined as the percentage preferring A minus the percentage preferring B. A table of Net Preferences is then formed for all pairs of products.

	A	B	C	....	Row Total (T)
A	–	A–B	A–C		
B	B–A	–	B–C		
C	C–A	C–B	–		
					0

The total (T_i) for each row of the table, divided by t (the number of products) gives the average net preference for each of the products A, B, C, ... etc. Let us denote these average net preferences by $\bar{A}$, $\bar{B}$, $\bar{C}$, ... etc.

The overall test of significance that all these average net preferences are equal is given by the following criterion

$$F = \frac{n \Sigma T_i^2}{100 pt(t-1)}$$

where p = the overall percentage of people, over the whole test involving all pairs, who express a preference for one product or the other.

n = the average number of people testing a particular pair. This is often constant from pair to pair.

This quantity F will follow the statistical distribution known as the F Distribution. Table 12.3 on pp. 334–5 gives the 5% and 1% significance levels for this distribution and it can be seen that two values of degrees of freedom are required to specify significant values of F. In the case of the round robin design of pairs the appropriate values of the degrees of freedom are $(t-1)$ and ∞.

If this test reveals that the null hypothesis of no difference between products is false, then individual differences between average net preferences may be tested for significance. To test the difference between two average net preferences (e.g. $\bar{A} - \bar{B}$) in the usual way, the standard error of the difference is given by:

$$\text{S.E} = \sqrt{\frac{100p}{N/(t-1)}}$$

where N = the total number of respondents over all pairs in the test.

The value $N/(t-1)$ is known as the Effective Sample Size as it is the sample size that would be needed to give the same standard error on a single paired comparison of two products.

Example. Three variants of biscuit A, B, and C were tested in pairs by adults in a round robin design involving all three pairs. Each pair was tried by a separate sample of approximately 400 people. The following results were obtained in terms of numbers of respondents.

	A–B		A–C		B–C
Prefer A	200	Prefer A	176	Prefer B	114
Prefer B	120	Prefer C	144	Prefer C	152
No Pref.	80	No Pref.	70	No Pref.	114
	400		390		380
Net Preference	20%		8%		−10%

Forming the table of net preferences yields

	A	B	C	Total	Average Net Preference
A	★	+ 20	+8	+28	+ 9.3
B	−20	★	− 10	− 30	− 10.0
C	− 8	+ 10	★	+2	+ 0.7

$$p = \frac{100[320+320+266]}{1{,}170} = 77.4\%$$

$$F = \frac{390[(+28)^2+(-30)^2+(+2)^2]}{100 \times 77.4 \times 3 \times 2} = 14.2$$

Looking up Table 12.3 for $t-1 = 2$ and ∞ degrees of freedom shows that the

Table 12.3   *Significant values of the F distribution*

v_2 \ v_1	1	2	3	4	5	6	8	12	24	∞
					5% points of F					
1	161.4	199.5	215.7	224.6	230.2	234.0	238.9	243.9	249.0	254.3
2	18.51	19.00	19.16	19.25	19.30	19.33	19.37	19.41	19.45	19.50
3	10.13	9.55	9.28	9.12	9.01	8.94	8.84	8.74	8.64	8.53
4	7.71	6.94	6.59	6.39	6.26	6.16	6.04	5.91	5.77	5.63
5	6.61	5.79	5.41	5.19	5.05	4.95	4.82	4.68	4.53	4.36
6	5.99	5.14	4.76	4.53	4.39	4.28	4.15	4.00	3.84	3.67
7	5.59	4.74	4.35	4.12	3.97	3.87	3.73	3.57	3.41	3.23
8	5.32	4.46	4.07	3.84	3.69	3.58	3.44	3.28	3.12	2.93
9	5.12	4.26	3.86	3.63	3.48	3.37	3.23	3.07	2.90	2.71
10	4.96	4.10	3.71	3.48	3.33	3.22	3.07	2.91	2.74	2.54
11	4.84	3.98	3.59	3.36	3.20	3.09	2.95	2.79	2.61	2.40
12	4.75	3.88	3.49	3.26	3.11	3.00	2.85	2.69	2.50	2.30
13	4.67	3.80	3.41	3.18	3.02	2.92	2.77	2.60	2.42	2.21
14	4.60	3.74	3.34	3.11	2.96	2.85	2.70	2.53	2.35	2.13
15	4.54	3.68	3.29	3.06	2.90	2.79	2.64	2.48	2.29	2.07
16	4.49	3.63	3.24	3.01	2.85	2.74	2.59	2.42	2.24	2.01
17	4.45	3.59	3.20	2.96	2.81	2.70	2.55	2.38	2.19	1.96
18	4.41	3.55	3.16	2.93	2.77	2.66	2.51	2.34	2.15	1.92
19	4.38	3.52	3.13	2.90	2.74	2.63	2.48	2.31	2.11	1.88
20	4.35	3.49	3.10	2.87	2.71	2.60	2.45	2.28	2.08	1.84
22	4.30	3.44	3.05	2.82	2.66	2.55	2.40	2.23	2.03	1.78
24	4.26	3.40	3.01	2.78	2.62	2.51	2.36	2.18	1.98	1.73
26	4.22	3.37	2.98	2.74	2.59	2.47	2.32	2.15	1.95	1.69
28	4.20	3.34	2.95	2.71	2.56	2.44	2.29	2.12	1.91	1.65
30	4.17	3.32	2.92	2.69	2.53	2.42	2.27	2.09	1.89	1.62
40	4.08	3.23	2.84	2.61	2.45	2.34	2.18	2.00	1.79	1.51
60	4.00	3.15	2.76	2.52	2.37	2.25	2.10	1.92	1.70	1.39
120	3.92	3.07	2.68	2.45	2.29	2.17	2.02	1.83	1.61	1.25
∞	3.84	2.99	2.60	2.37	2.21	2.09	1.94	1.75	1.52	1.00

Table 12.3 is abridged from Table V of Fisher and Yates: *Statistical Tables for Biological, Agricultural and Medical Research*, published by Oliver and Boyd, Ltd., Edinburgh, by permission of the authors and publishers.

required values of F for significance at the 5% and 1% levels are 2.99 and 4.60. The calculated value of $F = 14.2$ for exceeds this value and it can be concluded that there are differences in preference between biscuits. To test the significance of differences in preference between individual biscuits calculate

Table 12.3 *(continued)*

v_2 \ v_1	1	2	3	4	5	6	8	12	24	∞
					1% points of F					
1	4052	4999	5403	5625	5764	5859	5981	6106	6234	6366
2	98.49	99.00	99.17	99.25	99.30	99.33	99.36	99.42	99.46	99.50
3	34.12	30.81	29.46	28.71	28.24	27.91	27.49	27.05	26.60	26.12
4	21.20	18.00	16.69	15.98	15.52	15.21	14.80	14.37	13.93	13.46
5	16.26	13.27	12.06	11.39	10.97	10.67	10.29	9.89	9.47	9.02
6	13.74	10.92	9.78	9.15	8.75	8.47	8.10	7.72	7.31	6.88
7	12.25	9.55	8.45	7.85	7.46	7.19	6.84	6.47	6.07	5.65
8	11.26	8.65	7.59	7.01	6.63	6.37	6.03	5.67	5.28	4.86
9	10.56	8.02	6.99	6.42	6.06	5.80	5.47	5.11	4.73	4.31
10	10.04	7.56	6.55	5.99	5.64	5.39	5.06	4.71	4.33	3.91
11	9.65	7.20	6.22	5.67	5.32	5.07	4.74	4.40	4.02	3.60
12	9.33	6.93	5.95	5.41	5.06	4.82	4.50	4.16	3.78	3.36
13	9.07	6.70	5.74	5.20	4.86	4.62	4.30	3.96	3.59	3.16
14	8.86	6.51	5.56	5.03	4.69	4.46	4.14	3.80	3.43	3.00
15	8.68	6.36	5.42	4.89	4.56	4.32	4.00	3.67	3.29	2.87
16	8.53	6.23	5.29	4.77	4.44	4.20	3.89	3.55	3.18	2.75
17	8.40	6.11	5.18	4.67	4.34	4.10	3.79	3.45	3.08	2.65
18	8.28	6.01	5.09	4.58	4.25	4.01	3.71	3.37	3.00	2.57
19	8.18	5.93	5.01	4.50	4.17	3.94	3.63	3.30	2.92	2.49
20	8.10	5.85	4.94	4.43	4.10	3.87	3.56	3.23	2.86	2.42
22	7.94	5.72	4.82	4.31	3.99	3.76	3.45	3.12	2.75	2.31
24	7.82	5.61	4.72	4.22	3.90	3.67	3.36	3.03	2.66	2.21
26	7.72	5.53	4.64	4.14	3.82	3.59	3.29	2.96	2.58	2.13
28	7.64	5.45	4.57	4.07	3.75	3.53	3.23	2.90	2.52	2.06
30	7.56	5.39	4.51	4.02	3.70	3.47	3.17	2.84	2.47	2.01
40	7.31	5.18	4.31	3.83	3.51	3.29	2.99	2.66	2.29	1.80
60	7.08	4.98	4.13	3.65	3.34	3.12	2.82	2.50	2.12	1.60
120	6.85	4.79	3.95	3.48	3.17	2.96	2.66	2.34	1.95	1.38
∞	6.64	4.60	3.78	3.32	3.02	2.80	2.51	2.18	1.79	1.00

Table 12.3 is abridged from Table V of Fisher and Yates: *Statistical Tables for Biological, Agricultural and Medical Research*, published by Oliver and Boyd, Ltd., Edinburgh, by permission of the authors and publishers.

$$\text{S.E.} = \sqrt{\frac{100 \times 77.4}{1,170/2}} = 3.64$$

Compared with this value all three differences between Average Net Preferences are significant at the 5% level.

(b) *Ranking of three or more objects*

If a number of objects are to be compared, and the objects have obvious differences, then it is better to get respondents to do an overall ranking of all the objects instead of doing a number of paired comparisons. When t objects have been ranked by n respondents it is possible to test whether there is any agreement between respondents ranking by calculating *Kendall's Coefficient of Concordance* (W) and testing its significance. If significant agreement is found, it is possible to obtain the order of preference or acceptability of the objects. A description of the calculation of W is best done in the context of an example.

Example.   A random sample of $n = 100$ housewives are asked to rank $t = 4$ new designs for a breakfast cereal packet. The results of such ranking tests are usually given in the following form:

Cereal packet designs

Rank	A	B	C	D
1	40	10	25	25
2	30	20	40	10
3	20	30	25	25
4	10	40	10	40
	100	100	100	100

A design ranked first is given a score of 1, a design ranked second a score of 2 and so on. First calculate the sum of ranks R for each design:

$$R_A = (40 \times 1) + (30 \times 2) + (20 \times 3) + (10 \times 4) = 200$$

Similarly,

$$R_B = 300; \qquad R_C = 220; \qquad R_D = 280$$

Then calculate the average sum of ranks, $\bar{R}$:

$$\bar{R} = \frac{200 + 300 + 220 + 280}{4} = 250$$

Next, compute $S = \Sigma(R_i - \bar{R})^2$

R_i	$R_i - \bar{R}$	$(R_i - \bar{R})^2$
200	− 50	2500
300	50	2500
220	− 30	900
280	30	900
		6800 = S

S is the sum of squares of the deviations of the individual R_i scores from their average $\bar{R}$. If all respondents were in complete agreement, S would be equal to:

$$S = \frac{n^2(t^3 - t)}{12}$$

Kendall's W is the ratio of the observed value of S to its theoretical counterpart:

$$W = \frac{12S}{n^2(t^3 - t)} = \frac{12 \times 6800}{(100)^2(4^3 - 4)} = 0.136$$

The coefficient W may vary from $W = 0$, when all respondents are ranking at random, to $W = +1$, indicating complete agreement between respondents. To test whether W is significantly different from zero, use has to be made of tables of significant values of the statistical distribution known as the F distribution. Table 12.3 gives the 5% and 1% level values for this distribution, from which it will be seen that two values of degrees of freedom are required to specify significant values of F. It can be shown that a transformation of W given by:

$$F = \frac{(n-1)W}{1-W}$$

will have the F distribution with degrees of freedom approximately equal to

$$V_1 = t - 1 \quad \text{and} \quad V_2 = (n-1)V_1$$

In the example,

$$F = \frac{(100 - 1)0.136}{0.864} = 15.6$$

with $V_1 = 4 - 1 = 3$ and $V_2 = 99 \times 3 = 297$ degrees of freedom. Reference to Table 12.3 of the F distribution reveals that the calculated value of $F = 15.6$ is at least significant at the 1% level. There appears to be a small but real agreement between respondents in their ranking of the new packet designs.

The rank order of acceptability of the new designs is given, when W has been found to be significant, by the individual sum of ranks R_i for each design. A low score indicates a high preference and a high score suggests a low level of acceptability. To test whether one design is ranked significantly higher than another the sign test, previously described, may be used. If design B is to be compared with design C in the above example, the following two-way table involving the ranks of these two designs must be produced.

Ranking of design B

		1	2	3	4	Total
	1	0	5	10	10	25
	2	5	0	25	10	40
Ranking of design C	3	3	12	0	10	25
	4	2	3	5	0	10
Total		10	20	40	30	100

the number of times C ranked above B($+$) = 70;
the number of times B ranked above C($-$) = 30.

$$\chi^2 = \frac{(|70-30|-1)^2}{70+30} = 15.21 \text{ with one degree of freedom}$$

Looking up Table 12.2 of the chi-square distribution for one degree of freedom shows that $\chi^2 = 15.21$ is significant at the 0.1% level. Design C is significantly preferred to design B by respondents.

Tests on measured data

Testing the difference between the means of two independent samples

A frequent comparison, which is needed when assessing the results of a market research survey, is that between the means of two rating scales, where the scales have been given simple numerical scores. As explained earlier, if one is prepared to assume that the scores represent meaningful values on an underlying continuous distribution, then the test about to be described, which is applicable only to measured data, may be used. As an example of how more than one type of significance test may be used on the same set of data, the data previously used in describing the Kolmogorov-Smirnov test will be examined again for significance. This time a scoring system will be attached to the scale positions, and the frequencies are used in place of the percentages.

Rating on new brand of sherry

	Score	Men	Women
Very sweet	+2	37	30
Sweet	+1	45	35
Neither sweet nor dry	0	58	50
Dry	−1	40	45
Very dry	−2	20	40
		$n_1 = 200$	$n_2 = 200$

The main assumption being made is that the scoring system is an interval scale and that the numerical distances between the scale positions are valid. The Kolmogorov-Smirnov test makes no such assumption.

To test the difference between two means $\bar{x}_1$ and $\bar{x}_2$ based on two independent samples of size n_1 and n_2 it is necessary to calculate the variance of each set of data. From the two variances $s_1{}^2$ and $s_2{}^2$ the standard error of the difference between two means is calculated as:

$$\text{Standard error } (\bar{x}_1 - \bar{x}_2) = \sqrt{s^2 \left[\frac{n_1 + n_2}{n_1 \times n_2} \right]}$$

where s^2 is a pooled estimate of the variance based on both samples

$$s^2 = \frac{\Sigma f_1 (x_1 - \bar{x}_1)^2 + \Sigma f_2 (x_2 - \bar{x}_2)^2}{(n_1 - 1) + (n_2 - 1)}$$

This average value of the variance is used as this test assumes that the two samples come from populations where the variance is equal. The null hypothesis usually states that there is no difference in the means. If this is true then the quantity:

$$Z = \frac{\bar{x}_1 - \bar{x}_2}{\text{standard error } (\bar{x}_1 - \bar{x}_2)}$$

will have the normal distribution (except when the sample sizes are very small). Tables of the normal distribution may, therefore, be used to test the significance of Z calculated from the two samples.

Example. The data on sherry are used in the example calculations given below. Subscripts 1 and 2 in the formulae refer to the sample of men and women respectively.

Score

$(x_1 \text{ or } x_2)$	f_1	f_2	$f_1 x_1$	$f_2 x_2$	$(x_1 - \bar{x}_1)$	$(x_1 - \bar{x}_1)^2$	$f_1 (x_1 - \bar{x}_1)^2$
$+2$	37	30	74	60	1.805	3.2580	120.5460
$+1$	45	35	45	35	0.805	0.6480	29.1600
0	58	50	0	0	-0.195	0.0380	2.2040
-1	40	45	-40	-45	-1.195	1.4280	57.1200
-2	20	40	-40	-80	-2.195	4.8180	96.3600
	200	200	39	-30			305.3900

$$(x_2-\bar{x}_2) \quad (x_2-\bar{x}_2)^2 \quad f_2(x_2-\bar{x}_2)^2$$

$(x_2-\bar{x}_2)$	$(x_2-\bar{x}_2)^2$	$f_2(x_2-\bar{x}_2)^2$
2.150	4.6225	138.6750
1.150	1.3225	46.2875
0.150	0.0225	1.1250
−0.850	0.7225	32.5125
−1.850	3.4225	136.9000
		355.5000

$$\bar{x}_1 = \frac{\Sigma f_1 x_1}{n_1} = \frac{39}{200} = 0.195 \qquad \bar{x}_2 = \frac{\Sigma f_2 x_2}{n_2} = \frac{-30}{200} = -0.150$$

$$s^2 = \frac{305.39 + 355.50}{199 + 199} = 1.661$$

$$\text{Standard error } (\bar{x}_1 - \bar{x}_2) = \sqrt{1.661 \left[\frac{200 + 200}{200 \times 200} \right]} = \sqrt{0.01661} = 0.1288$$

$$Z = \frac{\bar{x}_1 - \bar{x}_2}{\text{standard error } (\bar{x}_1 - \bar{x}_2)} = \frac{0.195 - (-0.150)}{0.1288} = 2.68$$

Table 12.1 may be used to determine the significance level obtained by a difference in means which is equal to $Z = 2.68$ standard errors. Such a value is greater than the 2.58 standard errors needed for the result to be significant at the 1 % level but less than 3.29 standard errors needed for 0.1 % significance. It is actually significant at the 0.74 % level. The conclusion which leads from this significance test is that men rate the new sherry to be more sweet than do women.

When scores are attached to the semantic rating scales used in market research and the data are assumed to have the properties of measured data, significance tests such as the one just described may be used to evaluate differences. The gain in doing so may be seen by considering the results of the present significance test on the sherry data along with the analysis of the same data using the Kolmogorov-Smirnov test. This latter test was unable to detect any significant differences between men and women's ratings, whereas the present test between the two means was able to show that a real difference was present. On the debit side the two-means test requires a lot more calculations than does the Kolmogorov-Smirnov test. However, most modern computer programs for survey analysis have facilities for automatically calculating means, variances, standard deviations and standard errors for scales which have been scored.

Testing the difference between the means of two matched samples

When the same sample of respondents rates two separate items, or rates the same item on two separate occasions, the ensuing data are often presented in a form which may suggest that the test for two independent means may be employed. The test, if applied to such matched sample data, would give too few significant results due to the matching. The correct test for this situation will now be described using the data on after-shave lotion previously analysed by means of the sign test. These data consisted of a sample of $n = 200$ men rating two new versions, X and Y, of an existing after-shave lotion, by means of a semantic scale. It will give another example of how ranked data may, if certain assumptions are made, be treated as measured data by attaching a numerical scoring system to the scale positions. The scoring used in the example will be:

	Score.
Like very much	5
Like	4
Neither like nor dislike	3
Dislike	2
Dislike very much	1

The matched sample test uses the two-way table, presented previously, of version X's score (denoted by x_1) analysed by the score for version Y (denoted by x_2). From this table the difference in scores, $d = x_1 - x_2$ may be calculated and a frequency distribution of the d value can be formed. If the null hypothesis that there is no difference in the ratings of the two versions is true, then the expected or mean difference score ($\bar{d}$) would be zero, with a standard error of:

$$\text{Standard error } (\bar{d}) = \frac{s_d}{\sqrt{n}}$$

where s_d = the standard deviation of the difference scores,

$$d = x_1 - x_2$$

The null hypothesis that $\bar{d} = 0$ may be tested by calculating the criterion:

$$Z = \frac{\bar{d} - 0}{\text{standard error } (\bar{d})} = \frac{\bar{d}\sqrt{n}}{s_d}$$

Z will follow a normal distribution, when the sample is not too small, and Table 12.1 may be used to evaluate the significance level.

Example. Scoring the two-way table of version X's ratings against the ratings on version Y gives the following table.

Rating on version X
(x₁ score)

		5	4	3	2	1	Total men
Rating on	5	20	20	4	4	2	50
version Y	4	30	20	10	5	5	70
(x₂ score)	3	(18)	10	8	3	1	40
	2	10	(7)	5	4	4	30
	1	4	0	(2)	2	2	10
Total men		82	57	29	18	14	200

From this table a frequency distribution of difference scores is easily obtained; for instance, the score $d = x_1 - x_2 = +2$ is obtained from the cells circled in the above table.

$d = x_1 - x_2$	f	fd	$(d - \bar{d})$	$(d - \bar{d})^2$	$f(d - \bar{d})^2$
+4	4	16	3.725	13.876	55.504
+3	10	30	2.725	7.426	74.260
+2	27	54	1.725	2.976	80.352
+1	47	47	0.725	0.526	24.722
0	54	0	-0.275	0.076	4.104
-1	37	-37	-1.275	1.626	60.162
-2	10	-20	-2.275	5.176	51.760
-3	9	-27	-3.275	10.726	96.534
-4	2	-8	-4.275	18.276	36.552
	200	+55			483.950

$$\bar{d} = \frac{\Sigma fd}{\Sigma f} = \frac{+55}{200} = +0.275$$

$$s_d = \sqrt{\frac{\Sigma f(d - \bar{d})^2}{\Sigma f - 1}} = \sqrt{\frac{483.950}{199}} = \sqrt{2.432} = 1.56$$

$$\text{Standard error } (\bar{d}) = \frac{s_d}{\sqrt{n}} = \frac{1.56}{\sqrt{200}} = 0.110$$

$$Z = \frac{\bar{d}}{\text{standard error } (\bar{d})} = \frac{+0.275}{0.110} = 2.50$$

The calculated mean $\bar{d} = 0.275$ is 2.50 standard errors distant from the hypothesized mean of zero. Such a deviation is almost equal to the 2.58

standard errors needed to be significant at the 1 % level. It is, in fact, significant at the 1.24 % level. The sign test applied to these data gave a result which was just significant at the 2 % level according to Table 12.2 of the chi-square distribution.

Testing the difference between the means of three or more independent samples—the analysis of variance

A comparison of arithmetic means from several samples is often required when interpreting survey results. It is not good statistical practice to proceed immediately to carry out a number of individual significance tests on pairs of sample means. It is better first to do an overall test of the null hypothesis that the populations, from which all the samples have been selected, have identical means. The appropriate test for doing this is the *F* test. To carry out the test it is necessary to use a technique known as *analysis of variance* in which the total variance of all the data values in all the samples is split into two additive parts, that due to variance between samples and that due to variance within samples. The within sample variance in this case is equivalent to the pooled variance used previously, when testing two independent means. When these two parts of the variance, which are called mean squares, have been calculated, their ratio *F* given by:

$$F = \frac{\text{between samples mean square}}{\text{within samples mean square}}$$

will follow a statistical distribution known as the *F* distribution, when the null hypothesis is true. Table 12.3, which gives significant values of *F*, may be used to test whether the between samples mean square is larger than the within samples mean square. If the calculated value of *F* is found to be significant then it may be concluded that differences between the means exist.

Scale	Score	Young	Middle-aged	Old
	x	f_1	f_2	f_3
Very bitter	5	21	11	14
Fairly bitter	4	46	29	22
Neither bitter nor sweet	3	37	47	35
Fairly sweet	2	22	18	38
Very sweet	1	12	7	28
		$n_1 = 138$	$n_2 = 112$	$n_3 = 137$	$n = 387$

Example. Three samples of young men ($n_1 = 138$), middle-aged men ($n_2 = 112$) and old men ($n_3 = 137$) were asked to rate a new beer on a five-point scale of bitterness/sweetness. The results of the test are given above. The total variance has been previously defined as:

$$s^2 = \frac{\Sigma f(x - \bar{x})^2}{n - 1}$$

The numerator in this expression is known as the total sum of squares, and it is this quantity which is split into two parts, as below:

(a) square all $n = 387$ data values and sum them to give A;

$$A = (5^2 \times 21) + (4^2 \times 46) + \ldots + (1^2 \times 28) = 4132$$

(b) sum all $n = 387$ data values and square this total to give T^2;

$$T^2 = [(5 \times 21) + (4 \times 46) + \ldots + (1 \times 28)]^2 = (1178)^2 = 1\,387\,684$$

(c) divide T^2 by the total sample size n to give the so-called correction factor $C = T^2/n$

$$C = \frac{1\,387\,684}{387} = 3585.75$$

(d) sum the data values for each sample to give T_1, T_2, and T_3

$$T_1 = (5 \times 21) + (4 \times 46) + \ldots + (1 \times 12) = 456$$

similarly: $T_2 = 355$ $T_3 = 367$

(e) calculate the quantity B given by:

$$B = \frac{T_1^2}{n_1} + \frac{T_2^2}{n_2} + \frac{T_3^2}{n_3} = \frac{(456)^2}{138} + \frac{(355)^2}{112} + \frac{(367)^2}{137} = 3615.13$$

The total sum of squares is given by $A - C = 4132 - 3585.75 = 546.25$.

The between samples sum of squares is given by $B - C$

$$= 3615.13 - 3585.75 = 29.38.$$

The within samples sum of squares is given by $A - B$

$$= 4132 - 3615.13 = 516.87.$$

The calculations are summarized in the following analysis of variance table.

Source of variation	Sum of squares	Degrees of freedom	Mean square	F
Between samples (age groups)	29.38	2	14.690	10.91
Within samples	516.87	384	1.346	
Total	546.25	386		

Just as the total sum of squares is divided by total sample size less one ($n - 1 = 386$) to give the variance, so the between samples mean square is obtained by dividing its sum of squares by the number of samples less one ($3 - 1 = 2$). These divisors are known as degrees of freedom and, like the sums of squares, are additive. The degrees of freedom for the within samples mean square is, therefore, obtained by difference. If the null hypothesis of equal means is true, the expected value of the ratio of the two mean squares will be $F = 1$. The calculated value of $F = 10.91$ with $V_1 = 2$ and $V_2 = 384$ degrees of freedom may be assessed for significance by referring it to Table 12.3. For $V_1 = 2$ and $V_2 = \infty$, F must exceed 4.60 to be significant at the 1 % level. The calculated value $F = 10.91$ is therefore significant and it may be concluded that differences in means do exist between age groups.

After finding a significant value of F, one is justified in comparing pairs of means for significance using the test for two independent sample means given previously. If the number of samples is large, then so is the number of pairs of means that can be tested, and this leads to some of the comparisons being significant just by chance, as explained in the section on paired comparisons. *Multiple comparison tests* have been developed to overcome this and a good summary of them is given in the book by Snedecor and Cochran.[5]

The analysis of variance described above was concerned with data classified in one way only, i.e. by age. Often, data appear in a two-way table, e.g. age by sex, or in multi-way tables. The technique of analysis of variance may be applied to such data to highlight the effects of the various classifications and the interaction between them. A full treatment of this is beyond the scope of this chapter and the reader is referred to chapters 10, 11, 12, and 16 of Snedecor and Cochran,[5] the latter chapter giving an account of analysis of variance as applied to percentage data. A related technique to analysis of variance is the *analysis of covariance*. It enables comparisons between classifications to be made using analysis of variance when the effect of an unwanted classification has been eliminated. Details of how to use this technique may be obtained from chapter 14 of Snedecor and Cochran.[5]

Some general points on significance testing

Significance tests on small samples

When the data collected are based on small samples, many of the significance tests given in this chapter need modifying or replacing by special alternative tests. As a rough rule it is recommended that, if the sample size is $n = 50$ or larger, the tests given may be all applied without serious error. On this point, it is worth mentioning that the first two tests given for measured data are often referred to as 'the t-test for two independent sample means' and 'the paired t-

test for two matched sample means'. This is because the significance test criteria Z, in both cases, will follow a statistical distribution known as the t distribution. This distribution which is applicable for small samples becomes more and more like the shape of the normal distribution as the sample size increases. The convergence may be illustrated by considering the number of standard errors difference that are needed between two means to achieve a 5% significance level. In the case of large samples, where the normal distribution is appropriate, the value is 1.96. For small samples leading to the t distribution, a value of 2.04 is required for $n = 30$ and 2.00 for $n = 60$. This shows that the normal distribution may be used for samples of $n = 50$ or more in such significance tests.

Interpretation of significant results

The fact that a survey result is found, by carrying out a statistical significance test, to be significant often leads to confusion when such a result is presented to people unfamiliar with research methodology. The layman, when told that something is significant, often assumes that the researcher considers the result to be 'important'. As explained in this chapter, such an inference is not necessarily true. In statistical terms, if, for example, a difference between two percentages is declared significant, it simply means that this difference, no matter whether it is a *large* or *small* difference, cannot be explained by sampling errors. With very large samples, where the sampling distributions of the null and alternative hypotheses will have small standard errors, small differences in percentages will be significant. Whether these small differences are important to the researcher and his client depends on the subject matter of the survey, previous survey results and any number of other practical considerations. The example that follows gives some idea in one particular case how small differences in percentages may be viewed. A random sample of 1000 housewives owning washing machine brand A is found to contain 48% who claim to be 'very pleased' with the machine. A further random sample of 1000, who own brand B, contains 56% who are 'very pleased'. The difference in percentages $56\% - 48\% = 8\%$ is comparatively small and might be regarded as unimportant, even though it is a statistically significant difference. However, if it is known from previous surveys with samples of 1000 that differences between brands of washing machine are always insignificant, then the observed difference may be thought of as being an important finding.

This chapter has been presented in terms of simple random sampling. Most surveys use more complicated sampling methods where the standard errors are usually larger than the standard error formulae given here. The amount by which they are larger is known as the *design factor*. In those cases above where a standard error has been given, this standard error should be increased by the design factor of the survey being analysed, when carrying out a significance test (see chapter 4).

On this point about simple random sampling it is difficult to give much advice to users of quota samples. Strictly speaking, it is not possible to calculate sampling errors and, therefore, carry out significance tests on data from quota samples. In practice, researchers quite often assume that the data are as if they had come from a random sample and proceed to carry out significance tests as described above. The limited research that has been done in quota sampling methods indicates that, in some cases, the sampling errors may be higher than for random sampling. For this reason, some researchers increase the standard error by an arbitrary factor such as 1.5 or 2.0 when carrying out significance tests on quota sample data.

Appendix A

The chances are 95 in 100 that the percentage being estimated by the survey lies within a range equal to the observed percentage plus or minus the number of percentage points shown in the table.

Sampling errors on percentage in survey reports:

| | Sample size | | | | | | |
| | 100 | 250 | 500 | 750 | 1000 | 1500 | 2000 |
Observed percentage	± %	± %	± %	± %	± %	± %	± %
50	9.8	6.2	4.4	3.6	3.1	2.5	2.2
40 or 60	9.6	6.1	4.2	3.5	3.0	2.5	2.1
30 or 70	9.0	5.7	4.0	3.3	2.7	2.3	2.0
20 or 80	7.8	5.0	3.5	2.9	2.5	2.0	1.8
10 or 90	5.9	3.7	2.6	2.2	1.9	1.5	1.3

The usual formula for sampling errors of simple random sampling given below, was used in the calculations.

$$\pm 1.96 \sqrt{\frac{P(100 - P)}{n}} \quad \text{where} \quad \begin{array}{l} P = \text{the observed percentage} \\ n = \text{the sample sice} \end{array}$$

Appendix B

Significant differences between survey percentages

The following five tables may be used to decide whether observed differences between two survey percentages are statistically significant at the 5% level.

How to use the tables

To compare two percentages $p_1 \%$ and $p_2 \%$ based on sample sizes of n_1 and n_2 respectively, where n_1 is the smaller sample size:

(a) if the two sample sizes are approximately equal, calculate the average of $p_1 \%$ and $p_2 \%$

$$p\% = \frac{p_1\% + p_2\%}{2}$$

if the two sample sizes are very different calculate

$$p\% = \frac{n_1 p_1\% + n_2 p_2\%}{n_1 + n_2}$$

(b) look up the table corresponding to $p\%$ (the table closest to $p\%$);
(c) find the cell of the table corresponding to n_1 and n_2, approximately;
(d) the observed difference between the two percentages $p_1 \%$ and $p_2 \%$ must be equal to or greater than the value given in this cell to be significant at the 5% level.

Example. Is a value of $p_1 = 46\%$ based on a sample of $n_1 = 500$ significantly different from a value $p_2 \% = 54\%$ based on a sample of $n_2 = 500$?

As the sample sizes are equal, $p\% = (54\% + 46\%)/2 = 50\%$.

The first table corresponding to $p = 50\%$ shows that for $n_1 = n_2 = 500$ the observed difference must be 6.2% or greater to be significant.

The observed difference of $54 - 46\% = 8\%$ is thus significant.

Differences needed between two percentages around 50% to be significant at the 5% level:

$$p = 50\%$$

Sample size n_2	Sample size n_1						
	100 %	250 %	500 %	750 %	1000 %	1500 %	2000 %
100	13.8						
250	11.6	8.8					
500	10.7	7.6	6.2				
750	10.4	7.2	5.7	5.1			
1000	10.3	6.9	5.4	4.7	4.4		
1500	10.1	6.7	5.1	4.4	4.0	3.6	
2000	10.0	6.6	4.9	4.2	3.8	3.4	3.1

Differences needed between two percentages around 40 or 60% to be significant at the 5% level:

$$p = 40 \text{ or } 60\%$$

Sample size n_2	Sample size n_1						
	100 %	250 %	500 %	750 %	1000 %	1500 %	2000 %
100	13.6						
250	11.4	8.6					
500	10.5	7.4	6.1				
750	10.2	7.0	5.5	5.0			
1000	10.1	6.8	5.2	4.6	4.3		
1500	9.9	6.6	5.0	4.3	3.9	3.5	
2000	9.8	6.4	4.8	4.1	3.7	3.3	3.0

Differences needed between two percentages around 30 or 70% to be significant at the 5% level:

$$p = 30 \text{ or } 70\%$$

Sample size n_2	Sample size n_1						
	100 %	250 %	500 %	750 %	1000 %	1500 %	2000 %
100	12.7						
250	10.6	8.0					
500	9.8	7.0	5.7				
750	9.6	6.6	5.2	4.6			
1000	9.4	6.3	4.9	4.3	4.0		
1500	9.3	6.1	4.6	4.0	3.7	3.3	
2000	9.2	6.0	4.5	3.8	3.5	3.1	2.8

Differences needed between two percentages around 20 or 80% to be significant at the 5% level:

$$p = 20 \text{ or } 80\%$$

Sample size n_2	Sample size n_1						
	100 %	250 %	500 %	750 %	1000 %	1500 %	2000 %
100	11.1						
250	9.3	7.0					
500	8.6	6.1	5.0				
750	8.3	5.7	4.5	4.1			
1000	8.2	5.6	4.3	3.8	3.5		
1500	8.1	5.3	4.1	3.5	3.2	2.9	
2000	8.0	5.3	3.9	3.4	3.0	2.7	2.5

Differences needed between two percentages around 10 or 90% to be significant at the 5% level:

$$p = 10 \text{ or } 90\%$$

Sample size n_2	Sample size n_1						
	100 %	250 %	500 %	750 %	1000 %	1500 %	2000 %
100	8.3						
250	7.0	5.3					
500	6.4	4.5	3.7				
750	6.3	4.3	3.4	3.0			
1000	6.2	4.2	3.2	2.8	2.6		
1500	6.1	4.0	3.0	2.6	2.4	2.2	
2000	6.0	3.9	2.9	2.5	2.3	2.0	1.9

Chapter 13

Multivariate analysis of market research data

C. HOLMES

Marketing is a complex process. It involves the evaluation of many different variables and the ways in which they interrelate in the marketing 'mix'. In order to try and make sense of a mass of data measured on a sample drawn from a population, more and more reliance is being placed on the use of a variety of statistical techniques. Some of these techniques, such as correlation analysis, are relatively well established; others, such as canonical analysis and cluster analysis, are not so well known, and their potentialities in terms of their problem solving abilities are only just being realized.

Statistical techniques which simultaneously examine the relationships between many variables are known as 'multivariate statistical procedures'. A major contributing factor to the upsurge of interest in this area has largely been due to advancements made in computer technology.

Most multivariate techniques require an immense number of calculations which, whilst not beyond the resources of clerks and adding machines, are more quickly and economically carried out by computer.

It is not my intention in this chapter to dwell at large on the theoretical properties underlying the basis of the varying types of multivariate procedures. The inclusion of statistical and mathematical formulae will be kept to a minimum. References to the appropriate literature will be quoted for the interested reader to pursue at his leisure. The main aim is to present a somewhat simplified overview of a rather complex subject matter in as nonmathematical a manner as possible.

It is useful to consider some of the typical practical problems with which multivariate analysis is concerned. Some may be well known and well documented, others may be of a specialist nature; all are pertinent to the field of market research:

(a) In a survey of television viewing a 'dependent' variable, quantity of viewing, is measured. A hypothesis is formed that this may be predicted by such variables as age, education, readership, etc. *Regression analysis* would assist in the construction of a model to fit the data. Variations in the parameters of the model would enable changes in viewing to be predicted.

(b) In an attitudinal survey about various companies and their products, it is of interest to examine the relationships not only between correlations within the battery of 'company' rating scales and within the battery of 'product' rating scales, but also the relationships between the two data matrices. *Canonical analysis* could provide an insight into the way the two sets of data are interrelated.

(c) Results are available relating salesmen's performances over various activities together with training observations and results. It is required to produce, from these data, criteria to evaluate whether salesmen may be classified into specific groups. The use of *discriminant analysis* will assist in this problem as it attempts to maximize the probability of correct assignment to groups.

(d) From the results of repertory grids a large battery of semantic attitudinal scales is drawn up and administered to a sample of the population of, say, 'cake-mix' users. Straightforward correlation analysis is applied to the results but the matrix of correlation coefficients is too large to facilitate an 'understanding' of the data. The researcher seeks to find a certain kind of organization in the data to identify fundamental and meaningful dimensions in the interrelationships. *Principal components* and *factor analysis* might be used to explore the underlying dimensionality of the data.

(e) A list of a hundred towns (qualifying on certain issues) is drawn up as potentials for test marketing operations. Statistics relating to population, retail sales, readership, etc., are collected. A limited number of towns are required to be representative of national characteristics. In what way can they be chosen? The application of some form of *numerical taxonomy* (*cluster analysis*) might reveal distinct homogeneous subgroups of towns. The selection of one town from each group would ensure that each stratum is represented in the overall test-marketing mix.

These, then, are just a few examples of marketing problems where the use of multivariate analysis may assist in finding the answers. It must be stressed, however, that the techniques of multivariate analysis are not able to solve problems by themselves. It is not good enough to have masses and masses of doubtful data, consult a textbook for an appropriate technique and feed the lot into a computer. You may be lucky enough to get an answer that 'makes sense', but if the original data are not the 'right' kind of data then you will not get the 'right' kind of answer. In fact, the use of multivariate analysis makes it all the more imperative to consider the hypothesis-making and question-forming stages of the research. To quote Collins:[1] 'Multivariate analysis systems make ever-increasing demands upon the question designer, the question poser and the question answerer. Questionnaires become not only lengthy but extremely monotonous. With so many analysis techniques based upon the search for non-random patterning of responses, boredom is clearly a major problem.'

It is not within the scope of this chapter to dwell at large on issues like these but, nevertheless, they are important and should not be overlooked.

Dependence or interdependence

So to the actual subject itself. What is multivariate analysis? It is broadly concerned with the *relationships* between sets of dependent variables.

Kendall[2] in a very clear exposition of the subject discerns two main branches of the multivariate tree, and subdivides multivariate analysis into whether we are concerned with dependence or interdependence.

Dependence

In this type of problem we are concerned with the way in which one or more dependent variables, often chosen by us or dicated to us by the problem, *depends* on the other (independent) variables. The simplest example of 'dependence' analysis is the regression of one variable on others often in the form:

$$y = a + b_1 x_1 + b_2 x_2 + \cdots + b_n x_n$$

An often quoted example of a multiple linear regression is the prediction of university degree results from the so-called independent variables (number of 'O'-levels, 'A'-level passes and so on). The phrase, 'so-called independent variables' is a choice one, since they are often genuinely correlated or they are fortuitously correlated in the data sample.

Interdependence

The second branch is that of interdependence: here we are not concerned with any dependent variables, but only with the relationship of a set of variables amongst themselves. No variable is selected to be of special interest. Correlation analysis is a clear example of this part of the subject.

Correlation analysis

Since multivariate analysis is concerned with the interrelationships between variables, the starting points of most analyses begin with the way in which the

VARIATES (Responses)

	x_1	x_2	x_3	$\cdots$	x_i	$\cdots$	x_p
1	x_{11}	x_{21}	x_{31}	$\cdots$	5	$\cdots$	x_{p1}
2	x_{12}	x_{22}	x_{32}	$\cdots$	4	$\cdots$	x_{p2}
3	x_{13}	x_{23}	x_{33}		6		
4	x_{14}	x_{24}	x_{34}		7		
5	x_{15}	x_{25}	x_{35}		2		
n	n_{1n}	x_{2n}	x_{3n}	$\cdots$	3	$\cdots$	x_{pn}

OBSERVATIONS (Respondents)

Fig. 13.1. *Data Matrix:* Generally x_{ij} stands for the jth observation on the ith variable. Thus, the column headed x_i could refer to a rating scale and, as an example, hypothetical ratings are illustrated for respondents.

variables correlate (or co-vary) with each other. A useful way of considering the various manipulations that can be carried out on data is to visualize the end results of a survey in the form of a data matrix (Fig. 13.1).

Whatever the subject matter of the research we can visualize it in this row-by-column tabulation. It is convenient at this stage to look upon the columns as variables and the rows as respondents. By considering each pair of columns separately we can see how each pair of variables correlates.

The most widely used measure of correlation is the Pearson 'product moment coefficient of correlation'. It is a coefficient ranging from -1, through zero, to $+1$ and is a measure of the degree of *linear* association between two

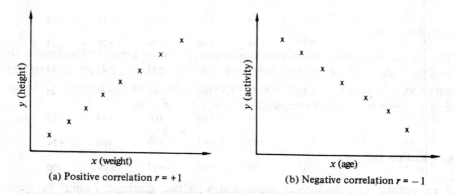

(a) Positive correlation $r = +1$ (b) Negative correlation $r = -1$

Fig. 13.2. Examples of scatter diagrams.

variables. We can illustrate varying degrees of correlation by means of a simple scatter diagram (Fig. 13.2). Positive correlation (Fig. 13.2(a)) means that increasing values of variable *y* are associated with increasing values of variable *x* and vice versa. Negative correlation (Fig. 13.2(b)) indicates that increasing values of *x* are associated with decreasing values of *y*. Zero correlation implies that there is no linear association between the two variables (although there could, of course, be a non-linear relationship). Essentially, Pearson's correlation coefficient, *r*, between two variables *x* and *y* is:

$$r = \frac{\text{covariance}(x \cdot y)}{\sqrt{[\text{variance}(x)][\text{variance}(y)]}}$$

where covariance $(x \cdot y) = \frac{1}{n}\Sigma(x - \bar{x})(y - \bar{y})$

and the variances are as defined in chapter 12.

From the data matrix we can calculate the respective correlation coefficients for each pair of variables across all sample members. The resultant correlation matrix (Fig. 13.3) is a useful starter in seeking relationships between variables. A.S.C. Ehrenberg[3] in a robust attack on factor analysts considers that in many cases the 'look at it' approach is equal to the so-called more 'sophisticated' types of analyses. However, it is increasingly difficult to sort out relationships since as the number of variables grows, the number of correlation coefficients increases rapidly. (For *n* variables, there are $n(c)2 = n(n-1)/2$ correlation coefficients.)

If variables are highly correlated, it does not follow that the existence of causation is proved. However, if the hypothesis of causation is postulated and

		1	2	3	4	5	6	7	8
	1	100	+31	−50	00	−35	−70	+40	−87
	2	+31	100	+37	−56	+21	+17	+10	−25
	3	−50	+37	100	+34	+40	−70	+25	−37
VARIABLES	4	00	−56	+34	100	−35	+45	+27	−55
	5	−35	+21	+40	−35	100	+05	−97	−43
	6	−70	+17	−70	+45	+05	100	+19	−17
	7	+40	+10	+25	+27	−97	+19	100	+24
	8	−87	−25	−37	−55	−43	−17	+24	100

Fig. 13.3. Example of a correlation matrix (the decimal point has been omitted for the sake of clarity). The 1's in the leading diagonal are conventional.

a zero or non-significant correlation coefficient is obtained, then the hypothesis may be rejected with a given probability level. Correlation analysis may disprove causation but it can never entirely prove it. Statistical tests may be applied to the resultant correlation coefficients to assist in deciding whether or not the variables show *significant* correlation as opposed to purely random (chance) correlation. In general we may test whether:

(a) the correlation coefficient is significantly greater than zero;
(b) the difference between the same correlation coefficient computed from different samples is significant.

In addition to Pearson's product moment correlation coefficient there are a number of 'non-parametric' measures, such as Spearman's rank and Kendall's tau which are often used on data which are not distributed normally, or where the measurement level achieved is only up to an 'ordinal' scale. For details of these and other coefficients the reader is advised to consult Siegel.[4]

Principal components analysis (PCA)

In the statistical analysis of relationships between variables it is often important that the variables are uncorrelated (orthogonal) with one another. This is particularly true in multiple regression techniques and in the interpretation of factors in factor analysis. The method of principal components analysis is a technique for obtaining new 'artificial' variables which are uncorrelated with one another. It is, therefore, a useful mathematical device as well as being central to the generally accepted method of carrying out factor analysis. Both Kendall[2] and Hope[5] describe the technique mathematically and it is only intended here to describe the mechanics of principal components analysis briefly.

Algebraic visualization.   If one considers the diagonal terms of the covariance matrix (or the standardized correlation matrix with '1's' in the leading diagonal) then the sum of the diagonal terms represents the total variance of the data sample. This total variance can be split up into N latent roots each of which has an eigenvector associated with it. The eigenvectors generate a set of principal components each of which has a variance associated with it equal to its latent root.

Geometric visualization.   Another way of visualizing principal components is to consider the data sample plotted in N-dimensional space. We may, for example, plot measurements made on three variables, say height, weight, and breadth as in Fig. 13.4. The first principal component is directed along the main long axis of the cigar-shaped cluster. Having extracted this component,

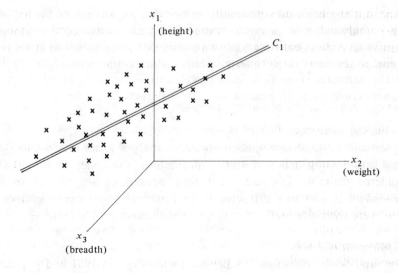

Fig. 13.4. Geometric visualization of the first principal component.

then the second principal component is along the next longest axial direction of the cluster, orthogonal to the first, and so on.

The main attraction of principal components analysis is that the components are extracted in descending order of the amount of total variance each one accounts for. There are as many components as there are original variables and the sum of the variances of all the principal components equals the sum of the variances of the original variables. In very simple terms, we may think of the principal components as weighted combinations of all the original variables. If we start with three variables, X_1, X_2, and X_3, then the three principal components, C_1, C_2, C_3 are given by

$$C_1 = W_{11}X_1 + W_{12}X_2 + W_{13}X_3$$

$$C_2 = W_{21}X_1 + W_{22}X_2 + W_{23}X_3$$

$$C_3 = W_{31}X_1 + W_{32}X_2 + W_{33}X_3$$

where W is a numerical weight determined by the analysis; (they are also termed the 'loadings' of the variables on the components). In practical terms, it is usually found that the first few components account for a large proportion (often in the range 70 to 90%) of the total variance. In certain circumstances the researcher ignores the remaining components in any further analyses and, thus, achieves a significant gain in data reduction.

Since each component is a weighted combination of the original variables, it is possible to calculate for each person (or object) in the sample a score on each component. Thus, not only does principal components analysis enable us to find out the basic dimensionality of our data, it allows the facilitation of further analyses to be made on scores which are measured on orthogonal dimensions. A practical drawback with principal components analysis is that the components are rarely interpretable in a marketing sense.

Examples of principal components analysis

Test market locations
Christopher[6] utilized principal components analysis in an attempt to classify towns into homogeneous clusters. Information was collected for 30 towns considered suitable for test marketing operations. A set of mutually independent factors was extracted using principal components analysis and towns were then clustered according to their scores on the factors.

Classification of towns
Moser and Scott[7] classified 164 British towns which in 1951 had populations of 50 000 or over. Four principal components were found to account for 60% of the total variance. The first component itself accounted for 30% of the variance and reflected social class differentiation.

Stratification of local authority areas
Holmes[8] similarly carried out experimental work relating to local authority areas in Yorkshire and Humberside. One hundred and forty local authority areas were analysed over seven variables using principal components analysis. Three independent components were found to account for over 70% of the total variance. This exercise was an attempt at optimal stratification for use in the selection of primary sampling units.

Factor analysis

A concise history of the development of factor analysis may be found in Harman.[9] Factor analysis embraces a set of statistical techniques which seek to analyse the intercorrelations within a set of variables. Developed originally by psychologists – amongst the early pioneers were such distinguished theorists as Spearman, Burt, Kelley, Thurstone, Holzinger and Thomson – factor analysis has gone through a controversial and turbulent history. To quote Cooley and Lohnes,[10] 'Each pioneer seemed .to feel his procedure was *the* method of factor analysis. Only recently have students of factor analysis begun to see that the different procedures are suitable for different purposes and usually involve different assumptions regarding the nature of human attributes.'

Factor analysis model

Factor analysis is different from principal components analysis (although the latter is often a prerequisite to the former) in that the factor analysis model attempts to describe the data in terms of a model with a number of new variables called 'factors', *less* in number than the original variables. The simplest formulation of the model is that the total variance in the data can be split into two parts, that due to the common factors and that due to residual factors, thus:

$$\text{total variance } (V) = \text{var.(factors)} + \text{residual variance}$$

In contrast to the principal components analysis model, the factor analysis model for three variables and two factors may be written mathematically as

$$X_1 = W_{11}F_1 + W_{12}F_2 + d_1R_1$$
$$X_2 = W_{21}F_1 + W_{22}F_2 \qquad + d_2R_2$$
$$X_3 = W_{31}F_1 + W_{32}F_2 \qquad\qquad + d_3R_3$$

where X_1, X_2, X_3 are the original variables; F_1, F_2, are the common factors, R_1, R_2, R_3 are the residual (sometimes known as the unique) factors. The coefficients W and d are frequently referred to as the loadings. Explained in words, the factor analysis model assumes that each variable may be represented as a linear sum of a number of orthogonal factors, usually less in number than the number of original variables, plus a specific residual factor unique to that variable. In other words, a hypothesis is formed that the total variance of a variable is made up of:

(a) a proportion of variance which the variable shares (or has in common) with other variables;
(b) an amount of residual (unique) variance which is uncorrelated with other variables.

Communality

The proportion of variance that is common to other variables is known as the *communality* of the original variables and is calculated as the sum of the squares of the coefficients (loadings) associated with the m common factors. This estimate of communality, strictly speaking, requires to be inserted in the leading diagonal of the correlation matrix but this cannot be achieved until the factor solution is obtained. This seemingly circular problem is resolved by estimating the communalities, carrying out a trial factor solution, readjusting the communality estimates and so on. The most widely used method of estimating communalities is the utilization of the squared multiple correlation between the variable and the remaining $(n-1)$ variables. It is worth noting that the problem of communalities is only acute in the case of small data matrices. In practice, it has been found that the larger the order of the correlation matrix the less it matters what values appear in the leading diagonal.

The most common methods of obtaining factor solutions are the 'principal factor solution' and the 'maximum likelihood solution'. Neither method will be explained here and the interested are directed to Cooley and Lohnes[10] for the former and Lawley and Maxwell[11] for details of the latter. The principal factor solution, based as it is on principal components analysis, has the important property that it produces factors in order of the amount of variance they explain. The maximum likelihood solution is probably more efficient and does not require any estimation of communalities although the number of factors required has to be stipulated in advance.

How many factors?

The problem of how many factors to extract has plagued factor analysts for many years but with advanced computer technology it is less of a problem today. There are, basically, two criteria for deciding on how many factors to retain:

(a) statistical;
(b) marketing meaningfulness.

Amongst the statistical criteria is the widely adopted Kaiser's[12] rule of retaining factors whose latent roots are greater than one. However, statistical considerations alone are not entirely satisfactory and in most market research studies the meaning and interpretability of the retained factors plays an important part in the decision process. A factor contributing only a small portion of variance may not be statistically important but it may prove a good discriminator for, say, degree of purchase.

Rotation

We now touch upon what perhaps has caused most controversy in the history of factor analysis, rotation of the factors. The rotation problem arises because of the indeterminancy of factor solutions. It is a mathematical fact that, given a set of correlations between variables, the estimating of the factor equations is fundamentally undeterminate; that is to say that the loading of the variables in the estimating equations may be chosen in an infinite number of ways, consistent with the observed correlations. Over the years, therefore, certain criteria have been established to limit the factor analysis solutions. The accepted criteria in the determination of new reference axes are Thurstone's[13] properties of 'simple structure'. The aim in rotating axes is to enable the factors to be more meaningfully interpretable. Amongst the many proposed solutions, two have stood the test of time, namely Varimax and/or Promax. The Varimax rotation still requires the restriction that the axes are orthogonal (uncorrelated) to one another. Promax, developed by Hendrickson and White[14] is an acceptable extension of Varimax such that the axes are allowed to become non-orthogonal or oblique (correlated). Over several studies, the writer finds that Promax usually gives the same factor structure but is slightly more interpretable. When the factor solution is oblique, knowledge of the degree with which the factors correlate with one another is required. A disadvantage of an oblique solution is that further analysis (such as cluster analysis) may prove to be more difficult to handle. Interpretability is gained at the expense of statistical simplicity.

Factor scores

A 'factor score' may be estimated for each respondent for each factor. These may be averaged for any sub-group in much the same way as ordinary rating scales. Thus, a typical factor analysis may involve 80 rating scales which produce some 10 to 12 dimensions (factors). On each factor we can estimate scores for rated products, brands, services, etc., which together with breakdowns by purchasing behaviour, age, social grade, etc., can provide useful marketing information. Charting methods such as simple 'profile charts' and two and three dimensional maps assist in the interpretation stage. Hill[15] gives clear examples of single and two-dimensional charts whilst Hope[5] devotes a chapter to 'spherical maps'.

Example of factor analysis

Frost[16] gives a clear example of factor analysis applied to seven-point rating scales. 750 television viewers rated 58 statements on two programs they had watched. In total, 61 programs were rated in this way, rotated randomly between the respondents, and the resultant factor analysis gave the following nine factors:

(a) general evaluation;
(b) information;
(c) romance;
(d) violence;
(e) conventionality;
(f) scale of production;
(g) noise/activity;
(h) acceptability;
(i) humour.

As Frost points out, 'It should be noted that, whilst names have been attached to these factors, this has been done simply for ease of reference and that the proper interpretation of a factor is to be found amongst the individual attitude scales which have substantial loadings upon it. Thus, for example, Factor 2 called "information" in fact describes a dimension of viewer differentiation which has at one end programs which tend to have much scientific interest, which make the viewer think and which convey educational information and which has at the other end programs which contain little scientific interest which encourage the viewer to relax being of a less informative and generally more entertaining type.'

Frost utilized these nine dimensions to compute program attitude ratings covered in the survey. An example in the paper illustrates that programs like 'Man Alive' and 'The Power Game' score highly on the 'information' factor whilst 'Juke Box Jury', 'Black & White Minstrels' and 'The Monkees' are to be found, not surprisingly, at the 'little scientific interest' end. 'These typical results', Frost concluded, 'confirm our original interpretation of this factor as being a dimension which differentiated between educational programs and entertainment programs.'

Numerical taxonomy

Cluster analysis

An integral part of the analysis of market research surveys is that of *classification*. Traditionally, analysis has been of the uni- or bi-variate kind : i.e., analysis by age, social grade, products bought, etc., and by combination of suchlike variables. Since data are collected for many variables, it seems logical that we should attempt to classify our repondents over many variables. The analytical procedures designed for this purpose of simultaneously assessing respondents over many variables may be subsumed under the heading of 'numerical taxonomy', the principles of which are clearly set out by Sokal and Sneath.[17] The term 'cluster analysis' strictly refers to part of the taxonomic procedure but has come into general usage to mean classification usually in a market segmentation context. Numerical taxonomy has as its objective the classification usually of persons, but not necessarily always so, such that persons within a cluster or group are more alike each other with respect to the measured variables than persons outside the cluster. If defined clusters exist then they may be described in terms of their 'profiles' and utilized as breakdowns in similar fashion to the traditional classification systems such as age within social grade.

Mechanics of numerical taxonomy

Figure 13.5 illustrates the steps required in the taxonomic process. Neither

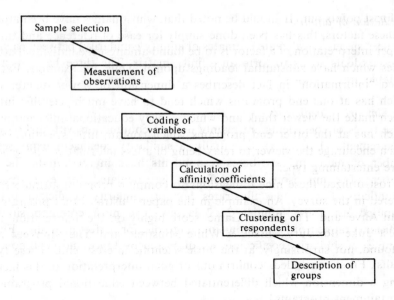

Fig. 13.5. Flowchart describing the steps involved in numerical taxonomy as applied to market research.

'sample selection' nor 'measurement' will be dealt with here since they are topics common to all types of multivariate analysis and, in any case, are dealt with elsewhere. Before proceeding to discuss the remaining steps it is worthwhile to reconsider the data matrix (Fig. 13.1) and the possible ways of analysing it. Traditional methods of analysis have always been based on the relationships *between the variables across the respondents*. Analysis of this kind leads to a clustering of variables and is known as 'R-technique'. However, there is another way of looking at the data matrix, and that is to look at the relationships *between respondents across the variables*, known as 'Q-technique'.[18]

Coding of characters

Once the information required has been measured on a sample of respondents, a coding operation is required before it is possible to calculate measures of affinity. Basically, there are three kinds of measurement:

(a) dichotomous characters (1:0 data);
(b) multi-state characters, of a *quantitative* nature;
(c) multi-state characters, of a *qualitative* nature.

The latter type of measurement presents the greatest problems and Sokal and Sneath[17] comment on the potential dangers involved in the coding process.

Calculation of affinities

The next step is to calculate estimates of affinity (similarity) between each pair of respondents so as to form an affinity matrix. The three basic measures available are:

(a) *Similarity coefficients*

These types of coefficients are mainly used in conjunction with dichotomous measurements (1:0) data). Essentially, a similarity coefficient expresses the number of 'matching' attributes respondents have in relation to the total number of comparisons. A coefficient is calculated for every pair of respondents. Figure 13.6 illustrates how a similarity coefficient may be computed using the familiar 2×2 layout. The most common similarity coefficients range from zero (non-similar) to one for perfect matching. Further examples of similarity coefficients are discussed by Joyce and Channon.[18]

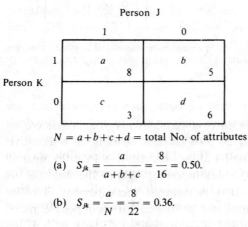

$$N = a+b+c+d = \text{total No. of attributes}$$

$$\text{(a)} \quad S_{jk} = \frac{a}{a+b+c} = \frac{8}{16} = 0.50.$$

$$\text{(b)} \quad S_{jk} = \frac{a}{N} = \frac{8}{22} = 0.36.$$

Fig. 13.6. Example of the calculation of two different similarity coefficients. The interpretation of the 2×2 table is as follows: code 1 for possession of an attribute: 0 for non-possession. Thus, comparing person J to person K in the numerical example – they each match on possessing eight attributes, person K possesses five attributes which person J does not, person J possesses three attributes which person K does not and neither person possesses six similar attributes.

(b) *Distance coefficients*

Measures of distance are based on a geometric model, and in special cases are related to similarity coefficients. The most common distance measurement is:

$$d_{jk} = \left[\frac{\Sigma(x_{ij} - x_{ik})^2}{N} \right]^{\frac{1}{2}}$$

x_{ij} is person j.s score on the ith variable and x_{ik} is person k's score on the ith variable, and $N =$ No. of variables.

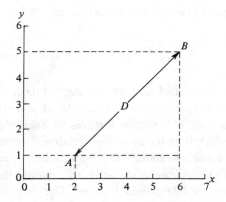

Fig. 13.7. Illustration of the calculation of a distance coefficient in two-dimensional space.

Figure 13.7 gives a simple two-dimensional illustration of the 'distance' concept. If the respondents are identical as regard to the measured characteristics then the distance between them and, consequently, the coefficient will be zero. The greater the disparity between two persons, the larger will be the distance measurement; thus, distance is complementary to similarity.

(c) *Correlation coefficient*
Just as a correlation coefficient between two variables may be calculated, so can a coefficient of correlation between two persons. This is an alternative method to the distance coefficient for handling quantitative data. Inglis and Johnson[19] in a studied paper on the developments in and the analyses of multivariate survey data consider that a distance measurement is often preferable since, conceptually, it measures distances between people more powerfully.

Cluster analysis

Having computed some form of affinity coefficient, the next step is to group together those respondents who are most similar to each other. In a paper read to an MRS course on 'segmentation analysis', Emmett[20] reviewed the new methods of 'clustering' and 'clumping'. Essentially, 'clustering' involves the formation of trial sets of clusters which are continually modified by successive iterations. The 'clumping' methods require the establishment of basic 'clumps', e.g. the two 'nearest' points, which are added to by the addition of nearest neighbours.

A review of common clustering packages/programs is provided by Punj and Stewart[21] and the authors also provide empirical comparisons of the performance of the clustering algorithms. Most clustering programs result in assigning respondents to *mutually exclusive* clusters. For an introduction to the concept of *overlapping* clusters the reader is referred to Van Ryzin[22] and Arabie et al.[23]

Naming the groups

Once the researcher is satisfied with the cluster solution the resultant groups can be tested for homogeneity using a variety of statistical tests including Holzingers B coefficient. The salient features of each cluster require to be summarized and described in terms of the variables/attributes involved in the analysis. As in factor analysis names may be attached to each cluster for ease of reference but, again, care is required to ensure that any 'shorthand' descriptions used are not later misinterpreted. The charting of simple 'profile charts' is a useful summarising aid.

Examples of numerical taxonomy

Political Party – Scientific Control Systems Limited

Morgan and Purnell[24] report on a cluster analysis using factor scores derived from a battery of attitudinal scales relating to electors' attitudes to political issues. Four factors were obtained and factor scores were estimated for each of 500 electors. A ten-cluster solution was considered to be the most appropriate. Each cluster was 'subjectively' named as follows:

Cluster No.	Name	Sample size
1	High Tory	45
2	Me first	34
3	Whig	36
4	Labour (little England)	70
5	Meritocrat	46
6	Me first (anti-Europe)	57
7	'One nation' Tories	44
8	Left-wing Labour	42
9	Meritocrat (pro-Europe)	43
10	Right-wing Labour	83

One of the aims of this case study was to see whether or not a 'new' political party could be discovered – a position analogous to seeking a new product. A program NEMO seeks to describe the existing products in a market in an *n*-dimensional product attribute space. The object of the analysis is to look for a point in the space which defines a new product which is as different as possible from existing ones.

Subjective clustering of television program similarities

Several papers in the Journal of the Market Research Society[25] concerned clustering procedures of television programs. An interesting paper by Green et al.[26] described the methodology and application of subjective clustering of television programs. Briefly, this procedure entails respondents sorting into groups various stimuli (television programs). One of the analyses reported is that of respondent configuration. For each pair of respondents a distance measure was computed, based on the degree of agreement in the pair's clustering of programs. The resultant distance matrix was submitted to a multi-dimensional scaling program. Whilst the authors report little relationship between the subjective clusters and other certain predictor variables such as demographic and socio-economic variables, the technique is mentioned here as being of particular interest in the area of defining markets and sub-groups in markets.

Multiple regression analysis

Multiple regression analysis is a technique for estimating the relationship between one 'dependent' variable and a number of so-called 'independent' variables. Since the technique is concerned with relationship — the way in which the variables are associated with one another — it is not unlike correlation analysis. Indeed, in practice both correlation coefficients and regression equations are generally desired in the same problem. The essential difference is that *regression analysis* is concerned with dependence; one (or more) variable is selected for study and we are concerned to find out whether the magnitude of the variable can be *predicted* from knowledge about the independent variables. *Correlation analysis* is concerned with the degree of association between sets of observations.

Simple linear regression

Let us consider the simplest case of regression, i.e. the way in which one variable may be related (and hence predicted) by another. A useful first step in such a problem is to draw a 'scatter diagram' (see Fig. 13.2). A line of 'best fit' through the points may be drawn visually. If there is a high degree of correlation between the variables then for any given value of x (weight) we can predict the likely value of y (height). Mathematically, we may predict y (height) by the equation;

$$y = a + bx$$

where a is the y-axis intercept and b is the slope of the line. The parameters a and b are known as the regression coefficients and they are chosen so as to minimize the sums of squares of the deviations from the regression line. This method is known as the 'least-squares' method. a is estimated by $\bar{y}$ and b is estimated by:

$$b = \frac{\text{covariance } (x \cdot y)}{\text{var } (x)} \left[\text{or } \frac{\Sigma xy}{\Sigma x^2} \text{ when } x \text{ and } y \text{ are standardized} \right]$$

Multiple regression

Multiple regression analysis is merely an extension of the simple case. Again, there is one dependent variable, but a number of 'independent' variables are used to try and explain the variations of the dependent variable. The addition of more independent variables means that the mathematical model can portray more realistically real life situations. It is rare that only one variable influences another. In a complex marketing situation, variation in sales may be associated with many factors, such as amount spent on advertising, distribution levels, national prosperity, etc.

The linear model for multiple regression is:

$$y = a + b_1x_1 + b_2x_2 + \ldots + b_px_p$$

where x is the independent variable and b the rate of change of the dependent variable y in each of the independent variables when the other independent variables are held constant. They are often called the *partial regression coefficients* and their estimation is carried out in similar fashion to the simple linear regression case. The mathematics is more complicated but the principle is unchanged, i.e. the coefficients are chosen so as to minimize the residual sums of squares. Those interested should consult almost any intermediate statistical textbook for details of the theory and Ferber[27] gives practical examples with detailed worksheets for simple cases. As the number of independent variables increases the computational aspect is considerable.

Additionally there are many alternative methods of 'finding' (economically) best fitting regression equations – the most common being the *step-wise* regression method. For a description of this and other methods see Draper and Smith.[28]

Example of multiple regression

Multiple regression is, perhaps, one of the most common statistical techniques used in marketing and yet, unfortunately, few case histories are available in the literature. This is probably because the greatest use of multiple regression is in the sales forecasting area, i.e. given sales data and a set of sales determinants such as economic data, household information, a forecasting model may be set up. The effect of changes in the parameters of such a model may be estimated by regression techniques.

Frank and Boyd[29] studied each of 44 grocery products (the dependent variable) and the way in which the proportion of product purchases related to nine household socio-economic characteristics and five measures of purchasing behaviour (independent variables). They found little association between household socio-economic or total consumption characteristics and *private* brand purchasing. The significant relationships which emerged were the obvious ones, such as households with members that shop in grocery stores with substantial private brand stocks spend a higher percentage of their purchases on private brands.

Canonical analysis

Canonical analysis procedures are designed to measure simultaneously the relationships between several dependent variables and several independent variables, all measured on the same set of persons (or objects). It is, therefore, a further extension of multiple regression, the main difference being that, whereas in multiple regression we have only one dependent variable, in canonical analysis we have more than one. Canonical analysis works in the following way. The variables are split into two sets, a set of criterion (dependent) variables and a set of predictor (independent) variables. Sets of coefficients are calculated such that the correlation between the weighted sum of the criterion variables has the maximum correlation with the weighted sum of the predictor variables. This equation is the first canonical regression equation. It is analogous to a principal component in that it maximizes correlation and thus facilitates prediction. A second canonical regression line is then found orthogonal to the first and yet has maximum correlation between the two (new) equations. There are as many canonical regression equations as there are variables in the smallest set.

Tests of significance may be applied to the resultant canonical correlations and one hopes that the first few will be large and the remainder negligible. Whilst Fornell[30] provides a framework for the application of canonical analysis, the lay reader is referred to Green *et al.*[31] for illustrative applications.

Examples of canonical correlation

Cooley and Lohnes[10] give an example which uses the technique to test general hypotheses that relate two sets of variables. The example is concerned with a set of seven predictor variables which are scores on scales relating to early home environment, e.g. how close was the respondent to mother and father in childhood. The criterion variables are scores relating to the respondents present orientation towards people, e.g. degree of curiosity expressed towards people. Those interested may consult the reference for actual results. A basic conclusion was that early home environment is related to orientation towards people and that the primary antecedent is early experience of social activities.

Multiple discriminant analysis

We are often concerned with the ability to predict a person's response given a set of different measurements about this person. We may wish to predict which car a person will buy from knowledge about his past ownership, his present situation and, say, his attitudes to cars in general. Discriminant analysis and, in general, multiple discriminant analysis is a technique for classifying persons into one group or another given certain information which is correlated with a multichotomous attribute.

In discrimination, the classes are predetermined and we are concerned with allocating a person to one of several classes. In the simplest case, that of two classes, the following example illustrates the technique. Suppose we have two groups of persons, purchasers and non-purchasers, and we have information for each person regarding attitudes, behaviour, socio-economic characteristics, etc. A discriminant function may be calculated by defining a new variable, 'propensity to purchase', as a weighted sum of the attitude, etc., variables. Assume we only have two pieces of attitude information, then we can plot the data as shown in Fig. 13.8. The discriminant function attempts to predict, by considering the weighted score for each person, whether or not he is more likely to be a purchaser or a non-purchaser. The problem is one of drawing the boundary so as to minimize the probability of misclassification.

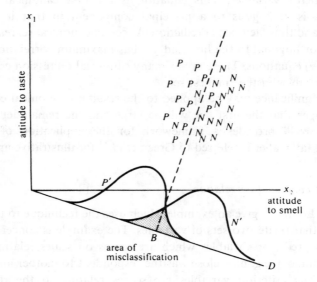

Fig. 13.8. Discrimination analysis: example in two dimensions. Purchasers (*P*) and non-purchasers (*N*) are plotted on two dimensions x_1 and x_2. A discriminant analysis generates a score (*D*), based on the two attitude scores. The problem is one of where to draw the boundary (*B*) so as to minimize the probability of misclassification (shaded area). Predictions may be made for 'new' observations by allocating persons to one or other side of the boundary by considering the score generated by the discriminant function.

Sands and Moore[32] illustrate the use of discriminant analysis as an operational technique to be routinely used in selecting sites for retail stores.

Sequential dichotomization techniques

One of the earliest new classification methods was developed by Belson,[33] who was primarily interested in attempting to find the best combination of independent variables which would predict a 'dependent' variable. The 'Belson sort' procedure examined all alternative dichotomizations of a sample to discover those which were significant predictors and then went on to examine in a sequential fashion the best combinations of independent variables. At each stage in the splitting process, chi-square values are calculated to test the predictive performance of the chosen dichotomies (Fig. 13.9).

Example of Belson sort

A recent example where an amended version of the Belson sort procedure was used is JICNARS Reader Categorisation Study.[34] In this study 15 candidate measures were tested as predictors of differences in reading behaviour. Part of the conclusions involved the qualified recommendation of including a question on 'provenance' in the standard questionnaire since this measure increased the proportion of explained variance.

Automatic interaction detection

This is a technique for dividing a sample into groups on the basis of demographics or other variables, again splitting on one variable at a time. The method arose because the authors, Sonquist and Morgan[35], were concerned with the inadequacy of simple cross-tabulations to reveal the complex interactions in survey data. It is similar to the Belson sort, splitting on one variable at a time except that the criterion for retaining the discriminating variables is based on analysis of variance. The first predictive variable is that which maximizes the between group variance and minimizes the within group variances.

Thompson[36] has succinctly summarized the differences between AID and the 'Belson sort' while Willson,[37] in a paper devoted to the computational segmentation of multivariate statistics, rightly notes that studies involving AID are typically concerned with market segmentation. In a brief note, Sampson[38] indicates how AID may be used as a preliminary to cluster analysis. Those independent variables which account for a high degree of variance on one (or more) criterion variable are chosen as the basis for cluster definition. The writer's own view is that AID will increasingly be utilized in the

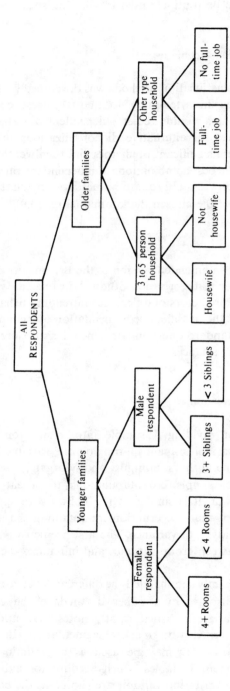

Fig. 13.9. Example of Belson Sort reproduced with permission of Dr.W. A. Belson. Matching and Prediction on the Principle of Biological Classification. The criterion variable in this case is the degree to which individuals participate with others in the home, i.e. joint activity. For simplicity's sake further dichotomization has been excluded in the example.

preliminary skirmishes researchers have when trying to reduce to sensible proportions large masses of data.

Examples of AID

Assael[39] gives two examples of the use of AID when other methods such as regression and cross-classification analysis have failed. The first example illustrates how a sample of respondents with a 'usual purchase' level of Brand X is segmented on these key variables; sex, geographical location, educational level, product usage, age, occupation and income. Surprisingly, product usage emerged only at a third iteration and after the fourth some 5% of the sample had a 62% Brand X purchase compared to the sample average of 16.5%.

A second example illustrates a perceptual market segmentation. A sample of 2000 housewives rated the degree with which a beverage satisfied each of thirteen criteria, ranging from 'good tasting' to 'pure ingredients'. The criterion 'restores energy' was the main predictor of the number of family units consumed in a week. A segment comprising 5% of the sample rating the product high on 'restores energy' 'year round drink' and 'easy to prepare' consumed 70.5 units compared to the sample average of 23.3 units.

Harris[40] in a notable contribution 'Recent Developments in the Multivariate Analysis of Market Research Data' at the 1981 MRS Conference discusses CHAID, a version of AID for use with a classified dependent variable.

Non-metric multi-dimensional scaling (NMDS)

The latest developments in multivariate statistics are concerned with the relative low-level degree of measurements achieved in market research data. Much of the data collected by researchers is of the nominal or ordinal kind (non-metric) and, in the past, analysts have indiscriminately applied the techniques described in this chapter which assume the conditions of metric measurement.

Statistical techniques are now available which require only non-metric data and yet yield results which are of metric scaling. These techniques may be subsumed under the heading of 'non-metric multi-dimensional scaling'. The input to a non-metric MDS is typically a ranking in terms of similarity *of all possible pairs* that can be obtained from a set of objects. The underlying statistical logic is that the consideration of all possible pairings *increases* the amount of information available. For example, 20 numbers describe 10 points in two dimensions whereas there are 45 pairings when considering 10 objects taken two at a time. Willson[37] illustrates this concept with the familiar example of the mapping of 11 cities by considering the 55 inter-city distances. A two-dimensional solution is obtained which adequately represents the original rankings. An examination of the derived co-ordinates is sufficient for the dimensions to be recognized geographically, NORTH to SOUTH and WEST to EAST. However, as Willson points out, MDS programs do not purport to reveal the nature of the resultant dimensions. A small-scale study by Doyle and McGee[41] explores the use of non-metric MDS applied to the convenience food market. An interesting paper which would serve as an introduction to this current development is by Neidell.[42] In this paper, Neidell introduces the notion of developing a multi-dimensional attribute space from a uni-dimensional data bank consisting of inter-object non-metric relationships.

The term 'conjoint measurement' is often associated with NMDS since conjoint measurement, at its simplest, is merely the response to pairs of objects such as two brands, or a person and a product, or a brand and an attitude. In other words, conjoint measurement, as defined by Green and Rao,[43] is concerned with the joint effect of two (or more) independent variables on the ordering of a dependent variable. The application of conjoint measurement is key to 'trade-off' models and research has been conducted into various methods[44] which shows that various algorithms, notable MONANOVA (either singly or pair-wise) and PERMUT, essentially generate similar concept and attribute utilities.

The advantages of NMDS are outlined by Guttman et al.[45] and may be summarized as:

no a priori assumptions as to population distributions;

no linear restrictions;

low-level (i.e. nominal data) can be handled; and

the techniques are user-orientated.

The key requirements of NMDS are that the analysis must 'recover' the original row and column scales (up to positive linear transformations) and a badness of fit measure known as the stress of the solution has to be computed. If stress is close to zero, then the recovery is effected.

The recent developments in NMDS have emphasized the role of 'mapping' techniques which facilitate comparisons of complex data to be made. Sampson[46] discusses the usefulness of mapping in this context and notes its implications for marketing especially in respect of market segmentation and gap analysis.

Multivariate analysis: concluding remarks

Inevitably this chapter on multivariate analysis can only touch the surface of the subject. It is hoped that the references provided will assist both specialist and non-specialist seeking to widen their knowledge in this complex field to a greater understanding of multi-dimensional space. Increasing use is being made of techniques like factor analysis, multiple regression, and so on, often in inappropriate situations on data that are not amenable to such analyses. The market researcher faced with such a toolbag of techniques must be familiar enough with the subject to utilize the right techniques. The mathematician/statistician must, likewise, appreciate the research problems and use techniques not for themselves but for their problem-solving capabilities.

The latest developments concerning *non-metric* multi-dimensional scaling are likely to continue with the awareness by analysts of the inadequacy of present-day data input. It is to be hoped that the introduction of 'time-sharing' computers and the advancement of higher level programming languages will enable researchers to utilize multivariate techniques to great advantage. Additionally, Sheth[47] suggests the availability of canned computer programs is a most important factor in the diffusion of multivariate methods.

The intial head-on plunge into new techniques and methodologies is always to be expected. As Green and Frank[48] point out: 'Despite the inevitable misapplication of techniques and over-selling (with the consequent failure to live up to expectations), the fact remains that quantitative and behavioural science are here to stay.' Multivariate analysis as an important sector of quantitative science should not be ignored simply because of its apparent complexities.

PART II

Use of consumer market research

PART III

Use of consumer market research

Introduction

The role of market research is to make marketing operations more efficient and profitable, by improving the quality of planning and decision taking. This is the only way in which market research can justify itself. The following chapters, therefore, illustrate how the research tools described earlier are applied to various problems encountered in marketing.

Market research is involved with a very wide range of activities directed towards helping an organization to supply, as efficiently and profitably as possible, goods or services designed so as to satisfy identified consumer needs. These activities cover not only distribution and selling operations but also many aspects of production and, indeed, company policy generally. Market research is certainly not the exclusive preserve of the marketing man. It has increasingly drawn in the laboratory scientist, the production manager, finance and personnel departments, and others. The contributions which follow reflect this broad view of market research.

In planning these chapters we had in mind a structure of the marketing process which explains their sequence. Like all such structures it is greatly over-simplified, but the reader may find it helpful to know the pattern. This is illustrated in Fig. 1, the bracketed figures being the chapter numbers. There are two additional chapters which do not fit so neatly into the pattern: the more specialized but very important field of financial research (chapter 22), and the broader and growing field of international market research (chapter 23).

There are four comments to make about this approach. First, the total material, to be manageable, has to be divided under sub-headings, i.e. chapters. This is inevitable but artificial; and it would be positively dangerous if, in real life, the different problems were treated as though in watertight compartments. A successful brand does *not* consist simply of a formula plus a pack plus a price plus an advertisement plus ... etc., where each of these elements has been developed in isolation. The whole is (or certainly should be) far greater than the sum of its parts. The various elements of the marketing mix, therefore, have to be interrelated and tested together at various stages. This point is emphasized at several points in these chapters, and is absolutely basic to successful brand marketing.

Second, market research and brand development does not often proceed in a neat and tidy time sequence from a study of market opportunities to the national launch of a new brand. It tends to involve a process of continual

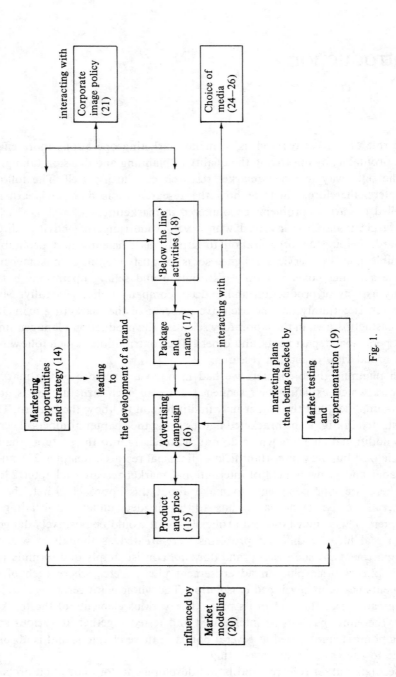

Fig. 1.

rethinking and adjustment of plans as more information becomes available. The elements of the marketing mix, and sometimes even the brand concept itself, may have to be modified as we progress towards the stage of market testing. This may mean going back on an earlier stage of market research and retesting.

Third, much of the following material is presented in the context of developing a *new* brand. This is the clearest, and in many respects the most comprehensive, method of illustrating the way in which market research is applied. Obviously, a great deal of market research is concerned with *existing* brands, particularly in recycling them to give them a new lease of life in changing and heavily competitive markets. The principles discussed in these chapters apply to such brands also, although not all the steps described will be needed. Probably the major difference is that an existing brand will normally have an established personality or image as far as consumers are concerned. This may sometimes be weak, and quite possibly be one we wish to change, but our research approach must take account of it, for in the market-place the existing image will condition consumers' views about any new developments (product, advertising or other) which we may plan for the brand. As chapter 15 points out, 'blind' testing can be particularly misleading in this context.

Finally, a substantial part, perhaps about a third, of the total expenditure on market research in the UK is devoted to market measurement (retail audits, consumer purchasing panels and barometers of different kinds). This is necessary both for drawing up plans and monitoring progress in existing markets and also to provide certain key background data for investigating possible new markets. Earlier chapters have described these techniques and discussed several of their key applications. The following chapters, therefore, do not make much reference to the more descriptive, background planning aspects of market measurement and similar research, since the latter's value in dealing with various marketing problems should already be clear.

One other general point is worth making. Most of the discussion in these chapters concentrates on the problems of frequently bought consumer goods. Even so, a lot of what is said applies equally to durable goods and to services, although some of the detailed mechanics of the research have to be adapted to fit the special characteristics of these products.

The chapters on media research call for some additional introductory comments. Media research is used widely, constantly and intensively and there is considerable similarity of objectives and methods among advertisers and their agencies in the continuous effort to secure maximum value per pound spent in allocating advertising appropriations both between and within media. Similarly, calibration of his audience or readership is the essential basis of any sales effort by a media owner. Accordingly, media research is one of the largest single areas of market research expenditure.

As a result of these factors, media research is (with the possible exception of the political polls) the most visible and generally scrutinized area of market research. Most media research is widely circulated since much of it is controlled by joint committees on behalf of the advertising industry generally; while privately commissioned media research projects are almost invariably published in attempts to convince advertisers and their agents of the particular merits of, say, one publication versus others. Such research is also widely used as a source of basic market data and demographic information and for dividing the country up into realistic marketing areas. Few other types of research come under this type of informed, users' scrutiny. And for this reason the standards achieved often tend to set the pace for the market research profession.

Ideally, one would wish for directly comparable techniques for assessing the value of different media, but this has so far eluded both the methodology and the cash resources of the industry. The characteristics of the various media and the differing feasibility of measurement (both technical and financial) have produced quite different ways of calibrating them. This particularly applies to comparisons between press and television. Thus, basic press research is typically based on large, national samples with relatively infrequent reporting periods, compared with small regional samples with more frequent reporting of very detailed data in the case of television. However, it is important to avoid the pitfall of assuming that because the research monitoring systems are so dissimilar this necessarily indicates fundamental differences in the way that the respective audiences react to the media.

A general question posed is that of the cost efficiency of traditional media research. Are we spending too much on what *can* be measured, as opposed to devoting more time, effort and money to that part of the iceberg beneath the surface? Little work, for example, has been done on inter-media effectiveness compared with the enormous volume of intra-media research. Another important question relates to the marginal efficiency of extra-media data in terms of the cost of obtaining it. In the early days of the move from simple circulation data to readership data based on research, the research payoff was manifestly obvious and large in terms of improved advertising efficiency. We now seem to be at a stage in media research where many potential avenues of enquiry, while of considerable theoretical interest, have much less attractive potential in terms of cost effectiveness. Reading intensity measures may be one example. Until recently, the emphasis rested heavily on getting as much data as possible – some would think too many data now that computer processing has made the marginal cost of extra tabulations so low. Possibly the most important step for media research to take is therefore to evaluate the uses of the data much more stringently. Also, given the many inevitable imperfections and gaps in the data, we need to be very cautious about attributing too much apparent precision to the measurements provided.

This leads us to another broader, but linked, issue. An important development during recent years has been the increasing use of 'econometric' techniques in attempts to measure the sales effectiveness of advertising campaigns – and thus to provide a sounder basis for setting the advertising budget and for allocating this between media, regionally and over time. Such approaches are still the subject of considerable argument, although they are gaining wider (if often very qualified) acceptance. The pursuit of this particular Holy Grail is outside the scope of the present book, but there is a growing literature on the subject which the reader can follow up if interested. A good starting point is the set of papers from the *Admap* 9th World Advertising Workshop in Berlin, October 1977, published in *Admap*, Volume 14, Nos. 1 and 2 (January and February 1978).

Turning back from the subject of media research to the general field, it is very noticeable that over the last two decades market research has moved from a stance of *providing information* to one of *solving problems*. This shift reflects not only the raised sights (and ambitions) of researchers themselves but also wider agreement that market research must be directed towards decision taking and marketing action. One aspect of this is that far more research briefs and plans nowadays include not only a discussion of the marketing background to the problem but also a clear statement of the action which will be based on the findings. In the extreme case this can be an action standard of the form, 'If the findings show A, we will take action X; if B, then action Y'. Market research reports in their turn are increasingly concerned with discussing action instead of merely summarizing the information collected.

However, 'problem solving' does not by any means cover all the objectives of market research. Much research is intended to improve the general efficiency of marketing by increasing our *understanding* of the market. 'Understanding' is *not* the same as 'information', 'Understanding' implies knowledge of both the structure and the dynamics of the market and of the ways in which marketing activities achieve, or fail to achieve, their desired effects. Much of the research described in the following chapters is designed to secure such knowledge. Market research is in the last resort valuable only to the extent it can be used predictively, based on such understanding.

Inevitably, this leads in the direction of model building. Some of these models have relatively limited objectives, e.g. in media selection. More complex ones deal with issues such as consumer decision processes: how *does* a consumer come to choose a particular brand on a given occasion? The major contribution of market research in this area has probably been its emphasis on the value of studying the attitudes and behaviour of consumers *individually*, particularly through panels. This 'micro' approach contrasts with the longer-established 'macro' approaches, as used in econometrics, which involve studying consumers in the mass. At this point, it becomes increasingly difficult to draw any clear boundary between market research and disciplines such as operational research.

Another point at which market research tends to cross a boundary is in its concern with information as such. The higher-flying comments of the last paragraphs should not distract attention from this important, if apparently less glamorous, function. In looking at what market research has to offer we must remember that it is one among several sources of data. Within a company, market research information has to be integrated with sales data, trade statistics and much other material. Increasingly, therefore, we have as users to think of total management information systems into which market research data must be fitted. We also have to find better ways of getting the relevant information (and only this) to the right people, at the appropriate time, quickly, clearly and concisely. During the last ten years there has been a steady growth in the development and use of computerized marketing information systems, drawing upon extensive data bases both inside and outside the companies concerned, and often with direct on-line access available to the individual users of the system. This is another perspective against which to consider the material discussed in the next chapters.

The fact that market research is not the only source of market knowledge introduces a further issue. Knowledge normally costs money (and time). This is certainly the case with knowledge obtained through research. We should therefore weigh the cost of the additional knowledge to be gained through a particular research project against the pay-off (extra profit) we might expect to obtain as a result of having this knowledge. This is very much more easily said than done. It involves calculations not only of cost and potential payoff but also of the amounts and different types of risk involved and the probability of different research and marketing outcomes. There is a field of statistics — Decision Theory, based on Bayesian statistics — which attempts to get to grips with this type of problem. So far, very little practical work has been done (rather more in the USA than in the UK) in applying this to the buying of market research. However, the problem is so important that we shall inevitably have to continue trying to use this or some similar approach more effectively during the coming years: reference is made to it in chapter 19.

As market research has developed away from the simple 'nose-counting' of its early days, so the problem of effective communication between market researchers and their clients has also increased. When dealing with the more sophisticated approaches (such as those described in chapter 14) the user of research may need to understand at least the principles of quite complex techniques if he is to make good use of their findings. He may, on occasion, even have to rethink his own basic marketing approach, e.g. when considering market segmentation studies. This is a challenge to both researcher and user. The researcher must try to explain his methods and findings simply and directly, avoiding jargon as far as he can, but the user must also build his half of the bridge. He can no longer expect to cope adequately with market research (or with other modern marketing techniques) on the basis of a short briefing plus a skimming of the report's summary of findings. The subject need not be abstruse, except in its most specialized technical aspects, but it has to be worked at if it is to be applied effectively.

The following chapters aim to help with this, although they cannot hope to deal with all aspects of the topics discussed. They will be the more useful if the earlier, more technical chapters have also been studied and if some of the books and articles referred to are subsequently followed up for more detailed information on subjects of interest.

John Downham

Chapter 14

Segmenting and constructing markets

TONY LUNN

Since the publication of Wendell Smith's pioneering article,[1] segmentation has become one of the most influential and fashionable concepts in marketing. It '... has permeated the thinking of managers and researchers alike as much as, if not more than, any other marketing concept since the turn of the century.'[2] It has featured prominently at conferences and seminars and has given rise to a voluminous body of literature.* However, simultaneously with this surge of interest, segmentation has become less a single concept and more an umbrella topic covering a diversity of issues.

A fundamental distinction is between the perspectives of marketing men and researchers. To the former, segmentation is a *strategy*, whereby products are directed at specific target groups of consumers rather than at the total population. Researchers, by contrast, have tended to regard it from a *methodological* standpoint: that is, as a set of techniques; or as a type of survey, geared to the description of fundamental market differences.

Researchers themselves have differed markedly in their emphases. For example, some, mainly social scientists, have been concerned with conceptual issues, such as developing new forms of consumer classification; others, mainly statisticians and mathematicians, with methodological issues such as factor and cluster analysis. These techniques, which are referred to throughout the chapter, are described in more detail by Holmes in chapter 13 of this handbook.

A distinction has also developed between consumer-oriented and product-oriented segmentation. The former approach places chief emphasis upon ways in which consumers can be grouped in terms of their needs and other basic characteristics; the latter upon ways in which products can be grouped in terms of the benefits they offer.

---

* Segmentation is not without its critics: some problems and alternative approaches are referred to later in this chapter.

The purpose of this chapter is to provide an outline of some prominent issues in the area. There is particular emphasis upon marketing considerations and applications. The marketing man can be faced nowadays with bewildering volumes of data, gathered from mammoth surveys, and analysed by highly abstruse techniques. There is a danger of both marketing people and researchers becoming lost in a forest of complexity. The former may seek panaceas and, inevitably, become disillusioned: the latter may become entranced by methodological niceties. In the present chapter it is hoped to illustrate how even the most sophisticated techniques can have clear and practical applications for both long-term planning and day-to-day decisions.

Given the generality of the segmentation concept, some of the points discussed below are also dealt with elsewhere in the book, usually in greater detail. In particular, see the chapters by Holmes, Morton-Williams and Sampson. There is also a list of useful references at the end of the book.

Some marketing considerations

General

Segmentation is a new term but an old concept. Manufacturers have long been aware that certain products are bought mainly by certain types of people: gold watches and tonic wines are obvious examples. Again, take the motor car market. A Model T Ford and a vintage Bentley are just as illustrative of market segmentation as are more contemporary cars such as a Ford Capri and a Mercedes. Nevertheless, much early segmentation was accidental, i.e. the product was launched with no clear target group in mind, but, by its nature, turned out to attract certain types of people. Or, if not accidental, the marketing action was often highly speculative: target groups were based mainly upon intuition, and described rather vaguely in such phrases as 'The modern woman who cares for her children'.

The main difference today is that segmentation policies are pursued more purposefully, and are applied to a wider range of product fields. This development can be attributed to a number of interrelated factors.

As a result of fundamental changes in society, purchasing has become more discretionary and less concerned simply with the necessities of daily life. The most important changes for marketing men are the growth of affluence and the rising level of education. These have been accompanied by increasing social mobility and by an erosion of traditional class-determined patterns of behaviour: the typist, like the movie star, can afford to express her personality through the latest fashions; the factory worker may take his holiday in Greece. As the constraints stemming from low incomes and traditional social values have lessened, so individual patterns of requirements have flourished. The result has been an ever-widening range of consumer tastes and needs for the marketing man to satisfy. Thus, in an era of social change, manufacturers are paying much more attention to consumer differences in their general planning. This consumer-orientation is a matter of necessity in an era of mass production and mass marketing, when the financial penalties of failure to produce the right kinds of goods and services can be ruinous.

The harsh economic conditions prevailing in the mid 1980s may, if prolonged, lead to changes in consumer needs and other market variables, but they are unlikely to have a fundamental effect upon the trends outlined above. The whole climate of marketing has become much more 'scientific'. The individual entrepreneur is being supported or replaced by teams of specialists; product life-cycles are more carefully planned and monitored; manufacturers are increasingly concerned with maintaining complementary ranges of products within any one area, and also with diversifying into related areas.

The increasing sophistication of technological development in the physical sciences has more and more been harnessed for the production of consumer goods, e.g. convenience foods, in-home computers. But the resultant new products rarely meet with instant and universal acceptance. Many may be dead ends. To be successful, a new product type usually has to make its appeal, at least initially, to a particular market segment, perhaps broadening its appeal to wider elements of the population as time goes by. Frozen foods are a case in point, where initial widespread rejection has been replaced by almost universal acceptance.

The combination of technological development and mass marketing has meant that basic physical products in certain fields have become almost uniform in composition and scarcely distinguishable by the consumer. As a result, marketing men have sought to establish clearer identities for specific brands, e.g. toilet soaps are given different perfumes and colours, toothpastes special ingredients such as fluoride. These extra product characteristics may well offer to the consumer benefits over and above the basic function of the product. A particular toilet soap may offer cosmetic benefits, a gold fountain pen may act as a status symbol, video games may satisfy a need to feel up to date. In some product fields secondary benefits of this kind have become the primary reason for purchase: Swiss watches may be valued more as fashion accessories than as time-pieces; the majority of Virginian tobacco cigarettes are indistinguishable on blind product tests, yet often command striking preferences in their branded form – the motivation for purchase may be identification with the branding personality. Discussion of this fourth point makes it important to distinguish between at least three levels of segmentation, namely where:

(a) totally different *product types* are produced for different consumer needs, e.g. toothpaste rather than some alternative means of cleaning teeth;
(b) different *product variants* are produced within the same overall types, e.g. special benefits such as fluoride are built in;
(c) different *brands* are produced within the same specific product variant.

A further corollary of mass production has been the neglect of certain minority tastes. These tastes have often been identified in product concept research, and have subsequently formed the basis of new product developments. The growth of delicatessen and health food product ranges provides a contemporary illustration.

Recent years have seen an interconnection between developments in marketing thinking – which have led to demands for more detailed descriptions of consumers – and developments in research techniques, which have themselves opened up wider possibilities for marketing action. At a time when complex data analyses can be carried out with increasing speed and economy by computers, marketing men have much sharper tools at their disposal for the derivation and implementation of segmentation policies.

To summarize the effects of these changes: there has been a growing recognition that consumers may differ in ways that are exploitable by marketing operation, and that to concentrate on producing 'universal products' for the 'average consumer' is to run the risk of missing significant marketing opportunities. Increasingly, therefore, marketing men have become concerned to identify target groups of consumers with distinctive patterns of needs, to develop products with the appropriate benefits, and to promote and distribute these products in optimum ways.

Different types of marketing problems

The segmentation approach to marketing can provide the cornerstone for a company's total planning. It helps to set the basic objectives for the whole marketing operation, and to indicate strategies for implementing these objectives. There are, of course, many different kinds of marketing objectives and strategies, which, in turn, give rise to different types of segmentation problem. It is important to distinguish between these. The particular problem posed will determine the kind of research necessary, including the sort of data that will be most relevant, and the ways in which the data should be analysed. Characteristic types of marketing problem are listed below, and illustrations of research designed to solve them are given later in the chapter.

Define the market

Consumers do not necessarily perceive the market in the same way as do manufacturers. From the consumer's standpoint, a market may be thought of as a set of products (or brands) which are considered equally suitable for the same need – or set of needs. These products may come from product fields which manufacturers would treat as quite distinct. In one project, for instance, it was discovered that the main substitutes for a particular type of frozen food were not rival brands in the field, but two quite different kinds of tinned food on the one hand, and poached eggs on toast on the other. That is, the consumer's concept of what constitutes a product field may range quite widely.

Moreover, the repertoire of brands considered suitable for a particular need will not necessarily include all the brands from any one field.

Rationalize policies for existing brands and products
This problem can be posed at two levels. At one level are questions of optimum strategies for specific brands (or products) marketed by the company. A variety of questions arises, such as how can market share be maintained or improved; how can inroads be made into the position of competitive brands; how best can brands be protected from competitive activity; and so on. In the light of research, attempts may be made to increase the purchasing of current buyers, to convert buyers of competing brands, or to attract new buyers to the product field.

The second level is discussed under the third type of objective, namely:

Position ranges of brands and of product varieties
Where in a given market there are different segments of consumers with differing needs, a company may be advised to market its brands in such a way that in total they satisfy as many as possible of the more important segments, at the same time minimizing direct competition between the company's own brands as far as any one segment is concerned. The same point applies to ranges of product varieties.

Identify gaps in the market which offer new product opportunities
Here the object is to identify consumer segments whose needs (at least in their eyes) are not being adequately met by any existing product. These needs may be met by launching a totally new brand (or product) or by modifying an existing one.

Underlying all four types of problem is the fundamental issue of competition. Segmentation studies usually include amongst their objectives the location and specification of competition from rival manufacturers. Resultant marketing strategies may, of course, be essentially defensive – particularly in relation to new entries in the market – or more aggressive in nature.

Segmentation and research developments

It has been emphasized that although segmentation can be regarded as an approach to marketing it has, nevertheless, stimulated a variety of developments in consumer research. Some of these are discussed below under two main headings: criteria for defining market segments or consumer classifications, and research methodology. For ease of exposition, the following sections on criteria and methodology are written from the standpoint of consumer segmentation: subsequent sections deal with product segmentation and the relationships between the two approaches.

Segmentation criteria

Requirements from criteria

Market segmentation is disaggregative in nature. To produce a 'universal product' for the 'average consumer' is to run the risk of missing important marketing opportunities. Likewise, for the researcher to represent data in aggregate form rather than analysed by relevant variables is to provide information that may well be misleading. These variables are often referred to as segmentation criteria.

But what types of criteria are relevant? This will depend upon the particular market being examined. There are, however, a number of general considerations determining relevance; namely that criteria should:

(a) be feasible to measure under normal market research conditions;
(b) be unambiguous and meaningful to both researchers and marketing people;
(c) discriminate between consumers themselves;
(d) provide adequate discrimination in the market, for instance, in respect of:

  (i)   product field usage or purchase,
  (ii) weight of usage or purchase,
  (iii) brand usage;

(e) increase the understanding of the market, particularly by indicating consumer needs;
(f) be fully exploitable in practice – i.e. marketing people should be able to take effective action in the light of the discriminations achieved. That is, the variables should, if possible, provide links between different data sources, e.g. media and purchasing panel data.

Different kinds of segmentation criteria

Consumers, and markets, can be described from numerous standpoints. The possibilities of several different kinds of variable have been examined over the years. Those most commonly used in segmentation are discussed below.

Consumer behaviour

Conceptually, the most straightforward way of classifying consumers is in terms of their behaviour, e.g. heaviness of buying and/or usership in a product field, solus versus multiple brand buyers, lapsed buyers, different ways of using the same product.

Head[3] has suggested a series of refined classifications based on different combinations of behavioural variables.

For some purposes – e.g. tests assessing formulation changes in an existing product – sample selection and/or data analysis by variables such as user versus non-user of the product in question may be all that is required. The same consideration can apply with the use of single source systems to relate purchasing and media data.

One research approach has gone further than this, arguing that behavioural segmentation in its own right is a single and logical policy. The heavy-half theory popularized by Twedt,[4] for instance, asserts that, granted that in many product fields 50 % of the consumers account for 80 % of consumption, these high-volume groups should command maximum marketing effort.

There are, however, two strong arguments against taking this reasoning too far. They are given by Haley[5] and Frank.[6] The former points out that people do not always buy products for the same reasons. Consequently, some heavy buyers may be better prospects than others. The latter points out that in any case, the heavy half is already the heavy half and may offer little scope for expansion.

Another interesting approach is 'backward segmentation'. To summarize, this involves applying techniques such as factor and cluster analysis to purchasing data across a variety of product fields, in the search for patterns of complementary and substitutable products.[7,8] Two main applications of this approach are to:

(a) guide future research and stimulate ideas, e.g. by raising questions as to why sets of products group together as they do;
(b) simplify marketing strategies, e.g. by suggesting common policies of couponing and distribution for related products.

In addition, groupings of consumers in terms of common purchasing and usage characteristics may delineate market segments of value in their own right: they may, for example, indicate meaningful 'life-style' segments. Cross-tabulation of these groupings by other variables, such as attitudes, will help build up profiles to guide marketing action (see next section).

Geographical region

Historically, geographical segmentation was probably the first in the genre. Small manufacturers who wished to limit their investments, or whose distribution channels were not large enough to cover the entire country, would segment national markets by selling their products only in certain areas. This phenomenon is much less prevalent today, especially in more advanced countries.

Nevertheless, regional differences do exist in some product fields. For instance, water softness/hardness varies by region. In addition, cultural differences still persist despite the phenomenon of mass communication and increasing travel — especially where there are immigrant sub-populations.

Demographics

Perhaps the most popular form of segmentation has been in terms of demographic characteristics. A comprehensive list can be found in Frank *et* al.[9] They include sex, age, occupation, income, social class and household composition. These characteristics have become the basic terms in which many marketing men and researchers think about the consumer. This is reasonable up to a point. Demographic variables describe important aspects of people's circumstances which give rise to purchasing needs. They also act as moderators upon the translation of these needs into behaviour, e.g. a low income household may have expensive tastes, but little prospect of indulging them. Moreover, because they have been studied over a long period of time their relationships with other market factors, such as media patterns, have become well known. They have, however, been subjected to considerable criticism in recent years, mainly through lack of brand discrimination, and because, giving as they do only indirect reflections of consumer needs, they may be of limited value in the formulation of marketing strategies.

There are also some definitional problems with certain demographic variables. Social class, for instance is a somewhat ambiguous concept, and has been shown through factor analysis to contain at least two components, which were labelled social values and income.[10] Moreover, income itself can be interpreted in different ways (e.g. head of household, total household, discretionary). It also presents data collection problems, with respondent refusals estimated at between 15–20%.

Some criticism may be overcome by a more critical and imaginative treatment of demographic criteria, as illustrated by the *life-cycle* concept. This is essentially a composite of length of marriage and age of children. It has an obvious logic as a classification tool, as changes in these variables in combination give rise to different needs and attitudes in many product and service fields, such as financial services and tourism.

A comprehensive scheme has been advanced by Wells and Gubar (see, Jain, ref. 11), with the following 9 categories:

bachelor stage (young single people not living at home);
newly married couples (no children);
full nest I (youngest child under 6);
full nest II (youngest child 6 or over);
full nest III (older married couples with dependent children);
empty nest I (no children living at home, head in labour force);
empty nest II (head retired);
solitary survivor (in labour force);
solitary survivor (retired).

In practice, it is customary to operate with fewer categories.

Life-cycle classification also has its critics. For instance, there may be problems over deciding the optimum nature and breadth of categories. And, given the changing nature of society, some people and or households do not fit neatly into conventional schemes; for example, households headed by widows,

widows with young children, couples who have never had children and single parent families.

A related new classification – labelled *Sagacity* – has been described by Cornish.[12] The basic principle is to interlace three dimensions, namely life cycle, income and socio-enonomic grade. Various levels of each are combined to produce a total of 12 sub-groups. There are as yet few published applications indicating the practical value. However, like life-cycle, it represents an interesting approach to what might be called 'extended demographics'.

Background and social environment

The term 'demographic' is itself somewhat ambiguous. And there are a number of additional ways of describing the consumer's background and social environment which may prove valuable for segmentation policies. These include the possession of complementary products. An obvious example is the relationship between the ownership of a refrigerator and frozen food purchasing. For a useful list of such variables, see a paper by Agostini.[13]

Situational variables

Recent developments in buyer behaviour theory have emphasized ways in which personal characteristics interact with situational factors. Situations relevant to purchasing, consumption, and the acquisition of information designed to influence these activities, are receiving increasing attention. However attempts to develop meaningful taxonomies of situations are still at an early stage.

Physical attributes

There are many products which either cater for, or are affected by, the consumer's physical attributes, e.g. skin and hair texture; and such characteristics are increasingly being used in segmentation.

Psycho-sociological characteristics

A promising development of the past two decades has been segmentation by *psycho-sociological* characteristics. This has been accelerated by advances in psychometrics, which allow such variables to be measured effectively in day-to-day market research projects. Segments identified by this approach have a compelling diagnostic quality. They indicate not only who buys a particular product but also why they buy. Target groups are described in terms of 'real people', and can be immediately appealing to research users – particularly copywriters in their search for appropriate ways of communicating with the target group. Diagnostic advantages can, however, be offset by weak relationships with purchasing and consumption data. It is important, here, to distinguish between different kinds of psycho-sociological characteristics.

When these variables were first introduced to market research the tendency was to use rather general characteristics borrowed from other fields such as clinical phychology. Sometimes total personality inventories – such as the Edwards Personality Preference Schedule – were adopted; sometimes individual traits such as introversion, neuroticism, and inner/outer directedness.[9,14,15] Not surprisingly, the results of applying these in market research have proved disappointing. They are at once too abstract and, in many cases, of doubtful relevance to consumer behaviour.

In recent years, the emphasis has shifted towards characteristics more obviously geared towards people in their roles as consumers. Considerable attention has been devoted to the merits of 'life-style' and psychographic variables, typified by the activity, interest and opinion batteries (A.I.O.) pioneered by Wells[16] and as exemplified by the Values and Life Style (VALS) approach.[17] Claims and counterclaims about the value of this approach abound in the literature.

A major criticism is that even these batteries are too abstract and lack discriminatory power. The criticism has been particularly severe in relation to the use of broad stereotypes – such as 'The Quiet Family Man', 'The Ethical Highbrow' – derived from carrying out factor and cluster analyses of the total set of items (e.g. ref. 16). In response, some researchers have changed their approach to life-style analysis. Segnit,[18] for example, has found more value in clustering people in terms of their purchase and consumption behaviour which are themselves life-style groupings of a kind – and in subsequently deriving diagnostic profiles by cross-analysing the clusters by individual life-style statements. Wells[16] provides an illuminating review of the life-style area.

The main problem with psycho-sociological classification lies in undue reliance upon generalized characteristics of any kind when attempting to account for specific and widely varying types of choice behaviour. Experience suggests that the most fruitful approach is to derive classifications empirically for the product field in question. The resultant characteristics vary in nature from specific consumer requirements in the product field, such as preference for a strong flavour in a toothpaste, to more general traits, such as traditionalism and economy mindedness.

These later characteristics have often been found relevant to several different product fields. But it is rare to find a segmentation project where more specific assessments of consumer needs do not play a vital role. See also Haley's work on 'benefit segmentation'.[5]

The value of generalized characteristics may well be less for studies of particular markets than in basic research designed to advance our understanding of consumer behaviour. Traits such as propensity to take risks, selfconfidence, innovativeness and cognitive style come into this category.[19] In the same context, the author carried out a project in which over 50 attitude scales derived from specific projects were brought together in the same questionnaire, which was given to 4000 female respondents. The **results were** treated by both factor analysis and cluster analysis, and eight groupings were identified, which were labelled:

(1) Young sophisticates (15% of the sample);
(2) Traditional working class (12%);
(3) Cabbages (12%);
(4) Middle age sophisticates (14%);
(5) 'Coronation Street' housewives (19%);
(6) Self-confident (13%);
(7) Homely (10%);
(8) Penny pinchers (10%).

In similar projects, four fundamental themes were found to underlie consumer attitudes and values, namely experimentalism, extroversion, anxiety and involvement. These findings are a valuable backcloth against which to view more specific action-oriented classifications.[20]

Other kinds of socio-psychological variable may be relevant for particular kinds of problem. For instance, empirically derived life-style indices concerning entertaining, interests, division of role in household tasks, and family influence on purchasing decisions have helped with longterm product planning.[21] In addition, six empirically derived shopper categories, e.g. 'the inefficient extravagant shopper', 'the reluctantly well-organized shopper', have been valuable in work designed to understand the effects of point-of-sale marketing variables.[22] Seaman *et al.* have pointed out the practical value of the kind of classification in developing strategies in the retail area.[23]

ACORN – a locational classification

ACORN represents a radical departure from previous types of geographical classification (see earlier section). It was conceived by Webber, previously working at the Centre for Environmental Studies and now at CACI. The concept, namely a national classification of residential neighbourhoods, is based upon UK census data, e.g.:

household composition;
occupation grade of each household member;
nature of occupation;
unemployment;
mode of travel to work;
number of cars owned;
household size;
household facilities;
degree of overcrowding.

By means of cluster analysis, the fundamental district units in the Census are grouped in terms of their similarity in terms of the major variables.

Thirty-six types of district emerged from this process which could be identified as distinctly different sorts of neighbourhood. It was decided that for most practical purposes 36 neighbourhood types provided an unnecessarily fine level of detail. Consequently these were reduced to a simpler set of 11 groups which still retained an apparently satisfactory level of homogeneity. These have been described as follows:

Group	Title	% of UK population
A	Modern family housing for manual workers	9.6
B	Modern family housing, higher incomes	7.4
C	Older housing of intermediate status	10.4
D	Very poor quality older terraced housing	9.2
E	Rural areas	5.8
F	Urban local authority housing	20.6
G	Housing with most overcrowding	2.9
H	Low income areas with immigrants	4.2
I	Student and high status non-family areas	4.3
J	Traditional high status suburbia	19.1
K	Areas of elderly people (often seaside resorts)	6.4

ACORN is being applied with claimed success by an increasing number of organizations, including those in finance and the media. It is basically a method of mapping geographically the concentrations of particular types of people where those types of people are those characteristic of their district. A major commercial use of ACORN has been in terms of 'hunting' people. It can indicate on a probabilistic basis the best places to go to find certain types of people and thus help you to site pubs, branches of building societies and so on.

For a further description of the method, and reported applications, see reference 24.

The topic of consumer classification is still a centre of active development. Work in buyer behaviour theory (e.g. ref. 19) has suggested a number of criteria worthy of attention, including involvement in the product field, specific self-confidence in brand choice, size of brand repertoire and decision-making styles and strategies.

For a more detailed review see references 9 and 20. Illustrations of the practical application of some of these variables are given later in the chapter.

Changes in approach to deriving criteria

The previous section discusses some of the main criteria used in past and present segmentation research. There have been three main changes in research approach to deriving these criteria. First, there has been a move from an essentially *a priori* to an empirical approach. That is to say, through the use of a stage of qualitative exploration (see below under Research Methodology), criteria are increasingly tailor-made for particular markets rather than imposed on the basis of researchers' preconceptions. Second, there has been an increasing emphasis upon *explanatory* criteria which provide a direct measurement of consumer needs and motives. Third, there has been a move away from the search for one single kind of variable, a search which dominated much of the early work on segmentation. It has been recognized that purchasing behaviour is determined by a multiplicity of factors, some of them being 'internal' to the consumer such as specific needs and general attitudes, others being 'external' to the consumer, e.g. background and circumstances, and the situations in which the product is purchased and used. Consequently, segmentation projects are increasingly concerned with using *multiple* criteria, i.e. with including all kinds of variables that are relevant to the particular market.

Segmentation and research methodology

Marketing problems giving rise to segmentation studies are of different kinds; the nature of the specific problem will determine the methodology to be adopted. There is no best technique, or set of techniques, for all circumstances. It is, nevertheless, possible to map out a broad sequence of stages applicable to many consumer segmentation projects. Four characteristic stages are:

(a) background clarification;
(b) qualitative exploration;
(c) developing measuring instruments;
(d) defining target groups.

This does not mean that all projects must pass inexorably through all four stages or that additional stages may not, on occasion, be appropriate. These four do, however, provide a useful means of categorizing consumer segmentation methodology.

Stage 1. Background clarification

The first stage in a segmentation project, as in any other major research activity, may be a thorough review of all existing knowledge and assumptions about the market. Most of this will probably consist of desk research. Information reviewed may vary from the findings of past motivation research to purchasing patterns derived from consumer panel records. Prominent issues will probably include:

(a) the nature of the market – is it expanding or contracting?
(b) the number of brands in the market and their respective shares;
(c) any rising or falling trends shown by individual brands;
(d) the proportion of the population buying the product, and the frequency of purchase;
(e) ways in which the product is used.

This information may, in itself, lead to hypotheses about the nature of the market and its basic mechanisms, which will help to guide subsequent research stages. It may also identify distinct behavioural sub-groups which will provide a valuable focus for qualitative exploration (see stage 2).

This is a crucial stage with respect to the relationship between client and researcher. Discussions between the two parties can lay the foundation for the mutual understanding which is a prerequisite of a successful segmentation project (see final section of this chapter).

A useful example of how a behavioural analysis can help to set the scene for subsequent research is given by Winkler,[25] with reference to the German toilet soap market. One finding reported by Winkler is the close correspondence between behavioural analyses of consumer panel data and consumer ratings of brand similarities. The same point is made by Stefflre,[26] and in several unpublished projects known to the author small-scale analyses of consumer similarity and preference data have provided valuable supplementary indications of market structure.

Stage 2. Qualitative exploration

This stage is often the cornerstone of the entire segmentation project. It has, however, been neglected all too often in the published literature, and also tends to be devalued by researchers whose particular skills and predilections are towards quantitative methods (see stage 3). The author's position is clear. Having identified, at stage 1, the main behavioural patterns in the market, it is then important to explore the various factors determining or influencing these patterns. Behavioural data may, in themselves, suggest hypotheses, but it is only by a thorough stage of qualitative research that these hypothese can be fully pursued and amplified.

The techniques of qualitative research have been described by Sampson in chapter 2. Any or all of these may be appropriate to an individual segmentation project. The objectives of this second stage can be summarized as:

(a) to build up a set of hypotheses about the consumer characteristics relevant to purchasing in the market;
(b) to develop a feel for the language used by consumers holding these characteristics, in order to guide the development of attitude scales and other appropriate measuring instruments (see chapter 5).

Qualitative research may not always be carried out as one single phase. Hypotheses may be progressively refined and developed during successive waves of interviews; some interviews may be carried out on the population at large, others on specific behavioural sub-groups of particular relevance to the problem.

In recent years, there has been a boom in the amount of qualitative research and some researchers would argue that segments devised from this approach are valuable in their own right.

A published example of qualitative segmentation is in the area of political research.[27] Extended Creativity Groups, using a range of projective techniques, such as psychodrawings and role playing, were used in an exploration of the UK Social Democratic Party in its formative years. A two-level segmentation emerged, in which SDP voters were found divided into 'mainstream', 'liberal' and 'protest', in terms of their basic motivations. 'Mainstream' voters, in turn, were partitioned between 'idealists' and 'depressives'.

Subsequent qualitative research has confirmed this segmentation, but, as the SDP has developed as a party, an additional level of motivation has emerged, namely 'core identifiers' and 'fragile proxy'[28] (see Fig. 14.1).

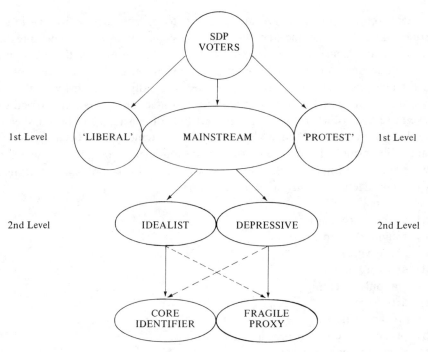

Fig. 14.1.

Stage 3. Developing measuring instruments

Content analysis of the interviews and other procedures used at stage 2 will have provided a set of hypotheses about the main forces relevant to consumer behaviour in the market. The next stage is to express these forces in quantitative form, i.e. to develop appropriate measuring instruments so that they can be applied feasibly in day-to-day market research enquiries. This stage is especially important for psycho-sociological variables. Ways of translating attitude dimensions into sets of statements are discussed in chapter 5. Techniques for analysing the responses of these statements, such as factor analysis, are described in chapter 13. An important issue is that of *how many* factors to extract from a given set of items. There is not necessarily a single best factor solution, and a variety of guides are available to help the researcher to select the best number of factors for the problem in question. The objectives at this stage are basically three-fold:

(a) to confirm or modify the nature and number of consumer characteristics already hypothesized;
(b) to clarify the meaning of each characteristic in terms of the statements that link together in practice, and also of those that do not;
(c) to produce subsets of statements that will serve as measuring instruments for each characteristic.

Measurement problems are not confined to psycho-sociological variables. Concepts such as income and life cycle, or behavior in relation to 'prestige products' and 'socially embarrassing' activities, may all involve the creation of special questions and indices. Two illustrations are given below of cases where factor analysis helped to clarify the picture originally provided by qualitative exploration. The first is from a study of the confectionery market, carried out several years ago, where twelve general attitude dimensions had been indicated by the qualitative research, and where sets of statements had been derived for each dimension. There were some 80 statements in all, to which a representative sample of 300 adults responded on a five-point agree/disagree scale. The twelve dimensions were labelled:

(a) sweet-toothedness;
(b) weight consciousness;
(c) conservatism;
(d) extravagance;
(e) compulsive eating;
(f) activity;
(g) gregariousness;
(h) preoccupation with personal appearance;
(i) social self-consciousness;
(j) impatience/impulsiveness;

(k) self-indulgence;
(l) ability to plan ahead.

Responses to the 80 statements were factor analysed. A final solution of eight attitude dimensions was arrived at, comprising 40 statements in total. Basically, the first six dimensions listed above were confirmed. Several of the second six, however, were shown to merge with other dimensions, to produce the following picture:

(a) sweet-toothedness;
(b) weight consciousness;
(c) conservatism;
(d) extravagance;
(e) compulsive eating;
(f) activity;
(g) self-organization;
(h) self-consciousness.

This picture was confirmed in a further factor analysis in a follow-up stage involving a sample of 2000 adults. As will be shown later, the eight dimensions helped to define important market segments.

The second illustration is from a study of general attitudes towards thrift. Initial qualitative exploration had suggested one broad dimension. Twelve statements were drawn up. Factor analysis of these revealed two separate dimensions, namely economy-mindedness and bargain-seeking. Further qualitative research carried out on high and low scorers on each of these two scales indicated that up to five separate attitudes were involved, namely economy-mindedness, extravagance, quality-consciousness, bargain-seeking and price-consciousness. Appropriate statements were derived for each dimension. Factor analysis confirmed the picture but indicated that bargain-seeking and price-consciousness were so closely related as to be scarcely worth separating in practice.

This picture has been confirmed in subsequent factor analyses, and these four separate attitudes to economy have played a valuable part in many segmentation projects.

Stage 4. Defining target groups
This stage provides the culmination of the previous three. Having identified the seemingly most relevant variables in the product field, and having developed new measuring instruments where necessary, the objective is now to pinpoint target groups on whom to concentrate maximum marketing effort. A search is made for sub-groups of consumers who are as similar as possible to each other in terms of important characteristics, and who are, in the same respect, as different as possible from consumers in other subgroups. The

techniques employed here have undergone radical development in recent years, and will undoubtedly advance still further in the future. At the risk of oversimplification, it is possible to distinguish four main historical phases of development in this area:

(a) simple cross-tabulations;
(b) regression-type techniques;
(c) sequential dichotomization;
(d) cluster analysis.

In the first phase researchers simply examined cross-tabulations between pairs of variables, e.g. the tendency to go on a packaged holiday to Europe would be analysed separately by age, social class, income, adventurousness, and so on. This approach is most appropriate when only a few variables are being analysed. Take the position in the UK floor polish market several years ago. There were two main product types: wax polish, a long-established product which, amongst other characteristics, demanded considerable effort on the part of the user; liquid, no-rub polish, a relative newcomer, and very much a labour-saving product. In recent years, wax polish had been on the decline, and liquid on the ascendancy.

The client had a brand in each type. He wondered whether the position of his wax brand might be improved by giving it more of the characteristics of a no-rub polish. No help had come from analyses by demographic variables, which failed to show any differentiation between buyers of the two types. However, a scale measuring the extent to which women are traditional or modern minded in their approach to housework was developed specially for this market. As shown in Fig. 14.2 this scale neatly segmented the market, clearly discriminating between buyers of the two types of polish. In the light of further analyses of the traditionalism scale, the client reversed the previous policy decision for his wax brand. Instead, through changes in both product characteristics and advertising themes, he further emphasized its current appeal. Likewise, he re-emphasized the labour-saving and other charateristics of his liquid brand. The wax brand subsequently increased its share, and maintained its sales volume despite the continuing decline of this market, and the liquid brand improved its share in the other market, which continued to expand. Moreover, an attempt by a competitor to launch a brand combining the characteristics of the two product types was a failure.

Cross-tabulations run into difficulties when several segmentation criteria are important. Take the packaged holiday case referred to earlier. Let us assume that there was a marked positive relationship with adventurousness and income. An inference might then be made about the existence of a target group for this kind of holiday amongst, say, highly adventurous people with a high level of income. The inference is, however, invalid. It can only be made through carrying out a cross-tabulation with the two characteristics interlaced; and

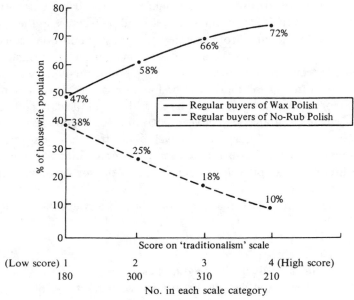

(Low score) 1   2   3   4 (High score)
180   300   310   210
No. in each scale category

Total sample = 1000   Fig. 14.2. Score on traditionalism scale.

there is, of course, for practical reasons, a strict upper limit to the number of such cross-tabulations that is feasible, especially when three or more variables appear to be relevant.

There has been a growing awareness that consumer behaviour is determined by a multiplicity of factors, some combining to precipitate or reinforce it, others to deter it and, consequently, of the need to analyse behaviour in terms of multiple characteristics. This led to the second phase, namely the popularity of multiple regression, multiple discriminant function, canonical correlation and similar techniques (see chapter 13). This was the kind of approach used by Massy *et al.* in their study of the relationship between purchasing and personality variables.[15] However even these techniques fail to take adequate account of interactions amongst the independent variables. In the packaged holiday example, for instance, adventurous people with high incomes may have quite different preferences from adventurous people with low incomes.

The third phase has attempted to deal with the disadvantages of the first two, i.e. by taking into account interaction and by examining 'automatically' a large series of cross-tabulations. The approach referred to is sequential dichotomization (see chapter 13) exemplified by the AID programs developed by Sonquist and Morgan.[29] An illustration of successful application by the author is quoted below (and another is given in chapter 13). It should be emphasized that the technique is appropriate for only certain segmentation problems. It is most relevant where the objective is to explain *one* particular variable, say heaviness of purchasing, in the product field.

There are many problems where this would prove too constricting, where, for instance, the objective is to examine the basic need structure in the market, or to define target groups from among the most important consumer characteristics, without gearing these groups to one particular variable. Here the collection of techniques known as cluster or profile analysis (see chapter 13) are more relevant. These constitute the fourth phase of development.

The search for target groups may well be carried out on the data collected at stage 3, i.e. where a sample of between 150 and 300 respondents will be interviewed with the main purpose of developing attitude scales, etc. It is, however, more customary to use a larger and fully representative sample. The size and nature of the sample will de determined by the sorts of consideration discussed in chapter 4.

Let us assume, for simplicity, that the data collected on our full-scale sample are of five kinds:

(a) demographics;
(b) specific consumer needs in the product field;
(c) specific attitudes to the various brands in the market, i.e. brand image data;
(d) more general values and attitudes;
(e) consumer behaviour such as brand purchasing and usage.

In the light of the above, it is unlikely that cross-tabulations or regression techniques will be used, at least initially, but a decision will have to be made between sequential dichotomization and cluster analysis.

An instance where the former method seemed more appropriate was in the confectionery project referred to on p. 402. The main marketing problem posed had been to provide a description of current purchasing in the product field, with a view to guiding strategies for reinforcing existing buyers, and suggesting ideas for new product development. The sample of 2000 respondents was roughly divided into two equal halves on the basis of heaviness of purchasing in the field. An AID analysis was run, using all independent variables considered relevant. Ten clear sub-groups of consumers were identified. Only three will be described here. The first, which contained 12% of the sample, contained 85% heavy buyers and 15% light buyers, compared with 50–50 in the total sample. It was defined in terms of four main characteristics:

(a) sweet-toothedness;
(b) low conservatism;
(c) highly compulsive eaters;
(d) DE social class.

It portrayed the typical buyer of the product in question and was used by marketing and advertising men to reinforce current purchasing. The group turned out to have distinguishing habits of buying the product at certain types of outlet, a finding which guided distribution policy.

By contrast, a second group, consisting of 11 % of the sample, had a very low propensity to purchase, namely 21–79. The defining characteristics of this group – low sweet-toothedness, low activity, older respondents without children – indicated that it was unlikely to respond to marketing action, and should, therefore, not be given special attention.

Particularly interesting was a third group, comprising 20 % of the total sample, which had a buying propensity of 55–45. Some of the characteristics of this group, e.g. their low sweet-toothedness, strongly deterred them from purchasing; other characteristics, e.g. the fact that that they were predominantly young married couples with children, and of DE social class, were factors which might be expected to encourage purchase. This was a group sufficiently large to be of interest from the marketing point of view; and analysis of their requirements guided the development of a totally new confectionery product which, among its other characteristics, was designed to be less sweet than other variants in this sector of the product field.

For many segmentation problems, however, cluster analysis is a more appropriate means of treating the data, at least initially. A key decision to be made then concerns which variables should be included in the cluster analysis itself, and which should be used subsequently in building up profiles of the groups obtained. Various positions have been adopted by different researchers.

One extreme approach is to cluster respondents in terms of all available data, including behavioural variables and attitudes towards brands. This approach, although comprehensive, may lead to difficulties in interpretation: the groups produced may be something of a hotchpotch, rather than clearly delineated descriptions of people. The second extreme involves clustering respondents only on data directly representing specific consumer needs. This has the advantage of clarity and precision, but may often be too limited.

Several years of experience with cluster analysis suggest that it is difficult to lay down hard and fast rules. There is no single, absolute way of looking at a market. In some recent segmentation projects guided by the author, data have been cluster-analysed more than once, using different variables, e.g. specific needs only the first time, general attitudes the second and both sets of data the third time. On each occasion fresh and valuable light has been thrown upon the market. Much depends upon the purpose of the study. For instance, where the main objective is guidance concerning the *physical* development of existing products, specific consumer needs are probably most suitable; where *advertising* themes are sought, or insights for new product concepts, more general attitude variables assume greater importance.

A sound general principle is to omit behavioural and brand image data from the cluster analysis, and to concentrate upon characteristics describing the consumer and his circumstances, e.g. general attitudes and values, specific needs, and demographic variables; and to select any variables of this kind which exploratory work has indicated will interact with each other to influence behaviour. Other variables can be used to provide profiles of the groups.

It was pointed out above, in referring to input data, that there is no unique way of looking at a market. This also applies to the number of groups that should be extracted from cluster analysis. In fact, most methods allow us to inspect a *range* of cluster solutions. They either start with each individual respondent, progressively combining those who are most similar, until, say, only two groups of respondents remain; or they start with the total sample and break it down into progressively smaller sub-groups. The issue of selecting the optimum set of sub-groups can prove a taxing one for researchers. A number of criteria can be brought to bear on the problem.

First, *size*; there is a limit to the number of groups which marketing men can seriously consider: moreover, once a cluster contains less than a certain minimum proportion of respondents, it ceases to be of marketing interest. The minimum proportion acceptable will vary with the product field; for instance, 5% of the population of cigarette smokers is an acceptable level, given the differences and low level of purchasing in the market, whereas 5% of the owners of dishwashers is not. Second, *homogeneity*; that is, at certain levels of generality, clusters may become too diffuse. Criteria have been suggested (e.g. ref. 30) for assessing the tightness or compactness of clusters. These can be at each level of a cluster solution. Third, *meaningfulness*; inspection of a range of cluster solutions usually leads one to reject several on grounds of interpretability. They just don't ring true; they are not describing meaningful stereotypes. Fourth, *discrimination*; the most valuable cluster solution is generally considered to be that which discriminates consumer behaviour most sharply. This is true up to a point, but clusters which do not distinguish between current purchasing patterns may indicate sets of needs currently uncatered for. That is, they may indicate marketing opportunity groups.

Cluster analysis provides a convenient means of describing subgroups in terms of shared characteristics. But these groupings are not fixed entities with rigid boundaries. They are relative, not absolute. Products directed at one particular group may be expected to attract sales from other adjacent groups – those which are most similar to it in terms of key characteristics. Furthermore, within a given cluster, individuals will usually vary in their strength of membership; some will be central, hard-core members; others will be more peripheral. It is not uncommon to find certain repondents who are so peripheral to all clusters that they are better removed from the analysis altogether and treated as non-classifiable. In one study of a specialist market, cluster analysis of the total sample proved hard to interpret, but a very clear set of groups was revealed once 25% of the sample, all outliers, had been removed from the analysis.

In the context of the relativity of clusters, it should also be pointed out that cluster membership may change over time, because the clusters themselves change, e.g. different combinations of needs become relevant, as happened to the UK detergent market after the launch of enzyme products. Moreover, individuals themselves may change, perhaps developing different needs with changes in their background circumstances.

Despite the usual proprietorial constraints, published examples are in the literature. For instance, Heller[31] describes a project where consumers in the automobile market were grouped in terms of both relatively general attitudes:

(a) attitudes towards travel;
(b) social activities and mobility;
(c) attitudes towards highway safety;
(d) liberalism – conservatism;
(e) self-image;
(f) attitudes towards automobile buying and maintenance;
(g) driving habits and patterns;

and more specific consumer requirements from automobiles:

(a) styling;
(b) size;
(c) economy;
(d) driving characteristics;
(e) special features;
(f) prestige factors.

Four groupings were produced. First, a group of consumers who like to travel a lot in their car and are generally safe drivers. They take good care of their car and they are not at all economy minded. They require large cars and are not overly concerned about style, power or speed. Second, a group which does not like to travel a lot by car. They are socially active and fairly reckless, being unconcerned about safety, care of their car and conservative behaviour. They desire a car that is stylish, and has power and speed. Third, a group which tends to be socially inactive, conservative and economy oriented. They are unconcerned about automotive styling, power, speed or the size of their car. Fourth, a group of drivers who are primarily interested in a conservative car that is expensive but stylish, powerful, fast and roomy. Their view of travel is neutral, they are neither socially active nor inactive and they care little about their car or about safety. Other published examples in this market are given by Grosse and Watson.[32,33]

Sherak[34] quotes a detailed description of consumer segments in the American beer market, based on such variables as benefits to be found in the 'ideal' beer, e.g. quality, prestige, smoothness, youthful image, mildness, robustness, dryness; and also more general personal characteristics, e.g. gregariousness, self-consciousness, price-orientation, masculinity. Nine clusters were identified, three of which he labelled 'the sociables', 'the rugged individualists' and 'light beer drinkers'.

The definitions of groupings such as these are based in part on the variables included in the cluster analysis, in part on additional personal characteristics against which the clusters are cross-analysed, and which provide extra profile data. These data may be obtained in successive stages, as illustrated below.

Some recent research in a different motorist market clustered 1000 respondents in terms of five types of variables — general attitudes, specific needs, demographic variables, descriptions of the product, and behaviour in relation to the product in question. Nine clusters were produced. Figure 14.3 indicates the proportion of respondents coming into each cluster.

The main purpose of the study was to show where the client's brands were positioned *vis-à-vis* competitive brands, in order to suggest both aggressive and defensive advertising strategies, and to indicate gaps for a new brand launch. The first cross-analysis gave brand shares for each cluster. Substantial brand discrimination was obtained (see, e.g., Figs. 14.4 and 14.5). This information in itself suggested a number of marketing and advertising strategies. Further analyses incorporating brand image data sharpened the picture of the structure of the market, including the strengths and weaknesses of the various brands within each cluster.

The next step was to attempt to determine the relative importance of the

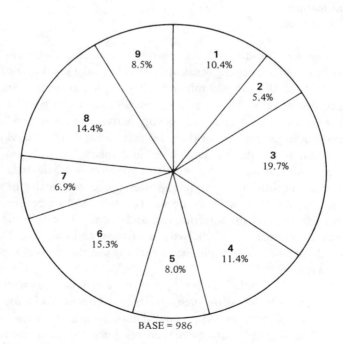

BASE = 986

Fig. 14.3. The nine clusters.

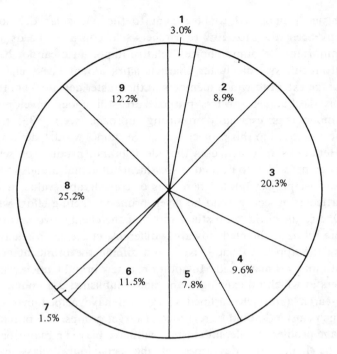

Fig. 14.4. Brand 'A' (Base = those claiming Brand 'A' as usual brand = 270).

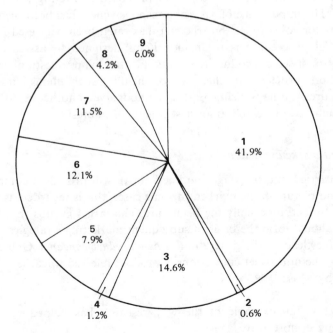

Fig. 14.5. Brand 'B' (Base = those claiming Brand 'B' as usual brand = 165).

consumer needs indicated to be salient to the particular decision. It has increasingly been recognized by researchers that consumer needs are not all equally important for brand choice. Relative importance cannot be obtained directly from analysis of cluster characteristics alone. These characteristics only show the extent to which members of the cluster deviate from the general population. Techniques for this purpose are still under development. The trade-off model is an especially promising approach (see ref. 35).

The one employed in this project was the St. James Model, developed in the UK by Hendrickson, which uses the 'ideal' brand, product or service as a yardstick against which to evaluate assessments of actual brands etc.[36] Its use in the motorist project quoted here was of considerable value in indicating which particular aspects should be given prime marketing effort within each cluster. One result of the total study was that the client's two existing brands were more clearly directed towards different clusters, in each case by reinforcing the appeal to one cluster, and aiming the brand at an adjacent cluster with many similar needs. In addition, a new brand launch was aimed at two clusters in which no existing brand had established a dominant position.

The research approach outlined so far will have helped marketing men decide which clusters should be regarded as target groups. The purchasing and brand image profiles of different clusters will have played a major part in this; so will the hypotheses developed at the behavioural classification and qualitative exploration stages. An acid test, however, is the likely *responsiveness* of the various clusters to proposed marketing and advertising strategies. The importance of assessing responsiveness has been recognized by researchers for some time,[2] but the step has often been neglected in practice. One way of proceeding is to include items designed to assess consumers' reactions to specific product concepts in the main questionnaire of the segmentation project: another is to include such items in follow-up questionnaires, perhaps using postal methods; yet another is to carry out further qualitative research amonst segments of interest.

Subsequent marketing action

Properly carried out, the stages outlined above will provide a comprehensive background picture of the market. In some cases, this is regarded as the end of the story. In fact, it is really the beginning. The target groups that have been identified should form the basis of subsequent marketing strategies. They may in themselves lead to the generation of *new product concepts*. One example is the case of the non-sweet confectionery product referred to earlier. Another is provided by Moss.[37]

Let's take an example of the way research has helped us to spot a marketing opportunity.

When we examined the usership of Fish Fingers, we found that the housewives who were the heaviest buyers were mainly of a particular type. They tended to be very conservative in their food purchasing habits; they were very concerned about the nourishment or goodness value of food; and they tended to be down the market in terms of social status.

But there was another large group of housewives, in many ways similar, but who were much more willing to experiment with new products, and were much less concerned about the nourishment value of food.

To them, tastiness was all important. Compared with the first group, these people tended to be either light or non-users of Fish Fingers. The research seemed to suggest that there was an opportunity to sell the second group an entirely new and novel fish product — a product that was very tasty but concerned itself less with nourishment value. This seemed likely at first to get a high level of trial, because we would be appealing particularly to the experimentalists.

The result was the launch of Crispy Cod Fries in the UK.

In addition, these groups should now figure at the centre of research designed to test the effectiveness of marketing strategies. It is the ratings, attitudes and preferences of the target group that matter, not those of the population in general. This applies to product concept tests, product tests, advertising copy tests, brand image research, media research, and so on.

Product segmentation

The discussion so far has concentrated on consumer segmentation, with particular reference to the identification of target groups. During recent years researchers have paid increasing attention to a different, if related, concept, sometimes known as product segmentation.

Barnett[38] gives a useful account of issues which stimulated early developments in this area, although he does, in the author's opinion, adopt a rather extreme position.

Barnett begins by discussing some traditional consumer segmentation criteria, e.g. demographic and personality variables, points out that none of these, individually, has shown much success in brand discrimination and goes on to argue that researchers should concentrate instead on deriving product-field-specific criteria by which consumers themselves distinguish between brands and products. He then goes on to imply that researchers should turn away from grouping consumers and should, instead, confine their efforts to grouping brands and products. Here the argument breaks down. Barnett's critique of traditional approaches is just as effectively answered by the developments in consumer segmentation outlined above, namely, that the criteria elicited should be relevant to the product field in question, and that techniques such as cluster analysis should be used to deal with the multiple influences on consumer behaviour. It is just as valuable to cluster consumers in terms of their requirements from product-field-specific variables as it is to cluster products in terms of the extent to which they are perceived to satisfy these requirements. The criticism being made here is not of the value of clustering products, which is, in fact, illustrated below, but of the extreme position exemplified by Barnett's paper. A more balanced view is that both consumer and product segmentation are valuable, often for different kinds of marketing problem. The former is important for questions about the kind of consumer who should be appealed to. It can throw light upon brand positioning through examining which brands are bought by the same types of people and can also indicate new product opportunities by identifying clusters of consumers whose pattern of needs is not currently being closely matched by existing products.

Product segmentation, too, can identify gaps for new product opportunities. Another application is market definition. Consumers do not always perceive markets in the same way as do manufacturers. Consequently, it is important, for market planning, to establish which brands and products are seen as substitutable. Manufacturers can then check which brands or products are competing with each other and in what respects, and whether there are any sections of the market where they might usefully reposition a brand – either to attack competition, or to fill a current gap.

Product segmentation has been the subject of several different methodological approaches. Three main categories are outlined below. For a fuller description and a critical appraisal see Beazley.[39] The first is a logical extension of traditional brand-image research. The basic methodology closely resembles that used for consumer segmentation as described above, and has been labelled the *factor/cluster approach*. Consumers are asked to rate brands or products along a series of double-ended scales, e.g.

Soothes the skin......irritates the skin
Makes you feel more feminine......doesn't make you feel more feminine

Preferably, the phraseology of these scales, like those used in consumer segmentation, will be based on qualitative research (stage 2 above). In many cases, individual scales will have been selected, by factor analysis or similar procedures (stage 3), as instances of underlying attitude dimensions, such as medication or cosmetic-benefit.

The simplest analysis is to compare the various brands or products along each factor, e.g. set of highly correlated scales, separately. The 'ideal' brand, say, for a particular usage occasion, may be used as a yardstick, as below.

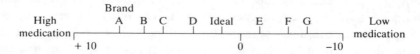

This step can provide valuable diagnostic information in its own right. It is

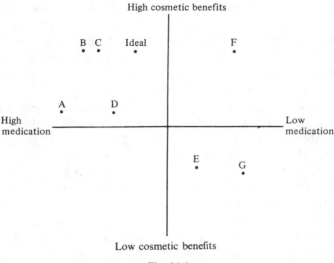

Fig. 14.6.

more illuminating, however, to compare brand ratings on pairs of factors. Where feasible, each pairing is examined in turn. Figure 14.6 gives an illustration. This second step portrays a series of 'contextual maps' of the product field, which provide:

(a) an indication of which brands are competitive in the sense that consumers perceive them as closely substitutable – in this case, brands B and C;
(b) market gaps, in that no brands are judged by consumers to provide this particular combination of characteristics – in this case the combination of high medication and low cosmetic benefits.

If products have been rated on a small number of factors, say three or four, it is relatively easy to examine contextual maps for all possible pairs. In many projects, however, more factors will have been included; quite often more than ten. Here, it is no longer feasible to inspect all the maps. A further problem is that each pairing deals with only part of the total information. Full knowledge about both substitutability and gaps can come only from a procedure which attempts to examine data from several factors simultaneously.

A next step, therefore, is to use cluster analysis to summarize the total set of ratings for all the brands. An example is given below from a food market project.

The main research objective was to guide marketing and advertising planning by showing how each of the client's products fitted into the wider context of all the products competing for the housewife's attention at certain meal occasions. Some twenty products were selected as characteristic of the meal occasion in question; most were manufactured products but others were home produced alternatives; some were essentially 'hot-served' products, others 'cold'; some were fruit-based, others savoury. Ninety scales were elicited (stage 2) and reduced to twelve factors (stage 3), using a pilot sample of 300 housewives. A sample of 1000 housewives rated the twenty products on the twelve scales. The cluster analysis progressively combined the twenty products into two main groupings. Each grouping, from the nineteen product solution to the two, was examined for its defining characteristics.

The four-cluster solution was judged to be the most meaningful, and was also the most compact statistically (see Consumer Segmentation above). One finding was that four out of the five client products came into the same cluster, a grouping which was, on the whole, assessed rather unfavourably by consumers. Several leads, in both product development and advertising terms, were obtained for repositioning two of the client's existing products, and for launching two totally new products.

The second main approach to product segmentation has been labelled the *brand associations/pattern analysis method*. In many ways similar to the first, it is marked both by a relatively simple means of data collection and by a certain novelty in data analysis. In summary, respondents are not asked to rate brands along attitude scales – instead they are presented with a matrix of brands and attributes, and asked to specify simply which of the nominated brands they believe to be associated with each of the listed attributes.

Patterns of responses can be examined from a number of standpoints. For example, taking each attribute in turn, it may emerge that:

(a) No brands are associated – this may imply that the attribute is irrelevant or not currently being delivered.
(b) One brand only is associated – i.e. the attribute is unique to that brand.
(c) Several brands are associated – i.e. the attribute is unique to that sub-set of brands.
(d) All brands are associated – i.e. the attribute is not differentiating between brands.

These data can then be treated by cluster analysis in which either attributes, brands or respondents can be the basis for seeking homogeneous groupings. For a practical case history see a paper by Buckle and Hughes-Hallett.[40]

The third main approach makes use of non-metric multi-dimensional scaling. Descriptions and applications of this branch of methodology have been extensively documented (see chapter 13). A distinctive feature is the derivation of maps of brands and product relationships directly from respondents' assessments of the degree of brand similarities – and from respondents' preference judgements – rather than by using attribute data. Attribute dimensions characterizing the market are subsequently inferred from the ways in which the brands and products are grouped together. This procedure for identifying attribute dimensions has sometimes been attacked, on the grounds that it relies too much on the subjective interpretation of the researcher. One means of answering this criticism is to include attribute data in the questionnaire and to derive attribute profiles of the obtained clusters. This approach is also closely related to consumer segmentation: consumers can be clustered in terms of the 'points of view' they hold about brands and products on the market derived from similarity and preference data.

Practical experience suggests that all three types of product segmentation yield broadly similar results. Beazley[39] suggests several criteria for choosing between them on particular occasions. For instance, the factor/cluster method is most appropriate for major, comprehensive market investigations: the brand association/pattern analysis method is a valuable, intermediate method when economy and ease of communication are of the essence: non-metric methods are valuable exploratory tools for hypothesis formulation, especially where consumers may have difficulty in verbalizing their attitudes.

Linking consumer and product segmentation

Like many aspects of research, consumer and product segmentation are better regarded as complementary rather than competitive. Each can throw light on a different aspect of the market. An illustration of this was provided by a recent study of the food market. The research involved the four stages of consumer segmentation described above, as well as product segmentation, in which the various brands in the market were clustered in terms of empirically derived attribute ratings. Two findings of the consumer segmentation were of particular interest. First, research failed to confirm certain strongly-held marketing convictions. It was assumed that the market was roughly divided into nourishment and economy segments, and that consumers would be grouped accordingly. Cluster analysis on specific consumer requirements failed to find any evidence of this. A number of clusters were, in fact, identified, but they had very different characteristics to those hypothesized by the marketing team; moreover, they did not show any distinctive patterns of brand usage. Second, when the cluster analysis was re-run with the addition of more general attitudes, a much clearer picture emerged. The clusters were more readily identifiable as 'real people', and showed pronounced discrimination between current brands. This illustrates the value of characteristics additional to product specific requirements, a point ignored by some researchers. The nature of these clusters, combined with an assessment of the relative importance of the product attributes, formed the basis of the relaunch of two existing client brands and stimulated thinking for two possible new brands. It is worth adding that the two re-launched brands achieved significant differences in product, pack and copy tests, within the target clusters and in terms of the attitude dimensions selected as most important.

Returning to the first point, the product segmentation did, in fact, confirm the marketing presuppositions in one respect. The twelve brands in the market grouped together into two clusters, one a mainly nourishment cluster, and the other a mainly economic one, defined in each case by distinctive attribute ratings. The point of this comparison is that the manufacturers had been successful in their policies: brands in this market were perceived in the intended ways; but their success had not had a full marketing pay-off, for the benefits conveyed did not correspond to consumer needs as revealed by the consumer segmentation analysis.

The whole area of linking consumer and product segmentation presents an important challenge to researchers. One means of attempting this is to superimpose actual and ideal brand clusters in the same spatial representation. Examples can be found in Green and Tull.[41] Another means is to carry out product clustering *within* previously established consumer segments.

Some general research issues

A few comments of a more general nature before leaving this section on methodology. Although in itself a relatively simple concept, segmentation has been the focus of some highly sophisticated research developments. Some of the techniques such as factor and cluster anlysis and the various nonmetric procedures are now widely used in consumer research; their strengths and weaknesses are well known.

This wealth of different approaches may sometimes lead to a certain feeling of arbitrariness; to a fear that quite different marketing inferences might have been drawn had other techniques been used. But, as was pointed out earlier in the chapter, different techniques have different properties and underlying models, and should, strictly speaking, only be applied to problems and data which meet the assumptions of these models. It is often possible to cross-check the results of any one technique by the use of another, e.g. by the combined use of qualitative and quantitative methods in attitude research.[42,43]

Different marketing problems require different types of analysis technique. Here the writer echoes the warning given by Holmes in chapter 13 about the dangers of standard packages. The marketing man should be wary of the researcher who encounters him armed with an all-purpose set of segmentation procedures.

The very complexity of segmentation methodology can lead to a total rejection by marketing men in favour of a much more simple approach. One school of thought, for instance, confines research for new product development to the following three stages:

(a) group discussions;
(b) the development of new concepts in the light of these group discussions;
(c) an assessment, on a national sample, of the proportions of the population responding favourably to each concept.

Such an approach may sometimes be justified, for instance if budgets are tight;

but the marketing man should be aware that he may be adopting a rudimentary, hit or miss approach. For his medium term strategic planning he will derive much more value from identifying consumer groups of varying potential defined by the needs they are seeking to fulfil by purchasing in the product field, and also from the richer assessment of the competitive situation which a segmentation study provides. Moreover, it is important to regard projects of the kind described in this chapter as contributing towards banks of data which can be used for re-analysis on several occasions. This is not to deny that there will be occasions when projects which are relatively modest in scale will be adequate. Increasing use of the brand association method referred to above reflects a concern to use simple methodology where this can be justified.

A more specific research issue concerns the *ideal brand* concept. This has been referred to several times in this chapter. It is widely used as an anchor point on semantic differential scales, and as an index of specific consumer requirements; for instance, as illustrated on page 414, respondents can be asked to rate not only particular brands but also 'the ideal brand' in terms say of cosmetic properties. Many researchers hold considerable misgivings about this concept. It is thought to be rather artificial and prone to ambiguity – what exactly does the respondent understand by an 'ideal' brand, something purely fanciful or something highly desirable but 'realistic'? There are many product fields where a respondent might be expected to have several ideals, according to the mood or usage occasion: for instance, would it be helpful or meaningful to ask a woman to conceptualize her ideal dress?

In practice, however, the concept often appears to work well, especially where use is made of appropriate scenarios. For instance, women might be asked about their ideal dress for a formal occasion, for going shopping, and so on. The ideal should, however, only be used in contexts where it is meaningful, and care should be taken in the interview to provide a precise, operational definition to the respondent, thus minimizing dangers of ambiguity. Furthermore, it is better regarded as a reference point indicating consumer needs on specific attributes, rather than as a general concept in itself. That is, we are not asking consumers to describe their 'ideal' brand in a total sense.

This chapter has emphasized the need for an empirical approach to market segmentation studies. It is equally important that these projects should be guided by appropriate theories and models of consumer behaviour, especially those which deal with decision processes in a dynamic manner.

A segmentation study can only provide a snapshot of the market at any one period of time. For a full understanding, and for effective marketing action, we require a consideration of the changes that take place over time. Some relevant insights can be found in the work of Howard and Sheth.[19]

Conclusion

There is still considerable scope for improvement in segmentation methodology. In some respects it has already outrun the practical value being derived by marketing and advertising men. This final section summarizes some problems arising from – or inhibiting – the application of this type of project.

There is still a basic suspicion by some marketing men of the whole segmentation philosophy. To focus upon specific target groups seems to imply a deliberate rejection of certain sections of the market. To a certain extent this is a question of facing up to issues raised earlier under 'Some Marketing Considerations'. Consumers do have different needs, and there is more to be gained from identifying and catering for these needs than from ignoring them. Moreover, segmentation is not always a matter of focusing down. Certain products may start with a minority appeal, and steadily capture sales from large sections of the population. In this context, the author has already suggested 'market construction' as a more positive term from the marketing standpoint one, which does more justice to the range of marketing activity that can stem from a 'segmentation' project. Hence the title of this chapter. From the research standpoint, 'market description' or 'market structure' might be preferred to the term segmentation.

To illustrate the potential superiority of the segmentation approach, consider three alternative approaches to market planning, listed by Sheth.[44] First, *planned obsolescence*, which is more of a technology-orientated concept. The fundamental assumption is to introduce new products according to technological programmes, by stimulating additional demand in the market place. 'Innovate or perish' is the watchword. Second, *aggregate modelling* of market responses, where it is assumed that the market place is composed of homogeneous customers who deviate from the average response only in terms of the law of statistical error. Third is the concept of *market variety*, which takes essentially a short-term approach. It is argued that a company is better off simply to produce a large variety of the same product or service, market them equally, and let the market place decide which variety is most desired by the consumers.

Some of the early segmentation studies produced disappointing results. Little discrimination was achieved at brand level, or even, at times, at product level. The picture has improved considerably with the incorporation of less restricted input data and more appropriate analysis techniques. At the same time, there are circumstances where it would be unrealistic to expect clear-cut results. For instance, consumers may be largely homogeneous in terms of determinant needs in the market; there may be considerable overlap in brand purchasing (although it must be remembered that quite different motivations may underlie similar purchasing behaviour); where involvement in the product field is low, purchasing may be more a matter of chance or of easily changed habit than of strongly motivated habit or conviction; and finally, there may have been little systematic marketing or advertising policy in the past in terms of either established or even hypothesized consumer needs.

Given the volume and complexity of segmentation research findings, a particular strain is placed upon client credibility and client-researcher relationships. Undoubtedly, it is important for marketing and advertising men to be involved in and committed to a segmentation project from the outset, to understand its possibilities and limitations, and to specify the problems they expect it to illuminate. It cannot be emphasized too often or too strongly that a client should commission a problem-solving project, not a set of techniques. Ideally, close liaison between client and researcher will be maintained throughout the project, and special attention will be given by the researcher to the ways in which the data are presented and communicated. A variety of devices can be brought to bear here.[45] Effective use can also be made of cartoons, pen-portraits, and other visual aids. The company research officer has a crucial role to play, as described by Hill in a paper which also gives several valuable examples of the practical value of segmentation research.[46]

Media constraints still present a problem. Some marketing people feel that segmentation projects are only of value where the target groups identified have distinctive readership or viewing patterns, thus laying the foundation for differential media scheduling. This is a somewhat extreme position. Absence of distinctive media profiles does not lessen the purchasing potential of a target group, or its value in product development and copy formulation. Research on selective perception suggests that consumers will respond to information that is congruent with their needs and filter out that which is not. At the same time, distinctive media profiles undoubtedly help marketing men to extract the fullest possible value from segmentation research.

Discovering distinctive media profiles is complicated by the recent trends in segmentation criteria described earlier in this chapter. In the days when demographic variables formed the major criteria it was relatively easy to find corresponding media profiles, but these chances have lessened as target group definitions have become increasingly tailor-made for specific markets. However, the discovery of fundamental psychological or life-style variables, relevant to a wide range of product fields, might still emerge as a possibility, and would open up promising avenues for media–buyer behaviour links.

There are still issues to be resolved in identifying target groups quickly and cheaply in everyday market research projects, where there is little opportunity for extensive batteries of questions. Methods currently under experimentation include asking respondents to allocate themselves to pen portrait profiles, based on cluster analysis descriptions, and the use of shortened batteries of attitude scales.

Finally, the question of change. It was pointed out in the previous section that a segmentation project produces a static picture. There is, however, a need to be aware of and to anticipate market changes. This may be helped both by the use of motivational variables as segmentation criteria, and by reference to theories and models of buyer behaviour. The crucial point is to recognize that target group profiles are not fixed for all time. Markets evolve naturally: they may also be changed by manufacturers. Segmentation and construction projects can indicate some of the means for achieving this.

Postcript

The first edition of this chapter was prepared in 1971, when large-scale market structure studies were enjoying a boom, and their potential was still being explored. Several years later it is possible to bring a fresh perspective to the scene. Many more such projects have been carried out (e.g. ref. 47) and a fuller assessment can be made of benefits and problems associated with their design and execution and with the implementation of their findings. In particular, the author has been associated with a major, unpublished review for a multinational corporation of market structure projects from several European countries.

The picture emerging from their review was an encouraging one. In all cases examined in the review, marketing men volunteered the information that the benefits derived more than justified the time and expenditure involved. In some cases the findings were held to have contributed to substantial gains in market share, in others to arresting an anticipated decline in share in the light of fierce competition. All the facets of marketing strategy discussed above have been influenced, to a greater or lesser extent, in different projects.

In certain cases, the results of a single project carried out five years or more previously were held to have influenced marketing thinking to the present day. The minimal benefit claimed was an enriched understanding of consumer and market behaviour, which was held to be of value in itself.

At the same time this particular review highlighted a number of extraneous factors which influence the extent to which 'good' research is related to market-place 'success'. There is not a simple one-to-one relationship because, to quote:

(i)   Marketing decisions are frequently complex and depend on many factors other than research (e.g. competitive activity, production considerations, financial considerations, marketing judgement, etc.). *Similarly marketing success is a function of complex circumstances, in particular the nature and effects of competitive activity.*

(ii) The personnel involved in the commissioning, execution and application of research change jobs with such frequency that the situation is often encountered in which *a study will not be used by the same people* (e.g. marketing or advertising executives) *who initiated it.* This may be an obstacle to realizing the full effectiveness of a research study.

(iii) Marketing decisions based on previous research are not necessarily pre-tested in order to establish whether the solution is consistent with the recommendation – this could result in inexplicable differences between forecast and observed effects in the market-place.

These factors are not, of course, confined to market structure studies although they are especially applicable to them.

Moreover, additional experience has led to certain changes of emphasis. Perhaps the major one has been towards simpler, smaller-scale projects with a more flexible and discriminating approach towards methodology. Large-scale market structure studies, involving extensive batteries of attitude statements and the combined use of several types of multivariate analysis, will continue to play their part. But they will be carried out less frequently and more purposefully – for instance where there is reason to believe that the basic patterns of the market have undergone a pronounced change.

Their value will be as periodic base-line studies, to be supplemented by small-scale surveys designed to monitor specific aspects of marketing activity. Both sets of data will be appropriate to feed into Management Information Systems, and to feature in attempts to stimulate and forecast future patterns and opportunities, as described in chapter 20.

Finally, too much emphasis cannot be placed on the need to communicate the findings of segmentation with simplicity and clarity – however complex the data.

Chapter 15

Research for new product development

COLIN GREENHALGH

It would be convenient, not only for the purposes of this chapter but also for marketing companies generally, if new products were developed by a logical step-by-step approach — by surmounting a succession of hurdles which remained constant from product to product, so that new product development could be 'learned by rote'. The facts, of course, are quite the opposite. The majority of new products are developed by a series of fairly unordered steps, the order and the degree of attention paid to each varying from company to company and from project to project.

There are many reasons for this lack of formality. Principal amongst these are:

(a) the large contribution which is undoubtedly made by sheer creativity to most new products which have much chance of success;
(b) the interaction of all the elements in the total 'marketing mix' (product, price, pack, name, advertising, etc.);
(c) the cost and time-scale pressures which are ever-present in most competitive situations.

Nevertheless, despite the difficulty of pursuing a thoroughly logical procedure, in practice it is well to have one constantly in mind, to avoid going too far off the charted course. This chapter, therefore, is written in terms of such a formal structure, though it is recognized that, once studied, this may well often have to be amended in the face of practical difficulties.

Note: The references quoted throughout this chapter are restricted to those which are likely to advance the reader's understanding of research techniques as they apply to the NPD function. There are, in the marketing and research literature, numerous case histories and passing comments which touch on these techniques without setting out to increase understanding. Many of our references contain their own extensive reading lists. We have not, in general, duplicated their efforts in this direction.

Coverage

Many of the steps in a new product program are ones in which market research has no part to play. Several publications are available to take the reader through all these stages (refs. 1–8 are some relevant sources). We are concentrating here on the contribution of consumer research to new product development, and are only describing those other, non-research, elements to the extent to which it is necessary to put the whole into context.

There is a stage at the very start of any new product program which can be described as 'selecting the product field'. This is not covered here for a variety of reasons. Firstly because, rightly or wrongly, many companies are in one product field (or a small number), feel themselves constrained to stay within those product fields and, as a matter of policy, work at new product introductions in each of them concurrently – so there is no problem of selection. Secondly, where a pre-selection stage *is* necessary it usually rests on considerations of company capabilities – such as finance, technology, the sales force – and familiarity, backed by market-size and market-trend information of the desk and sales research type. And thirdly, insofar as *ad hoc* consumer research does play a part in this fundamental decision to 'look at' a particular product field, this can come about in many and varied ways which are rather outside the scope of this chapter, ranging from small-scale group discussions and structured usership and attitude surveys, to long-term social trends research. (See chapters 2, 8, 9 and 10 of this book, and ref. 9, in particular, if further reading on this use of consumer research is required.)

This chapter is also essentially restricted to low price, pre-packed and branded consumer goods (so-called 'fast moving consumer goods'). In other words, even within the context of consumer goods, it excludes specific discussion of durables and services. The major contribution of market research to new product development undoubtedly continues to be in this area of 'fmcg', but marketers and researchers working in the area of durables, services (and even industrial goods) will certainly find much of relevance here and will, no doubt, amend and adapt the techniques described when necessary.

This chapter also has nothing to say about researching new products amongst the trade. It is well known, nowadays, that the power of large buying points (multiple chains and wholesale–retail co-operatives etc.) is such that they can spell failure for a new product regardless of consumers' attitudes towards it. Some pre-testing amongst buyers is, therefore, carried out, but (a) it is a difficult universe to research and (b) such research as is done in this area is really an adaptation of concept tests, product tests, and pricing research (see later) to samples of trade buyers.

Finally, the research contributions described in this chapter stop short of the market place (whether national, test market or mini-test market) because these later stages are dealt with in chapter 19. It also precludes detailed discussion of elements of the marketing mix except the central ones of new product concepts, their physical realization, their price, and the resultant 'total product'. This is not to say that the other necessary elements — packaging, name, advertising, etc., often called the 'communication elements' – are less crucial to ultimate success, but that they also are covered elsewhere, in chapters 16 and 17.

Why new products?

It is, perhaps, worthwhile dwelling for one moment on why new product development is so important in the first place, and why so much market research effort is dedicated to this particular end-use.

Mass-marketed products undoubtedly go through a life cycle*. The excact shape of the life cycle is irrelevant; its length is certainly very variable from product to product, but it is almost axiomatic that any product will eventually start to decline in the face of competition, advancing technology and changing consumer tastes. Various devices can be resorted to to postpone the effects of this decline on profits, e.g. a cut in advertising or increase in price. Such devices, however, are generally self-defeating in the long run. More promising is 're-cycling', i.e. finding and promoting new uses for the product, attacking new segments of the market, or straight product improvements, designed to hold up sales in the face of the inevitable life cycle. Even re-cycling, however, will wear thin in the long run and profits will start to decline.

It follows that most companies need to develop new products regularly, so as to phase in their profit contributions as those on existing products start to decline. The new products which are developed may be new brands in an existing product group, they may be 'new, new products', of which the like has never been seen before, or they may be range extensions, companion brands to existing company products. Which of these they turn out to be is for the new product program, allied with the necessary research, to determine.

It is for these reasons, though — that the changing demands of consumers, allied with the spur of competition, technological change and the urge to grow, force innovation on most companies – that new product development is so vitally important to the prosperity and, even, survival of most companies.

Generating new product concepts

While 'product concept' is a term which is often used at the initial 'ideas' stage of a new product program, there is no universally accepted definition of what a

---

* King[5] has argued forcefully, and justifiably, that most companies market much more than products, they market brands. It is, strictly, *brands* which go through a life cycle and we ought really to talk of new *brand* development: however, the use of the word 'product' to connote 'brand' is so ingrained that we propose to continue to use it in this sense in this chapter.

concept is. One definition which has been used elsewhere is 'A description in words of a product: the vocabulary employed should be non-evaluative and descriptive'. This would not seem to cover all cases, however. For one thing, many concepts (particularly in the fmcg markets which we are considering here) cannot be adequately conveyed in *non-evaluative* words, if they can be conveyed in words at all. These are the concepts which depend not so much on what the end product looks like or what it does but on the way people *feel* about it. The rational justification for a new toilet soap, for instance, may be 'A soap which contains an ingredient which will eliminate blemishes and restore the skin's natural softness'. It may be that a more profitable concept for marketing purposes, however, is that of 'A soap which makes you feel young again!'

The most important characteristic of successful concepts is probably that they are based on the *consumer's* point of view, that they express what consumer benefits will be offered, what consumer needs will be satisfied, even if this means they cannot be expressed in words at all! Perhaps a fairer definition, if a definition is needed at all, would be that a concept expresses the 'essentials of the product idea – that collection of consumer benefits by which it differs from other available products and which are believed to be essential to its portrayal to enable it to achieve its desired position in its target market'.

Where do new product ideas come from?[6, 10–13]

The majority of new product ideas are generated in one or more of the following ways. The task of consumer research is to take its appropriate place amongst these different routes:

(a) creative flair;
(b) R & D (Research & Development) breakthroughs;
(c) deliberate procedures to search for or invent new products:
   (i) consumer based,
   (ii) non-consumer based.

While there is only sketchy evidence (see below) on the relative effectiveness of these different sources in generating *successful* product ideas, it is likely that the continuing growth of the marketing philosophy throughout industry will result in an increasing proportion of new product ideas being directly consumer based. Therefore, while all these sources will be briefly described in this section, the particular contribution of consumer research will be stressed.

Creative flair

Marketing men, advertising agency people – particularly those in 'creative' jobs – salesmen, laboratory workers – all are likely to think of new product ideas out of the blue – 'I wonder what consumers would think if we gave them …?' This creative flair is not, however, necessarily accidental and it can be cultivated and stimulated in various ways. One of these is deliberately to expose such people to consumers and to relevant consumer research.[14] If a copywriter attends group discussions on an existing product group, it exposes him to the possibility that a chance remark may suggest the germ of a new idea. If an R & D scientist reads the detailed results of a product test, it increases the chances that a new way of satisfying a minority segment of the market will occur to him.

Doing consumer research at all – almost any type of consumer research – exposes the lively minds of marketing, advertising and technical people to consumers' behaviour, attitudes, needs and aspirations and increases the chances of a *relevant* inspiration.

R and D breakthroughs

Another fruitful source of new product ideas may certainly be investment in R & D.[15] Sometimes, though rarely in the type of packaged consumer goods which we are considering here, these ideas are the results of basic research in the natural sciences; more often they come from the accidental or deliberate application of well-known technologies and processes in new areas.

The major contribution of consumer research is probably in keeping the R & D technologists, and those who direct their efforts, constantly aware of consumers' needs. In this way the company's R & D effort can be directed into the potentially most rewarding areas, and ideas for new product breakthroughs, when they occur, will be more readily recognized as relevant.

Deliberate procedures for searching or inventing

These are broadly of two types. Those which are:

(a) conducted amongst and about consumers and are therefore, to a greater or lesser extent, consumer research based;
(b) not amongst and about consumers.

We will take the latter (historically the more usual) first.

Non-consumer based procedures

These differ in kind from 'flair' and 'breakthroughs', in that there is a conscious effort to go out and look for possibilities, or to invent new products, rather than waiting for them to arrive 'out of the blue'.

There is also a difference in degree between – at the one extreme – searching for products to copy those which already exist 'out there', and – at the opposite extreme – inventing something the like of which has never been seen before. But the majority of procedures combine both these ingredients to a greater or lesser extent, that is *searching* for an idea or opportunity which then needs an element of *invention* to realize. So, no clear dividing line has been drawn between 'searching' and 'inventing': the following procedures are arranged roughly in order from the one to the other:

(a) routine vetting of the home market for new entrants to copy, or improve on;
(b) similar observation of overseas markets;
(c) routine observation of the home market for potential growth areas;
(d) reading of technical periodicals and journals (and those of consumer testing organizations);
(e) regular searches of the register of patent applications;
(f) morphological, gap and spectrum analysis[16,17]

(The latter has much in common with 'mapping techniques' based on consumer surveys (see below). In this context, however, it refers to a conscious search for gaps in product technology rather than in consumers' perceived images of products.)

(g) asking R & D people, inside or outside the company, to 'invent something';
(h) suggestion schemes amongst employees;
(i) 'brainstorming' amongst employees and other groups.

A development of the latter is 'synectics'.[18] This is a form of advanced brainstorming, which brings together experts from several different, and apparently unrelated, disciplines and, by making them aware of the nature of the creative process, attempts to turn them into highly original inventors. Synectics has not been much used in the marketing of everyday products (whose success does not often depend on the solution of difficult technical problems) but it is a technique which may be worth experimentation in particular cases. As with most new techniques, synectics has itself undergone development and adaptation with experience in use: at the very least, it appears to have encouraged more structure and discipline into company brainstorming.

Consumer-based procedures

Probably the cheapest and simplest search procedure amongst consumers is the regular vetting of correspondence on existing products; though, in truth, new product ideas from this source will generally be very unformed and needing astute recognition and nurturing. Von Hippel[19] has described methods of improving upon this passive receipt of suggestions by, for instance, soliciting them and running competitions.

But now, arriving at the kernel of this chapter, the use of *consumer research* based attempts to find new product ideas, the first is quite straightforward. It is simply to read previous qualitative and quantitative research (usership and attitude studies, product tests, advertising tests, etc.), very comprehensively and with a very detailed eye, in a conscious attempt to look for openings via, for instance, likes and dislikes of existing products.[5,20] As with many procedures, some researchers and commentators have proposed that this type of search is likely to be much more productive if it is set into a formal framework. For instance, Tauber[21] suggests the use of a 'problem inventory'. He lists 134 possible problem areas for consumers in food and drink markets, e.g. physiological (weight / hunger / thirst), sensory (taste / appearance), buying and usage (portability / spoilage), psychological / social (eating alone / self-image) etc. By reviewing the standing of existing products against this checklist – and such a review is likely to lean heavily on previous product research – then the chances of finding an opening for something new must be enhanced.

However, the odds are that, if consumer research is to be increasingly productive in generating new product ideas, it will ve through 'tailor-made' studies. The following techniques are worth describing.

Qualitative research

This involves the use of group discussions and individual depth interviews to explore consumers' behaviour, attitudes, needs, wants and, particularly, problems in the selected product group or need-area (see chapter 2 and refs. 16, 21, 22). (The expression 'need-area' is used here, and later, in preference to 'market', because in really forward-looking cases no recognizable selection of brands or products may as yet be on sale for that purpose.) Being qualitative, the research can be comprehensive and reasonably exhaustive and, in this way, unsatisfied needs and aspirations can be looked for. Once found, these aspirations can become the starting-point for a deliberate attempt at new concept invention.

The reasons for using qualitative research are (a) that, at this stage, we are only searching for possible ideas, not evaluating their potential, and (b) that most of the need-areas we shall be looking at are already exploited to a substantial extent – latent aspirations will be lurking beneath the surface, to be patiently winkled out, by discursive questioning. 'Qualitative' research, however, is not necessarily synonymous with 'small scale' research. If our marketing criteria are such that we are prepared to look for latent needs in a very small segment of the total market, then we may well have to employ substantial sample sizes, minimizing the cost of researching the interesting segment by filtering out the remainder at an earlier stage of the recruiting procedure – as long as we know in advance how the potentially interesting segment will be defined!

A development of qualitative research which has sometimes been used for suggesting new product ideas is 'action studies'. These generally take the form of very detailed studies of consumers' behaviour in a need-area of interest to the manufacturer. A panel of women, for instance, might keep a detailed diary of their use of toiletry and cosmetic products over a period, or a sample of housewives might be filmed throughout a working day in their kitchens. These records can be used to draw conclusions about possible needs or, more productively, they can be used as recall aids when informants are subsequently interviewed in depth about their feelings and frustrations at each point in the 'action'. These are helpful devices to increase the chances of latent needs being recognized; any other productive or cost-effective device is open to the researcher at this ideas generating stage (providing, of course, it complies with the accepted professional and ethical standards).

Conventional quantitative research

This is the next logical progression in the use of research to look for possible new product ideas. If the company has no, or inadequate, previous research in a market or need-area in which it is currently interested, then it might consider it worth its while to specially commission usership and attitude studies, product tests on existing brands and so on. Then, of course, to use these as previously described, to sift and search for new product possibilities. Kuehn and Day[23] in particular describe how product tests can be used this way. However, such specially commissioned research may be something of an exception and a luxury *for this basic inventive purpose*. (It must be clearly distinguished from the very frequent use of market surveys *after* the product idea is available, to optimize the way in which the new product is to be marketed.) Structured consumer research may be productive of product ideas if one needs it for other purposes anyway and, obviously, it is then very cost-effective. But if one wishes to commission research specifically to generate new ideas, then the odds are that one would be better off moving in one direction or the other – either back towards less circumscribed qualitative research, or forwards towards more tailor-made quantitative techniques, such as 'mapping'.

'Mapping' techniques

There are numerous variants on this whole family of techniques, varying according to the data they collect and to the analysis methods they employ. In essence, they collect either detailed ('multi-attribute') data about consumers' perceptions and/or attitudes towards existing products, or detailed descriptive and attitudinal information about the consumers themselves or, more often, about both of those. They then construct multi-dimensional 'maps' of that market in terms of the data they have collected – mapping either the products, or the people, or the one allied with the other. These maps then lead to the identification of potential new product opportunities in terms of the original, very detailed, information which was collected.

The range of available techniques can, perhaps, be most easily represented by their two extreme forms, from which subsequent variants have grown, namely 'gap analysis' and 'segmentation'.

Gap analysis

This approach is also sometimes known as 'product segmentation'. In general, a representative sample of consumers in a broadly defined target group is interviewed about existing products in a broadly defined market. ('Broadly defined', in both cases, because the end-product of this whole search procedure may well be a concept which has the potential to attract new types of users to the product group. Such a concept may be at, or beyond, the fringe of existing products and existing consumers.) The vital information collected in these interviews is consumers' perception of the existing products, either in terms of their overall similarity to each other, or along relevant attitudinal dimensions, i.e. their 'image' of each product (see chapter 14). In some of the adaptations this is also supplemented by consumers' perceptions of their 'ideal' product in the same terms. Appropriate multivariate analysis techniques are used to analyse this image data and to 'look for gaps'. These gaps are empty spaces in the multi-dimensional attitude space, where no existing product represents a particular set of attitudinal characteristics as seen by a significant segment of the population covered, or where a significant number of consumers would position their (non-existent) ideal product.

Such gaps in the attitude space represent potential areas for the positioning of a new product with significant appeal. They *are* only potential areas at this stage, because such a procedure inevitably throws up obvious but impractical gaps (e.g. a cheaper product than any existing brand, but using only the highest quality ingredients), and 'nonsense' gaps (an expensive product using poor quality ingredients). Such gaps are thrown up simply because no manufacturer is able (or would be foolish enough) to market such a product: their existence is no great disadvantage to the outcome of the research because they can easily be eliminated on sight.

Since most consumer markets have a substantial number of relevant attitudinal dimensions, certainly if they are sufficiently broadly defined, such a gap analysis will often throw up a large number of attitudinal gaps. Each of these could, if wished, be subjected to the next stage of the new product programme (concept evaluation), but the available gap analysis techniques often have built-in devices for ranking the gaps in approximate order of their potential – or even for predicting their likely sales levels – so that the least interesting can be passed over without further ado.

Segmentation

This is more exactly known as 'consumer segmentation', to differentiate it from the 'product segmentation' described above. Again, data about the need-area of interest are collected from a large and representative sample of the possible target group, very much as above. There tends, however, to be a greater emphasis on descriptive information about the informants themselves; demographic, personality, behaviour in the relevant need-area, and attitudes to the need-area itself. Appropriate multi-variate analysis techniques then enable the informants to be clustered into groups which are homogeneous within themselves, but as different from each other as possible, in terms of the descriptive and attitudinal data collected about them. Simple tabulation of existing product-use and attitudes for each of these clusters can now help to identify significant segments of consumers who appear to have a (possibly latent) unsatisfied need. Examples are quoted in the literature; a hypothetical one might be 'Elderly women who worry about their health, who believe that a particular ailment can be cured and not just relieved, but also believe that existing remedies might not be entirely safe'. If, in addition, a high proportion of this hypothetical segment currently uses no proprietary medicine (or has very fragmented brand-use – another way of saying their needs appear not to be very effectively met by currently available products), then they would appear to present the necessary potential for a possible new product.

By drawing an 'Identi-kit picture' of potential consumer segments, such a technique clearly goes a long way to suggesting possible product concepts which might attract those segments.

Gap analysis and segmentation are but two of the battery of multi-variate techniques which are increasingly used by market researchers, and about which there is an awesome volume of literature. Shocker and Srinivasan[24] have published a comprehensive review which, in its turn, includes a very extensive list of references. We could do no better than to direct the student to that, and to chapters 14 and 13 (in that order) in this book.

Invention by consumers

Getting consumers themselves to invent products is by no means easy. Attempts which have been made tend to be qualitative in nature and in scale. At their simplest they involve brainstorming in a group discussion context. All the evidence, however, is that consumers are not very productive or inventive when being handled in this way. Various approaches have been tried to get over this reticence: one manufacturer,[25] for instance, is reported to have tackled it by what he calls 'reverse brainstorming', that is by putting the emphasis in his groups on the discussion of problems with existing products. Others clearly do the same, while giving their techniques different names.[22] But, of course, this is likely to generate potential opportunites for functionally new products, not for ones which depend on their 'communication elements'.

A few practitioners have attempted to go rather further and to apply such knowledge as we have about creative processes to ordinary consumers – even to try the full synectics approach. From their attempts, they claim to have at least learnt how to *encourage* inventiveness in consumers; for instance, Sampson[26] says that the principal lessons are:

(a) not to expect consumers to spell out potential new products in all their detail, but to get ideas to ᴛhe prototype stage where they can be recognized and carried forward by experts;
(b) to allow much more time than for conventional group discussions, and even to hold repeat sessions;
(c) to have materials and props available, rather than expecting informants to discuss too much in the abstract;
(d) not to hope for much *technical* inventiveness from ordinary consumers, even in a synectics environment.

Holmes and Keegan,[27] too, provide guidance on this type of consumer research. In particular, they emphasize:

(a) the value of recruiting creative informants, with suggestions on how to find them;
(b) the desirability of continuous panels or, at the least, of an 'incubation period' between repeat sessions;
(c) the value of having two researchers to alternate in leading the group.

Conclusion on this stage: generating concepts

These, then, are the principal sources which have generally been used to generate new product ideas. As we have seen, they are many and various. But, this is a chapter about the contribution of consumer research to new product development, so let us briefly summarize those which adopt that route:

(a) Exposure to research which is already on file or is newly commissioned – including attendance at interviews and group discussions – is always likely to stimulate ideas, and maximise their relevance, amongst marketing, creative and R & D people.
(b) Deliberate attempts can be made to search for new product ideas by a careful reading of all past research in a need-area.
(c) Qualitative research – group discussions or individual 'depth' interviews – can be commissioned specifically to search for new product ideas. These can even go further by asking participants to 'invent' something. They can be made more productive by the use of developments such as action studies, synectics etc., but all the evidence is that the final step – of turning a consumer need or dissatisfaction into a product concept – will need to

be taken by marketing and technical people, rather than by consumers themselves.

(d) Conventional quantitative research – usership and attitude surveys etc. – is unlikely to be very productive for this purpose. But specialized developments of them, e.g. mapping techniques, are likely to be more so: whether they are, as yet, more productive of succesful ideas than other techniques it is impossible to say.

It is for the individual manufacturer to decide how comprehensive he can afford to be in setting up new product search procedures. In doing so, however, he should remember two things. The first is that, despite what ought to be, and what the future may hold, the vast majority of new product ideas do not, at present derive from specially commissioned consumer research. The author in fact, demonstrated[11] some years ago that, at least for supermarket-type products, about 40 % of new products introduced in Britain were claimed to have derived from some form of market-searching (including accidental 'one-offs' as well as planned investigations), about 25 % from consumer research (only a half specially commissioned, the rest already on file), about 15 % from R & D, with the balance from other sources. Other types of surveys, on other types of products, in other countries,[12] have shown different proportions, but the share of consumer research has always been modest. Its principal contribution is to act as a catalyst, to prompt creativity, and to help the recognition of valuable ideas when they are otherwise suggested.

The second thing is that none of the above procedures (with the possible exception of some of the mapping techniques) can produce a unique or 'best' new concept in a particular product area: most of them will produce several different ideas. It is the principal function of the next stage to evaluate concepts and to sort the more promising from the less promising.

Evaluating and developing new product concepts

When new product concepts have been generated, by whatever means, they need to be:

(a) evaluated; and, in most cases,
(b) developed.

'Evaluation', in its turn, has two meanings. First, assuming there is more than one possible concept to pursue, putting them into a likely order of interest, so that the available management time, R & D expense and financial investment (which are never unlimited) can be devoted to the most promising idea(s). Second, determining whether that concept, or the best of them or, even, which of all of them, deserve time and money put against them at all.

Then, these new concepts will probably need 'developing', because no product idea will be complete and optimal in every respect as it comes straight off the 'ideas production line'. It will need rounding-out: some aspects to be pronounced, others to be suppressed or amended, before it stands a good chance of success in the market-place. The marketing man will also need guidance, at an early stage, about which segments of the total available market appear to offer the easiest target including, for instance, which competing products might be most profitably attacked; and which concept will best complement, rather than compete with, existing company products. Such 'diagnostic' information contributes to the development of the new product concept, before the manufacturer gets down to the serious job of specifying the physical product, its packaging, advertising and other detailed elements of the marketing mix.

Initial screening

The first stage of the evaluation process has, again, little or nothing to do with consumers or consumer research. It is the stage of 'initial screening'. Is the potential new product compatible with the company's strategic aims? With its financial objectives? With company know-how? And plans for the salesforce? Are there any legal constraints on its marketing? Or any relevant social or environmental considerations?, and so on.

While this initial screening is a vital stage in weeding out concepts which never could lead to marketable products *for this company at this time*, it does not generally involve consumer research and is not, therefore, expanded on here. (Several of the 'comprehensive descriptions of NPD procedures' listed at the end of this chapter cover this stage.)

Evaluating new product concepts

After initial screening, new product concepts are generally evaluated by one or other form of 'concept test'. But, sometimes, all that is required at the outset is just 'a steer' — a rough idea for the marketing man whether he should recommend going on or not. In that case, consumer research can sometimes help in quicker and cheaper ways. A very simple behavioural check (perhaps two or three questions on an omnibus survey) can, maybe, demonstrate that the available market is nothing like big enough to support the potential new product at a level which would be acceptable to the manufacturer. (A typical example might be a new medicine, where a simple check might demonstrate that the number of sufferers in the market could never support a product which was compatible with the company's financial objectives.) Goldsmith[10] has described a refinement of this approach in his 'System 651' for evaluating new ideas for frozen foods, in terms of the eating occasions for which they would be seen as appropriate. In rejecting a potential new product on these grounds, however, it is vital to ensure that there is no question of a blinkered approach; that there is no possibility of stretching the proposed product to encompass more interesting and extensive end-uses.

Concept testing

Useful though a simple usership check, or even a full usership and attitude survey into the existing market, may be in its own right — for general 'orientation' throughout the whole of the development program — the majority of new product concepts will *not* be amenable to go-no go evaluation in such a quick and easy way; some form of concept test will generally be called for.

But, here, we must write in another couple of provisos. For the reasons explained at the beginning of this chapter, we are still writing in terms of a fairly formal step-by-step approach to new product development. Over recent years, there has been a move towards rolling-up the whole program into fewer, though more complex, research steps — usually offered as proprietary packages by particular research agencies, or developed by large manufacturing companies on their own account. Indeed, we hinted at such a development in the previous section, when we said that 'the available gap analysis techniques often have built-in devices for ranking gaps ... or even for predicting their likely sales', in other words, for *evaluating* new product concepts at the same time as *generating* them. Added to this, is the fact that proprietary services have been introduced for subsequent stages in the program — for concept and product testing and pricing — sometimes all rolled up into one 'package'. These techniques generally provide information which one-off tests, mounted in isolation, cannot hope to do — specifically forecasting market share or, even, absolute sales levels. But, concomitant with that, they have their own particular requirements about, for instance, the form of the test material (whether concepts or products), and about the particular questions to be asked. We shall return to these 'proprietary' developments later on, after describing the more traditional 'one-off' approach, since this is what most of our readers are likely to find themselves using most of the time.

Concept tests, then, can provide guidance in all of these areas:

(a) which of these ideas looks most interesting?
(b) does it (do they) warrant further investment of time and money?
(c) in what ways can it (they) be further developed?
(d) which segments of the market look most interesting to aim for?

If these are the *aims* of concept tests, let us discuss how they are *conducted*. In general, concept testing works by exposing the test concept(s) — in one form or another — to a sample of consumers, and then asking appropriate questions about them. A detailed description of concept testing *techniques*, then, must embrace the following:

(a) in what form the concepts are exposed;
(b) to whom;
(c) where, and how;
(d) in what particular experimental design;
(e) what questions are asked, and how are they analysed.

In what form are the concepts exposed?

The expression of the concept(s) to be tested can vary from, at one extreme, simple oral statements (sometimes tape recorded for uniformity from interview to interview) through written statements ('words on cards') and line drawings, to dummy packs and mock advertisements (press or video-taped television). If there is no heavy investment involved, or if a 'cribbed' product will do, the dummy pack might even contain a prototype or a close approximation to the real product, as it is envisaged at this stage. It goes without saying that this is an ideal way to express the physical elements of the concept if it is possible.

It is widely argued (the 'holistic' argument, as opposed to the 'atomistic')[28] that the saleability of a product depends so much on the *interaction* between different elements of the total marketing mix, that the nearer we can get to testing 'the whole thing' the less likely we are to make errors in predicting the success or failure of new concepts. However, carried to its logical conclusion the holistic approach introduces three major difficulties into research design:

(a) any testing short of the market-place (with real advertising, real media, actual retail outlets, point-of-sale material etc.,) may produce deceptive answers;
(b) component parts of the marketing mix cannot be developed and tested independently;
(c) *every* element in the marketing mix must be optimally executed before *anything* can be tested.

In other words, the holistic approach would argue that the concept itself cannot be evaluated until all the other elements of the marketing mix have been optimally developed and yet, if *anything* needs to be changed after this initial evaluation, then *everything else* might have to be changed and re-evaluated because of their interactions.

While such a thoroughgoing holistic approach is never seriously commended, there is wide agreement that the diametrically opposed atomistic approach — testing elements of the marketing mix in isolation and only bringing them together ready for the market place — can lead to serious errors, certainly in products where the 'communication' elements are likely to play a large part. The most practical approach would seem to be to build into the concept testing stage those elements which are necessary to convey the proposed new product idea adequately (bearing in mind its possible novelty and uniqueness) and seem likely to *interact* significantly. And to leave out those which, on judgment, are unlikely to interact to any significant extent. This suggests that the concept test should often include:

(a) the emotional aura surrounding the product, as well as its functional claims;
(b) the creative execution up to a fairly advanced stage;
(c) its expression in the chosen main medium;
(d) and (very possibly) its proposed name and price.

This would argue, in such cases, for expressing the concept in a fairly finished advertisement. In other cases, we can probably get near enough by using a 'concept statement' (a description with or without illustration) and/or mock pack and, in rare cases, a new product idea may be so functional that 'words on cards' will be adequate. No hard and fast rule can be laid down. Much depends on the perceived risk in missing out some elements of the marketing mix which could significantly affect consumers' evaluation of the proposed new product, against the costs and time involved in building these other elements into the initial concept testing stage. Balancing these constraints must generally remain a matter of subjective judgement tempered with experience.

To whom is the test administered?
Quite simply, the test should be administered to a representative sample of the target market. This should be defined as those consumers who are likely to have any part in affecting the purchase decision: it would probably, for instance, include the users of many day-to-day products as well as their (housewife) purchasers. The target market should certainly not be defined too restrictively, however. Bearing in mind that one of the objectives of most concept tests is to provide guidance on how the product might be developed, and on which segments of the market it will mostly appeal to, it is highly desirable to include in the sample all consumers who could be in the market for the proposed product – perhaps in an amended and improved version. (Then, of course, it becomes necessary to analyse the results by relevant characteristics of the testers – particularly current behaviour and attitudes to this need-area – to establish the acceptability of the concept to different segments, their likes and dislikes and so on.[29])

It is often suggested that the definition of the target group, for recruitment to concept (and other) pre-tests, should employ attitudinal characteristics, as well as demographic and behavioural characteristics, and a segmentation approach will almost certainly imply this (e.g. chapter 14 of this book). In theory this is obviously desirable, provided – as so often in this particular area of marketing – (a) we already have relevant attitude definitions as a result of previous research in this market, or (b) the commitment to the project is such that the time and cost of refining the target group in this way makes sense, and (c) we do not allow it to restrict our vision of how the concept might be re-positioned and re-targetted *as a result of the test*.

Some researchers believe that in-depth, qualitative concept testing[30] on small samples is likely to be more helpful than straightforward quantitative testing – certainly for developmental purposes, if not for straightforward evaluation – and, indeed, there is often a strong case for both. For such tests, the participants are often recruited purposively and they might comprise, for instance, heavy users of the product group, recent brand switchers, known innovators, extreme acceptors and extreme rejectors of the new concept, without too much regard to strict representative sampling.

Some researchers have also suggested that all new product pre-testing should be restricted to 'innovators' who, they claim, determine the success or failure of new ventures.[31] However, this is rather dubious advice, because the evidence is also that innovators vary from product to product, so that we cannot identify a valid group of innovators for *this* product in advance of at least concept testing it.

Where, and how, is the test administered?

This depends very much on the type and quantity of stimulus material which can (economically) be made available. Thus, with 'words on cards', or a concept statement, or an oral description, we might well conduct the whole test in-home, i.e. by personal call by an interviewer. Even this, though, can have its variations: concept statements can be placed by post, with informants responding on a postal questionnaire; postal placement of the concept can be followed up by a telephone interview; or, with an oral description of the concept, the whole exercise could be conducted by telephone.

Mock advertisements might also be tested in-home if they were economical enough to reproduce (press ads probably, though even video-taped TV ads if the test can be restricted to video machine owners); as could mock-up packs and/or prototype products if enough of them can be economically acquired. However, the more we depend on real products, real packs, or real advertisements to express the concept, the more we are likely to be constrained by costs. In this case, we shall probably have to move towards some form of central location testing – theatre tests (as for TV ad pre-testing), test halls (in permanent locations, or transient), or even mobile test vans. Finally, qualitative tests often imply the use of group discussions, and they will be held in typical discussion locations.

In other words, concept tests can be administered in almost any location, and the concept exposed in almost any manner in which stimulus material is used in consumer research generally, limited only by the economics of producing enough copies or samples.

In what experimental design?

If there is only one concept to be evaluated then there is little problem about experimental design: it has to be monadic – which means that everybody sees and tests just one concept (with rare exceptions (see below)).

It is well to remember, though, that a one-off test, conducted outside one of the proprietary services to which reference has been made, cannot forecast the absolute viability of a new product idea, i.e. whether or not it will make a profit, nor even what level of sales it is likely to achieve. Therefore, the only reliable uses of such a test for *evaluative purposes* are to ask:

(a) is the idea so utterly rejected by testers that it is highly unlikely to be viable at all (even to a minority segment)? (In truth, however, this is a very rare finding for any sensible idea which has passed initial screening);
(b) how does it compare with other concepts which have been similarly tested in the past? (This implies really comparing like with like, in a comparable research design, with comparable questions.)

If there were plenty of such comparable cases from the past which had subsequently been marketed, then we would have 'normative' data to set the latest concept against; but it is unlikely that many individual manufacturers will have accumulated such norms for particular product groups.

However, if several new product ideas are to be evaluated *comparatively*, then it is possible to use well-known experimental designs such as matched monadic tests (separate sub-samples of testers evaluating one concept each, their 'ratings' then being compared – an example of a 'split run'); paired comparisons (testers expressing a preference between two concepts); complete ranking (each tester putting *all* the concepts into an order of preference) etc. – see chapter 3 and many specialized textbooks for a more extended discussion of these designs.

It goes without saying that such tests should still be trying to compare like with reasonable like. Indeed, as with all tests, concept testing is probably on safest ground when it is trying to choose between alternative *treatments* of the same basic idea, different creative claims, different end-uses, different prices etc.,[32] than between fundamentally different ideas.

In this context, particular attention may be drawn to the 'trade-off' approach (also known as 'conjoint analysis') which has been described by several authors.[33–35] This is essentially comparative, testers being asked to choose between concepts which, as in other forms of factorial design testing (see chapter 3), contain all combinations of the relevant product attributes at different levels (or, in complex cases, a balanced sub-set of all possible combinations). An example might be, say, a new paper tissue which could come in any one of three different colours, several different sizes and different thicknesses, but where some of these combinations might need to cost more than others. The trade-off approach would not only predict the winning combination of these attributes but would also estimate how much consumers value changes in one attribute against changes in the others – in other words, to what extent they are prepared to 'trade-off' size against thickness, colour against size, and all of these against price. Such an approach clearly provides understanding, flexibility and (hopefully) validity to the evaluation of alternative treatments of the same basic concept. Equally clearly, it is always likely to be on safer ground when dealing with the rational, factual elements of a new product idea than with the intangibles – say, in the case of those tissues, size or colour which are quite easy to convey 'conceptually', rather than texture, which is not.

Sometimes, new concepts are tested comparatively against existing marketed products. Theoretically, this does build in the necessary point of reference to predict an approximate level of sales in the market place, but such a procedure is obviously of less certain value if the existing product is known to testers; like is not, then, being compared with like. It could, however, be of real value in those rare cases where the test can be conducted amongst a universe to whom the existing product is itself new; e.g. the existing product may still be in test market, so that it can be used as a new concept – but with a known level of sales – in other parts of the country. The trade-off approach could be particularly valuable here and Westwood[35] describes (admittedly for a more functional, industrial product) how hypothetical developments of *competitors'* products can be built in, to deduce this manufacturer's best strategy under conditions of uncertainty about other brands' intentions.

What questions are asked, and how are they analysed?
The questions that are asked in a concept test, as in any piece of research, depend on the marketer's informational needs.

For the evaluative aspects of concept tests it is certainly necessary to ask one (or more) questions which will provide a measure of 'overall acceptability'. Such questions can range from simple rating questions, 'How would you describe this product: excellent/very good/good ...?'; through propensity to purchase, 'How likely are you to buy this product at 30p?' and, maybe, 'How often?'; to mock purchasing situations, 'Would you like to buy a pack for 30p?' A danger to avoid, however, is that of rejecting the concept because of the stated price at which it was put into the test. Price is, after all, one element of the marketing mix and the proposed new product may well be marketable at other prices, something which could be tested by putting alternative prices into the test.

The most important point about such questions, even those of a mock purchase nature, is that they cannot be used just as they stand to predict sales. Any test is a highly artificial, heightened situation and quite unlike real life. Therefore, their major use must be for comparative purposes and, for this, they should be as comparable as possible from test to test within a given product group. In the case of comparative testing against competition, or for choosing between alternatives, particularly paired comparisons, rankings, etc., the problem of meaningful questions is eased. Any sensible questioning technique would probably be acceptable, e.g. 'Which of these products would you be most interested in trying?', or 'Which of them do you think you would buy most often?', and the usual arguments for using the most *discriminating* questions would apply. Some commentators, however, claim that this sort of simplistic question is always likely to provide invalid data — even for comparative purposes. Iuso,[30] for instance, believes that concepts should be assessed by trained researchers working from 'discursive reactions', i.e. semi-structured interviews. Tauber[36,37] correctly emphasizing that 'adoption includes a sense of product commitment', believes we should measure importance and involvement. And Twedt[38] is specific that this can be done by 'tri-variant analysis', i.e. by rating the desirability of the claim × its exclusiveness × its believability. It is one of those areas where it would be nice to have concrete *evidence* that the more sophisticated approaches are actually more valid (i.e. more likely to lead to profitable products) than the simpler ones.

The diagnostic questions which can be asked in a concept test are obviously many and varied, and specific to the particular concept involved. Typical questionnaires have much in common with those of advertisement testing, e.g. in studying:

(a) comprehension of the new concept;
(b) perception of its attributes (particularly its differences from existing products);
(c) its believability (as a possible new product);
(d) its perceived advantages and disadvantages, again with particular reference to existing products;
(e) its ratings on relevant specific attribute scales, to establish its strong and weak points;
(f) what situations it might be used in;
(g) how often/how much at a time;
(h) which existing products it might replace;
(i) what sort of people it might appeal to.

Note that all such questions are amenable to personal interviewing — whether conducted in-home or in a central location, and whether face-to-face or by telephone. But, if postal interviews are used — possibly on grounds of cost — then it may be necessary to truncate the interview, and to recognize that, in effect, some questions cannot be asked 'unprompted'.

It is in these *diagnostic* areas that qualitative concept testing mainly comes into its own, and ingenious techniques are often used for learning how best to develop the new product idea. Typical examples are 'creative group discussions' and 'word-of-mouth chains', in which successive informants pass on the idea to each other in their own words, and discuss it together, their conversations being tape-recorded and subsequently analysed. This is sometimes found to provide new insights into the most promising appeals of the potential new product. And, of course, if this evidence is to be used constructively to *develop* the new concept, it must be ploughed back and re-evaluated. Quite often, this results in a feedback procedure – test, evaluate, diagnose, develop, re-test[2] – with the marketing man 'carrying on a dialogue' with his potential consumers.

Reverting to quantitative tests, how are the results analysed? Many tests, at this stage of the new product program, need to be modest in scale on account of their cost. Such tests lay themselves open to little more than straight counts on the total sample (which, of course, has already been restricted to a putative target group). However, if we have been able to be more generous, so that particular sub-groups can be reliably looked at, then it would probably be helpful to analyse in terms of conventional demographics (e.g. age, family composition) in order to pinpoint those groups which appear to be most interested in the concept. Even more helpful may be analysis by life style or attitudinal segments – so that we understand better how to present the concept persuasively to its most interested potential users. It can also be helpful to look at the answers to the diagnostic questions for those who are most interested in the concept. This may seem tautologous (trying to appeal more to those people we already appeal to). But, in truth, the vast majority of new products do only attract a small proportion of their *potential* target group – at least, in their early days – so there is much to be said for maximizing our chance of capturing this limited number of users, rather than spreading our grapeshot too far and too wide.

Another method of evaluating new product concepts

Some variants in concept testing depend less on asking consumers directly what they think of the possible new concept, and more on asking them to provide ratings relative to existing brands and, sometimes, relative to an 'ideal' product. They are rated along the image dimensions which are known to be relevant in their market: indeed, such techniques are often directly derived from the mapping analysis which may have invented the new concepts in the first place.

The alternative concepts are now evaluated by their nearness, in the image space, to the ideal product and/or to their distance from existing brands in the market. The number and the characteristics of the consumers they could hope to attract are deduced by the relative distance between each concept and each existing product in the image space. Several interesting examples of this method of concept evaluation (known as 'multi-attribute pro-active techniques') are described in the literature, e.g. ref. 39, and Shocker[24] has reviewed this approach exhaustively.

Earlier in this chapter, we made reference to new product research 'packages': these packages sometimes use these multi-attribute techniques. At their simplest, they 'bolt on' the type of forecasting model, which we have just described, to one of the mapping techniques for concept generation, which we described earlier. With rare exceptions, they are standardized services which are offered by particular research agencies: therefore, an intending user will need to approach one of these agencies if he wants to embark on such a project.

Evaluating and developing new products

In our idealized model of the new product process we have, at this stage, an idea (or ideas) for product(s) which we believe to have potential saleability but which must be *developed* into a physical product before there is anything available to test, let alone to sell. The first stage of development will tend to be in the laboratory, the R & D chemists, engineers, designers turning an agreed blueprint, based on the concept testing stage, into something physical. (Again, we stress that this *is* idealized because, as we saw earlier, we may have started with a finished product or, at least, something to copy.)

Business analysis

This laboratory development is often an expensive process, in terms of both management time and out-of-pocket expenditure. For this reason, a full 'business analysis' is often undertaken at this stage of the programme. The marketing man has the benefit of a fully developed concept and is to turn this into a business proposition – forecast sales, cost of goods, advertising, selling and other marketing costs (and, therefore, anticipated profit), proposed channels for distribution, advertising strategy, etc. Only on agreement of this business analysis can he expect to get top management approval to invest in physical product development. (Several of the 'comprehensive descriptions of NPD procedures' listed at the end of this chapter cover this stage.)

Product testing

Once there is a physical product to progress, the next step is usually one or other form of product testing. As with most types of research the exact boundaries of product testing are somewhat vaguely determined but, as a working definition, we can say that 'a representative sample of the target group will be exposed to the physical product under controlled conditions, will use it under realistic circumstances, and will then express their opinions about it in a structured way'. But the degree of control, of realism, and of structure, can vary substantially from test to test – as, indeed, can the particular manifestation of the physical product – as we shall go on to describe.

Some researchers would include, as product testing, the type of technique where the principal measure is the extent to which consumers purchase, or *re*-purchase, the test product – the 'mini-test market' or 'laboratory test market' type of technique. The deciding line is arbitrary but, for the purposes of this chapter, we are excluding techniques where participants *buy* products in real or simulated shops, with their own money, in the belief that these are 'real' purchases. (These techniques are mentioned in other chapters). But we are including, as product testing, techniques which depend on *simulated* purchases, where participants realize that they are involved in a piece of research (and where therefore, at least according to the UK Market Research Society's Code of Conduct, any money which changes hands ought to be restored to the tester).

A great deal of what has been said about concept testing is entirely relevant here. Product testing, too, has two basically different purposes:

(a) to evaluate, and, often,
(b) to develop,

the proposed new product.

However, there are differences in emphasis which often affect the research design. At this stage of the program, the manufacturer will generally have homed into one or a very limited number of concepts. Everything up to this stage (initial screening, concept testing, business analysis) will have served to weed out non-runners, so that those which are still left in are *all* candidates for marketing. If there is more than one of them, this will be because each of them seems to have adequate potential: they will, therefore, be treated as separate projects from now on (possibly being handled by different people in the marketing/advertising group).

This does not, however, mean that we are necessarily left with only one *physical manifestation* of each concept. As a result of R & D work, or of borrowing or copying physical products from elsewhere, we are quite likely to have different variants of that product – different formulations, ingredients, manufacturing methods, strengths, tastes, smells, colours, shapes, designs – all of them (on the face of it) compatible with the concept. (For simplicity, we shall refer to all of these as different 'treatments' from now on.) The manufacturer's aim is to market the optimum treatment. So evaluation may, again, have two meanings. First, putting the alternative treatments into a likely order of acceptability to the target group. And second, determining whether that treatment (or the best of them) deserves continuing time and money put against it.

In summary, then, the areas in which product tests provide guidance are:

(a) which of several alternative treatments is likely to be most successful?
(b) does the potential new product (now in its physical form) live up to its concept, which has already been shown to be potentially saleable?;
(c) does it warrant further investment of time and money?;
(d) in what ways can it be further improved?;

(e) (if there is still any doubt) which segments of the market look most
     interesting to aim for?

Just as for concept testing, discussion of particular product testing techniques
must embrace the following main headings:

(a) in what form the product is exposed;
(b) to whom;
(c) where, and how;
(d) with what instructions;
(e) in what particular research design;
(f) what questions are asked, and how are they analysed.

(Much more has been published about product testing techniques than
concept testing: see, for instance, refs. 40-44).

However, *unlike* concept testing, there are often distinct differences between
the way these elements of the research design are resolved according to the
purposes of the test. In particular, a test intended to evaluate the product in
terms of its *absolute* potential ('determining whether that treatment ... deserves
continuing time and money put against it') is likely to have several differences
of design from one intended to 'put the possible treatments into a likely *order
of acceptability*' – for reasons which we shall explain. The former (absolute
evaluation) is probably the more sensitive to good research design, so our
discussion will, first, be on the basis that that is an important part of the
objectives. And, as a reminder, we are still concentrating on one-off tests – not
the proprietary services which we have mentioned, and to which we shall
return later.

Tests designed for absolute evaluation

It is highly desirable that the product be tested in a reasonably complete form
under reasonably realistic conditions. But we are involved in the holistic *v.*
atomistic dilemma again – whether a product can be correctly evaluated unless
it is surrounded by *all* the other elements in the total marketing mix, including
specifically the 'communication' elements.[45]

Again, there is no categoric solution to this dilemma, though it would still
seem that a thorough-going atomistic approach could lead to serious errors in
some cases, e.g. the packaging of many day-to-day products certainly
contributes a great deal to their acceptability to consumers, both in practical
and aesthetic terms. It is quite likely that a test product placed in an unsuitable
and unpleasing package would be misleadingly assessed by testers, no matter
how acceptable they found the product itself.

On the other hand, it is also true that many of the elements of the total marketing mix cannot be faithfully reproduced except in the real market place. The only sensible solution is much as for concept testing, namely to build into the test those elements which are necessary to convey the product and its performance adequately (bearing in mind its possible novelty and uniqueness) and seem likely to *interact* significantly.

As a broad generalization, then, the elements which it is often found necessary to put into the test include a reasonable approximation to the final packaging, and enough copy (on the package and/or contained in accompanying material) to make clear the benefits which will be claimed for the product. This copy will, of course, itself be based on the optimally developed concept from the preceding concept testing stages. As the product itself moves from the 'functional' towards the 'emotional', e.g. from a staple food towards a luxury cosmetic, so the creative execution of the claims becomes of greater significance in expressing the product benefits. It may become necessary to execute a finished pack design, to accompany the test product with a mock advertisement, even to give it the aura of a suggested price, in order to be confident that the product has a realistic chance to 'express its point of view' in the test.

Conversely, if the communication elements become overwhelmingly important, it may be that the product itself becomes almost an irrelevancy – any competent formulation, e.g. a copy of an existing brand, may perform as well as any other. In extreme cases, there might even be a case for getting the communication elements right, by concept, advertisement, name and pack testing, and then going straight into the market place without product testing at all!!

A particular problem in deciding what to include in the test is whether to use the proposed brand name or not, whether to test 'blind' or 'branded'. Bearing in mind that we are considering potential new products here, and not going brands, it is probable that in many cases the name on its own serves a relatively unimportant part in 'expressing' the product. On the other hand, it is usually difficult to present realistic pack copy without a brand name, and impossible to do with mock advertisements. So, as a general rule, the test will be conducted 'branded' if those other communication elements are judged to be desirable, but 'blind' if they are not.

In some cases, judgement may suggest that the name *is* an important conditioning element in its own right and then it is essential that it be included if consumer acceptability is to be reliably assessed. The most obvious example is where the new product is an extension to an existing, familiar brand range. Perhaps the manufacturer's name is more often important in this respect than the proposed brand name itself.

To whom is the test administered?
Again, the test should be administered to a representative sample of the target market. However, it may now be possible to specify the target market in rather

more specific terms – for instance, those consumers who, in attitudinal terms, are seeking the particular benefits which the product has to offer – that, indeed, was probably one of the objectives of the previous concept testing stage. Care should still be taken, however, not to recruit too restrictively for fear of eliminating potential consumers who would find the product acceptable if it were amended in accordance with their opinions as expressed in the test. Testing is often to provide guidance on which segments of the market the product will appeal to most, *including* consumers who might become users if it were amended in certain ways.

Unlike concept testing, in most cases there is probably little point in testing a new product, in use, on people who are expected to be purchasers but not users, e.g. on housewives who buy for their husbands. The original concept and its presentation may well be highly relevant to such purchasers but the performance of the product *in use* probably is not (except at second-hand).

Where, and how, is the test administered?

In-use tests are generally administered in-home, unless there is something very specific to the product which makes this inappropriate. Even products which are used out of the home (handbag cosmetics, cigarettes etc.) are generally placed and testers re-interviewed in their homes, because this is the most efficient way to contact and re-interview a representative sample of testers.

Sometimes, however – and this is particularly true if expensive stimulus material is needed at the placement (e.g. mock advertisements to 'position' the product), or when attempting to recruit a target group which is very much of a minority – it is more economical to recruit testers and place the product(s) in a central location (a test hall etc.), but then to re-call at their homes for the subsequent re-interview. Wherever the products are placed, re-call interviews are often conducted by telephone nowadays, rather than by personal call.

It is not unusual for in-use product tests to be conducted by post, since relatively simple questionnaires are often involved. Some organizations have standing panels specifically recruited to test products by post in this way.[44] Since the panel members get an element of practice in completing tests, and appreciate the supply of test products, response rates can be much higher than with other postal research. However, since conditioning is a latent problem with all panels, product testing panels are probably much safer for choosing between alternative treatments (see later) than for absolute evaluation.*

Products are sometimes tested – not just placed – in a 'hall test' (as they are for concept testing).[44] A sample of testers is invited into a test room, e.g. a

---

* The justification for postal panels depends very much on the relative costs of the postal service (together with the necessary clerical back-up) compared with, for instance, the telephone and/or interviewers. This comparison, over recent years, has told against postal panels in the UK – at least, for product testing – so they are now rarely used for this purpose. However, this does not necessarily apply in other countries where interviewer costs are higher than in the UK.

public hall, an advertisement testing theatre or a specially equipped test centre or, even, van, and exposed to the test there-and-then. Apart from the limited exposure to the test product in these circumstances, however, we must bear in mind that it is an artificially controlled exposure, fixed as to time of day, methods of preparation, etc. and this could be a distorting influence. On the whole, such hall tests *for absolute evaluation* should probably be restricted to initial screening, to eliminate obvious failures before full in-use testing.

With what test instructions?

The instructions to testers should say, simply but unambiguously, what they are expected to do with the product(s). Therefore, they generally embrace the essence of the instructions which will accompany the marketed product, *less* any unnecessary 'blurb' but *plus* any additional clarification for the purpose of the test itself. For instance, the marketed product may eventually say 'Whenever you feel jaded and under the weather, a teaspoonful of delicious X, stirred into a glass of cold water, will give you that get-up-and-go feeling'. The comparable product test instructions will probably say something like 'Use this product whenever you feel a little tired and would like a refreshing drink during the next week. Please try, in any case, to take it at least once during that time. To prepare, stir one teaspoonful into a glass of cold water'.

There is one particular trap to avoid in writing product test instructions. Testers are generally very co-operative and will try to do just what they are asked. If one of the developmental objects of the test is to encourage experimentation and provide information on different ways testers find of using the product (different end-uses, different modes of preparation) then they should be clearly invited in the instructions to experiment. For instance, in the example above, by adding statements such as 'Stir one teaspoonful, or more or less according to taste, into a glass of cold water'; 'Use it also on other occasions when you feel like a drink'. Otherwise, the test will stand in danger of simply demonstrating that the product was used as specified in the test instructions and consumers in the real market-place will probably not feel so constrained.

The length of time over which participants in an in-use test should be invited to use the products is sometimes a problem.[44,45] The pressures are often to produce a result quickly. Against this should be set the fact that many products are used infrequently 'in real life', or take some time to use up, while opinions can and do change after continued trials. A flavour or perfume which was initially acceptable can pall after repeated exposure. Yet all the evidence is that the majority of successful products depend for their long term health on achieving adequate repeat purchase over several years. Certainly, it must be a danger to base important decisions about a potential new product on an unrealistically short test period and, if in doubt, the researcher should always veer towards extending the period rather than curtailing it, even if this means providing a larger supply of samples for each individual.

One interesting application of extended-use tests – 'controlled consumer choice' – is to place several packs of the test product (and, if relevant, another existing product) after the short-term re-call interview and then, at a later date, to observe how much has actually been used up when the pressure of a short-term test is off. This, it is suggested, can provide a worthwhile estimate of the off-take the test product might achieve in the market place, other things (shop distribution, advertising, etc.) being equal.

In what experimental design?

All that was said above, about concept tests, applies here and, particularly, the general lack of normative data – outside the proprietary services – which would enable us to project results to the market place. Penny et al.[44] have shown in a comprehensive paper which discusses many of the different aspects of product testing techniques – often with evidence to support particular procedures – that monadic rating scores do correlate quite well with subsequent market place performance *within one particular food market where product quality is believed to be important*. This gives rise to the hope that the development of norms for different product groups (or need-areas) might be valid, but the task is clearly formidable for individual companies. (Also see ref. 46).

However, unless a product is really 'new new' it can more often be tested against an existing brand. Whilst it is difficult to take an existing product and express its basic *concept* in truly 'blind' form (except in the rare case where it is still only on sale in part of the country), it is much easier to repack a competitive *product* so that this does effectively become 'blind'. Provided the product itself does not have peculiarly recognizable physical characteristics then 'like' will reasonably well be being compared with 'like' and we shall have *some* sort of benchmark against which to judge the test results. Considerable ingenuity can be used in order to introduce competitive benchmarks into the test validly: Brown and Millward[47] have described various of the devices they have employed to do so.

Having settled on a suitable benchmark of this type (or more than one, if that is possible, to increase the reliability with which the results can be interpreted), then paired comparisons or complete ranking can generally be used for establishing relative preferences.

Occasionally, paired comparisons do have drawbacks peculiar to the product or to the particular circumstances of the test. It may not be possible, for instance, at least within a sensible time scale, to test two products on an equal footing. The first medicine may cure the ailment, so that there is no opportunity to test the second realistically. The first application of a cleaning product may remove the dirt for good. Even if the use of the first test product does not make the second irrelevant, it may so affect the condition of the test material that the second cannot be tested under comparable conditions. Ingenuity can sometimes overcome these difficulties, for instance by dividing the test material into two and using one product on each half. In some cases, however, there are no ingenious solutions to such problems and then a matched monadic design – or a 'sequential monadic' (i.e. with each informant having two products, but testing and rating the first before receiving the second) – is inevitable.[40,45]

Sometimes, too, the researcher will judge that there is something inherent in the products to be tested which could make paired comparisons invalid. This is usually because of the danger of consumers being too 'sensitive' or too 'rational' in the test situation. As an example: a 'marketing mix' test in which retail prices were stated, and they differed as between products, might tempt consumers to choose the more expensive in a paired comparison situation ('because it must be better quality') where, in a monadic situation – therefore being oblivious of the differential – they might choose the cheaper (because, in truth, they judged it to be better value). Similar situations could arise with other elements of the marketing mix, e.g. with particular product claims which lend themselves to a degree of rationality or sensitivity on the testers' part which *would not exist* in the actual marketing situation: again, see ref. 45.

No *general* rules about this can be laid down. The researcher must be on his guard to recommend paired comparisons or complete ranking for their greater sensitivity, where they are practicable and are not likely to distort the results, but to recommend a matched monadic design where one tester cannot sensibly use more than one test product or where a multi-product design might actually distort the results as they would relate to 'real life', and with the sequential monadic as a compromise between the two.[40]

In the absence of normative data *and* relevant benchmarks from amongst existing brands, however, the only reliable use of a one-off test for absolute evaluation, just as for concept testing, is to ask:

(a) Is the product so utterly rejected by testers that it is highly unlikely to be viable at all (even to a minority segment)?
(b) How does it compare with other products which have been similarly tested in the past (with a comparable research design and questions)?

What questions are asked, and how are they analysed?
The form of the questionnaire for most product tests follows fairly routine lines. There is usually a measure of overall acceptability which, in the case of monadic tests, will be similar to those used in concept testing, described earlier. Just as with concept tests, and in the absence of norms of the type described by Penny,[44] the answers to such questions cannot be used directly to predict sales. Their major use is, again, for comparative purposes, to compare against an existing brand within the test, or against other products which have been tested on earlier occasions. As before, they should be made as comparable as possible from test to test within a given product group for this latter purpose.

Side-by-side testing – paired comparisons and ranking tests – eases the problem of designing reliable questions and any sensible comparative questioning technique is likely to be acceptable. 'Which product did you prefer?' is probably as valid as anything, but some researchers prefer to bring the decision nearer to the market place by asking, for instance, 'Which of these products would you be most likely to buy for 50p?' Unless there is likely to be an *interaction* between the variants being tested and the price at which they might be sold, it seems unlikely that such a device adds anything to the validity of the test. Some researchers have suggested various questioning methods which are more *sensitive* (and, maybe, more predictive of market place performance) than simple preferences etc. One such is the 'constant sum' method, e.g. 'Out of 10 purchases, how many do you think you would devote to each product?'[40]

Mock purchase situations are sometimes introduced further into the test design. Since the long-term health of most products depends on their level of sustainable repeat purchase, an offer is made to sell another pack (or packs) of the product at the end of the in-use test. The reasoning is that the proportion of testers who do purchase will approximate to the proportion who will repeat purchase in the long-run in the market place. This is an ingenious and promising use of product tests which comes very close to mini-test marketing (see chapter 19) – and it is, indeed, the approach which is used by some of the proprietary services to which reference has been made. But, while a measure of repeat purchase in the test situation is enlightening, it does need the modelling facilities which those services provide in order to turn it into a reliable prediction of market-place performance.

As well as appropriate overall acceptability questions, most product tests also ask diagnostic questions for developmental purposes – questions of the type, 'Why did you prefer that product? What did you like about it? What did you think were its good points? Was there anything you disliked about it? Any other way in which it could be improved?', and so on. There will also usually be preference or ratings questions, as appropriate, on specific attributes of the test product(s), 'Which of the two products did you prefer for its flavour?' or 'How would you rate this product for its flavour – excellent/very good, etc?'. These, too, will sometimes be followed by more specifically diagnostic questions, 'Why did you prefer that one for its flavour?'. On the matter of questionnaire design, Brown et al.[45] have contended, with some evidence, that there are definite advantages in asking at least some of the other evaluative and diagnostic questions before overall ratings. This appears to increase the discrimination between products (in other words, to improve the chance of picking the 'winners' from the 'losers') on the very reasonable grounds, as they claim, that to do otherwise is to ask testers to give the verdict before the evidence!

While the specific attribute questions can prove of great value in suggesting where to look for product improvements and even, in some cases, for determining 'the winner', like many other measures they must be treated with caution. Some effort will have to be made to attach relative importance weights to the different attributes asked about. This may have been attempted at an earlier stage of the new product program, as part of the basic market survey or of preliminary qualitative research. On a quantified scale, the St. James or Fishbein models may have been employed (see chapter 3) or Twedt's tri-variant approach.[38] The discursive nature of qualitative research is often thought to be more conductive to the reliable attribution of importances (see chapter 2) and some support the use of projective techniques – though their interpretation has the disadvantage of being very personal to the individual researcher.[30] The attribution of importance weights may also be built-in to the product test design itself – as it is in the 'trade-off' or 'conjoint analysis' approach (see the next section on choosing between alternatives). But often it must be based on the rather dubious approach of simply asking informants about the relative importance of each attribute to them: dubious because it is not usually a matter of having one attribute rather than another – it is a question of *how much* of one attribute he/she would rather have than *how much* of other attributes.

It is also obvious that large 'halo effects' exist in product testing. The product which is preferred overall will often also be preferred on every individual attribute, including those on which it does not, in fact, differ from the others. In the present stage of our knowledge, the most defensible procedure to isolate the effects of different attributes on overall evaluation, should it be necessary, is to build different 'levels' of these attributes into alternative versions of the test product in the first place.

A different problem to do with specific attribute questions is that of semantics. It is very important to ensure, for instance, so far as possible that the attributes described in the questionnaire mean the same thing to typical consumers as they do to R & D technologists and others. Much has been written about the necessity for prior qualitative research into the relevant semantics and reference should be made to the relevant papers (e.g. refs. 48 49).

The final diagnostic questions, as with concept testing, will often deal with the way consumers perceive this particular new product – what situation it might be used in, how much at a time, etc. These can obviously be catered for as appropriate within each specific test.

It will be remembered that we suggested various characteristics by which the results of concept tests might be analysed for 'developing' those concepts, to home in the more accurately on an appropriate target group –ranging from demographic and usership sub-groups, to attitudinally defined segments. The same remains true of product tests, though the scope for refinement will usually be somewhat less: we are down to 'fine tuning' at this stage. If we think of 'development' in the sense of improving the product itself, then analysis of the diagnostic questions by overall attitude (i.e. overall ratings or, in a paired comparison against a competitive benchmark, overall preference) can prove

C. Greenhalgh

instructive. It is important that we hold on to those who, *overall*, like our product: there is no point in putting them at risk by changing things about it which are disliked by those who dislike it in toto. Such analysis can help to sharpen up either our formulation work, or our communication support, or both.

Tests designed to choose between alternative treatments[43]

Let us make one thing clear: product tests are often mounted, during a new product development program, for *both* evaluative purposes: (a) to choose between alternative treatments, and (b) within the same test, to attempt absolute evaluation. The latter has, in general, the more rigorous design requirements if it is to produce a useful prediction. All that has been said in the preceding section ('Tests Designed for Absolute Evaluation') would, therefore, apply to these dual-purpose tests. We now go on, then, to discuss the *additional* or *different* requirements of 'alternative treatment' tests.

In what form are the products exposed?

What is needed are the different versions of the test product, each incorporating one of the alternative treatments. If the test is to be combined with absolute evaluation, these versions will need to be 'dressed' in whatever way had already been deemed necessary for that purpose. But, if the test is *only* to choose between the alternatives, then the products can (if it is more convenient – as it often is) be tested 'blind', with no dressing at all.

The exception to this general rule is if we believe that the treatments may themselves *interact* with, i.e. be influenced by, any of the communication elements – maybe with the name, or pack design or, even, the proposed price but, more likely, with the copy claims and general 'positioning'. The optimum colour and perfume of a cosmetic product, for instance, will often depend very much on the positioning of the brand. In this case, it will be necessary to surround *all* the test variants with such dressing as is judged necessary, in order to convey this intended positioning to testers.

To whom is the test administered?

The sample of testers should be much as described in the previous section, except that we usually don't need to agonize about whether or not to recruit potential consumers at the margin. In choosing between treatments we are obviously going to have to satisfy the bulk of our proposed market and, even if consumers at the margin would disagree, we would not let their opinions override the majority anyway. So, recruiting these marginal consumers is something of a dissipation of our research resources.

Where, and how, is the test administered?

A full in-use test may be judged necessary to choose the optimum treatment, and this will usually be so if the factor(s) under test are to do with the product's performance – the cleansing ingredient in a shampoo, the efficacy of a medicine, the preparation qualities of a convenience food. It will also probably be so if the family's opinions are likely to influence preferences, not just those of the 'provider', e.g. the taste of a breakfast cereal, the texture of a toilet tissue. If an in-use test is judged desirable, then all that was said in the previous section applies – including the observation that panels are probably safer for this purpose than they are for absolute evaluation (because conditioning is less likely to be a distorting influence).

But, quite often, 'hall tests' are judged to be reliable enough for choosing between alternative treatments: a 'sniff test' for choosing a perfume, a 'look-and-handle test' for a shape, or a 'taste test' for a flavour. While advising caution in the use of such truncated tests – the physical attributes of a product can interact substantially, and 'snap judgments' may sometimes be misleading – Penny[44] has produced evidence that they can often be valid and, certainly, they are widely used for such purposes.

With what test instructions?
Again, all that was said in the previous section applies. Since we are choosing between alternative treatments, we are more likely to be using a paired comparison design, or even one in which each informant tests more than two products. In that case, they will also need to be instructed as to how to use those products, e.g. 'use this one for a week, followed by that one for the second week', or 'use them both at the same meal' or 'on alternate occasions' etc. Which of those particular instructions is given is a function of the experimental design.

In what experimental design?
If we are choosing between alternatives then, by definition, there is going to be more than one product in the test. If we want to choose 'the winner', then it makes sense to start off with the most sensitive experimental design so that, for a given research expenditure, we have the maximum confidence that we have correctly identified it. This argues for paired comparisons or, even, complete ranking of the alternative treatments. But various contra considerations then come into play, as they did for testing against a competitive benchmark. (E.g., the application of the first cleaning product may remove the dirt for good; the first toothpaste may whiten the teeth, so that the second one starts off on a different footing; the stronger flavoured soup may swamp the taste of the weaker one if it is tested first, but not vice versa; there may not be the time available for informants to give two or more products a fair trial.) Ingenuity – dividing the 'test material' into two and using different products on each half (e.g. one shampoo on the left-hand side of the head, the other on the right) – may get over those problems; if not, there may be enough time for a 'sequential monadic' design – with a long enough gap between products for the

test material to revert to its original condition. Failing those possibilities, though, we are forced back on the matched monadic design, with 'matched' samples of informants each testing just one of the alternative treatments, and then comparing attitudes towards them in order to establish the 'winner'.

Some researchers argue that paired comparisons etc. ought *never* to be used, because products are used monadically in real life. While this argument is important in relation to absolute evaluation, it would not seem to be a particular cause for concern when choosing between alternatives. Most testing of the latter type is only to determine the *direction* of preferences (which treatment is most preferred, which next, etc.) and it must be rare for the test design actually to reverse the direction of a preference.

It goes without saying that, whatever design is chosen as appropriate for a particular test, full use should be made of the principles of experimental design (see chapter 3) to get the maximum information for a given research expenditure. Thus, for instance, a 'round robin' (all possible pairs of products tested by an equal number of informants) is more efficient than a 'common control' test (everybody testing one of the variants against the same product) — provided we are equally interested in all of the products in the test. And, for instance, if we believe that informants can sensibly test several, but not *all*, of the variants, then equal sub-samples of informants should be allocated to 'balanced sub-sets' of the products. (For instance, with four products, and informants only sensibly able to test three each, one-quarter should test each of ABC, ABD, ACD and BCD.) Good experimental design is, indeed, a study in its own right.

There is another important aspect of this subject: if there are alternatives for several different factors in the product — say flavour, texture, and smell — then, whether the test is to be multi-ranking, paired comparison, sequential monadic, or matched monadic, it is not only more cost-effective to test all the variants at once in a 'factorial design' but information can be obtained which might not otherwise be available. Information on the interactions between the different factors — flavour and smell perhaps — allows the optimum *combination* of these to be marketed and not a simple addition which might be less than optimum (see chapter 3). Factorial design testing is the basis of 'conjoint analysis', the attribution of 'utility values' to the factors which are varied in the test product (e.g. see refs. 50, 51). This enables us to deduce how much a given change in one factor is 'worth' (in increased consumer appreciation) compared with given changes in the other factors. This, in its turn, leads to the refined use of such tests for developmental purposes — not only choosing between the treatments which were actually put into the test, but indicating (probably with greater precision than simple diagnostic questions) how the product might be *further* changed to improve even on the 'winning' treatment.[40,48]

What questions are asked, and how are they analysed?

Nothing needs to be added to the previous section – questions for absolute evaluation – at least, insofar as that dealt with evaluation testing against a competitive benchmark. All that we need to note is that, since we are generally comparing like with like here, we can usually use simpler rather than more complicated forms of question – ratings, preferences, strength of preference, constant sum methods etc.

Bowles[48] has suggested a useful way of analysing preferences in choosing between alternative treatments, and that is to look separately at that sub-sample of testers who claim to be interested in *any* of the variants. They may be more discerning than all testers, and their preferences more relevant to the choice of treatment to market.

This section, then, has dealt with the ways in which tests to choose between alternative treatments might differ from those designed to evaluate a new product absolutely. As we have seen, the main differences with testing alternatives are likely to be in the areas of: the product form (more often 'blind'); where the test is conducted (more often 'in-hall'); and experimental design (more often multi-product and, even, factorial design with 'conjoint analysis').

Proprietary concept and product testing services

We made reference at the beginning of the Concept Testing section of this chapter to 'proprietary testing services' and again, in passing, at the beginning of the previous section on Product Testing. These services have over recent years been introduced by particular research agencies or, occasionally, by large manufacturers on their own account. They depend on the general notions that: (a) if we can build a high degree of standardization into our test methods, and (b) if we can derive a 'model' to convert results derived from the test into forecasts of the real market place, and (c) if we can validate that model from several (hopefully, many) cases where test products have gone on to be marketed, then we can forecast the real market place from future tests.

Exactly *what* we can forecast depends on the particular service: at one extreme, simply comparing the concept or product under test with 'norms' derived from previous tests; at the other, providing forecasts of penetration, repeat purchase, and resultant sales for Year 1, Year 2 etc., under variable assumptions about advertising expenditure and distribution achieved and, therefore, with the ability to answer 'What if?' questions. Factor[52] and Wind[53] both describe a very wide range of the available models, and Godfrey[54,55] has discussed the practical application of one in particular (see also chapter 20).

Some of these services are specifically geared towards real products, others to concepts, and some have different variants for concepts and products. However, the essence of these services is that they *are* standardized to a greater or lesser extent. So, intending users must obviously approach their suppliers to discuss exactly what information they will provide and their requirements in terms of stimulus material etc.

Some final comments on product testing

What has been described so far has been, on the whole, quantitative product testing, i.e. the design of tests in which numbers can reliably be attached to the results. *Qualitative* product testing can also be very valuable.[10] Sometimes this is conducted on independent samples of testers; sometimes on sub-samples of previous testers, say those who expressed extreme favour or disfavour with the new product in a quantitative test. In either case, the test procedures are much the same, except that sample sizes are generally much smaller (for cost reasons) and the final interview is much more discursive and unstructured. Such qualitative testing can prove valuable for gaining insights into product performance which more structured tests cannot do, and for suggesting product and creative leads which might not otherwise have been forthcoming.

Sometimes, the concept testing and product testing stages are collapsed into one, by placing a test product with the sample of consumers who have just carried out the concept test (e.g. see ref. 56 and many of the 'proprietary' services). While such a procedure can save research costs it can also have limitations and potential dangers. Diagnostic leads from the context test obviously cannot be taken into account in designing the test product itself. It also follows that the test product must be exposed in the concept of the original 'unrefined' concept, without the benefit of any improvements in presentation which might have resulted from a prior concept test. There is everything to be said for testing a new product in the context of its claims but two separate stages of concept and concept-plus-product would seem to be both safer and more productive.

Just as with concept testing, and most other aspects of new product development, successful projects are always likely to result from feedback – the willingness to test, evaluate, diagnose, develop and re-test. For this reason, some commentators (e.g. refs. 5 and 9) recommend starting off with small-scale, possibly qualitative, tests (even 'workshop' tests, where the communication elements – prototype advertisements, etc. – may be inserted and amended as testers react to them), gradually working up to larger and more structured tests as certainty grows that the project is on the right lines.

Pricing new products

As stressed earlier, the physical product is only one element, although a vital one, in the total marketing mix. Development and testing techniques for the more important of the other elements – packaging and advertising – are described in chapters 16 and 17. There is one element, however, which is so vital to the whole *business proposition* that it must be considered almost as fundamental as the concept and the product itself; namely, its price. Indeed, so fundamental is price that it will almost certainly have been built into the preliminary business analysis, because it is only by converting anticipated sales into approximate revenue that management could evaluate the whole project at that stage. However, despite the fact that an approximate unit price must have been in mind at a very early stage of the project, there will probably be a need later in the development process to refine and firm up on this price.

How is price determined?

Techniques for determining an optimum retail price ahead of actual marketing are probably less well developed than for other elements of the marketing mix. As a result, retail prices are very often determined as a fixed mark-up on the cost of goods (or cost of sales). Such a procedure, however, though it may limit the possibility of loss, is unlikely to result in an optimally profitable price. There is certainly evidence that a 'just' price, from the consumer's point of view, has little relationship to the manufacturer's costs and, indeed, why should it when these costs are generally not known to consumers?

An examination of the ruling price structure

When a new product is going into an existing market, or even into peripheral competition with existing products, its price must bear *some* relationship to competition. Exactly what relationship is up to the manufacturer to decide in the light of his marketing strategy. He may have decided, on judgement or, better still, in the light of his research into the existing market, that he wishes his new product to be seen as relatively premium-priced. Then an examination of existing brands, their retail prices and brand shares, will obviously help to set his own lower limit. (And, clearly, vice versa if his intention is to be seen as relatively cut-price.)

Occasionally, the manufacturer may feel that the ruling price structure determines his own price exactly; perhaps all brands sell at one price and he cannot afford to be different.

Such an examination still, to some extent, begs the question because the decision to be seen as premium-priced, cut-price or average-priced is, in itself, a pricing decision, and *marginal* differences in price thereafter can affect volume sales and profit significantly. Therefore, the manufacturer of a new product would usually like assistance in determining its price fairly exactly, not in the sort of broad range which an examination of the ruling price structure generally affords. What assistance, then, *can* research provide? Overviews of available techniques have been provided by Aspden et al.[57] and Frappa et al.[58] and they cover most of the following methods.

Concept and product tests incorporating price

Let us dispose of this approach first, because it is the most straightforward and, probably, the most reliable approach. If we only have a limited number of prices from which to choose, and if we use one of the concept or product testing techniques which can reliably predict sales (probably one of the proprietary services), then we can put those alternative prices into such a test and, therefore, predict the sales they would generate – hence choosing the 'winning' price.[54,55] But such an approach will be costly (these services are not inexpensive), so it is generally reserved for the final stage of the pricing programme, when there are very few – probably only two – prices between which to choose.

Thus, (a) we may, rightly or wrongly, feel we cannot afford an ambitious price testing method like this, and/or (b) we shall, in any case, find it necessary to short-list a very limited number of alternative prices to go into such a test, from amongst a broad range of initial possibilities. So let us go on to discuss other techniques which can help to satisfy these requirements.

Propensity to purchase

Price questions are often asked as an integral part of concept and product tests, as indicated earlier in this chapter. Generally, they are of the type 'What do you think you would be prepared to pay for a 250 g size of this product?' or 'Do you think you would buy a 250 g size of this product for 50p?' Sometimes, too, they are asked as rating questions; 'How likely would you be to buy a 250 g size of this product for 50p – very likely, fairly likely ... etc?' (The latter two approaches need, of course, to include a range of alternatives if they are for choosing between prices.)

It is dangerous, however, to apply the answers to such questions, as they stand, directly to 'real life'. Consumers probably tend spontaneously to understate the price at which a new product will subsequently establish itself in the market place; in other words, a smaller proportion tends to nominate the market price than will actually become regular purchasers at that price. Yet, perversely, when the question is asked the other way the evidence is that a much *greater* proportion tend to claim to be interested at a nominated price than ultimately do buy regularly at that price. This would not matter if the answers to such questions had a direct, pro-rata, relationship to market place performance – which, in general, they do *not* – or, alternatively, if we had a reliable formula to convert them to 'real life'. However, as we have already said, it is unlikely that any one manufacturer will have such a 'model', so that such an approach is likely to have severe limitations in its applications: (a) to eliminate non-runners – prices which produce results very substantially below other prices in the test; (b) those rare cases where a higher price is the 'winner' in *volume* terms (maybe, for instance, a cosmetic); (c) if – rather perversely – the marketing plan calls for maximum volume sales *regardless of revenue*. These three cases are exceptional because it is not necessary to convert the test results to estimates which are at least pro rata to market place sales in order to evaluate their meaning. In practice, it tends to leave (a) – the elimination of non-runners – as the most frequent purpose to which simple propensity-to-purchase questions are put.

It goes without saying that if we *are* going to use this approach – maybe because we *do* have a reliable forecasting model, or because one of the cases (a)–(c) may apply – then the nearer the test product can be to its market place presentation (including its packaging and advertising) the more reliable it is likely to be, since price undoubtedly creates an 'image' of its own which may well interact with other elements in the mix.

A development of propensity to purchase

Gabor and Granger[59] suggested two developments of simple 'propensity to purchase' in order to find the optimum price (as opposed to choosing between a limited number of alternative prices). In their first variant, which is said to be more relevant to completely new products, a representative sample of the target group is shown a sample of the proposed product (either in illustrative, conceptual or, better, its physical form). Each tester is asked whether or not (s)he would be prepared to buy it at each of a range of prices, up to about nine in number, from one which is obviously too high to one which is obviously too low, at equal intervals throughout the range, but asked in a random order. For those prices at which they would not buy, they are also asked why – because it is too expensive, or too cheap to trust? But a subsequent paper,[60] based on their work, suggested that this supplementary question is redundant, and that the 'buy-response curve' – which is the end-product of these questions – can be deduced simply from willingness to buy at each price: this takes us back to simple propensity-to-purchase, but with a range of possible prices instead of a limited number of alternatives. The summation of these data over the total sample gives the proportion who claim that they would be prepared to buy at each point within the range and, from this 'buy-response curve' appropriate pay-off conclusions can be drawn – though, for this to be reliable, its users would say that 'interpretation' (based on past tests and normative data) is still necessary.[61]

In the second variant, which is said to be more relevant to a new entrant in an existing product group, each tester is asked what would be the *most* (s)he would be prepared to pay, and also the *least* before (s)he would suspect the quality of the product. A cumulative calculation then enables a similar buy-response curve to be drawn for all possible prices – though, again, this needs interpretation, based on experience, to indicate the optimum price.

These two Gabor–Granger approaches retain many of the difficulties associated with simple propensity-to-purchase — specifically the need for interpretation if they are to be used reliably. Given those prerequisites, however, they obviously provide more comprehensive data for choosing between all possible prices, since they produce a continuous curve (or virtually so). They also illustrate the peaks and plateau-edges which are typical of 'natural' and 'threshold' prices. Whether or not the curve, as it stands, is predictive of actual sales for a potential new product, there must be a presumption that these *patterns* have relevance to penetration (i.e. to first-time trial). For instance, that in pricing the product, troughs in the buy-response curve should be avoided; and that it makes sense to price towards the expensive end of a plateau rather than 'over the edge', on its down-slope. This should, at least, enable the manufacturer to find a localized optimum which will maximize trial, within a narrow range which has been limited in other ways (e.g. by the cost of goods, or the ruling price structure). (See ref. 62 for an interesting application.)

Further developments

Apart from the need for interpretation, other researchers have suggested possible shortcomings in the Gabor–Granger approach. These have led to suggestions for yet further improvements (as mentioned at the outset of this section pricing research is an area where techniques are 'probably less well developed than for other elements of the marketing mix'.) Blamires,[61] for instance, has suggested that:

(a) the testing environment should at least approximate to a mock shopping display (i.e. that it should be more realistic for informants than the rather abstract context of most Gabor–Granger tests);

(b) testers should judge the test product against competition (because they need a point of reference to make their price judgements realistic);

(c) but each tester should only have the test brand and their usual and/or most preferred brand(s) included in their propensity-to-buy questions (since the other competitors would, in practice, be irrelevant to their purchasing decisions);

(d) this/those referent brand(s) should be priced for each informant individually, at the level (s)he thought they were on sale in their usual shop (since recommended, or average, retail prices would not represent a realistic benchmark for most testers);

(e) (s)he should be specifically directed towards a 'typical' purchase occasion (since shoppers are often prepared to pay more for occasional, or stop-gap, purchases);

(f) (s)he should have the option of not buying at all, or 'shopping elsewhere' (and not be forced to 'purchase' if (s)he found the test prices unacceptable);

(g) an attempt should be made to identify — with appropriate attitude questions administered before recruitment — and then to eliminate 'steady state' consumers, i.e. those who would not buy the test product at *any* price in the range to be tested or would buy it at *every* price (because they simply act as 'deadweight' for the pricing question).

Blamires claims that, if those improvements are incorporated, then the results of the Gabor–Granger approach become much closer to a real market place demand-curve and, as such, they do not need normative data and interpretation in order to home in to the optimum price for the proposed new product.

Trade-off

Another avenue which has been explored — indeed, fully developed — by other researchers is the 'brand-price trade-off' approach.[57,63] We have mentioned trade-off, allied with conjoint analysis, previously. For this particular application, the variables incorporated in the test are brands (say six of them) — including, obviously, a realistic representation of the proposed new product — and a range of possible prices (say 12 for each brand). Testers — again in a simulated shopping situation, which can use actual products or, for instance, pack photographs — are asked to make 'purchases', i.e. to say what they would be likely to buy when confronted by all of the brands at the lowest of their possible prices. The one they would buy is then gradually increased in price until they would switch, or decline to buy at all, and so on, up the full range of prices. These data, subjected to conjoint analysis, can provide a complete purchasing model for each informant, across *all* possible combinations of prices for all brands: these individual models are aggregated ('inside the computer'), and we then have a complete pricing model for the market.

This is another way of selecting the optimum price for our proposed new product (at least, for generating first-time trial), but it is claimed — in common with other trade-off applications — to do much more: to answer 'what if?' questions of the type 'what if we increased our price by 5p?' or 'what if the leading competitor dropped his price to match ours?'.

This trade-off approach is another of the 'bolt-on' options which is made available with some of the proprietary concept/product testing packages.

Postscript

One important limitation of these pricing techniques must be stressed. A new product with an innovatory formulation or communication elements could markedly change consumers' expectations of, and judgements about, what constitutes a suitable price in a particular product field. The techniques referred to above tend, in the main, to provide answers based on the current market price structure, and (especially at the concept stage) do not easily cope with innovations which may upset this.* The (proprietary) techniques which use a 'product test incorporating price' get over this shortcoming – or, at least, move towards solving it – by basing themselves on experience of the proposed new product in use; it is possible to adapt the other techniques so that they are *also* applied after experience of the product. This obviously needs a real test product, packed in a real way. It is not logistically easy, nor cheap, but it does come closer to forecasting an optimum price for sustained repeat-purchase, not just for maximizing initial trial.

Re-cycling

As indicated at the beginning of this chapter, a process which frequently goes on in parallel to new product development is the re-cycling of existing brands, i.e. the attempt to prolong their profitable life by finding new uses, attacking new segments of the market, reinforcing existing appeals or incorporating new ones, and generally combating competitive and other market changes. This may involve making product and pack improvements, using more persuasive advertising claims, altering the price, and other marketing activities.

Of course, devices such as these designed to increase or maintain profits are the *constant* preoccupation of marketing men, but we are concerned here with something more than a new copy line, a revamped pack design, a revised trade price structure or increased advertising expenditure. Recycling, to warrant the title, implies a significant change in what is on offer *in the consumer's terms*, together with a thoroughgoing examination of all the other elements of the marketing mix to ensure that they optimize on that change, whatever it is. The really significant change, therefore, will generally be in the product itself (or, occasionally, in its packaging where this is an important element of the product) and/or in its creative claims and 'positioning'. An example of the former would be the addition (or retention) of fibre in ready-to-eat breakfast cereals; of the latter, their re-positioning as a snack throughout the day.†

---

* There must, too, be difficulties in interpretation at a time of rapid inflation – which will be more of an issue at some times, and in some markets, than others.

† We are also concerned with something more than the substitution of ingredients, or change in manufacturing processes, for simple cost-saving reasons. This may be a very effective way to revitalize profits, and it certainly calls for careful product testing. But it probably does not represent a discernible product improvement in the consumer's eyes.

Similarities with new product development

Expressed in this way it is clear that re-cycling has a very great deal in common with new product development. To re-cycle a going brand, some or all of the following will be necessary: to generate a new concept for it; to evaluate and develop this new concept; and/or to evaluate and develop the product itself in the context of this (new) concept.

The first really major difference between re-cycling and new product development, however, is that some of these stages may not be appropriate in any given case and they may, therefore, be eliminated. It may, for instance, be decided that the basic concept (and all that this implies in creative treatment) should be unaltered. What is really required is a radical product improvement. Maybe what was the 'whitest' washing powder is now only 'white' compared with its competitors – then we might go straight to the product development and product testing stages.

Maybe the product itself cannot easily, or economically, be reformulated; what is needed is that it should be repositioned. Then it will be necessary to generate, test and develop a new concept for the brand, and although the product itself will almost certainly need to be *evaluated* in the context of its proposed new concept, product development will be irrelevant.

What is needed from the marketing man and the researcher is that they think of their re-cycled brand *as though* it were a completely new project, eliminating only those stages in our idealized program which are clearly inappropriate or unnecessary.

Branded and blind tests

There are, however, two other major differences between re-cycling and new products. One is that, as far as the consumer is concerned, existing brands already have a wealth of associations from the full range of marketing elements which have been deployed in their support: pack, name, price, advertising, promotion, etc. Since it will be impossible to divorce the re-cycled product from these associations, it will often prove not only desirable but quite essential to carry out concept and product tests in a 'branded' rather than a 'blind' form.

The principle for the researcher to remember is basically the same as that for new products. If the new element being tested – concept or product – is likely to interact with other existing elements of the marketing mix, then these other elements should be introduced into the test: this generally involves the introduction of the brand name because of all its prior associations.

Research design

The other major difference is that of research design. Re-cycling of a brand implies that there is almost always a built-in 'norm', namely the brand as it is now. Instead, therefore, of often having great problems in evaluating the proposed new concept or new product in any absolute sense, this becomes comparatively easy; it can be evaluated against its current self. Many of the tests in such a program will, therefore, be paired comparisons or (in the circumstances described earlier) matched monadic tests against the current brand. Even if that does not permit a prediction of absolute sales, it does help in making a reasonably reliable 'more–less–or about the same' projection. Such testing does not, of course, necessarily remove the requirement also to test against competition; we will often still need to check that improvements to our own brand have gone sufficiently far to match, and preferably beat, it (or them).

Companion brands

Allied to re-cycling is the strategy of range or variety extension or companion products, in which increased sales and profits are derived not from the existing product (though that may well benefit in the process) but by *adding* new products under the umbrella of the same brand name.

Companion brand development has so much in common with completely new brands that the test program outlined above may well be adopted in its entirety. Again, there are two special considerations. In the first place, the brand name, with all its associations with the existing product, is vital. In this respect, the companion brand is in much the same position as the re-cycled product and its correct evaluation by consumers will almost always depend on the use of branded tests. Second, the introduction of a companion brand may well have a 'knock-on' effect – either good or bad – on the parent product. It is highly desirable to try, through research, to anticipate this effect, because of the importance of the existing product. The techniques for doing so are not appropriate to this chapter but are, indeed, very much akin to those of advertising research on existing brands.

Another postscript

Both re-cycled products and companion brands are amenable to evaluation by the proprietary techniques to which we have made frequent reference: these will often incorporate a prediction of the 'knock-on' effect on the present product and so become doubly useful.

Conclusion

The outline program described in this chapter has been very much idealized.

Apart from the fact that several important elements of the marketing mix have been left to elsewhere in this book, a new product program will rarely be so logically pursued 'in real life'. At the simplest the whole program will often *start* with a product – from R & D or from market searches – rather than starting by looking for a product concept. The structure of the program can, however, easily be adapted. The important thing is to appreciate that, apart from the mechanics of evaluating and developing the concept and the product, such a research program has other, less tangible, benefits.

The first is to *understand* consumers better, in their relationship to the proposed new product. This basic understanding acts as a general 'orientation': it constantly conditions the activities to do with the development of a new product, in directions which are favourable rather than unfavourable.

The second is that it provides a continuing series of checks, that all the elements of the marketing mix are satisfying the original concept in a *consistent* way. Even if the whole research program cannot be 'holistic', it is certainly desirable that each element is pulling in the same direction, towards the ideal specification rather than (unwittingly) away from it. In this way, a program of research and testing acts like a compass: a constant source of reference that the new product, during its development, is not straying too far away from its intended path.

Chapter 16

Advertising research

MARK LOVELL

Introduction

This chapter examines research into *advertising*. Although media researchers regard much of their work as 'advertising research', media research generally is left to the next section. Anyone engaged in advertising research presupposes that there is, in fact, something about advertising that can be studied, and is worth studying. From time to time, in a given instance, he may question either assumption. Researchers who have limited contact with advertising research often voice these questions, critically, for various reasons.

Given the total amount of money spent on advertising, it must logically pay people handsomely to conduct research into it, but attempts to hold various factors under experimental control, in order to isolate the effects of advertising, prompt two lines of argument against this.

First, that a campaign should influence the consumer's mind, in the face of heavy competition for attention, is important, but we are unlikely to know *how* important it is, relative to other factors. Why not simply judge that the direction of the advertising is right, examine the expected advertising/sales ratio to find a reasonable level of pressure, and assume that all will go more or less according to plan? Why try to calculate what may be incalculable?

Second, markets change, as to consumers, products, needs, and interests but the advertising scene in a product field can change more quickly, more dramatically than anything else. This tends to make advertising research data *historical*. Does it do any more, then, than satisfy academic curiosity?

Advertising researchers have been known to touch the extremes of confidence and despair. Assurances have been given from time to time that a particular technique, or interpreter, has been proved beyond reasonable doubt to provide utterly reliable indications of advertising effectiveness. This has applied to pre-tests and post-tests alike, but no sooner has the new sun appeared over the horizon than clouds of doubt have blotted it out. There is then a reaction, which can be summed up in the words by Peat and De Vos as a statement of 'Murphy's Law': 'If something can go wrong with advertising research, it will'. Someone with a new technique, then, appears little better off than a huckster preparing bottles of cure-all medicine in his cellars.

A presentation of advertising research results can sometimes be notable for this individual feature: cynical eyebrows are raised not only at explanations of what preliminary depth interviews suggest but also at percentages indicating differences of 'shifts' based on respectably sized samples. The terms of reference are suspect; the context of the interview is suspect; the questions are suspect; the analysis is suspect; the people, even, are suspect.

Why cannot the research world develop, agree, and validate set procedures for advertising research? Advertisers, and some advertising agencies, have often demanded this. It is good that they do so. The result is progress, up to a point. To expect a complete answer, however, is unrealistic. *Why* this should be so, is important. Formalization of advertising research is difficult because:

(a) advertising itself works in different ways — *or* achieves a range of effects with varying degrees of emphasis;
(b) the marketing context within which advertising is expected to work is itself variable — between brands and products and over time;
(c) the demands placed on advertising research vary, according to the interest of the parties concerned;
(d) the relevance of certain survey data (whether collected in a pre-test or in a campaign evaluation study) to the end results of advertising is a matter of dispute.

These factors need to be looked at separately, before proceeding to techniques.

Advertising theory
The case has often been put that anyone who is doing research into advertising must consider, first of all, how advertising works; i.e. he must have some theory or model in his mind, and his research activity should be consistent with that theory. It seems, on the surface, a sensible requirement.

There have been several attempts to systematize advertising theory. Stepwise models have been constructed, like these:

$$AIDA = \begin{array}{l} \text{Attention} \\ \text{Interest} \\ \text{Desire} \\ \text{Action} \end{array}$$

What AIDA suggests is that advertising works by inducing each of these four effects in sequence.

A slightly more complex scheme was put forward by Colley in the early

1960s;

DAGMAR = Defining Advertising Goals
for Measured Advertising
Results

The steps up which advertising was expected to take the consumer corresponded to:

Awareness	*Comprehension*	*Conviction*	*Action*
(of existence of brand or product)	(of what the product is, and will do)	(mental preparedness to purchase)	

It seems straightforward. A consumer needs first to be made aware of the brand and what it is; then there is understanding of its advantages, its characteristics; 'conviction' is a matter of persuasion that the brand delivers these goods and that he wants them; 'action' speaks for itself.

The big problem is that step-wise models of this kind do not take time and experience into account. Various studies, particularly of buyer profile and buying pattern data, have pointed to one main finding — that much advertising effort that can be judged to be successful succeeds by virtue of marginally increasing the frequency of purchase of the brand among consumers who already have experience of it. A further finding is that attitude changes are not necessarily measurable when this advertising effect occurs. There are situations, in fact, where the progression shown in Fig. 16.1 seems to be more likely. In

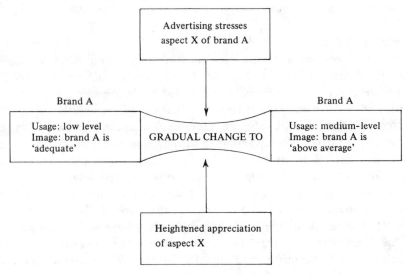

Fig. 16.1

this situation, it may be very difficult to observe subtle differences in attitude until after the increased usage has developed into a strong trend of which the consumer is conscious.

There are, of course, special cases, such as product launches, or when advertising is being put behind a near-dormant brand for the first time, that make DAGMAR seem much more realistic. Here, advertising must develop awareness, understanding of what is special about the brand, and so forth, but even then, the various stages of a DAGMAR progression may happen all at once; and the item 'conviction' in an impulse purchase will be something very elusive by contrast with a consumer durable buying situation. Time, competition and other marketing support make advertising seem even more complex in its ways than any of the above models suggest.

Time. Advertising input is rarely, if ever, separate from a stream of past and future activity. Reactions to a new campaign are conditioned by past advertising.

Competition. A competitive market means competitive advertising. One brand's claims are not judged in limbo. There is *other* advertising, *other* promotion.

Other marketing support. If a campaign succeeds in sales terms – how far was it the work of a banded offer, or the advertising that told people about it? (This point is expanded below.)

In our present state of knowledge, there is no reason why a particular advertising theory should be regarded as central to all or even most advertising research. There are, in fact, good reasons why only a very flexible theory could be regarded as allowing for many different cases. This makes the experienced researcher more likely to be eclectic than systematic.

The marketing context

The point has been made above that advertising does not happen in a vacuum. Special provision may have to be made to study other influences, in parallel with the analysis of how a particular 'above the line' campaign has performed. The success or otherwise, for example, of that campaign may be affected by the extent to which promises about a reformulation of the brand are borne out by experience of it. Copy tests combined with product tests may be one means, before the event, of seeing that results are in line with expectations raised. During and after the campaign, comparisons between trialists and non-trialists may be necessary. This argues a need to choose or adapt advertising research techniques according to the circumstances of the market. Even where standard methods are used, judgement may have to be applied as to what the resulting figures mean. This applies both to the question of whether a particular score is 'good' or 'bad' and to the problem of disentangling the elements that have produced such a score.

What people demand from advertising research

Sometimes the purpose of an advertising research study seems to undergo changes as it moves from planning to presentation. This has encouraged some researchers to analyse the motives behind particular tests. Here is a list of possible reasons, any number of which may be operative when a research brief is delivered:

(a) *information* about advertising that is developed; about possible improvements to advertising; about the market (as a substitute for formal consumer research);
(b) *justification* to make sure one's judgement has been right;
(c) *conformity* e.g. because the managing director is expecting it to be done;
(d) *litigation:* to settle an argument;
(e) *mobilization:* in search of a weapon to use against the agency.

The interesting section is 'information'. It is enough to recognize the others when they occur.

Information is required by different people at different stages. In the early stages of creative development, the value of advertising research lies mainly in providing the creative team with indications of advantages and disadvantages in particular approaches and in presenting data about consumers' comments on the product field, the brand, past advertising, etc., that helps the team *create* approaches.

When finished advertising is being pre-tested, most clients will want some indication of its absolute value. The account executive may want the same. A choice may have to be made – in which case all parties will want research that is sensitive enough to discriminate between reactions to alternative advertisements. The creative team will be interested in evaluation but will usually want to know more about *why* a particular effect has been achieved.

When a campaign is being tested in the field, other specialist needs may have to be catered for. Whoever is responsible for marketing and media planning will be concerned to know what sort of response function data are available. That is to say, how many exposures to the advertising are required to get the consumer to register, understand, or buy something?

The emphasis put on special information needs in advertising research will vary according to the nature of the individuals involved, and the efficiency of the communications that connect them. Not everyone will see the same value in the data he is given. The researcher must be aware of how this affects his brief, and plan accordingly.

Relevance of advertising research measures

A great deal, still, has to be taken on trust. Commonsense suggests that, if after heavy advertising pressure there is still no demonstrable awareness of a new brand's name, something is likely to be wrong with the creative content;

but if there is moderate awareness, how much *latent* awareness is there that may be raised to the surface by sight of the product at point of sale? How good are question and answer methods at uncovering the amount and the value of material that has been registered as a result of advertising?

There is a lot of evidence, from psychologists as well from market researchers, to suggest that the deeper you dig the more you will find. Dig deeper, then; but the more intensive the interview, the smaller are the chances that it will be administered in a standard way.

Awareness data should be treated as symptoms, not achievements in themselves. Those claiming they first learned about a newly launched brand when they saw it on display might or might not have noticed it if advertising had not helped. A new campaign for a well-known brand may, paradoxically, remind some consumers of previous advertising, a question mark against figures for 'claimed' and 'proved' advertising recall alike. Irrespective of what may be the most sensitive or the fairest way to gauge awareness and recall, it has been claimed by some that neither of these measures has much relevance anyway. When advertising is very successful indeed, awareness is usually high along with most other measures. At the other extreme, one of the features of a dead loss is lack of any evidence that anyone has noticed the campaign. Between the extremes, however, recall data can mean practically anything. For a fuller exposition see Lovell and Lannon.[1]

Some attempts have been made to observe what kind of measures, in pre-tests or in post-tests, have results that correlate well with sales change data in test markets, where other marketing factors can be kept more or less constant. The most sensitive and stable measures and the best predictors are those which prove to be the most useful *on average*. They will not be appropriate in every case.[2]

The more that is known about question forms and interview situations, the greater the choice seems to be for the individual who is planning and interpreting a particular advertising study.

Who does what

If standardization is suspect, the responsibility for briefing, planning, and making sure that what gets presented in the end is what people need to know, quite apart from being accurate, is all the greater. The past 15 years can be looked upon as ones in which individual advertising research experts have evolved, who adapt and choose from the techniques available. This is a move away from a more technique-oriented era, in which advertising researchers tended to be made use of by organizations who had pet systems. It is also very different, however, from what might be called the 'age of the wizards', in the fifties, when advertising research was often the province of an intuitive virtuoso whose analogies were drawn from Viennese consulting rooms. The advertising researcher today knows that there are various kinds of evidence,

Table 16.1   *Communication in advertising research*

Advertising agency	
A Research executive	is responsible for day-to-day communication with creative team. Plans internal work, to B's brief. Plans formal work jointly with D (or E); and with F (or G) as required, by agreement with D (or E).
B Creative team	asks A for help; gets answers from A, and (by arrangement) from F and G.
C Account executive	observes that communications are working. Combines with B and E to deliver brief for formal pre-tests, and post-testing.
Advertiser	
D Research executive	liaises with A to ensure advertising research fits without duplication into overall research programme. Discusses with A plans and results; commissioning work from F and G; presentations to C and E.
E Brand manager	draws on D's advice for briefing input; for considering interpretations of results.
Independent research consultant	
F	may be retained by A or D, either continuously or 'ad hoc'. He may do planning; perform small-scale work; provide objective assessment of large-scale work.
Research agency	
G Advertising research specialist	as F; but conducts large-scale work as well.

which can be gathered in different ways, and he judges their relevance and importance according to marketing circumstances. He can be found in four places:

(a) in an advertising agency;
(b) in a research agency;
(c) in an advertiser's research department;
(d) on his own, as an independent consultant.

The proportion on the client side (the third category) is growing, only slowly. The biggest increase has been in the fourth category. This analysis is important because it has an effect on communications, which are crucial if advertising research is to be meaningful, understood, and acted upon.

A communications system is suggested in Table 16.1. It works, but it is expensive, in that it demands the presence of certain people whose time is valuable. It may, of course, save time and money in the long run. Alternatives can be worked out by doubling-up certain of the functions.

Several large advertising agencies have developed 'creative workshops', whose prime purpose is to apply research in such a way that it actively helps creative people to develop campaigns. Sometimes a creative team actually commissions such work. Usually, it has at least got direct access to the researcher. Close involvement by the creative team often leads to a sequence of qualitative studies, rather than one single job, as the creative team gains and elaborates new ideas from the research.

Problem analysis

A careful distinction often needs to be drawn between two things:

(a) *creative strategy*, the effects that advertising is intended to have on the consumer;
(b) *creative tactics*, how the creative team intends a specific advertisement to work.

Failure to observe the differences between these two is often at the root of any frustration that follows a presentation of copy test results. It also thickens the blanket of fog that may surround the advertising component in a test market study.

An example of this difference is afforded by a television campaign for Cadbury's Whole Nut. The *strategy* included, as one of the basic advertising aims, that the brand should be made distinctive, differentiated from other chocolate bars in a desirable way. Since the confectionery market is kaleidoscopic, the need for a clear-cut identity is particularly important. But the identity has to be relevant to confectionery eaters, as well as sharply defined.

A campaign was developed (see Fig. 16.2) in which the creative *tactic* was to dramatize the unique product feature of Whole Nut: the fact that it contains entire hazel nuts, not the results of chopping or grinding. This was achieved creatively by introducing a zany recognition scene into certain ordinary situations, where sudden observation of a bar leads a protagonist to exclaim 'Nuts! Who-ole Hazel Nuts! Cadbury's take em and they cover them with chocolate!' in a chant which is vaguely reminiscent of a Harry Belafonte number.

The first pre-testing work on this campaign, which ran successfully for several years, was concerned with the reactions of the target to the first film – *in terms of its execution of the tactical principle*. This was *not* a test of the advertising strategy. What was at stake was the question whether, when shown in a reel of other commercials, it established clear awareness of Whole Nut; and whether people were made to react positively towards the product, by accepting its unique feature as well as by appreciating the fun.

Further pre-testing, on follow-up ideas for further commercials, revealed that some of them were more powerful than others in securing the right balance of tactical effects. It helped the creative team to find that those situations which included an element of conflict between the participants (before the Whole Nut recognition moment) had a stronger result in terms of dramatizing the product and its benefit.

Research into the evaluation of the campaign was a very different matter. Here the brief was, basically, to investigate the links between the advertising

Fig. 16.2.

and sales; and to analyse how far the evidence here was consistent with efficient execution of the strategy. Audit data from test areas showed the extent of sales increases that accompanied the advertising. Consumer data showed the extent to which, for example, chocolate bar buyers showed awareness and recognition above the level of other competing campaigns.

The point of the example is to underline that certain aspects of the campaign evaluation brief *could* have been put into the pre-test brief. This might have shown, for example, that, after exposure to this film, very few were prepared to regard Whole Nut very differently from the way they looked at it before. This is because with a well-known brand the response to advertising must be understood to be gradual. A good campaign *could* have come under suspicion; an irrelevant part of a pre-test *could* have condemned it to be jettisoned.

Pre-testing – at different stages

A pre-test may happen once in the development of a campaign or there may be a pre-testing program. There may be cases where preliminary work on rough creative material is ruled out because of a conviction that the kind of advertising envisaged demands finished or near-finished treatment if it is to have any appreciable effect on the consumer. A similar case can be made out against testing at an early stage on the grounds that reactions to rough material may be misleading. The two arguments are not quite the same. When this happens, the campaign may be discussed with the advertising researcher who is required to give his views, based on the other research or experience of the brand, of the campaign's likely success. This may be useful or not, depending on the people concerned: but it should be recognized that it is discussion *not* research.

The preliminary stages of a pre-test program are often explorations of basically different advertising approaches. The concept test is sometimes used in this context, except by those who have taken a public stand against formalized concept testing, in which case they may use other phrases to describe the same thing.

The problems of concept testing are very real. The main ones can be stated briefly. The essence of a concept may be easy to describe, logically, on a plain piece of card but it may seem very bald; it may provoke the response 'So what?' among the same people who would react positively to an emotionally loaded presentation of it. How, then, do you interpret the 'So what?' Any attempt to present concepts in forms that approximate to advertising, on the other hand, may lead to difficulties in disentangling response to the concept and response to the treatment. There is both the difficulty of deciding what constitutes a meaningful but undistracting illustration of the claim, and the difficulty of avoiding an interview situation where the informant has clearcut but misguided ideas that his job is to improve advertising.

Nevertheless, many find it useful to put a rough advertising treatment in front of some consumers and analyse their reactions in order to assess the viability of an advertising platform or approach. The data are, perhaps, no different from any other advertising research data, in that they require interpretation to sort out what influences are at work. There is a question of degree of obscurity, however: this makes it more often a matter for qualitative research, and for psychologists, than for using a pre-coded questionnaire. Disagreement among advertising researchers is frequent at this stage.

In North America both Burke and Eric Clucas · (using mainly recall measures and communication measures respectively) have suggested that for most TV commercials there is little difference between the results of testing the same campaign in rough or finished form. This includes anything between a hand-held storyboard with the audio played on a tape recorder; a videomatic or a photomatic treatment; or a finished commercial without opticals, or with the audio on a separate tape. There are sometimes problems with, e.g.:

drawn pictures of cooked food;
inability to reproduce a complex visual effect, or joke;
distinction between 'tranquil' and 'sombre' scenery

in rough commercials. But given appropriate introduction Clucas (from experience on both sides of the Atlantic) maintains that only the more extreme 'mood commercials' are genuinely hard to test in rough form.

It is true that there may be a bias in this argument stemming from the fact that a rough commercial that pre-tests *badly* will probably not be made into a finished film without radical changes, which makes comparisons impossible in some cases. However practitioners over the past decade have tended towards greater optimism concerning pre-tests of rough material.

Yet partly because of cost considerations, and partly because of experience, the tendency has been to increase the amount of work done on potential campaigns at this stage. Some have gone about this more by concentrating on improving *qualitative* examinations of the material. Others have tried to make this testing more 'accurate' and 'sensitive' (if not always 'positive') by validating and adapting *quantitative* methods, concentrating both on test situation and measurement.

Some believe that concept research is of most use when the primary features of the possible campaigns are rational, rather than emotional. The point here is that strength of an effective rational theme is more likely to be apparent despite crude representation, since it depends on logic. An emotional theme may depend on the suspension of logic, and it may only be by use of elaborate professional treatment that the right mood for this can be established. (Of course, very little advertising is *entirely* rational or *entirely* emotional.)

A second limiting point sometimes made is that valuable *negative* information is more likely to emerge from concept testing than any meaningful indication of the degree to which an idea may be a good one. That is to say, concept testing is allowed the credit for pointing out what probably won't work, and saying why; but sorting out the good from the average is another matter. This is the territory of opinion. Practitioners will disagree about how positive, as well as about how sensitive or accurate, concept test work can be.

Example

The development of an advertising campaign for National Benzole petrol is a case in point. In 1968, a new campaign was prepared with the purposes of projecting National as a big, dynamic brand, a technological leader in tune with modern idiom, having a recognizable style of its own. Any number of advertising platforms, in theory, could achieve this. In practice, the limitations imposed by the nature of the target market are severe. The advertising concept for National needed to be new, distinctive, re-echoing past success, making desirable points, and above suspicion; all at once. The task of advertising concept research was, therefore, as much one of suggesting *how* a concept might best be developed, as *whether* it should be encouraged at all. Figure 16.3 shows three press ad layouts. These were tested in parallel with pilot film material to investigate the concept. 'National is the Motorway Petrol' ought, basically, to make an association. Was this association, in which the fastest, most modern, most technically admired means of road travel was pre-empted for the brand, desirable, noteworthy and without danger? What possible aspects of the association were likely to work hardest for National?

Layout A shows an attempt to provide a technological background to the motorway claim. Layout B shows a 'human interest' approach in stressing that the 'motorway petrol' is right irrespective of the road, picking up a commonly experienced motoring situation. Layout C makes a dramatic, if imprecise announcement of the 'motorway' theme.

Consumer reactions in group discussions suggested that, despite criticism of certain aspects of motorways, motorists admired them and acknowledged their superiority and necessity, but the argument attempted in Layout A aroused suspicion. Building the campaign around one octane rating (99) was also limiting. Further concept work suggested that *any* logical approach was

Fig. 16.3A
Reproduced with permission of Leo Burnett Ltd.

Fig. 16.3B
Reproduced with permission of Leo Burnett Ltd.

Fig. 16.3C
Reproduced with permission of Leo Burnett Ltd.

likely to be self-defeating. Motorists appreciated a sense of power and 'motorway performance' that appealed to them in Layout C. If they were not made to work it out, they did not query it. The attempt to widen the motorway theme in Layout B merely achieved bathos. This underlined the importance of capitalizing on the dynamic aspects of motorways, to achieve interest and meaningful association. Concessions to normality were resented.

Television commercials were created and produced with the concept research in mind. They aimed at associating positive emotions with 'The Motorway Petrol', leaving rational arguments strictly to one side.

Subsequent research showed that the campaign had registered very strongly with the target market; and that National buyers in particular spoke of 'the Motorway Petrol'. This illustrates the point that concept research must be directed towards development opportunities of a concept in order to aid judgement about the viability of the concept itself. Putting up a sheet of paper with 'National is the Motorway Petrol' on it would have put research informants into an intolerable situation if asked to react to it.

Once a campaign theme has been established – tested or not – the advertising material developed from it may be tested in any state of finish. At this point it is worth observing that advertising researchers (as in the case of product development research) incline to either end of this spectrum:

Holistic ——————————— Atomistic

The more 'holistic' they are, the more likely they will be to:

(a) test only finished material;
(b) test campaigns, rather than individual advertisements;
(c) examine specific elements using techniques that allow breadth of expression of consumer reactions.

The more 'atomistic' they are, the more often they will:

(a) test individual advertisements, as individual queries arise, using material in any state of finish;
(b) test headlines, illustrations, other details;
(c) examine specific elements using techniques that allow precise reflection of the effect of those elements in consumer reactions.

It is not necessarily *bad* to be more one than the other. It is a matter of dispute which research approach will succeed in providing more useful diagnostic data that can help improve creative work. Possibly, however, it is easier to observe cases where a holistic approach allows greater insight into the real business of advertising than it is to see where an atomistic approach has a clear advantage. Questions of detail, e.g. which of several recipes attract sufficient interest to warrant including in a food advertisement, tend to be those at which the atomist shines.

Pre-testing techniques

Several techniques are common to market research in general. The depth interview, group discussion, the use of structured questionnaires, are all involved in advertising research, but scarcely need separate comment here. This chapter will concentrate only on features of such basic tools that require specific attention in the advertising context.

For convenience, techniques for testing television commercials will be covered separately from press and other media. There are first, however, some considerations which apply in all cases. These are stressed, because they show exactly why it is impossible to expect anything like absolute truth from any of the techniques outlined here. Figure 16.4 shows the relationships between the actual situation – consumers (C^1) actually exposed to real advertising (S^1) in its media context (M^1), and reacting to it (R^1) – and the pre-test. Any broken line

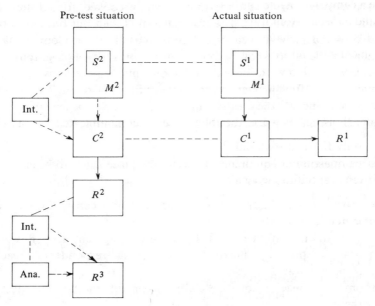

Fig. 16.4

Note: The point at issue in pre-testing is the extent to which R^3 is an aid towards calculating R^1. This figure shows the influences and possible differences, that can make the relationship between R^3 and R^1 uncertain.

C^2 is a sample selected to be representative of C^1, S^2 is advertising that may be in any state of finish. M^2 could be a theatre test, or a folder, etc. ... Int. (interviewer) is an important component of the exposure to test advertisements. Both Int. and Ana. (Analyst) mediate the direct response to S^2, (which is R^2) and record and/or interpret it as R^3.

indicates a relationship that will vary in closeness; a broken arrow shows that there is an influence by one factor on another, that also varies in nature and strength.

It is rather unlikely that the pre-test result will show *how* successful the advertising will prove, but what one can demand from pre-testing is direction, with a rough indication of extent – other things being equal.

Television commercial tests

The first problem in a TV commercial test is to choose the form in which the material can best be shown; and what equipment to use to expose it to a sample of informants. Filmed storyboards are usually preferable to showing the raw storyboards themselves, in that they give a sense of what the medium is all about. Animatics (showing a sequence of drawings) or photomatics (in which there is a sequence of photographs) can be used. A combination of these two kinds of material can be filmed on videotape. Incorporating photographs may be important when, for example, known personalities are used as presenters, or it is important to show cooked food (often rather unappetizing in drawn form). The test material is then put onto cassette, for use in a VCR machine. A cheaper option is to use La Belle Courier machines (or similar models) to show a series of pictures or photographs with a synchronized audiotape to individual respondents or to groups, quickly and economically. The final arbiters on the state of finish of rough TV commercial material should include the creative director: he needs to believe that the basic ideas of his commercial are capable of being communicated by the chosen means.

Once the question of equipment is solved, the place needs to be chosen. The alternatives are, for the most part:

(a) a theatre (or large hall) in which large audiences can be exposed to the commercial;
(b) a group discussion facility with built-in equipment for showing TV material: a one-way mirror for observing respondents' reactions; recording apparatus, etc.;
(c) a room in a house or hotel, specially equipped for a particular test to be run there;
(d) a mobile unit (test van);
(e) respondents' own homes, using easily portable equipment.

A number of research companies have developed systems for testing television commercials in theatres or halls, but anyone can organize his own theatre tests, using a fieldwork agency to recruit an audience and to supply projector and projectionist.

What happens at a theatre test depends on the kind of interview situation and questions favoured by the research agency or the executive who is organizing the test. It also depends on the degree of flexibility with which the test is approached.

The sample size has an influence on what can be done. Small audiences of say, 12 to 50 have been split up into groups, after exposure to the commercials, and separate group discussions in separate rooms conducted. Alternatively, this size of audience can be considered a 'large group', in which informants use self-completion questionnaires, and are then led by an interviewer into discussion. When there is disagreement, the interviewer can ask the informants to write down their personal views or to give a show of hands or to use Votometer machines.

Some of the best-known standardized test procedures are shown below.

Burke	—	'DAR' for 'day after recall', and adaptations of this technique for rough material or finished commercials that have yet to be broadcast. Available in many countries.

PEAC	These are examples of communication tests in
McCollum –	which the intent is to diagnose the kind of
Spielman	communication that is being effected, rather
Clucas	than a net recall store; they include attitu-
Comtest	dinal measures too.

Those offering standard commercial testing services vary in the extent to which they accommodate particular, 'custom-designed' questions that are inserted to test a commercial in terms of the *specific task* that is has been set. By analysing the results of many such tests, norms have been developed against which the scores achieved by individual test commercials can be compared. Because some types of commercial perform better than others on certain measures, and because the target market varies in the precision with which it is defined, e.g. 'analgesic users' as opposed to 'all adults', norms can be built up for product fields, or market segments, and used for comparison as well. Most companies nowadays favour having a range of standard measures within each test. Those who buy tests of this kind appreciate the fact that there is a combination of the standard and the specific. Comparison with the norms they see as supplying a perspective against which to examine individual features of the commercial.

Critics will be found to say that a norm has, in fact, little relevance. This is because the commercials for a product field may have been made for products at very different points in their life cycle, and with very different creative aims in mind, both at the strategic and the tactical level. How far any standard question can be relevant to many such aims is a matter for conjecture. The average of different commercials' scores is unlikely to be *more* relevant.

The search for a single measure that discriminates infallibly between commercials in terms of their overall selling effectiveness has long occupied the minds of researchers. The ground is strewn with the remains of systems that have been promoted on this basis. There is no reason whatever why such a measure should exist anyway; the problems of relating R^3 to R^1 (see Fig. 16.4) suggest that evaluation must be complex, and must be relative to a specific advertising context.

One alternative to standard questions for quantified pre-tests has been to make use of brand image batteries. This can mean administering attitude scales before and after exposure to the commercial. The scales may be established in advance, separately, for each product field (sometimes for each brand) as being those which are critical for choice between brands. Comparison between the rating scales before and after exposure can be both evaluative and diagnostic. Objections to this practice centre on the question of how attitude formation *really* happens. Attitudes to well-established brands, in particular, are unlikely to change after one 30-second commercial. When informants react to scales the second time round, they may mislead by trying to be helpful.

Brand image questions can be useful in pre-tests, more so for lesser known brands, but comparison ought to be between measures taken on separate matched samples, which is expensive.

Possibly the most controversial question about TV commercial testing is still the same one that has vexed marketing researchers for decades: how much value should be put on *recall*?

Recall certainly has a significance, but one which varies with the advertisement being tested and which requires interpretation. Recall *as such* has been shown to bear little relationship to advertising success, but the *kind* of recall may be important. Such questions are dependent, to some extent, on informants' ability to verbalize their impressions. Some people are more articulate than others, or more imaginative. The nature of the target market, and samples drawn from it, obviously affects the answers that result; but so does the nature of the advertisements. Jingles, slogans, with obvious meanings, are easily repeatable, but consumers may well be deriving the desired information and emotional colour from a television commercial that lacks these recall aids without being able to put these into the neat, elegant language of the creative *rationale*.

Several techniques have been developed to avoid this kind of problem. In one of these, informants are asked to note down what were the main thoughts that occurred to them while they saw each separate section of a commercial. Analysis shows whether the thought processes that the creative team imagined would be set in motion were, in fact, forthcoming. Supplementary questions check on whether informants agree that they were given a particular communication, or not. Clucas' technique involves showing the commercials in small 'reminder' sections, as well as in their complete form.

This yields a mass of diagnostic data. Criticisms are sometimes made that this procedure is unnatural, and leans heavily towards the 'atomistic' end of the spectrum described on page 486. The detial of the diagnosis sometimes, however, serves as a useful corrective of creative ways and means.

Testing TV commercials on large screens can be misleading. Most consumers have (relatively) small television screens in their homes. An eating shot, for example, on a large screen may seem remarkably unpleasant to anyone who is not used to a large close-up of incisor activity. For tests taking place in halls, shopping centres or theatres, a series of (smaller) TV monitors is often used in preference to the large screen.

Theatre tests organized for quantified research have been criticized for the unrepresentativeness of the samples who appear there. A considerable proportion, varying according to incentive, of those who are invited refuse to come. An extension of this point is that those people who *do* attend may be rather unsociable people, who ordinarily have little evening life. The kind of products and commercials that appeal to them may be atypical. Day-time interviewing in a hall by a busy shopping precinct can avoid this. But frequent users of the same shopping centre are often re-interviewed. This produces a learning effect in advertising research samples, because certain questions are then anticipated. Choice of centre, and then screening of potential respondents, are important.

Private houses are sometimes preferred for television commercial tests, because this is closer to normal viewing conditions; but trying to achieve greater reality in this way is an expensive business unless one limits oneself to small-scale qualitative work.

Qualitative vs quantitative

Much of the time the main argument about research into TV campaigns concerns the question of *whether* to use qualitative techniques; and *how much attention* should be paid to the results of each of these two kinds of test, in cases where both are done. It is more pragmatic to avoid looking at different tests as competitors, and to consider them more like complementary operations. Each can be applied to examine different aspects of a TV campaign. The information required from each of them is different but linked. The quantitative work will supply a frame of reference within which the attitudes and feelings probed in the qualitative work may operate. Raw facts established in the quantified test will be elaborated in the interpretation of the qualitative study.

In Canada, the advertising for Sunlight Liquid had depended since May 1981 almost exclusively on two TV commercials called 'Wedding' and 'Graduation'. These commercials are an expression of a strategic approach called 'Celebration'. In brief, this approach aims at giving an impactful combination of emotional as well as rational reasons for preferring to use this

Lever Detergents Ltd.
Sunlight Liquid
30 sec. T.V.
"Wedding"

SFX: Live party sounds,
concertina music.
ANNCR: When the Rossini's
have something to celebrate...

there's dish after dish to eat.

And of course, dish after
dish to wash.

The Rossini's use Sunlight
Liquid.

Because for a sensible price,
Sunlight gets brilliant results.

When you've got a lot on
your plate, when half
measures just won't do

Sunlight's the bright choice.

Lemon fresh Sunlight.
A little does a lot.

Fig. 16.5A

Lever Detergents Ltd.
Sunlight Liquid
30 sec. T.V.
"Jennifer"

ANNCR: On the day of
Jennifer's first birthday.

There was lots of sunshine,
lots of food and lots of

dirty dishes. And there was
Sunlight, shining in the
kitchen.

Hardworking, sensibly priced.

Washing dishes

sparkling clean and bright.

Just like that. Lemon fresh
Sunlight liquid.

It'll be right at home in
your kitchen too...
You'll take a shine to
Sunlight.

Fig. 16.5B

particular brand of dishwashing liquid. It adopted at the same time a confident, 'brand-leader' stance. The years 1981–3 were marked by a very satisfactory sales situation for the brand.

In 1983 the campaign was examined again, along with a new commercial, 'Jennifer'. This was an execution of the same strategy, and (logically enough) it featured a baby's christening party as opposed to the in-home wedding reception of 'Wedding'. Both were calculated to inspire a happy sunlit atmosphere, as well as suggesting a valid reason for having a lot of washing-up to do. Several questions were asked:

Had 'Wedding' begun to wear out?
Was 'Jennifer' communicating the same messages as 'Wedding'?
How effective would each of them be, in 1983, at communication; at achieving share of mind in terms of advertising consciousness; at helping to make users and non-users feel positively about Sunlight Liquid's characteristics, and about making it their choice of dishwashing liquid?

In the meantime, it may be noted, 'Graduation' had not shown itself in tracking studies to be as impactful as was required from the campaign. About 'Wedding' it was questioned whether the balance of emotional to rational communication was not top-heavy, perhaps leaving the viewer with not enough concrete reasons for choosing Sunlight Liquid. Might not 'Jennifer' fall into a similar trap?

A straightforward communication test conducted in a theatre situation showed that the right kinds of information were being picked up by homemakers in a controlled viewing situation. The figures were not, however, as high (in the case of 'Wedding') as might have been expected for an established commercial. Doubts persisted about the balance of what was getting across to the consumer.

A series of 20 individual depth interviews, split between:

background brand image;
advertising recall *before* exposure;
reactions to 'Wedding', then to 'Jennifer' separately and in detail (order alternated);

showed that both commercials had considerable appeal. 'Wedding' was widely recognized, but had by no means lost any of its charm. 'Jennifer' was believed to offer a more realistic explanation of a need for a really effective product; but in 'Wedding' the picture of the bridesmaid (who has caught the bouquet) and her boyfriend joining in the dishwashing scene in the kitchen *together* made for a strong emotional appeal.

Both commercials were shown to be on strategy by the qualitative work. It was true that the emotional side dominated – but for users of premium brands this seemed a strength, not a weakness. A problem of branding was underlined – suggesting the need for greater use of a 'sunlight' visual device, and the possibility of a different media scheduling pattern to secure share of mind.

The results of the two pieces of research were complementary, and the conclusions needed interweaving, not an adversarial approach.

Distrust of the meaning of question-and-answer has driven some researchers to want physiological measures. These may be applied in a theatre, or a mobile unit, but they are mainly used in laboratories. Their basic purpose is to provide objective indications, that are not subject to interpretation, of the extent to which an informant is emotionally aroused by a commercial. Either the total effect of the whole commercial is observed or the separate effects of the constituent parts as well.

The psychogalvanometer, which provides a measure of the sweat response – an autonomic indicator of emotional arousal – is the tool most often used. In the US an eye camera was developed to measure pupil dilation, another autonomic indicator. The latter, it was argued forcibly for some years, was superior to similar devices for two main reasons – sensitivity and direction. Very precise, minute measurements make it possible to have fine discrimination between reactions to successive parts of a commercial. At the same time, the *nature* of this particular response encouraged some to consider that it showed direction, i.e. not just emotional arousal was being measured, but *desirable* reaction which could be related to likelihood of purchase behaviour. Efforts to substantiate this suggest that whatever diagnostic value the tool may have the evaluative promise that it held out has not really been fulfilled.

Physiological psychologists have noted that different people react emotionally in different unconscious ways, e.g. some turn white with anger, others red. A polygraph is an instrument developed to account for this by taking a range of arousal measures, including galvanic skin response and pupil dilation. The costs are, needless to say, very considerable. It seems likely to remain a matter more for experiment than for consistent commercial use.

More recent experiments have concentrated on:

measuring tension in the eyebrow;
measuring voice pitch analysis (pioneered by VOPAN in the USA);
examining hemispheric activity (in the left brain vs the right brain, to contrast emotional and rational responses to advertising stimuli).

In theory many such physiological devices could be applied to test advertising other than TV commercials. But it has been here that their proponents have been anxious to demonstrate their value. This work continues, but none of it has been definitively adopted for particular purposes by the trade.

An alternative objective measure is to test on a large scale, near a supermarket, and offer informants money-off coupons which can only be used there. A matched control panel needs to be interviewed. Even with fast moving consumer goods, such a test can be very slow, and very insensitive.

Unexpected re-interview with commercial test informants, or signing them up for diary panels, might be more fruitful avenues.

An on-air pre-test demands small, localized operations if it is not to be a contradiction in terms. In the UK (as opposed to the USA) it is impossible to make use of areas as small as cities. Smaller TV areas can be used to secure exposure of just a small (yet hopefully representative) section of the target population. Local consumer research services are usually available for evaluation.

On-air tests, e.g. 24-hour recall, together with Starch tests, or reading and noting tests for print media, have tended to be more popular in the USA than in Europe. They take place, by definition, after a finished film has been developed. It is therefore too late to make radical alterations to it economically. The counter argument is that it is useful to apply to all finished products, rather like a quality control screening. It also has appeal to those who want a realistic exposure situation rather than employing a test where the respondents' attention is artificially focused. There are elaborate procedures for determining who, and how many, constitute the potential audience for a particular screening of a particular commercial, and then measuring its recall. Recall of ads is not above criticism (as explained above) as a criterion of effectiveness. But the method appeals to advertisers who aim as a basic rule to communicate simple, easily verbalized sales points.

Another standard form of testing that is sometimes used for finished commercials is to arrange a situation in which some kind of pre-post attitude shift is measured. The technique first advocated by Horace Schwerin, of finding out how many more people expressed a preference for the test brand after exposure to a test commercial compared with before exposure, is now used as one of a number of measures by Audience Studies Inc. in the USA. As a rough quality control mechanism for isolating a commercial that seems remarkably poor or remarkably good, it has its appeal. Some research work has however demonstrated that in practice there is a rather worrying amount of 'random' switching of choices in this test situation, and it is very difficult to establish a correlation between sales effectiveness and this measure. But this is not the only type of pre-post measure. Specific attitude changes are also studied. It is important to accept that since in many types of test the respondents often are aware, at least in part, of what they are doing, the attitude shift is in fact a communication measure. That is to say, it shows how many people have taken the point that they are being told a product is (e.g.) more healthy, and are prepared to play this back. This is particularly so where the *same sample* is used for the pre and the post measurements. Alternatively, a *parallel sample* can be used, as control: this parallel sample is *not* exposed to the test commercial. Another possibility is to have a *baseline* sample, as a reference point for the attitudes to the brand of the population at large, against which comparisons with test samples can be made. None of these methods is in fact perfect. To use the same sample for pre and post is somewhat obviously artificial: people do not undertake the same task twice without at least some of them having an idea of what they are doing. Where a baseline sample is used, there is the problem of allowing for changes over time which may be affecting the population at large. But using separate parallel samples means that there are problems of sample matching to be overcome and that shifts have to be large if statistical significance is to be read into them. Although they give one better experimental control they also tend to be expensive. Nevertheless, this latter procedure is the one to be recommended where possible.

Press advertising tests

There is a problem of definition of pre-testing that tends to occur more when press advertisements are being discussed. What, exactly, constitutes a 'pre-test' as opposed to a 'post-test'?

The standpoint taken here is that 'pre-testing' may include any situation in which a deliberately restricted proportion of the target population is exposed to the advertising. This includes cases where a magazine or newspaper actually appears, with the advertisement inside it, provided this is on a restricted scale. (The point here is that a check of advertising is being carried out prior to putting the bulk of media expenditure behind it.)

Folder test

Probably the most frequently-used technique of pre-testing a press advertisement is to expose the sample of informants to an advertisement included in a folder containing control advertisements. The classical version of this is described below, but in passing it should be mentioned that there are several variations. The first of these is where specially prepared copies of magazines are used for the same purpose as the folder. The main advantage claimed for this procedure is that the advertisement appears in a natural, rather than a contrived, context. It also becomes possible for the informant to consider the advertisement in a more realistic situation, e.g. the magazine may be substituted for his normal magazine in a particular week, when it is left to be read at home for a period of time before the second interview. Another variation is where a folder, as such, is not used but a number of advertisements are shown to the informant, (e.g. on boards, or projected on a screen) and the informant's reactions are observed.

In a sense, these two variations represent a deliberate movement in opposite directions: towards greater realism in the research situation, and away from it on order to concentrate attention on particular items. The advantages of either approach are matters of dispute. Some claim that greater realism in the research situation allows for greater meaningfulness in informants' response. Others argue that realism is illusory in the context of advertising research, because getting insight into likely reactions to advertisements depends, to some extent, on focusing attention.

A typical folder test will proceed as follows. Informants are allowed to look through a folder containing press advertisements. Included among them is a test advertisement. The folder should preferably be not too bulky, so it can be flicked through easily and the state of finish of all the advertisements should be roughly similar. It is sometimes claimed that only advertisements of comparable size or nature (black and white with black and white, or colour with colour, etc.) should appear in the folder. In fact, this seems less important than that the kind of advertisement included should be calculated to have roughly comparable appeal in terms of subject matter and style to the target group. At the same time, it is obviously undesirable to have all the control advertisements in black and white and only the test advertisement in colour. At this stage, the informants should not realize which is the test advertisement. Sometimes the interviewer will be instructed to pay attention to the amount of time spent looking at each advertisement. Occasionally, a time limit is imposed for looking at each advertisement but this procedure has been known, on occasions, to unnerve informants. Allowing the informant to browse through *ad lib* seems better practice. The folder is then withdrawn, and informants are asked a variety of questions, usually designed to elicit evidence of 'impact', 'involvement', 'interest', and the like. These questions are often favoured: 'We have only time to talk about two or three of these advertisements. Which would you prefer to discuss?', or, 'People sometimes like to turn back to a particular advertisement and have a closer look at it. Do you feel that about any of these? Which?' The questionnaire may often proceed: 'Which products can you remember seeing advertised here? Can you remember the brand name?'

The importance and relevance of these and other questions depends very much on which aspects of the advertisement are being researched, and what they are intended to do. This is particularly to be borne in mind when considering questions about the message received, e.g. 'What was the main point of the advertisement for...?'

A check list of adjectives is sometimes offered to the informant. This aims at getting evidence of the *kind* of message received, and the *way in which* it has been received. Informants may be asked, for example, to choose from a list including 'attractive', 'childish', etc. In themselves, the choices of adjective may be puzzling, bearing in mind that different people read words differently; therefore, reasons for choice of adjectives are often probed.

At some point in the interview, some kind of recall question, demanding playback of detail, is often included. The extent, or often the nature, of the recall of details may not in itself tell very much. It may, however, indicate the degree to which, in the short term, an advertisement tends to dominate attention or to be swamped by other advertising. It can also suggest which features of an advertisement are dominant; but careful interpretation is needed here, because some features may be simply easier to describe than others.

Coupon response

Arrangements can be made for advertisements to be included in local media, or in restricted issues of national media, in order to check how the advertising would work *in situ*. As opposed to relying on consumer research to show what the results are, behavioural measures can be used. The main ones in this group are:

(a) coupon response – redemption at local shops;
(b) coupon response – sent to advertiser/agency;
(c) 'hidden offer'.

These measures are valuable only to the extent that the behaviour itself is the result that the creative work is designed to achieve. It is easy to visualize a short-term effect being contrived, possibly among consumers outside the target, which risks cheapening expectations of the products among the best long-term prospects.

The total number of people who send in coupons from couponed advertisements may give an impression of precision in advertising evaluation that is entirely illusory. Where durables or services are concerned, it is the total number of *conversions* that is of interest. It is one thing to encourage twice as many to send in coupons for a brochure or a salesman's visit; it is another to do so without leading to disappointment. Relying on conversion data makes the assumption that the brochure and the salesman are standard items, with a fixed value. This may not be true.

When coupon response is a matter of detaching a coupon and handing it over as part-payment for the brand, certain other considerations apply. Some housewives collect coupons of this kind, as a matter of principle. They are continuously defraying the costs of their basic household purchases. In the shops they need to get the brand name right, but beyond this, they are simply thinking in terms of commodity. Coupon-combing is a habit with many women, to the extent that they ignore the advertisement itself. There is also the question of 'malredemption' whereby retailers accept coupons indiscriminately. without strict reference to the brands concerned.

'Hidden offers' are said to provide evidence that consumers have really penetrated as far as the body copy. (A coupon, of course, may just have been seen as a coupon.) Insofar as the consumer must have read deep into the advertisement in order to know that the offer exists, and how to get it, this is a fair assumption; but the principle that some people are more likely than others to be 'offer-hunters' is still an influence on results.

There is one variation that should be mentioned, i.e. research that is appropriate for much department store advertising: advertisements which describe the bargains available at the time can be varied so that they include different combinations of bargains. Some combinations are then proved to be better at getting people into the store to make a purchase.

Some have found that these measures distinguish better between *media* than between the advertisements themselves. This is an important consideration for interpretation. All these measures are best regarded as telling part, but not all, of the story. Qualitative research among matched groups of coupon senders – those who are converted into buyers and those who are not – can often indicate far more about the advertisement's *role* and *how* the advertisement played it.

Laboratory methods

The equipment used to make physiological measurements discussed under 'Television Commercial Tests' (p. 495) is used for testing press advertisements too. The same comments apply. Tachistoscopes are also used to determine the thresholds at which features of one or more press advertisements are registered. Two points can be of interest here – the degree of legibility, or recognition that the advertisement is for brand 'A', and the *order* in which certain features are recognized.

There are few things as unlike real media contexts as a tachistoscope, which is a large box used for exposing material for small, controlled periods of time. If it suggests or confirms, however, that an advertisement is not communicating identity, or a basic point, efficiently, then its evidence needs to be considered alongside data from more 'natural' sources.

The eye movement camera (as opposed to the eye observation camera used for measuring pupil dilation) is capable of showing *how* people look at advertisements. It traces the path taken by the eye when it passes over a printed page. The PRS method developed in the USA has become a standard tool for checking the performance of finished press advertisements, among several large national advertisers. Here the time spent on particular detail is important in interpretation of results, just as much as the eye movement track.

Post-testing

There is little point in describing all the pitfalls to be avoided in consumer surveys, which are covered elsewhere. Essentially, post-testing tends to be a matter of finding out, by means of *ad hoc* consumer survey work, what effects of advertising can be found among consumers. For anyone to want to do this, he must have good reasons for supposing that other, simpler steps that could be taken will not give all the information necessary. These simpler steps include:

(a) counting sales changes, retail audit;
(b) coupon return analysis;
(c) playback from sales force;
(d) consumer audit;
(e) standardized post-test services.

Sales data, in the final analysis, must be relevant, but the point has already been made that advertising is one of many things contributing to sales and that the relationship between these factors is more likely to be dynamic than additive. It is like testing fertilizer by observing whether the flowers come up big and strong from a packet of seeds. If the results are good, perhaps the product (the seeds) is so good that advertising (fertilizer) is scarcely necessary. Comparison with what happened last year, with a different fertilizer, is difficult, because the weather conditions may have been different. The metaphor can be extended indefinitely.

Coupon returns have their limitations, which have been discussed in the previous section. The opinions of the sales force are subject to remarkable bias.

Consumer panel data are a half-way house between retail audit work and sample surveys. On both sides of the Atlantic there are panels in existence which can be used to assess changes in purchasing behaviour by households within a particular campaign area and outside it, *or* by households with different likelihoods of exposure to an advertising campaign according to media exposure data about those same households.

In the USA and Canada the BCR method (developed by Bruzzone Research, California) makes use of panels to conduct post-testing of advertising campaigns by concentrating on reactions to campaigns, not on purchases of the brands advertised. This can be criticized for putting the consumer into the position of expert witness: she has to say which of the storyboards that she receives in the mail with her questionnaires, she recalls seeing on television; how interested she is in that message; how relevant she feels it is to *her*; etc.

The two uses of consumer panels outlined here are almost at opposite extremes. Any purchase behaviour variations have to be *assumed* to link up with advertising; but any variations in the BCR storyboard ratings have to be *assumed* to have some relevance to eventual purchase behaviour. Where it is economically feasible, a more complete answer can be obtained by:

a sequence of consumer surveys ('tracking studies') which will check purchase behaviour, advertising awareness and attitude change, as well as including media exposure questions in the classification (basic data) section;

a qualitative follow up among users who show awareness of the advertising; and non-users who also show awareness of it.

This will provide both evaluation and diagnosis. The use of telephone surveys or syndicated services can make the first part economically more accessible.

Very often the worst aspect about planning a post-test for the researcher is matching the practical need for speedy information to aid forward planning, and the likelihood of getting meaningful results while the campaign is still new. The timing of a post-test must take into account:

(a) How much advertising pressure is being put behind the brand – in absolute terms and in relation to competitive activity?
(b) Over what period is the money being spent?
(c) When was there advertising behind the brand before? At what level? On the same theme?
(d) How far is advertising trying to introduce a new thought, about new or generally reformulated products? How far is it a matter of trying to amend the image of a well entrenched product, which has near commodity status?
(e) What is the repurchase rate for the product?

All these points, which are obviously interrelated, can decide whether a clear picture is likely to emerge from survey work done earlier or later. Most researchers tend to advise later research. They do so for a number of reasons. They are less sanguine, as a rule, about the chances of consumers really seeing a product in a new light, when that product has already been around a long time. They also prefer to judge a campaign once they have seen how appreciation of the product in use ties in with expectations derived from advertising; for this it helps if time has been allowed for a repurchase rate to establish itself. The classical approach is to conduct identical checks before and after a campaign appears. This allows one to evaluate how much progress has been made. There are problems, however, in that several factors may not be the same, before and after the campaign break. The product may be seasonal or dependent on epidemic conditions, etc. The sales force activity may be heightened by the campaign. Competitors may have started to retaliate. This makes it desirable, in some cases, to have a control area, as below.

	Pre-campaign	*After campaign break*
Test area	Check 1^A	Check 2^A
Control area	Check 1^B	Check 2^B

Some prefer to take the rest of the country as the 'control' on the principle that a particular control area may be rendered unsuitable half-way through the test, by competitive activity.

Sometimes no pre-check is possible, because the decision to post-test comes too late. In this case, a control area is most desirable. Long-term effects, or campaign wear-out, can be studied by repeating post-checks.

What to measure? Recall measures will certainly figure among what is measured, although relatively uncomplicated things such as purchase and the presence of the brand in the pantry, etc., can also be covered. These question areas are sometimes useful:

(a) brand saliency (first mentions of brand when product field is mentioned);
(b) spontaneous awareness (any mentions of brand);
(c) prompted awareness (recognition of brand);
(d) trial and repurchase (for new brands);
(e) purchase and frequency of purchase (established brands);
(f) spontaneous awareness of advertising;
(g) prompted awareness of advertising;
(h) detailed recall of advertising;
(i) impressions of the advertising;
(j) brand image questions;
(k) attitudes to purchase (possibly using 'constant sum' technique);
(l) media exposure data.

A long questionnaire already, and no mention has yet been made of specific questions that may be important to establish the penetration of a particular campaign, e.g. 'How does brand A compare for price against brand B? Is it more, or less expensive, do you think?', where an economy platform has been used. The optimum question order must be expected to vary.

Some of the questions above, it has been suggested, are better indicators than others that a campaign has succeeded, or is succeeding, in increasing sales – 'brand saliency', 'spontaneous advertising awareness', and 'constant sum' have support here, e.g. Axelrod.[2] Certain useful cross-analyses stick out a mile. Ability to recall advertising detail can be usefully crossed with trial, repurchase, and intentions to purchase. 'Brand image' can be crossed with 'frequency of purchase' groups. The value of this is fairly obvious.

A lot can also be done with media exposure data. Given analyses of media questions a series of cells can be built up as follows:

Likelihood of advertising experience:				
Very high	*High*	*Medium*	*Medium/ Light*	*Light/ None*
Definition:				
Television	Watches ITV every night	Watches ITV 4–5 nights a week	Etc.	Etc.	Etc.
Press	Reads daily	Reads daily	Etc.	Etc.	Etc.
	two out of three publications on schedule	one publication on schedule; occasionally sees others			

(Note: ITV = relevant commercial television stations)

These groups can be considered separately on such questions as 'brand saliency', 'advertising awareness', etc. Figure 16.6 shows two very simple examples of the value of this. The example assumes that 'brand saliency' is a crucial measure as it may be for a fragmented market. Brand A has achieved no significant increase in brand saliency, given that heavier ITV viewers were very much aware of it already. Both the media choice and the creative content need to be critically examined. Brand B has fared better. The fact that the response function seems to be linear could be important. Briefly, this suggests that the *more* advertising received, the *greater* the effect. One implication could be that greater advertising pressure would be useful.

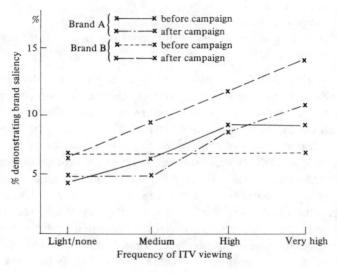

Fig. 16.6

The story is still incomplete, however. Large-scale quantified work usually yields hypotheses about advertising effects, e.g. 'Those who were exposed to the advertising message were made aware of the brand, but not of its advantages; this is reflected in disinclination to purchase it'. The paradox of advertising research is that one is often forced, then, to go below the surface and examine hypotheses by means of qualitative work. Campaign evaluation studies can often be considered as establishing which sub-groups need intensive interviewing. This stands much conventional market research procedure on its head but advertising research is territory where the practitioner needs to develop and follow his own rules.

Market modelling techniques have been invading the territory of advertising research over the past few years – with some success. Opti-Concept, for example, developed by Clancy Shulman Associates in the USA, makes use of an advanced conjoint analysis programme to identify optimal combinations of concept elements in an advertising approach. But in the area of post-testing, their LITMUS II model deserves a mention as an example of a test market simulation that takes into account the apparent effects of exposure to a campaign for a new product (within the context of an 'as-marketed' test incorporating actual purchase in a store) when assessing the likelihood of success and failure in terms of purchases and share of market. Part of the output is an analysis of the 'sensitivity' of the advertising component – as represented by the particular campaign – on a comparative basis with other variables under control. For example, in a given instance, the sensitivity may be calculated to be marginal, showing that this advertising campaign should be regarded as a minor element, deserving minimal expenditure. In another instance the sensitivity might be very high, suggesting that it works well enough to justify considerably greater expenditure than planned so far. The advertiser, of course, may decide (on *all* evidence) that his campaign needs changing, just as he may decide to go with the advertising that has been tested at the optimal weight indicated by the model.

It is often useful to observe the progress of a brand's advertising penetration, compared with other brands' performances, and broken out by usage and media exposure groups. Standardization of interviews means it is easier to note significant changes over time.

To be satisfied with standardization presupposes that one is confident that certain questions, repeated every few months, will continue to get at reactions to a brand's advertising in the most meaningful way, despite campaign changes and possibly altered strategy. For some brands, in some situations, this may, almost, be the case, but to understand what a specific campaign is achieving, it is usually necessary to add specific questions. The same argument can be applied to the standardization of the sample.

While many advertisers will find it easier and cheaper to buy into a continuous survey, say twice a year, to get data of this kind on brand saliency, awareness, comprehension of messages, brand image, and forth, a larger advertiser with a number of brands often reaches a different solution. This is to buy fieldwork direct, at appropriate intervals, from a fieldwork agency. The sample will be structured to suit his purposes, and there is no risk of 'interference' from questions on other advertisers' product fields.

There is another approach to campaign evaluation in the USA – the AdLab – which has attracted the interest and hopes of advertising researchers for some years. Even in the USA it is only in the 1980s that the approach has developed on any scale, and in Europe such systems are only just starting to grow. It is also somewhat expensive to administer, and demands more time to measure results than many advertisers can afford. The system involves setting up matched panels of homes within the *same* geographical area and controlling their reception of advertising (e.g. with a split cable for commercial television reception). The effects of exposing comparable groups of homes to alternative advertising can then be measured. The system is described further on pages 556–7. The principle seems above criticism, provided there is accurate panel matching (in terms of shopping behaviour and access to different outlets) and provided the test area is reasonably typical. Control of media exposures will never be perfect so long as people visit each other, but this is a minor problem.

American experience suggests that a lot of time is needed before getting clearcut trends, whether it is advertising pressure or scheduling or campaign content that is the subject of the test. Nevertheless, many European advertisers and researchers would probably appreciate having a similar realistic campaign evaluation opportunity available – if it did not cost too much and if it could aid judgment sufficiently quickly.

Advertising Research Program

There is no perfect advertising research program, but here is an example of one, taken from work done to re-launch Silvikrin Shampoo in the UK in 1966–8, which introduces many of the points made in this chapter.

In 1968 Silvikrin Shampoo was re-launched as a range of shampoos based on natural ingredients, called 'The New Naturals'. The outline of research is given below.

(a)	Summer 1966	Concept of 'New Naturals' tested on small scale in group discussions.
(b)	Winter 1966	Reactions to 'New Naturals' concept (adapted since summer, 1966) tested on larger scale, in parallel with tests of optimum balance of shampoo variants, names and packs.
		(1967. Product and packaging development.)
(c)	Winter 1967/8	Tests of four advertising approaches for the 'New Naturals' introduction.
(d)	Spring 1968	In light of the above, two press advertisements in finished form. (One 15-second announcement commercial was also prepared, using the features that came out best in winter 1967/8.) These press ads were tested on a small scale.
(e)	Summer 1968	Tested on a large scale, in a folder test, against other toiletry and cosmetic advertising.
		Autumn 1968. Advertising broke (national launch). Mainly press and television in support.
(f)	Autumn 1968/70	Tests of further individual press advertisments, featuring each shampoo variant separately. Mostly small-scale, to check for negatives and appropriateness to specific hair types; occasional larger-scale tests to check the strength of the continuing campaign.
(g)	Spring 1969	Large-scale national usage and penetration study, checking inter-relationships of:

brand use;
advertising awareness;
understanding of 'New Naturals' theme;
appreciation of 'New Naturals' theme;
media exposure.

The length of time spanned by this whole program is a function of the fact that the re-launch involved a re-vamping of the whole brand. The right formulations, colours, bottles, and names for each of the four Silvikrin variants – 'Natural', 'Protein', 'Lemon and Lime', and 'Almond Cream' – had to be developed in parallel. As the creative work was developed, it had to take into account any new turn taken in the presentation of the range.

The first stage showed that the idea of the 'New Naturals', as a means of reintroducing a well-known brand, was arresting, intriguing, and pleasing to the target market. The natural ingredients featured seemed to carry considerable promise, and were consistent with the brand image idea, 'beauty through health' (see original concept board in Fig. 16.7a). The work in the winter of 1966 (b) confirmed this impression. It also showed which names, colours, packs were consistent with the promise of the 'New Naturals' theme, and which were not.

The 'Natural' theme inspired four creative routes, one of which is illustrated in Fig. 16.7. Of these, one featured a headline 'Once Upon a Time', recalling the days of childhood when hair was naturally attractive. This had significant negatives for some women, who saw it as a reminder of advancing years, and was abandoned; but the one illustrated in Fig. 16.7b 'Silvikrin Goes Natural', combined emotional arousal with communication and appreciation. The other two were workmanlike, rather than inspired.

Figure 16.8 shows the two advertisements that were tested at (d) and (e). Both were significantly more likely to arouse comment, interest, and remarks suggesting relevance to consumer need than the other advertisements tested in the folders at (e). Further, they succeeded in securing the attention and enthusiasm of both the younger and the older parts of the target market, which earlier creative work had never quite succeeded in achieving. The sales results of the re-launch thoroughly vindicated the whole operation. The close inter-relationship of all factors in the marketing mix made it extremely difficult to apportion results to causes. (Note that the original concept research was as much product concept as advertising concept research.) The comparison of awareness, usage and media exposure in the post-campaign evaluation at (g), however, showed that advertising must have played a considerable part.

Fig. 16.7A
Reproduced with permission of Leo Burnett Ltd.

Fig. 16.7B
Reproduced with permission of Leo Burnett Ltd.

Fig. 16.8A
Reproduced with permission of Leo Burnett Ltd.

Fig. 16.8B
Reproduced with permission of Leo Burnett Ltd.

Chapter 17

Packaging research

WILLIAM SCHLACKMAN and DAVID CHITTENDEN *

The areas in which packaging research can help most

Packaging is the *key* vehicle in the passage of many products from the manufactured state to the point of consumption. At the very least, it has to:

contain the product physically;
protect it from contamination or degradation;
stand up to transportation and storage by the trade;
present the product to the consumer;
allow consumer transportation and storage;
allow the product to be dispensed (and perhaps resealed) whenever needed; and
stimulate purchase and repurchase.

Good packaging does all this at low cost and in a way which allows of easy disposal and minimal wastage.

Nevertheless the most frequent use of, and greatest opportunity for, packaging research is in assessing how packaging *presents* the product – first to the retailer and more importantly to the consumer. As James Pilditch[1] has said in 'The Silent Salesman', with the growth of self-service and self-selection: 'The package as salesman ... is the connecting link between company and consumer .... The final step, from shelf to shopping basket, depends on the package.'

The research methods outlined in this chapter therefore, are concerned primarily with assessing the acceptability of new or existing packaging at retailer and consumer levels, and with how effectively the packaging presents

* In this third edition of the Handbook this chapter has been completely revised and up-dated by David Chittenden.

the product it contains, so as to stimulate purchase or encourage repurchase.

If the analogy of the pack acting in the role of salesman is taken a little further we can identify four important functions:

(a) getting one's foot in the door;
(b) making a *very quick* sales pitch which will interest the potential consumer;
(c) following up with an effective presentation of the sales story;
(d) closing the sale.

It will be important, then, to consider research methodologies which measure:

(a) the ability of the pack to stand out from competition in retail shop displays;
(b) what the pack is able to communicate quickly;
(c) what ideas and associations are communicated overall by the packaging;
(d) what is the overall effect on likely intention to purchase.

Before going on to consider these methodologies, however, certain other areas of research should be considered, because the need to undertake them usually occurs early on in the total packaging development process.

Laboratory tests of pack performance

Although such tests do not fall within the area of consumer research, many manufacturing organizations carry out their own in-house tests on packaging materials (e.g. tests of the ability of a package to resist heat, pressure, or handling; or, more frequently, to maintain the quality and characteristics of the product contained, without allowing deterioration; and without any adverse interactions between the product and the packaging material).

Where such tests are not able to be conducted internally by Quality Control or Research and Development Departments, they may well be undertaken (in Great Britain) at the Packaging Industry Research Association in Leatherhead, Surrey, from whom further details may be obtained.

Functional considerations

Functional innovations in packaging which facilitate actual product usage are welcomed by consumers, who now expect effective, convenient packaging from manufacturers and when they do not get it may express hostility toward the brand. In your own experience as a consumer, think of all the times you had difficulty opening a can or bottle. Try to remember how aggravated you got. Then multiply your experience by thousands and you can easily realize the sales effects such experiences can create for a given manufacturer.

The familiar closure problem, however, is only one of the many in the area of usage. Consider such things as cartons that cannot easily be disposed of and bottles which are cumbersome to use, and/or difficult to hold.

Packages which overcome such problems are attractive to consumers. Research on usage is able to locate such consumer difficulties and suggest new directions for packaging development.

The functional features of a pack are best studied under in-use conditions, in a way which avoids any concentration on the pack as such. A useful procedure is to adopt a *pseudo-prduct test* research design, where the product is kept constant while the package construction or graphic design varies for each sample tested.

Example: This study comprised a pack test for a hand-rolling tobacco, in which two alternative types of pack construction were tested ('R' and 'T'). These were placed with informants, separately and in sequence, with the placement order rotated; informants were allowed two days to smoke each of the two samples of tobacco, and then were called upon and interviewed to find their reactions to the tobacco. At the end of the test, when the informants had tried both products, they were also asked to express a preference between the packs, and to give reasons for this. This emerged as follows:

$$N = 200$$

Preferences between the packs	%
Prefer pack 'R'	31
Prefer pack 'T'	68

When asked the reason for their preferences, the informants replied as follows:

Base: Informants who:	prefer 'R'	prefer 'T'
Reasons	%	%
Just like it, for no particular reason	2	4
Easier to open	7	43
Easier to get at the tobacco	4	31
Better sealed	26	2
Easier to reseal	9	6
Keeps the tobacco fresh	42	10
A stronger pack	19	8
Easier to use	0	9

These comments centred upon two aspects of the packs, convenience and protection. Those who were convenience-oriented preferred pack 'T' and those who were protection-oriented preferred pack 'R'.

In this case, although the test was introduced to respondents as a *product* test, the actual questions (answers to which are shown above) are clearly directing respondents to consider the packaging itself, and to comment on it, whereas in most pseudo product tests the aim is to establish the *effect* of different forms of packaging on *perceptions of the product*, and questioning is almost entirely directed to that aim, as will be discussed later.

It should also be noted that in such a test, the information produced depends on the respondent reporting back to the interviewer in his/her own words, and at some distance (in time and space) from the actual occasion on which the product was used. In order to get nearer to actuality, an observational approach is needed, so that the interviewer can *see* what is happening, and record his/her observations accordingly.

Such observation tests are usually conducted in the home or at central locations, in which potential consumers are introduced to a particular form of packaging which they are invited to use, so that their behaviour and any difficulties they may encounter may be observed. In the successful development of ring-pull cans Metal Box conducted a number of such research exercises. In that case, experiments were mainly concerned with difficulties in opening the can; other more recent experiments have been concerned with the consumer's abilities to drink directly from cans with different openings.

Another obvious example where such observational studies are of crucial importance is that of testing the ability of pilfer-proof packaging to resist the attempts of young children to open it. Such tests are particularly relevant to pharmaceutical products which might be dangerous in the hands of children.

Typically such tests are concerned with the length of time taken to achieve a particular objective (e.g. to open the actual pack), with the incidence of failure to complete the required task, and the observed degree of difficulty experienced by consumers.

Research with retailers

There is much evidence to suggest that if a package fails to meet the retailer's needs he will behave in such a way that distribution of the product will be severely inhibited. He may not display the product or he may discourage consumers from making a purchase, or he may simply not carry the product because its packaging creates too many problems for him. Of course, such decisions may well be taken at the Head Offices of multiple retailers, rather than at individual store level, but they are still based on an appreciation of how the package will perform in store.

There are a number of questions, the answers to which will help in the development of pack design which is effective and appealing to retailers, for example:

(a) What kind of package will be most convenient for retailers to stock and maintain?

(b) What kind of package will minimize the cost of handling?

(c) What kind of package will minimize breakage and pilferage?

(d) What sizes and shapes will fit into normal displays, and what kinds of outer or point-of-sale display will be welcomed?

(e) What kind of package does the retailer think consumers will buy?

(f) With what types of packs currently on the market has he experienced difficulty?

(g) What are his personal preferences and how do these influence his buying practices?

Either personal or telephone interviews with shop managers or owners can yield useful answers to these questions, the telephone interview perhaps being more appropriate for situations where large numbers of retailers need to be contacted quickly, and the personal interview for situations where some visual contact is needed for the interviewer or retailer to explain a particular point. However, when there is so much concentration of package goods sales through a relatively small number of large multiple retail organizations, it is often more appropriate to conduct personal interviews with the senior buying personnel at Head Office. Since such personal interviews are difficult to arrange and fairly expensive to undertake, it is probably more likely that investigations relating to packaging will only be made in the course of a much wider ranging interview, perhaps concerned with the whole of the manufacturer's reputation with the retail trade, his perceived ability to provide good service, the likelihood of his producing future innovations, etc.

On occasion however very specific retailer pack studies are undertaken. In one case, a spirits producer found it worthwhile to interview bartenders on their views about bottle shapes, since it was found that (other things being equal) bartenders expressed a strong preference for a bottle neck which allowed them to pick up a bottle quickly and without fear of mishandling whilst mixing cocktails. Although it was impossible to quantify the effect of changing bottle neck shape to one which was ergonomically correct, there seemed no reason not to include such a requirement in a design brief.

Research at the point of sale

While retail attitudes are generally well understood by marketing management and/or the design team, what is sometimes less clear (in spite of frequent personal store checks) is the exact set of conditions at the point of sale under which packaging has to perform effectively in presenting the product to the consumer. For example:

(a) What are the store lighting conditions under which the packaging has to be easily seen?

(b) In what context is the brand's packaging normally placed – in outers? on lower or higher shelves? alongside other brands immediately competing in the same product field? or alongside totally different product fields? against competitors which appear to be using the same basic colours, shapes, or graphics to communicate the generic qualities of the product field? or against competitors which are extremely varied in colour and design approach?

(c) How frequently is the product being purchased? Is there a core of loyal buyers who only buy that brand? or of loyal buyers with a small repertoire of brands? or is the concept of brand loyalty irrelevant?

(d) Whether purchase of the product is very infrequent (for example, less than once a year) or not, what are the conditions leading to the purchase? Is the purchase *predetermined*? If so, is the preselection one of product type? or of brand? Is it an *impulse* purchase? Or is it simply a matter of *replacing* a product which the housewife has run out of?

(e) How much time and consideration is given by the buyer to the product and its packaging before the purchase decision is made? Is the process almost instantaneous (as with washing powder)? or is it more deliberate? Do people appear to examine each pack carefully before they buy? Do they look at the front, back, top, or sides? Is time spent looking at weight, size, price, etc.?

All of these points have to be carefully considered before going too far with design development. For example, in a recent pack test the objective of which was to screen ten different pack designs, it was found difficult to recruit buyers of the product category within the previous year, although almost twice as many housewives actually had the product in their larders and used it from time to time for specific purposes. Once it was found that such long time periods elapsed between purchases, it was clearly imperative to establish how much predetermination there was to purchase and in what terms the purchase was thought of e.g.:

(a) 'I must buy some more (BRAND – PRODUCT FIELD) before I run out'

(b) 'I'm going to get some fresh (PRODUCT FIELD) to use in cooking a meal I'm planning now'

(c) 'Help! I've run out of (BRAND), I'm lost without it'

In this particular case it was established that a major objective of pack design was to stimulate usage of the product once it was in the home, while a second important objective was to communicate more effectively that the product was suitable for a *particular* end use. In other cases strength of communication of brand name or ability to reinforce the basic generic qualities of the product field may be more important.

At this initial stage of design development, then, it is first of all essential to establish as far as possible from existing research (syndicated, omnibus, or *ad hoc*) just what is the background to the purchase decision-making process. Secondly it is usually of importance to conduct some research (formal or informal) at the point of sale itself.

One of the most obvious research exercises which can be useful at this stage is a photographic survey of displays of the product field in a cross section of retail outlets, large or small. Such a survey conducted by specially selected interviewers can provide voluminous data on:

the lighting conditions and geographical situations (e.g. lower shelves, end on, upside down) under which the brand's packaging has to work;
the products forming the visual background against which the brand is displayed;
the colours and graphic design styles of the immediate competition.

Secondly observation and interviewing of shoppers at the point of sale should confirm the amount of time spent deliberating before making a purchase decision, and the extent of any examination of individual pack elements.

Two experimental studies designed by the authors, and conducted at the point of sale, showed the value of collecting information close to the point of purchase. The first of these[2] involved the personal interviewing, outside large multiple grocery outlets, of some 400 housewives, both before and after their trip round the store. The questionnaire was structured, and designed to establish, prior to entry into the store, what brands or products the housewife intended to purchase there; while the re-interview, subsequent to purchases being made, established which products and brands had in fact been bought, in five major product categories.

As expected, impulse purchase turned out to be higher in some product fields then others, with confectionerty being tne notable example: but of interest also were the findings on failure to purchase due to the product not being found in the store (usually because it was genuinely out of stock, but sometimes because it had not been *seen*); and decisions to go elsewhere because of the price or (occasionally) because of the condition of the product or packaging as seen in the store.

The second study[3] was intended to gain a better understanding of the processes going on in the shopper's mind, both before and during her visit to the supermarket. Thirty-four in-home depth interviews were undertaken with pre-recruited shoppers who were then asked if they would agree to the interviewer accompanying them on their next major shopping expedition. No refusals were met with, and on the next occasion, outside the store, the interview established what products/brands the shopper expected to buy, and at roughly what prices. The shopper's in-store behaviour was then observed, and on completion of the trip round the store, the interviewer noted the items bought, and what they cost, and asked for any comments on discrepancies between the amount paid and any amount previously stated as expected for that item.

Apart from suggesting that many shoppers tend to shop primarily at one store and are not particularly price-conscious, this study identified three different effects of special offers, depending on product category:

(a) Categories (such as toothpaste) where the repertoire of brands the housewife is willing to consider is of at least 2–3 brands, and where one of these is always on special offer. In this situation the housewife can afford to wait until she really needs the product field before purchasing.
(b) Categories where only one *brand* is favoured, so that when it comes on special offer, as much of it as possible is bought.
(c) Categories where the addition of a special offer *increases* the temptation for a shopper to buy, particularly in self-indulgent product fields such as cakes, chocolate, etc.

The need or otherwise for on-pack promotion and the likely interaction with shopper's purchasing behaviour is clearly an important part of the packaging design brief.

In-store observation has been covered in a highly relevant article by Wells and Lo Sciuto.[4] Their direct observation of (not pre-recruited) shoppers in-store produced purely observed data (i.e. on what shoppers were *seen* or *heard* to do). It suggests strongly the inconsequentiality of much shopping behaviour and the many different criteria that are under consideration by the shopper, particularly in a product field with which she is unfamiliar. Examples of coded observational data taken from the study are shown below:

	Products considered		
	Cereal	Candy	Detergent
Clear evidence of intention to purchase	55 %	38 %	72 %
Difficulty in finding or deciding brand	30 %	18 %	12 %
No purchase made	15 %	44 %	16 %
Occasions on which considerable handling of pack took place	22 %	16 %	22 %

These data agree with those derived from the British studies previously referred to, in that confectionery ('candy') may well be an impulse purchase or simply not be bought; detergents are purchased in a fairly decisive manner; while breakfast cereals, on the other hand, cause the shopper some difficulty in deciding what to buy (examination of the breakfast cereal packs available suggests this may be partly due to the emphasis given to appetite appeal and on-pack promotion, rather than to branding).

Direct observation of this kind has been used in the United Kingdom to confirm the speed and directness of purchasing behaviour in the detergent field whilst aiming to find the best ways of conveying perceived value through to the consumer. The same study successfully identified certain on-pack promotion ideas which were highly appealing to the consumer, and are still in use today.

Research on key elements within the overall pack design

Again, before proceeding too far with design development, it is usually desirable to establish what ideas and associations are conveyed by certain elements of pack designs. In the case of an existing product with several strong competitors it may be essential to conform sufficiently to reinforce the idea of being acceptable within the product field, but be sufficiently different in one or two ways to form a basis for brand differentiation and thus present a unique proposition. A very strong brand leader within a major market may find it almost impossible to change pack design greatly without upsetting a proportion of its existing buyers; but a completely new product with a strong story to tell, or a similar product which has not yet established itself, has much more freedom of movement.

It is not only *graphic* design which communicates ideas or impressions. Some years ago it was found that buyers of stock or gravy cubes like Oxo or Bovril could easily ascertain from glancing at a small red cardboard box that the product it contained was in the form of *cubes*. There was therefore little point in using the *word* 'Cubes' on the outside of the packaging to describe the product format, and this space could therefore be used for other purposes.

More generally within the food product area the use of *foil* can be expected to suggest airtightness, freshness, and perhaps a need for refrigeration.

In the field of motor oil, a comparison between 5 litre cans made of metal and of plastic showed the consumer as still perceiving some greater quality attached to the oil in the metal can, whilst recognizing and appreciating the possible advantages of lightness and lower cost in the plastic container.

In a similar comparison between glass and plastic containers for hard and soft drinks, it was found that glass was very highly regarded by the consumer and almost irreplaceable as a container for certain types of drink (particularly wine and quality beers), but that cheaper beers and certain types of carbonated or squash-type soft drinks could safely be packaged in plastic packs since any perceived detriment in quality was more than offset by expectations of lower prices, lightness in the packaging itself, and increased safety (particularly for children's products).

Colour may also strongly affect product recognition and acceptance within a product field. For example the gold on black pack style adopted for John Player Special cigarettes and the purple long used as a background colour for Cadbury's Dairy Milk chocolate must strongly convey both a brand name and a product field. Similarly, the green glass generally used for Moselle wine bottles imported into the UK is for those who know their wines an almost essential sign of the authenticity or heritage of the wine – irrespective of the brand. Green glass would not have the same effect if applied to lager bottles but might be expected to suggest a paler, less *strong-tasting* but possibly higher quality product. Still other forms of bottled lager rely heavily on colour graphics applied to labels or foil, to communicate their presence, and their authenticity, in a particular market sector.

How far is it possible to change pack design for an existing product without losing strong and immediate identification? Sometimes the answer is surprising. Key elements of colour or of design detail may be more important for recognition purposes than the brand name or logo itself. And other pack elements – a line drawing or symbolic device – may be important communicators of key product characteristics. For example, it was found in relation to a small but exclusive brand of canned soup – Frank Cooper (a name more commonly associated with traditional marmalades) – that a unique device within the graphic design area was able to communicate the brand identity even more quickly than the written brand name itself.

Because of all these possibilities, research undertaken prior to final formulation of the design brief is highly desirable. But what form should it take? Group discussions are one obvious answer, because of the need to find a way, in the interview itself, of establishing *in what context* of behaviour and attitudes the pack has to do its job; and forcing out some consensus views on what is being communicated by each pack, and by which elements within each pack (as opposed to the basic imagery of the brand derived from previous usage, word of mouth, advertising, sales promotion, etc.). However, it is important to define brand usership or loyalty extremely carefully in the recruitment for such groups, and to give much thought also to the definition of potential buyers of the brand or product field.

It is also worth considering, when pack communication is all important, setting up a *larger* number of groups of 4–5 people for shorter periods of interview (say 15–20 minutes). One advantage is the opportunity to talk to *more* people for the same research cost about exactly what a particular pack suggests to them. Another is the reduction in contamination or group consensus effects. The main disadvantage is the slightly superficial level at which interviewing takes place.

In addition to such qualitative investigations of key element communication using the pack designs in their entireties, it may sometimes be possible physically to break up an existing or new pack design into its component parts or elements so as to see what is communicated by each such element alone. The Frank Cooper soup label design mentioned previously was tested in this way, the individual pack design elements being transferred to overhead projector transparencies and then shown to individual respondents in sequences rotated so that all possible permutations were covered.

An example in the course of new product development has been cited by Vineall and Origlia[5] in relation to the development of packaging for Twyford Amber Ale in Italy. In this case the 'minigroup' approach was used, and various design elements were transferred to transparent overlays which could be superimposed onto a board representing a 33 cl bottle. Items represented separately were:

the name;
the shape of bottle;
basic elements of the label in different colours and shapes;
emblems;
different lettering (in black and white) for each name;
additional elements that would identify the beer as imported into Italy.

As that article points out, to do this properly requires a very close liaison between marketing, creative, and research personnel.

When a pack design for an established product is already well known in the market it is equally important to investigate which elements of that existing pack design are key recognition features. In order to provide information on which elements are key, one approach[6] requires the respondent to build up a physical representation of the pack *as she recalls it*, using a recessed board to represent the pack shape and up to thirty plastic strips on which are mounted pieces of the pack or its label. Thus the respondent has to select the correct form of brand name, recall its position on the pack, select the correct colour background, remember which pictures (if any) are featured on the pack, and so on.

Clearly such a study can be of particular relevance at an early stage, prior to the briefing of pack designers, when it provides clear guide lines on which pack elements are important recognition features, and which areas are available for design change.

In *summary*, then, we are suggesting that before design development goes too far, a responsible research approach should:

(a) give careful consideration to any already available information on consumer behaviour and attitudes which may affect the ways in which the pack has to perform, and particularly at the point of sale;
(b) mount some formal or informal study of the visual conditions at the point of sale and consumer behaviour at the point of sale;
(c) set up qualitative research to establish as far as possible how elements of pack design including materials, shape, weight, colour, texture of finish, logos, and other design elements affect brand recognition and registration of the product category, and support communications of key brand/product type characteristics;
(d) consider the practicality or otherwise of setting up some form of 'key

element' test, to measure more efficiently the information communicated by each element, and its recognition value.

Pack design screening

Although not all pack designers work the same way, most pack development programmes include a first stage at the end of which a number of different ideas are presented to the client in flat artwork form, to ensure there is reasonable agreement on the further direction of design development. Some designers we know present 30 or 40 such ideas to clients, but even if more than one designer is involved, it is usual to reduce the main alternatives (by subjective judgement) to perhaps 12 or 18.

At worst, such ideas are produced before research has been involved in the process at all, the requirement then being for qualitative (i.e. group discussion) research to be conducted not only to deal with all the preliminary research areas previously outlined but also to screen the consumer 'acceptability' of the various pack designs put forward. Unfortunately this approach is open to criticism on several grounds: first, the need to look at a large number of alternative designs takes over priority from the need to look at issues likely to affect design development; secondly, asking any respondent to consider many designs for the same brand makes it clear to him/her that packaging and pack design for Brand X are the subjects for discussion, and casts him/her in the role of art director. Thirdly the group discussion interviewing situation clearly is far from ideal for the investigation of what an individual pack communicates to any individual person, since that person's views are so quickly contaminated by those of other respondents who speak first in the group.

On the other hand it is possible to conduct, at a similar cost to that of a series of group discussions, a Pack Communication Test with individual respondents, in which they are asked to state their views first about one example of the test product (i.e. in one of the test pack designs), and then about another, before going on to compare the two. If one believes that two is the maximum number of 'products' (i.e. pack designs) which should be considered by any one respondent at any one time, then the problems of permutation may be acute. For example, 10 test pack designs give rise to 45 combinations of 2, or 90 if the order of presentation is taken into account.

Nevertheless this approach, on samples of 200–300 respondents, can be very effective in screening alternative designs, producing (as it does) not only evidence on which designs *appeal* most to actual or potential consumers of the brand, but also what brand *positioning* is suggested by each design. In one case, a study designed to screen down 18 alternative pack designs for a new toiletries product was able to eliminate 14 because they suggested the product was either too masculine or too feminine to suit a Unisex product. In a more recent case two alternative new packs were shown to be appropriate to replace the existing design for an established food product, and both appeared equally appealing: however, one clearly communicated product qualities appropriate to one particular end use for the product which brought it directly into competition with another brand owned by the same client, so the decision on how to develop these pack designs further had to reflect the overall strategy for the client's brands.

Visual communications testing

With the established importance of self-service merchandizing, creating pack displays which will easily be singled out by the consumer has become an important criterion in packaging success. However, measuring this dimension in a meaningful way is difficult.

Our primary aim in this phase of research is to establish the extent to which a pack will 'stand-out' in a visual display, but there are other important 'identification' factors such as legibility and brand recognition, which should not be confused with the problem of 'stand-out'.

Most people automatically think of tachistoscopes* whenever visual testing is mentioned; but what is a tachistoscope test like?

Example of tachistoscope test

The aim of the research was to provide some measurement of the:

(a) ability of a new pack design to convey the brand name for a frozen food, and its identity *as a frozen food*;
(b) relative visibility and legibility of the various messages contained on the pack.

The method employed in the research was a tachistoscopic procedure (using two matched samples of 50 respondents). Either the existing pack, or the new test pack featuring a rectangular panel, was exposed to the respondent in a series of controlled-time exposures, by means of a mirror tachistoscope. Eight progressively longer controlled-time exposures were used, ranging from 10 ms (1/100 of a second) to 2000 ms (2 s). After each exposure the respondent was asked to say what, if anything, she saw, and her responses were recorded verbatim. Responses were probed to ensure that maximum available data emerged after each exposure. If, at the conclusion of the full series of eight controlled-time tests, the respondent had not fully verbalized all the messages

---

* A tachistoscope is a mechanical or electronic device for exposing stimuli (packs, advertisements, etc.) to a viewer for strictly controlled periods of time.

contained, the pack undergoing test was exposed to her for such a period of time as was necessary for her to do so. This constitutes the ninth (infinity) trial on the table of results included in Table 17.1.

Table 17.1   Summary of responses. Trial at which design component/element first mentioned

Sample base: 36		Design component code (see key below)						
Trial No.	Controlled time exposure	A	B	C	D	E	F	G
		No.	No.	No.	No.	No.	No.	No.
1	10 ms	–	–	–	–	–	–	–
2	20 ms	1	–	–	–	–	–	–
3	50 ms	4	–	1	2	–	–	–
4	100 ms	9	2	–	2	–	–	–
5	200 ms	12	8	3	3	–	–	–
6	500 ms	5	8	6	3	–	–	–
7	1000 ms	1	6	3	6	4	8	–
8	2000 ms	–	3	1	3	12	4	11
9	infinity	–	–	–	–	–	–	25
		–	–	–	–	–	–	–
Total responses on each design component		32	27	14	19	16	12	36
Median score – in trials		4.17	5.44	5.5	5.83	7.66	6.75	–

Key to coding of design components:
Noting of, reference to ...
A: Brand name
B: Product type/field
C: 'New' flash
D: Price
E: Slogan
F: Ingredients list
G: All of these

Comparison between these results and those for the existing design confirmed that the new pack was significantly better than the existing one in terms of its ability to communicate brand name, although its definition of product type was weaker.

Such tachistoscope tests can be reliably carried out on between 30 and 50 respondents. One approach suggests that the larger number, selected from potential purchasers of the product, and screened to exclude those with colour blindness or other obvious visual deficiency, will be sufficient to ensure comparability between samples of respondents testing two different packs, while another suggests that if more stringent measures of visual acuity are taken to exclude poor performers, it is possible to obtain valid results on matched samples of perhaps 30 respondents.

There are also differing views about the suitability of the tachistoscope for measuring shelf stand-out or impact. Some researchers argue that the tachistoscope can be successfully used *provided* that the respondent is asked to identify which pack is seen by *pointing* at a display of product set up beside the tachistoscope, and this certainly overcomes the problem of the need for what is seen in the tachistoscope to be verbally reported by the respondent. However, other problems have convinced many researchers that alternative methods need to be employed.

Some problems encountered in tachistoscope testing

If a respondent is exposed to a display of packs under tachistoscopic conditions i.e., where she is exposed to the display on 8 to 10 occasions, with the length of time she is allowed to search being approximately doubled on each occasion, it is often the case that she will follow the normal reading pattern, i.e., top left to right followed by centre left to right, followed by bottom left to right. However, this search pattern is likely to be disturbed whenever the respondent recognizes *something* (a shape, a colour perhaps) which promises to assist in clearer identification of the object focused upon. A number of respondents will then aim to home in on this sector of the total display given any subsequent opportunity to look at the display. This tendency to 'home-in' on a particular area or object will obviously be increased if any of the packs in the display are particularly familiar to the respondent since concentration on this particular sector may well allow her to 'win' in the test situation by reporting more information to the interviewer than if she had continued to scan the display.

Several conclusions can be drawn:

(a) there is an in-built 'familiarity bias' operating in most tachistoscope tests which makes interpretation of the results rather difficult;
(b) there is need to match very carefully samples recruited to test new and existing packs not only in terms of their familiarity with the test brand, but also with its main competitors, which may themselves attract attention away from the test pack;
(c) it is best to use the tachistoscope only where one pack is on display and where the problem addressed is one of on-pack detail.

We therefore conclude that a tachistoscope may legitimately be used in considering the visibility or legibility of on-pack elements; and also to measure 'shelf stand-out' under certain conditions; but that a different approach may be more appropriate to shelf stand-out testing specifically.

The shelf stand-out test

The procedure is a variation on what is known as 'disjunctive reaction time'. In essence, the respondent has to search for an item in each of a series of displays, knowing that it will sometimes be in a given display, and sometimes not. If she finds it, she gives one response; as soon as she decides that it is not there, she gives an alternative response. Basically the measurement is of how long it takes to find a pack when it is there. Prior to the main task each respondent should be tested for normal vision (with glasses if worn), and undertakes a practice run on an unrelated product area and series of displays.

Let us say there are two test variants, 'A 1' and 'A 2'. These might be two (competitive) current packs, a current design and a proposed new design, or two possible designs for a new product. The type of display should correspond to the actual market environment as far as possible, given the probable shortage of test packs to make up the display.

Although the number is arbitrary a frequent pattern is, for any one test series, to use six displays with a given test item present (in six different positions, with detailed control over the pack adjacencies from display to display) plus three displays with the given test item absent. A separate closely matched group of, say, 50 people will see each different test series (on nine displays). One series will differ from the other only in respect of the test variant which appears (in six out of the nine displays).

After screening and the practice run, each respondent (individually) is shown her particular test item and is allowed to familiarize herself with it as she wishes, and she has it in front of her during the rest of the session. She is instructed to press a small response-key (situated immediately beneath her fingers) as soon as she sees the test item in any display or as soon as she decides that it is not present in any display (speed and accuracy both being emphasized). She is then asked to state whether the test item was present or absent from the display.

Each display is projected by means of a pre-loaded, pre-focused, automatic projector (the order of test item present/absent being determined by the experimenter in advance), which is electronically linked with a timer, and the response key. Exposure time continues from the start of the projection (which starts the timer) until the response key is pressed, stopping the timer. Having recorded the reaction time (or 'find time' as it is often called) and reset the timer, the start button is pressed to start the next display (and the clock).

The data derived from the test consist first of records of whether the respondent said 'Yes' or 'No' on each occasion, indicating that she believed the test item was present in or absent from that display; and secondly of the time taken for her to reach that decision on each occasion. If there are nine slides in the series, six of which have the test item present, a sample size of 50 will provide 300 opportunities for respondents to be right in saying the test item is present; while there are a corresponding 150 opportunities (3 per respondent) for them to be right in saying that the test item is not present.

In the course of the series of tests conducted since 1971 various measures have been taken to increase the level of accuracy of response (brand presence or absence correctly reported) so that the expected normal performance of any given sample is 95 % or better; and, where this is achieved, direct comparison of the mean reaction times or 'find' times of the total samples is appropriate, the statistical significance of any differences registered between packs or products being calculated by use of a *t*-test procedure.

Where this accuracy figure is considerably reduced, however, it is necessary first to consider whether the interview conditions have affected results in some way; and if not, what other causes there may be. Clearly, if one particular pack continually fails to be identified as present (when it should be), one strong hypothesis must be that it has little visual impact. On the other hand, if it is often said to be present when it is not, the most appropriate hypothesis may well be that there is some other pack which is continually being mistaken for it in the display situation – in other words the problem is confusion not lack of impact.

Occasionally, however, series of displays are tested in which accuracy of response is very low indeed, either because the pack styles adopted by competitive products in the display are very similar to one another, with the test pack following a similar path; or because the problem is one of variety identification where the main visual cues to brand identification have intentionally been subordinated to other pack design requirements. In such cases more attention has to be paid to the relative performance of each variety in establishing a minimal level of correct identification, and speed becomes less relevant.

Stand-out testing of this type would normally be preceded by a photographic survey of retail outlets to confirm for an existing test product the most representative positions and types of display, the number of end or front facings normally found, the products most often displayed alongside it, and the lighting levels in which the pack will have to make its impact. In the case of a new product, a similar investigation among its potential competition at the retail outlet is desirable.

Whether or not such a photographic survey is undertaken, however, the displays represented in the stand-out test should be as realistic as possible especially in terms of the likely number and disposition of test and competitive packs. Within this context, it is possible to set up a more complex series of tests specially adapted to the investigation of ease of identification of individual varieties within a range (for example, by the use of colour coding, symbols, or emphasis upon the written word); or to problems of confusion with a competitor's packaging.

Example of 'stand-out' problem. The aim in this research was to assess two variations of a new pack design for a confectionery product in terms of stand-out effectiveness relative to the current pack. The research involved the use of the find time technique. The test material comprised:

(a) variation 1 of a new pack;

(b) variation 2 of a new pack;
(c) the current pack 'P'.

Table 17.2   Stand-out results

| | | | | Accuracy levels | |
| | | | | Pack present (%) | Pack absent (%) |
Packs	Mean reaction times (s)	t-test value	Significance level	Pack present (%)	Pack absent (%)
'V 2' Current 'P'	1.77 1.59	1.99	Not significant Current 'P'	98	97
'V 1' Current 'P'	1.98 1.59	3.71	$P < 0.001$ V1	96	96
'V 2' 'V 1'	1.77 1.98	2.05	$P < 0.05$ V2	94	97

The total sample of 150 respondents was split into three quota-matched sub-samples of 50 respondents each, corresponding to the three test items. After visual screening, and a full practice run, each respondent was given the test pack appropriate to her sub-sample. She was then shown, sequentially, a series of nine slides showing displays of confectionery items. In six of these displays the test pack was present and in the other three displays it was not present. The respondent was required to press a response key, according to whether or not she found the test item present in the display. The length of time taken to find the test pack when it was present comprised the data for this research, summarized in Table 17.2. The 'V 2' packet was thus significantly better in stand-out than 'V 1' at the five per cent level. However, there was no significant difference between 'V 2' and the current pack, which was also significantly better than 'V 1' at the 0.1 % level, suggesting the desirability of remaining with the current pack design.

Perhaps the central virtue of the stand-out test, apart from its sensitivity in terms of discrimination between test items, lies in the fact that it appears to overcome the familiarity bias found in most tachistoscopic tests[7] – which nevertheless remain the most appropriate way of measuring communication of product type, brand name, and other detailed elements within a total pack design.

Assessing what the pack communicates and whether its sales appeal is effective

The pack has to project the brand image. People buy products for the promise of the gratifications offered and these gratifications are not simply physical but emotional and social as well. So the pack, seen as clothing for the product, must communicate in visual symbols the promise that what is within the container will fulfil these satisfactions.

The second critical consideration is the degree to which the package activates purchase behaviour. If, for example, you are selling ice cream and you want to create an aura of 'abundance' and 'traditional qualities', it would be necessary to measure the degree to which the package does, in fact, induce this image. An example relates to a brand of dandruff remover. Here, it was found that, although women were the most frequent users and invariably those who bought the product, men used the product as well. However, the package being used was extremely feminine and many potential male users were reluctant to use the brand. With these factors in mind, the company dropped the use of a flower pattern but retained all the other design elements. This made the package less feminine and tended to make the product less cosmetic in its appearance This simple change resulted in increased usage by men while, at the same time, holding its female users.

Most of the packaging research done today concentrates on this aspect of a pack's performance. A number of examples of how this can be done usefully are given below.

The pseudo-product test procedure

The pseudo-product test procedure is the 'ideal' method for evaluation of symbolic influences on product judgement. The method consists of either double placement or sequential placements of the same product but in alternative pack designs. Allowing respondents to act as their own control, i.e. by testing and comparing more than one pack, is somewhat more efficient than the monadic design for this purpose because the use of one sample to provide data on both pack/product combinations undergoing test allows a smaller sample size to provide the same efficiency.

Since the manufacturer usually has a clear idea of the desirable characteristics for the product and as he knows which sectors of the market the product is aimed at, the dimensions for measurement are normally predetermined. A simple illustration is from a beverage study where two alternative labels were studied. A sample of 200 drinkers of the beverage were recruited. The client who was not currently a producer of such a version wanted to launch a new brand into this section of the market. The problem was to indicate which of two alternative labels would be most appropriate.

The same product formulation was presented in two differently labelled bottles (it was a simultaneous double placement test). Respondents were instructed to use one bottle first and, on completion, to use the second bottle (this sequential instruction was rotated). Respondents were simply told that they should consume the product and that the interviewer would return in four days and ask them some questions about their experience.

The results from pseudo-product tests are sometimes dramatic, as in this case. Consumers experience differences where chemically and physiologically no differences could possibly exist. Here are some results from the pack test.

	'L'	'M'	Don't know	N = 200 Total (%)
Product found most acceptable	20	75	5	100
Product which was mild	25	65	10	100
Product most bitter	70	28	2	100

This very brief abstract illustrates a clear difference in the perceptions of the same product presented with two varying labels. Version 'M' moves the product more effectively in the direction of the marketing intention than does 'L'.

In another area, it was found that of two identical margarines, that which was packaged in blue was significantly more likely to be regarded as sharp and salty in taste, when tested (in an in-home placement test) against a margarine packaged in gold packaging (seen as smoother and more bland).

However, pseudo-product tests do not always produce usable results. On one such test (on a powdered drink) conducted in the UK in the early 1970's, 32 different combinations (2 product names, 4 physical pack formats, and 4 graphic designs) of packaging were introduced into a paired comparison test. 95% of those interviewed had a clear preference for one of the two drinks tested as against the other; but only two graphic designs produced a preference split significantly different from 50%/50%.

For this reason, tests of the communication and appeal of packaging are usually conducted by giving the respondent the *impression* that the products contained are the subject of the interview, but without giving an opportunity for product trial (this is especially the case if the product has strong characteristics on which the respondent can readily comment, while the differences in packaging are slight).

Projective imagery tests

The most common procedure used to deal with this aspect of the problem is what might be described as the 'Projective Imagery Test'. This is a *projective test* procedure in which the respondent links concepts with the pack. There are a number of versions that can be used but the principle is usually the same, depending to some extent on the context of the research. In a nondirective-type interview, for example, there would be little structure. The respondent might simply be asked to free associate to the pack i.e. simply relay all the thoughts that come to mind as he/she looks at the packet or in slightly more structured form to imagine:

(a) the kind of product that would be in the packet;
(b) the kind of people who might use it or not use it;
(c) where the product might be used and seen;
(d) the types of shops in which it would be sold.

Still within the framework of an unstructured interview the respondent may be required to make up a story involving the stimulus pack, or make-believe that the pack is a person and describe what sort of person the pack would be. All these procedures are projective in nature and based on associative procedures. This type of research principle is easily extended to quantitative surveys.

In either case (whether at the qualitative or quantitative stage) it is important *not* to concentrate solely upon the evaluative ('I like it') or aesthetic ('It looks pretty') aspects of the pack, but upon the way in which it works to project desirable imagery and associations on behalf of the product it contains.

While in an unstructured interview such associations may be produced by nondirective questioning, the requirement of the quantitative interview that every respondent be asked the same question in the same way leads one to introduce a series of statements dealing with aspects of the product, its qualities, and likely appeal to its different types of user. Each such statement can then be considered by the respondent before she is asked to express her view:

(a) by applying that statement (e.g. 'This would be a good quality product') to as many as it seems appropriate of several brands on display before her; or
(b) by checking the most appropriate answer from a series (e.g. agree strongly, think I agree, think I disagree, disagree strongly) in relation to one particular product.

In the first of these cases, where a statement can be applied to as many or as few of the products displayed as the respondent thinks appropriate, a matched sample is required for each alternative design as it is compared with competition. Although the competitors may have well-established images the results of this test have not been found to be biased against the new design (even though an unknown is being compared to a known). This monadic research design is useful in that we emerge with a score for each design against its normal competition and the relative imagery effectiveness of the designs can be seen. One answers the question 'Given the image we want to create which one of the proposed designs does best against competition?'.

However, this exercise may prove fruitless if there is very little difference between the packs in terms of the ability to convey different ideas about or associations with the product. It is still a valid research exercise to attempt to find aspects of differentiation between the packs in aesthetic or projective imagery terms; and the next alternative therefore would be to display several of the test packs, again asking respondents to apply a series of statements to as many of the pack/product combinations as they think appropriate. It is particularly important in this case not to ask for a single 'forced choice' response since this is liable to distort response in what is already an artificial situation in that the consumer will never be confronted in the market place with all the designs to be tested in the research.

It should also be borne in mind that in this forced 'head-on' comparison situation there is a tendency for any pack which is very different from the others to attract to itself a great deal of both favourable and unfavourable imagery precisely because it is different from the rest; and it is generally advisable to set up 'head-on' comparisons using a *paired* comparison design, AB, AC, AD, BC, BD, CD, if four different test packs are to be compared.

A further refinement increasing the precision of the projective imagery data uses a simple scaling technique, the respondent being asked to consider only one pack/product combination at a time, and to indicate her agreement or disagreement with each statement read out by the interviewer by checking the answer category closest to her own view (e.g. 'Think I agree' or 'Strongly disagree'). Such a technique is, however, more exhaustive in its demands on the respondent, and will only yield more sensitive data provided the number of scales and the complexity of their verbal cues are kept under strict control.

In practice, such monadic rating scales are usually restricted to between 6 and 8 in number: they are of particular relevance where the action standard adopted is that packaging will not be changed unless the new design enables the *product* to be seen significantly more frequently or more strongly as performing as required by the brand strategy.

It should be noted also that the scaling and association tests described above serve only to provide information on the acceptability of the imagery produced by each pack without giving any idea (except by inference) of 'why'. In order to provide such diagnostic data within the context of these projective imagery test procedures it is necessary to adopt further probing questioning techniques in relation to the test pack, using phraseology such as 'What is it about (NAME TEST PACK) which makes you say it is … (READ OUT STATEMENT PREVIOUSLY APPLIED TO TEST PACK)?'

Testing the sales effect of new packaging

While the processes so far described should have led to the selection of the best possible pack design, marketing management will often wish to be convinced about the likely effect on sales of adopting that pack. Where a new product is concerned, this need will be accommodated in plans to measure the effect of the total new product launch; but where an existing pack is already in the market, it may be desirable to undertake a research project in which consumers see the product in its new packaging in a relatively real display situation where they can make a choice to buy or not to buy it.

Obviously the most realistic situation is one where the new pack is in finished form and is used to contain real product which is actually sold from a selection of stores. Although it is certainly possible for individual manufacturers to make arrangements with multiple retailers of their own choice, it should be noted that the test does depend to a very large extent on equal conditions of sale operating for both the existing form of packaging and a new form of packaging. This in turn may well imply twice weekly or perhaps daily visits to each store in order to ensure that no out of stock positions occur, and that the appropriate display space is in fact occupied. If such a responsibility is left with the individual store managers, it has been known for the more enthusiastic to give favoured conditions to one of the test pack designs. Neither is it always satisfactory to involve the manufacturer's sales force in this responsibility. For these reasons it may well be best to entrust such an exercise to a specialist organization with the appropriate connections with multiple outlets and the appropriate field force. Some years ago, in the United Kingdom, the A. C. Nielsen Company ran a panel of 20 stores for just this purpose, and it is perhaps worth noting (in 1984) that the Fine Fare organization are co-operative in setting-up such in-store retail tests, although they do not normally undertake the audit work associated with it. However, certain specialist research organizations exist which do cover this area of research comprehensively.

At the same time, there are a number of problems which may be encountered. In the first place the test is public so that security is less than with a normal market research survey or test; in particular the manufacturer's competitors will certainly know of the test, and the possibility of sabotage does exist (hence part of the need for an independent operator to ensure that stocking and displays are as they should be). The exercise itself is expensive in research terms, but it is even more expensive because it requires the new form of packaging to be finished and to be actually applied to as much product as is likely to be bought over a period of at least twelve weeks.

Another less realistic alternative which avoids some of these problems is to set up a 'simulated shop' in local halls or other central locations in town centres. In this case potential buyers are recruited from the street and asked to go through the 'shop' as if on a shopping expedition, possibly with instructions to make purchases in certain product categories. The test packs can be finished to such an extent that the consumer can physically pick them up and put them in her shopping bag along with other 'purchases'; or may be only part finished, in which case the 'purchase' can be recorded by the consumer at the time she makes the decision. Such 'simulated shop' studies offer the opportunity of observing consumers whilst they are going through a purchase decision, and of interviewing them shortly after that decision on what was going through their minds at the point of decision. However, when used to test the incremental sales level likely to be achieved by the introduction of a new pack as against an existing pack, our experience is that results are unlikely to be statistically significant if sample sizes are less than approximately 400 respondents for each pack design or other variable tested.

Both real and simulated shop testing can be quite valuable in providing reassurance that a pack change will affect sales for the better rather than for the worse; in practice they are perhaps most used in situations where the brand's position is already strong, and where there is no need to change pack design unless a real advantage can be gained by so doing.

Summary: the programme recommended

Areas where research has been found to be of considerable value include:

(a) in-use tests aimed at assessing consumer difficulties with packaging;
(b) assessing the retailer's views on packaging;
(c) providing an objective method of screening down from a large number to a small number of alternative pack designs;
(d) measuring the sales effect of new forms of packaging.

However, this chapter suggests that packaging research can be at its most effective if it is undertaken early in a programme of pack development; and if careful consideration is given to:

(a) any previous research which may be available on frequency and other circumstances of purchase of the product category and the brand;
(b) conditions operating at the point of sale;
(c) key pack design elements which identify the product within its product field or as a brand, and which need to be retained;
(d) measurement of the visual communication abilities of each pack;
(e) most importantly, measures to establish what is being communicated to the consumer by each pack design, and how far each pack design motivates the consumer to purchase.

Chapter 18

Research on 'below the line' expenditure

MARTIN SIMMONS

This chapter deals with the contribution of research, both in the planning and evaluation, of 'below the line' activity. Any definition of 'below the line' assumes a false dichotomy since many promotions are dependent on media advertising. This would be so, for example, when reduced offers are backed by national press advertising. In the current context 'below the line' expenditure is defined to include the following, whether or not they are supported by media advertising:

(a) any in-store promotional activity to the consumer such as premium offers, reduced price offers, stamps and coupons, competitions and banded packs;
(b) any trade incentives or discounts to the retailer;
(c) all display material whether in support of specific promotions or not;
(d) any point-of-scale aids such as leaflets, brochures, store demonstrations;
(e) any direct promotion to the consumer such as couponing or free samples.

Expenditure on items such as sales force incentive schemes and sponsorships is excluded for the purpose of this chapter.

The growth of 'below the line' expenditure

There are three trends in British retailing which have placed increasing emphasis on 'below the line' activity. The first is the development of self-service techniques, especially in the grocery trade. Self-service retailing now accounts for 90 % of grocery turnover and is becoming increasingly important in other retail outlets such as chemists, confectioners, hardware stores and off-licences. Any self-service operation lends itself naturally to 'below the line' activity. The manufacturer has to ensure that his goods are noticed and subsequently purchased. The second trend is the internationally increasing concentration of trade into a smaller number of outlets, in the UK 2% of stores accounting for about half of the grocery trade. Manufacturers spend vast sums of money to secure a favourable position at the point of sale, particularly at these key outlets. The third trend is the ever-increasing range of brands from which the consumer has to choose. To identify his brand from the competition, the manufacturer resorts to varied forms of promotion as well as media advertising.

There are no validated figures for the size, in monetary terms, of 'below the line' activity but the growth has been substantial in the last decade. If all 'below the line' activity is included, expenditure now probably exceeds that of media advertising.

Planning 'below the line' activity

The problems facing an advertiser in planning his 'below the line' activity can be classified into four broad categories:

(a) *Budget allocation* – he has to decide for, possibly, a range of products on the optimum allocation of limited resources. What part of his promotional expenditure should be made on television, press, and other media and what part should be spent 'below the line'?
(b) *Setting promotional objectives* – what exactly is the aim of the promotional activity? It is necessary to distinguish between retail objectives which can be regarded as 'intermediate' such as increasing shelf space, and final consumer objectives which are 'ultimate' in the sense of actual sales?
(c) *Pre-testing* – the next problem involves pre-testing the promotional plan in order to evaluate its likely success, or which of several possible tactics should be adopted. In practice, this normally means pre-testing the components of the promotional plan, i.e. the individual promotions.
(d) *Post-assessment* – having decided on a certain level and form of 'below the line' expenditure, how effective has this been? The manufacturer will want to assess whether or not his objectives have been achieved.

The allocation of budgets for 'below the line' expenditure is often not planned on any scientific basis. Because of the difficulty of creating a marked division above and below the line, there is a tendency to consider an overall promotional budget. Then portions are hived off for 'below the line' activity as and when needed. This philosophy is encouraged by the reluctance of some advertising agents to fit 'below the line' into their services and functions.

Budget allocation and the setting of promotional objectives for 'below the line' activity are inseparably linked, and equally liable to neglect in forward planning. Many marketing executives would have difficulty if asked to define exactly what a specific promotion is designed to achieve. It can be argued that the aim of any promotional activity is to increase sales, either short-term or long-term. The advantage of more precise objectives is that they can determine the most appropriate promotional techniques to be used. Some examples of possible promotional objectives and techniques are shown below.

Promotional objective	Technique
(a) To encourage consumer trial of a new product or pack size.	Product sampling.
(b) To clear old stock prior to brand re-launch or main promotional campaign.	Consumer offer, e.g., plastic daffodils for two packs.
(c) To widen retail distribution prior to commencement of media advertising.	Trade discounts.
(d) To obtain prime display position in key outlets.	Trade bonusing backed by special display units.
(e) To maintain display space in key outlets.	Self-liquidating consumer offer.
(f) To encourage consumer purchasing across a range of, e.g., soup flavours.	Money-back consumer offer, e.g., 20p postal order for five packs of different flavours.
(g) To emphasise a new variety, e.g., a flavour of soup.	As above, requiring two of the packs to be of the new flavour.
(h) To combat competitive pressure; blocking the competition.	Price cuts.
(i) To stimulate repeat purchasing.	On-pack coupon, i.e., money off on next purchase.
(j) To widen consumer interest in a brand.	Competition.

The contribution of research

While many stages of marketing activity are scientifically planned and researched, the influences on consumer purchasing have been widely neglected at perhaps the most vital point of all, the point of sale. A survey on point of sale carried out in 1966 by Industrial Facts and Forecasting on behalf of Abbey Goodman Display Limited revealed that fewer than one company in ten had ever assessed point-of-sale effectiveness on a systematic basis; twenty years later the situation has hardly changed. Relatively little research is being conducted on promotional activity despite the fact that 'below the line' expenditure now exceeds traditional media expenditure. Decisions still tend to be based on experience, competitive activity, and hunch. Some reasons for the slow development of research into promotional activity are:

(a) lack of clear promotional objectives to measure;
(b) vested interests; i.e. those with the function of promotional planning at advertiser and agency level resisting the entry of research into a traditionally creative area;
(c) the *ad hoc* nature of many aspects of promotional activity which does not allow for long-term conclusions to be drawn for future promotional planning;
(d) the apparent limitations of time and confidentiality when pre-testing any parts of a promotional plan. This is due to the tight schedules (or lack of forward planning) operating and the fear of any 'leak' to the competition.

There are also doubts about the validity of research on promotional activity coupled with the failure of research agencies to develop and convincingly market appropriate techniques. These techniques, their applications and their limitations are described under the following headings:

(a) budget allocation;
(b) pre-testing;
(c) post-assessment.

Research: budget allocation

The problem here is what part of advertising expenditure should be made 'below the line' or, more specifically, on point-of-sale activities. Research has contributed very little to this decision and certainly no available technique can give an exact figure for the appropriation to be allocated to point-of-sale activities. The decision is clearly not a simple matter of statistics. Media advertising is often an important strategic weapon to use with retailers to gain distribution. Also point-of-sale advertising can act as a reminder of a message previously got across by other media. We are back to the extreme difficulty of introducing an artificial line between media and other promotional activity. Nevertheless, a premise which is gaining acceptance is that point-of-sale activities should be concentrated on product groups where the impulse sector is high. That is where the brand, and often the product purchased, is decided inside the store. Research can contribute by assessing the magnitude of the impulse sector. Shoppers can be interviewed before and immediately after purchase.

The expenditure on a product can then be divided into four sectors:

(a) *Specifically planned* – product and brand known before the shopper arrives at the store;

(b) *Substituted* – specifically planned but brand substituted in the store;

(c) *Generally planned* – the shopper knew the product, but not the brand, before arriving at the store;

(d) *Unplanned* – the shopper had no intention of buying the product when arriving at the store.

This information establishes the relative influence on the purchase of store factors. Research conducted by the Gallup Poll in conjunction with the Association of Point of Sale Advertising showed the level of impulse purchasing across a range of products illustrated in Table 18.1. A limitation of this method is that it can only be applied to 'quick-moving' product categories, otherwise the expense of interviewing shoppers at the retail outlets is prohibitively expensive. For less frequently purchased products research methods relying on a reconstruction of buying behaviour at a single-call interview can be used to establish the importance of impulse buying. Before deciding how much to spend at the point of sale, it seems relevant for a manufacturer at least to find out what part of brand expenditure is decided

Table 18.1

	Product expenditure	Specifically planned	Substituted	Generally planned	Unplanned	Impulse sector
Breakfast cereals	100	52	19	13	16	48
Brown bread	100	38	10	24	28	62
Butter	100	65	13	13	9	35
Cakes and pastries	100	17	4	37	42	83
Canned cat food	100	61	11	17	11	39
Canned dog food	100	62	9	18	11	38
Canned milk pudding	100	45	6	17	32	55
Canned soup	100	55	10	12	23	45
Chocolate confectionery	100	16	5	29	50	84
Frozen foods:						
Burgers	100	45	5	11	39	55
Fish fillets	100	43	5	24	28	57
Fish fingers	100	43	7	21	29	57
Green beans	100	45	5	18	32	55
Mousse	100	39	2	16	43	61
Peas	100	61	4	18	17	39
Instant coffee	100	59	9	12	20	41
Instant milk powder	100	60	4	5	31	40
Margarine	100	73	6	10	11	27
Meat and vegetable extract	100	48	8	6	38	52
Paper handkerchiefs	100	18	20	25	37	82
Paper kitchen towels	100	48	12	23	17	52
Soft tissue toilet rolls	100	33	9	29	29	67
Tea (not tea bags)	100	70	8	9	13	30

there. This information can only be used as a broad guideline, indicating whether more attention is warranted to 'below the line' activities in a particular market or not. It can be used to avoid the situation where 60 % of consumer brand decision is made at the point of sale and 15% of the promotional budget is spent 'below the line', and vice versa.

Another consideration in budget allocation is whether the brand is growing, static or declining. With a growing brand, promotions have an element of investment in encouraging trial and, thereafter, repurchase. With static or declining brands, this is unlikely to be true and promotions may have to justify themselves in terms of short-term payoff. A further factor determining 'below the line' expenditure is the marketing situation. Again, there is an investment element in a new product launch or a major product relaunch, compared with the continuing activities connected with an ongoing brand.

Research: pre-testing

There are various techniques which exist for pre-testing, either with the consumer or the retail store, the likely success of promotional activity. These tests can be carried out on a wide variety of materials ranging from verbal concepts to actual examples of the promotion. These techniques can be classified into:

(a) group discussions;
(b) hall tests;
(c) van tests;
(d) mini-van tests;
(e) postal and door-to-door- tests;
(f) pre-testing the advertising of promotions;
(g) in-store tests.

The first six of these methods are consumer based for the very good reason that they tend to be easy, quick and cheap to operate. They are designed to give a reliable indication of the relative levels of likely consumer acceptance of a given set of promotional ideas or propositions. This may be further divided into two parts; first, which is the most likely to succeed of a list of possible ideas; and second, how successful is the best one likely to be.

Group discussions. Before considering any kind of quantitative research, a company will often make use of group discussions with their likely target group to test concepts and ideas. Groups may be used to:

(a) glean ideas for promotions which could warrant further consideration and research;

(b) assess which of several promotional ideas should be pursued, and which
     should be discounted as completely unacceptable.

Group discussions should be used only as a first filter and never interpreted as
a final quantified result.

Hall tests.   Hall tests can be used to sort out which one is the most likely to
succeed out of several similar possibilities. The hall test would usually
be employed to pre-test such offers as free gifts, extra-size packs, on and in-
pack premiums, and with-pack premiums. The methodology usually involves
bringing a sample of target consumers into a hall or theatre and asking them
to rate alternative offers in rank order. Briefly, the procedure of hall tests to
pre-screen promotional items is as follows: for a ranking of, say, six possible
items, consumers are invited to take part at the hall on a particular day; the
interviewers ask the respondents which items they like best, which second
best and so on, and which they would not be interested in at all. The sample
size is usually 100 to 150, which is sufficient to indicate the favourably and
unfavourably considered. In the items to be tested it is advisable to include a
control item, an item that has performed well in the past and, consequently,
will give a relative measure of success and failure. The following points need to
be built in to the test for the results to be of value:

(a) a maximum of eight items – large numbers would confuse the housewife
     and produce distorted ranking;
(b) the items to be tested should be of a similar cost to give the company a
     basis for decision;
(c) items should be of a similar nature – gimmicky items should not be tested
     against practical ones. Although the housewife may prefer the gimmicky
     items, she will be reluctant to admit so in the interview situation;
(d) only certain types of promotional ideas may be tested in the hall test.
     Money-off offers, for instance, will always be ranked the highest
     alongside other ideas.

The hall test may also be used effectively to test differing designs of the same
proposed offer, e.g. drinking glasses or table mats.

Van tests.   In this instance a motorized caravan can be parked in a busy
shopping area. Respondents would then be invited into the van to take part in
similar tests to those carried out in hall tests. The advantage over the hall test
for this technique is that larger samples of respondents can be obtained for the
same field costs.

Mini-van tests.   A more sophisticated method was pioneered by Research
Bureau Ltd. Promoted items are sold through vans calling at homes and the

extent of buying each item is recorded to assess their likely success. The mini-van sets out to provide as closely as possible an actual retail sales situation within which promotions can be tested. To that extent, it is similar to store testing.

Postal and door-to-door tests.   The postal method consists of a panel of consumers to which the promotional offer is sent by post. It is then possible to assess the likely success of an offer or the relative success of offers by recording the extent to which the panel members buy the offer or offers. Information would also be collected on the types of consumers who are liable to take up a particular offer. This type of test does not necessarily have to be carried out by post. It is possible, for example, to place by distributing door to door and then measure the effects of couponing, sampling, etc., by recording returns or by re-interview.

Pre-testing the advertising of promotions.   It is useful before embarking on a large-scale promotion to pre-test supporting advertising and display material which may have an effect on the success or failure of a promotion. The aim of this is two-fold:

(a) Is the advertising and what it has to say readily understood?
(b) Is the approach attracting the target consumers ?

Tests can be carried out with consumers to assess these aims and can check whether the advertising is likely to have an adverse effect on the brand's image, even though it may persuade people to buy in the short-term. These tests may involve using the same pre-testing techniques as for ordinary display advertising (referred to in another chapter).

In-store tests.   In-store tests are offered by a number of research companies in this country. The in-store test is a natural progression from hall tests and van tests, in that the items for offer that did well in these tests may now be put on the market place. This will provide a useful indicator in a realistic situation of likely market sales. These are two main methods which can be employed both based on the technique of retail auditing:

(a) two panels of stores, one with the promotion or particular activity that is being tested and the other panel as control. The success of the promoted item is measured by the sales achieved compared with the control item;
(b) alternatively, the two items (promoted and control item) are rotated within the same panel of stores. This reduces any error which may arise from using two matching panels. The disadvantage is the extra administrative work involved in switching the items so that both are tested in the same store within the test period.

In-store tests, unlike hall tests, can also be used to assess the effect of price changes, different shelf space allocations, changes in display material and variations in display position. The tests can involve a particular promotional activity versus no promotion, e.g. a banded pack tested against the normal marketing situation. Or they can involve an assessment of two possible promotions, e.g. two different self liquidators, or $1^1/_2$p off tested against 1p off normal price. Most forms of promotional activity can be tested in-store but there are certain limits. It is not possible to take account, in the pre-test situation, of promotions which, when they go national, are going to get media backing. The test, if carried out, cannot measure the influence of television or press support. It is also difficult to pre-test competitions and contests, since this involves giving away the prizes which can result in an expensive piece of research. Additionally, the main practical problem in these tests is to ensure that all other variables are controlled throughout its duration. It is essential that each test item is examined in exactly equal competitive situations. To achieve this, complex designs have been developed using, for example, Latin squares. These are more complicated to administer but achieve a tighter control of outside variables.

Research: post-assessment

The case for not assessing the effect of promotional activity is that it cannot be measured quantitatively because there exist in the market place too many other variables which are difficult to isolate. This is a somewhat defeatist attitude emphasizing the problems and dismissing any possible solutions. Provided the objectives are clearly defined, measures can be found to assess their achievement. Outside variables may blur any assessment but allowance can be made for them, where necessary, in the interpretation.

Rather than have no assessment of promotional activity, it is preferable to develop research techniques whilst recognizing their uses and limitations. As in pre-testing of promotional activity the research methods are retail and consumer based.

Store checks

Measures of effectiveness obtained from store checks can include:

(a) penetration achieved by the promoted product in the retail outlet, i.e. the number of stores handling the product;
(b) shelf space achieved by the promoted product in relation to competitive brands;
(c) penetration of display material; and its type and position.

All these statistics are relevant to a manufacturer who wants to assess his return on point-of-sale investment.

Retail audits

All the above data can be obtained from retail audits. Additionally, sales data are collected from retail audits providing accurate information over specific time periods. However, identifying the sale of promoted items is generally very difficult because the timing of the retail checks may not fit in with the promotional activity, while competing promotions may overlap.

Consumer research

Consumer research on aspects of 'below-the-line' activity must not be considered as an alternative to retail research. The retail research can be used effectively to answer a number of important questions on distribution, sales and stock cover but it provides no information about the target audience. It then becomes necessary to research the important questions of, for instance, who are the buyers taking up the promotion?, are they existing or new buyers?, will they or have they repeated their purchase of this brand or product?, is there an increase in the rate of buying per buyer resulting from the promotion?, how did buyers come to take up the promotion in the first place?, does the promotion affect the shopper's attitude towards the brand? These are some of the numerous questions that the manufacturer will ask when planning his promotional strategy and the consumer techniques available at the present time can, and do, provide some of the answers.

Consumer panels

The consumer panel is one of the more important methods of obtaining the relevant data and has a great advantage over other methods in that the information is continuous over time. Parfitt and McGloughlin [1] described the use of consumer panels in evaluating promotional activity. They state that the consumer panel is valuable for three basic reasons:

(a) It measures consumer purchasing behaviour accurately and sensitively.
(b) It measures this on a continuous basis to gain information over time.
(c) It is possible to ascertain accurate information on when purchases are made.

They also outline the practical difficulties involved which may obscure the relationship between promotional activity and sales. Again, three factors are basically involved:

(a) Consumer purchasing behaviour is extremely complex in that individual rates of buying a product may change continuously in what appears a relatively static market.
(b) Competitive activity may have a blurring effect and, for one brand, individual promotions can and do overlap with each other. This makes it more difficult to isolate the effect of a particular promotion.
(c) The objective of a promotion, as in advertising, may not **be to *increase***

sales in the short-term but rather to maintain a share or halt a declining share of the market.

It may be necessary to measure the extent of repeat purchasing some time after the promotion to establish whether the initial purchase has been followed up by a repeat purchase, and the relationship of repeat buying by 'new' buyers to those original buyers already using the brand. This can be observed from consumer panel data. The model developed by Ehrenberg and Goodhardt [2] is based on a theoretical framework. Basically, it states that in a 'stationary' market the average rate of buying per buyer is constant. The model takes actual sales and predicts what would have happened without the promotion. The difference is the effect of the promotion. The limitation of this method is that it can only be applied in 'stationary' markets, and in a market undergoing change a control panel would be needed. One advantage of this method is that it eliminates the necessity of controlled experiments and consequently reduces the expense.

Impulse buying

The share that a brand achieves of impulse purchases is largely determined by its point-of-sale activities – its retail distribution, shelf space, display, pricing and other promotional activities [3]. One measure, therefore, of the success of these activities is the share taken by a brand of impulse purchases in the product category. Expenditure on a product group can be segmented as described earlier. We can look at the brand's position in the two broad sectors of the market – the planned sector and the impulse sector where the brand is decided in the store; for example, a brand may have a 24 % share of the impulse sector. This can be taken as a benchmark *prior* to promotional activity; and a similar look can be taken at the market at a later date to assess the brand share of impulse purchases *after* the promotional campaign. The advantage of this technique is that it removes the planned sector, which is largely dictated by media advertising, from any evaluation. This argument is rather tenuous in markets where promotional activity is supported by media advertising.

Appraisal and limitations of these techniques

Pre-testing

Qualitative and quantitative research should be regarded as a means, despite their limitations, of reducing the risk of failure. Relatively small expenditure on research, prior to embarking on the expense of the promotional campaign, can enhance the likelihood of success. The consumer and retail pre-tests are complementary rather than competitive in the sense that ideas and offers that have been successfully screened in group discussions, hall tests and van tests may then be tested in stores. The limitations of consumer pre-tests are:

(a) The methods do not measure accurately what is likely quantitatively to take place in the actual market situation. They cover preferences and attitudes but should not be used to forecast potential sales.
(b) They cannot be used for certain types of promotional activity, e.g. price changes, display positions, shelf space allocation, etc.

The limitations of in-store pre-tests are:

(a) They are difficult to control.
(b) They tell you nothing about the consumer, e.g. whether the promotion is attracting new buyers or people who would have bought the item anyway. This limitation can sometimes be overcome by linking in-store consumer interviews to the test.
(c) There is also a limit to the type of promotional activity that can be tested, as described earlier.

Despite these limitations, the present pre-test methods do go a long way in helping the manufacturer to assess the likely success or failure of promotional activity. It is a small price to pay for what could turn out to be an expensive failure.

Post-assessment

The main problem in any post-assessment of promotional activity is that of isolating all other variables such as seasonal effects and competitor activity. Controls can sometimes be set up but these are normally expensive and not always appropriate. The practical answer to this problem is to deal with outside variables in the interpretation of the results, making due allowances according to the particular circumstances.

The retail audit has limitations:

(a) The timing of a retail audit, e.g. bi-monthly, may not fit in with the promotional activity. Promotions often last only two to four weeks.
(b) Retail audits are highly organized and inflexible. It may be impractical or expensive to adapt an ongoing service to the specific needs of promotional assessment.
(c) Retail audits provide no information about the consumer, e.g. on repeat buying behaviour.

Consumer panels do not provide information on certain in-store activity, e.g.:

(a) retail distribution;

(b) display penetration;
(c) the penetration achieved by a promotion.

The objectives of the promotional activity and the criteria for success must, therefore, be defined. The criteria taken determine whether retail checks, consumer panels or both are appropriate to measure the effect.

Future development

The contribution of research to 'below-the-line' planning and evaluation has not progressed in recent years mainly because of the resistances outlined earlier. Investment in new research techniques has been at a low ebb in the last decade either because the demand is not apparent or because research companies are unwilling to invest in order to stimulate a possible latent demand. Possibilities that still remain to be explored are as follows.

Shelf space allocation
What is the relationship between shelf space and brand share? It would be very useful for a manufacturer or a retailer to be able to assess what shelf space he requires to achieve a target level of sales. The evidence of some work carried out suggests that in high-impulse markets shelf space tends to equate with brand share or, putting it very simply, to get 20 % brand share you need 20 % of shelf space. In low-impulse markets however, e.g. margarine, a high brand share can be achieved with a relatively low share of shelf space. In such markets, consumer brand loyalty is high and impulse purchasing is low. The shopper knows what she wants before she gets to the store and the manufacturer must get his brand across at that stage. In the store, the manufacturer does not necessarily require shelf space exactly pro rata to brand share provided his brand is currently one of the leaders. Shelf space allocation requires a great deal of researching and could be rewarding.

Data bank
Another important question (the answer to which depends upon the particular situation at the time and also the creative aspect) is what type of promotion seems to work best for particular objectives in a particular product field. If a sufficient backlog of information were available about different types of promotional activity in different product fields, it would be possible to draw some useful conclusions about what type of promotion seems to achieve a particular objective best.

Trade reaction
Research can also help to avoid waste by getting trade reaction to a new promotion at an early state. Many promotions have failed, not because of lack

of appeal to the consumer, but because the trade would not accept them. Too often this is found out when large sums of money have already been spent.

With the growth of promotions 'tailor made' for specific major multiple retailers, the most fruitful area for research development would appear to be an independent research means of testing trade reaction at chief buyer level to their suppliers. Promotional activity would be one of many aspects of trade relations that could be monitored.

Chapter 19

Market testing and experimentation

JOHN DAVIS

One major function of market research is to provide a feedback of information from the market to the manufacturer or distributor. This information shows the state the market is in as a result of the marketing strategies currently being applied to the various competing brands. Taken together with other relevant data, such as the observations and impressions of the executives concerned, this provides the basis on which the company can take its decisions about continuing or changing the strategies for its existing brands, or developing strategies for new brands.

As long as possible alternative strategies remain mostly within the company's existing field of experience, the likely outcome of changing from one strategy to another can sometimes be assessed sufficiently accurately for the purpose of making a decision *without* conducting extensive additional research. It may be possible to base the decision on judgment alone, but more often it will be necessary to supplement this by various types of pre-testing research. However, problems can still arise even where the company knows the field well and, once it moves outside its existing range of experience, pretesting is very unlikely to provide a sufficient guide to the likely results of introducing a given change into the market. The company will then need to carry out some form of market testing or experimentation in order to gain the additional experience required to make its marketing decisions, in some cases merely to form an initial assessment of whether a project is worth carrying further; in other cases major planning and investment decisions may depend on the results. Some may be concerned with comparing the relative effects of two or more alternative courses of action open to a company, others only with assessing the effects of a single proposed course of action. Projections of the scale of effects in a wider market may be required, or merely a 'better, no-change, worse' result. A whole new product and its marketing plan may be involved in a test-launch, or only a single factor in the marketing mix of an existing product.

The difference between this type of experimentation and the various forms of pre-testing is that the changes and innovations are generally introduced into the market through the normal channels of communication or distribution – through normal advertising media and retail stores. Any effects are then measured among a population who have been exposed to the media and who have made their preference and purchasing decisions in the normal way. Experimenting under these conditions is generally expensive, and there is a marked rise in costs as a project moves out of the pre-testing stage into a marketing experiment. As a result of this step in costs, a number of attempts have been made to provide 'mini-testing' marketing facilities which, while sacrificing some of the benefits of full-scale testing, provide the means of obtaining some key information and measurements at much lower costs. One development has been the establishment of panels of housewives who are visited by a mobile shop or van from which they can make purchases of a range of foods and household products. By calling on the same housewives regularly through time and recording their purchases on each occasion, details of their buying patterns, and any alterations in them through an experimental change or innovation, can be built up. Hence, for a comparatively small outlay on stocks and research a manufacturer can gain information on such key factors as the rate of repurchase among triers of a new product. While the results may not be adequate to provide a firm forecast for the total market, they will indicate whether the project is worth proceeding with in its present form, either through immediate introduction or through more extensive testing in the market. Similar limited testing facilities are also available among retail outlets, special panels of stores being set up in which to experiment with new products, pricing, packaging and promotions, with sales being recorded using normal store audit methods or electronic scanning of barcodes.

The remainder of this chapter is concerned with the principles and problems of the more general larger-scale forms of marketing experiments, but as will be seen later, considerations of the costs and risks involved may frequently indicate the advisability of moving through some form of initial exploration before becoming committed to a major experiment.

Practicability of testing

With some projects a company may not have the option of testing in the market, since production or other constraints may preclude the possibility of introducing the proposed changes into only some parts of a market in advance of a total market decision. It may, for example, be impossible to produce a new product in quantities sufficient to supply a test area without building a plant capable of producing on a national basis; or of adapting the style or design of an existing product without changing the whole output. It may be impossible, because of overlapping and interlocking channels of distribution, to vary trade terms or prices within test areas without serious repercussions on the total market, and so on.

The competitive situation in a market may frequently inhibit any experimentation, because this will reveal company planning or product formulation. Competitors may then react and, if the time necessary to take counter-activity or even copy the product is short, be the first to launch on the wider market. In any case, much of the experience to be gained from an experiment by one company can be frequently acquired by competitors if they merely observe and measure the effects for themselves. One advantage of some forms of mini-testing referred to above is that they preclude competitive access to the results.

If such problems cannot be overcome then the possibilities of mounting specific experiments do not exist. For the purposes of this chapter, however, it is assumed that an experiment is not precluded by such constraints.

Definition of the problem

Seldom is the initial request for an experiment or test framed in a way that can lead to an effective plan. Frequently a great deal of questioning has to be done to establish the proper objectives of the experiment, and to quantify them sufficiently to determine such factors as the scale of the experiment or the precision required in the results. A client, for example, recently asked for help in designing an experiment to see whether a proposed display stand would be worth introducing into stores. The first question was whether the experiment was to cover the rate of trade acceptance and use of the stand, and possibly its life expectancy, or whether it should only cover the in-store effect of the stand when it was there. This is a vital planning question, since an experiment of the first type would have involved normal distribution through the sales force, large numbers of the stands, and heavy expenditure on display checks and store audits. The second type of experiments could have been carried out, in this market, with two matched panels of 20 stores and 20 display stands, and for a modest expenditure on auditing. The question had not previously been considered explicitly by the group concerned, and discussion immediately showed that some members were expecting only an in-store test, others the wider experiment.

A major problem area concerns the precision and type of results required and the uses to which they are to be put. A simple feasibility study to assess whether some project holds sufficient promise for further limited investment in it should not be allowed to become large or elaborate. At the other end of the scale, an experimental launch from which estimates are to be made of the likely effects in a wider market must be mounted with a great deal of careful planning, executed under properly managed conditions and measured in ways which will provide the required data. Dangers frequently arise when a modest experiment, designed perhaps merely to assess certain aspects of a complex situation, is then expected to provide forecasts for which it was not originally intended.

Examination of existing experience

Given that any experiment is a means of gaining experience, before any experiment is undertaken the question should be posed whether additional experience is necessary in order to arrive at an adequate decision. Because of the costs involved in a major marketing experiment, it should only be considered as a last resort when all other means of reaching a firm decision have failed. Consequently, before an experiment is started a rigorous reassessment of all available data and experience should be made, including the subjective assessments of those who know the market, to establish the range of the possible profits or losses which might arise from the marketing activity under consideration. Not infrequently this rigorous assessment based on existing experience shows that the entire range of possible results is profitable, or that the entire range is unprofitable. The latter result must mean that testing the project in its present form will be a waste of time and resources which would be better spent on some other activity. The former result (that all outcomes of the project would be profitable) should lead to immediate marketing without testing if the proposed course of action can only take one form, but there may still remain a need for experimenting if there is scope for variations in the project which would lead to different levels of profitability. If the optimum level cannot be prejudged but there are marked differences between the optimum level and other levels, further investigation of the value of experimenting is needed. If a manufacturer of a packaged product, for example, is considering whether or not to add a 2 kg pack above his existing range of sizes, and all assessments of the outcome are profitable, there is no point in an experiment. If, however, he is considering the more open question of introducing a new larger pack which could take one of a range of sizes, there might still be a case for experimenting in the market to get as near as possible to the most profitable new size.

Where the expected range of possible outcomes shows that some will be profitable but some will lead to losses, the company has three options. First, introduce the course of action fully into the market in the hope of success, but with the risk of losses. Experience is then gained after the event. Second, experiment by introducing the proposed course of action into one or more small parts of the proposed market, thus limiting the risks while experience is acquired, but at some cost. These costs may well include the loss of profits through delaying the introduction of a beneficial change into the wider market or the losses through the sacrifice of any lead time the company has achieved or even pre-emption by a competitor. Third, postpone or shelve the project, thus avoiding the risk of direct losses through failure, but accepting the risks that profits are being foregone through delay, and may be lost altogether through pre-emption.

At this stage we assume a decision to test, and examine some of the problems involved.

Types of experimental design

Basically, the normal principles of experimental design as described by Rothman in chapter 3 apply to marketing experiments, although there are frequently some practical limitations which prevent the full application of some more complex designs. Hence, experimental designs tend to be simple 'before and after' or 'side-by-side' designs, and generally without replication, so that each treatment and control appears only in a single area.

In 'before and after' experiments the relevant results are measured in the selected area before and after the introduction of the innovation or change, and comparisons are made between the readings. Since other conditions in the market may cause changes beyond those due to the experiment itself, a control area (in which the experimental measurements are made but no experimental action is taken) is normally needed to arrive at a sound interpretation of the results. Hence, even simple 'before and after' experiments tend to become comparative or 'side-by-side' experiments anyway. Not infrequently a control area can be found among marketing areas already being measured and analysed in normal continuous research.

Comparative tests, where the relative merits of two or more different 'treatments' are to be assessed, call for designs in which the treatments can be run side by side in different areas although there is no need for the selected areas to be contiguous. To avoid wrong conclusions a control area free of any experimental stimulus is again needed, as one recent set of results showed. Here, the introduction of two experimental methods of promotion into separate areas was followed by uniform increases in sales of about 10%. Without further information the conclusion would have appeared to be that the introduction of either method into the market would be beneficial. Fortunately, a control was used, because this showed a rise in sales of the same magnitude but without any experimental stimulus. Some other factor, in this case probably the weather, was affecting the market, and this could only be detected, at least in the short-run, by the inclusion of a control area in the design of the experiment.

Because the individual areas used in experiments, whether towns, television areas or other units, may vary in their initial pre-test states and in their reactions to an experiment, the ideal design of any type calls for the placing of each experimental treatment in a number of areas. This is particularly so in comparative tests. However, in the great majority of marketing experiments such replication of the design is not administratively or financially possible, and operations are limited to single areas. This is a condition which generally has to be accepted – although every opportunity should be taken to use multi-area designs – but it should never be forgotten. To some extent, and given adequate background data, some of the risks involved in single-area tests can be reduced in the later stages leading to forecasts (referred to later in this chapter) but this again is only a poor substitute for proper multi-area testing.

An alternative method of attempting to overcome the problems posed by the variability of sales or other factors between areas has been to create facilities for mounting some types of test with the different treatments, or treatment and control, within the *same* geographic area or market. The method is particularly applicable to experimenting with different advertising campaigns or media schedules, and much of the early development was undertaken by the Advertising Laboratory which operated in Milwaukee up to 1971. There, by split-running and then controlling the distribution of the local newspaper within its distribution area, and (more importantly) by using an electronic device known as a 'muter' to cut out reception of certain television commercials in selected households, matched panels of households or people living close together in the same general environment could be subjected to different advertising campaigns or schedules. Any effects on purchasing patterns could then be measured, and they would be free of any inherent 'between-area' difference.

The muters used in the Milwaukee Ad-lab suffered from a number of disadvantages which imposed severe constraints on the design of experiments in the area, and although research workers in other areas considered their use they were never widely adopted. Instead more flexible systems were developed in other cities in the USA, making use of the Community Antenna Television (CATV) systems and their associated cables distributing the incoming signal to sets in homes. Here it was realized that if, instead of the normal single cable system linking homes to the antenna, a double or split cable was used, alternate blocks or individual homes within an area could be fed from each. By introducing appropriate switchgear and signal generators into the system it was possible to feed different schedules or different campaigns into homes on a chequer-board pattern throughout a city. Measurements of results could then be made with a sufficient reservoir of people for any combinations of diary panel research or successive surveys on independent samples of the population.

The development of research facilities linked to cable television has differed from one country to another, due to varying combinations of research needs, physical systems, and legal requirements. In some countries cable operators are free to change the advertising carried in broadcast programmes to meet research (or other) needs, and it then becomes possible to design useful experiments using two or more versions of advertising content or schedules within small geographic areas. In other countries, where 'tampering' with a broadcast signal is illegal, the same advertising must be carried to all sets tuned to a channel and there is little more opportunity to experiment than is possible with normal broadcast transmissions. The current interest in the development of more flexible and more widespread cable networks, with the additional facilities for measuring local store sales via electronic scanning or for immediate viewer response via the connecting cable or by telephone, should lead to enhanced opportunities for experiments at all levels. Market research companies are working closely with cable TV contractors in many countries, and although secrecy surrounds such activities in the planning stages each new facility will be adequately publicized as it becomes commercially available. Then the facility of being able to run two or more different TV schedules or campaigns within the same community will permit the application of more powerful experimental designs than is possible using geographically separate areas. There may well, however, be complications if a multiplicity of channels leads to severe fragmentation of the audience, and to very small numbers of potentially atypical viewers being exposed to any experimental situation.

The scale of experiments

Three main sets of factors operate to determine the appropriate scale for an experiment. These are the physical requirements to mount the experiment at all, the research requirements to provide adequate measurements, and the risks and costs of success or failure.

Physical requirements include such factors as availability of advertising media, the use of administratively coherent sales or depot areas, or that the experimental areas shall absorb a given proportion of capacity if production or packaging lines have to be modified to provide the necessary material. Such factors may place either upper or lower limits to the scale of an experiment, and may, on occasion, rule out the possibility of an experiment of the desired type. Thus, an experimental launch heavily dependent on television advertising may not be possible if available production facilities could only supply a few dozen stores.

The *research requirements* will set lower limits to the scale in terms of the number of areas needed and the populations of consumers or stores within them. Hence, they will depend on the extent to which the market varies between areas, on the current or expected levels of distribution and consumer usage, the magnitude of any expected changes or results, and the precision with which the results are to be measured.

Where the research requirements call for experimentation on a scale above the limits set by the physical factors, then the experiment must either be abandoned or its objectives modified. On the other hand, the research need not, and often should not, cover the whole area into which the experimental stimulus is introduced; e.g., in test-launching a new product using television in the area covered by a single transmitter, it will normally be considered necessary to allow – if not impossible to prevent – distribution of the product to extend to the limits of transmission. If, then, research measurements are carried out over the whole transmission area, and this includes some overlap areas, the results will be diluted through the inclusion of outer areas in which the advertising is not achieving full impact. Hence, the research should be limited to the primary area, however far distribution may be carried.

The *risks and costs* of success or failure seldom receive the attention they merit in planning the scale of an experiment. The costs of research usually receive some attention, and they can normally be estimated in advance from quotations, whether for *ad hoc* work or for the use of the increasing number of packaged facilities. Such costs tend to depend far more on the design of the experiment than on the scale or the size of the area used.

There are two other sets of possible costs, one of which will have been incurred by the end of the experiment (although in certain cases the costs may prove negligible). If the experiment leads to the project being introduced into the wider market, then there may have been some *loss of profits* during the period in which the project was held back from the main market awaiting the test result and a decision. This is not inevitable, e.g. when a test launch is carried out using pilot plant production and where the timing of the main launch depends on the completion of production facilities already under construction irrespective of the test; but whenever the introduction into a market of a profitable project is held back by the decision to test, there will be some loss of profits chargeable against the costs of the test. Taking time to test projects which are profitable always costs profits; but these opportunity costs can be reduced by carrying out the experiment, and thus avoiding this loss of profits, in a wider area.

Conversely, if the test results lead to the project being abandoned there will generally be *pull-out costs*. In some cases, such as in a test of a revised television schedule which has not affected media or production costs and which has failed to move the market share away from the line it would normally have followed, these may be insignificant. However, if the same experiment had led to a fall in market share, there would have been some loss of profits during the test and for such time afterwards as it took the market share to recover, plus the costs of any additional efforts put into the area to aid recovery. With the test launches that fail, there may be considerable losses on plant and equipment, on materials and labour, and such costs as cleaning-up operations and uplifting stock in the areas used. These pull-out costs can be reduced by keeping the size of the experimental areas as *small* as other requirements permit.

It follows that, where the project is believed to have a high probability of succeeding, the ultimate costs of testing may be reduced by allowing the sizes of the areas used to increase. Where a project is believed to have a high probability of failure the area involved should be kept to a minimum or key factors in the situation tested first on some more limited basis.

In some cases a rolling launch, in which the project is introduced through time into successive marketing areas across the country, may be the appropriate form for an 'experiment'. A company may be certain of gaining a profit, for example, from a new product if production is geared to the right level. Underproduction may kill the market, overproduction may kill the profit, and there may be a wide range between the available estimates of the upper and lower limits of potential sales. In these circumstances, if other factors are favourable, a logical plan would be to install capacity to meet the lowest estimated total sales level, and to launch in a part of the market which could still be adequately supplied if the highest level of demand was reached. Treatment of this area as an experiment would then provide the data for planning any necessary expansion of production as the product was 'rolled-out' into the remainder of the market. As a corollary to this, if for other reasons concerned with production, manpower, cash-flow or whatever, a rolling launch is imposed on the marketing planning, then again the patterns of development in the initial areas should be researched in the same way as for a test launch, to provide bases for forecasting and indications of failings or weaknesses in the marketing processes.

The selection of areas

The problem of selecting areas to be used in marketing experiments presents some difficulties. In an ideal situation the major market would be divided into areas on some suitable basis, and an adequate number of areas for use in the experiment and the control would be drawn at random. Unfortunately, this ideal method can seldom, if ever, be applied to marketing experiments for two major reasons. The first is that many of the areas which would appear as natural sub-units of the market are for one reason or another not suitable for particular experiments, e.g. in any experiment using television advertising in a country the natural sub-units of the market tend to be the respective areas covered by the various stations or program contractors. Some of these serve too large a part of the population to be generally economic as test areas, and they may put too large a slice of the market at risk in the event of a failure. Other areas may exhibit other characteristics which would make them unsuitable for use in particular tests. Consequently, only three or four may remain which can be classified as suitable. When towns are considered as test areas, a number may be rejected as too large or too small, or possess other features deemed unsatisfactory; the number remaining can again be very small.

The second reason is that random selection of the single areas within which most testing is conducted, or even two or three areas in exceptional cases, is too 'chancy' to be acceptable. The selection of only one or two areas at random for a test to be carried out only once does not allow the chance factors in random sampling to operate effectively. Hence, it becomes preferable to sample on a purposive basis, selecting each area for what it is known to be or to contain.

Logically, this leads to attempts to select areas for use in experiments and controls which are typical of the wider market, and which reflect within themselves the major characteristics of the wider market. This can be extended, where more than a single area is used, to selecting one typical of the north, one typical of the south, one hard-water area and one soft, and so on. In practice, however, it is doubtful whether there is a completely typical area in any market, because even after the usual comparisons have been made on demographic or economic bases it may still be found that particular relevant market parameters differ in the area from any 'national' pattern. Normally then, the most that can be done is to ensure that the areas finally selected for an experiment are not widely atypical, and then to cope with moderate degrees of atypicality through more sophisticated methods of interpretation and projection.

In some situations where there is a choice between a number of areas, such as towns of medium size, some form of cluster analysis may be useful (see chapter 13). This has been used to divide towns into groups with similar characteristics, and one set of such clusters has been devised and published by Christopher.[1] If, then, a spread of towns is required to provide a range of results from a single set of experimental conditions introduced into a range of different environments, this can be achieved by selection from as many of the different groups as the resources permit. On the other hand, when comparing two or more alternative projects, or selecting pairs of towns for experimental and control use, selection is made *within* the groups.

A wide range of test market research and other facilities is offered by media owners in many countries, sometimes at specially favourable rates to users of the media concerned. Lists of such facilities available are published from time to time by the media owners themselves, by trade journals and advertising agencies.

Timing

Many tests and experiments suffer from being run over too short a time. Often, this is a condition imposed by other considerations, but not infrequently it arises from an inadequate appreciation of the time which may be needed for a project to produce an effect on the market at all or, having produced one, to reach a stable level. Where a new product is introduced into a market or where some additional activity is added to an existing marketing program, it is frequently found that sales will move to an initial level from which they subsequently decline before stabilizing. If, then, the experiment or the measurements associated with it are discontinued prematurely the final readings will still be above the stable level and misleading results may be obtained. An analysis of 141 test markets in the UK and USA, for example, carried out by the A.C. Nielsen Co., suggests that, after the first six months of testing, the chance of adequately predicting the final test market share (achieved at the end of 12 to 18 months) is only about 1 in 2. This rises to about 2 in 3 after eight months of testing. In the opposite situation, where some factor is being removed from a marketing program or is being diminished, such as the advertising appropriation or the frequency of representatives' calls, there can be an inertia effect, and the market can continue unchanged for some considerable time before any movement can be observed. In one case there was an interval of fifteen months between the complete withdrawal of advertising for an established brand and any fall in market share in the test areas.

When both sets of factors may occur together, as in experiments where one type of activity is substituted for another, extreme care is needed in interpretation and in deciding when an experiment can be terminated. If the benefits of introducing the new type of activity appear quickly and before any detrimental effects from removing the old activity, sales or other measures will show a rise irrespective of the real strengths of the two activities. Conversely, if removing the current activity leads quickly to a detrimental effect but it takes time for the effects of the new activity to appear, early sets of measurements will show falls from the previous level. In either case, the initial results may be seriously misleading and time must be allowed for the position to stabilize. In the ideal situation, apart from using a suitable area as a control in which the existing activity will continue unchanged, a further area should be utilized in which the existing activity is removed and not replaced by the new one, in order to observe the decay of the current activity effect. This, however, may be too drastic a solution to be acceptable.

Apart from endeavouring to ensure that adequate time is allowed for experimentation, two further points relating to the time factor should be considered during the planning and execution of the research. The first is concerned with saving time by making provision for projections from the early results to provide estimates of the way the market is likely to move in subsequent periods. For consumer goods, such projections are based on analyses of the build-up of penetration of the product concerned (either from scratch in the case of a new product or from base levels for existing products) and of the repeat buying patterns among buyers of the product concerned. For details the reader is referred to chapter 8.

The second point is that the experiment and its associated research and measurement should continue in the test areas after any decision to introduce the project into a wider area is taken. Then some warning will be obtained should any detrimental movement occur in the market at a later stage, and appropriate action can be initiated. There is also a supplementary benefit from such a procedure, in that experimental areas may then be used for further experiments for which they are uniquely suitable, such as testing the second year's advertising for a new product in an area which has already completed its first year, or in testing other forms of follow-up activity.

Projections, predictions, and forecasts

The problem of converting the results observed in an experiment in a limited area into an assessment of what can be expected to happen if the project is introduced into the wider market is one of the most critical in marketing experimentation.

There is a range of experiments in which it may not be a vital concern, as in early feasibility studies of a new project or in some forms of pilot marketing where the emphasis is on ensuring that the more mechanical aspects of an operation will work efficiently. Even in those cases, however, where the development of wider market estimates may not have been part of the original brief, demands for some form of estimate will almost inevitably be made at later stages in the operation. In other cases the development of estimates of the likely effects of introducing the proposed course of action into a wider market is a prime requirement.

It is useful to differentiate between projection and prediction, and between the results of these processes and a forecast.

Projections are essentially simple means of obtaining estimates from test results. A brand share of $x \%$ in a test launch is merely projected to an estimate that $x \%$ of the wider market will be obtained; a rise in sales of y points as a result of an experimental promotion is projected to a rise of y points nationally, and so on. Straight projection is easy, but highly fallible, because there is an underlying assumption that 'all other things' will remain equal. Almost inevitably differences will be found between test areas and the wider market in such factors as demographic characteristics and the size of the target group, the existing penetration and rates of consumption of the product group, market shares of existing brands, shop populations, media coverage and so forth. These and other factors will tend to render the simple processes of projection inaccurate.

Predictions are the result of more complex series of càlculations, in which some attempt is made to take account of the factors which vary between the test area and the wider market. An attempt is made to construct a 'model' of the situation in the experimental area from the relationships found between the level of sales, or whatever criterion is being used, and the other market factors such as the demographic structure of the population, the store population, the shares held by competing brands before and after the experiment and so forth. Once these relationships are established in the test area, then predictions of the likely results in a wider market can be calculated by inserting the wider market values of the other factors into the relationships. One simple model which has proved useful is based on calculations of the proportionate changes in existing brand shares before and after a test launch. The predicted new brand share is then calculated by applying these proportionate changes to the wider market shares held by the existing brands and subtracting from 100%.

If x_0, y_0 are the market shares held by brands X, Y in the test area prior to the test; x_1, y_1 are the test area brand shares after the test; X_0, Y_0 are the wider market shares of X, Y, when the new brand is introduced there; then T, the expected wider market share of the test brand, is given by:

$$T = 100 - \left(\frac{x_1}{x_0} \cdot X_0 + \frac{y_1}{y_0} \cdot Y_0 + \cdots \right) \%$$

Normally, only simple models can be built up from the results of a single experiment because data to quantify many of the possible relationships are lacking. Where, however, a company has been able to bring together larger amounts of data, either from experiments or from observations in the main market, and to establish relationships between the main marketing factors and the levels of sales, the resulting marketing models can be invaluable not only in the interpretation of the results but in the planning stages of experiments as well.

A *forecast* should be developed from the projections or predictions as a joint effort between the research team and the marketing team involved. At this stage the whole history of the experiment should be reviewed and allowance made in the forecast so far as possible for any factors which may have detracted from the integrity of the experiment – difficulties in maintaining supplies, the effects of competitive activity, problems with major multiple organizations and so forth. Beyond this, there may be elements in the situation whose effects are wholly 'unpredictable' however sophisticated a model may be used, such as knowledge that a new competitive product is to be launched, and allowances for such factors can only be made at this final stage of turning projections or predictions into forecasts.

One point which is often overlooked in forecasting from the effects of test launches or other experiments is that a time element should be incorporated. This is because the forecast needed for the main operation should be pitched at some point in the future, while the information on which it is based is inevitably historic. Failure to take due note of time trends has led to significant differences between projections and results in the past, and the need to have information on movements outside the test area, in other parts of the main market, calls for the establishment and measurement of a control – a factor which is often left out of the design of experimental launches.

It follows that, since results from test areas may not be related to the results likely to occur in a wider market by a simple relationship, comparisons between the results of different strategies tested in separate areas should only be made after forecasting to a national level. There is always the risk that, if comparisons are made between raw area results, different conclusions may be drawn. The only safe procedure is to produce forecasts from each individually before comparing the results, in order to remove as far as possible any specific area influences.

Establishing the appropriate test conditions

The application of experience gained in experiments to wider markets or at later periods depends for its justification on the experience being valid. To be valid the experience must, among other things, have been generated under appropriate conditions, and setting up such appropriate conditions is probably one of the more difficult aspects of many marketing experiments.

In bald terms, the object of experiments is to create in a small area a prescribed set of conditions. In a full-scale experiment this normally means establishing as nearly as possible the conditions under which the project will be introduced into a wider market, in order to measure the effects. In the most complex case of an experimental launch this involves introducing the proposed product with the proposed advertising material used in the proposed media, and backed by promotions, offers, the activities of the sales force and any other factors at appropriate levels. If the experiment is to succeed it is necessary to look at each of these factors carefully to see precisely what is needed in the test areas and what can be achieved.

With the physical factors, such as the product or the pack, achieving comparability with what will be marketed on a wider scale may not be difficult – although it is not always easy. The product from a pilot plant may differ in some ways from the product which will eventually come off the main production line. An imported product used in anticipation of setting up a production line domestically may differ in its formulation, in the nature of the ingredients, in the form of packaging, or even only in the fact that it may bear the name of the country of origin, but any of these factors could be significant in affecting results achieved.

With advertising and promotion, the material to be used in the wider market may already be available for use in the test area, although even here the media selection problems may make changes necessary. The increase in split run facilities among newspapers and of tipping-in and other facilities among magazines is reducing the extent of such problems, but they still exist for many experiments and should always be looked for. With television advertising the problem appears simple, but this is deceptive and it is a good example of how an apparently simple solution to the problem arising in experiments can be damaging.

Consider an experimental launch in which television is the only form of advertising and the national appropriation has been set at £300,000 for the first six months. The problem is to assess the advertising appropriate to a test area containing, say, 5% of the population. One approach is to put 5% of the appropriation into the test area but this, of course, will take no account of variations in 'costs per thousand' between stations. A second approach is to put into the test area the national schedule of advertising which would be run in the event of a wider launch. However, because of the ways in which companies allocate their budgets after taking account of differences in card rates and other conditions between television areas, there may not be a 'national' schedule as such but only a series of differing area schedules. If there *is* a national schedule, or if an approximation to one can be constructed, this achieves comparability between the test area and the expected national pattern in terms of transmitted advertising − but still not necessarily the national pattern in terms of received advertising or opportunities to see. There appear to be quite marked differences between viewing habits in different parts of the country so that to attempt to set up a pattern of received advertising which will be 'typical' it is necessary to consider the reach and frequency schedule which is being aimed at on a national basis, and to reproduce this in the test area.

Even if comparability is achieved on this basis it may still leave problems unsolved, because of the relationship between the advertising for the experimental brand in the test area and advertising for brands already existing in the market. If there are area variations in the weights of advertising generated by competition it is quite possible that, whereas on a national basis the effort put behind the new product X may leave it below the effort put behind existing product A but above that for existing product B, variations in spending by A and B between areas may provide a quite different set of relationships in the test area. The main point is that a very detailed approach to the establishment of the appropriate experimental conditions is needed, not only in the media field but in others as well, both in an attempt to set up an appropriate set of test conditions, and also in order to know how far the conditions actually achieved may depart from the ideal and may need to be specifically allowed for in forecasting.

Beyond setting up the appropriate conditions at the beginning of an experiment, it is necessary to maintain them during its life. This involves such factors as ensuring that the sales effort is not unduly augmented either by the activities of the personnel normally working in the area, or by the attention or the visits paid to an area by head office personnel, acting on the best of motives of gaining experience but possibly influencing the experiment in some way at the same time. Hence, rigid discipline must be maintained over any company activities which might impinge on the experimental results.

Outside the company other factors may come into operation. The general effects of exogenous factors should have been catered for by setting up an adequate system of control areas in designing the experiment. Beyond this, however, competition may introduce counter activities into the test area which may affect the results. To maintain the integrity of the experiment, these activities must be carefully monitored and appropriate action taken. If, for example, a new launch is countered in the test area by increased advertising or other activity on the part of competitors, this may, in fact, enhance the value of the test operation if it is the type of activity which is to be expected on a wider scale in a wider launch. Further, if in the wider launch plan a contingency reserve has been set aside for use should such counter activity develop, then it is logical to use similar appropriate resources in the test area for this purpose.

However, if the counter activity mounted by competitors is specifically aimed at wrecking the test, such as flooding the area with coupons or samples or advertising on a scale which could not be supported nationally, then it may be necessary to abandon any hope of obtaining a projectable result from the test area, and to proceed as seems best with more limited objectives; for example, competitive couponing or sampling may have so distorted the market that any immediate estimate of brand share is unlikely to be valid but it may still be possible to gain a great deal of useful information from the test. Valid data may still be obtainable on the extent of awareness of the new product, the comprehension of the content of the advertising, the types of people who have bought and, in particular, the repeat buying patterns of those who have tried the new product at all. Some of these measures may have become suspect as a result of the competitive activity but almost certainly something can be gained from any test, whatever the interference, and any opportunities of gaining useful information should be taken rather than allow the whole operation to be written off.

This raises a point on the advisability of attempting to interfere in tests run by other manufacturers. In general, it would appear that far more is gained by watching and measuring the test oneself, and possibly using it in order to test any logical counter activities, rather than by becoming involved in a wrecking exercise.

The cost-effectiveness of experimenting

While there are numerous cases where hindsight shows that prior experimentation would have enabled a company to avoid losses incurred in launching some unsuccessful project, there are also many examples to be found where experiments were needlessly undertaken with a subsequent increase in costs or loss of profits. One large company, since taken over by another, for years prided itself that it never took a major decision without proper experimentation, and time after time it lost heavily because competitors had pre-empted the market by the time the experiments were completed. The problem of whether a particular experiment will justify the full range of costs involved is therefore vital.

The first requirement is for the likely range of outcomes of launching the project to be assessed in the light of existing knowledge and experience, together with assessments of the probabilities of the various outcomes occurring. Some such assessments are normally made anyway in considering a new project, although few take the process as far as attaching probabilities to the outcomes. This, however, is easily achieved by, in effect, carrying out an opinion survey among executives who know the project and the market, and deriving mean assessments of the probabilities, weighted perhaps to allow for different degrees of experience (or different weights of authority).

The outcomes normally need to be assessed in terms of profits or losses. In some cases, any effects resulting from the project will be immediate and of short duration, such as with a short-term promotion in a market with little brand loyalty. The effects will appear within a limited period and there will be little carry-over into the future, and there is little difficulty in putting a profit figure onto any set of market conditions which may arise. At the other extreme, if the project is one of launching a new brand which may be expected to have a life of some years ahead of it, it may be preferable to discount future profits in some way to provide figures of current net worth.

Where the assessed range of outcomes shows some probabilities of profits and some of losses if the project is put directly into the market, the first point to consider is the size of maximum loss and its assessed probability of occurrence. If the loss is one which the company, the marketing group, or the executives within it, could not survive, then the only logical options open are to 'test' or 'abandon', irrespective of all other factors. If the maximum loss would not be crippling in this way, then all three options of 'launch now', 'test', or 'abandon' are still open and further calculation is required.

The next stage is to consider whether a test operation would lead to a more precise assessment of the range of outcomes, allowing for the problems of measurement and forecasting. Measurements can be made more precise by increasing sample sizes at a cost, and forecasts can be made more firm by increasing the number of areas into which the experiment is introduced, but again at a price. If the original assessments of possible outcomes were based on solid information and experience, the range may already be so narrow that further testing may do little to provide additional information. On the other hand, if existing experience is sketchy and the possible range of outcomes developed is wide, then even a simple experiment may help in refining the estimates of outcomes.

The problem of balancing the costs and the benefits of market testing is one of Bayesian Statistics, and a full discussion is beyond the scope of this chapter. For the general theory readers should consult Schlaifer,[2] and for an application to market experiments, Davis.[3]

In essence, the procedure involves balancing the costs against the improvement in the probability of avoiding losses or of gaining profits, as a result of testing. Hence, apart from the estimated outcomes and their probabilities, calculations of the costs already mentioned are needed, and some estimate of the accuracy likely to be attained by the possible methods of testing and forecasting. In many cases, where experimentation could proceed at more than one level, separate calculations need to be made covering the various options open to the company.

If the whole range of assessed outcomes is profitable two situations arise. On the one hand, if the investment required to introduce the project will remain flexible and can be adjusted to meet the market requirements as they develop, then clearly there is no point in incurring the costs of a separate test operation. An immediate launch, nationally or on a rolling base, is logical. On the other hand, if there are severe penalties involved should planning and investment proceed on a level which is not subsequently matched by market performance − even though that performance in itself would have been profitable had it been properly planned for − then testing may be called for. Thus, an achievement of selling 400 000 cases of a product a year in a market may be profitable if the whole planning was on the basis of achieving that level, but it may prove to be *un*profitable if the original planning and investment was based on achieving a level of 800,000 cases. This is a further complication which can be brought into the calculations if required.

Exploratory experiments

In the past, it has probably been true to say that most market experiments have been carried out to secure information relating to some specific immediate problem − whether a new product will gain a viable share of a market, a new campaign will increase sales, changes in an appropriation will be profitable, and so forth. With many aspects of marketing this is the only way in which experiments can be conducted at all, because until the new product has been formulated and its marketing mix agreed, or until a new campaign has been developed or a new pack designed, there is nothing to experiment with. On the other hand, there are some areas of marketing in which useful experience can be gained through exploratory experiments at almost any time and added to the company's fund of knowledge for future use. Such areas include the level of the advertising appropriation, the way it is allocated between media, the ways in which it is scheduled; the representative journey cycles and the frequencies of calling on customers of various types; the effects of display bonuses and so forth. With these factors it is not necessary to wait until a particular decision has to be taken before beginning to collect experience by introducing planned changes into different parts of the market and measuring their effects. This type of experimentation becomes more important if the company is attempting to build marketing models, when all too frequently it is found that some factor which may well have a bearing on sales or profitability has hitherto been running at a steady level so that no information can be gained about the effects of variations from a study of past data. In these fields, then, it is possible to anticipate needs for experience and to carry out a comparatively inexpensive program of experiments accumulating the information through time, either in order to increase the running efficiency of an operation or to be able to provide more specific data when faced with future problems.

Collecting data

Linked with this is the idea that whenever any changes are made in the way a product is being marketed — whether in limited areas or on a total market basis — as much relevant information as possible should be collected. In general, most marketing experiments suffer from a lack of resources applied to the collection of data. The results of test launches, appropriation tests, campaign tests, and so on, too often tend to be assessed only in terms of changes in retail sales measured through some form of store panel. Such measurements may be adequate to answer the immediate direct question of whether the test produces beneficial results or not, but they fail to cover two other vital aspects.

The first is that if the experiment does not generate an improved level of sales or profitability then unless the failure is due to some in-store conditions, such as a lack of distribution, there will be no information to show where the marketing process broke down. If, for example, in an experimental launch only store audit data have been collected, there will be no means of diagnosing many possible causes of failure — or even of detecting weaknesses in a project which is in most respect successful. There will be no way of knowing whether the advertising failed to achieve attention or to create awareness; whether awareness was created but interest in the product did not develop; or even whether adequate numbers of the population did, in fact, buy the product but did not repeat their purchases. Thus, even though some of these measures may not be needed in order to assess the profitability of the project they are vital in any attempt at diagnosing weaknesses or causes of failure.

Second, in a more general way, the lack of this type of information, whether collected during experiments or when changes are introduced into wider markets, means that our knowledge of marketing is more restricted than it need be. There is, for example, little information about the way in which awareness of a new product or of a new advertising campaign develops. Too often, research in this area is merely confined to a single *ad hoc* survey some weeks or months after the launch which will then show some existing single measure of awareness. There will, however, be no indication of whether the level found has only just been reached, whether it was reached some time earlier and has merely been held since, or whether the level has been higher in the past and is now declining. It is also then difficult to assess whether the achieved level is a satisfactory one or not. Increasing the amount of research to collect this information will, of course, involve additional expenditure in most cases, but this need not be unduly high. Against this the benefit of being able to plan future launch advertising against a more secure knowledge of the way in which awareness develops could well lead to significant increases in the efficiency of such operations.

Any collection of additional data beyond that necessary to assess and interpret the results of the particular experiment must, however, be done within the context of the experiment itself. Attempts to use or modify an experiment being run for a specific purpose, in order to test some other quite different factor at the same time, must normally be resisted. The bits and pieces tacked on are likely to jeopardize the main experiment. However, arranging for a more comprehensive set of measurements to be made within the context of the experiment should normally enhance the value of the results as well as adding to the company's fund of experience.

Summary

To sum up: marketing experiments need to be carefully designed and measured in order to answer the questions being posed – and this applies whether the experiments relate to immediate problems or are being mounted in order to gain long term experience. Before embarking on any experiment, four basic questions should be answered:

(a) Is it possible to get the information required in this experiment from any other source, such as re-analysis of existing data, comparisons with other markets, or the accumulated experience of the company?
(b) Given what is already known about this situation, will an experiment add to that experience in a way which will lead to a better-based decision?
(c) Will the benefit expected from the better decision be sufficient to cover the costs of the experiment, taking account of the full range of costs which may be incurred?
(d) If this experiment is run can it be used as a source of other useful information and experience?

When an experiment or test is to be run, four major considerations should be coverd as far as is possible:

(a) The experiment should, wherever possible, be conducted in more than a single area.
(b) The integrity of the experiment must be established and maintained, and all decisions relating to the way it is handled operationally must be made in the light of the objectives and needs of the experimental situation.
(c) Adequate time should be allowed for the effects of the changes to be developed and to reach stable levels.

(d) An adequate amount of measurement should be undertaken, not merely to provide measures of performance, but also to provide for diagnosis of the causes of weaknesses or failure and to increase the general understanding of the market.

Chapter 20

Market modelling

TONY LUNN, CHRIS BLAMIRES and DAVID SEAMAN

Introduction

Modelling is a diverse and complex area. It is also a controversial one. For more than two decades, researchers have developed and adapted models of widely differing kinds, ranging from econometric systems designed to forecast changes at the global market level to theories about individual decision processes. There has been considerable activity and enthusiasm, among research practitioners and marketing managers as · well as marketing academics.

On the other hand, some researchers and marketing men have reacted with either indifference or scepticism. Models have been condemned as too complicated, both conceptually and methodologically; as necessitating long and costly procedures of data collection and analysis; as being difficult to implement; and as irrelevant for practical decision making. These criticisms have stimulated protagonists of the modelling approach to pay more attention to building usable models and to finding ways of getting models used. Successful case histories have been reported and two are quoted later in the chapter.

The purpose of this chapter is to draw attention to some major issues in the area. Space restrictions do not permit anything approaching a comprehensive overview and the reader wishing to learn more should consult the literature references contained in the text. Fuller discussions can be found in these. Particularly relevant for an introduction are references 1–9.

The chapter is complementary to that by Rothman in this handbook (chapter 3), which is written from a more mathematical standpoint. Emphasis is given here to certain models of individual choice behaviour which have received increasing attention from researchers in recent years. Allied to developments in computer simulation, these are already demonstrating considerable potential as tools for management decision making. The first part of the chapter deals mainly with issues at a general level: the second part gives illustrations from two successful published case histories.

Definitions

The term 'model' covers a multiplicity of constructs, some of which, it has been alleged [8], have little in common except that they share the same label! However, there would be general acceptance for the definition given by Zaltman,[9] namely that 'A model is a simplified but organised and meaningful representation of an actual system or process'. It specifies both the key elements in a system – such as consumer beliefs, situational factors and purchasing behaviour – and the relationships between these elements. It is a replica of the real world and not the real world itself: it is simplified in that usually only a sub-set of the total pool of possible elements is incorporated – those critical to the nature and objective of the model in question. Where the phenomenon under investigation is relatively complex, as is the case with market and consumer behaviour, it becomes especially important to ensure that an adequate number of variables are included without, as a result, producing models that are too unwieldy to be of practical value.

A more colloquial definition has been suggested by Westwood *et al.*[10]

> Models may be regarded as essentially views of how things work. As such, we all use models all the time. In everyday life we need models in order to act at all, and effective models in order to act successfully – in preparing a meal, catching a train, etc. Likewise, every market research project implies a model or series of models of one kind or another. We assume that our questions reflect phenomena in the real world; that the variables we cross-analyse are linked in a meaningful way, that our questions and analyses have relevance to the problem in hand. All of these assumptions imply models – views of how consumers operate and how they are affected by marketing action.

The same point holds for managers in their planning and implementation of marketing strategies. It cannot be emphasized too strongly that even the most unsympathetic critics of formal models in practice base their management decisions upon implicit models, which may well be totally misleading. As discussed more fully elsewhere,[10] a particularly important function of a modelling exercise is to make explicit the implicit assumptions held about market structure by both marketing men and researchers, thereby enabling these assumptions to be criticized, tested and developed.

The value and role of models

The function of marketing models has been discussed extensively in the literature.[6,11,12] Particularly important considerations are that models are valuable in:

(a) Providing an improved understanding of how particular markets, or markets in general, work, of how consumers arrive at purchasing decisions, and of ways in which these decisions may be influenced by marketing action.

(b) Enabling better predictions to be made of the nature of future market structures. This refers both to circumstances outside the direct control of marketing management but also, and more importantly, to the likely outcome of alternative marketing strategies, re-launching an existing brand with a revised formulation, putting more expenditure into below-the-line promotional activity, etc. The main benefit here is to enable management to ask 'what if' questions – e.g. what would be the effect of repositioning a minority brand in a certain way? – while avoiding the time, expense and practical problems associated with traditional research approaches such as experiments and test markets.[8]

(c) Helping to integrate the plethora of disparate concepts and findings which exist both in market research generally and also within the information systems of individual marketing companies.

(d) Indicating gaps in our knowledge of marketing structures, thereby helping to generate relevant basic research projects; likewise models help to indicate gaps in the knowledge about particular markets, thereby guiding the commissioning and implementation of specific market studies.

(e) Improving communication between researchers and marketing management, partly by establishing a common language in which research planning and findings can be linked to management decisions.

(f) Improving specific research projects by identifying the kind of data required and ways in which these data can be operationalized, and by indicating the most relevant analysis techniques.

Typologies of models

Several researchers have advanced typologies of models as a basis for comparison and evaluation.[13–15] Some major categories are outlined below.

Micro – macro

The distinction refers to the level at which the market is considered during the model building process. A macro-model focuses upon the market at a global level and treats it as a total system. An example would be an econometric model which aims to predict market share as a function of differential weights of advertising expenditure.

In a micro-model every unit is treated separately: as an example, the characteristics and responses of consumers are examined on an individual basis. These individual responses can then be aggregated either to form subgroups of consumers sharing common characteristics or to produce an average response for the total sample. For instance, the likely market share of a new product could be forecast by aggregating the reactions of individual consumers.

Statistical – behavioural

In a statistical model, market behaviour is represented as a mathematical function of the variables included which, in turn, are often selected by statistical procedures such as regression analysis. The consumer is usually treated as a 'black box', the mechanics of which are not explored. Stochastic forecasting models are typical examples.[2]

In a behavioural model the aim is to illuminate the mechanisms within the 'consumer black box'. The model may be based upon knowledge or assumptions about consumer behaviour and choice processes, and will typically incorporate theory drawn from the behavioural sciences.

In contrasting these two approaches, Nicosia[16] draws attention to their limitations when pursued separately. Statistical models tend both to make sweeping assumptions about behavioural processes and also to contain a somewhat parsimonious number of variables. Behavioural models, by contrast, sacrifice formal precision to richness of content and may, as a result, be regarded as too insubstantial as a basis for decision making. Nicosia argues strongly for 'substantive models' which combine the two approaches.

Attitude-orientated – behaviour-orientated

A development of this division is a distinction between behaviour-orientated models and attitudinally-orientated models: the former using behavioural measures as inputs (actual choice, actual repeat-purchase, actual shares), the latter inferring a link between attitudes and subsequent behaviour in monitoring attitudes yet modelling behaviour.

This distinction is a useful one in developing a schema of models, encompassing the wide area which comes under this heading and which will be discussed further in the ensuing section.

Explanatory – predictive

Some models are essentially descriptive, in that they are concerned primarily with providing descriptions rather than explanations of market behaviour. An example is the work of Ehrenberg[17] who, in analysing purchasing data, has identified simple general rules or laws such as the Logarithmic Series Distribution. 'Starting without any formalised preconceptions of how or why people behave or feel as they do, the emphasis is on inter-relating simple empirical patterns, in cases where these are known to hold under wide ranges of observed conditions.' Interest is in both the laws themselves and in deviations from them: the latter are regarded as cases where special marketing action may be called for.

There is a grey area between description and explanation. As descriptions become more detailed and sophisticated, so a model becomes more diagnostic in nature and provides explanation of the phenomenon of interest. Many models, especially behavioural ones, are essentially diagnostic.

Prediction of how markets will react under specified circumstances is also a feature of many models. This is certainly the case for econometric models[2] and is increasingly so for the consumer choice models which are described later in the chapter.

A schema of model characteristics

At this juncture the authors would like to offer their own classification of models. It is submitted that models relevant to traditional and current applications in market research fall into two basic categories.

Ad hoc research derived models – Models here are those for which the parameters and data input are specifically collected with a modelling objective in mind. A programme of *ad hoc* research is constructed which will supply sufficient data for model building. Within this category lie micro-anlytic behavioural models, the Fishbein model and the various Simulated Test Market models (*STM*) such as *ASSESSOR*, *SENSOR* etc.

A common feature of these models is that data are likely to have been collected with each single individual respondent as the supplier of a number (often the majority) of the inputs to be used in the construction of the model; the model inputs are largely 'single source'.

Such a feature means the model is able to exploit the fact that these data inputs can be cross-related in a way that would be impossible with data collected from independent sources.

Thus, for example, in micro-analytic behavioural modelling, a key feature of the model is its ability to relate each individual's beliefs to the importance weights held by that individual.

Historically based models – This group can be regarded as *post-hoc* models; they are imposed on data collected initially without a modelling end in view.

Of necessity, such models do not attempt to relate the various inputs back to the individual, and can be classified as truly macro-models. They take measurements such as advertising spend, brand share, price relatives etc. and attempt to relate them in format which 'explains' movements in the dependent variable (often brand share).

These two fundamentally different groups of models will be discussed in turn.

1.   Ad Hoc research derived models

The nature of an *ad hoc* model is necessarily determined by the objectives of the model builders. This will follow intensive discussion of the marketing issues that management wish to explore. Thus models can be designed to indicate likely new product performance, share movements resulting from price shifts in existing brands, the efficacy of alternative promotions or the impact of an increased/reduced advertising budget. Such questions are addressed by defining the consumer decision to be modelled, and the parameters (or influences) that affect that decision. Subsequent measurement of those parameters and study of their relationship with the dependent variable (the consumer decision) result in a model of that decision. This enables the researcher to trace and replicate the choice process.

Early *ad hoc* – based models tended to be fundamentally divided into those which were attitude-based (e.g. the Fishbein Model), and those which were behaviour-based (e.g. Simulated Test Market models). The former sought to 'explain' consumer choices by studying consumer attitudes while the latter utilized actual behaviour in an attempt to predict behaviour in an alternative or enlarged context (e.g. by relating test results to likely national success). More recent models have combined the two approaches. However, even these later models tend to have their roots in one or the other traditions.

(a) Attitude-orientated models

These are models which lay emphasis on the attitudes (images, beliefs and importance weights) of individuals in predicting/explaining their subsequent choices and behaviour. In the case of micro-analytic behavioural models, for example, elements such as brand awareness and weight of purchase by those 'choosing' a specific brand are now frequently monitored and included in the model, but they are secondary to the attitudinal elements, which remain the 'core' element of the model.

Attitude-orientated models, by virtue of their reliance on measurements of attitudes and beliefs require a theoretical base on which to make projections about likely behaviour; that is, such models require theories which link the attitudes and beliefs monitored to the ultimate result – the actual behaviour in the area of interest (frequently brand choice). A discussion of the theoretical bases now follows.

Theoretical bases for consumer models

As mentioned in the previous section, behavioural models in particular are characterized by an explicit theoretical basis. In fact, few consumer models are totally devoid of some kind of conceptual foundation. The literature on this subject is extensive, and there is space here for only a few brief comments concerning aspects especially relevant to current developments in modelling.

For the most part, theory has been drawn or adapted from the behavioural sciences. The potential of many different approaches has been explored. Many of these have dealt with states and processes internal to the consumer; for instance, those dealing with motivation, attitudes, learning and perception. These theories throw light on issues such as how people develop needs for different product characteristics, how they evaluate alternative products in terms of these needs, how information about products is acquired, structured and stored, and how predispositions towards buying different products are developed and changed. To quote just one instance, the work of social psychologists such as Rosenberg and Fishbein has been incorporated in a variety of multi-attribute models, as reviewed by Wilkie and Pessemier.[18]

Attention has also been devoted to theories concerned with influences upon the consumer, such as his reference groups, the situations under which he buys and consumes various products and the nature of family decision making. These external factors have two main kinds of influence. First, they help to formulate consumer states such as awareness, needs, attitudes and buying intentions. Second, they help to mediate or modify the translation of predispositions into actual behaviour. For instance, a housewife may herself be highly inclined towards exotic foods, but may buy other foods instead because of her husband's traditional tastes.

Much model building is concerned with representing the consumer in his social environment. And, increasingly, the importance has been recognized of incorporating theories dealing with both internal and external factors. At a specific level, the work of Fishbein,[19] with its emphasis upon social normative beliefs, has been implemented here. At a more global level so have the comprehensive theories, such as those of Howard and Sheth,[12] Engel et al.[20] and Nicosia.[21]

Comprehensive theories are one development. They represent the emergence of buyer behaviour as a discipline in its own right.[22,23] Somewhat ambitiously, they aim to integrate a number of social science theories purportedly relevant to consumer behaviour, as well as the findings of published empirical studies. As a result, they tend to be too complex to provide a direct basis for consumer modelling, but indirectly they have considerable practical value, indicating ideas and concepts which might be embodied in particular projects. One example is the concept of evoked set. This distinguishes those brands in a product field which a consumer would consider buying (or in some cases, also those he would definitely *not* buy) from those of which he is either not aware or would not seriously consider. The size and nature of the evoked set may vary over time according to factors such as experience and confidence.

Another important feature of comprehensive theories has been their dynamic property. This is manifested in Nicosia's argument for shifting the emphasis away from the purchasing act itself and towards the decision processes which both precede and follow this act. As he points out, 'the act of purchasing is only one component of a complex, on-going process of decision-making – a process of many interactions amongst many variables over time'.

One of the most influential recent developments upon modelling has been the information theory approach to buyer behaviour, e.g. refs. 24, 25 and 26.

> Information Processing Theory is concerned with the mind and the way it is organised. It postulates that people think and make decisions by processing information according to some mental structures. The information will be certain cues or stimuli received from the person's environment and stored in memory as verbal concepts. The structures comprise fundamental processes that in the end result in some observed behaviour.[25]

This information theory approach is concerned with ways in which consumers acquire and process information and how they use this information in making purchasing decisions. It has provided a fresh perspective for understanding existing research findings, and has also been the starting point for new conceptualizations.[26]

An important development deriving from information theory has been the identification and operationalization of different types of decision rule used by consumers in their handling of cues about alternative brands, products and services. Many models have assumed that consumers normally use a compensatory rule; that is, they will choose brands which are perceived to have the best overall balance of favoured characteristics across all attributes. In some of these models, attributes have been weighted for importance in arriving at an assessment of purchasing probabilities.

Increasingly, alternative rules have been identified and applied in consumer modelling projects. For example:

(a) a *threshold* rule, where brands are eliminated from further consideration when they are perceived to have unacceptable characteristics or an insufficient score on favoured characteristics;

(b) a *disjunctive* rule, where a brand with a single overwhelming advantage is chosen;

(c) a *lexicographical* rule, where the brand most perceived to demonstrate an advantage on a sub-set of key attributes, considered in order of importance, is chosen;

(d) a *compensatory* rule such as trade-off, where the basic contention is that consumers are not as a rule faced with alternatives which they can meaningfully judge against some hypothetical ideal. Instead they usually have to choose between a series of imperfect options: and to obtain a desired level of a particular product quality (say efficiency) they will have to sacrifice, i.e. trade-off, a certain level of some other product quality (say, gentleness).

There has been much discussion in the published literature of the relative merits of different decision rules, the circumstances under which they are most appropriate, and the ways in which they may be used by consumers in the same choice situation either sequentially or in combination.[27-30]

Micro-behavioural models have gained significant popularity, largely as a result of their ability to explain and describe markets and market-related decisions in greater detail but also, to a limited extent, by their ability to predict events using the data collected. A brief description of two such models is given below.

The first, an example from the dry shaver market, reviews the stages involved in building the model, and the ultimate use to which it is put; the second, from the grocery market, highlights the use of the model created in both a predictive and explanatory role.

Model 1: The dry shaver market

Stages in the model building process

Each modelling project should proceed at its own pace, depending upon the problem in question and prevailing circumstances. A characteristic series of steps is outlined below. Brief illustrations are given from a project carried out in the UK dry shaver market, which is reported in detail in reference 31.

Problem definition

Modelling is a problem-oriented activity, and obvious first steps are to clarify both the problem to be solved and the objectives of the model. A task force should be established at the earliest moment, and criteria agreed for evaluating the results of each stage of the project. In the dry shaver study, a project team was established with members drawn from the initiating company's headquarters, the research agency, and outside consultants. Some objectives are mentioned in the next sub-section.

Developing a macrostructure

The next stage is the development of an overall representation of all relevant elements in the market and their interrelationships. At first this 'macrostructure' would be highly descriptive and qualitative: it can be progressively refined in the light of experience and research findings. The objective is to provide task force members with a common language, and to ensure that they share a common perception of the main issues involved.

In the dry shaver project, the macrostructure represented the flow of information available to consumers, and the role of this information at various stages in the buying process. Various elements in the decision-making situation were specified, each of which could be the subject of a sub-model.

(a) *Wet/Dry choice model:*   representing the factors which influence whether an individual will become a customer in the dry (electric) shaver market or in the wet-shaving market.
(b) *Pre-store choice model:*   representing the interplay of brand awareness, beliefs about brands, and the individual's value system in the development of purchasing dispositions, prior to active shopping.
(c) *In-store model:* representing those distributional and point-of-sale factors which may interact with 'pre-store choice' dispositions in the determination of actual choice.
(d) *Retailer model:* representing the attitudes and requirements of the retailer and how these influence stocking, display and sales activities.
(e) *Theme advertising model:* representing the content and delivery of advertising messages.
(f) *Gift model:* representing that part of total buying which arises from the purchase of electric shavers to be given as unsolicited (i.e. non-requested) gifts.

These elements are represented in diagrammatic form to show the inter-relationship between the separate parts (Fig. 20.1).

Where several elements can be identified, priorities will have to be established over where to concentrate initial effort. In the dry shaver study the 'Pre-store choice' area was selected, mainly because it was judged to hold most immediate benefit to the Company in making various marketing and advertising decisions. Objectives for this sub-model were set – e.g. 'To identify when an existing brand or type is approaching the limit of its appeal to consumers, i.e. has been bought or considered by all who value its attributes' – and a flow chart was produced to represent its main characteristics (Fig. 20.2).

Operationalization
The next stage is to operationalize the various elements within the structure. For instance, in the shaver project measuring instruments were developed for variables such as awareness, beliefs and values, and for the various decision rules hypothesized to be relevant to consumer choice in this area, for example the threshold, disjunctive, lexicographic and compensatory rules referred to earlier in this chapter. Exploratory research conducted during a preliminary phase of this project had suggested that consumer decision making in this

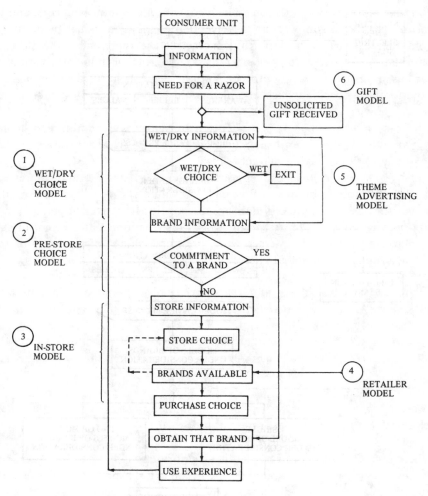

Fig. 20.1. The macrostructure.

product field was based upon a combination of these rules. To quote:

> In effect the brand choice model can be thought of as asking the following sequence of questions:
>
> (i) Which brands is the respondent aware of?
> (ii) Do any brands have completely unacceptable attributes (i.e. Threshold Rule)? If so, reject them.
> (iii) Does any brand have a unique advantage on any important attribute (i.e. Disjunctive Rule)? If so, accept it as the predicted choice.
> (iv) Are any remaining brands inferior on any particular important attributes (i.e. Lexicographic Rule)? If so, reject them.

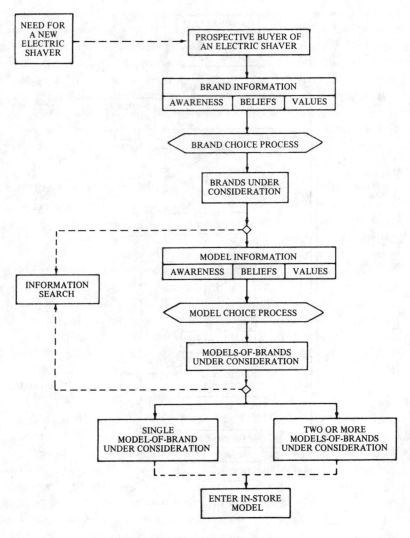

Fig. 20.2. Pre-store choice model.

(v) What is the total utility associated with the characteristics of each
    remaining brand (i.e. Compensatory Rule)? Select brand with most
    utility.[31]

Validation

Models will be used by management only if they are comprehensible and
relevant to decision making. In addition they should have face validity: that is,
they should provide a representation of the market that makes sense to the
managers concerned. However, there is also a need for validity of a more

stringent kind, namely that models should provide accurate representation of the markets under investigation in particular cases. A thorough review of issues involved in the validation of marketing models is given by Faivre and Sanchez[32] who describe a case history of a relatively complex model where there was an impressively high goodness-of-fit between results predicted by the model and those observed in the market place: the variables on which comparisons were based included awareness, attitude measures and market shares.

Validation of the dry shaver model was also encouraging. Three basic forms were used:

(a) comparison of the model's prediction with measures of purchasing intention. Correct predictions were obtained for over 90% of respondents;
(b) comparison of the model's prediction with individual consumers' measured reactions to a set of new shaver concepts, obtained on a re-interview of the original sample. A satisfactory brand choice was obtained from about 75% of individual respondents;
(c) 'process validity' where, through the analysis of questions answered by the original sample but not used in building the model, comparisons were made between the choice processes used by individuals as suggested by the model and what was actually purchased by the respondents themselves.

Application

Consumer models of the kind discussed above have already begun to demonstrate their value for management decision making. Two aspects are dealt with below, namely explanation and prediction.

An example of their explanatory power lies in the illumination of the choice processes adopted by individual consumers. For instance, it is possible to identify how many respondents reject each brand on threshold characteristics, and which attributes lead to a brand being rejected in this way; likewise, for people who choose each brand, it is possible to identify how many make disjunctive, lexicographic and compensatory choices, and also to indicate the determinant attitudes. Moreover, it is possible to classify consumers in terms of the way in which they use different combinations of these rules.

Their predictive power lies in the mechanism they offer marketing management to estimate the effects of alternative strategies. The procedure is for the marketing man to formulate 'what if' questions and for answers to be obtained through computer simulation. Typical 'what if' questions (from ref. 31) include:

(a) What formulation changes, effectively communicated, would increase the frequency with which our brand is selected?

(b) What attributes should be stressed in our advertising?

(c) What are the characteristics (attitudinal, demographic, behavioural, media, etc.) of the people who are likely to be attracted by a new strategy?

(d) Does our current advertising platform have continuing potential, or is there a case for a new one?

(e) What is the likely effect on brand choice of our competitor's change in his advertising positioning?

(f) What would be the most effective response to protect our brand from competitive activity?

(g) Which combination of attributes would be the strongest basis for a new brand? From where would a new brand, of a given specification, attract its customers?

Simulation can take place at both micro and macro levels. The description of the dry shaver case provides illustrations of both. Computer print-out is obtained under both the pre-simulation and simulation conditions. First, at the micro level it was shown how, for instance, a particular respondent would currently choose a Ronson razor, given his perceptions of the various brands available. The print-out also showed how this decision was a function of the threshold and disjunctive rules, and which attitudes appeared to be determinant. It was then assumed that marketing action could change his perceptions of the brands in terms of a certain key attribute. Given this assumption, a simulation run showed that he would now choose a Philishave. The print-out also indicated that, under the changed conditions, he would use four decision rules in sequence, namely threshold, disjunctive, lexicographic and compensatory.

At the macro level, effects of marketing action are provided by aggregating the total set of individual results. One means of showing these is by a brand switching matrix, as in Fig. 20.3 below.

Brand Choice Pre-Simulation		Post Simulation					
		Philips	Philishave	Boots	Remington	Ronson	Braun
Philips	21	17	4	–	–	–	–
Philishave	30	–	30	–	–	–	–
Boots	4	–	–	4	–	–	–
Remington	21	–	–	–	21	–	–
Ronson	12	–	2	–	–	10	–
Braun	12	–	2	–	–	–	10
	100	17	38	4	21	10	10

Fig. 20.3. Shaver brand switching matrix.

In this example Philishave seems capable of achieving an 8% increase in brand choice if a particular attribute can be effectively communicated and if other factors are constant. It would appear, however, that 4% of this increase would come from the Philips brand, thus giving only 4% increase in the combined share of Philips and Philishave. The results of macro simulations may also be represented in terms of brand choice percentages.

Model II: The grocery retail market

The second example quoted shows how a micro-modelling project assisted the strategic marketing planning of the Co-operative Wholesale Society in the highly competitive grocery retail area. A fuller account can be found in reference.[33] Collective marketing activity, including advertising, promotions and research is undertaken by the C.W.S. with Co-op retail society involvement. It was felt that marketing planning could be greatly assisted by a model with both diagnostic and predictive qualities. The model concentrated on the 'main' (as opposed to the 'secondary') shopping trip, as not only did this represent a considerable proportion of grocery expenditure but also tended to be based on a rational decision process. Using as inputs store availability, shop imagery and attribute saliency (as shown in Fig. 20.4), a model was constructed which was validated by checking predicted main trip shopping choice against known referent behaviour. The internal predictivity of the model achieved the highly acceptable level of 81%.

With the confidence that the model could satisfactorily replicate consumers' store choice, the model could be used in a predictive way whereby simulations were conducted on the basis of artificially altering the model's parameters. During the course of each simulation, each respondent's most likely choice was processed, and the numbers of respondents 'choosing' each option simulated accumulated as 'choice shares'. This provided the useful facility of answering marketing management's 'what if' questions.

In translating marketing 'what if' type questions into a format compatible with the model, two broad classes of simulation arise; the first attempting to make predictions corresponding to real-life events in the market, and the second designed to 'diagnose' the underlying relationships between variables. More 'diagnostic' simulations may, for example, include the systematic variation of shop images to determine those areas in which theme advertising can be most profitably applied.

Use of the model in prediction
As an example, the following illustrates how the C.W.S. Shop Choice Model was used to simulate and predict the effects of real activity in the market place.

In the early 1980s a major competitor launched a price initiative which was

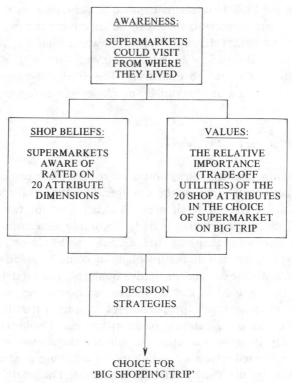

CHOICE FOR
'BIG SHOPPING TRIP'
(Also measured: 'referent shop' = Supermarket used most often on their 'big regular trip').
Fig. 20.4. The grocery main trip shopping model.

to have a substantial impact on the grocery market. Immediately the details were known a simulation was undertaken to assess the likely impact prior to packaged grocery share data becoming available.

Competitive price initiative was amongst the simplest simulations possible in that it involved only an improvement in the rating for price competitiveness of that retailer amongst all those holding an opinion about it. This resulted in a new set of 'market shares' being created by the model. The model, of course, simulated only main trip share, but this was regarded as a good indicator for the final impact on the market.

An abridged list of changes with regard to four major retailers in the market can be seen in Table 20.1. Given the relative size of the initial shares, the model was predicting major gains for Retailer A at the expense of major losses for Retailer B and smaller losses for Retailer C, with no change for Retailer D.

Without quoting actual share figures, Table 20.2 below give the change in packaged grocery share experienced by the same major retailers in the four weeks of the initiative as a proportion of the share immediately before, and the same figure for six months afterwards.

Table 20.1   *Competitive price initiative simulation*

Retailer	% Point change of 'main' trip share	Proportionate change against initial 'main' trip shares (%)
A	+1.7	+14.4
B	−0.6	− 4.5
C	−0.3	− 3.2
D	n/c·	n/c·

Table 20.2   *Changes in packaged grocery share*

Retailer	Model prediction	Actual proportionate change against base share for retailers (TCA)	
		Immediate (%)	Six months after (%)
A	Substantial gain	+ 14.5	+8.7
B	Substantial loss	− 2.1	−5.6
C	Minor loss	− 1.2	−1.8
D	No change in trend	+ 0.8	+3.4

Packaged grocery shares, while only indicative of the total situation, were the best available monitor of market shares. It was noticeable that following the successful initiative by Retailer A, Retailer D continued its trend of long-term gains; Retailer B began a long-term decline and Retailer C suffered marginally. The 'six month after' figure confirms these results, which can be seen to be reasonably closely in line with model predictions.

The variable data used in a model can also provide a wealth of basic information when selectively aggregated. For example, the C.W.S. Shop Choice Model examined the value system (i.e. utility values from trade-off analysis) and shop usage for main trips by those who have a superstore available to them but do not use it. Additionally those who regard price as more important against those who regard price as of lesser importance can be analysed. From this, data on the attributes that mattered more to those who attach a lower value to price *per se* could be obtained.

Similarly, the model was able to identify those retailers which are likely to be patronized by housewives who vary according to their attitudes towards price. A division of the sample on this criterion can show main trip shops visited in a new light as can be seen in Table 20.3. Thus retailers (iv) and (vi), for example, were in the potentially limiting position of appealing strongly on price. Others such as retailers (i) and (iii) had an advantage or disadvantage depending on their desired marketing positions.

Access to the shop choice model provided C.W.S. marketing management

Table 20.3   Source for main trip: price value analysis

Housewives believing price:		Share of main trips	
		Relatively less important	Relatively more important
		(%)	(%)
Retailer:	(i)	6.4	2.7
	(ii)	10.0	14.3
	(iii)	6.2	2.6
	(iv)	1.8	6.0
	(v)	17.4	14.9
	(vi)	9.8	17.8

with an aid and prompt to their creative marketing thinking. It was used to assist strategic planning by evaluating the likely effectiveness of different forms of marketing activity. It gave an indication of the possible effects of competitive action. It highlighted the advantages and disadvantages of various retail formats from a consumer standpoint. It was used to help make tactical decisions on advertising and promotions. The late 1970s and early 1980s were a period of great change for the Co-operative movement which was in a transitional phase of re-structuring its business by closing down small, uneconomic shops and developing larger hypermarkets and superstores. The Shop Choice Model played a part in guiding these very considerable changes.

(b) Behaviour-orientated models

In contrast with attitude-orientated models, behaviour-orientated models seek to monitor actual behaviourally-linked reactions to test situations in order to apply these behavioural findings in wider contexts.

Because of the more robust nature of the data input (i.e. actual or intended behaviour readings) such models are used more in the area of prediction (e.g. new product launches) than in the area of explanation, reversing the situation described above for attitude-orientated models. (Ref. 34 develops this theme in relation to a range of widely used models.) These models, however, frequently play a strong role in explanation too. Two examples are described in detail from different fields below:

(a) Simulated Test Market models
(b) Pricing research using conjoint analysis

Simulated Test Market models

Actual test marketing of new products can pose problems of cost, confidentiality and accuracy (though a number of existing methodologies aim to minimize these, for example, The RBL Mini Test Market).

Simulated Test Market models are used as an alternative to actual test markets, providing a quicker and cheaper method of examining likely new product performance, with some concomitant loss in 'realism' of a test market situation.

Since such a methodology is a 'laboratory' version of a real-life test market, certain crucial components of the test must be made as realistic as possible. Robinson[35] effectively divides such elements into three:

(a) *Product-related attributes* (where the product formulation/specification, packaging and price should be close to, or identical with, the final product).
(b) *Market-related attributes* (where advertising, promotional elements, the media mix and sampling opportunity should be as close to reality as is feasible).
(c) *Environment-related attributes* (i.e. the marketing mix into which the line is to be introduced should attempt to reflect reality in terms of competitive brand positioning on all the above points, together with realistic representation of buyers' own attitudes and values).

The emphasis on this wide range of elements differs between models, with some models highlighting the importance of certain elements to the near-exclusion of others – one key example being given below in the distinction between 'full' and 'partial' models.

Inputs to the final model produced vary, but are likely to take the form of two separate strands, each providing an independent 'model' in their own right of ultimate market share estimation.

(a) *Brand preference*; brand rating data are collected for the new brand and compared with similar measures obtained for existing brands on the market, usually restricting comparison to each individual's own 'evoked set' of brands. This frequently involves a 'constant sum' competitive preference ('chip game') approach. The rating scale, however applied, can be used to project share for the brand by comparison with scores achieved by existing brands.
(b) *Trial/repeat purchase*; here, specific elements of behaviour are monitored during the test, relating to the existing and test brands.

   These behavioural elements relate to two key factors in determining any brand's ultimate share:
(i) Initial trial rate (the % actually trying the brand);
(ii) Repeat purchase (the degree to which those trying it decide to repurchase). The former is dependent upon a number of factors in addition to the appeal of the concept itself – price, advertising support, in-store support, distribution, competitor activity, etc.

The latter is concerned with the proportion repurchasing and the depth of re-purchasing (how many, how often).

The brand shares projected by use of the second strand of the total model (based on trial/repeat purchase) are then compared with those projected by the earlier 'Brand Preference' Model, and a final share projection for the new brand is made on the basis of these two independent forecasts. (One version of STM also has a *third* predictive element based on a Price Trade-Off Model – see below.)

Most Simulated Test Market models aim to provide an overall *market share* prediction based upon measurements which allow estimates of these or equivalent variables. Some versions can be used to predict market *volume* in cases where share is not a meaningful concept (e.g. in new or ill-defined markets).

The methodology adopted for achieving such estimates varies substantially from model to model in terms of the weight given to each element and adjustment factors applied, but there is one useful division relating to this genre:

'*Full*' *Test Market Simulation models* – These typically involve hall tests where the new product is set out in a supermarket-type display in the context of competitor brands. Individuals (pre-recruited on product usage criteria, demographics, etc.) are asked questions about brand awareness and preferences, and then exposed to brand advertising and asked to make purchases using 'seed' money or vouchers supplied. Those choosing the new product (and, in some cases, some or all of the remainder of the sample as well) are given the product to try at home.

Follow-up call(s) monitor the degree of liking for the product following actual trial in-home, interest in repurchasing it, etc.

'*Partial*' *Test Market Simulation models* – These models dispense with the simulated point-of-purchase element and simply establish the degree of interest in the concept via the showing of advertising, support material, product descriptions, etc., that would appear with the product on-shelf, to the respondent.

Interest levels in purchase are established and those respondents showing an appropriate degree of interest are provided with samples to try in-home. Subsequent visits again establish the degree of liking post-trial, etc.

The two alternative data collection methods can be seen to differ significantly mainly in the earlier stage of initial exposure which provides the 'Trial Purchase' reading in the subsequent model created. The 'Full' Test Market Simulation version provides a direct 'shopping' comparison with competition, while the 'Partial' version relies on the respondent's own assessment of the 'current' market situation at the point at which she 'decides' her level of interest in the new product.

Each approach has its own benefits and drawbacks, but both are well validated as methodologies in the literature (see ref. 36 for a more general review, and ref. 37 for a discussion of STM Models in particular).

The mathematics necessary to construct a brand share or volume from the various components collected is necessarily complex, and differ depending upon the model chosen (*ASSESSOR*, *SENSOR*, *BASES*, etc). However, the differences between models stem largely from:

(a) The list of individual components that are included in providing an estimate of the ultimate market share.
(b) The weight given to these components (e.g. downweighting for over-claiming, and other adjustments justified on the basis of past validation exercises).

Such differences lead to a range of alternative statistical formulae whose parameters and weights differ from model to model.

A wide range of alternative marketing scenarios can also be examined via changes in the parameter values (e.g. levels of distribution, awareness, etc.).

The parameters and weights of the models themselves can usually be justified as appropriate on the basis of market-place validation of previous use of the technique. Most models of this type claim some degree of such validation, the *ASSESSOR* Model in particular having a large amount of historical data available. (See, for example, refs. 38, 39.)

A detailed description of the principles and methodologies involved in the often very sophisticated STM approaches is beyond the scope of this chapter. For a useful discussion of the more frequently used models, see refs. 40 (ASSESSOR), 41 (LTM), 42 (COMP – a model which encompasses both STM techniques and some of the more attitudinal measures discussed earlier) and 43 (SENSOR). See ref. 35 for a useful if technical overview.

Pricing research models
Pricing research is a second, completely independent area in which behaviour-orientated models are applied.

Here again, the early pricing research techniques relied solely on behavioural measures (choice of different brands at different prices). However, the 1970s and early 1980s have seen increasing awareness of the complexity of the decision process under study and additional attitudinal elements have often been added, e.g. consumer attitudes to the purchase decision, image batteries, use context, etc. (For a review of pricing techniques in a wider context see ref. 44). *All* pricing research is nevertheless fundamentally behaviour-orientated modelling in so far as the key variables recorded are consumer responses to alternative brand/price combinations, in terms of intention to buy at that price level/combination.

The technique described below as an example makes substantial use of modelling, in contrast with a number of other pricing techniques which, though still models in their own right, are much more limited in the number of market price structures they can examine or model.

Pricing research is also discussed in chapter 15, so is referred to only briefly here.

'*Trade-off pricing models* – In more traditional pricing models the data collected, in the form of respondent choices between brands/sizes/varieties at given prices, can be reproduced as models *only* of market situations to which those actual price combinations appertain. That is, for a new product or size launch, or for an investigation into the effect of a price increase or decrease for existing lines, the model created can generally only reflect the price structure actually facing the respondent at the time of fieldwork and for which choices were recorded. With these traditional approaches, the model consists solely of perhaps five or ten alternative prices for the client brand at a single price structure for competitors, or possibly with one or two variations in competitor prices.

The Trade-Off methodology, while not without its critics, supplies a great deal more information than such models by allowing the examination of a large range of alternative market price situations and the calculation of price elasticities.

Briefly, it requires the respondent to choose a brand at a range of price combinations selected such that a complete hierarchy of all possible brand/price alternatives, for all brands present/prices tested, is obtained. Using conjoint analysis, that hierarchy can be 'solved' and replaced with a series of values associated with each brand and each price level, for each respondent. (Note that the analysis works on the basis of *individual* members of the sample rather than aggregating across all members.)

The nature of the value calculated for each element has one simple characteristic: that when the values of each individual price and individual brand are added together, the order created replicates the original order in which that specific respondent placed the options (i.e. the individual hierarchy). The programme itself simply searches for a solution (i.e. a set of values) which most nearly replicates that hierarchy.

Results for *any* specific price combination (simulations) are now calculable. Other simulations are also possible – removal of a given line, for example, to simulate restricted distribution in a particular retail chain, or removal of a particular size or variety to identify the degree of trade lost out of a brand as against conversion to another size or variety.

The above is merely an outline of the approach, with many variations and considerable sophistication available. Micro computers have, for example, been successfully used for data collection here as in other fields of modelling (see, for example ref. 45). However, in all cases the basic principle remains the same.

Thus the modelling element in Trade-Off Pricing Models is a particularly powerful tool, but it should be noted that the technique itself is merely a (very powerful) extension of the modelling capability of all pricing models rather than an entirely new approach to pricing research. In common with other pricing techniques, 'Trade-Off' relates a behavioural measure (choice, intention or likelihood of purchase, dependent upon technique used) in a test situation to likely occurrences in the real world.

2. *Historically based models*

Historically based models form a completely separate genre, where data are collated from a number of sources. Such data are likely to have been originally collected as *monitoring* information (consumer panel data, industry data, retail audits, etc.), and are only brought together to build a 'macro-model' of the way a specific market (however defined) operates *after* the data has been collected.

Here, as in the behaviour-orientated *ad hoc* models, the emphasis is on *prediction* rather than *explanation*, though Causal Models (to be discussed) by their nature must explain relationships prior to prediction. (For a not overly technical review see ref. 46).

Such models are 'macro-models' in two senses.

(a) The data sources are completely independent of one another and model use is based on aggregates rather than individual readings.
(b) Of necessity, the data deals with *total* markets – simply because it is multi-source, information is often likely to be comparable only at the broadest level – e.g. that of total national market. In some instances (e.g. test market monitoring) data can be compared and correlated within, for example, geographic region, but even here elements of non-comparability (different definition of regions for example) and problems associated with sample size often militate against successful modelling and mean that output must be interpreted with care.

Despite the fact that macro-models must be wide in scope they can be of any degree of detail or sophistication. Thus while one is often constrained to looking at the total market share nationally, for example, this can be examined in relation to one independent variable alone (e.g: relative price v. share) or a wide range of variables, dependent upon the information available and the degree of sophistication of the model.

Equally, the data on share trend alone can be subjected to simple techniques for establishing historical patterns or extremely complex computer-based ones.

This brings us to the central distinction to be made within the range of macro-models available to the market researcher: that of Time Series models v. Causal models. In both cases we are examining historical data on a macro level, to establish patterns and thus to be able to forecast future values.

Time Series forecasting – Within such models we are relying on movements in the variable under study (e.g. share) *alone* to predict what will occur in the future.

Causal models – Here, by contrast, we are seeking to *explain* how a given value of the dependent variable (share) occurs by reference to a number of independent variables (price relative, adspend, distribution, etc.) in order to be able to forecast future values.

Historically, this has been the single overriding distinction between model types (i.e. time series v. causal), though there are certain increasingly applied advanced techniques of macro-modelling which bridge the divide (Transfer Function models).

(a) *Time Series models*
Conceptually, Time Series models are simpler to understand and easier to interpret.

If we chart the share of a given brand and can visually observe certain seasonal variations (e.g. peaks in summer), and an underlying upward trend, we can use such elements to make an approximate estimate of the next *x* points on the Chart before they occur. Nothing about the series is being explained directly (though assumptions are being made about the relationship of the summer months with share, and the stability of the long-term trend), yet we are able to 'forecast' the ensuing periods with some degree of accuracy.

That is, the model is 'self-enclosed': if we believe that the historical share series adequately reflects the brand's *actual* past performance, the prediction we make based on that trend is then as good as our forecasting methods can make it. Different methods of calculating the forecast shares are available and the choice between them depends largely on the skill of the forecaster in being able to identify the appropriate model based on the way the trend series has behaved historically.

Briefly, there are two basic forms of Time Series forecasting.

Smoothing – Here nothing is assumed about seasonality or any other individual influences on historical share; the aim of the exercise is to 'smooth' the curve in a way which will supply an 'average' forecast of future values. This can be achieved by either:
(i) simple averaging of the data. Applying a moving annual average, for example, will 'smooth' out the seasonal factors, while alternative and additional moving averages will further 'smooth' the data. This method gives each value in the series the *same* weight: no one value is deemed to be 'more important' than another.
(ii) alternatively, it is possible to assume that the most recent values are the more important and should be given a higher weight than those, say, five years ago.

The usual method of weighting is one which exponentially declines as values recede into the past. This method is therefore known generally as 'exponential smoothing'.

Decomposition – This alternative approach avoids the relatively naive assumption that patterns in the data (which may be important in the ultimate derivation of forecast values) can be smoothed away, and instead investigates the presence of:

a *seasonal* pattern
a *cyclical* pattern
an underlying *trend*

within the single time series (e.g. share) under study.

Standard statistical methods exist for establishing each of these (and other) factors which can not be reviewed here. They vary in sophistication from the classical decomposition approach to the Census II methodology and Box-Jenkins applications.

(b) *Causal models*

As this name suggests, there is an alternative battery of techniques available which seek to relate a given time series (e.g. share) to independent factors which might influence that series.

Thus, instead of making the assumption that 'history repeats itself', this range of techniques seeks to *explain* how the historical values occurred in relation to these independent measures (e.g. price relative, adspend, etc.) and to allow forward projection on the basis of information known about the independent variables (e.g. likely pricing policy, advertising budget, etc.).

The basic concept behind such models is that of *regression*. Regression simply provides a measure of the degree to which one variable (the dependent variable) moves in a pattern which is related to movement in other, independent, variables – i.e. the degree to which the dependent variable is correlated with the others (e.g. how far share, for example, is correlated with relative price.

Various techniques exist which provide measures of correlation between two or more variables.

Relationships may exist between the dependent variable (share) and one other variable only. In such a case, share would be 'explainable' by movements in this one other variable. Here *simple* regression between the two series would create a working model.

More realistically, however, share tends to be determined by a wide range of variables such that *multiple* regression, inputting a range of independent variables, is required.

The relationships that do exist are not always easy to identify, and here again a wide range of techniques are available to the forecaster in his search to 'explain' movements in the dependent variable. 'Econometric models' (despite the fact that the term is sometimes used to signify *any* multiple regression-based model) are generally acknowledged to be models where a *number* of multiple regression equations, using some common variables, require 'balancing' simultaneously. That is, the variables used are interdependent.

Those wishing to make serious study of the area of forecasting are recommended to read the comprehensive account of the field to be found in ref. 46.

Conclusions

A number of general conclusions may be drawn:

(a) The construction and building of a model is a vitally important and beneficial stage. At its best it is a collaborative and interactive process between marketeers and researchers. The process of building the model makes explicit the implicit reasoning and mental models of the participants and provides a common basis for decision making.

(b) Models can act as a catalyst to creative marketing thinking and can generate hypotheses on the workings of the market under consideration.

(c) The limitations of a model are a function of its design. No individual model is likely to give a globally satisfactory account of a complex process such as decision making, and the researcher needs to decide at the outset the parameters of the model bearing in mind the marketing question to be explored.

(d) It has been conclusively demonstrated that most decision processes can be modelled, whether they be related to specific products or to services. Modelling thus offers a valuable aid to both strategic planning and tactical development for a wide range of organizations.

The emphasis within the modelling areas as a whole is changing in line with the pressure on the research industry as a whole. There is a greater requirement for research specifically applicable to identified problems at as low a cost as possible. Modelling has, as a result, moved from providing 'global' pictures of markets and presenting grand theories produced to meet a 'general' objective of greater market understanding, to a position where it provides *specific* answers in a more comprehensive way than non-modelling approaches can achieve. This is especially true in the area of pricing research, but it is increasingly true in areas such as micro-behavioural modelling, where the model produced can be regarded as providing an extra dimension to an existing need for market data. STM models, similarly, are designed to meet a very specific need – the desire to know how a particular new product will fare. Given the failure rate of new products this is a very important aid to successful marketing activity. Equally, macro-modelling using existing historical data is a means whereby data collected (and paid for) previously can be made to 'work harder' for the company.

The trend is therefore towards a greater focus on specific objectives and decisions and a more critical appraisal of the ways in which modelling can help. New applications are likely to be those which can truly justify themselves on a 'value-for-money' basis, a key requirement of research in the eighties.

Chapter 21

Corporate image research

ROBERT M. WORCESTER

Corporate research encompasses all aspects of research conducted among publics of importance to the corporation, company or organization in their direct role other than as customers. Consumers are obviously the primary target of marketing research, but there are many other publics of importance to the corporation. Industrial customers, while not included as such in this handbook, are of prime importance to a company selling industrial products. The financial community, including shareholders, are another important audience; financial relations research is covered in the next chapter.

There are other publics of importance as well. Employees are perhaps the most important, but the general public are becoming increasingly influential as 'consumerists' (as opposed to consumers) and are for this reason a vital audience to be researched. Opinion leaders, senior civil servants, the press, students, people living around manufacturing plants, suppliers, and trade union officials: all impinge on corporate actions to a greater or lesser degree. In the complex world in which we live, it is likely that a prudent senior manager will demand to know as much as he can about the attitudes and behaviour of those he wishes to influence and so corporate research will be demanded. It is for this reason, and because it is likely that (while corporate research is perhaps out of the mainstream of the average market research manager's usual activity) the company's market research manager is the one to whom public relations will turn for a study amongst the general public and personnel will turn for assistance on an employee attitude study, as will others for research into their areas of interest, that the research function should be involved.

In succeeding sections this chapter defines and puts into perspective the role of corporate image research and discusses research among a number of the other publics of importance.

Over the last four decades, a great deal of research has been carried out into the images of companies, institutions, products and brands. It may be said that generally there are four major categories of image influences. There is *the image of the product class* as a whole, *the image of the brand* as opposed to other brands within the product class, *the image of users* of the brand, and *the corporate image* of the company that stands behind the brand.[1] Of course, there are other influences at work on image as well, such as the time and place that the product or service might be used.

In some industries and in some countries the image of the country of ownership of the company can be important. In Britain, for instance, there is no difference in favourability between British-based oil companies and oil companies known to be American-owned. Yet a food company thought to be British is more favourably regarded than the same company by those who believe it to be American.

Research has shown that the crucial image influences sometimes occur in one of these dimensions and sometimes in another. This situation varies from product class to product class, brand to brand and company to company. Substantial variance also occurs during the life cycle of a product of some manufacturers; witness the prominance given the corporate identity of Procter and Gamble during the first eighteen months of their new product introductions in America.

The product class image is that collection of image attributes shared by all the brands of a particular product class, such as motor vehicles, cigarettes, textiles or a certain sort of machine tool. Every class of product exists for a reason, meets certain needs and desires, plays a certain role in the lives of its users, is associated with certain kinds of people and competes directly or indirectly with other product classes in various ways, most often for disposable income, increasingly frequently for leisure time.

Brand images are the unique characteristics of a brand that distinguish it from others. These include how, and how well, the brand is seen as fulfilling the functions of the product class, its appearance and style, package, price, and the degree to which it is believed to be economical and of good value.

Alan Brien's comment in Punch some years ago related brand images to the third category of image, the brand user image. He said:

> When I was a boy, men would talk about their cigarettes as they now talk about their cars. Brand loyalty was as strong as class loyalty and the two were often linked. Park Drive, de Reszke, Black Cat, Balkan Sobranie, Passing Clouds — they were clues in a detective story. It was possible to deduce the sex, the income, the accent, even the favourite fantasies of the last person to dump a fag in your ashtray just by reading off its name. For a gent to be discovered smoking Woodbines was as suspicious as a tramp lighting up a fresh cigar.[2]

Especially when there are few clear and demonstrable functional differences among brands, brand user images can be crucial to a brand's success.

The fourth source of image is that of the corporation or other institution that stands behind the product or service. This includes the company's general familiarity and favourability and many specific corporate image attributes that can be categorized as relating to product reputation, customer relations, employer role, ethical reputation, and others.

In 1967, David Lowe-Watson set out a theory of advertising based on the concept of a set of relationships between the buyer, the 'personality' of the brand, and the 'personality' of the seller, or company.[3] This theory, he suggested, is more useful than standard advertising theories because it can satisfactorily account for a number of discrepancies between existing theory and empirical observations.

Lowe-Watson provided a model that distinguished three key factors involved in effective advertising: a customer's image of the company, his image of the product, and his perception of the advertising. He said that the company image is related to advertising effectiveness and this underscores the concept of 'total communication' which includes the coordination of policy in every part of the company's communications activity, advertising, sales promotion, packaging, product planning, public relations, and corporate identification. He concluded that the advertiser who can build up a strong and favourable relationship with his customers will establish a fund of goodwill from which he can derive future benefits. These benefits include not only a greater readiness on the part of the customer to pay attention to his advertising, and a predisposition to put a favourable interpretation on the message received but also a favourable attitude toward the product itself and expectation of satisfactory product performance and a greater willingness to try a new product.

The late Leo Burnett was quoted as saying 'We feel that proliferation of brands and mergers have brought on a growing need for corporate advertising. No brand can be given the support it needs and corporate identity is becoming more important as a seal of approval';[4] and in speaking about industrial purchasing, William Paterson of Tube Investments said 'The reputation of the company is an important factor and it is in this area that subjective decisions tend to be made'.[5]

Definition of corporate image

What is a corporate image? Corporate image may be defined as 'the net result of the interaction of all experiences, impressions, beliefs, feelings and knowledge people have about a company'. The sources of image are extensive. These include the product, its packaging, both product and corporate advertising, distribution, and promotion patterns. Also, all the other manifestations of its communications, such as its letterhead, brochures, public relations, the impressions left by the company's employees and salesmen, its factories, offices, lorries and activities of the industry in which the company operates, frequently have important effects on the corporate image. Opinions of other people and messages from competing companies also play an important role in forming a person's image of a company.

The role of the corporate image

A strong corporate image influences the predisposition to buy a company's products, speak favourably of it, believe its statements, apply for a job with it, and the like. It is important for industrial goods companies with listed shares. It is important to companies seeking highly technical staff in a tight staff availability situation. It is important to a consumer goods company whose very life is dependent on successful new product introductions. Just how important it is to a consumer goods company is illustrated by recent findings that show that a sizable proportion of the British public are less than enthusiastic about any new product, and yet still show faith and trust in companies they feel they know well – in spite of a dip in confidence over the past decade that 'A company that has a good reputation would not sell poor products' (Fig. 21.1).

The importance of a good reputation (Great Britain)

	Strongly/tend to agree				
	1969 (%)	1971 (%)	1975 (%)	1982 (%)	1985 (%)
A company that has a good reputation would not sell poor products	75	68	65	65	70
Old-established companies make the best products	48	52	51	51	55
I never buy products made by a company I have not heard of	37	33	33	39	39
New brands on the market are usually an improvement over old-established brand	37	33	37	25	31

Fig. 21.1. Source: MORI Cooperative Corporate Image Study.

And how important a company's reputation is to a housewife's propensity to try new products is shown by research which found women 14% more likely to try a new product from 'Heinz' than from 'a large (unspecified) food company'.

The context of corporate reputations

The detailed image profile of a company or organization as seen by external publics can best be understood within the perspective of overall attitudes towards business; attitudes towards specific industries, not only the industry in which the client is involved but other industries as well; and then towards the client company versus its competitors and in the context of many companies, some better known and some less well known. Images cannot be measured in a vacuum. All images are relative and must be comparative.

That favourability increases with familiarity is an important finding indeed to a company with a low level of public awareness, Companies are most highly regarded by those that know them best. The scatter graph (Fig. 21.2) shows the correlation between familiarity (on the horizontal axis) and favourability (on the vertical axis) and also illustrates clearly how the car companies in Britain are going through a particularly bad patch. The car companies as a group are well below the 'line of best fit' which is the graphic representation of the general rule that 'familiarity breeds favourability, not contempt'.

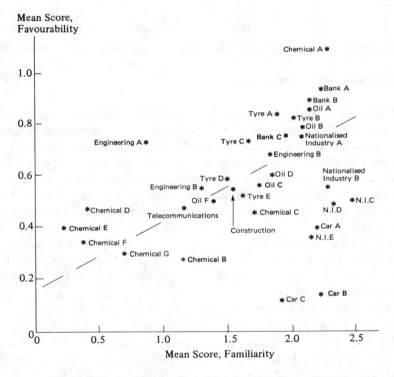

Fig. 21.2 Company familiarity and favourability. *Source*: MORI.

This correlation is shown in another way in Fig. 21.3, which shows that across 32 companies studied in 1983 there is an almost straight-line relationship between how *well* a company is known and how *favourably* it is regarded.

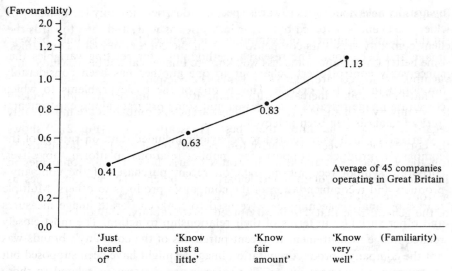

Fig. 21.3 Companies are *usually* highly regarded by those who know them best. Source: MORI

The ingredients of corporate image

What goes to make up a good corporate image? When the British public were asked 'Which two or three things do you consider most important to know about a company in order to judge its reputation?' over a third (34%) mentioned quality of products and services provided by the company. One in five (21%) said customer services industrial relations, 10% honesty and integrety of the company, 10% fair and competitive prices, 13% said such things as good/sound management and 14% mentioned efficiency and 17% profitability.

For over a decade the interrelationship between familiarity and favourability has been clear. This has led to a concept of the 'Three generations of corporate advertising: (1) here's who we are, (2) here's what we can do for you and (3) here's what we think'. Thus increased awareness is the first step on the road to increased favourability, all things being equal.

Extending the understanding to how companies can increase favourability, detailed measures were taken of the source of knowledge for 12 major companies in Britain. If the average favourability is equal to 100%, then those people who are aware of having seen their ads gives a 'lift' of 1% over the average, or 101% favourability. Those people who have heard or read about them in the news are 7% more favourable to them on average, those people who are conscious of often seeing their name on buildings and lorries reached to 108%. As might be expected, those people who have used their products and services got a 'lift' of 16%. But the importance of the employee as goodwill ambassador is measured by the fact that to actually know someone who works at the company on average gives a favourability 'lift' of 22%.

Image and behaviour

In this chapter a number of examples are introduced to suggest links between image and behaviour. The research methodology for relating variables that conceivably control overt behaviour to one another has been considerably developed in the last decade. This is one of the basic problems to which corporate image research is addressed and some progress along experimental lines of analysis has been achieved.

Variables which were related to behaviour included data on ratings of the company's products, support for public relations platform objectives, corporate symbol recognition, data on recent purchases of the company's products and recommendation of the company's products to others. Multiple regression analysis techniques were used to rank corporate image measures and other variables in terms of their relationship to action. The most closely related image measurement to recent purchases of the company's brands was not the company's product reputation image as might have been supposed but the customer treatment image. The same image dimensions related to those who had recommended the company's products. On the other hand, willingness to listen to a company spokesman on an issue was most closely associated with having a favourable attitude towards big business.

The actions people take with respect to a company depend on far more than whether or not they like or dislike the company. Yet, complex and subconscious as a person's feelings and beliefs about a company may be, they can often be synthesized into ranked data that may be examined statistically. Images differ from company to company in important ways. While they are undoubtedly rooted in general value systems, each company has its own strengths and weaknesses among various segments of the population. With objectively measured knowledge of corporate strengths and weaknesses, companies can organize their efforts in appropriate directions, capitalizing on their strengths and, where possible, identifying and taking steps to correct their weaknesses.

One of the most useful findings from a study of corporate image is where the facts of the situation contradict the image. One large, very well known and well respected British company had a price earnings ratio far below where its management believed it ought to be. In fact, it is a well diversified and reasonably profitable company. Yet nine out of ten AB British men think of it as selling only one product and that product is traditionally a low profit item. Thus, the company has a blueprint for communications action based on objective knowledge of the facts, *as seen through the eyes of the shareholding public.*

Measuring the effectiveness of corporate advertising

A number of companies augment their product advertising with corporate campaigns designed to benefit the company as a whole. In doing so they are attempting to do considerably more than just sell their products (though a laudable ambition in, and of, itself). When one is trying to build a corporate reputation the results are sometimes subtle and often have a wide effect.

For example, in 1975 Woolworth launched the 'That's the wonder of Woolworth' campaign, principally on television. One per cent of the general public attributed 'That's the wonder of...' to Woolworth before the campaign broke, seven months later the figure had rocketed to 64%. In conjunction with this, awareness of the range of goods stocked increased and respondents were visiting Woolworth stores more frequently.

Research in another case showed television to be a very powerful medium for putting across corporate communications. In a campaign for Philips in 1973–4–5, which centred around the slogan 'Simply years ahead', television and the press were used equally during the first year of advertising, but by the last of the three annual campaigns this had been changed to 100% television. Research showed that television was much more forceful in getting across the message.

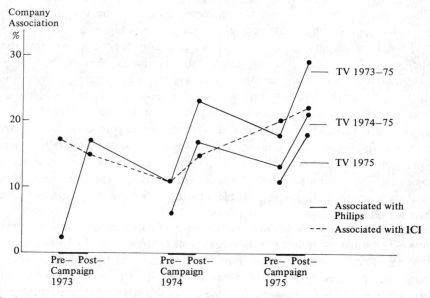

Fig. 21.4 Awareness of 'Simply Years Ahead' 1973–1975. Weight of TV Campaign Exposure. Source: MORI

Figure 21.4 shows how Phillips, over a period of time, built up and sustained its slogan awareness. At the same time it also demonstrated the value of ICI's image building over the years. Although 'Simply years ahead' is unconnected with ICI, 17% of the respondents initially associated the slogan with ICI. It took considerable effort to overtake ICI as the 'natural' recipient of a slogan awareness such as Philips'. Also vividly shown is the effect of repeated exposure on television versus the effect of national press advertising in the first two years of the campaign.

Several years ago Trust Houses Forte built a campaign around the slogan 'The biggest smile in Europe', which was designed to show THF as a large, British-based company offering good service in several different fields. The success of this campaign could be seen from the results of a pre-post corporate image survey' in the Thames Television area which also showed how their reputation had increased, particularly as an employer and in the quality of their management. [6]

ICI has for many years believed in developing and maintaining a good corporate image. Its 'Pathfinders' campaign on television together with press followed years of steady effort in press advertising, a well developed public relations effort, and generally good corporate activities in providing good products, having low-key product advertising (e.g. the Dulux dog), treating its employees well and generally behaving in many ways as a good corporate citizen. The success of its policies is tracked regularly by a series of studies among publics of importance to the company, but the 'flagship' of their research program is a regular measure of the general public's image of ICI. One analysis of interest examined in 1976 was the effect on the public of living in an 'ICI area', defined as areas in which ICI has a physical presence such as a manufacturing plant or chemical works. This analysis showed that there is a substantial and measurable difference in attitudes to ICI between those who live in 'ICI Areas' and those who don't. Figure 21.5 illustrates a few of these differences.

Response	ICI areas–non-ICI areas %
Say they 'know' ICI well	+8
'Favourable' towards ICI	+6
Think ICI shows an interest in people as well as profits	+6
Think ICI have excellent benefits for employees	+12
Think ICI is fair in the wages they pay	+19
Think ICI have good relations in communities where they operate	+7
Think ICI makes too big a profit	−9

Fig. 21.5 Source: MORI.

The corporate 'publics'

Any company has a number of masters who must be served. The prime public of concern to every manager is the customer. Certainly without the customer the company must fail; but there are a number of other groups without which the company could not live, much less prosper, and chief among these are the company's employees. Yet there must be literally thousands of consumer research studies conducted each year for every study conducted amongst employees, or even, if the truth be known, amongst *all* of the other corporate 'publics' put together. The company 'publics' generally include:

(a) consumers;
(b) shareholders;
(c) the 'City';
(d) opinion leaders;
   (i)   parliamentarians;
   (ii)   senior civil servants;
   (iii) local government officials;
   (iv)   trade union officials;
   (v)   press;
(e) potential employees;

(f) community;
(g) suppliers;
(h) the 'trade';
(i) employees
   (i)   management;
   (ii)   sales force;
   (iii) administrative staff;
   (iv)   scientists and engineers;
   (v)   production workers.

Consumers

Much that has been said above relates to work with consumers, yet so often, as Lowe-Watson has pointed out, the relationship the consumer feels with a company is overlooked or ignored[3].

There is considerable variability in the image influences that determine the brand commitment of the consumer. Each product field differs in the way in which brands are discerned and in the criteria that consumers use to compare brands. Conducting corporate image research to determine the effect of an image on a brand, the researcher seeks to determine the image of the company that stands behind the brand as differentiated from the companies that provide other brands.

As Pilditch put it in his excellent book, 'Communication by Design',

The pertinent question is not when to adopt the brand policy, but how to see this in corporate terms. In the soap business, the archetypal product or brand structure, an important change is taking place.

Marketing men have thought in the past that the brand name was the important thing to get across. They felt that the company making the brand was unimportant, and didn't help sell the product. Who cares who makes Tide as long as Tide has what the shoppers want?

This view is now less strongly held. In front of the author now is a bottle of Square Deal Quix. Which is the brand name? In a prominent place it states: 'A Lever Product – guaranteed'. Below it is written: 'Lever quality and performance guaranteed or your money back'...

A corporation needs to become well known in the interests of attracting shareholders and employees, and developing good relations generally. Three points emerge. First, the relationship between brand and corporate identity is being reassessed. Second, the requirements of a corporate identity are different from those of a brand. This difference must be understood and preserved, and the problem of relating the two will then be much easier to solve. Third, relationships must vary to suit the situation, particularly the comparative strength of brand name to corporate name, the ubiquity of the corporate name, and the appropriateness of the product to the corporate identity.[7]

Another use is in product compatibility research. This type of study determines whether a new product is compatible with the company's existing image. Where it is not, different brand names are often used so that these names will *not* be identified with the company. Where it is, the company can use the corporate name to help sell the product. Research can help determine the compatibility of prospective new products with established brand and corporate names.

Corporate image research may also be used to uncover new products people think are compatible with an established corporate name which may not be those that management expects. Consumers judge product compatibility from a personal point of view that may differ drastically from that of the manufacturer. The manufacturer may reason that he should keep within his special areas of manufacturing competence. Consumers may see this in a different light entirely.

Shareholders and the 'City'

These groups are receiving increasing attention from companies in recent years. While consumer research techniques in the main apply, there are special problems one may encounter in researching these publics. The next chapter is devoted to financial relations research.

Opinion leaders

Much misleading work has been done in the name of opinion leader research in the past. Many studies of AB men have purported to represent opinion leaders' opinions. Yet for all the work that has been done in this area, none has shown that there is any constant segment of the public that can truly be termed 'opinion leaders'. Other studies have been conducted with parliamentarians, the press, with business executives, and even with clergy, in the belief that they are in a position to mould public opinion: *so they are* but what is most often forgotten is that this ability to mould public opinion varies enormously, depending on the subject. The big businessman, for instance, may wield enormous influence among his contacts when he recommends an industrial product, or a share to buy; he may also influence the son of a friend seeking career advice; but it is unlikely his word on washing powders or washing machines, or even for whom to vote, would swing much weight, for the thing that is often overlooked in this sort of study is the selective perceptions of those led, and selective indeed they are.

Precise sample selection and careful attention to ensure full and comprehensive interviews (nearly always personal if to be most useful) is of prime importance. A key is the thought that the most valuable image study, probably by a factor of ten, is the second one, after the facts have been obtained from a first study and action has been taken based on the facts uncovered. It is necessary to structure the study so it may be replicated a year or two hence. This requires a sample construction that will enable comparisons to be made and more attention to sampling than 'ten of those and twenty of those'.

Potential employees

Potential employees generally fall into three categories: managers, staff and workers. In each category there are a number of factors that affect the two elements of successful recruitment, attracting appropriate applicants and convincing the desired applicants to 'sign up'. Factors potential employees consider important to know about a company, media they value and remuneration expectations may be researched. Hundreds of thousands of pounds are spent each year on recruitment activities, yet the amount of research to improve the effectiveness of recruiting is practically nil.

Community studies

Consumers, employees, potential employees, opinion leaders, a prime source of shareholders, suppliers, and others gather in the community in which the company is located. Some companies have looked at residents of these local areas as a separate audience to be researched. Especially interesting to factory managers and other executives concerned with community relations are social issues and the concept of corporate citizenship. Do the townspeople regard the company's offices and factories as assets or liabilities? Is the company blamed for pollution? Is the company regarded as a good place to work? If not, why not? These and many other areas of general interest become especially relevant in communities in which the company is a major force.

Suppliers

Another audience of importance often overlooked is the company's suppliers. A few companies have realized that if they can help their suppliers serve them more economically and effectively, the company will itself reap rewards in lower prices, better delivery and service, and generally more effective purchasing.

The 'Trade'

Other important, but also often overlooked, links in the chain are the company's distributors, dealers, or agents. These are, to many companies, the only contact with consumers, and yet often go unresearched. Within the trade, corporate image – dealer relations, delivery practices, payment policies and the like – are very important and sometimes the key to success or failure. This is a group usually easily, if not inexpensively, researched. As in any 'image' study, it is most valuable done periodically, so that the effect of changes that occur can be reliably measured over time.

Employees

And finally, employees. How much 'upward communication' is there? Management attention is overwhelmingly devoted to telling employees what to do and rarely listens to what employees, at all levels, think about the company and how it can be made more effective. As a letter to the Editor of the Financial Times [8] put it,

> However much it spends on the introduction of modern management techniques and up-to-date equipment and machinery, a company still depends for its success in the end on recruiting and holding sufficient staff of the right calibre at all levels from the boardroom to the shop floor. In these days, this can be a difficult enough process without the added drawback of a poor employer image. Anyone who has had anything to do with the operation of confidential reply or box number services must be able to compile a list of firms to which candidates frequently request their applications should not be forwarded. In the closer knit professional groups, a whisper on the grapevine can mean death to successful recruitment. How many companies even take the trouble to find out what their employees think about them – as employers? The attitude survey technique is still too little used. Perhaps some employers prefer not to know just how bad their image is. Sometimes, no doubt, the bad employer's image is a deserved one in which case the remedy lies elsewhere than in improved communications; but employers who take more trouble in talking (by word of mouth or in print) to their employees in a language they can understand, who take pains not to create mystery where none exists, will find the rewards in terms of improved recruitment and reduced staff turnover are well worth the trust and effort.

Still too few companies have made employee attitude measurements a regular aspect of their research program.

How to do it

Corporate images don't exist in a vacuum; they are affected by the company's activities, its industry's image and by information from competing companies. All images are comparative; therefore, wherever possible, and this means in most studies of corporate 'publics', one must study a company's image in the context of other companies. This, in the case of image studies of 'publics' outside the company itself, leads to the development of cooperative studies and the dual advantage of the reduction in the demands made on the public under study and the price to the client.

There are such surveys conducted by a number of market research organizations. These include semi-annual surveys of corporate image amongst the general public and annual corporate image surveys amongst AB men and final-year male undergraduates in universities. Also, technical staff recruitment surveys are undertaken periodically, as are various trade surveys. Employee attitude studies are more difficult in that comparative studies are impossible (except of course over time) without access to data collected from a cross-section of other studies and few agencies have done enough work in this area in the UK to provide a sufficiently broad data base of 'normative' information.

As there are a number of special considerations as to the methodology of internal studies, it may be useful to devote a few paragraphs to how employee attitude studies are carried out.

The goal of an employee attitude survey is to produce an accurate and detailed picture of employee satisfactions as well as their dissatisfactions, their knowledge and understanding of the company and its operations, any 'road blocks' which may be limiting employee productivity, reactions to company communications and the like.

It is important, whenever possible, to have access to previous studies which have developed data on important aspects of employee attitudes and thinking. These accumulated results can serve as norms against which to judge survey results in any given company.

In order to develop the necessary understanding of the specific company's employee relations practices and objectives, to discuss current operating problems and to explore employees' ideas to 'what the survey really should cover', the research agency normally conducts preliminary interviews with members of management and representatives of all groups to be surveyed.

Depending on such factors as the geographical dispersion, levels to be included, the number of employees who can be taken off the job for the survey and the budget available for obtaining and processing data, the procedure may be as follows.

Ideally, survey all employees – a survey based on 100 % coverage takes maximum advantage of the morale-building potential of employee attitude research. It also permits detailed analysis of results department by department or unit and an analysis of the thinking of small groups of employees whose functions or problems may be deemed especially important. If a census is not possible, all employees at a single location, of like job classification, should participate in the survey. If half are sampled, the half that are selected tend to say 'Why pick on me?' and the half that are left out say 'Don't my opinions count?'.

Alternatively, if a representative sample of employees is surveyed, the sample can be so planned that an adequate number of interviews is obtained from both supervisory and non-supervisory employees and that enough interviews are taken in major departments to permit separate analysis of the results for key employee groups.

Some employee surveys have been very satisfactorily carried out by mail. In 1975 a ten-country employee attitude survey was carried out among salesmen, service engineers and managers from a large multinational company. A response rate of 75% overall was achieved while response rates from individual countries ranged from 65% to 91%.

The following list suggests possible questioning areas that might be considered:

(a) How is the company regarded as a place to work?
(b) How do employees regard their supervisors?
(c) What do employees think of the employee benefits provided for them?
(d) How do employees evaluate the various methods of communication used by the company?
(e) What is the attitude toward promotion practices and policies?
(f) How do employees feel about job security?
(g) How do employees appraise working conditions?
(h) What is the extent of employees' knowledge of important economic facts?
(i) What is the appraisal of the management of the company?

In addition to this type of question, the survey should include some questions that give employees the opportunity to say, in their own words, whatever is on their minds.

Also included on the questionnaire are background questions designed to permit analysis of the replies of various groups of employees. Frequently, special tabulations are made by departments, sex, length of service, occupation, location, etc. This detailed type of analysis enables the company to isolate sources of dissatisfaction wherever they exist. Results are reported only for groups of employees, of course, not for individuals.

Conclusion

Corporate research differs from most other forms of market research being carried out here today because it is at the same time both tactical and strategic. It is geared both to finding out gaps between the facts as they are and as people believe them to be – immediately actionable – and to pointing the way for the future.

Corporate research can take many forms among the 'publics' under research. Corporate research can be carried out with all 'publics' of interest to a corporation, all 'publics' having influence over its destiny, including consumers, employees, potential employees, the plant community, parliamentarians, opinion leaders, shareholders, and so on.

The importance of the corporate image is just beginning to be felt here. It will become even more important in the future than it is today. It is the responsibility of research to help management to understand and measure its importance and effect on the future.

Chapter 22

Market research in the financial field

JOHN F. SWIFT and ROGER J. STUBBS *

Financial market research covers two main types of work:

(a) Survey research for *financial institutions* among audiences of relevance to them. This includes surveys among customers, both personal and corporate, and potential customers of banks, building societies, insurance companies, credit card organizations and finance houses.

(b) Survey research among the financial community, on behalf of any organisations. Frequently abbreviated to *'City' research*, this part incorporates studies among stockbrokers, merchant banks, pension funds, insurance companies, investment trusts and others responsible for investing large sums of money, and surveys of the financial media and among private shareholders.

Market research came relatively late to the financial sector. In the first edition of this book, published in 1972, it was stated that 'the financial community made little use of market research until recently'. The following decade has seen increasing use made of research by the financial sector, particularly by the major banks. Insurance companies and building societies were slower off the mark and will probably develop rapidly over the next decade.

Research for financial institutions

The basic techniques of market research which are applied to survey research for financial institutions such as banks and building societies are the same as those which are applied in other fields. Segmentation studies, usage and attitude research, product development research, all using variants on the range of techniques available are all of value to the researcher in this market.

* The section on Research for Financial Institutions is by John Swift, and that on City Research by Roger Stubbs.

There are, however, a number of characteristics of the market which, whilst not unique, do lead to the need for care in the planning, design and interpretation of research studies in this field.

The most evident difference is that the financial industry is a service industry, and a service industry which is dealing with a product which is important yet which many people find difficult to discuss.

> Money, or the lack of it, is something which affects our lives in one way or another nearly every moment of our waking day and, if we are to believe the psychologists and psychiatrists, for a good deal of our nights as well... Because money is so important in our lives it is difficult to pin down... In psychological terms, it can be viewed as a general incentive, as a compensation for feelings of deprivation, as a substitute for lack of love, as a focus within a world of shrinking values — a concrete anchor, and so on. By its nature it is both tangible and, at the same time, completely meaningless.[1]

The service provided will, of course, differ from one sector of the financial field to another. For example, the banks provide a service which is ever present. The large majority of the population hold an account with a bank and for these people, whilst most of their transactions are by cash, the larger part of the value is disbursed and received through the medium of the bank and its instruments: the cheque, the bank giro credit, the standing order and so on. There are in addition, branches of one or more banks in every shopping centre worthy of the name. On the other hand, decision-making about a choice of bank is, for most people, a once-in-a-lifetime process.

The individual's relationship with the insurance industry is different. Policies are likely to be held with a number of companies. It is, in the eyes of most policy holders, a highly technical subject, hedged round with legal jargon. Only when demands are made upon the insurance companies, usually as a result of some misfortune such as death or theft, is the relationship reviewed in any real sense. Between these two points all you do is pay.

The second characteristic of the market which affects the way in which research is conducted is the sensitive nature of money. At the simplest level there is a reluctance to discuss one's income, whether earned or unearned. The growth of the black economy has not helped in this area. In addition there is both a reluctance to reveal, and an ignorance of, many financial holdings. For instance, many respondents will find it very difficult to recall the full range of insurance policies held and well nigh impossible to recall any but the simplest detail about them, even confusing the names of the insurance companies, let alone correctly defining the type of policy or the sums involved. This reluctance to discuss financial matters is as common among businessmen as it is among private individuals.

The following sections discuss how the particular research needs of financial institutions are met, outlines the difficulties in practical terms and indicates how these can be overcome. No attempt is made to discuss in detail the research techniques since these are fully dealt with elsewhere in this volume.

It should be remembered that while there is a tendency to treat this as one market, in fact it is made up of many disparate markets all of which have their own characteristics. Apart from the basic division between the business and the personal market, one can divide each into many sub-markets: for instance, on the personal side there are banking, insurance, unit trusts, executor and trustee services and so on. One bank claims to have three hundred services.

Basic market data

As in all markets there is a need for basic data required for a proper analysis of the market and the opportunities which are offered. The main problem with most of the major financial markets is that they have the characteristics of both mass markets and minority markets, and they are interlocking. There is thus a necessity for comprehensive market data to be based on very large samples. The most extensive is the omnibus-based Financial Research Survey carried out by NOP, which has a total annual sample of approximately 50,000 respondents in Great Britain.

The necessity for a sample of this size is well illustrated by considering the problem of monitoring the simplest market fact, the share of new business which a particular bank is acquiring. This is clearly crucial to all market planning; for while internal data on new business is presumably easy to acquire, the strength of the institution in the market place must be determined by the extent to which it acquires an adequate share of the relevant pool – a pool which in this case includes both those who are opening an account for the first time and those who are either transferring business from another bank or who are opening an additional account. The following table, based on 6 months' data, shows how quickly the very large sample is reduced to sub-samples of a size which are the minimum to provide an adequate period-to-period monitor of market share, let alone to monitor changes in new-customer profiles.

	Samples	%
Total adult population (England and Wales)	28,647	100
Hold any current account	18,618	65
Opened any current account in last 12 months	1,545	5
Opened first current account in last 12 months	885	3

Source: NOP, FRS (October 1983–March 1984)

When market share data of *any* current accounts opened are examined, the sample sizes amongst the big four banks range from 331 to 191; for those *new* to current account banking the samples are in the range 209 to 110.

It can thus be seen that analysis of socio-economic profiles of new customers, and their comparisons between banks and between periods, will be resting on insecure statistical ground.

But of course, holding of accounts and opening and closing them is only part of the information that is required; equally important are the values of the accounts themselves, the flow of money through them and the methods of payments from and recepts into the accounts which are used. This, the important dynamic element of the market, has a crucial importance in marketing planning.

It is possible to collect information on standard sample surveys which, when taken in conjunction with published data, provides information on the total values held by personal customers; but this cannot give information on cash flows.

To obtain dynamic data on cash flows a panel operation is necessary. One example of such a panel which operated in the UK for several years was based upon a quota sample of 10,000 adult respondents. After completion of a recruitment questionnaire which identified their account holding and credit usage, respondents completed a monthly diary on payments in which were recorded all sums over £3 – whom they were paid to, for what product or service, and the method used to make the payment. At quarterly intervals the respondent recorded balances on accounts held and outstanding debits, and also indicated any changes in accounts held and credit commitment.[2]

An example of the use of the data generated by this type of survey is indicated by the very marked changes in the savings market in recent years, as more and more financial institutions paid higher rates of interest with little or no interest penalties. These were data that cannot be obtained from published financial statistics and would not necessarily be apparent to the financial institution if it were not already participating in this market.

Liquidity of savings – personal market
(% held in liquid form: bank current and deposit and building society ordinary accounts)

	%
1980	65
1981	58
1982	49
1983	45

Source: AGB Index.

The collection of financial data, be it in the personal or the corporate market. points up the difficulties of providing totally comprehensive data which will match internal company statistics. As so often, the majority of savings and especially corporate borrowing are held by the large investors or businesses. These are often the individuals or organizations most difficult to approach and least likely to divulge financial information. In the personal market this is an acute problem as many of the wealthy are reluctant to discuss their finances even when they do not happen to live abroad.

External research information is only part of the picture. For many financial institutions a key part of the research process is the analysis of their own customer base. In some cases the internal data base provides all the information that is necessary directly from computer records. But in many instances it is not possible to consolidate customer data, and in this case it is necessary to sample the customers and consolidate the usage of the services available, from both computer and manual records. Once again this often has to be carried out on large samples to provide an adequate level of statistical accuracy amongst the sub-groups in the customer bases.

In summary, basic data can be expensive to collect on a scale that is likely to be of real value as

(a) many sub-groups of interest are very small;
(b) financial holdings are dominated in value terms by a small number of wealthy individuals and large corporations.

Service development research

The opening up of financial markets and the increasing pace of technological development in the last decade has led to an increasing rate of introduction of new services and new and improved systems and hardware. There has been a consequent burgeoning of the use of research in the evaluation of such factors as the relative importance of service features, e.g. notice of withdrawal as against interest rate; in establishing the acceptability of the service; and in deciding on the service name.

The techniques which are used are in no significant way different from those used in other service industries. For example, qualitative research techniques, structured and semi-structured interviews are used as is considered appropriate to the service which is being studied.

There is, however, a major difficulty in research in this area which is again common to all such service fields: it is difficult, if not impossible, to pre-test the service in a real sense (other than on a test market basis). The processes which are involved in opening an account, in taking decisions as to where to invest money or which type of insurance policy to take and with which company, or who to turn to for financial advice or consultancy, can only be broadly conceptualized. Thus it may be possible by careful questioning to evaluate the general response to a new service but it is difficult to translate this evaluation into a realistic forecast of actual demand. Financial market research has still a long way to go in this field.

Qualitative research

Both group discussion techniques and depth interviews are used in research into financial markets. The latter are more common than in many other fields for two reasons. First, as pointed out above there is a degree of sensitivity in discussing financial matters in public; and second, the minority nature of many of the markets which are surveyed makes the convening of a group even of four or five individuals very difficult and consequently expensive.

There are a number of other issues which also have to be taken into consideration when recruiting group discussions. There are extremely wide ranges of sophistication in financial awareness and behaviour even within fairly tightly defined demographic groups. The psychological positioning of finance can mean that the group opinions are dominated by a minority. Again, the roles of partners can be critical: some financial decisions are made jointly, others as individuals. Care should thus be taken to define the partner's role when discussing such topics as mortgage finance and life assurance for families. These constraints often also lead to quite lengthy recruitment questionnaires covering a wide range of behavioural and psychological aspects of financial activity.

Attitude and image research

For service organizations such as those in the financial field the standing or image of the institution is of key importance in the development of the industry sector and of the individual company in the market. This has been clearly demonstrated by the erosion of the banks' share of the savings market by the building societies. Not only have the building societies had for most of the period an interest rate advantage, but they have built up an image amongst the general public of being more welcoming and less stuffy. They are clearly more favourably regarded now than are banks and this must increase their likelihood of success if they move into related financial markets.

Consequently there has been extensive research among customers and non-customers, both personal and business, into their attitudes to financial institutions and the services they offer. Research of this type is not easy as there is the necessity to distinguish between the industry image and that of the individual company. In the more fragmented sectors of the financial field, such as insurance and unit trust companies, there may also be difficulties in identifying the individual financial institution.

Regular surveys of corporate image and attitudes to company services are carried out by most of the major companies in the financial fields. With some building societies and banks the very skewed regional distribution of their activity leads to non-national research being carried out. The regional biases and the nature of the distribution network should always be taken into account when setting up and interpreting research of this type.

Those institutions which rely to a large extent upon branch networks (i.e. banks and building societies) often use the branch itself as the base for research into attitudes to service and services. This type of research should be used with caution as it is possible to obtain a very atypical sample. More and more customers never have to cross the branch threshold in order to conduct their business: the increasing custom of paying wages and salaries directly into an account, the growing use of cheques and the increased availability of automatic teller machines (ATMs) have reduced the customer's direct contact with the branch network.

An effective and relatively inexpensive method of surveying customers is by the use of postal questionnaires. By the very nature of their activity most financial institutions have an up-to-date address for their customers, and most of them can produce addressed communications easily and quickly. The response rates for such postal surveys are probably higher than for unsolicited postal questionnaires – one always looks at letters from one's bank. Response rates in excess of 50% are not uncommon. In addition, most financial institutions have sufficient data on their total customer base to accurately evaluate the behavioural and demographic representativeness of those replying.

Research into business markets

The problems of research into business markets for financial institutions have been mentioned in passing, above. The nature of the problems of sampling, selection of respondents and interviewing are common to all research which is carried out with individuals in their capacity as a representative of a business entity. These are discussed elsewhere in this book.

Here it is only necessary to mention a few specific problems. First, there is the dominance in many markets of a few, often very large companies, the officers of which are under considerable and constant pressure to co-operate in surveys. When they do co-operate, by the very nature of the size of the business the questionnaire is likely to be very long. Second, there can be particular difficulties in defining the correct respondent: responsibility is often spread, particularly in larger organizations. Some parts of a questionnaire may therefore have to be referred to other officers of the company. Third, terminology. In some areas this is not very clear and it is therefore very important that interviewers are well briefed about the precise meaning that should be put on such concepts as 'medium term loans' or 'swaps and options'. Finally, of course, there are the perennial problems of obtaining the hard financial data which may often be required.

City research

Major companies are becoming increasingly aware of the importance of the financial community to them. Stockbrokers produce extremely detailed analyses of their performance and prospects. Financial journalists and City editors write about them. Fund managers buy, hold, or sell their shares. Merchant and other banks may help finance them. Other organizations may attempt a takeover bid on them. Rumours based on misinformation can wipe millions of pounds off a company's valuation literally overnight. An adequate understanding of the views of these audiences can therefore be of crucial importance.

Thus the demand for City research is increasing rapidly:

(a) What are the criteria on which investment managers evaluate a company?
(b) How is the 'quality of management' assessed?
(c) How useful and relevant is the information put out by the company? Where are the gaps?
(d) What profit levels are the experts forecasting, and why?
(e) Who is ripe for a takeover bid?

As the value of such research is becoming more evident, the scope is widening, too. Stockbrokers now commission research on the reasons why institutional investors use one stockbroker rather than another. Merchant bankers try to find out how large pension funds select an organization to manage their portfolio (frequently running into millions of pounds). Dealers in the Eurobond market have commissioned surveys designed to sound out the opinions of corporate clients (and potential clients) on their services worldwide. In short, it has been a real growth area of the 1970s and early 1980s.

Contact and interviewing

Respondents in the financial community are usually as busy and brusque as any in industry, and probably less willing to suffer fools gladly. However, if the subject interests them, and if the interviewer is well-briefed and intelligent, they can be more courteous, better informed and more helpful than most people.

In these situations the quality and character of the interviewer is of fundamental importance, and there is persuasive evidence that, even in the City, an intelligent, mature, and experienced female is far superior to a male! An intelligent woman may listen more sensitively, probe more delicately and record what she hears more objectively, perhaps because she has fewer preconceived opinions. Male interviewers are expected to know more about the subject than female interviewers, and can therefore be judged – and treated – more harshly in an interview. Good male interviewers can be very good but they are not easy to find or to keep, as interviewers, for long.

One important characteristic of City audiences is the importance of the telephone in their day-to-day work. They are therefore very at ease with the telephone medium, and many surveys – even with complex and fairly lengthy questionnaires – can most successfully be conducted by telephone. (It also prevents the frequent telephone interruptions which are so much a characteristic of in-person interviews with such audiences!)

This continues to hold true with multi-national audiences. Not only do virtually all executives in this field speak English but the knowledge that someone is 'phoning from another country can boost response rates.

A danger in financial research, as in the industrial field, is that the very small number of potential respondents will become over-interviewed, and permanently alienated by over-persistent, ill-briefed, dull interviewers struggling through a long, highly structured questionnaire more suitably designed for pet-food purchases.

All institutional investors' surveys want the views of the top 100 or 150 institutions: the stage is already well-past when a decent response rate can be obtained on an *ad hoc* study with these key people. The comparable situation with the 30 or 40 key financial journalists was reached at least a decade before that.

That is why the trend is towards conducting such surveys on a once-a-year-only, multi-client, basis. Although this means a long interview, excellent response rates are obtained, it is relatively inexpensive for each sponsor and it offers a sometimes welcome cloak of inconspicuousness.

Qualitative research has an important role to play in City studies. In a quantitative survey of a company's reputation it is essential to know the right questions to ask (and the right terminology to use), and these may vary from company to company. A small group discussion (4 or 5 participants, over dinner) among broking analysts specializing in the appropriate industrial field provides essential material. Indeed, such is the depth of knowledge of these analysts that a group discussion or two can form a valuable study in its own right.

Sampling

There are many reference works in the UK for major companies: The Times 1000, Kompass Management Register, Dun & Bradstreet's Key British Enterprises. But these – quite apart from the seemingly inevitable problems of inaccuracy and outdatedness – tend to focus on companies, and in City research we are often interested in banks, insurance companies, investment trusts, stockbrokers, etc, which are generally excluded. Even the pension funds of large companies are not always located at the same place as the head office. We tend, therefore, to use rather specialized sources.

(a) *Stock Exchange Official Yearbook.* In addition to listing companies, this also gives banks (including foreign), insurance companies, but not stockbroking firms. A separate publication, 'Stock Exchange Members and Firms', is available.

(b) *Crawford's Directory of City Connections* is a valuable source for many categories – self-investing pension funds, investment trusts, unit trusts, investment management departments of merchant banks, investment advisers, specialized industry analysts (i.e. named individuals) in stockbrokers. But care is required because of the extensive overlap between categories: the same organization can appear under numerous headings, so careful cross-checking of samples is needed. Crawfords is also updated only infrequently, so particular caution is needed.

(c) *City Directory.* This, like Crawfords, has only been published within the last decade, and is a useful alternative source for banks (by type), insurance companies, discount houses, stockbrokers, managed funds, commodity funds, etc. It is especially good for addresses.

(d) *NAPF Yearbook.* This publication of the National Association of Pension Funds gives more comprehensive coverage of pension funds than does Crawfords, but does not distinguish the self-investing from the managed. Nor does it include the minority of funds which are not members of the NAPF.

You can begin to understand that each survey must be treated separately: the best source for one may be inappropriate for another. In fact, full use should be made of the client's knowledge of his market. Very often he has the best sampling frames of all, and in some cases (e.g. Eurobonds) these constitute the only available source. Personal knowledge and extensive recent experience of these markets are clearly tremendous assets when conducting such surveys.

Private shareholders

Although only a quarter of quoted shares are held by private shareholders, this statistic conceals wide ranges for individual companies. For many the proportion exceeds 70%, and for most companies the *number* of private shareholders greatly exceeds the institutional investors.

Surveys of these audiences are sometimes associated with takeover bid situations. In such situations speed is the keynote. Fortunately, most shareholders have telephones and it is possible to conduct a few hundred telephone interviews during an evening, hand-count the findings and report to the client first thing the following morning. Then, if necessary, a further set of questions can be devised, depending on recent developments in the bid (an improved offer, advertisement in the press, letter from the Chairman to shareholders, etc.), for administering to a further sample of shareholders that evening. One prerequisite for being able to undertake such work is a reliable, up-to-date and rapidly available shareholder list. (It is frequently less rapidly available than the company initially believes!) It is a real problem if these records do not give telephone numbers, since many shareholders are women, and Mrs A Smith may be listed under her husband's initials in the telephone directory.

Private shareholder research is not restricted to takeover battles, however. There are a number of ways in which companies can benefit from a better knowledge of the perceptions and opinions of their private shareholders. It can help determine who (in demographic terms) the shareholders are, what their expectations and aims are from their investment, what their wishes are in terms of future company direction, how useful they find the annual report, etc.

Far from offending shareholders, as some companies fear such research might, most shareholders are flattered that 'their' company cares enough about their views to commission such research: goodwill is the invariable result.

Chapter 23

International market research

JOHN DOWNHAM

International research can be defined as research carried out in a country other than that of the sponsor. This covers a very wide variety of situations. At one extreme, the sponsor may be interested in whether or not he should move into some market with which in the past he has had no dealings of any kind. At the other extreme, he may already have a substantial local operation — agency, associate or even branch — active in the market concerned, but nevertheless wishes for reasons of international policy himself to carry out research there. On a different dimension, international research may be concerned with a single country exclusively; or with several countries simultaneously, or in sequence; or even with research carried out regularly across a number of countries on a more or less continuous basis. International research thus comes in many different shapes and sizes. It is *not* synonymous with 'export' market research, or with 'multinational' studies — although both these types of activity form part of the total.

This chapter looks at a number of the key issues which are encountered in such research. Certain of the issues are peculiar to the international field. Many of the problems are, however, to be found in national or domestic research also, although on the international front they tend to appear on a larger scale and sometimes in a rather different guise.

The development of international market research

The development of market research generally is bound up with, and depends on, the development of modern marketing methods. The same is even more true of international market research. Although international *trade* pre-dates history, international *marketing* in any full sense is a very recent development indeed. Systematic and scientific international research did not really get under-way until the 1950s, the breakthrough coming during the 1960s. For a long time the majority of such research was sponsored by the larger multinational companies, particularly American, British and a few Contir.ental firms operating in fields such as consumer durables, detergents, food, oil, pharmaceuticals and tobacco. A great part of this work was in fact carried out for local rather than international planning purposes, since many even of the multinationals have marketed brands on a genuinely international (and internationally researched) basis only in comparatively recent times.

It is worth emphasizing that the growth of international manufacturing and service organizations does not in itself necessarily lead to an equivalent growth in international research. The majority of marketing planning and operating decisions are still carried out at national rather than international level. As a result most market research work is also commissioned at national level. International surveys form a relatively small proportion of all the market research carried out, even for the international companies. [1]

As Keegan [2] has pointed out, there is a range of different strategies possible in multinational marketing:

(a) The same (or virtually the same) product can be sold in different countries, using the same advertising approach.
(b) The same product may be sold, but using a different advertising approach in different countries.
(c) The product offered may differ in some way but be sold with the same advertising approach.
(d) Both product and advertising may be varied to suit the needs of the local market.
(e) Finally, in the extreme case the company may market completely different product concepts and formulations, differently advertised, in different countries.

These alternative strategies may of course be associated with differing degrees of centralization or decentralization in the company concerned. Multinational research policies vary all the way from completely standardized approaches and methods, centrally specified, to complete independence of the local branches to decide what to research and how to do it. Whatever the situation in this respect, the requirements for international research as such are likely to be quite different (in both amount and type) from one strategy to another. Any discussion of international research approaches thus makes sense only when it is related to the sponsoring company's strategy and operating methods. [3]

Problems of international research

One basic difficulty of much international research is the element of *unfamiliarity*. Compared with his home market, the sponsor may know relatively little about the characteristics of the country and its people, the local customs and ways of life, the market structure and marketing methods, etc. He may know even less about the possibilities and problems of carrying out research in the country. This situation can lead to uncertainty and insecurity on the one hand, and the danger of false assumptions and conclusions on the other. The sponsor must accept the need for even more help and careful pre-planning than in the case of domestic research.

Even for a company experienced in international marketing and research, however, there are still many additional hazards. The first is the vastly greater problem of *communication*. This is not just a question of different languages, although these undoubtedly complicate the issue. Nor is it due only to geographical distance, although this may add to the time, difficulties and cost involved in setting up the research. More basic problems stem from differences in customs, ways of thought and experience between different cultures, in addition to the more obvious range of local market differences, which can complicate and confuse the planning of a research project. It is easy to fall into the trap of assuming that someone from another country is working to the same (unspecified) assumptions as yourself, or is using words in the same way, when this is not the case. A shake of the head, or the word 'yes', mean different things in different cultures: it is even easier for misunderstandings to arise with the more subtle issues of research design and logic.

Further problems arise in connection with the *organization and administration* of international research, sometimes at long range. In the case of multinational projects, there is the issue of which research organization(s) to select and how to coordinate their work. Even where only one country is involved, how do we best ensure that the research on the spot is adequately set up and efficiently carried out? Effective control of an international research project is liable to be much more difficult than that of a national project.

Further difficulties sometimes arise from the *nature of the client company* itself. It has already been pointed out that international companies vary greatly in their international management style. The degree of centralization or decentralization is likely to affect the way research is initiated, planned and carried through. It may be difficult for a highly decentralized organization to arrange for closely comparable multinational research, given widely varying interests and requirements of its local operations. Conversely, there are sometimes occasions on which the regional or international headquarters wishes to carry out research without directly involving its local operators in the project – where for example the findings of the research are concerned with confidential international planning, diversification issues, etc. Problems of these kinds complicate effective international research.

All these problems, and others, are normally in addition to – or at least a magnified version of – the kinds of research problems discussed in other chapters. They must not be overstressed. It is perfectly possible to carry out effective market research in most countries of the world, given adequate planning, often using fairly advanced techniques.[4] Adequate planning does, however, mean full awareness of the difficulties which are likely to be encountered, knowledge of how these are most likely to be overcome, and acceptance of the fact that certain kinds of research information cannot practicably be obtained in certain countries for cost, technical or other reasons. Before turning to the practical issues of how to set about international market research in ways which minimize these problems, we should therefore first look more closely at some of the problems themselves.

Market differences

The problem of unfamiliarity referred to above reflects many different factors. Most of these are obvious ones but some of their effects may not be. Certain can operate even *within* countries such as the UK, but on the international scene such differences are magnified many times. The fact that we are probably more likely to anticipate them in international research does not mean that it is easy to deal with them when they turn up.

Language

This obviously can produce considerable complications for market research, especially where a number of different languages are used within the same country. It causes problems in the wording (translation) of questionnaires, in the organization of fieldwork and in the analysis of open-ended questions. We therefore have to decide, for example, how far we should attempt to cover all the different language groups in a given survey. Unless we are concerned with some specialized study of, say, crofting we can usually afford to exclude Gaelic speakers from a study of the UK market. But in the case of Switzerland, for example, should we ignore the minority of Italian speakers living in the Ticino region? In the Republic of South Africa, most general market studies will be involved with both Afrikaans and English; but how many of the Black African languages ought we to use in order to cover the key sectors of this increasingly important part of the total market? Worst of all, probably, how many of the fourteen key languages is it necessary to use for a national survey in India? The fact that in a number of countries one particular language – Swahili in parts of Africa, for example, or even on occasion English – acts as some kind of *lingua franca* does not really offer a solution. Except in the very simplest forms of research, or research among special groups, effective interviewing involves using the language normally spoken in the home by the person we wish to interview. We are unlikely to get the right information on (for example) attitudes towards different products if the housewife is having to express herself in a tongue which is not her customary one. This in turn calls for the use of interviewers who are completely fluent in the relevant language(s) – not always easy in a multi-lingual society.

Fieldwork is the most critical part of any international survey. The problem of language also enters into other key sectors of the research project, however – most obviously when it comes to communication between the client and the local research agency which will carry out the survey in the country concerned. In the best of all possible worlds, the client or his research representative will be fluent in the key local language, so that all discussions with the local researchers are carried out in the latter's language. A number of international market research organizations quite rightly make an important point of this. However, we ignore reality if we try to make this a rule of operation. It is a fact of life that sometimes researchers in other countries will speak English much better than we can speak their own language. This is generally true of, for example, Scandinavia. It is almost invariably true of Japan.

Ethnic differences

To some extent this point is associated with the last one: but language may well not be the most important difference between ethnic groups. Obvious major examples are the differences between white and black groups within the USA, or between the various regions of Brazil. Such differences are often reflected in consumer habits and attitudes, especially in food, and need to be very carefully considered when planning research in a foreign market. They may call for different interviewing approaches, and often for different interviewers.

Religion

This factor also can radically affect a range of habits and attitudes, most obviously again with food and drink. Differences with respect to the use of meat and alcohol are very clear as between Christians, Muslims and Hindus. Religious festivals and fasts can also completely distort the patterns of food consumption at certain times of the year. There are many more subtle differences, however, which carry through into various aspects of lifestyle. These may be reflected in differing attitudes towards newer or more 'permissive' patterns of thought and behaviour, as well as in such aspects as the differing roles of men and women. For example, in some countries where the influence of Islam is strong there may be severe problems in interviewing women: in Saudi Arabia in general women cannot be interviewed by men but it is virtually impossible to employ women as interviewers for ordinary door-to-door fieldwork.

Social structure

In developed 'western' markets we are accustomed to talk in marketing terms of ABs, C1s etc., as being appropriate target groups for specific products or services. It is extremely dangerous to attempt to translate socio-economic concepts of this kind to other types of society. Even within Europe it can be difficult – social class is by no means the same concept in Italy, Sweden and the UK. Various attempts over many years to reach a generally agreed and consistent set of social class definitions in Europe have at last begun to achieve some success, [5] but in other parts of the world the European approach frequently does not relate at all realistically to local social structures. In many countries there is no substantial middle class in the European sense, and it may be necessary (as in India or other parts of Asia) to classify households by factors such as the sources of income, ownership of land, lifestyle ('traditional' or not), etc. This again affects the design and analysis of surveys.

Culture and tradition

To some extent the preceding headings already cover cultural differences. There are, however, many other aspects of local cultures which can affect marketing. International studies of certain markets in Latin countries which ignored the 'machismo' factor would be incomplete. 'Face' is an important consideration to take into account in both the content and the manner of market research – and not just in the Far East. The role and significance of 'gifting' is a key element in many markets: perfume or jewellery in Western countries, but much more apparently mundane products such as toilet soap in Japan. Examples of such cultural differences are easily multiplied.

Literacy

Even in parts of Europe, literacy levels may be well below 100%. Official statistics are likely to be particularly misleading in this connection. Often the definition of 'literacy' implies no more than the ability to sign one's name. For marketing and research communication in written form to be effective, very much more than this is required. Visual aids, let alone self-completion questionnaires of various kinds, do not work well unless people have reasonable facility in reading. This problem is much more acute outside Europe. It obviously reduces our research options, particularly for techniques such as diary panels and postal product testing panels.

Income patterns

Differing levels of average per capita income clearly influence the kinds and amounts of goods and services bought by the local population. In planning research, equally important considerations are the pattern of income *distribution* and also the ways in which incomes are *earned*. Much wider variations in income between the top and the bottom of the economic scale frequently mean much more variability in buying behaviour – and consequently additional sampling problems. Another important issue is the difference between urban and rural populations. In many parts of the Third World some of the rural population may hardly be in the cash economy at all − or if they are, only at certain times of the year. In such countries the geographical spread and particularly the timing of research must take these points into account. In East Africa, for example, some sections of the rural population do most of their buying of many products during limited periods which vary from one part of the country to another, depending upon the harvesting and sale of the particular type of cash crop grown in the area.

Geography and climate

Air conditioners and fur coats are clearly products which are likely to have different market potentials varying with the climate. There are many other less obvious but nevertheless fundamental differences resulting from geography which have a profound effect on marketing − and therefore research − possibilities. Such variations very often do not conform to political frontiers. Within Europe a good example would be the 'olive oil frontier'. The availability of oil in Mediterranean Europe as a medium for cooking, and the traditionally greater difficulties of producing and marketing butter in hot countries, mean that there are major differences not merely in the cooking oil/butter/margarine markets themselves but in a whole wide range of cooking and eating habits also, within as well as between countries. The planning of multi-country research in particular is often affected by such differences − not just of latitude but also of altitude, soil, water hardness and many other factors − which cut right across the pattern of national boundaries.

Institutional factors

Differing types of market background in different countries frequently call for changes in the research approach. For example, consumers' needs in personal and clothes washing are often similar over broad regions of the world, but the ways in which these needs are met can be considerably affected by factors such as the nature of the local washing facilities available − domestic water supplies, heating arrangements, the ownership of washing machines of different kinds, the predominant use of baths or showers, etc. Different research approaches will be needed to deal with washing habits in Northern Europe and rural Asia. Again, cooking facilities (and not just the foods eaten) vary enormously across countries: kerosene stoves pose different cooking problems and opportunities to gas or electricity.

Distribution

Distribution channels vary greatly from one country to the next: the rapid development of large supermarkets and hypermarkets is a key feature of many developed countries, but small stores, bazaars and markets still predominate in other countries. The degree of concentration of the grocery trade also varies enormously. Differing emphasis on competition through pricing, convenience in location or facilities, credit terms offered, etc., all affect the ways in which people carry out their shopping.

Media and advertising

The level of literacy is only one factor which affects the relative importance of different media in different countries. Commercial television does not exist at all in some countries even though in general television tends to be the dominant medium in most advanced – and even many of the developing – economies. The quality and geographical spread of press media vary enormously, especially the relative importance of national and regional newspapers. The quality of advertising agency facilities is highly variable. And so on. Such differences affect not only the way in which consumers learn about products, but also the *nature* of the information and impressions they receive.

Legislation and regulation

The rules within which marketing operates vary from country to country. Legislation relating to fair trading issues, pricing, different types of promotional activities, the content of advertising, labelling, date-stamping, the sales of drugs and a hundred and one other marketing activities are still far from harmonized even within the EEC. Alongside the law as such there is a growing body of 'voluntary' codes, restrictions and procedures which affect the ways in which marketing operates. International research into (say) a possible advertising campaign for a food product based on a health claim could very quickly go off the rails if it failed to take account of local differences in regulations of these kinds.

This list of differences between markets is only illustrative, and far from comprehensive (see also ref. 6). While it indicates some of the ways in which marketing has to adapt to local situations, its purpose here is to emphasize how many different issues are liable to influence the design and carrying out of marketing research internationally. All the factors mentioned can, and do, affect the design of a research project. They should, of course, be very much part of the stock-in-trade of an international market researcher. They call for considerable local knowledge and awareness of where the (often hidden) differences may lie. Much more extensive examples, including case-histories, are quoted in the literature – see for instance the paper by Berent.[7]

Differences in market research

Market differences of the kinds referred to all influence the design and carrying out of international research projects. There are a number of other factors which even more directly affect the possibilities for market research and the way in which it is handled. These include the following.

(a) *Differences in the basic data* available for use in designing the sample of people to interview. Some countries have better basic data than the UK, many have much worse. Quota sampling may be quite adequate for many commercial research purposes in countries such the UK; but in certain other parts of the world – particularly in developing countries – it is virtually impossible to design an adequate quota sample, either because the necessary data about the relevant population characteristics cannot be obtained or because the structure of the population is in any case such as to defeat appropriate quota setting. In such cases some form of random or quasi-random sampling is called for. Even here the necessary information, for example suitable lists or maps, may not be easily available. It is generally possible to find some way round these problems, but to do so often involves considerable ingenuity and improvization, together with a good local knowledge of where and how appropriate help might be obtained.

(b) *Local legislation or social customs* which may make it difficult to obtain interviews, particularly among certain sectors of the population. Sometimes the researcher will run into problems in trying to interview people living in 'protected' upper- and middle-class housing blocks or in areas where entry is restricted. In some countries it is necessary to obtain central or local official authorization to carry out research at all – in Indonesia this may have to be obtained at three different levels before interviewing can start. It is essential for the researcher to know about such problems in advance, and how they may best be solved, in order to avoid gaps and delays (or worse) in carrying out the research.

(c) *It may be necessary to use different types of interviewer.* For example, in countries such as the UK many research organizations tend to be wary of employing students as interviewers except for certain special types of project, on the grounds that they may be too much a 'floating population' which does not repay the effort of training, or may not have the right motivation for the work, etc. In some other countries, however, there may be few suitable alternatives to using students, whose position is in any case very different to that of students in countries like the UK. Travel and accommodation problems (sometimes even physical dangers) mean that it is preferable to use men as interviewers in some countries, especially in rural areas. On the other hand it can be impossible for men to interview women in some Muslim cultures. Our choice of potential interviewers is very often severely limited by such problems of education levels, ethnic groupings, mobility, etc. It is important therefore not to export our domestic views and prejudices about the kinds of people who make suitable interviewers into quite different cultural situations.

(d) *The interview situation* itself may differ radically. The possibilities for postal surveys or for telephone interviewing obviously vary enormously from country to country, even within the 'developed' world, depending on the efficiency of postal services, literacy levels, etc. The personal interview situation will also differ. In many countries it is much more difficult to obtain privacy for an interview, and at the extreme (for example among rural communities in developing countries) a personal interview frequently takes on the characteristics of a very large group interview session.

(e) *People may also react quite differently* to the interview situation. In Western societies interviews are generally accepted as a familiar and normal situation in which interviewer and informant can interact on reasonably level terms, and on the whole with sufficient frankness. This is certainly not the case in many countries where market research — indeed, any kind of contact with people from outside the local community — is still relatively unknown and where the conventions of social intercourse may be quite different. Question and-answer interaction with a stranger can sometimes seem strange, even uncomfortable or threatening. Depending upon the local culture, informants may turn out to be more or less frank than would be the case in the West. In the Far East politeness and 'face' can be dominant elements in the interview situation. In a country such as Nigeria, on the other hand, it may be possible even on fairly personal issues to get an uninhibited response which would surprise many interviewers in the UK. Local differences in cultural or social customs may also affect the handling of other forms of research. Informants in a discussion group situation can behave differently. Even more than in the West certain topics may turn out to be taboo; members of the group may be less inclined to disagree with other members; they may try harder to give the socially acceptable or most 'favourable' answer; etc. Once again, there is no substitute for close familiarity with the local culture.

(f)   *In some countries interviews may need to be much shorter* if we are to avoid the danger of respondents mentally — if not physically — withdrawing from the interview. This too requires awareness and sensitivity on the part of the researcher since the innate politeness of many cultures towards a stranger means that the more obvious signs of interview breakdown are not apparent.

(g) *Rating scales and visual aids* may not work in the same way, or as effectively, in different countries.[8] It is not easy to develop scales which are 'culture-free', while the problem of 'top-boxing' (respondents tending to choose the most favourable position on a scale simply because of a desire to please the interviewer or for some similar inappropriate reason) varies across cultures.

(h) Another problem that must be watched for in this context is that in some cultures people are simply not accustomed to *thinking in abstract or conceptual terms* — a fact which makes it more difficult to carry out attitude research, for example brand image surveys. A typical example is the greater difficulty which may be found in obtaining images of brands which the informant has not personally tried — a frequent and quite natural response being 'I have not tried it and so I don't know what it is like'. While such problems are by no means restricted to overseas markets, they are often more acute there.

(i) In a slightly different context, it is notoriously difficult in many countries to obtain information on matters relating to people's finances. This is particularly a problem in attempting to organize retail audits: not only may traders not be accustomed to keeping efficient records, they have for taxation reasons a very marked antipathy to *any* kind of recordkeeping.

These are examples of differences between countries which affect the mechanics of carrying out research. In addition, *market research organizations* themselves differ tremendously from country to country. Clearly technical knowhow and experience are likely to be less in countries where market research is a more recent and still relatively limited activity. Apart from this, the standards of professional conduct also vary. While in a number of less developed countries market research standards are as high as in most of Europe, in many they are not. It is often necessary to look very much more closely into the quality of fieldwork, and at field control and supervision procedures; editing, coding and analysis work may be less systematic and accurate; confidentiality of the project is liable to be more of a problem; and 'cutting corners' — whether deliberately or unwittingly — needs to be carefully watched for.

Finally, *the costs of market research* vary sharply between countries. Exactly comparable data are difficult to obtain, but based on surveys carried out by ESOMAR in 1982 and 1984 and supplementary calculations made by Research International it appears that within Europe costs can vary by a factor of 2 or more between the cheapest and the most expensive countries.[9] Interestingly the cost ranking of countries differs for qualitative and quantitative research. Even in many developing countries where in the past market research costs used to be low — mainly because of relatively low salaries — charges have been rising steadily, in many cases to European levels. This is one further factor calling for additional thought and care in planning international research, and putting an extra premium on skill and experience in finding economical answers to the various other problems described earlier.

Standardization and comparability in international marketing and market research

From what has been said so far it might seem that the scope for standard approaches and methods is extremely limited in both marketing and market research. The various national or regional differences outlined above should certainly lead us to be cautious in transferring ideas and techniques from one country to another without checking how they may be affected by factors of these kinds. There is, however, no need to become obsessed by the differences. In practice a considerable degree of standardization is often possible.

Any discussion of the principles, procedures and problems of international marketing falls outside the scope of this chapter. However, some indication of the extent to which standardization internationally was developing in the 1970s is given in an article[10] by Sorensen and Wiechmann. This study was based on about 100 interviews with executives from 27 major multinational companies in the food, soft drink, soap-detergent-toiletries and cosmetics industries, and refers to marketing operations in Europe and the USA.

The Sorenson and Wiechmann study showed that the differences between market conditions in different countries should not be over-emphasized, at least in the case of developed markets. The article argues that many marketing programs are standardized in spite of significant differences in these conditions, and that 'a widespread rule in multinational companies seems to be: When in doubt, modify only those parts that *must* be modified because of insurmountable barriers to standardization'. Among the reasons why companies would follow such a policy, the authors suggest that:

(a) To people at the centre, standardization may well appear a much simpler and more straightforward approach than the need to deal with innumerable permutations of programs for different countries. It is also easier to monitor and control. (This point is clearly linked to the degree of centralization of company operations referred to earlier.)

(b) Standardization can sometimes lead to significant savings in the design of products and of their advertising and promotion. While, as the authors comment, it is not very often that this argument is backed up with hard facts, it is certainly true in principle that the relatively scarce and expensive resources of technical research and top level creativity will yield a bigger pay-off the more they can be exploited internationally.

(c) Standardized marketing programs may lead to more economical use of local man-power (and, it might be added, can simplify international training and transfer of staff.)

(d) There is a general feeling that if a successful marketing formula has been found in one country the sensible thing is to try to transfer and exploit it elsewhere rather than laboriously work out a new solution for each new country.

Against these arguments there are plenty of examples where a relatively unsophisticated and uninformed approach to standardizing international marketing has led to disaster. (The case for adopting a more cautious approach towards standardisation is also made in another study of multinational corporations' experience, by Hill and Still[11]). The authors refer to the example of three US food companies in their earlier attempts to break into the UK and subsequently the Continental markets. The conclusion they draw is that:

> The experiences of these three companies lead us to believe that managements of multinationals should give high priority to developing their ability to conduct *systematic cross-border analysis*, if they are not already doing so. Such analysis can help management avoid the mistake of standardizing when markets are significantly different. At the same time, systematic cross-border analysis can help avoid the mistake of excessive custom-tailoring when markets are sufficiently similar to make standardized programs feasible.

This is the classic argument for taking the international view of international research; and it is not confined to multinational companies. From the market research point of view, it implies starting from the position that international research should be handled similarly in different countries *unless* there is good evidence in a particular case to show that local variations are needed. Against this is the still strongly held view which emphasizes the many differences between countries and the over-riding importance of very carefully tailoring research techniques to the local market situation. The latter approach concentrates on the end-result of the research – the interpretation of the information provided – as ultimately the only issue where full comparability is likely to be critical.

The problem of what international 'comparability' really means has been usefully discussed by Day.[12] He argues that in practice comparability in research is important only insofar as it 'allows or facilitates *marketing* decisions to be reached for the *totality* of countries under consideration'; that comparability may either 'direct' (i.e. using very similar research methods in the different countries) or 'indirect' (using different approaches in order to achieve essentially the same marketing objective); and which type of comparability should be sought in any given case depends on:

(a) the freedom of marketing action possible in the individual markets;
(b) the type of research under consideration;
(c) the degree of homogeneity or heterogeneity between the marketing situations in the different countries.

This distinction between the need for *comparable information* and *standard research methods* assumes that for the purposes of international planning the user of research is mainly interested in having *findings* which are comparable, and he should not be unduly concerned if varying methods are used in different countries in order to obtain these. More than this, given the kinds of differences between countries discussed earlier in this chapter, we sometimes *have* to use differing research approaches if we are to get genuinely comparable data. For example, using the identical questionnaire in different countries can in practice sometimes produce information which is *not* comparable.

All this is true. There is no point in pursuing standardization merely for the sake of standardization if this runs us into other problems. A key argument of this chapter is precisely that the researcher has to be especially alert to the risks of miscommunication, and the possible need to adapt his approach, when working internationally. The validity of the local information obviously must not be sacrificed to a simple-minded pursuit of standard techniques and (even more) of standard questionnaires. Good examples of the possible dangers are to be found in papers such as the one by Berent. [7]

This said, the more exaggerated versions of these arguments considerably over-stress the need for local adaptations to take priority over the use of standard approaches. Some arguments based on the mystique of local research know-how are not always entirely disinterested. They are also not the whole story. There are in fact several very strong arguments in favour of the standardization of research methods wherever possible:

(a) The use of standard approaches can *save time and money* internationally (as they do nationally), especially at the project briefing and design stages.
(b) They *simplify life for the user* of the research – whether he is trying directly to compare research findings from different countires or is moving from one country to another during the course of his work. If the research methods used are similar, it will be much easier for him both to discuss research proposals and also to absorb the background to the findings.
(c) Marketing people are not necessarily closely interested in – or do not have sufficient time for – the more esoteric aspects of market research technology. They feel *greater confidence* in using research findings based on standard approaches, provided of course that the latter are soundly designed.
(d) The *international training and transfer* of market researchers is simplified by the use of standard methods.
(e) There are in any case certain types of information where *absolute uniformity* internationally is essential and where this can only be obtained by rigorously standard approaches in the field. A good example is the kind of data required for technical development work, such as information on the detailed routines followed in clothes washing.

One particular issue raised by Day in the article quoted is worth returning to, in pointing to difficulties for research arising from the fact that markets themselves are heterogeneous. He gives as an example the problem of designing an international research project to help in a marketing decision as to whether or not it would be a viable proposition to introduce an international brand into three adjacent markets which differ fundamentally in the stages of development reached, but which would be supplied from one (new) factory. In one market the type of product under consideration is already well established, with many well known brands; in the second market the product type has only just been introduced, with one or two brands in the process of trying to establish themselves; and in the third market the product type is as yet completely unknown. What international research, he very reasonably asks, could give us 'comparable' information in this situation? The question asked in fact underlines not so much the risks of trying to use standard research approaches internationally as the much more general danger of trying to answer quite different problems with the same approach. It is as vital (but often much more difficult) with an international research project to define our problem clearly in each country in order to establish what research is relevant as it is in the case of a domestic project.

It is also important to point out that the problem of comparability is not confined to surveys which are explicitly 'multi-country'. It is often just as important in the case of a survey carried out in a single country where the results may at some time in the future need to be compared with findings from equivalent surveys in other countries.

To sum up this section, comparing and interpreting research data from different countries is already sufficiently complicated without also having to make allowances for variations in the techniques used. The assumption that the soundest market research approach to a given problem could be reached by first examining it from each national viewpoint involved may in many cases be theoretically correct. In real life it is often inefficient and even unpractical. For most problems it is better to start from a well planned international approach – preferably one which has been piloted already in one or more countries – and then to modify this for other countries *only if* good evidence is produced for doing so. The stress here should be on the word 'evidence' – market research is no freer than other disciplines from prejudices of the 'not-invented-here' type or from anecdotal evidence and folklore of the kind 'someone tried it once some years ago and it didn't work'.

Which countries should we research?

Often there is no choice in this – the answer is dictated by the marketing problem. On other occasions, however, there may be quite a long list of possible countries of interest. The question then is how to select the most appropriate ones to research. This is typically the case, for example, with a firm which is seriously planning to export on a significant scale for the first time.

There are several approaches which can be considered before starting any new and more extensive research:

(a) The different markets can be ranked in order of potential importance to the company. 'Desk research' on production, imports and exports, consumption, income trends, etc., can often be used for this purpose. The approach is similar in many respects to desk research in the domestic market, although the sources of information will be different: the reader is referred back to chapter 1 and its comments on the international scene. (Other useful articles are by Foreman[13] and Hibbert,[14] which also quote various UK sources of information) Such classification and ranking of countries can sometimes involve quite extensive sets of data[15,16] and more sophisticated forms of statistical technique such as regression or cluster analysis; but relatively simple and straightforward approaches are likely to be quite adequate in most cases.

(b) It may be possible to categorize countries into groups or clusters, each of which has various characteristics (economic, social, marketing) in common which differentiate it from another group. Thus the Scandinavian countries, or certain of the Latin countries, are sometimes held to share important characteristics which mean that research findings for one member of the group can up to a point be projected to the others. Research can then be concentrated on a 'typical' or key member of the group. This can be a dangerous procedure without further evidence to support it – as the Scandinavians themselves are the first to point out, the national character and customs of Denmark, Norway and Sweden are far from identical. Nevertheless, there are certain criteria which can provide a valid basis for categorizing countries into groups along such lines. Dependence upon different types of food grains (rice, wheat, etc.); different methods of cooking (margarine, butter, olive oil, ghee, etc.); different types of clothes washing facilities (front-loading automatic machines, twin-tubs, tanque, bowl, etc.) – these and similar criteria have been used to categorize countries or regions in this way, along with the other more conventional variables such as per capita income or consumption levels.

It is worth stressing again that such groupings often do not follow national boundaries. In some respects northern Germany differs more from southern Germany than it does from other northern countries; while the 'olive oil line' mentioned earlier sharply distinguishes southern from northern France and for many purposes puts it into a different group. An overall national average is always a dangerous statistic, and this context is no exception.

(c) Many attempts have also been made to classify countries on the basis of whether in any given field of activity they are trend setters (innovators or early adoptes of new market developments) or come towards the tail of the new developments queue. It is naturally very tempting to try to find the international equivalent of 'what Manchester thinks today, London thinks tomorrow'. For many types of new product innovation in the affluent society, it used to be assumed that North America would lead the way, with Northern Europe (particularly Sweden) following and providing a bridge for the diffusion of new ideas to other less prosperous or more conservative parts of Europe. While it is true that a great deal of marketing innovation has in the past occurred in the USA, it is certainly not correct that diffusion of different new ideas follows more or less similar geographical paths internationally. Any international market research program founded on such a premise is likely to produce misleading results.

Whether or not different countries are grouped or ranked in some such way before starting on a full-scale study, there are two alternative strategies which can then be pursued in actually carrying out multi-country projects. Both strategies have their obvious advantages and disadvantages, and sometimes it is possible to combine elements of each.

The first strategy is to follow a *selective* (or *sequential*) approach. Although from time to time particular countries, e.g. Belgium, have been put forward as suitable test markets for a much wider group of countries, for most research problems it is extremely unlikely that any single test country can be found which is sufficiently representative to provide an adequate answer internationally. It is however often very sensible to carry out a major international project in only a few key countries (perhaps 3–4) at the outset, either simultaneously or in sequence – the results being looked at partly from the point of view of projecting them to other similar countries but also as a form of sensitivity analysis: what important elements in the situation are likely to vary in practice between different countries, in what directions and how far? Depending on these findings, the decision can then be made whether or not to extend the research to additional countries, and which ones.

The second strategy is to start by carrying out relatively limited *broad spectrum* research over a larger number of countries, before going into any of the individual countries in detail. Such research can be limited in one or both of two ways. It can confine itself to a restricted set of key questions asked of reasonably large national samples, perhaps using omnibus surveys, in order to get a 'first feel' of the major dimensions of the problem and the likely extent of differences between countries. Or it can be a more intensive survey carried out on a total international sample which is large enough to provide the opportunities for more detailed analysis and understanding of the sample as a whole, but where the individual national sub-samples are too small to provide anything more than first rough indications of differences between countries. In either case further research can be carried out subsequently to complete the picture in more detail for some or all of the countries previously 'dipped into', depending on the findings of the first stage.

A very different way of looking at the problems of where to research is illustrated by the concept of various 'international cultures' which have been identified for marketing and research purposes. Major city/smaller city/rural life styles are an example of one such trans-national concept. Another is that of the typical teenager (with international tastes in clothing, pop music, etc.). A third is that of the international businessman and traveller. For certain research purposes such international strata may be perfectly valid, although it is obviously unwise to assume that they are not also strongly affected by purely national or local factors. Where such strata exist, it could well be useful to direct market research at such groups right across countries rather than set out to conduct a series of separate national surveys. This would of course argue for a multi-national study early on, and so indicate a different research approach to that involved in selecting certain key or representative countries. Even in cases of an international target group of this type, however, it is usually necessary to take some measure of the differences between countries for the purpose of marketing decision and action.

Preliminary steps

Once we have decided that we want to research a particular market in a given country, what steps are then involved? Many of these are naturally similar to those we would take in researching the domestic market, and the following comments therefore concentrate on points where there are more likely to be some differences.

First, and most obviously, we should pull together any relevant *published or otherwise available information* (secondary data) there may be which bears upon the market we are studying.[14] This may already have been done in the course of selecting which country to research, but probably not in great depth. We can commission a research agency to carry out this work for us; or set out to collect as much data as possible for ourselves. Chapter 1 has described the possibilities open to us. A considerable and growing volume of published information on different markets in different countries has become available in recent years – some of it for a fee, much of it free. In addition to the more obvious government statistics on population, production, trade, etc., in many countries other data (e.g. consumer budgets) may be available from official surveys, on request where it is not formally published. Other likely sources of information include international organizations of many kinds, university departments, banks, media organizations, etc.

The standard warnings about using such data apply, and even more strongly in the case of data relating to foreign countries. It is essential to establish how, and on what basis, the data were collected, and what definitions were used. It is not possible to use data published even by reputable international agencies without very carefully reading the small print, and even then it is unwise to assume that figures which appear to be comparable in fact necessarily are. [17] Also it is sensible to remember that sometimes governments or other bodies have an interest in presenting information in a particular light which can mislead the unwary. Retail price indices are notorious for this, but even fundamental data such as the population census are not immune in some countries. Wherever possible it is advisable to check such figures with people who know the country and its statistics well and who can warn if there are liable to be serious inaccuracies or distortions in the data.

It is also worth checking at this stage whether there are any *syndicated market research services* available on subscription which could provide all or at least some of the information required. There is a growing number of such services, especially in the more developed markets – some of them run on a continuous or periodic basis, others 'one-off' jobs. An alternative approach is to buy questions in *omnibus surveys* (see chapter 9), which are now available in most parts of the world. It is generally possible to track down the major services of these kinds with the help of an international agency (market research or advertising) or a body such as the British Overseas Trade Board. There are also directories of these services published by organizations such as the UK Market Research Society or the BOTB itself [18] – although since the situation is constantly changing these directories inevitably find it difficult to be completely up-to-date or comprehensive.

Once again it is necessary to sound a loud warning note. Some of the syndicated services on offer are technically inadequate, at least for certain purposes; and before subscribing it is vital to check the detailed specifications of the study, and also wherever possible its likely accuracy either with other subscribers or by asking for a few sample figures which can be cross-checked with other information. Failing these possibilities, it is worth trying at least to get an informed and objective opinion of the technical competence and general reputation of the agency producing the service. Above all beware of syndicated services which promise the earth at a bargain basement price. Sound work costs money, even on a shared basis, and if the price quoted looks commercially unsound this can be evidence of corner-cutting in assembling the information. The argument that 'We can't lose, after all it costs so little' simply does not hold water: inaccurate or misleading information may cost a great deal of money in terms of a wrong decision based on it.

Setting-up the research

The preliminary background work completed, how should we organize any new research needed? There are basically four main ways in which a client can arrange for a research project in a foreign country:

(a) He can – using his head office staff or his local branch or associates –
     directly organize and control the necessary fieldwork and other facilities
     in each country concerned ('do-it-yourself' research).
(b) He or his associates can select a local research' agency to carry out the
     work in each country.
(c) He can commission an international research chain to organize the
     project through its local branches or affiliates.
(d) He can commission a market research company or consultant in his own
     country to control the project on his behalf, either (a) sub-contracting the
     on-the-spot work to a local agency in each country concerned or (b) itself
     organizing the necessary field and other facilities for the job.

There are a number of possible variations around these main themes.

Not all these options are available in every case. Some clients do not have
the resources or skills themselves to arrange for an international project. Many
countries around the world still do not have adequate (or perhaps any) local
market research agencies, so that it is necessary for someone to go in from
outside on each occasion in order to set up the facilities. Even where the client
does have appropriate internal market research resources and some familiarity
with international research, it is sometimes more convenient or more efficient
to work with an outside research supplier based in his home country or in a
regional centre.

The pros and cons of the different routes have been debated on public
platforms almost *ad nauseam*, and the alternative cases made out at length by
sometimes not-entirely-disinterested protagonists. It is not intended to replay
all the arguments here, and the reader is referred to the literature (e.g. refs. 13,
3 and 19). Among the more important questions which a client needs to
consider in choosing his best course of action, however, are:

(a) How can he most effectively shorten the length of the communication
     chain, and minimize the risks of miscommunication between the research
     user, the research planner, the questionnaire designer and the field
     frontline (both down the chain and back up again) – and how are any
     language hurdles best crossed?
(b) Which course will make for the most effective contact with local research
     personnel, tapping their skills and local knowledge of the market?
(c) How can the necessary local facilities – especially fieldwork – be most
     effectively and efficiently selected/controlled/evaluated?
(d) How can comparability between countries best be insured?
(e) How can time delays be minimized?
(f) What are the alternative *total* costs? (For example, planning and
     coordination by a UK agency mean money on top of the on-the-spot
     costs, but so will the additional efforts of client head office staff in dealing
     with a series of local agencies.)

In answering such questions there are a few considerations worth mentioning among the many others. First, even though at first sight it may not seem the most cost-efficient solution it may be well worthwhile on many more important and complex jobs for the client to incur the cost and time penalties of himself travelling to the countries involved in order to benefit from the additional local knowledge gained, the direct contact with and feedback from the local researchers, and improved communications generally: third-hand impressions at long-range do not often give a real 'gut understanding' of the market situation.

Second, when is a chain a chain (or perhaps, how long is a chain)? Some international research chains have a common ownership, standard international systems and research methods, international training and exchange of personnel, tightly organized briefing and control methods across countries; others have relatively loose affiliation arrangements, changing membership, little direct personal contact, limited standardization in their approaches. The first are not *necessarily* better than the second, but they are certainly different − and the client needs to understand the facts of the situation.

Third, research agencies which work on the principle of having no fixed affiliations but of 'selecting the most appropriate local agency for the particular job' often appear to have a good case going for them (e.g. ref. 20). The strength of a chain is that of its weakest links; few if any chains are equally strong in all their links for every type of job. This is particularly true in qualitative and 'industrial' research. On the other hand, the 'horses-for-courses' approach may at times just be a case of making a virtue out of necessity.

It is quite impossible to generalize about what is likely to be the best solution in any given case. Apart from reading and considering the arguments put forward in the literature, the most sensible procedure is to talk to a number of different research suppliers and users and where appropriate apply their international experience to your problem; and to seek such disinterested advice as you can find. For a variety of reasons − such as the way in which the research industry developed, the home locations of many multinational companies, language, etc. − the UK and the USA have long been the major coordinator countries for international research projects. This situation may gradually change, especially with the increasing use of the telephone for various types of international survey,[21] but for the moment these two countries inevitably contain the largest reservoir of experience in coordinating international projects.

Choosing a local market research agency

If an international project is being handled through a UK market research company, the latter will normally be responsible for selecting suitable local agencies. If, however, the client is involved in choosing the local agency, he is faced with the question of how best to appraise the various available alternatives.

In many respects the problem is similar to that of selecting an agency for research in the home market, and this chapter does not set to deal with this in detail. (For anyone who wishes to follow up this issue, there is an exhaustive checklist approach suggested by Mayer[22]; other advice and suggestions are contained in publications by Marsh,[23] ISBA,[24] the Market Research Society[25] and IMRA.[26]) Lists of research agencies operating in various countries are contained in several of the references already quoted, and in directories published by the Market Research Society[27] and by ESOMAR.[28] Further information and advice can be obtained from the British Overseas Trade Board and equivalent bodies elswhere and also from the local professional associations such as those listed in the Market Research Society Yearbook[25] and the book by Douglas and Craig.[29]

Although similar principles apply, the difficulties of choosing a research agency in an overseas country are likely to be considerably more acute than in selecting a domestic agency. Unless the client himself has a good understanding of what is involved in carrying out sound market research, and is fully aware of the pitfalls and shortcomings which may lie beneath an imposing commercial veneer, he would be well advised to seek professional help in making his selection. There are however a number of checkpoints which it is often useful to have in mind in looking at a potential overseas research supplier. For example:

(a) Does it belong to any international market research chain or group? If it does, there is then the possibility of checking further with the chain headquarters or local representative about the particular experience, skills and other aspects of the local company.

(b) Which clients (particularly international ones) has it worked for during the last two years? And which has it worked for *regularly*? There may be an opportunity to check with such clients for their experience. The fact of working regularly for larger or more sophisticated clients provides some evidence of the standing of the research agency – although it is necessary to check what kinds of work it has carried out for such clients.

(c) What is known in the client's own country about the agency? Some information may be available through the relevant professional organizations, or from other companies operating in that part of the world.

(d) How long has the agency been in business as a market research company? Is market research its *only* business? What is its financial standing? Newly formed companies, and ones offering a range of non-research facilities such as 'marketing consultancy', 'import agency facilities', etc., need additional probing since market research may be just an occasional sideline.

(e) Does it belong to any group of companies with other interests outside the market research field? If so, which – and how independently does it operate? In some cases there may be links with other types of commercial organization which could pose problems of competing interests or lack of objectivity (e.g. sales agencies or media).

(f) Are there any possible conflicts of interests with other existing clients?

(g) Does it in its work conform to accepted Codes of Standard and Practice in market research (in particular the joint ICC/ESOMAR International Code [30])? What guarantees can it give of confidentiality?

(h) What experience does the agency have of tackling the *type* of market research problem under study? Some companies specialize only in certain fields of research, or at least have had little or no practical operating experience in many fields they may claim to cover.

(i) What procedures does the agency follow in drawing up and submitting research proposals? What form of reporting does it normally use – is an example available? What language(s) will the research proposals and reports be written in?

(j) What is the system of payment expected – in instalments or on the completion of the project?

In addition to questions of these kinds about the agency and its general methods of working, it is naturally important to check the qualifications and experience of the key members of staff – and particularly of the research executive who would be handling the particular project. Apart from the fact that the level of technical research skill varies considerably between countries, especially outside Europe, language difficulties and/or a lack of *marketing* knowhow can lead to problems in research design and interpretation. It is also vital to check certain of the research facilities operated by the agency – in particular its field organization. The latter is often the weakest link in the whole operation. What are the qualifications and training of the fieldworkers; what supervision procedures are carried out (and can they be checked by the client); can the client meet the fieldworkers and see them in action? On the office side, is it possible for the client to see how much, and what kinds of, editing and checking of questionnaires is carried out, and the control procedures used at the analysis stage?

This summary list of checkpoints should not be regarded as comprehensive – or as necessarily essential in every case. In the case of international research, however, checks of these kinds are likely to be more necessary than they are when commissioning research in the UK.

Some further considerations in organizing international research

The operating conditions for market research vary so much in different parts of the world that it is impossible sensibly to discuss in a single chapter the detailed aspects of how to carry out research in other countries. The kinds of local factor which affect the design and conduct of surveys have been referred to earlier. Dealing with them efficiently and effectively calls for experience, determination and imagination; but in an increasing number of countries around the world, not just in the main developed markets. research is now sufficiently well-established for the major local problems to have been identified and solutions found.

As far as technical issues are concerned, it is inevitably a question of steering a course between underrating local differences and over-reacting to them. We should not automatically accept an 'it won't work here' opinion without checking the evidence for this assertion, whether or not the view comes from a local researcher. Much received wisdom of this kind is based on quite inadequate or out-of-date information. Conversely, it is clearly dangerous to assume that a particular research approach or technique used successfully elsewhere will work in a new country without carefully checking it out first. The fact that interviewers succeed in obtaining answers and completing the questionnaire does *not* indicate that these answers are meaningful or valid.

The most difficult field for international research is that of attitude measurement. Techniques and standards differ widely between countries. The concepts we are trying to measure are not always easily defined, and may well vary greatly but in unknown ways between different cultures; the measuring devices we use are often not very precise or robust, and may sometimes themselves be culture-specific; and the problems of language and semantics are at their most acute. Some work has been done to get grips with such problems (e.g. ref. 31), but qualitative work generally is a minefield for those inexperienced in international research.

Without plunging into the detailed aspects of research in particular countries, there are certain general points which it is again worth underlining in connection with international research projects. The first is *the crucial importance of precise communication*, especially in briefing the local agency. There is much more scope for misunderstandings to occur than in the case of domestic research. Where some at least of the communication between client and local research agency is indirect or at long range all details of the research approach and methods must be clearly set down and agreed on paper. It is safer to go into possibly too much detail than to take anything for granted: research experience and practices differ from country to country and it is essential that any underlying assumptions are brought out into the open. Quite apart from affecting the efficiency with which the research is carried out, such breakdowns in communication often lead to unfortunate arguments over the costing of international research projects.

A second requirement, particularly with multi-country projects, is the need for *firm coordination*. There must be a clear and generally recognized central point of responsibility for decisions affecting the design and conduct of the research if comparability is to be achieved, and time and money not wasted. It is especially important that the respective roles, contributions and involvement of the centre and of the local units – in *both* client and research organizations – is agreed from the outset. Confusion about this is a frequent cause of delay and even friction.

An excellent discussion of the issues involved in international briefing and coordination is contained in the article by Barnard;[32] several contributions at the 1984 ICC/ESOMAR Symposium[21] deal with the need for appropriate checklists; and the ICC and ESOMAR have jointly published a relevant guide and checklist for commissioning research.[33]

Among other issues which are peculiar to international research, and which need particularly to be watched, are the following:

(a) Who is to be responsible for any *translation* work involved, and how will this be paid for? This can be a major item in certain types of research, especially qualitative work involving group discussions and/or extended individual interviews. Is such material going to be digested and analysed by local staff in the local language(s), so that only the final report needs to be prepared in English; or is it (also) going to be necessary to translate the basic questionnaires and transcripts into English, so that they can be read and if necessary worked on in the UK? The author has come across cases where translation charges have added 50% to the basic cost of carrying out the study; and if several countries are involved this could be a major consideration in the original design of the research project.

(b) Is the *analysis of the data collected* to be carried out locally or in the originating country? The likely advantages of the latter are in helping to ensure comparability of the analyses (and their layout) across different countries; in the existence of better computer facilities and programs compared with certain other countries; in providing further checks centrally upon the quality of the data; and on occasions it can be cheaper. Against these arguments, central analysis adds to some of the logistical problems. It is often expensive to ship all the original field material back to the coordinating country and may be dangerous. There are too many examples of such material being lost in transit, temporarily or even permanently, and usually it is safer to copy any basic information of this kind before despatching it – which also can cost a lot of money. If on the other hand the information is part-processed, on to punchcards or tapes, we have to be confident that the local processor can provide a reasonably clean and accurate job, otherwise additional time, money and frustration will be involved before the final tabulations can be carried out.

(c) How is the actual *report* to be prepared? Should this be written back at the base country; by the agency actually carrying out the research in the country concerned; or by some combination of the two? A case can be made out for each of these courses, depending on the nature of the study. Where a number of countries are involved in the same project, there is certainly a strong argument for an overall report to be prepared centrally. Conversely, even where the main analysis and reporting is being handled centrally and not in the individual country or countries concerned, it is foolish to forego the opportunity of potentially valuable local comment on the data collected. The organization actually carrying out the fieldwork will in most cases be well placed to suggest why particular findings come out the way they do; and a local research agency of any insight and experience will be able to contribute usefully to the interpretation of findings. It is generally sensible at least to invite their comments on any central interpretation of the local research results in those cases where they are not asked themselves to prepare a full report.

(d) How much will the *total bill* be – and *how will it be paid*? Which currency will payment be in, at what rate of exchange? Are there any arrangements for inflation-proofing or hedging against currency fluctuations? It is very easy to leave out of account certain types of local tax, costs of international transfers, etc., or to overlook the importance of cost or currency adjustment clauses.

One final possibility which also should not be overlooked is that of obtaining some form of grant or subsidy for research into export markets. In the case of the UK, for example, the British Overseas Trade Board can contribute up to 50 per cent of the cost of approved export research costs.

This by no means exhausts all the problems and 'tricks of the trade' which arise in planning and carrying out international market research: the reader who is interested in going further should consult the references at the end of this book, and the additional follow-up suggestions contained in some of those. (The book by Douglas and Craig,[29] and the paper by Barnard[32] are strongly recommended in this connection.)

Chapter 24

Print media research

MICHAEL BROWN

Introduction

This chapter is concerned with research into print media in the sense of newspapers and magazines, whether aimed at a wide, general audience or a narrower, more specialized one. This introductory section comprises, first, a brief review of the several purposes to which research in this area is put and, second, a synopsis of the order and content of the other parts of the chapter.

Media research is often interpreted as being synonymous with audience measurement, particularly in the case of newspapers and magazines, and, further, as providing data solely of relevance to advertising agencies or, in some cases, for direct use by the advertisers whose accounts they handle. Both of these concepts are oversimplifications. From the point of view of the advertiser or his agency, the requirement from research into any medium is to provide information that will assist both in choice between media – between newspapers and magazines, for example, or between magazines and television – and as regards intra-media choice: the selection, for instance, of individual advertising vehicles, such as the *Daily Express* or *Woman's Own*. The criterion of both inter- and intra-media choice will be, at base, one of cost-effectiveness: a relation between the price of using a particular advertising medium and the 'effects' of the campaign concerned, however defined.

The contribution of media choice itself to the overall variation in effectiveness, from campaign to campaign, is largely a matter of opinion and contention, rather than one of fact; some authors [1] would rate the creative content of advertising ten times as important a factor as media selection.

Well-documented cases in which the media contribution may be unequivocally partialled out are not common; but in the case of newpapers and magazines, direct response advertising provides an exception. Here, different media vehicles can be very clearly shown to generate varying responses in the marketplace. [2]

More generally, given that the impact of media choice, even if not fully documented, is certainly not completely negligible, one factor of obvious relevance to effectiveness is the size and nature of the audience delivered by an advertising schedule. At the same time, to enumerate the audience that has opportunity to come into contact with advertisements is far from providing a complete assessment of a campaign's likely results. There are thus many other aspects of 'effectiveness' beyond audience size and composition and some of these fall into the proper area of media research.

Turning to the publisher's viewpoint, the advertisement department of a newspaper or magazine will, in common with the advertiser and agency, require from print media research data on audiences and other criteria of effectiveness; the difference in application of the results is the self-evident one that the publisher will be seeking to demonstrate a competitive advantage for his vehicle vis-à-vis others, both generally and in relation to the particular marketing and advertising briefs of a potential client. However, the publisher has also other interests, since he is operating in a situation of joint supply in two markets: not only is he selling advertising space or a potential audience, but also copies of his actual newspaper or magazine to readers. He thus requires marketing research, in all its aspects, which treats the publication as being just as much a 'product' as any other one. Under this heading may be included investigation of readers' preference for and reaction to editorial material – a particular form, relevant to media, of 'product content' research.

Within the total area of media research, there are thus a number of measurement requirements, some overlapping, from advertisers, agencies and media owners. The next section of this chapter covers audience measurement: after consideration of the relevant concepts, research methods and problems in the measurement of issue, page and advertisement audiences are discussed. The section ends with a review of the sub-groups identified in audience research – demographic, geodemographic, attitudinal and behavioural, including, under the latter heading, audience breakdowns by product/brand purchasing and the research requirements of 'single source' and integrated data.

The third section turns to the use of audience measurement and other data as input to computer programs designed either to construct print media schedules or forecast their performance on certain prespecified criteria. The objectives, broad lines of development, advantages, and limitations of such programs are described, but full mathematical treatment of methods is outside the scope of the section.

In the fourth section, criteria of newspaper and magazine advertising effectiveness other than audience measurements are discussed. Requirements and difficulties peculiar to media research are highlighted, fuller treatment of relevant techniques being provided in other chapters.

The final section deals relatively briefly with the applications of market and marketing research to print media as a product field and to individual newspapers and magazines as 'brands', rather than as advertising vehicles or providers of audiences.

The bibliography for this chapter is not comprehensive. Books aiming to cover the total area of print media measurement are non-existent and, as far as the narrower topic of readership is concerned, texts are rare. [3,4] One seminar [5] and three more recent international symposia [6] have provided valuable overviews of 'the state of the art'. There is a massive and ever-growing journal literature on the validity of the alternative readership measurement methods and the effects of research design variables on the estimates produced. The interested reader is recommended to the selected references we have cited, which deal with some of the more important technical aspects in greater detail than this chapter can accommodate.

Audience measurement

Audience concepts

Given that the overall requirement in the implementation of any advertising brief is to achieve optimum cost-effectiveness, a sub-objective is to select advertising vehicles in such a way that the size and nature of the audience, and the pattern of their opportunities for contact with the advertisements, are 'best' on some agreed set of criteria. There thus exists a need for audience measurement, so that the performance of alternative schedules, on these criteria, may be evaluated; but before dealing with the practical problems involved, it is necessary to consider what is implied by 'audience'

Issue audience may be defined as the number and kinds of individuals that come into contact with either a specific issue of a given newspaper or magazine or with the 'average' issue. People counted within the issue audience are often referred to, loosely, as 'readers' and their total is frequently labelled the 'readership' of the publication concerned. Further, being an issue reader is said to provide an 'opportunity to see' (OTS) an advertisement carried by the issue. Any definition of issue audience is essentially an operational one, as will be seen below; but irrespective of the exact definition selected, it will not reflect differences, within the total issue readership, between individuals and between different occasions as regards the amount that is read or looked at within the issue. A narrower definition thus exists of the *page* (or double-page spread) *audience* as comprising the number of people who look at anything on a page or spread, or on the 'average' one.

Being counted within the page audience obviously confers on an individual a higher probability of contact with an actual advertisement than does merely being a member of the issue audience. However, it is possible to refine the concept yet further and define, as falling within the *advertisement audience*, those people who have contact with the ad itself.

The main points to note from the brief discussion of audience concepts

above are two: there exists a hierarchy of increasingly narrow definitions; but
at each level – whether issue, page, or advertisement – the interpretation of
'contact' is not an unambiguous one.

Issue audience

Having dealt briefly with basic audience concepts, attention is now turned to
the practical problems of issue audience measurement. The most common
research requirement here is to provide an unbiased estimate of the audience
for the *average* issue of a newspaper or magazine. Meeting this requirement
raises two essential problems: defining 'readership', in the sense of contact with
an issue, and selecting an appropriate data collection method.

Audience definition.   As already noted, *any* definition of issue readership is an
operational definition; there is no absolute standard against which it may be
assessed whether a person is or is not a reader. As an example, in Britain the
National Readership Survey takes a reader to be a respondent who claims to
have read or looked at any copy of the newspaper or magazine concerned,
anywhere, within a period equal to the publication interval of the title prior to
the date of interview. (That is to say, a reader has to have seen a daily paper on
the day before the date of interview, a Sunday paper or a weekly magazine
within the seven days ending on the day before the interview, and so on.)

Three points within this definition serve to illustrate the contention that
'readership' is not an absolute concept. First, a respondent qualifies as a reader
irrespective of the proportion of an issue they have seen at all and of whether
they have read intently or merely glanced. In fact, people labelled as 'readers'
in the NRS sense do have a high probability of having looked at the average
page within an issue, as experimental work preceding the 1968 Survey [7] shows;
but it would be possible to count within the average issue audience only those
with some 'proved' level of 'within the issue' reading intensity.

Second, the definition allows readership of current and outdated issues to
count equally; but it is possible, if it is relevant to the application of the
research, to consider only those reading occasions that occur within some set
interval of an issue going on sale. This would produce, naturally, a numerically
different estimate of average issue audience.

Third, readers defined in this way are not necessarily those who actually
purchased the newspaper or magazine – they may equally be people, within or
beyond the purchaser's household, to whom the issue was passed on; nor, to
be counted within the average issue audience, must they have read the issue
concerned at home or in some other, specified, circumstances. Clearly,
audience definitions may be framed which take a different view on these points.

Research techniques.   Turning to research techniques relevant to average issue
audience measurement, a first, major choice lies between relying, on the one
hand, on a person's recall of a previous reading occasion or previous occasions

or, on the other hand, on a person's recognition of a specific issue of a newspaper or magazine as one they had read before (the *average* issue audience estimate then being derived by measurement, in this way, of a number of different issues).

The 'recall' approach subdivides again into two alternative routes. We may ask people when they last read an issue – any issue – of some newspaper or magazine (using an open-ended question or one precoded in terms of time periods); this is conventionally referred to as the 'recency' or 'recent reading' approach. Alternatively, we may ask how often a person claims to read or page through different issues of a stated title, either phrasing the question in terms of usual, habitual behaviour or in terms of a stated, historical time period, such as 'the last four weeks' or 'the last six months'; this is the so-called 'frequency' method of average issue audience estimation.

In relation to the recency method, the average issue readership (AIR) estimate is then the number of people claiming to have read any issue in a period of time, preceding the day of interview, equal to the publication interval. In the frequency method, by contrast, the responses lead to a person-by-person estimate of the *probability* of contact with the average issue; a weighted average of these probabilities, across the sample, allows an AIR estimate. Reading frequency measurement methods are discussed in more detail later in this chapter.

If a recall-based technique is to be employed (whether in relation to a single, most recent reading occasion *or* the number of issues seen in a specified, historical period *or* habitual behaviour), the question arises whether the respondent should or should not be prompted (in relation to the names of the newspapers and magazines being measured) and, if so, in what way.

Prior to 1984, the British NRS (following widespread practice) utilized, as prompts, reproductions of publications' mastheads – their titles, that is, in the type style used on the cover or front page. However, there are many examples of average issue readership measurement using other forms of prompt – from actual covers of magazines to just the names of the publications, whether shown to the respondent or only read out – or of not using prompting at all. We comment below on the effect of variation in the form of prompting; but to employ completely open, unprompted questioning on the recall of readership certainly tends to result in underclaiming of issue contact, particularly for titles which the respondent sees infrequently or irregularly.

Turning now to the basic alternative to estimating average issue readership on the basis of the recall of reading occasions, the recognition approach as originally developed in the US in the 1930s involved using a complete issue of a magazine as a prompt and then, when a person had perused it fully, asking them whether they had read or paged through it previously; the title by which the technique is universally known, 'Through-the-book' (TTB), naturally follows. However, findings that, to some small but measurable degree, spurious claims of previous readership could arise if an issue that had not yet been distributed was tested led to a modification of the original approach, termed the 'Editorial interest' method.[8] Here, respondents are first taken through an issue and asked, in relation to items of its contents, whether they would find them of interest. As a final question, intended to appear an incidental and unloaded one, it is established whether they think they have seen the issue in question previously.

This is, basically, the TTB technique variant currently in use; but, under the commercial pressure of having to measure an ever-increasing number of magazines in the same, reasonably priced survey, later modifications have led to not using a full, unadulterated issue as a prompt aid but a heavily 'stripped down' version, hopefully retaining sufficient of the key items of cover and/or index and/or main editorial contents so as to be unambiguously identified.

In parallel with the choice between recall and recognition approaches, there are options of average issue readership measurement via personal interviews, telephone contact and self-administered questionnaire. Whilst readership research has, very largely, grown up in a face-to-face personal interview setting, there is a growing volume of evidence that satisfactory estimates can be obtained from self-administered questionnaires; comparisons between NRS results and those from the Target Group Index[9] provide an example. At the same time, once questioning is beyond an interviewer's direct control, there may be problems in adequately conveying to a respondent the precise definition of 'readership' that is being employed; in what prompts may be used; or in controlling the order in which the respondent answers similar questions on different publications.

With respect to readership measurement via self-completion questionnaires, a particular note should be added regarding publications with narrow and specialized audiences. Here, in the interests of sampling economy, it is not uncommon practice to obtain self-completed data on a sample drawn from a magazine's list of subscribers, or to insert a questionnaire in all copies of a particular issue. Whilst there is nothing intrinsically wrong in a well conducted readership survey by mail – given that, with or without follow-up, a satisfactory response rate can be obtained – the characteristics of readers who choose to return a questionnaire inserted in the actual publication can often be markedly different from those of its total audience. Further, pass-on readership clearly cannot be directly measured in any 'one copy, one questionnaire' design.

Readership measurement by telephone[10] is widely established in the US, particularly in relation to newspapers, but relative to personal interviewing or self-completion questionnaires it is less frequently used in Europe. Adequate penetration of telephone ownership in the population of interest is an obvious requirement; and the impossibility of visual prompting may be a limitation. On the other hand, there is evidence of being able to achieve commendably high response rates from specialized audiences.[11]

Turning to another dimension of survey design, the majority of readership surveys tend to provide either 'one-off' estimates or regularly published reports based, in the latter case, on fresh samples on each occasion. However, panel techniques may also be employed. A readership diary panel would appear to avoid the limitations imposed by inaccurate recall of reading events (*if* the diary were kept up-to-date and completed soon after each reading occasion); also, it can potentially capture more detail than other techniques – for example, the issue date of each newspaper and magazine seen, or multiple pick-ups of the same issue. On the other side of the balance sheet, however, are such questions as bias-free recruitment to a panel, cooperation rate over time and costs. A number of excellent discussions in depth of panel advantages and limitations have been published.[12] The Netherlands offers one of the few examples of a major, syndicated readership measurement service which is panel-based.[13]

Reliability and validity. Any complete discussion of the comparative or absolute accuracy of the readership estimates obtained by the technique alternatives outlined above is completely beyond the scope of this chapter; it is only possible to touch on some of the main topics at issue – many of them not fully resolved – and to direct the reader's attention to fuller discussion elsewhere.

Readership measurement results are *highly* technique dependent and research design changes which may appear comparatively minor can have marked effects. Noted below are some of the principal variables.

Filter questions are commonly employed at the outset of a readership survey interview, to determine to which respondents will be put the critical question or questions which categorize a person as a reader or non-reader of a particular title. Results may prove highly sensitive to the number and wording of such filter questions.[14] For a recall-based survey, the form of prompt aid used may be of importance,[15] although the balance of evidence suggests that other variables have far larger effects.

At the analogous stage in a Through-the-book interview, it has long been contended that the age of the issue used as a prompt is of some considerable importance: if it were too 'young', the issue's audience would not have grown to its maximum by the time the interview was carried out while, if it were too 'old', some reading events could well be forgotten. However, the evidence on this point is not clear-cut.[16]

The number of titles included in a readership questionnaire will certainly affect the estimates obtained,[17] but so, very dramatically, will the way in which the presentation of a long list of titles is varied from interview to interview.[18] Randomization of title presentation order does not, of course, cure this problem – it simply conceals its effects. Some authors favour a fixed order of groups of publications and, in a recall-based interview, there is some logic in dealing with the most difficult cases (from the respondent's viewpoint) – monthly magazines – first, and the simplest – daily newspapers – last.

The readership questions themselves are, of course, of importance; [19] an outstanding example is provided by South African experience, where a change in the definition of the reading event from 'read or paged through' to 'read' led to a loss of nearly 50 % in the audience estimated for monthly magazines. [20] But it is not just question *wording* which is at issue here. Asking all questions about one newspaper or magazine before moving on to the next title – a 'horizontal' approach – may produce different results from a 'vertical' one, in which questions are applied, sequentially, to the whole title list. [21] Even more interestingly, German work has clearly shown that, in the recency method, the estimates obtained will markedly depend on the number of permissible answer categories that lead to a person being labelled 'reader', relative to the number leading to a 'non-reader' coding. [22] This effect still shows through when the question asked on the last reading occasion is an open-ended one, with the responses *interviewer*-coded. A likely explanation thus lies in a degree of uncertainty, on the respondent's part, as to the dating of the last reading event, but with an unbalanced tendency as between reporting it more recently than was actually the case and less recently.

Turning from the reliability of readership measurement techniques and their robustness (or lack of it) to validity as such, the recall technique is subject to a number of potential biases, such as the overclaiming of reading events, on the basis of habitual behaviour that did not take place in the specific period at issue; underclaiming, often through forgetting; confusion of one publication with another; [23] and the mental displacement of a reading event in time, usually forward, this last-mentioned error being often referred to as 'telescoping'. [24] The work of Belson in Britain [25] marks the first, classic investigation of the validity of the recency method, but the literature is a growing one, particularly recently. [26]

One particular problem of the recency method lies not in the accuracy of the data gathered in the field but in the estimation model: the number of people reading *any* issue of a publication within a period of time equal to the publication interval provides an unbiased estimate of the average issue audience if, and only if, each of the reading events represented a *first* reading occasion for the person and issue concerned. Unfortunately, readers' behaviour is not as conveniently neat as this. If a person re-reads an issue over two or more publication intervals ('replication'), overestimation of the AIR occurs; if they read two or more different issues in the same publication interval ('parallel readership'), then the audience estimate is understated by the recency technique. The 'model bias' problem, as it is commonly termed, has been long recognized, and a very full treatment is provided by the published papers submitted for the Thomson 1962 awards; [27] there have been a number of later contributions. [28] Eliminating this particular bias calls for a considerable complication of the basic recent reading technique; one of the first UK attempts is seen in the Odham's work on women's magazines. [29]

The recognition-based, Through-the-book technique is no less subject to sources of potential bias, most of which have already been touched upon: the injudicious use of inappropriately aged issues as prompts; overclaims arising from their perceptions of habitual behaviour by regular readers; and, perhaps, poor pick-up of out-of-home reading events. TTB generally returns lower levels of estimated readership than does the recency technique, but one author at least contends this to be solely dependent on the detailed formulation of the questioning in the two cases. There is a growing literature. [30]

Before leaving this all-important area of technique reliability and validity, it must in all fairness be said that, at the time of writing – and the research area is quite a fast-moving one – there is no certain solution of the problems that have just been sketched in, at least on the near horizon. Some fascinating, very preliminary work has been conducted on the 'automatic' detection of proximity of a reader to an issue using ultrasonic or electronic scanning and sensing, [31] but enormous investment would be required. Much more modest but, perhaps, more promising of an early benefit are attempts to measure accurately the readership of an issue or issues 'yesterday' (to minimize recall problems) and, on that day, reading it or them for the time (to eliminate replication bias). [32]

Reading frequency. The discussion of issue audience measurement above may have conveyed an oversimplified picture of a population divided on a black and white basis into 'readers' and 'non-readers' of this or that publication. In fact, of course, the situation includes shades of grey. For a particular newspaper or magazine, there will be a group of people who, to all intents and purposes, never come into contact with it; another set of people who see virtually every issue; and, in between, those who are irregular readers to a greater or lesser degree.

The regularity with which an individual is in contact with the 'average' issue has come to be known colloquially as his or her *reading frequency* for the title concerned. The importance of measuring reading frequency lies in the fact that readership research results are used not only to forecast the potential audience for one insertion in one issue, as discussed above, but, more generally, to investigate the full pattern of contacts arising from a schedule of several insertions in one or more publications. This pattern will depend intimately on the reading frequencies involved. Consider, say, five issues of one magazine, having an average issue audience of one million. On the simplifying assumption of there existing only 'readers' and 'non-readers', each of the million will see five issues and the remainder of the population none. On the more realistic model of issue-contact probabilities other than zero or one occurring, somewhat more than one million people will read at least one issue, because the audience from issue to issue will not comprise always exactly the same individuals. On the other hand, the average number of issues read, amongst those who see any, will now be less than five.

There are at least three distinguishable approaches to reading frequency measurement. First, consistent questions on issue readership can be repeated twice or more to the same individuals in a panel context. As previously discussed, this will normally involve a self-administered questionnaire depending on respondents' recollections of historical reading occasions. Recognition of distinct issues will not normally be involved. Note, therefore, that it will not in general be known whether a given individual's claim, for example, of two reading events in relation to two successive publication intervals relates to the two issues respectively current in these periods, to some other two issues or, indeed, to the same issue, unless a diary is in use which records issue date in relation to each reading event. The panel approach to reading frequency estimation has, in practice, been little employed in the UK outside the work by Attwood. A much fuller consideration of its possibilities and limitations than is given here is provided by the Thomson award papers [33] on the general problem of panel use in audience measurement.

As a second method the recognition of two or more difficult issues of the same publication (as having been read before) can be measured on the same sample at successive interviews; the logistics of the amount of material to be carried by the interviewer probably precludes the use of one interview only. This approach has, traditionally, been widely used in the US. The information directly obtained is the 'turnover' of audience from one issue to the next; from it, the cumulative audience reached by several issues may be mathematically modelled. A decision has to be taken whether there is any material gain in accuracy in measuring audience turnover across *more* than two issues. [34]

Third, and most commonly other than for North American recognition-based surveys, a reader is asked, in effect, to make a subjective estimate of their reading frequency, using some form of scale. Again most commonly, this scale will be numerical; for example, the French CESP survey asks, in respect of weekly magazines, 'How often do you personally read or flick through a copy of... either at home or elsewhere?', the possible responses being 'Every week', '2–3 times a month', 'Once a month', '5–6 times a year' or 'Less often'. Again, the German Media-Analyse formulation was (until 1983) for all publication groups 'How many of the last 12 issues did you read?' Naturally, the use of a numerical scale raises the problem of the optimum number of scale positions. [35] It is also to be noted that exactly the same reading frequency claims are unlikely to be obtained from the three different formulations in common use: the number of different issues read in some stated period (e.g. 'the last six weeks'); the number read out of the *last n* published; and the number 'usually' read out of each *n* published.

Purely verbal reading frequency scales are less common, although they have been employed in France. The British NRS changed in 1984, after many years, to a verbal form, but with the intended meaning of the scale positions explained semi-numerically. An excellent review of frequency scale formulations across 24 surveys has been provided by Meier [36] — although, like all such reviews, it is now slightly out-of-date.

The difference between the use of a numerical and a verbal scale is not so great as may at first appear. The intention in both instances is to segment the population in such a way that within-group differences in true frequency of issue-contact are smaller than between-group ones. Responses to a verbal scale have, clearly, to be given a quantitative meaning; but so, in fact, have those on a numerical scale. Answers here cannot be taken at face value: individuals, generally speaking, tend to *over*estimate their reading frequency, so that a claim to see 'six issues out of six' implies, in fact, a probability of contact with the average issue not of one but of some smaller number.

In the NRS case, the scale of reading frequency is 'calibrated' by use of the data on average issue readership obtained in the same interview, e.g., if, for some weekly magazine or Sunday newspaper, 90 % of those claiming to see the publication 'almost always' actually qualify as 'average issue readers' on the definition used, then the *adult probability*, as it is termed, for this group will be taken as 0.9. It will be noted that there is an implicit assumption that the true reading frequency is the same for all respondents making a given frequency claim. The developmental work behind the orginal NRS scale and its application are fully dealt with by Corlett,[37] whilst there have been a number of later contributions on scale construction, calibration and validation.[38]

It is equally possible, of course, to give numerical values to each position on some frequency of reading scale by research quite separate from the readership survey in which the scale is to be employed; e.g., a verbal scale might be put to the individuals providing readership data on a panel.

As noted earlier, the practical application of reading frequency data involves using it to forecast the pattern of contacts over several issues and publications. With panel data, individuals' claims of issue contact in successive periods may be used directly for this purpose, assuming only that the pattern of claimed reading actually observed is stable over time. With NRS-type information – providing, in essence, average probabilities for groups of individuals – further assumptions are involved, principally that successive issue contacts for a given individual are independent events. Given such an assumption then if, say, the adult probability for some group and title is 0.6, the Binomial Theorem can be employed to calculate distributions such as:

Number of issues read	Probability
3 out of 3	$1 \times (0.6)^3$
2 out of 3	$3 \times (0.6)^2 \times (1.0 - 0.6)$
1 out of 3	$3 \times (0.6) \times (1.0 - 0.6)^2$
0 out of 3	$1 - (0.6)^3$

To obtain the forecast pattern of issue contacts resulting from a schedule, calculations of the above type would have to be performed, person by person, for each newspaper or magazine involved and the results then accumulated. Clearly, this is a time-consuming process, even in computer terms. A number of mathematical techniques have thus been developed which approximate, with adequate accuracy, the results of a full binomial expansion. Some further consideration of this aspect is included in the later section on the use of the computer for media schedule construction and evaluation. It should, however, just be noted here that the use of frequency-scale-based data for the purposes of mathematically modelling cumulative audience is not without its critics; some American researchers would maintain that the European approach underestimates issue-to-issue audience turnover and thus cumulative audience build-up and would aver that calibration/validation via the 'two-visits-issue-recognition' approach is essential [39].

Spread, page and advertisement audiences

If an individual qualifies as a reader of the average issue, or of a particular issue, of a newspaper or magazine, this clearly confers on him a better chance of contact with an actual advertisement in that issue than would be the case if he were outside the audience for the publication. However, only wide limits can be set on the probability of such ad contact actually occurring: even if they see an issue, some people will read more of its contents, some less. Given that the media selection objective is essentially to put an advertisement economically before a relevant group of people, a more refined measurement than issue audience seems desirable. Exactly the same two basic problems occur here as have already been noted in relation to issue audience: selecting a workable operational definition that is sensible in relation to the basic concept; and devising the best technique for measuring an audience against this definition. It is convenient to consider these problems first in relation to the audience for a particular page of a newspaper or magazine.

Conceptually, the audience for a page comprises those individuals for whom, at some time, the page was in their perceptual field, i.e. those who were in a position to perceive some particular item on it or, colloquially, had 'open eyes in front of the page'. Unfortunately, it is extremely difficult to frame an *operational* definition, suitable for large-scale audience measurement use, which well mirrors this concept. On the one hand, evidence may be sought merely that a given page in a publication has been opened, using the 'glue-spot technique', first introduced many years ago. [40] Here, a small spot of glue, hopefully imperceptible to the reader, fixes together each pair of pages near their edge. Copies specially prepared in this way are placed with a sample of people and collected again after a period. A person is then counted within the audience for a pair of pages if the glue seal between them is found to have been broken. Setting aside the practical difficulties of neither making the glue spot so weak as likely to be broken accidentally nor so strong as to interfere with normal reading behaviour, the technique is clearly more suited to limited-scale use. It is artificial to the extent that the respondent will be receiving the copy to be measured in an 'abnormal' way. It is necessary to check that the issue has only been handled by the respondent between placement and recall interviews. Finally, and most importantly, the evidence is, literally, of a pair of pages having been opened – whether or not as a prelude to the reader giving attention to anything on them is not known just from the glue-spot break.

On the other hand, far more complex observational techniques may be employed; e.g., it is possible to take a continuous record on film of a respondent in a reading situation – unavoidably, a somewhat artificial one – that can show not only which pages were opened and for how long but also the direction of gaze in relation to the page. Equipment for this purpose, originally developed in Germany, has been employed in the UK by the British Market Research Bureau. The technique is known as the Direct Eye Movement Observation System (DEMOS) and is referred to again below.

Whilst it may be possible, by such approaches, to obtain relatively direct evidence of page contact on a small scale or under 'laboratory' conditions, survey measurement of page audience has, in practice, come largely to rely on an operational definition where a respondent is counted as within the audience if, on their own report, they have looked at one or more items on the page in question. For this purpose, unprompted *recall* is little used; to ask a respondent, without the use of any recall aids at all, what items they remember having read or looked at will produce generally low scores and ambiguous data, in view of the peripheral importance to the reader of many reading events. Instead, *recognition* is largely employed. In Gallup's Field Readership Index, for example, having established that respondents claim to have seen a particular issue at all, they are taken through it page by page and asked to indicate each item – whether editorial or advertisement, text or illustration – that they have previously looked at. *Page traffic* is then defined at the proportion of the issue audience claiming one or more items on the page in question.

There is little doubt that, unavoidably, the recognition approach leads to some bias in page audience estimation. In the interview situation, there may be strong internal pressures on a respondent to report, even if it can be recalled, not exactly what he or she did when previously looking at the issue – which is the answer sought – but what they think they did or think they 'ought' to have done. Faced with a dominant item on a page which now seems unavoidable to the eye, it is not easy to say 'I didn't look at it'. Equally, reading some items may seem less socially desirable to the respondent than other ones: comic strips (or, for that matter, advertisements) as against leading articles. To this extent, to deduce page contact from *claimed* self-exposure to an item on it is far from straightforward.

There is another approach to page audience measurement, distinct from the recognition technique just discussed. Here, a respondent is presented with some form of scale indicating degrees of thorough or less thorough reading within the issue of a particular title and asked to choose that scale position which best describes their own behaviour. The scale itself can take a number of forms. In the National Readership Survey, a pictorial scale was employed for some years; however, many other formulations are possible. People might be asked, for example, how many pages out of ten they look at on average or, in verbal rather than numerical terms, whether they read 'all' of an issue, 'most', 'some' or 'little'. Some of these alternatives were investigated in the developmental research preceding the introduction of the NRS scale,[41] while their relationship to page audience and that of some other, indirect, measures of issue reading 'intensity' has also been reported.[42]

A comprehensive listing of a number of 'thoroughness' questions currently in use is provided in the review by Meier already mentioned.[43]

Irrespective of the exact form of scale employed, this technique will require actual numerical values of probability of contact with the average page to be ascribed to each scale position, if the data are to be of practical use in choosing between print media vehicles in planning schedules. In the National Readership Survey case, the scale of reading intensity was 'calibrated' (so far for groups of publications only rather than individual titles) by taking a page traffic measurement amongst people opting for each of the scale positions, but using a postal survey rather than personal interview approach.[44].

It will be seen that there is an important difference between deriving page audience data from claims of what was read or looked at previously and using a scaling approach of the type just described. The former is applicable to one or more specific issues; the latter can use questions phrased in relation to a respondent's 'usual' behaviour. This raises a basic problem in the application of the data, if it is desired to forecast the probability of contact between a given person and the 'average' page in a particular publication: it is likely that not only will people differ between themselves in the amount they 'usually' read of this newspaper or that magazine, but also that, for any one reader and title, the amount they look at will vary from issue to issue, dependent on content and reading circumstances.

The same qualification applies in the case of the third alternative approach to page audience measurement — direct questioning on recent behaviour, but without using an actual issue as a prompt. The objective here might be to estimate ad page exposure per issue period[45] and one might question people about the number or proportions of pages looked at in issues that had been read 'yesterday'.[46]

An excellent overall review of the research problems and possibilities in moving from issue audience to page audience has been provided by Noordhoff.[47]

So far, the discussion of this section has been entirely in terms of *page* audience. However, the various measurement methods touched on can equally well produce data in relation to the double-page spread formed by two facing pages; and operational definitions of 'spread audience' follow naturally from those for 'pages'. Indeed, it has been strongly argued that the spread is the more natural unit relation to audience measurement, in the sense that it is difficult to imagine a reader having no opportunity to perceive an item on a given page if the evidence is that they have focused some attention on the facing one. In fact, the validity of this argument may be seen very much to depend on definitions of 'reading' and 'attention'. All too little is known about the mechanisms of perceptual organization of complex stimuli as applied to newspaper and magazine pages. However, it does seem likely that a large amount of scanning – probably subliminal – will be involved before the eye fixes on this or that item. Thus, everything on a double-page spread may have been 'seen' in a subconscious sense; but the items later reported – quite honestly – as 'looked at' may be far fewer. This point brings one directly to the final topic of this section – measurement of audiences not for issues or spreads or pages, but for advertisements themselves.

It is to be stressed immediately that this subject lies on the borderline of 'media research' in the sense taken throughout this chapter. *Post facto*, the number and sorts of people whose knowledge, attitudes or opinions have been modified by anything transferred to them from a particular advertisement will heavily depend on its content – its product or brand subject, the ideas the advertisement expresses and the way it expresses them. This variation of advertisement audience with ad content is not the province of media research. There are, however, a number of 'media' variables which *are* relevant at this level. An advertisement's size, absolutely or relative to the page; its position on the page; the position of the page in the issue; whether the page is left- or right-hand; whether the ad faces editorial matter or is amongst other advertisements; whether it is surrounded by a margin or 'bled' to the edge of the page; and whether it is in monochrome or colour, are all characteristics which may, in principle at least, affect the size of an advertisement's audience and render it distinguishable from the audience for the page on which it appears.

Conceptual and operational definitions offer even more difficulty at this stage than before. In terms of '*opportunity* to see', the advertisement audience is virtually equivalent to that of the page carrying it; refinement must invoke some idea of communication. Whilst the principle may be to count only within the ad audience those with some proven opportunity to be affected by it, the practice is far more difficult; what cut-off point of behaviour in relation to the advertisement should be taken, and how is unbiased evidence of this behaviour then to be obtained?

In practice, methods already mentioned are the ones in use. Unaided recall of advertisements read can be employed. For an exhaustive treatment of comparisons of recall and recognition results, the reader is referred to the Advertising Research Foundation's Printed Advertisement Rating Methods (PARM) study.[48] Regarding recognition methods themselves, the Field Readership Index referred to above has the measurement of claimed readership of individual advertisements as a prime objective, its page traffic results being a byproduct. Here, reported ad contact is researched at three levels, respondents being categorized on whether they claim to have 'noted' the advertisement, to have 'read most' of its text and to have registered the brand name concerned.

As already noted, claims regarding previous advertisement reading behaviour are not unbiased, and the work reported by Fletcher[49] with the DEMOS equipment well illustrates the difficulties.

In conclusion, it is to be stressed that the techniques currently in use for measuring contact with advertisements have primarily been developed for assessing the apparent, comparative effectiveness of the ads themselves, as influenced by their content and its creative expression. Quite apart from the difficulties of definition and technique, considerable reprocessing of the data is needed to render it of relevance to media decisions; e.g., noting scores from many individual advertisements may be examined to see if the effects of such factors as ad size may be partialled out. Considerable work in the UK by the now-dissolved Agencies Research Consortium, reported by Twyman,[50] had as its objective the development of more immediately 'media-oriented' ad audience research, but did not lead to basic changes of the recognition method.

Audience classification

A rationale of audience breakdown

In the preceding sections, the concentration has been on the measurement of total audience – whether for the average issue, a page or an advertisement. However, the sub-groups which are to be examined within this total are of considerable importance; and their identification may call for considerably more than gathering straightforward 'classification' data in the usual sense of that term.

There are two basic concepts which underlie the need for audience breakdowns. First, people differ between themselves in their value as prospects to a given advertiser. This leads to a search for criteria which meaningfully segment the population both as regards their actual or potential purchasing behaviour and also in respect of their contact with media and vehicles.

Second, the effectiveness of a particular campaign may be thought to depend – holding creative content constant – on the vehicle which carries it. This variation, again, may derive from the characteristics of the audience and their interaction with the newspaper or magazine.

Demographic classification

The most commonly occurring audience breakdowns utilize demographic criteria, including sex, socio-economic class, marital status, household size and composition, employment status, and geographical area. The collection of data on these criteria does not call for special comment here, except in two cases.

The objective of any socio-economic classification is to group individuals in a clear-cut and unambiguous manner into segments which may be expected to display differing patterns of consumption of goods and services. Such an objective is difficult to meet in practice. A simple, robust, reproducible coding framework for social class is hard to find, but the efforts to date of the ESOMAR working group on the harmonization of demographics are encouraging.[51] The classification developed originally for the National Readership Survey and still the most widely used one in Britain is occupation-based. Reasonably stable results are produced, but the method is still criticized; however, the investigation by the Market Research Society produced little evidence of a decline in discriminatory power over time, or of an obviously preferable alternative classification.[52]

Regarding age, there is a school of thought that favours replacing age group classification with stages in the life cycle. Whilst there has been no general move in this direction (at least in Britain), the 'Sagacity' approach is of interest,[53] combining, as it does, elements of life cycle, affluence and occupation.

Geodemographic classification
A comparatively recent development has been the classification of individuals in terms of their areas of residence or, more strictly, by the *type* of area where they live. These types are arrived at by some form of clustering of small areas on the basis of a large number of socio-demographic variables, usually Census-based. The British development of the technique grew out of social geography but was rapidly 'adopted' by market research.[54] A comparable US system has developed.[55] Geodemographic classification may be shown to discriminate sharply in terms of the use of certain products and services.[56]

Attitudinal classification
The demographic breakdowns of print media audiences covered briefly above have, as their basic objective, the identification of population sub-groups with varying actual or potential behaviour in the market place. However, on turning to attitudinal classification of audiences, both of the two distinct concepts noted in the beginning of this section are relevant. On the one hand, brand or product-oriented attitudes of members of the audience of a newspaper or magazine may be measured. Such criteria may yield a more meaningful segmentation of the population than demographics alone can provide, in terms of 'value as prospects' for a given campaign; and it will be desired to ascertain media coverage within the attitudinally defined segments.

Within the last few years there have been considerable advances both in quantitative attitudinal measurement techniques for market research purposes and in market segmentation methods based on such data. Despite this progress, however, there has been very limited introduction, so far, of attitudinal classification into print media research, at least as regards syndicated or other generally available work as distinct from private surveys. One likely reason is that, quite apart from many remaining difficulties on the prediction of *future* purchasing behaviour from measurement of attitudes, in the cases where some success has been achieved by an advertiser in developing measures of demonstrable relevance to his market the scales in question will have tended to be specific rather than general. By contrast, the objective of much print media research is to provide market-actionable data to a wide variety of users, operating in many different product fields. Few attitudinal scales are likely both to be general enough to offer 'something for everybody' yet also 'sharp' enough to provide actionable data in specific marketing and advertising planning instances. There may be exceptions: conservatism versus experimentalism (as affecting behaviour towards new brands) or attitudes to price may be cases in point. The Target Group Index[57] provides instances of including general attitudinal, as well as demographic, audience classification.

One solution to the problem of the likely specificity of any highly predictive attitudes-to-products (or brands) has been to seek generalized, psychometric segmentations of the population – based on the responses to a large battery of attitudinal and/or behavioural questions – and then to measure media use within these segments, it being hoped that the segmentation will be predictive of market-place behaviour. Since these questions of psychographics and consumer typologies receive attention elsewhere in this volume, they will not be pursued in any depth here, but the reader's attention is directed to a number of fuller discussions in the readership research literature.[58]

There is in fact another consideration relevant to classification of audiences in attitudinal terms. Such data can certainly provide a 'richer' portrait of an audience group; and 'pen portraits' of this or that set of readers are to be welcomed in a situation where media selection decisions, increasingly, jointly involve both creative considerations and viewpoints equally with 'traditional' media department opinions.

So far, the attitudinal measurements discussed have been market-oriented; but, quite separately, attitudes to vehicles – to newspapers and magazines themselves – are measured. The thought here is that, in addition to behavioural aspects of the interaction between a reader and a print media vehicle, what the audience thinks of and feels towards the publication is of importance to the likely effect on them of advertising it carries.

The classification of audiences according to the 'image' the medium or vehicle presents to them, whilst not common practice as far as syndicated or 'industry' research surveys is concerned, is quite widespread in publisher-sponsored research. Examples of measurement of perceptions of newspapers or magazines on such dimensions as their prestige, sophistication and modernity are provided by the work of the National Magazine Company,[59] the Evening Newspaper Advertising Bureau[60] and *TV Times*.[61] Another common dimension to measure is the perceived utility of newspapers or magazines as aids to purchasing decisions.[62]

One particular instance of 'attitudes to media' has received quite considerable attention, though more on the Continent than in the UK. It argues in favour of a generalized dimension of reader's 'involvement' with a newspaper or magazine and thus of the importance they attach to it; an example is provided in research by Gallup for the *Reader's Digest.* [63] A common question format here is to ask how vital it would be to a reader if he or she could not obtain a particular title – the so-called 'regret at loss' question.

In conclusion, it seems a reasonable assumption that readers hold definable attitudes towards print-media vehicles, largely (though not wholly) determined by their perceptions of the contents of the various publications. Whether, as a result, the editorial environment in which an advertisement appears has a material bearing on its effectiveness is, at present, a more debatable point. Research in support of this contention – and thus justifying attitudes-to-media classification – is limited. Experiments by Winnick [64] are often cited but, as Broadbent [65] has pointed out, the evidence they provide is not strong. We ourselves tend to the position taken by Joyce: [66] that it is not difficult to demonstrate these attitudes, but that they have limited relevance to communication effectiveness.

Behavioural classification

Just as in the previous section, there are two separate aspects to the classification of members of an audience in terms of behaviour. On the one hand, measurement of a person's behaviour towards a particular newspaper or magazine may be used as an indicator of the likely effectiveness of an advertisement it contains. On the other hand, the 'behaviour' in question may be in the market place and of importance in grading people as more or less valuable advertising targets.

Under the first of these headings, the dividing line between attitudes to media vehicles and behaviour towards the same publications is a narrow one; e.g., measures of a person's 'involvement' with a particular magazine or newspaper, or of the importance they attach to it, or of their interest in its editorial contents will correlate highly with many of the behavioural criteria dealt with below. A danger to be avoided, therefore, in media research design and the application of its results, is the use of a number of audience classifications as if they each provided independent evidence of vehicles' values when, in fact, their information is largely redundant.

Apart from actual criteria of issue, page, or ad contact, dealt with above, a common behavioural measure is of claimed time spent reading, usually in relation to the 'average' issue and thus asked about in terms of habitual behaviour. Whilst usually seen as an indicator of probability of advertisement exposure, reading time is equally a likely correlate of the importance the reader attaches to the title and thus, possibly, of the degree to which its editorial authority 'rubs-off' on advertisements.

Adding another dimension to people's reading behaviour is a measurement of the number of separate occasions a particular issue is looked at. (This criterion is to be distinguished from reading frequency, where the concept is one of regularity of contact taken across *different* issues.) Apart from observational techniques – impracticable economically and otherwise on other than a small scale – readers' recall of their previous reading behaviour must be relied on. This in turn normally limits research to the measurement of the number of different dates on which a particular issue was looked at, a variable that has come to be known as 'reading days' from the first, American, research on the subject. UK examples of investigating issue reading occasions are provided in work by *Radio Times*[67] and *TV Times*.[68]

Next, the reading locale may be measured by asking, for example, whether the newspaper or magazine concerned was read 'at home', 'during a journey to work', 'at work', and so on. Similarly, the time of day when reading took place may be questioned. The common rationale in both cases is that the circumstances surrounding a reading event, such as the degree of distraction or relaxation or concurrent preoccupations of the reader, are of likely relevance to the effectiveness of advertising in general or of a particular campaign carried by a vehicle.

Finally in this list of aspects of behaviour towards a newspaper or magazine, audience members may be classified according to how they acquire it: whether it is delivered to their home and, if so, whether wholly or mainly for them or for some other member of their household; or, if not delivered, whether copies are personally purchased by a respondent or passed on to him or her.

Data of this kind have relevance for circulation marketing problems of a publication treated as a 'brand', discussed later in this chapter. In the present context, the justification of the measure is again that being a 'primary' reader of a publication is likely to be a correlate of a person's general attitude to it and thus of the effect on him of advertising it contains. Caution in the interpretation of the above measures of behaviour-towards-the-issue and the likelihood of correlation between them is to be re-emphasized.

For example, non-buyer-readers, or readers who come into contact with an issue other than in a buying household, are likely to display notably lower 'time-spent-reading' scores; but consequently to downweight their value as advertising prospects may not be justified, since it can be that they are characterized by page traffic figures that are almost as high as those for primary readers.

The above paragraphs have listed various aspects of people's behaviour towards newspapers and magazines that may identify meaningful audience sub-groups. In a print media survey, it will also be common practice to collect at least relatively simple data on respondents' contact with other media, such as television, radio or the cinema. The objective here is not so much to provide audience estimates in their own right (which may better be achieved by research techniques tailored to the task) but again to allow breakdowns of the readership of publications which are relevant to print media selection, e.g. to demonstrate the penetration of a particular magazine amongst those who view little commercial television.

Turning, now, to the other area of behavioural classification of audiences mentioned at the head of this section, demographic and attitudinal measurements noted earlier provide indirect evidence of whether a reader is a better or worse prospect from an advertiser's viewpoint, as regards their present or prospective purchasing behaviour. Self-evidently, readers may also be classified directly in terms of what they buy.

For the provision of single-source data ('single-source' in the sense of providing both media contact and purchasing behaviour information for the same sample of individuals), the number of technique alternatives is large. In principle at least, any appropriate audience measurement method can be linked to any one of several approaches to collecting purchasing data, including single contact versus continuous (panel) reporting, and personal interviews versus self-completion questionnaires. Examples of single-source data are provided, in Britain, by BMRB's Target Group Index and, in the US, by the syndicated services offered both by Mediamark Research and Simmons Market Research Bureau. However, a large proportion of the readership surveys in Europe and elsewhere also carry at least a modest number of questions on purchasing behaviour. [69]

The great advantage of single-source data is that it may lead to a more exact matching of media to markets than is possible by the 'indirect' route of using demographics as the linking variables. [70] However, the technique is no panacea. Being able to classify media survey respondents in terms of their purchasing behaviour does not of itself solve previously existing problems of whether vehicles should be so selected as to reach heavy or light buyers of a product, buyers or non-buyers of a brand; and fine distinctions between newspapers and magazines in terms of the buying behaviour of their respective audiences may, in practice, be swamped by gross differences in their advertising rates, as largely dictated by the sizes of their total audiences.

Schedule construction and evaluation programs

Program types and objectives

In parallel with the refinement of audience measurement methods, a notable feature of the media research scene in the last 15 years has been the development and application of computer programs which take as their input, partly or wholly, the data discussed in earlier sections of this chapter. Whilst such programs are usable, in principle, in relation to any measured advertising medium, in practice they have related most frequently to newspapers and magazines and therefore should be briefly covered here, although the subject is by now a wide one, with a very considerable literature.

Computer media programs may be divided according to objective into three groups.

Ranking (or *cost-ranking*) programs concern themselves only with the relative value-for-money of a single insertion in each of a number of newspapers or magazines, taking into account costs and readerships within some defined audience sub-group.

Evaluation programs take as input an existing schedule or schedules of insertions in a number of vehicles and provide, as output, measures of schedule performance — notably full data on the pattern of contacts that should be produced and indices of the 'effectiveness' of this pattern.

Construction programs by contrast have, as input, audience data and much other information and produce an actual schedule on the basis of given instructions and assumptions. The term 'optimization' (of schedule selection) has been and is still often applied to these routines. It is more accurate to regard them as producing, within stated constraints, a selection of vehicles and numbers of insertions in each of them which is 'best', if at all, only under the assumptions made. Further, the schedule can often be guaranteed to be no more than 'very close to the best', for technical reasons of the programming method employed.

In the next section, the input requirements and calculation methods of these programs are described in bare outline only. No detailed comparisons between specific commercially available programs are drawn, but several general reviews are available, [71] which also serve to underline the extent to which different programs will provide varying evaluations of the *same* schedule. A later section turns to some consideration of the advantages and limitations of using evaluation and construction programs.

Methods

It is convenient to consider first schedule construction programs, although it is to be stressed that evaluation routines are, almost certainly, finding wider day by day use at present.

The first input requirement is a list of *candidate vehicles* from amongst which a schedule is to be selected. Different programs will accept lists of varying lengths. For each vehicle, the cost of the sizes of insertion associated with it is to be specified. Some programs are able to take series discounts into consideration. The audience data included in the input will usually relate to issue contact, often but not invariably in the form of reading frequencies. It is required for each population sub-group to which the program is instructed to ascribe a different 'value'. Unless the schedule is to be constructed on the assumption that all people are equal in their worth as prospects for the advertising concerned, a full set of *market weights* is to be specified, comprising the relative values — whether based on assumption or measurement — of each type of individual to be separately considered by the program. Such groups may be identified by any classification covered by the audience research data used, but are most commonly demographic ones. Some programs require the user to specify weights separately for each criterion he nominates – to say, for example, that upper social class individuals are twice as valuable to him as lower class ones and that, separately, younger people should carry three times the weight of older ones. Other input formats may call for weights for groups identified by interlaced criteria; thus, for instance, a figure might be attached to mothers with children under 16 living in the South-east and to other mutually exclusive groups similarly defined.

Quite separately from market weights, most construction program inputs will allow the optional use of *media weights*, which are quantitative expressions of the varying values the program user attaches to a contact between one individual and the different vehicles within the candidate list. In the calculations the computer subsequently performs, these media weights are almost always treated mathematically as probabilities; but in fact they may reflect either of two different concepts.

On the one hand, a media weight may express the probability of advertisement contact (or, at least, of opportunity of such contact) conditional on contact with an issue of the vehicle. Clearly, data on page traffic, or its correlates such as time spent reading, could be utilized to provide weights in this sense. On the other hand, a media weight may be an attempt to express a judgement on the relative strength of impact delivered to a reader by exposure to an advertisement in one vehicle rather than another; e.g. it might be felt that the editorial authority of some magazines was greater than others, that this 'rubbed off' on their advertising and, therefore, that the former should be given higher media weights.

Data input requirements are completed by a statement of the budget available for the schedule to be constructed – some programs will call for a single figure, others a range – and by a set of constraints which limit the pattern of insertions the program may choose. These may be partly 'environmental' in the sense that, for example, if a rule of 'one insertion per issue' is being followed and the schedule period is a year, the computer must be instructed that there are only 52 issues of a weekly magazine available for selection; or constraints may again reflect purely the program user's wishes that, say, no more than half of the total budget is to be expended in one media group.

Given the type of input data outlined above, the objective of a construction program is then to arrive at a schedule which is permissible within the constraints laid down and is also 'best', in some sense, amongst all feasible alternatives. This simple statement of the problem raises three basic issues: what criterion is to be nominated, against which any given schedule may be evaluated? How is this evaluation to be achieved in practice? And how is the program to arrive at a candidate schedule for evaluation?

The type of criterion most commonly adopted is the weighted number of contacts a schedule delivers for given expenditure. The weighting involved comprises the varying values of individuals as advertising prospects, as expressed in market weights; the differing worth of contacts effected by this vehicle against that one, or media weights; and, usually, a third weighting expressing a view that successive contacts with a given individual are not of uniform value. This last-mentioned set of weights is termed, collectively, a *response function:* a numerical expression of the marginal or cumulative value of the first, second, third... contact with a given individual. It may be in-built into a program; or it may be variable at the user's choice and form part of the required input. Different response functions may be chosen to reflect viewpoints that the first, tenth, and hundredth impact are of just the same value; that several impacts are necessary to gain any effect at all but that, beyond this critical point, nothing is added by further ones; that cumulative effect rises slowly at first with number of contacts, then more rapidly and later tails off once more; or that early impacts in a series are the relatively most forceful, diminishing returns then applying.

In evaluating any given schedule against such a criterion of market, media, and response function weighted impacts, a program's central task is to calculate a frequency distribution of issue contacts – to calculate the numbers of people, in total or within relevant sub-categories, seeing varying numbers of issues. Here two basic approaches are possible. First, the program can consider each individual in a population (or, more strictly, each member of a sample of that population) in relation to each vehicle concerned and 'decide' on the basis of the data provided (reading frequency information, for example) whether a contact will or will not occur. This *respondent probability* approach may use up much program running time where a large sample and many vehicles are involved. Alternatively, a program may estimate a distribution of contacts, through the use of appropriate formulae, by considering reading patterns for the population or groups as a whole, rather than one by one; data typically taken into account would be vehicle readerships within the target group, together with pair-wise duplications between vehicles and issues. This technique has come to be known as the *formula* approach.

Turning to the third essential problem, even given a meaningful criterion on which schedules' values can be compared and a calculation method for such evaluation, a program has still to arrive at a feasible schedule in the first place; and, even given the very high calculation speeds which attain, it will not be economically practicable to generate and evaluate every one of the myriad alternative sets of vehicles and numbers of insertions that derive from even a short candidate list.

A common approach is to build up the 'best' schedule in a series of steps. Such a *stepwise* program first ranks candidate vehicles on a value for money basis, comparing market and media weighted audiences with costs; selects the most economical; examines the value-weighted patterns of contacts formed by this first insertion combined with each possible addition to it; again makes a choice on value against cost; and so continues until the budget is exhausted.

Any form of such a procedure is properly subject to the criticism that it cannot be guaranteed to produce a schedule which is optimum. However, the shortfall is likely to be small and can be further reduced by refinements which allow the deletion of insertions as well as their addition or permit the program, in effect, to 'look back' and compare, in terms of value, the point it has currently reached with branches of its path that it rejected earlier.

The discussion of this section has, so far, been entirely in terms of schedule construction programs, but it will be seen that the essential problems of evaluating an existing schedule have also been covered. The calculation of a frequency distribution of contacts, together with the application of market, media and, probably, response function weights are, on the one hand, intermediate stages in most 'optimization' routines but are equally the core of evaluation programs.

Advantages and limitations in program use

The period which saw the introduction of computer programs for the construction or evaluation of print media schedules was characterized by considerable over-claiming of resultant benefits; but subsequently and currently, the gains from the use of the computer remain hotly debated. This section summarizes some few points on both sides of the argument. A longer and very balanced review is provided by Broadbent [72].

It is unquestionable that computer use permits fast, numerically accurate comparative consideration of far more schedules, permissible within the budgetary and other constraints, than could ever be reviewed by manual means within economic time and cost limits. Equally, a program may 'consider' simultaneously a large number of factors held to be relevant to a schedule's value. However, the program of itself adds nothing to the logic of its constructor. What factors are to be considered and how they are to be traded off the one against the other must be specified in its instructions. There is no genie in the hardware bottle, only a totally obedient, incredibly fast-working slave. Further, 'garbage in, garbage out' is no empty truism. If the logic of the program's construction or the quality of the input data are indefensible, so will be the output. Even so, the availability of only limited data is no argument against using sophisticated analysis techniques on it.

The two areas of input information most frequently criticized are media weights and response functions. It is properly said that, in relation both to the contribution of vehicle environment to advertisement impact and to the marginal effect of successive impacts, judgement must currently largely stand in for knowledge.

On the first of these areas, if any 'qualitative' factor, beyond intrinsically quantitative audience and cost data, would be taken into account in selection of advertising vehicles by non-computer means, it seems hardly logical to ignore it when writing a program. At the same time, the hard task has to be undertaken of turning generalized 'feelings' about relative media values into overt, quantified judgements the computer can note.

As regards response functions, the advent of the computer has merely given a name to a problem existing long previously. Every hand-constructed schedule, in which reaching many people was traded off, to some purposeful degree, against contacting a smaller audience more frequently, concealed an opinion on the planner's part regarding the relationship between cumulative number of impacts and cumulative 'effect'.

In relation to both these areas of 'doubtful' input, it is to be noted that computer use allows – and should ideally always include – investigation of the effect on the schedule constructed or evaluated of varying the assumptions that have been made. Such sensitivity analysis cannot answer the question of whether this media weight or that response function, assigned on judgement, is 'right' or 'wrong'; but it can indicate, quickly and relatively inexpensively, how critically dependent a particular media decision is or is not on some unmeasured factor.

Finally, there are those who are happier only to use the computer to evaluate rather than to construct schedules and who, further, stop short at weighted distributions of impacts; they point out the uncertainties of whether (for mathematical reasons) a strictly 'optimum' schedule can be arrived at, and stress the non-knowledge regarding response functions. The counter-arguments are that a handful of trial schedules constructed outside the computer can, equally, not be guaranteed to contain the 'best', or even 'nearly best', one possible; and that two or more tables of the numbers of people subject to varying levels of contact can only be compared when, for example, '70% receiving eight opportunities to see' and '60% with 10 ots each' can be put on a common denominator. This reduction to common coinage involves, inevitably, a response function concept.

Measuring print media effectiveness

Media effect and content effect

This section is concerned with the measurement of the effectiveness, as advertising vehicles, of media at large and newspapers or magazines in particular.

Taking a mass media advertising campaign as a whole, it is neither theoretically desirable nor practically possible to separate its effect (however 'effect' is defined) as between contributions from the content of the campaign – the advertising theme and its creative expression – and from the media in which that content appears.

On the theoretical point, the contributions to effectiveness of advertising content and media vehicles are unlikely to be straightforwardly additive; they will interact. Even holding advertised brand and audience constant, a given medium or set of vehicles may be more effective carrying one campaign than another. Hence, any concept of a fixed 'pecking order' of media effects, irrespective of mode of advertising use, is somewhat sterile.

On the practical point, media effectiveness cannot be measured *in vacuo*; an actual campaign, or advertising created for test purposes, must enter into the research. The ability then to generalize from one particular set of circumstances to the intrinsic, forecastable value of the medium under test is limited by a total lack of any comprehensive model of 'how advertising works'.

These somewhat pessimistic comments are intended to point up some overall limitations of media effectiveness measurement. The following paragraphs firstly review criteria of 'effect' and then comment on some aspects of research design and method. These are not explored in depth since many of the relevant points are covered in other chapters of this handbook.

Effectiveness criteria

One half of the problem of media effectiveness research is the question 'what to measure?' There exists a continuum of variables which may be utilized. In one direction this runs from data which are relatively easy and inexpensive to collect to more complex and more costly measurements. Unfortunately, however, the ranking of measures in terms of relevance runs in the opposite direction.

At the one extreme lies a measurement of consumers' purchases or of retail sales. Given that the objective of advertising, and thus of the use of some particular medium or vehicle, is to increase or maintain sales, there is no doubt here of relevance. (The admitted fact that achieved sales will depend on many other factors besides advertising complicates research design and interpretation but is not, *per se*, a reason for measuring achievement against some other criterion only.) However, accurate purchases or sales measurement is costly. Manufacturers' deliveries may, occasionally, be an adequate substitute, given no complications of alternative distribution channels, varying stock levels or inability to break out delivery figures just for the area required.

Midway in the continuum lie measures of attitudes to the brand advertised and of their change. Research costs *may* be lower than for sales measurement, although very considerable developmental work may be involved if relevant attitudinal dimensions have to be established from scratch and scales for their measurement built up and tested. The major question is, however, of relevance, since the link between attitudinal change and subsequent purchasing behaviour is far from unequivocally established.

Questions in the general area of communications effects are the easiest to formulate and probably the least expensive to administer: they include recall and recognition of product, brand name, attributes and copy points. Unfortunately, an individual's knowledge of an advertised brand or its campaign is but tenuously connected to his behaviour towards it in the market place. The relevance of communications measures is thus considered the lowest of those here mentioned.

It is, of course, possible to move completely away from attempting to measure advertising or advertising vehicle effect on brand awareness, say, or on attitudes or behaviour towards the brand, and aim instead for direct evaluation of the newspaper or magazine by its reader; we can ask, for example (as mentioned earlier in the discussion of attitudes to media) how influential a person rates a publication in its effect on their buying behaviour. [73] The validity of such an approach rests heavily first, on a person's ability to assess such an influence accurately and, second, on their reporting it honestly.

Effectiveness research design

In parallel with the choice of criterion measure discussed above, research into media effectiveness can be conducted under controlled 'laboratory' conditions, at some cost, unavoidably, of realism, or in the field. The latter alternative subdivides according to whether data are collected in parallel with an ongoing advertising campaign or whether a special pattern of exposure is imposed for experimental purposes.

'Laboratory'-scale research may constrain costs and allow at least some of the many unwanted, confounding variables to be controlled. It will typically involve exposing relatively small samples of individuals to advertising in the vehicle or vehicles under test and taking measures on these people of the chosen 'effect' variable. A simple 'before and after' measurement approach is often used but more complex experimental designs may be introduced. An example of this general category of media research is provided in work by the *Daily Mirror* aiming to demonstrate its effectiveness relative to that of television. [74]

The main limitations of 'laboratory' work are two-fold. First, the conditions of exposure to the media vehicles concerned and of contact with the test advertising are often far different from those naturally occurring and, if a comparison of widely dissimilar media is involved, the bias thus introduced regarding their relative 'effectiveness' may not easily be assessed. Second, the measures that may be taken obviously stop short of any actual expression of brand preference in the market place.

Turning to field research, one approach to effectiveness measurement in the context of a normal, ongoing campaign is to monitor both levels of exposure and 'effect' amongst the same sample of individuals. At the analysis stage, weight of purchasing of the advertised brand or changes in attitudes towards it, for example, may then be compared as between a sub-sample with low numbers of OTS and a group exposed to many issues. Whilst some success has been reported with such a method, [75] there is a major danger to be avoided in confusing correlation with causation when interpreting the results. Even if high levels of 'effect' are found to be associated with high exposure, it is quite possible for some third variable to be responsible, which predicates both 'effect' and exposure.

More commonly, the advertising plan will be tailored to research requirements. The simplest design will be to run a press schedule in one area only, and to take measurements of the chosen variable(s) before and after the advertising period. The problem of other uncontrolled factors also affecting the observed difference between the 'before' and 'after' readings leads naturally to the addition of parallel research in another control area, in which there is no advertising. This device cannot, however, solve the problem completely; in general, neither will it be known what other factors it is important to take account of, nor in practice will it be possible to select two areas which are comparable in all aspects thought likely to be relevant. More complex experimental designs may, therefore, be sought (as discussed in chapter 3), using several areas and allowing statistical estimation of the contributory effects of the actual media being researched, of between-area differences, of time effects and of residual factors. Examples of elaborate experimental projects are provided in American work by General Foods research, [76] aimed at comparing the effectiveness of magazines and television, and in a *Time/Seagram* project on print media only. [77]

Another practical problem in the application of experimental designs to print media effectiveness measurement is that the regions available will be dictated by the areas in which part or all of the circulation of a publication falls, which may not be ideal, in size or nature, on research grounds.

One alternative to using naturally occurring circulation areas for experimental purposes is to so arrange matters that, amongst two otherwise comparable samples, one receives copies of a publication containing a test advertisement and the other sees issues which are apparently similar but do not, in fact, carry the campaign. The method of achieving this result will depend on the realism demanded and the level of permissible costs: an extra advertisement may just be 'tipped-in' or, at much greater trouble and expense, a whole section of four or more pages may be 'doctored'. Whilst unwanted inter-personal and inter-regional differences may thus be eliminated, it will be administratively extremely difficult to supply specially prepared copies through normal trade channels. The artificiality may have to be accepted of having respondents receive the test publication other than by the delivery to the home or purchase at a newsagent as would normally be the case. However, these difficulties are not insurmountable; and the work by *Time*, referred to above, involved providing magazine subscribers with experimentally prepared copies so perfect that no suspicion would arise at all; the cost, though, was very high.

The use of coupons or keyed write-in addresses as a means of evaluating media vehicles is also to be noted. The analysis only of enquiries resulting in actual sales may be preferable to looking just at total enquiries received by the advertiser. Clearly, a *media* comparison properly results only from the use of the same couponed or keyed advertisement in two or more newspapers or magazines. Note that, as in virtually all attempts to evaluate media effectiveness under 'real-life' conditions, the overall level of coupon response actually derives from the combined effect of many factors, including the size and nature of the issue audience, intensity of reading within the issue, the contents of the advertisement itself and interaction between vehicle and ad.

Finally, we should mention the emergence (or re-emergence) of an econometric approach to effectiveness measurement. Here, typically, a mathematical relationship is modelled between sales, advertising weight and, say, relative price. However, there is then no reason in principle why an attempt should not be made to relate discrepancies between predicted and observed sales to media variables, as has already been done for advertising content. [78]

This section has provided a very brief overview of some approaches to print media effectiveness assessment. A useful (if now somewhat dated) summary of American methods and case histories has been published by the National Industrial Conference Board, [79] whilst Corkindale [80] has more recently reviewed effectiveness measurement, although not solely in a media context.

Circulation marketing research

Introduction

The research problems and methods discussed so far in this chapter have been concerned almost entirely with newspapers and magazines viewed as advertising vehicles. However, as already noted, a publisher is often operating in a situation of joint supply. He derives income not only from offering an audience, or opportunities for advertisement contact, but also from selling actual copies to readers. Clearly the relative importance of the two markets will vary from case to case. At the one extreme, a free sheet or controlled circulation magazine depends entirely on advertisement revenue. At the other there are periodicals (although few, if any, now, in the consumer area) carrying no advertising and deriving all income from copy sales. In practice, in the UK at least, less research effort is devoted to publications as 'brands' in their own right than as advertising vehicles; but some mention is to be made of the techniques relevant to the former.

Note that the concept of a newspaper or magazine as a 'brand' is often questioned, on the argument that 'product content' is entirely variable from issue to issue. However, a publication is unquestionable seen by its readers as a continuing entity: and those needs which a title seeks to satisfy are no more impermanent than for other fields.

Circulation market measurement

Nearly all newspapers and magazines provide a figure of their net sales. Often, this will be one endorsed by the Audit Bureau of Circulation (ABC), a body calling for sales returns in a set format and carrying out spot-checks of publishers' internal auditing procedures. ABC figures usually relate to a net sales' average struck over all publishing days in a six months' period; monthly data are also published, in arrears. Some publishers not in membership of the ABC will appoint their own auditors to produce net sales figures, or offer merely a 'publishers statement' of their sales. Audited circulations lie somewhere between ex-factory sales data for other product fields and a true, unbiased estimate of net consumer offtake. They do take into account not only the quantities of copies supplied to the trade, but also the numbers unsold and returned for credit. However, in the UK at present, newspapers are *not*, in general, supplied ex-publisher on a 'sale or return' (SOR) basis; and whether SOR applies to a magazine, either as a permanent feature or a limited period, will vary from case to case.

There is a further complication to audited circulation figures. Even if SOR applies, the promptness and speed with which unsold copies are returned through the trade channels will vary. However, an audited figure for a given period will be based on ex-publisher supplies for that month or months and on returned copies recorded in that same period, but representing outdated issues of varying age. Thus the audited figure may well provide a biased estimate of short-term variations in net consumer offtake. The problem can, of course, be overcome, at some trouble and expense, by sorting returned copies according to their cover date.

Seeking fuller information on sales to, or purchases by, the final consumer of newspapers and magazines, there are at present no continuous, generally available measurement services analogous to those for many other product fields. However, techniques employed in other areas can be applied – with some modifications – and are in use by some publishers on a limited or experimental basis.

Purchase data can be derived both from single-contact surveys (either using personal interviews or self-administered questionnaires) or by panel techniques. Two problem areas are to be noted. First, the casual, irregular purchase of a particular title will not be a highly memorable event to a respondent. Second, publications are acquired through more than one channel. Separate questioning may be required to cover copies received on direct subscription from a publisher (of negligible proportions in the UK, save for some few magazines); copies delivered to a household by a newsagent; copies purchased at a retail outlet – whether newsagent, station bookstall, other type of shop or street vendor; and copies passed on by an initial purchaser to someone else. Loose questioning can lead to copies in this last category erroneously being counted more than once.

Retail audits are also possible with, again, some special problems attaching to newspapers or magazines as product fields. Street sales will be unmeasured if the universe sampled is only of newsagents and bookstalls. Newsagents' normal recording of 'deliveries' may need to be specially supplemented, particularly where they receive supplies not only from wholesalers but also by publishers' representatives 'filling-in' their additional requirements. Far more than in other product fields, 'outdated stock' — yesterday's newspapers, for example — are waste and will normally be disposed of unrecorded. Finally, if sales data are required issue by issue, the audit period becomes as short as a week or a day for some publications, which would clearly lead to astronomical costs if a normal stock-check approach were used. However, self-completion of a questionnaire by the retailer may be employed.

An excellent example of a publisher's use of retail audit is provided by the research on the launch of *Company*.[81]

Researches for publication launches

Formal test marketing of a major new newspaper or consumer magazine hardly ever takes place. Editorial, production and distribution economics are such that 'first copy' costs are high and pilot-scale production hardly feasible. This is not to say, of course, that 'dummy' issues are not produced, both for early circulation to advertisers and agencies and, sometimes, to gauge reaction to a new title from the wholesale and retail trade. Short of full-scale test marketing, however, the publisher can apply much of the methodology of other areas of consumer research to measuring prospective demand before committing himself to a new publication. Examples are provided by research for Thomson Regional Newspapers[82] and by the research for *Company*, mentioned above.

'Product' and pricing research

The individual newspaper or magazine, as much as any other brand, has definable 'product content' in the shape of the news, comment, fiction and features it carries. The actual items vary from issue to issue, but the satisfied reader is, nonetheless, buying a mix with a consistent shape imposed on it by editorial policy. Systematic product content research is relatively little applied to print media; a strong journalistic tradition makes more for a producer-oriented outlook than a marketing one. However, relevant evidence can be obtained.

Post facto investigation of claimed readership of individual items, discussed above, points to their apparent relative interest to different segments of a publication's readership. Reasons for an individual pursuing this item but ignoring that one can be probed by direct questioning, with the usual caveats that some degree of rationalization will be unavoidable. More elaborately, a market segmentation approach can be applied to mapping the consumer needs that print media satisfy.

The information needs of readers can also be investigated more generally, as in the Dutch 'Interest Priority Test',[83] whilst panels offer the possibility of regular monitoring of the reaction to editorial contents.[84]

The 'make-up' of a newspaper or magazine — the style and arrangement of its content on and through its pages — is in many ways the analogue of packaging in other fields. Again, research techniques used in other areas may be applied to measure the legibility of a particular typeface or the brand image conveyed by a magazine's cover design. Examples of research in this area that are generally available are few; some have been summarized by the American Newspaper Publishers Association Foundation.[85]

Finally, in this section, the special problems of pricing research may be mentioned. For British newspapers and magazines, resale price maintenance is the invariable rule so that experimental manipulation of cover prices for research purposes is not practicable; questioning on readers' attitudes to present or prospective prices must be relied on. The limitation is perhaps not a critical one, since print media do not occupy an essential 'price-market', nor is pricing often used as an aggressive marketing weapon.

Chapter 25

Television media research

W. A. TWYMAN

Advertising in the television medium

This chapter concentrates upon research to measure television audiences in relation to the use of television as an advertising medium. The general principles of audience research discussed here also apply to the measurement of programme audiences and television in its public service role.

The choice of research methods is affected by the way in which advertising is presented in the medium and the way in which advertising time is bought and sold.

Commercials may be screened in a number of ways

(a) as part of a sponsored programme, e.g. USA;
(b) isolated commercials, e.g. USA;
(c) as part of a short break of several advertisements, e.g. USA, UK;
(d) as part of a longer block of advertisements, e.g. Germany;
(e) within short pieces of entertainment material, e.g. Italy (Carousella).

These alternatives vary along the dimensions of how much advertisements are separated from programming, how predictable is their timing, and the extent of the total period of advertising offered for attention.

The advertiser can have varying degrees of control over the placing of advertisements

(a) to the nearest minute including position in break;
(b) to a break within a programme;
(c) as part of a sponsored programme;
(d) within broad time segments;
(e) day of transmission;

(f)   week or longer period of transmission;
(g)   as part of blocks with time roughly specified;
(h)   as part of blocks with time unspecified.

The amount of control over the placing of advertisements determines how far detailed audience measurement data are actionable.

The conditions under which advertising time is bought can vary

(a)   competition for best times, blocks or packages;
(b)   allocation without choice in a seller's market.

In selecting the appropriate research design for a particular set of conditions therefore it is necessary to consider what degree of frequency and detail of audience research data are usable in making decisions.

A further consideration is that the validity of different methods relating to advertising audiences may be affected by the way in which advertising is presented in the programme context. This should be taken into account when reviewing the evidence on techniques.

The changing nature of television viewing

The changing nature of television viewing has implications for the respondent tasks set by different research techniques.

Until recently television viewing has had the following characteristics. It has usually been

–   based upon regular habits as to time and place;
–   set in a family context.

Any viewing event has been uniquely defined along two dimensions, content and time. This means that the more memorable viewing events are accessible to recall by reference to programme title or description and even the less motivated viewing is likely to be recalled in terms of time. Research techniques which combine the dimensions of time and content as recall aids are thus likely to present a reasonable task to the respondent. Television is also an attention-attracting medium, using two dimensions of the senses, hearing and vision. To these might be added the third dimension, that of time, because the sequential presentation of information itself demands attention. Compared with other media, therefore, there are fewer brief, casual encounters with the television medium.

These characteristics have hitherto made the audience measurement research task theoretically easier for television than for other media.

There are, of course, some exceptions to these general rules. There can be confusion of titles between similar programming material at similar times on different channels. There are some casual encounters with the medium – entering the room briefly when others are viewing, for example.

Research needs to be carried out with care. To prompt memory by a careful reconstruction of time and programmes available is a lengthy task if done fully. In the absence of thorough reconstruction, the respondent may easily confuse regular, usual or intended behaviour with actual behaviour when making claims.

The simplicity of the television measurement task is thus only relative rather than absolute, and there are plenty of opportunities for error, but these should usually not be great in total for carefully conducted research.

A further special feature of the medium is the position of advertising. Because the medium presents material sequentially it is possible for viewers to treat the advertisements as breaks in the transmissions they have chosen to see. The unique definition of advertisements in terms of time of exposure makes it possible to consider measuring audiences to individual commercials or blocks of advertising. This creates an interest in data based on short time units such as minute-by-minute. Once audiences are considered in time-specific terms, and there is any week-to-week variability in programming and competition, then the demand for *continuous measurement* is created.

Thus, short advertising breaks create a requirement for minute-by-minute, continuous data. Variable programming could of itself create interest in continuous measurement but with less precise time units. From these reasons one can see that, in Europe, public service broadcasters without advertising have tended to go for regular recall surveys whilst commercial stations have tended to favour continuous meter-based panels. In the USA, meter panels have had a long history, supplemented by other intermittent diary research for smaller local stations. Unmetered diary panels represent a 'halfway house' where the diary is used to collect fairly precise (usually quarter-hour) time unit information and acts as a prompt to record the more casual encounters with the medium.

The feasibility of precise minute-by-minute continuous measurement arises from the unique relationship of transmissions to time and has been made easier by the fixed location family basis of most television viewing.

These are features which are changing rapidly with the advent of new developments in the electronic media and which will bring to television audience measurement many of the problems which already beset othe media, in addition to its own problems.

These revolutionary developments are not only satellite and cable, which mainly increase channel choice, but also:

- the growth of video cassette recording; bringing the possibility of time-shift viewing;
- the increasing number of television screens in the home; making television a more personal medium.

These developments have the potential effect of making television broadcasts more like newspapers or magazines: they can be delivered to the household (broadcast) but the viewers can then look at them when there is time (from the recording) and viewing can be in a number of locations. While these developments are small as yet in many countries, their rates of growth show signs of being very rapid. These changes may well modify data requirements and alter the feasibility of research techniques.

Another important development has been the growth of remote control devices which enable the set rapidly to be switched between channels by a viewer without leaving the chair. Particularly when allied to video recording and timeshift viewing this greatly increases the degree of viewer control which can be exercised over the reception of advertising. In a sense remote controls and video machines represent a change from 'the captive audience' to the 'captive medium' as the character of the television medium.

Further changes in the future concern the technology of the TV screen. Small battery portables are already marketed and very large flat screens are just around the corner. Both these directions of development further expand the range of conditions under which television may be watched. In particular they can take it further out of the purely domestic setting.

All the changes considered here can alter both the research data requirements and the feasibility of specific research techniques. In evaluating techniques, therefore, attention must be paid to their capacity to deal with changing conditions.

The measurement of TV set ownership and station reception, and definition of station areas

Purposes of the data

The measurement of set ownership and reception arises in two main types of situation: (a) to define all the media sources to which a household is potentially exposed; and (b) to define an area of coverage of a television station.

There are three aspects of defining a station's coverage:

(a) fixing the *potential audience* for a station. This means measuring the number of people or households effectively receiving the station, and their characteristics;
(b) defining the *areas to be sampled* for audience measurement. Theoretically, there need be no geographical limits. Since coverage of a station generally does have geographical limits and because of marketing needs, it has been usual to associate the media measurement with a formally defined area;
(c) defining the *area effectively covered* by the station. This can be used for

various marketing purposes such as retail distribution of the advertiser's brand in a regional campaign.

These three functions could be satisfied by three different definitions. Potential audience could be independent of area while audience measurement could be limited to an area of dense reception and the marketing area based on another criterion. In practice, however, there is sometimes a requirement to use the same basis for all three.

These issues become very important for highly regionalized television services, less so for national networks.

Researching station reception

There are two broad approaches.

Respondent-assessed reception

Respondents can be asked whether their household has a TV set in working order (and how many), followed by questions on which stations can be received. This can be done in surveys for both in-home and out-of-home locations. Questions about stations received are best approached from a prompt list. The accuracy of replies depends on the confusability of local stations. Some claims can be checked by asking questions about the viewing of programmes unique to specific stations. Such answers do not, however, cover stations which the respondent could potentially receive but to which the set is normally never tuned. Questions can be asked of the respondent on their subjective assessment of picture quality.

Interviewer-assessed reception

At a home interview, interviewers can inspect the switched-on TV set. The respondent can switch between known stations to demonstrate the household's range of stations and the interviewer can search for any others, perhaps unknown to the household. Trained interviewers can apply a quality-of-reception scale for each station. These can be based on technical standards available from broadcast authorities but are not always easy to apply and reception can vary by time and season. An alternative approach is to ask the respondents to assess their own satisfaction with the picture for each available station using an appropriate scale. While this is not an objective measure of quality, it is likely to be predictive of behaviour. A check in the UK has shown that, for comparisons between alternative stations, the subjective preference scale ranks them similarly to an objective picture scale.

Under some circumstances it may be necessary to establish which transmitter a household receives from among a number normally carrying similar programmes. In the UK, AGB have carried out surveys with electronic detection devices to establish such information.

Interviewer check on respondent-assessed channel preferences

An interviewer calling on a household may check the reception capabilities of the set and then ask the respondent questions about his viewing habits. This is concerned with the problem of respondent classification rather than just reception measurement. This extension has been regarded as particularly important in relation to the situation where several stations with similar programmes can be received. If one station were strongly preferred, there could be arguments for counting that home as 'belonging' to one station's potential audience and not to the others'.

A JICTAR study in the UK examined the viewing records of panel homes receiving two ITV stations. These were checked against their answers to the question 'Out of every 10 hours watching ITV how many hours would you and your family watch each of the ITV transmitters?'

The conclusion from the JICTAR study was that panel records generally confirmed the allocation of preference between stations in response to this question. There were, however, some 40% of households who divided their viewing fairly evenly between stations. A forced choice question would have hidden this fact.

General problems of classification

In assessing the *potential* audiences to stations there are alternative approaches.

Household classification. This can be based upon the capability of sets within the household. This can go beyond stations actually viewed, to those capable of reception. The classification of the household can then be applied to the individuals there. This does not take account of viewing outside the home.

Individual classification. If this is approached by a survey of individuals then it is likely to be based upon stations *actually* viewed from all sources. This can take account of out-of-home viewing.

There is thus a choice between seeking the potential or the actual coverage of stations. These are likely to be needed for different purposes. Major growth in out-of-home viewing would tend to make classification based upon household sets less realistic.

Defining television areas

A station area can be defined by a list of its smaller population units, such as administrative districts. Defining an area involves making decisions about possible districts, accepting or rejecting them on criteria which are usually based on the proportion of homes effectively covered by a station.

In the UK, ITV regional station areas have been based upon the inclusion of a district where 15% or more households have sets capable of receiving the station, whether by direct transmission or relay. A recent modification has been to exclude households claiming negligible actual viewing to an ITV station where more than one ITV station can be received. Definitions such as these generate overlapping station areas, since within a district, more than 15% of households may receive each of a number of regional stations.

Definition of areas by minimum signal strength boundaries

For technical purposes, authorities responsible for transmitters publish maps showing a contour defining the extent of a certain level of measured signal strength. How far this corresponds to a true reception boundary depends on alignment of aerials, which in turn is affected by the history of services available to the area. Ideally this approach should be tried first since it is far cheaper than conducting surveys.

Use of a sequential sampling approach to measurement for the reception criterion

A sequential sampling procedure has been used for determining whether or not a district qualifies for inclusion within an area boundary. This has involved surveying an initial minimum sample, usually 50. If the percentage of reception found can be regarded as above or below the criterion percentage at a pre-set level of confidence, the decision to include or exclude the district is taken. Otherwise, further samples are interviewed until the decision can be made at the pre-set level of confidence. This ensures considerable savings in sample sizes for districts with very high or low densities of reception. This method can only be used where the sole object of the survey is to make a decision about including a district rather than measure its absolute density of reception.

System of data collection

A television station is likely to require basic data describing the size and characteristics of its potential audiences and other features of its area. Often these data can be supplied from existing data sources by adding questions like those discussed above on TV reception. Otherwise it may be necessary to run special surveys for this purpose, sometimes known as Establishment Surveys. The possible functions of such surveys covering the catchment area of a TV station can be:

(a) to define the extent of reception of various TV stations in that area;
(b) to describe the characteristics of the station potential audience including demographics, exposure to other media and various marketing data as required;
(c) to provide targets for quota weighting or stratification purposes for other samples such as regular audience measurement surveys or panels;
(d) to provide a master sample from which TV panels can be selected.

If signal strength definitions cannot be used to define station areas, 'Boundary Surveys' using the techniques discussed above will have to be used. These tend to be expensive since decisions have to be made about many small districts accumulating to a large sample. Since these are usually peripheral to the main urban areas, the possibility of combining this research with any other is remote, unless a large national sample is available.

Where the object of such a survey is to record change in viewing possibilities, pilot or preliminary work is necessary to check that some change has in fact occurred and that the situation is stable. Guidance may be obtained from television dealers who are closely concerned with the problem.

Many data sources incorporate some form of measurement of potential exposure to television stations and can use differing approaches. When comparing between sources, therefore, it cannot be assumed that a 'TV station viewer' always means the same thing.

Techniques and sources of measurement for broad viewing habits or average media exposure probabilities

In the long-term planning of advertising campaigns, having identified those people who form the target market it is necessary to establish which are the media vehicles through which they are most economically reached. This is often done by a narrowing down process: deciding whether to use television, radio and/or press; which broad categories; and, finally, which specific vehicles. Computerized media selection models [1] could enable decisions to be made across a mass of vehicles in different media together, were it not for the lack of knowledge about the relative values of different kinds of media exposure. Such lack of knowledge also presents an equal problem for the stage-by-stage approach, but the greater opportunity for making personal judgements may make this a more efficient way of using unquantified experience and certainly more reassuringly conceals lack of fundamental knowledge about media values.

Either approach generates a need for data about an individual which represents a prediction about his behaviour in terms relatable to his probability of exposure to the medium. It is likely that the more computerized the media selection process, the more precisely defined in terms of vehicle (i.e. particular times in the case of television) the media exposure probability will have to be expressed.

In most markets the major research effort for television is often devoted to a ratings service. This will obtain data which can be expressed in terms of individual probabilities of viewing, within various possible time units: weeks, days, hours, programmes, advertisement breaks. These data are not always readily available to everybody while the classification of panel individuals may not include the most relevant marketing data.

Data about *purchasing habits* are frequently used to define marketing opportunities and target groups. The problem of how to reach these target groups then leads to simplified media measurements on product surveys and consumer panels. One solution is that detailed media and detailed product data could all be collected from a 'single-source' or easily integrable system. [2] Another possibility is data marriage from several sources. [3]

The following section discusses methods of obtaining broader estimates of probability of exposure to television including other than by collecting a detailed continuous historical record of all viewing. These measures can be used to link product and media data or as a stratification control in surveys where television exposure may be relevant, and in studies where the aim is to relate probability of exposure to the medium to some other attitudinal or behavioural variable.

Derivation from detailed viewing records

If detailed viewing records are available, which are likely to be from a TV panel, viewing probabilities can be computed for a class of individuals for a single viewing occasion or for a single individual averaged over a number of possible occasions, e.g. viewing three weeks out of four on Monday at 7 p.m. gives a probability of 0.75 for that individual. Looking at a number of similarly defined target individuals gives a further average and a distribution of probabilities, by putting TV panel basic data tapes through a computer. No purchasing or other media data may be known about the individuals. It is, however, possible to combine viewing data like this with other forms of data via demographic characteristics using various data marriage systems. [3]

It is also possible to obtain detailed viewing records intermittently for a short time period from respondents for whom purchasing or other information *is* available. Television diaries for a single week's viewing or seven-day aided recall interviews are sometimes applied to Consumer Purchasing Panel housewives in the UK. These techniques are discussed in the section below dealing with the measurement of audiences for time segments, programmes and advertisements. In both cases the data obtained are used almost exclusively to classify housewives into three viewing categories: heavy, medium and light ITV viewers. This kind of intermittent collection of viewing records precludes the use of meters and generally less is known about their validity. It is arguable that if only broad classifications are used these may be accurate enough even though the precise details of viewing might be at fault. Some findings reported by Buck and Taylor [4] suggest that seven-day aided recall, as used on a Consumer Panel, gives classifications as consistent as metered TV data whilst producing overall higher levels of viewing.

The use of questioning techniques for collection of exposure probabilities

This approach involves asking about *usual* viewing to time periods in the form of frequency claims. The precision with which the time periods are defined can vary from bookable segments through to very broad general claims. Generally, 'frequency of usual exposure' measurements in media research involve over-claiming for the more memorable and habit-based media. Respondents omit the exceptions to what they regard as their usual pattern and claim the intended, idealized or perhaps just simplified pattern of behaviour. This means that, to convert a frequency claim to a probability, some calibration of the scales against actual viewing habits will be necessary. Typical findings would be that a frequency of claim of 'three times out of every five' did not represent a probability of 0.6 but perhaps more like 0.45.

A set of questions which has been used and calibrated by CESP in France (and which can easily be adapted or extended) is of the following form, with the scale presented on a card for each relevant time segment.

> 'Normally do you personally view even if not at home between mid-day and one-thirty'.....
> Every day
> Nearly every day
> Once or twice a week
> Once or twice a month
> Hardly ever
> Never

This question can be asked for television as a whole and/or for each station segment by segment. With a calibration study, probabilities can then be attached, for each respondent, to each segment and station asked about.

The use of questioning techniques for general classification by weight of viewing

Media research often employs a classification of viewers into broad categories such as 'heavy', 'medium' and 'light' viewers, as already mentioned. These are basically simplified probabilities of exposure. Such categories can be based on taking more detailed actual viewing records or exposure probabilities and analysing them into broader groups. A typical approach would be to take the sample of individuals under study, arrange them in rank order of amount of viewing or exposure probabilities, and then divide the ranked list into equal thirds, quarters or fifths, etc., according to the number of categories involved.

A widely used approach in the UK is to ask a series of three questions which can be multiplied together to give an index of viewing.

Question 1: During an average week, on how many days do you personally watch television?

The respondent indicates whether it is nearer to seven days, six, five, four or three, two or one, or less often.

Question 2: On a day when you watch television, for about how many hours on average do you view?
The respondent selects an answer from a scale running from 'less then one', 'over one and up to two', 'over two up to three', etc., to 'over nine'.

Question 3: Out of every ten hours that you watch television, about how many hours would you spend watching each service?
(Show card listing services, i.e. stations, and allocate digits to each adding to ten.)

There are two ways of analysing the answers. One involves a response guide from which looking up the combination of answers given will lead to a viewer classification; this method enables instant classification. The alternative approach multiplies out answers to the questions, thereby creating an indicator of station-viewing hours followed by a rank ordering of respondents and a division defining heavy, medium and light station viewers. The values of the indicator figures occurring at the boundaries between categories can be used in subsequent surveys (subject to re-checking or adjustment for seasonality) to provide instant categorizations of individual respondents if the interviewer multiplies out the answers.

These two approaches can be calibrated to give similar classifications. A general problem is the validity and durability of viewers' assessments of their own broad viewing habits. Classifications as above can fall short of absolute validity because:

– respondents cannot adequately summarize their current behaviour in these, or perhaps any, terms;
– viewing habits are unstable and change with time.

This is one aspect of the important issue of the capacity of respondents to summarize normal media behaviour. JICTAR investigated this by comparing the answers to broad habit questions given by viewing panel members with their actual viewing recorded in the panel.[5]

One JICTAR investigation compared answers at a sign-up in January 1973 with subsequent average actual viewing levels from four weeks distributed through to 1974. This ensured that a single unusual week would not dominate the results and also gave opportunity for the passage of time to have affected usual habits. To check whether changes with time were responsible for any difference or whether 'usual' habits cannot be reported accurately anyway, the questions were also asked again in mid-1974. A further line of investigation was based on the idea that the answers, being in this instance given by the housewife about her own viewing, might inevitably be inaccurate because her viewing was affected by the viewing habits of other members of the household. This led to the consideration that the procedure might be improved by using questions about total household viewing (i.e. set usage). The results are summarized in the table of correlations in Table 25.1.

Table 25.1 Correlations between ITV weight of viewing estimates asked of the housewife and actual levels of ITV viewing

	Household actual viewing 1974	Housewife actual viewing 1974	Household questions new 1974	Housewife questions new 1974	Housewife questions est. survey Jan. 1973
Household actual viewing 1974	1.00				
Housewife actual viewing 1974	0.88	1.00			
Household questions new 1974	0.51	0.47	1.00		
Housewife questions new 1974	0.46	0.58	0.74	1.00	
Housewife questions est. survey Jan. 1973	0.42	0.43	0.42	0.44	1.00

The conclusions were:

(a) Housewife ITV viewing is very closely related to household ITV viewing; there were no very light housewife ITV viewers in very heavy ITV viewing homes.

(b) Answers at mid-year were better predictors of viewing in that year than answers from early in the previous year. This showed that viewing habits change and people are to some degree aware of the changed levels.

(c) None of the approaches to questioning gave a correlation with actual viewing better than 0.6. This shows that there are limitations to peoples' capacity to report their *usual* viewing levels and proportion of channel choice. There was some suggestion that housewives had a tendency relatively to underestimate their own viewing and overestimate their household's viewing.

(d) A major feature of the findings, not shown by the correlations however, was that radical reversals between usual claims and actual viewing were uncommon. Very few very light ITV viewers claimed to be heavy or vice versa, although there is no reason why this could not have occurred validly, given the passage of time.

It is known from other work that individuals are relatively stable in their tendencies to be heavy or light viewers. It appears that this is also accurately reported. What is less stable and must also be open to more distorted reporting is the finer detail of viewing habits. Even when questioned concurrently people do not accurately identify their exact viewing levels even in rank order terms.

The conclusions are that it may not be possible to measure usual viewing habits any more precisely than through something which correlates across respondents at about 0.6–0.7 with actual viewing, although it is worth experimenting with new forms of questioning in a national context. Later UK experiments have found similar correlations with actual viewing from questions based on regularity of viewing particular time-segments or programmes. The questions listed above are, therefore, still widely used despite the obvious difficulty of the task for the respondent.

Terms like heavy, medium or light viewers are widely used in media surveys. There are a variety of definitions, and when trying to understand results or compare between surveys it is worth checking the basis of the classification system:

(a) whether it relates to viewing for a single station or total television viewing;
(b) whether it is based on actual viewing records or usual-habits questions;
(c) for which period the classification data were obtained and to which period the classifications are being applied;
(d) whether they are individual or household classifications;
(e) the exact method by which the classification is derived from the original consumer data.

The measurement of audiences for time segments, programmes and advertisements

Regular data on the size of actual audiences are widely collected for both advertising and programming purposes. The emphasis here is for advertising purposes, but the total range of methodology common to both is considered and the two sets of needs do not usually dictate different research approaches.

Although the concept of audience size sounds unambiguous there is a problem in deciding how to define an individual as part of the audience for a transmission. Does the individual simply have to be in the room with the set on, or should some attempt be made to include *attention* in the definition? How much of the piece of transmission does the individual have to have 'viewed' (however defined) in order to count as being in the audience? Techniques for defining an audience vary, leading to problems of non-comparability of data.

It is generally felt that standard audience measurement techniques such as the meter-diary system are measuring something close to 'presence in the room with the set on'. To probe further into behavioural attention requires special questioning. This has generated a class of 'attention studies' which have been experimental rather than regular sources of data collection. [6,7]

Units of measurement can be *time*-based, expressed in minutes, quarter hours, or averages of separate minute readings; or *content*-based, covering commercials, breaks, programmes, or parts of programmes. Sometimes the technique determines this basis, as with meters which must measure by time, but some techniques can be adapted to cover any unit. Within a single unit of measurement the quantity criterion may vary both by design and in the way a viewer interprets instructions. The most commonly used approach is to ask viewers to count themselves as viewing a quarter-hour if they cover more than half the quarter-hour. On this basis, measured audience levels disregard brief absences from the room.

A measurement system based upon quarter hours or some broader time unit will therefore fail to record brief absence or presence, and such limitations could affect audiences for commercials or short programmes. This has led to a sub-class of audience measurement work concerned with establishing presence levels during commercial breaks and seeking to relate these to conventionally measured quarter-hour data.

The requirement for programme data can be met by any of the methods discussed. A minute-by-minute record shows both the detailed pattern of response to the programme and can provide a meaningful average. Similarly, quarter-hour data can show some changes during the programme. Direct measurement in terms of programme units leads to various definitions however, such as 'seeing any at all' (a cumulative audience), or 'seeing more than half' of either the whole programme or of each of various discriminable parts. Again when comparisons are made between surveys exact definitions should be checked.

Techniques of measuring audiences for time segments, programmes and advertisements

Interviewing: Coincidental

This technique is generally regarded as the most artefact-free and is therefore used as an expensive yardstick in validation studies.

It can be based either upon personal or telephone interviewing; the approach will depend on national audience characteristics. The use of telephone interviewing depends on the extent of telephone coverage, and personal interviewing upon ease of access to households during evening viewing. Where both techniques are viable the choice will probably be made on economic criteria unless any special interviewing requirement can affect the decision.

There are two distinct applications of coincidental interviewing to validation. It may be used on an independent matched sample to obtain estimates of viewing levels at different times which can be compared with those from the technique under test. Where the tested technique involves the respondent carrying out some task at the time of viewing, such as pushing buttons when viewing or wearing some identification device, the coincidental interviews can be carried out on the tested technique sample. The role of the coincidental interviewing there is to check that the task is being carried out correctly.

The basic coincidental technique involves calling at a household (personally or by telephone) and checking whether any television sets are switched on and to which channels and then, either which individuals were present or whether a preselected individual was present. These measurements all relate to the moment of the call which must be identified accurately. It is clearly an expensive technique, one interview yielding a measurement for just an instant of television transmission time. This makes it more suitable as a methodological check than as a regular method of data collection.

It is obviously efficient to keep evening interviews short and to maximize the number of effective calls an interviewer can make. This inevitably means clustering, which should be done as carefully as possible. A major limitation to the use of the technique is the hours in which it can be carried out, it being unacceptable to disturb respondents later in the evening or early in the morning.

It may be worthwhile to split a coincidental survey into two stages. At the first enumeration stage, by day, a sample of households is interviewed to establish those which can receive the appropriate television stations, and the household demographic details. The second call can be confined to the true universe for the study and questioning limited to 'who was viewing what'. It is possible to conduct about eight of these interviews per hour. Clearly, the home should not be forewarned at the first interview when a later check will be made.

There is a problem about the exact time period an interview covers. Unless all interviewers are issued with special watches it is difficult to keep a precise timing. This makes it a difficult technique to use in relation to commercials if time alone is to be relied upon with no reference made to what is on the screen. Time control is more precise in telephone calling.

There is a choice as to whether actual *viewing* is the question criterion, or just presence in a TV room. If respondents are asked about other activities, such as reading or ironing, as in attention studies, they may give answers which cover, say, five minutes, since these activities may be discontinuous.

A decision has to be made on how to treat refusals and non-contacts. Refusals at a second stage are rare if previously contacted respondents are interviewed. Ignoring refusals equates their behaviour with co-operators. An ARF study in the USA[8] found that refusals on a one-stage survey had different (lower) viewing levels than co-operators, but this may not be a general rule.

Non-contacts, or a sample of them, can be called back on the following day to check whether they were out, or viewing and not answering the door, which sometimes happens. In a UK study it appeared that around one-third of households not answering the door were actually viewing. This can be measured on a sub-sample and total figures adjusted accordingly, but the greater the incidence, the less the value of the coincidental data. Subject to re-dialling to check that the right number has been rung, the best assumption for telephone non-response is to classify the household as away and therefore not viewing.

The problems of coincidental interviewing and practical solutions are well displayed in UK industry studies by TAM[9], the IPA[10] and JICTAR[11]. Coincidental interviewing by telephone is the norm in the USA and is now being used more in Europe.

The absolute accuracy of normal telephone coincidental interviewing in the USA was challenged in CONTAM Study No. 4[12] where it was found to underestimate ratings slightly. This study showed that results could vary with the training and supervision of interviewers, procedural rules for dealing with contact difficulties, and rules for interpreting non-contacts. Telephone interviewing has increased in the UK and other countries as the proportion of telephone ownership has increased. The basic question is whether, in general, telephone owners differ in viewing behaviour from demographically similar non-owners. If they do not, then telephone interviewing would be possible if some means could be found for obtaining, economically, samples balanced to match the television universe.

When comparisons are made between results from a technique under test and coincidental interviewing using separate samples, then differences may reflect both the techniques and the samples interviewed. It is necessary to consider whether the samples are drawn from the same population and the implications of response rate. Many panels for example have relatively low response rates. This involves some self selection and, as mentioned below, unless this controlled for panel membership can drift towards higher viewers. Interpretation of differences between coincidental and other surveys should therefore take account of both technique and sampling differences.

Interviewing: Near-coincidental

This approach consists of making what is almost a normal coincidental interview and questioning back over the recent viewing periods. Interviews covering the last hour of viewing conducted during evening viewing time have been used by LPE [13] and TAM. [14] A version of this technique was developed in an industry study by BMRB for the IPA and ISBA [15,10] and JICTAR [11] where the objective was to measure presence in commercial breaks. The difficulty of precise timing was overcome by scheduling calls just after a commercial break, checking at the interview that the break had just occurred, and then effectively carrying out aided recall over the previous three commercial breaks and intervening programming. This procedure is best illustrated diagrammatically as in Fig. 25.1.

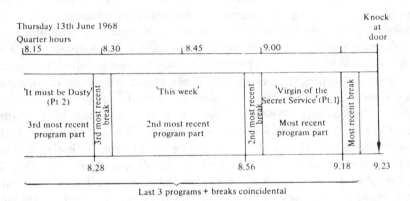

Fig. 25.1. The interview obtaining near-coincidental data.

The validity of this approach depends upon the care with which the interview is conducted and the form of questioning. In a 1968 study there were no significant differences between results for the same break or programme, and the viewing levels reported checked with the current meter diary panel data. A similar study in 1974 with slightly less uniformity in fieldwork, however, showed small differences occurring with time. [11] These differences were not great enough to invalidate all uses of the data, and the technique remains viable for some purposes. A small survey using a version of this technique, without the programme prompts, found big differences in quality of data back over an hour. [16]

The approach seems to depend very much on the interviewer creating a reconstruction of a programming sequence in the respondent's mind and thereby making a behavioural rather than an attitudinal measurement.

The telephone approach is also relatively costly and, as with personal interviewing, cannot be used late in the evening.

Interviewing: Recall: aided and unaided, next-day and seven-day
A variety of media research problems relating both to commercial and programme audiences have been approached through various kinds of recall techniques:

(a) *Day-after recall* (DAR) of specific commercials is used as a kind of on-air advertising testing procedure and, according to circumstances, may be used to measure attention and communication aspects of the advertisement. This is usually concerned with a dimension of advertising effectiveness rather than audience measurement.

(b) *Next-day aided recall* has been used in some experimental studies to measure the behaviour of audiences to television advertisements. A London Press Exchange next-morning-recall technique [13] showed a programme sheet with competing ITV and BBC programmes laid out side-by-side on a time scale, the ITV list showing where the commercial breaks came. Respondents indicated which programmes they had viewed and were then taken through the list with careful probing as to when they started and stopped and whether they saw the commercial breaks. After rating their liking for the programmes they were then asked what their behaviour had been at the time of each commercial break, classified into a number of possible activities. The LPE study compared results from the next-day recall technique with those from similar questions asked of a different sample on the actual evening about the most recent hour of viewing. *Housewives* in the morning recalled consistently less activity during breaks than those asked in the evening. The various kinds of activities were reported in similar proportions from evening or morning. *Men*, however, reported slightly more activity during commercials in the morning and there were some noticeable but non-significant differences in the kinds of activity reported. Despite the optimism of the LPE reports, these and other differences between next-morning recall and same-evening recall suggests that more methodological work would be needed before findings from next-morning data could be interpreted with confidence.

(c) Another technique used in the LPE studies was based on the ability of programme viewers to *identify commercials* that had appeared, from a list containing three commercials shown and three not shown in a particular break. This yields measures of correct responses for true and for false commercials and a 'no decision' score.

Results from the technique were also compared from evening and morning interviews. There were more 'no decision' responses from next-morning data but, of the decisions made, the proportions correct were mostly similarly related to factors like time, reported viewing behaviour and interest in programme, whether from evening or morning interviews. The use of these *recognition* procedures in relation to commercials seems promising but the technique has not had the necessary methodological development since the LPE studies.

(d) *Next-day aided recall* designed to cover all transmission times in a comprehensive service measuring audience size was used by the BBC for a number of years and is still used by a number of public service broadcasters in Europe.

The next-day recall interview can be:

unaided – spontaneous recall of what was viewed
aided by – programme titles: e.g. 'did you view any of these programmes?'
          programme schedules
          time reconstruction e.g. 'where did you start viewing?' etc.
          time reconstruction with programme schedules

These really represent a hierarchy of increasingly complex interviews. Undoubtedly the most thorough way to prompt memory is to reconstruct the respondent's day and to introduce programme schedules when viewing starts. Viewing can be recorded on a time grid to the nearest quarter-hour or by programme or segment of programme. Whatever the unit recorded a definition of viewing that unit, usually 'more than half', has to be adopted and made clear to the respondent.

Studies claiming to be 'reconstructive' range from those with well laid out questionnaires covering the whole day, full instructions and manageable visual aids, to a general instruction to go through the day's viewing, showing the programme list from a newspaper bought by the interviewer. The length of such an interview can range from 10–15 minutes or so down to 2 or 3 minutes, according to the amount of care taken. The less carefully the reconstructive process elicits real recall of yesterday then the more likely there is to be:

– some forgetting of less memorable or casually viewed programmes;
– some filling in of 'usual behaviour'.

The risk of programme titles alone as an aid is that the respondent may feel that if the programme is usually viewed but missed yesterday, he ought to mention it otherwise he won't be reporting the 'correct' behaviour. It is also absolutely essential that recall aids show all stations similarly. One danger is that, in research commissioned by a station, the quality of recall aids for that station may be better because they are able to supply fuller and better information. This can create a bias.

One basic issue with next-day recall research is the sample. By definition each day's sample is based upon those people who can be contacted in a day. This does not allow for call backs and makes a random probability sample virtually impossible. (It is possible in a methodological study to pre-select a sample and follow up non-contacts to establish likelihood of viewing rather like a coincidental survey.)

A version of 'next-day aided recall' tested in the TAM Comparison Survey [9] used simplified displays of programmes taken from the programme magazines printed out side-by-side in the questionnaire. The respondent was taken through the programmes and viewing recorded on the questionnaire by quarter-hours. This technique, using a random sample, was close to the coincidental results in the TAM Comparison Survey in peak time but significantly under-reported in early time (5.30 p.m. to 7.00 p.m.). This result has been interpreted as suggesting that a technique relying on memory may be less accurate when covering periods of low attention or less distinctive programmes.

(e) *Seven-day aided recall* is one of the most economical techniques in that a whole week's viewing is collected at a single interview. Each informant is taken back over programme aids such as the programme magazines or some derivation from them and questioned more closely about exact timing. The viewing record can be completed by the interviewer in terms of quarter-hours or half-hours viewed. This technique was used by Granada Television in 1959–60, studied in the TAM Comparison Survey 1961, and used by Marplan for JICTAR 1962–4 to produce data on more demographic groups than the meter-diary service.

Extensive, if somewhat perplexing, discussion of seven-day recall is given by Ehrenberg. [17] Evidence and interpretation from various sources is conflicting. It is reasonable to conclude that the data need not weaken over the seven days as the recall period gets longer, but that the technique does report relatively low levels of viewing in early time and off-peak time generally.

The suggestion of over-reporting in peak time depends on whether one expects exact correspondence with coincidental interviewing. The technique produced different deviations from meter-diary data on different groups of surveys, suggesting sensitivity to small variations in procedure.

A recall aid, discussed by Simmons, [18] with considerable potential for methodological work is a series of story-boards which can show the progress of transmissions through programmes and breaks.

Meter-based systems

The history of audience measurement has seen the development of several generations of meters which vary in their style of recording and the method of retrieving the data from them.

Devices like the Recordimeter (Nielsen, Attwood) or the Metrilog (AGB) have been referred to as 'meters' but these merely recorded the total time the set was on daily. The respondent entered a coded figure from the meter display and the total 'set-on' time could then be checked against the respondent's record which was otherwise an unmonitored diary. The total viewing record merely provided a check against gross error in diary completion and acted as a motivator. The technique appeared to work well in simple situations and was checked in the TAM Comparison Survey 1961.

The mainstream developments of meters have, until recently, been devices which were basically designed to provide a record, on a continuous basis, of the channel to which the set was tuned. Under the conditions of the past, knowledge of time and channel uniquely defined the context of the transmission. This had the advantages of:

– eliminating all possibility of respondent error as to what was being viewed;
– providing some information for otherwise unresearchable small time units such as advertisement minutes;
– providing an easily analysable source of continuous records within individual times for measuring schedule coverage etc.

Fig. 25.2.
Reproduced with the permission of AGB Research PLC.

Under current and future conditions however it is necessary for the meter design to become more sophisticated to identify:

– more channels;
– complex methods of tuning the set (e.g. through the VCR machine);
– the various modes of operation of the VCR machine i.e. recording only, viewing through VCR only, viewing and recording, playing back only;
– the content of time shift viewing;
– the use of video disc or pre-recorded VCR material;
– the use and content of teletext etc.
– other uses of the TV set, e.g. home computers, video games etc.

In addition the meter system needs to be able to deal with several sets in a household, some of which may be portable. Potential problems for TV meters include the development of very small battery-operated portable sets. These present problems, not only of size, but also lack of any easy access to a line connection along which a meter can pass information.

The function of the meter is now therefore much more complex. Meter panels have to represent a fast-developing electronic world and these developments challenge both the technical ingenuity of the meter and also the structure of long-running panels.

Meters have gradually been developed in relation to how the recorded information is stored, from heat sensitive tape to digital information on an audio tape, to solid state storage. Initially the meter record had to be collected or despatched manually. A major development in meter technology has been the capacity to retrieve the information stored in it directly by telephone line. (This is a primitive forerunner of the kinds of information retrieval which will become possible with multichannel cable services.) The availability of set-switching information by line to the computer is of little value if the *individual's viewing* information is not also retrievable with similar speed. This has led to the development of methods of recording audience presence directly into the meter. Operational at the moment are the 'push button' systems where the household members record their entry to, and departure from, viewing by pressing their own individual button on the meter. Set tuning information and individual presence are thus logged simultaneously and can be retrieved at the same time. Such push button systems have been operating for some time in Germany and Ireland and are now also operating in Italy, UK and Switzerland and piloted in the USA. A further development piloted by AGB in the UK is an electronic diary which is a mode of recording analogous to the paper diary, but using a light pen on a small electronic display also linked to the meter. This information can be entered or corrected at any time. It can however still be retrieved via the meter over the telephone line.

Other ways of retrieving information about individuals viewing include using a panel on a private viewdata network. Here questions can be asked (including the use of a viewing diary if required) on the TV screen or on a special VDU. Replies can be made via a small keyboard. This approach gives great flexibility in asking questions. This method is being piloted for obtaining qualitative reactions to programmes in the Netherlands. A similar small panel is being used experimentally by Granada Television in the UK (operated by AGB). The Granada panel has been used to ask opinions of the panel during discussion programmes.

In the long term, multi-channel cable systems would enable both diary type data to be logged by the individual and questionnaires to be applied to respondents on line and possibly interactively. This kind of system has already been operated on a limited scale in the US (QUBE) and in Japan.

Some limitations which can affect meter methods in the future include:

- they only measure viewing to metered sets, i.e. not viewing out-of-home or to small battery portables;
- the necessity of working with long-term panels for which it may prove difficult to maintain representativeness in a fast-changing situation as regards acquisition of new modes of media access;
- the tendency for an operational meter design to lag behind the state of development of electronic reception equipment, requiring frequent re-investment.

In particular, viewing *outside the home* presents a problem for research based on domestic sets. 'Guest viewing' in other homes can be accommodated by including guest viewing within panel homes. This may be limited by the number of push buttons. Guest viewing demographics can potentially be entered either by an electronic diary or expansion of the push button handset (this may be limited by the number of push buttons). Otherwise estimating procedures have to be used. Viewing other than in homes is currently not very significant. It is possible however that new technology involving larger TV screens might offer more opportunities for out-of-home viewing, particularly for special events.

Diaries: used in conjunction with meters
As already discussed, meters are designed to measure what the set is showing, to which has to be added a record of *who is present* (or possibly, defined as *viewing*). The methods available are:

(a) *Factors applied from data from another measurement system.* These have to be viewers-per-set factors, but the set data may be measured less precisely than by a meter and then applied to the meter. Nielsen in the USA have obtained audience composition data via diaries and set data from meters from different panels. There have been no potential advantages for this hitherto, apart from the possibility of higher response rates and maybe improved accuracy because of a reduced respondent load. In the future, however, factors for minority samples applied to detailed set switching data could be of greater interest.

(b) *Paper diaries kept by panel members.* These have been widely used in most meter-based systems before the arrival of overnight telephone retrieval. Since channel, and therefore programme, choice is measured by the meter the diary design is usually based on a time grid working to the nearest quarter-hour. Shorter time units based on 5 minutes have been used experimentally in the UK but there has been no systematic study of the effects of this design. Diaries would ideally be completed whilst viewing but realistically are, at best, filled in at the end of the day. Knowledge that a day is to be reported, however, is likely to help the remembering and retention of viewing behaviour.

This kind of diary has been used until recently in the UK (even on the meters accessible by line) and in the USA.

(c) *Electronic diaries.* This term has been used by AGB in the UK to refer to an analogue of a paper diary where recording is onto a small portable display screen using a light pen. This technique could replicate the paper diary procedure *and* make the information entered accessible to overnight collection over the telephone line to the computer. If the day's diary was not completed in time for collection that night a reminder can be signalled for next-day completion.

This method has the advantage of flexibility, being able to cover any viewing anywhere. The disadvantages are that it is a slightly more laborious task and requires working in quarter-hour units which reduces the precision of the record. Since respondents probably enter their data at the end of the day there is also a reliance upon memory.

(d) *Push button diaries.* These have also sometimes been called electronic diaries or 'people meters'. The key difference between push button diaries and any previous audience composition technique is that individual viewing must be recorded as it happens. The respondent denotes the start and finish of his viewing presence by pressing and depressing a button linked to the meter. Individual viewing is therefore recorded simultaneously with set behaviour. In theory this would produce conceptually 'perfect' audience measurement data if only the respondent can always remember to carry out the task at the correct moment. The degree to which this is possible is considered in the section on validity below.

The arrangement of push buttons has been considered in a number of forms, e.g.:

– on the meter at the TV set;
– on a remote control handset;
– at a door convenient for recording entering or leaving the room.

There is no real evidence to decide between these options.

Paper diaries used with meters are generally in the form of a time grid and can be designed for individuals or families. A separate diary or set of diaries is needed for each TV set.

The individual records only viewing and has no need to identify the channel. If the individual completes the records totally from imagination or fading memory the disparity with the meter record is immediately noticeable and an interviewer can call. Diaries can be read by machine and their data checked against and incorporated with meter records within the computer. This kind of system checked well against coincidental interviewing in the TAM Comparison Survey, and would not be affected by the complexity of services available, since the respondent does not record *what* he is viewing, only *when* he is viewing. Such diaries are usually retrieved by post.

Individuals ideally mark their diaries when they start and finish viewing sessions, filling in the quarter-hours in between. In practice, they may well fill in their diaries more in arrears than that, although grosser malpractices should be minimized by being part of a monitored supervised panel.

An issue with paper diary panels is whether the diaries are kept by all individual panel members or on a one-person-per-household basis. A cost-accuracy trade-off is involved. It is undoubtedly cheaper (and vastly so if meters are used) to collect data on an 'all persons' basis. However, the TAM Comparison Survey 1961 showed that because of the high correlations between the viewing of household members, the precision of the data from, say, 500 adults in 250 households is hardly greater than that from 250 adults in 250 households. The number of household units really represents the effective sample size for groups represented more than once per household. For other audience composition breakdowns, where there is rarely more than one per household, there is not likely to be any loss of sampling efficiency through collecting data from all persons in a household. The loss of efficiency applies to groups like adults, individuals or children.

TV Diaries: partially monitored

Diaries can be used in conjunction with devices like the Recordimeter or Metrilog which record total set usage in coded form which the respondent notes down. This provides a check on his other recording which is good enough to indicate serious malpractice in diary-keeping, and the resulting incentive to be accurate probably improves performance. This kind of technique was closest to coincidental interviewing in the simple two-channel situation in the TAM Comparison Survey. It requires that individuals record which channel the set is tuned to as well as when they are viewing, usually by quarter-hours. New problems may arise as reception possibilities become more numerous and difficult to distinguish. Whilst it seems likely that panel members could be trained to record channels accurately, further validation would be advisable before using the technique more widely in a multi-channel situation. One set of diaries will be required for each television set in the home.

TV Diaries: unmonitored

Unmonitored diaries are potentially the most cost-efficient form of audience research, particularly if they can be used by mail. Diaries can take a variety of forms. They may be completed by continuous panels, as has been the case in Finland, or for a single week. They may be placed personally, by telephone or by post and collected personally or posted. They may be individual or household diaries. The respondent must indicate the channel viewed and, minimally, the start and finish times of viewing sessions. Some possible formats include:

(a) *Time-scale diaries.* The channel to which the set is tuned can be recorded on one scale with further columns to be marked by individuals present; or individuals may indicate channel by the column used. Basically these diaries would be like the successful Recordimeter diaries without the Recordimeter. All entries are recorded on grids representing time units, usually quarter-hours.

Time-based diaries were used on the AMP's survey[19] and the results correlated reasonably closely to those from metered diaries. Studies by London Weekend Television have also shown unmonitored time-based diaries corresponding reasonably closely with meter diary results.[20]

A risk associated with unmonitored diaries is potential confusion of the channel viewed, and can be a problem if diaries are filled in retrospectively. The error patterns, if this occurs, are likely to be something like those for aided recall: possibly slight overclaiming on well-known and established programmes or viewing times, and confusion at times where programme titles are not unambiguously discriminable between channels.

(b) *Start and finish time diaries.* This form of diary has been used in the USA by ARB[21] and experimentally in the UK by AGB. The respondent records the start and finish times of viewing sessions, i.e. when the set is turned *to* and *from* a channel, the name of which is entered in another column. Individuals present are recorded in separate columns. Data from the ARB system in the USA have in the past correlated well with the Nielsen meter/diary data.[22,23] In the UK, a sample of 100 homes who had this form of diary, and a meter which they believed to be faulty, showed that they could keep accurate set switching records. It is possible, though, that the meter was still acting as a motivator.

This form of diary apparently gives minute-by-minute data although probably misses brief absences, and it has succeeded in US multi-channel conditions. Further validation may be necessary in other national conditions.

(c) *Programme diaries.* Diaries can be used which show the timing and titles of programmes for alternative services and require respondents to mark those which they view. The programmes can be split up into several parts. This form of diary is undoubtedly attractive to the respondent, providing as it does a miniature viewing guide. There are likely to be some considerable administrative problems, however, in producing such diaries with accurate programming information. However efficiently this is managed, there will inevitably be some last-minute changes and these create considerable confusion about the meaning of the data at times when they occur, because not all respondents will manage to obey instructions to enter programme changes.

A variant on the purely programme diary is the programme-break diary where validity has been substantially investigated in the UK. [10,24] At one time, this seemed the most economical and promising technique for establishing *presence* in commercial breaks with possible extensions to cover *attention*.

Programme and break diaries had been used at TAM [14] and BMRB [25] and produced very meaningful-looking results showing how the pattern of viewing varied between programmes and breaks. This technique was subjected to a rigorous programme of validation through an industry group. [15,10] The pilot stages involved the identification of certain 'wrong-looking' completion syndromes, with later evening calls on those homes to see how they were keeping their diaries. This established a number of patterns which had to be rejected, some arising from completion in advance as well as the more conventional completion in arrears.

On the main study the diary results were checked against coincidental data. Surprisingly, in view of the success of other unmonitored diaries, the viewing levels recorded by the diary were much too high compared with coincidental data (which were also in line with metered diary results). Furthermore, many of the most interesting findings from this kind of diary appeared to be artifacts. Whether such a diary could succeed if monitored by a meter and with greater training and supervision of respondents is untested.

Programme-based diaries were also subject to an experiment by broadcasters in the UK in 1979/80 and again produced exaggerated and unreliable audience levels. Errors likely to occur with programme diaries therefore include overestimation, particularly of well-known regularly viewed programmes. This is similar to overclaiming on most frequency-of-media-exposure claims and suggests some influence of usual or intended behaviour, in turn implying some completion in arrears. The role of the programme diary as a programme guide should also be considered in relation to possible effects on viewing. Further sources of error are likely to arise at times when programme titles can be readily confused between channels and where programme titles are obscure.

Observation techniques

Viewing behaviour can be investigated by the use of observers present in the television room and recording the behaviour of others present. Such techniques are obviously not appropriate for the regular collection of large amounts of data, but are suitable for experimental studies investigating patterns of viewing behaviour in greater depth than conventional measurement techniques. The use of observers can vary considerably as to the degree of awareness and obtrusiveness generated. One study by RBL for Lintas [26] placed selected interviewers in the homes of a recruited sample of households for two consecutive evenings. Useful information was obtained about family activities and attitudes to viewing, although clearly there must have been some influence upon the behaviour observed. By contrast a very well conducted American study by Steiner [27] used a wide range of college students to observe their own families and, by careful training, obtained quantifiable data with a negligible level of obtrusiveness. Other studies in the USA [28] have used students in this way and have included the recording of exposure to individual advertisements in press and television as well as the detail of conditions of exposure. [29] In the UK, the TAM experiment with programme-break diaries required other members of a household to keep a diary about the housewife where this was possible, although otherwise she completed it herself. [14] A further observation study has been carried out in the UK by Bates [30] again using students to observe the families. This was primarily used to investigate behaviour in commercial breaks and the use of video recorders.

There is a wide range of potential approaches to observation studies and the major problem is achieving a representative sample. Their unique advantage is that they can get a closer and more objective record of behaviour in relation to advertising exposure than can be obtained by direct reporting from an individual. The observation approach has considerable potential, therefore, for gaining understanding of the true meaning of more conventionally reported measurement. It is however difficult to conduct in representative circumstances and without bias.

Cameras

Cameras can be used with a television set to take pictures of the viewing audience and the screen itself via a mirror. This can be arranged to occur either programmed by a timing device or triggered by some transmitted signal. The technique could thus cover commercial breaks, or rather fractions of them because a picture covers a very short exposure time compared with most television measurements.

A major problem with the technique is clearly low co-operation rates and the probability that typicality of behaviour is affected even if the camera has a privacy switch-off device. A further problem is interpretation of pictures. They relate to a very short period of time and certainly it is almost impossible to assess level of attention from them. People adopt a wide range of postures during attentive behaviour which overlap with the postures of inattentive behaviour. The camera can record unambiguously presence versus absence at an instant, and this may have some methodological value. Video cameras mounted on the TV set are now being used experimentally to study viewing behaviour. A pilot study has been reported by Collett[31].

Detectors: external

Detection machinery is capable of registering that the television set is on from outside a house. The technique has been used by the ARF in the USA[8] as a means of establishing whether refusals and non-contacts in a coincidental survey had their television sets switched on. The machine used had limitations in that it could only be used unambiguously for detached houses. This would seem to be a technique with a clear but limited methodological potentiality. Since detection must take about as long as a personal coincidental interview, it is also not likely to be any cheaper than that technique.

Detectors: internal

It is technologically possible to operate some kind of electronic counters in the television room which would either count and record numbers present or even identify individuals if they could be persuaded to carry some electronically identifiable object. This kind of development would obviously require capital investment and there might be problems of respondent co-operation. No experiments of this kind yet appear on record, although various designs exist.

The validity of television audience research techniques

It is unfortunate that techniques which have never been subjected to any validation test are used with more confidence than those which have been tested and found to have some minor faults.

Tests which compare results from a technique under test with some specially set up 'objective' measure are somewhat rare, although data are sometimes compared between techniques without a control measure. The conventional yardstick for television viewing is the coincidental interview, personal or telephone, which asks people at an exact moment what they are doing in relation to television viewing. While this seems a very clear-cut yardstick, it presents some problems of interpretation. The following issues need to be taken account of in comparing coincidental results with those from other techniques:

(a) whether the techniques as used are sampling the same population and, if not, whether that should or should not form an element in the comparative test;

(b) whether at the coincidental interview respondents can correctly report the channel viewed. (In a past UK study it appeared that about 10% of the sample could give the wrong channel unless prompted with programme titles);

(c) how non-replies should be treated. In a UK winter-evening personal coincidental study a substantial proportion of non-replies were found at follow-up to have been in and watching television. If this problem is likely, some kind of call-back on non-replies will be necessary. For telephone coincidental checking the conclusions of the US CONTAM study apply;[17]

(d) is the coincidental measure definitionally comparable with the measure to be checked against it?

In the UK, the largest validation study was the TAM Comparison Survey[9] sponsored by an industry committee. This was in many ways a model of planning and covered coincidental interviewing, TAMmeter monitored diaries, Recordimeter-monitored diaries, 'one-day' and 'seven-day aided recall', all on sample sizes of 500 households for each quarter-hour comparison.

The recall methods showed under-reporting in early evening. For peak time, all the techniques deviated in the same direction, i.e. slightly above the coincidental level, but recall slightly more than diary methods. If comparisons are made with the coincidental survey, the recall methods show most significant differences – the interpretation made in the report. If the main techniques are compared among themselves, there are few significant differences between them – the interpretation offered by Ehrenberg.[17] Logically, being averages of instantaneous readings and therefore depleted by brief absences, coincidental ratings should be lower than those from other techniques which are based on seeing more than half of the units measured and consequently are *not* depleted by such brief absences. The results of all techniques should have been higher than those for coincidental interviews by an unknown amount and they were indeed higher for peak time. This leaves as the major findings that recall techniques were under-reporting in early evening and had a tendency to report higher for better known programmes with clear titles, compared with lesser known or ambiguous programme titles. Data from meter-monitored and partially unmonitored diaries were subsequently validated by the coincidental survey. There are further adjustments which can be made to the data to cover definition differences.[32]

All this illustrates the difficulty of establishing validity even with a large, expensive and well planned study. A further limitation in this study was that because of the enormous commitment of coincidental interviewing (500 interviews per quarter-hour added up to nearly 9000 interviews per evening), only three evenings could be covered between 5.30 p.m. and 9.30 p.m. It so happened that ITV ratings graphs on those evenings were fairly smooth and no exceptional programmes were screened. Thus, nothing could be discovered about the techniques in relation to late evening, sharply changing audience levels, or unusual programmes. Other gaps included children's viewing, since the TAM Comparison Survey covered only adults. Most techniques are used with children, sometimes with adults reporting for them. The validity of some of these procedures seems unlikely for the youngest age groups and little checking ever seems to be done on media measurements among children.

A further UK validation study was the IPA and ISBA Television Audience Presence Research in 1968 carried out by BMRB.[10] Many of the findings have already been mentioned. This study, concerned with more detailed measurements than normal ratings research, supported near-coincidental interviewing and largely invalidated the programme-break diaries. This result is a salutary one for market researchers because the data from the invalidated technique had a lot of 'face validity', i.e. they supported widely held views. The truth, if that is what was established, was much less interesting. For this study, too, there could well be some alternative interpretation of the coincidental findings.

Both this and a further UK study in 1974[11] confirmed that coincidental interview data broadly validated the standard meter/diary measurement. This is essentially a validation not of the technique alone, but the technique as operating within a system of long-term panels.

In the USA, a programme of validation was conducted for CONTAM,[17,22] an industry group representing broadcasters. There were four studies. The first showed that sampling theory applied to audience measurement which, although interesting, seemed to be a large hammer to crack an opened nut. The second compared Nielsen meter panel data and ARB diary sample data and found them basically in agreement. This implied that there were no conditioning effects on the Nielsen panel and no other mechanical fieldwork errors unless they cancelled out. The third demonstrated a bias in audience size-estimates because of non-co-operation, discussed below. The fourth examined the telephone coincidental technique and has already been discussed. Some smaller-scale validation studies are reported by Simmons.[18]

The Bureau of Broadcast Measurement (BBM) in Canada conducted an extensive development and validation programme for short-term diaries. For some time they operated a research system using a *postal, one-week, combined radio-and-television diary*. The Quantity Control Test published in 1973[33] compared diary sample results with a telephone coincidental check on another sample who were also sent diaries, enabling a comparison to be made between the coincidental ratings of diary co-operators and non-co-operators within the latter sample. The diary data from the coincidental sample were found to be affected by the telephone call in that they appeared to lower the diary TV ratings while not affecting radio.

The coincidental results showed that, in total, television viewing was correctly diary-reported but that this was because co-operators were very slightly lighter viewers than non-co-operators but overclaimed their viewing by 7%. Paradoxically the diary radio results, also correct overall, seemed to come from underclaiming by heavier listeners. These results must be viewed against the national situation with respect to media channels, but the most crucial points to note are that the diary followed telephone contact and the percentage of the population keeping diaries was around 30–35%. Since that time the BBM has carried out further development work and validation in relation to both single media and two media diaries. The findings were published in 1975. [34] They included reports on intensive interviews with people to whom diaries had been sent, about their reasons for non-response; and on interviews with people about their mode of keeping different forms of diary. The principal errors for television were failure to keep diaries up-to-date, failure to indicate viewing if not interested in a programme, and incorrect recording of parts of programmes. There was also some confusion about the definition of viewing (but not so extensive as confusion about the meaning of radio listening). For the dual-media diary there were more respondent problems overall, but radio appeared to suffer more than television.

In 1975 another comparison study was carried out of single- and dual-media diaries against a benchmark of telephone coincidental interviewing on an independent sample. A further coincidental check was carried out upon people sent diaries some weeks after their diary keeping was over, which again enabled a comparison to be made between responders and non-responders. The single-media diaries achieved a higher return (about 35–40%) than the dual-media diary (about 25–30%).

The coincidental survey measured exposure to television (and radio) at four levels at the moment of call: 'aware of TV set on', 'being in the same room', 'noticing what was on the set' and 'paying attention to what was on'. The 'TV only' diary gave viewing levels corresponding to being in the room while the set was on; the 'dual-media' diary was closer to the 'noticing' level, although there was less difference at peak times. Share was distributed similarly across the techniques. There were no significant differences in the subsequent coincidental measure between levels of TV viewing of responders and non-responders. The results were interpreted as 'calibrating' the TV-only diary as corresponding to 'presence in the room', and single media diaries have been adopted. Because two survey results produce the same level for different measurements, it cannot be concluded one measurement means the same as the other, but the findings provide a basis for taking action, and at least set up a hypothesis as to the meaning of different diary measurements. Results of this kind depend very much on the conditions under which they are obtained and while the methodological insights from this programme are valuable, the findings cannot be universally generalized. An interesting side observation, however, was that television audience measurement seemed fairly robust, relative to the technique used, and radio audience measurement much more sensitive.

Tests of the validity of push button meters

Push button meters represent an entirely new kind of research technique whereby respondents record events *as they happen*. Diaries are mostly filled in in retrospect from forewarned memory. Interview techniques always have to attempt the measurement of behaviour by the use of unforewarned memory. The push button technique requires the respondent to perform a not very arduous recording task at the time of the event recorded. This may be a forerunner of research techniques which monitor behaviour as it happens. The event to be recorded is starting or finishing a television viewing session. Because the behaviour measured and the research task have to match each other in time, validation is rather easier than checking upon memory for behaviour. Coincidental calling can be carried out on respondents with push buttons, and what they are doing (viewing television or not viewing television) should match the state of their buttons (pressed or not pressed). Evidence on push button meters has therefore come from three sources.[35]

> *Coincidental checks*, whereby the presence of viewers in the room with the set at any given moment is assessed by personal interview or telephone calls. This observation is then checked against the metered measurement for each individual. This is a particularly stringent test for, in order for the technique to be accurate in aggregate, it has to be accurate at each minute; there is no opportunity for subsequent correction.
> *Consistency of the data with other methods* from comparisons of the findings with those from other techniques.
> *Respondents' reports* on any difficulties they found with the technique.

The main published sources of evidence on push buttons come from checks upon the German system and experimental research in the UK in support of tenders and in preparation for setting up a push button system.

Typical results are reported from Germany by Bermingham and Liepelt:[36]

Table 25.2 Behaviour of individuals in households with sets on and the state of the push button meter. Coincidental check on German TV panels 1982

Total individuals in households with set on	762		100%
Total individuals found to be viewing	393	100%	
Individuals viewing with correctly pressed buttons	365	92.9%	
Individuals viewing with buttons not pressed	28		
Non-viewers with buttons pressed	18		
Net reported viewing level	383	97.5%	
Non-viewers with buttons not pressed	356		
Total correct buttons	721		94.6%

The degree of correspondence is quite close: only 5% of buttons are in error.

Most recording techniques are likely to be more than 5% in error, but the
degree of satisfaction with this result must depend upon where the errors fall:
if they are biassed towards any sub-groups in particular times (such as
advertising breaks) the implications could be more significant. Further
analyses of these data suggest that this is not the case.

Table 25.3 *Behaviour of individuals and state of push buttons by days, time segments and sub-groups*

		(%)
Total sample/interviews correct buttons		94.6
Days	Saturday	93.7
	Sunday	94.4
	Monday	95.6
	Tuesday	95.6
	Wednesday	95.6
	Thursday	94.6
	Friday	94.9
All week, times	17.30–18.29	93.0
	18.30–19.29	95.5
	19.30–20.29	93.7
	20.30–21.29	95.9
Sub-groups	Under 14 years	90.6
	14–29 years	95.0
	30–49 years	95.6
	50 years and over	95.2
	On panel 1979 and earlier	95.2
	Joined panel 1980	93.0
	Joined panel 1981	92.3

These findings suggest that there is a slightly higher error rate for children but
otherwise the results are generally consistent. An important finding was that, if
anything, longer term panel members gave more accurate results, suggesting
that panel performance does not deteriorate over time (or that less
conscientious panel members drop out). These results overall showed a slightly
higher level of accuracy than a similar check in the early days of the German
panel in 1975. [37]

In Germany a more total check on the system as a whole was also carried
out by means of an independent coincidental check on a parallel sample and
reported by Pfifferling 1982: [38]

Table 25.4 *Comparison of percentage viewing from Bremen coincidental survey and Teleskopie panels*

	Households	
	Coincidental	Teleskopie
TV usage	(%)	(%)
Households	46.6	46.5
Adults	32.2	30.7
Men	29.0	26.3
Women	35.0	34.5
14–29 years	23.3	16.6
30–49 years	25.9	23.6
50 years and over	44.1˙	46.5
Advertising blocks		
Households	16.6	17.6
Adults	10.9	11.6

Being from independent samples, greater discrepancies are to be expected. There are also some technical reasons why the Teleskopie figures might be generally lower. The results do, however, suggest two things for push buttons: (a) some under-reporting by younger respondents; (b) no under-reporting in the advertising blocks.

In the UK AGB ran some experimental push button panels for BARB[35] as follows:

First study: October *1981 – April 1982*
30 households formerly keeping paper diaries;
30 households newly recruited.
Second study: from end October 1982
60 households with children.

Some similar panels were also operated with electronic diaries. Like the German data these results show a high level of accuracy of button pressing and tendency for the small number of errors to be compensating. A number of unpublished test of push button meters in Italy and Switzerland appear also to have been satisfacwtory.

Results from the AGB experimental push button panels were compared with the records from matched samples with paper diaries. Obviously these comparisons were based upon small samples. Half the AGB experimental panels had previously kept paper diaries and this provided a further basis for comparisons.

It was thus possible to reach the following conclusions from a series of detailed comparisons:

Table 25.5 *Coincidental checks on panel households*

	Total people in H' holds with set on	Found to be viewing	Buttons correct	Reported viewing	Errors: on	off
First push button study			(%)	(%)		
Check November 1981	237	146	140 (92)	152 (104)	12	6
Check February 1982	248	153	149 (98)	152 (99)	3	4
Second push button study						
Check December 1982	484	249	237 (96)	247 (99)	10	12
Electronic diary panel						
Check December 1982	480	277	260 (94)	276 (100)	16	17

(a) Allowing for differences in household size the viewers-per-set levels appeared to be similar as between paper diaries and both push buttons and electronic diaries.

(b) Push button viewing data show more shorter-viewing sessions than paper diaries.

(c) Conversely, push buttons also appear to record more short gaps in viewing.

(d) In a number of cases there is a lag of 1 or 2 minutes after watching on the set before individual buttons are pressed.

(e) The push button data do not show a sharp drop in individual viewing at commercial breaks.

(f) Push buttons data appear to provide a more realistic estimate of audience size for short programmes.

A valuable part of the AGB experiments was discussions with respondents after the experimental panels were disbanded. A quantifiable questionnaire was administered and there were also free ranging interviews and some group discussions. This provided evidence on a number of issues. The answers given below are generally for housewives; some had previously kept paper diaries.

Discussions showed that people felt that they kept their push button records conscientiously for the purpose of recording precisely their viewing to programmes. They agreed however that they did not always record brief absences from the room and certainly might omit to record unplanned

Table 25.6 How acceptable is the oush button task to respondents?

		Push buttons
Total sample		55
How easy?		
Very or reasonably easy		54
Difficult		1
How long to adapt?		
Immediate or 2/3 days		47
A week		6
Longer		2
Does it interfere with viewing?	'No'	55
How good a record of viewing?		
Very good/good		54
Quite good		1
Fair/poor		0
Compared with paper diaries?		
Better		37
No difference		2
Worse		1
Preference for new technique?		
Prefer new		40
Prefer paper diaries		0

absence. This was reflected in their quantified answers. It was also confirmed by telephone checks, where individuals who left the TV room to answer the telephone were most often found not to have pressed their buttons. Some people were also aware of some time lag in pressing buttons.

Most people usually pressed their own buttons although others could sometimes press for somebody else when they had left the room without pressing, or when nearest the push buttons.

In the push button trials repondents reported finding no difficulty in getting guests to press buttons when viewing. This was reflected in higher levels of guest viewing being reported in this experiment compared with levels reported by paper diaries.

In the UK subsequent use of push buttons appears to have been associated with a substantial increase in the levels of individual viewing reported: whilst some of this increase is probably associated with other changes in the system, some arises from push buttons. The main identifiable source of change has been that levels of reported guest viewing are much higher, nearly double those from paper diaries.

Table 25.7 *When and by whom buttons are pressed*

		Push buttons
	Total sample	55

How often is button pressed to record a brief absence from the room?

Between programmes	
Always/mostly	17
Half	9
Quarter/Never	29
Answering telephone	
Always/mostly	14
Half	10
Quarter/Never	31

Do you press your own button?

Always		14
Sometimes		39
Rarely/Never		2
Other "presser": various	25	
Housewife	12	
Child	4	

The high relative acceptability of the push button task to respondents also demonstrated the converse laboriousness of the paper diary, with the suggestion that the inconvenience of its use for guests led to under-reporting.

Panel controls, sample design, and special problems in television audience research

The running of panels and designing of samples are topics dealt with elsewhere in this book. The present discussion concerns some problems particularly related to television research.

Short vs. long-term panels

The general suitability of TV panels for measuring change is reviewed by Buck *et al.*[5] Very different practical issues of operation arise, according to the length of time the panel is operated. There are two major differences between any panel and interviewer-administered questionnaire:

(i)   the load on the respondent is greater, involving some degree of continuing commitment;

(ii)   the respondent has to work mostly unsupervised by the interviewer.

There is a wide range of techniques, and major differences can arise from:

(i)   length of commitment (ranging from days to years);
(ii) frequency of recording;
(iii) onerousness of the task;
(iv) degree of interviewer instruction and contact;
(v)   feedback and supervisory checking.

When panel operations are reported, the results often ignore the need to consider conclusions separately for different kinds of panel. This produces apparently conflicting results which are resolvable if the *kind* of panel under discussion is taken into account. A particular source of differing conclusions is the distinction between short- and long-term panels, which can be radically different research approaches.

For *long-term* panels:

(i)   the respondent can have extensive training over a period of time in carrying out the recording task; but
(ii) the task must be so onerous that the respondent cannot keep repeating it over a long term; and
(iii) the research must not affect the behaviour under study.

For *short-term* panels:

(i)   normally, by definition, there is little training 'on the job'; training is normally by advance instruction;
(ii) respondents can be motivated to carry out a more extensive task for a brief period of time;
(iii) after the panel task is completed, questions can be asked of the respondent which, while potentially affecting future behaviour, can still usefully relate to an immediately past period of reported behaviour.

Clearly both approaches have their uses in particular situations, but they are approached rather differently. For *long-term* panels, the aim is initially to check upon and improve quality of reporting and subsequently to maintain this and avoid conditioning. For *short-term* panels, the aim is to get correct reporting from the beginning and to avoid an initial artificial response while recognizing that it may not be possible to maintain this level of responding. Successful long-term panel operations check that training in a running-in period improves quality of reporting; successful short-term panels check that the first week is not atypical. Only by recognizing these essential differences can findings supporting the benefits of a training period for long-term panels be reconciled with those showing no difference between the first and subsequent weeks for medium or short-term panels.

Conditioning and running-in for long- to medium-term panels
What little evidence there is suggests that conditioning is not a problem with
meter-diary systems. Newly recruited Recordimeter samples gave similar
results to existing TAM meter panels and both matched the coincidental
results.[9] Similarly, long running Nielsen panels gave similar results to fresh
ARB samples in CONTAM.[22] A Nielsen study and a number of ad hoc
survey results which match panel data also confirm these findings.[39]

Some published work by JICTAR in the UK[11] examined the relationship
between the viewers-per-set reported by samples of meter-diary members after
they had been on a panel one, two and three years, compared with matched
samples of newly recruited members. After panel membership of a year
viewers-per-set became about 5% higher than for new members. It was not
possible to trace the cause of this or to establish which was right, but the result
does set a limit of about 5% for any possible conditioning effects on long-term
panels under these conditions.

In the UK within the BARB system, there have been a number of
comparisons of the viewing levels of 'new' versus 'old' panel members with
other characteristics matched. No significant differences have been found.

It seems likely however that long-term panel respondents may learn a
simplified mode of carrying out the task over time which might alter the detail
of viewing records without affecting the overall level.

Related to conditioning is the question of running-in periods for diarists. *A
priori* it could be rationalized that diaries are kept most conscientiously when
people are fresh to the task, and they then tire; or that people have to learn to
fill in diaries and are best after a running-in period; or that people behave
atypically at first and then settle down. The evidence is scanty and conflicting.
Unmonitored diaries run by BMRB[40] and Research Services for AMPS[19]
showed consistency over their first 12 and 8 weeks respectively. This was taken
as evidence against the need for running-in periods. JICTAR experience has
been that monitored diary results on long-running panels are sensitive to
contact with interviewers and instructions: for example, in relation to the
recording of guest viewing. The high levels obtained by IPA/ISBA
programme/break diaries also support the view that diarists are more sensitive
to format and procedures than had been believed. The only deduction one can
make from a mixture of evidence is that individual cases need testing.

Fatigue in short-term panels
Short-term diaries represent a very different task for the respondent who is
asked for a brief, once-and-for-all effort with no training on the job.
Everything then depends on the clarity of the original instructions with less of
a commitment and no chance for a correct diary-keeping habit to have been
created. There is some suggestion from the BBM work[34] that, even with a
one-week diary, the accuracy of recording can change: there was relatively
higher reporting at the beginning of the week, declining a little at the end.

Co-operation biases, panel controls and stratifications

A number of studies in the USA [22,39,41] have shown that co-operators in samples and panels view television more than non-co-operators; the amount varies with co-operation rate. The effect may be partly compensated for by substitution procedures involving stratification controls. The Canadian work reviewed above, at rather lower response rates, did not suggest a significant co-operation bias for television with a dual-media diary. [33] With the TV-only diary, however, and a slightly higher response rate, there was a non-significant tendency for the diary co-operators to be heavier viewers. [34]

In the UK the JICTAR and BARB panels have been operated using a stratification procedure which applies a control by weight-of-viewing classification. On establishment surveys, respondent housewives are asked the questions discussed on pages 698–9 and divided into equal 'heavy', 'medium' and 'light' ITV viewing thirds. Recruitment to the viewing panels is equally divided between these thirds. At the initial sign-up of the AGB panels it was found that response rate increased with viewing-weight classification. Overall it varied between 65 per cent to 75 per cent of households originally selected for the AGB Home Audit. It was possible to compare viewing level results on the panel, with the viewing control operating, against what would have happened without the viewing control. For one area it seemed that ratings would have been some five per cent higher without the control. Table 25.8 shows how demographically similar groups viewed more in the initial sign-up group *without* the weight-of-viewing control than in the final balanced panel *with* the weight-of-viewing control. Other ITV areas examined showed less effect but in the same direction.

Table 25.8 *ITV viewing hours with and without weight of viewing control* (week ending 24 November, 1968: Midlands Area)

	With/without children		Social class		No. in household			Age of housewife		
	with	without	ABC1	C2DE	1–2	3	4+	−35	35–64	65+
S/U (without control)	19.3	18.5	14.1	20.5	16.8	21.2	19.7	17.9	20.2	17.0
Total balanced panel	18.9	17.1	13.3	19.6	15.1	20.1	19.4	17.7	18.9	15.9

Source: JICTAR/AGB

It was shown earlier, on page 700 that the weight of viewing classifications have only limited correlation with viewing. This section demonstrates how even an imperfect measure can be useful. Even an irrelevant stratification, correctly applied, cannot be harmful. [42] These results of controlling a panel by a direct forecast of what it is supposed to be measuring seem to be a promising approach to panel control where there may be a co-operation bias. In JICTAR panels normal demographic controls are applied [35] marginally and interlaced.

The BBC reported [43] that terminal education age was associated with ITV and BBC preferences, which suggests some measure of education as an appropriate control. Other stratification controls used in the UK include reception capabilities and geographical location in relation to ITV areas. BARB is reviewing the value of these.

There may be value in some form of multivariate analysis of television viewing which would group people by the similarities in certain aspects of their viewing behaviour and provide other data about the groups. This might establish either groups of people or factors which are as meaningful as the heavy-viewing syndrome and which could be used as a basis for stratification controls, perhaps in place of some of the less effective demographic controls.

With panels there is not only the problem of bias in sign-up but bias in drop-out. With the JICTAR panels after some initial drop-out from heavier viewers the regular pattern appears to follow sign-up bias, and lighter viewers drop out more frequently. Maintaining representative panels is a major issue in audience research.

Aspects of accuracy
Sample surveys and panels can be used very differently in relation to the accuracy of what is measured. Repeated surveys on independent samples, say for different months, can be added together to provide average data over a period of months. This means that, while monthly trends can be followed on the broad sample categories, with the cumulation of samples much smaller breakdowns can be analysed on an average basis.

The use of panels very often results in smaller samples on grounds of cost, and they are generally used for following trends on broad audience categories. There are a number of ways in which panels can be used which mitigate the prima facie limitations of sample size. For the measurement of trends panels give greater statistical efficiency, as discussed in Buck *et al.* [5] Basically, the sampling error of an observed change between two measurements is a function of the sampling error of each of the measurements reduced by a term which reflects the association between them. The variances of two measurements X_1 and X_2 and the difference between them have the following relationship:

$$\text{Variance } (X_1 - X_2) = \text{Variance } X_1 + \text{Variance } X_2 - 2 \text{ Covariance } (X_1 X_2)$$

Panel data can further be used to examine the *sources* of change as well as its size.

The association between readings reduces variance when measuring change. When averaging data, however, there is less efficiency than when samples are independent. Indeed the general tendency is to treat all data from panels, single readings or averages, as if their variance was simply that implied by the basic panel size. In the case of averages this is not true because different readings from the same sample are not wholly correlated and are to some extent independent readings. Averages over a number of times or days have lower variances than a single reading.

An empirical study of the sampling errors associated with averages from panels was published by 1974 by Arbitron in the USA. [44] A way of expressing their findings is in terms of the total sample size implied by the size of the variance associated with an average. This can be expressed as a multiplying factor termed the Statistical Efficiency Value. A Statistical Efficiency Value of 4.0 for an average would mean that the sampling error or variance for that average was equivalent to that associated with a single reading from a sample size four times as large as the actual panel. For that average, therefore, the panel sample is performing as if it was four times as large as it actually is.

These findings on the power of averaging panel data have been confirmed by work on the JICTAR panels in the UK.

The level of Statistical Efficiency for an average depended on the audience sub-group. The empirical efficiencies quoted by Arbitron ranged up to about 3 for averages based on 30 quarter-hours and up to about 18 for averages based on 420 quarter-hours. Some Statistical Efficiencies quoted for single readings were well below one. This showed that, for some sub-groups of individuals who may be clustered with more than one per household, the effective panel size for single readings is much lower than the actual panel size. A similar conclusion was reached in the UK TAM Comparison Survey where adults, of whom there are often two or more per household, had an effective sample size of about the same as the number of households. In other words the variance of data from 200 adults in 100 households would be about the same as that from a random sample of 100 adults in 100 households.

Thus panels and surveys which interview more than one individual per household may lose statistical efficiency if there is a correlation between the individuals' behaviour within households – as there is with television viewing.

The small sizes of panels can generally be offset for averages because there is not a complete correlation between viewing at all times, and the gains in statistical efficiency from broad averaging can be very large. This however only applies to following trends within a sample. A cumulative audience or 'reach' statistic is not an average and has the sampling error of a single reading even where it is a cumulative audience over many scattered times and days.

Systems of research

The demand for media research is often regular, leading to the creation of a total system of research which can comprise any or all of the following elements:

(a) research to define the boundaries of station reception;
(b) research to measure the size and nature of potential audiences to stations: these are likely to be sample surveys. They can be easily integrated with other research, and they can serve as an address bank for panel recruitment;
(c) regular measurements of TV audiences: this can be through regular sample surveys, or a continuously or intermittently reporting panel;
(d) a data bank for special analysis.

Around the world there are many variations on these ingredients. Overall, where television carries advertising, countries where the market is big enough are increasingly using continuous metered systems.

Measuring responses to television transmissions

The main approaches to audience research generate data related to the viewer's concept of watching television. For a number of techniques this is constrained into claims about viewing a time unit, such as the majority of a quarter-hour. In the case of push buttom diaries the individual is attempting to record 'viewing' to the nearest minute. In practice it seems that viewers may take a minute or so to press their buttons. They also appear not to record very brief or unplanned absences from, or presences with, the television set. This is partly because they do not see some of these events as discontinuities in what they are doing. In some cases, such as answering a ringing telephone, the task of first pressing a button may sometimes be beyond them.

When the respondent does record 'viewing' this says nothing about what else the respondent is doing, the level of attention being paid, the degrees of involvement or enjoyment being generated. Consequently all television audience measurement data, by varying degrees according to technique, leave unanswered a number of questions.

– whether the respondent is present for all of a particular time period?
– any other parallel activities engaged in?
– what degree of attention is being paid?
– how much the viewer is involved, interested or enjoying himself?

Concern about presence or absence over short time periods is of specific interest to advertisers. Reactions to transmission content are obviously of concern to programmers, but may also be of interest to advertisers if such reactions affect the reception of advertising.

These are therefore a number of areas of research very close to audience measurement which evaluate on various dimensions the audiences generated by the basic head counting measures.

These are briefly summarized in this section.

Measuring audience reaction

Programmers are interested in what people feel about the programmes they see, and who appreciates particular programmes, both as an aid to future success and in fulfilment of any public service role of broadcasting.

It is easy to assume that, because many people watch a programme, it must be enjoyed more than a programme seen by fewer people. A similar deduction may be made that people watch the kinds of programmes they like. These hypotheses are often not supported by the data. The mismatch between what people like and what they view arises from the following reasons:

(a) people cannot watch all the programmes they would like to because;
   (i)   in some situations other people determine what is viewed;
   (ii) the programmes may not be on at a convenient time;
   (iii) the programmes may clash with something equally liked on another channel;
(b) people sometimes watch programmes they like less because:
   (i)   in some situations other people determine what is viewed;
   (ii) they may just want to watch television and there is nothing on any channel which particularly appeals to them;
   (iii) they watch programmes which follow or precede programmes they like.

Deductions can be made from ratings research about the popularity of programmes, but they are likely to be in very general terms. These factors have also generated the lack of patterning found in the actual viewing of individuals, investigated extensively by Ehrenberg and his collaborators.

Studies of IBA audience reaction data in the UK by Ehrenberg[45] have shown however a broad correlation with audience size providing that the comparisons are made *within* broad programme type e.g. within entertainment programmes or within serious programmes.

In the UK there have been a series of regular studies of audience reaction:

(a) *TVQ*

During 1964, TAM in the UK introduced an approach to measuring simple audience reaction, based on the service operating in the USA, TVQ.

The TVQ system used postal questionnaires with lists of programmes against which people indicated whether they were familiar with the programme and how they rated it on a five point verbal scale – 'one of my favourites', 'very good', 'good', 'fair', 'poor'. Such data helped to explain ratings but were not such a strong predictor as had been hoped, probably due to the reasons for the liking and viewing mismatch suggested above. The data nevertheless represented a measure of enjoyment independent of ratings which could be of use to the programmer. It was suggested that one universal liking scale was not appropriate to the different kinds of programmes screened. In practice people do see programmes, apart from news broadcasts, as part of a continuous stream of material rather than separate categories. The TVQ service ran for several years and was bought by the ITA and by several programme companies and for an experimental period by some advertising agencies.

(b) *The IBA research programme*
The IBA (then the ITA) commissioned a programme of exploratory research in 1967–8 ending in a pilot panel operation in London for a limited period. This was fully described by Frost.[46] The research programme started by seeking the terms in which viewers described programmes using the Repertory Grid technique (Kelly triads). The constructs obtained were converted into seven-point semantic differential scales. These were then applied to programmes by another sample and the results factor analysed. This yielded nine factors upon which any programme could be rated. A programme typology was then built up by cluster analysis. Following this pilot work a further large-scale pilot study, covering three areas over six months, was commissioned by the ITA and ITV programme companies from a consortium, Television Opinion Panel Ltd. (TOP). A variation on the earlier procedure was used to establish eleven factors and a general evaluation factor. Programmes were again clustered and the importance of factors within cluster determined in some cases. Panels of 300 in each of the three areas then reported fortnightly by mail on the programmes they chose to view. The data covered an appreciation index for all programmes, detailed factor scales for a limited list, spontaneous comments and, occasionally, special questions. Another approach to forming a programme typology is given by Kirsch and Banks,[47] and a viewer typology, in terms of programmes liked, by Rothman and Rauta.[48]

More recently the IBA has operated a less complex audience appreciation service for ITV, AURA, measuring programmes on all stations by rotation using intermittently reporting panels of adults filling in self-completion diaries/questionnaires.

(c) *BBC research*
For many years the BBC collected audience reaction data from a 'viewing panel'. This comprised some 2000 people recruited from those interviewed on the daily listening-and-viewing survey who reported weekly by postal questionnaire. Respondents were asked to comment only on programmes seen in the normal course of viewing. The questionnaire covered both detailed aspects of the programme's content and evaluations on a number of dimensions such as 'funny – unfunny', 'entertaining – boring'.

(d) *The BARB audience reaction service*
In the UK, the BBC and ITV companies now collaborate in joint systems both

for the measurement of audience size and audience reaction. The latter service is based upon 5-day diaries/questionnaires left with individuals, interviewed on a daily survey of 1000 respondents. The basic measure of appreciation is a scale applied cross all programmes as follows:

How interesting and/or enjoyable did you find the programmes you watched today? (please ring one code for each programme watched).

extremely interesting and/or enjoyable	very interesting and/or enjoyable	fairly interesting and/or enjoyable	neither one thing nor the other	not very interesting and/or enjoyable	not at all interesting and/or enjoyable

Also in the booklet are rating scales and questions relating to specific programmes. For a description as to how these data are used in programme production see Meneer.[35] This service is moving over to a panel basis in 1986.

(e) *Other approaches*

Most broadcasters find it necessary to take some measure of audience reaction to programmes. This may be done on an *ad hoc* basis. At other times it is based upon continuous, or regular intermittent, surveys or panels. In some countries combined research for viewing and opinion has been undertaken on the same samples although this may be thought potentially to influence the audience measurement data. In the Netherlands, programme reaction questions were put to a viewdata panel via the television screen when these were called up by the respondent. A similar small experimental panel has also been operated by one of the UK television companies.

Programme audience reaction in relation to advertising

An advertiser would be interested in any programme reaction data which could be used as a basis for predicting ratings. It is probable that no reaction data would do this perfectly because of factors affecting viewing other than an individual's preference, i.e. timing, competition and other people.

There is evidence that attitudes to the surrounding programme context are correlated with some measures of commercial effectiveness. There may be different principles at work with programme sponsorship, where the attitude to a programme may represent an additional message-source relevant to the advertising, compared with spot advertising, where commercials are more clearly unrelated to the programmes and seen as separate from them.[49] With spot advertising it seems likely that the mediating link between a positive attitude to a programme and response to its commercials is reduced competing activity or even increased probability of staying with the set during the break, rather than any kind of editorial mood association. The source of the effect remains to be demonstrated. That there is an effect, although sometimes a weak one, is shown by studies by TAM [14] and Unilever, [50] while a number of American studies are briefly mentioned by Bogart [51] and some further data reported by Corlett and Richardson. [52] Generally, those viewers liking a programme show higher levels of behavioural attention and/or recall for advertising breaks within it than those viewers liking it less.

A review of context effects by Twyman [53] also included some JICTAR evidence that brief absences by the stable (non-switching) TV audience did not seem to vary in extent from programme to programme in UK conditions. The more recent observation study by Bates [30] however has shown both variations by time of day and by programme type. It seems likely that, as the amount of programme choice increases and the range of viewing conditions widens, then the possibility of editorial or environmental context effects increases.

Studies of behaviour during television advertising

Whilst there is a general sociological interest in what else people do while watching television programmes, great commercial interest has been focussed upon behaviour during advertising breaks.

Observations of viewers reported by Steiner [27] represent the most detailed attempt to study what happens when people view commercials. Krugman [54] has attempted to extend this further into studying their thinking about commercials while viewing.

Observation has been used again in a study by Bates [30] in the UK with students reporting on their families, and by Collett [31] using video.

In the UK, the findings on *presence* in breaks are most relevant to evaluating advertisement audience size. An early LPE [13] study showed that more programme-viewing housewives were missing from breaks early in the evening than later on. The IPA/ISPA [10] and later JICTAR [11] studies conflict with this, showing virtually no time effects for presence in breaks, and some limited evidence against programme effects. There was little difference between centre and end breaks for adults but more housewives were missing in end breaks. An overall level of absence in breaks of around 20% appears in both American and UK studies. Programme audiences are based on seeing more than half of the programme so that an unknown proportion of viewers will also be missing from programme audiences for short time periods. UK evidence suggests that some of the commercial audience loss is associated with the timing of set switching between programmes. Where there is a metered measurement of set switching, therefore, the unrecorded audience loss at breaks may be considerably less than the 20% found with other techniques. In contrast with these studies, the Bates [30] study in the UK did claim to find variations in presence for and attention to advertisements by time of day, programme type and end versus centre breaks. These effects were, however, relatively small. Further work is needed to resolve these issues.

Advertisers have also been interested in the *quality of attention* paid to advertisements but this has often been approached by asking about parallel behaviour during advertisements.

Early studies, including unpublished data from the IPA/ISBA,[10] generally agree that *behavioural attention* levels rise from early to peak time although relatively little is known about late-night viewing. Evidence for the importance of behavioural attention rests solely on its correlation with higher levels of recall. There is evidence of programming effects, particularly in relation to programme interest or liking, from studies by LPE,[13] JWT[25] and TAM.[14] Work by BMRB has shown that indications of attention-level, additional to time effects, can be deduced from frequency of viewing or loyalty to television programmes.[52] This approach may still offer the greatest accessibility to the concept of attention since it can be deduced from regular audience measurement rather than by expensive coincidental surveying.

A number of later studies have used telephone interviewing to check activities while viewing, sometimes asking a respondent to report on activities of other members of the family. There are frequently methodological problems with this kind of study:

- nothing can be directly observed, only reported by the respondent;
- questions are often related to a time period rather than just 'the instant when the telephone rang'. The respondent, in a search to understand the purpose of the question, may then refer to recent memory to look for any activities mentioned by the interviewer.
- a number of intermittent and overlapping activities can occur over a period of time. A respondent perceives these as 'happening' and will report them if they seem appropriate, even if they did not occur at the precise moment of time under investigation. Results from activity surveys depend very much upon what the respondent perceives the interviewer to be interested in. It is very difficult under such circumstances not to 'lead' the respondent if the classes of behaviour under investigation are to be specified clearly. It is thus very difficult to devise unbiased questions;
- respondents often see it as more socially acceptable not to be 'just watching television'. It is probably socially unacceptable however to admit to being asleep;
- people perceive the viewing of commercial breaks, which are seen 'incidentally', as involving a different kind of attention from that involved in watching programmes which are the subject of motivated viewing. Thus if programmes are an implicit yardstick, many respondents feel obliged to downgrade any assessments of attention to breaks.

Having made these points, it is clear that there are different levels of behavioural activity whilst viewing television and these may be associated with level of commitment to the programme, time of day, or certain kinds of respondent. The distinction between such ongoing activities ('having something to do') and more discrete events ('having to do something') is relevant. While the former will affect the general probability of lapses of attention, advertising breaks will be particularly vulnerable to the latter. The difficulty lies in obtaining an unbiased estimate of the extent of these types of behaviour and in assessing their impact on advertising reception.

The nature of attention involves the monitoring of partially unattended information sources and rapid switching between sources. It is therefore not unreasonable that findings show that levels of commercial recognition are not as sharply different as between varying levels of behavioural attention as might be expected. Since the nature of selective attention is to select what is relevant, it is possible that perceived *relevant* advertising might survive better under conditions of competing activities when viewing than *irrelevant* advertising.

An unresolved question is whether there are classes of respondent for whom most television viewing is under more variable conditions of attention. If so then another issue is the degree to which it is the proportion of these in the audience which determines variations in *average* levels of behavioural attention and how far time of day and programme content are the significant factors.

Thus it is not clear how activities affect reception of advertising nor how this interacts with different segments of the audience. This and the level of bias in some studies often makes such qualitative data difficult to use.

This is an area which urgently needs further investigation. An approach which could help to resolve some of the conceptual problems would be a high quality unobtrusive observation study. Such a study could show how far various factors affect behavioural attention *within the individual* over time and how far different levels of behavioural attention affect the reception of advertising. These are the important issues currently obscured by 'average' findings. Although subject to problems of representativeness, further observation studies could potentially make average findings more interpretable and usable.

As with context effects, it seems likely that changes in the television media (e.g. more programme choice, more television sets, video recorders, breakfast television) can create a wider variety of attentional states than formerly and these are likely to need more investigation in the future. One of these issues, video recorders, is discussed below.

Indirect evidence on behaviour in advertising breaks

Variations in the consumption patterns of water and electricity supplies have often been quoted as reflecting television viewing behaviour. This evidence has not generally been made public nor examined systematically. Bunn 1982 [55] has however examined a period of demand for electricity in relation to programmes and advertising breaks and developed a regression model for one week to forecast surge of demand at advertising breaks.

The programme period shown in detail included a long, much publicised mystery television film shown with a news break in the middle. Clear rises in electricity consumption are shown at breaks and particularly during the 15 minute news break. These could be caused by turning on lights, kettles etc. and must largely (but not wholly) reflect brief absences from the TV room by some individuals amongst those watching.

The conclusions reached were consistent with some previous presence research in that the variables associated with programme type and programme appreciation were not significant. The proportionate increases in electrical demand for the breaks shown in detail were usually under 5%. Some findings however suggest new hypotheses. There is the suggestion that absence in breaks is higher for longer programmes, and for longer periods of involvement where the previous programme also had a high rating.

More significantly, however, the analysis was extended to cover 15 minute Party Political Broadcasts shown on all channels. Here the rise in electrical demand seems much sharper and is higher the greater the popularity of the previous programme. The audience data used in this part of the analysis were, however, from qualitative programme appreciation diaries rather than the meter measurement system, so some caution is needed.

Behaviour when recording and playing back video recordings

A number of surveys have shown that some viewers fastwind through commercials when playing back video tapes and a much smaller number edit out advertisements at recording. This was also observed in the Bates study.[30]

Measuring the precise extent of this behaviour is however difficult: survey questions are likely to be answered in very general terms. The most reliable approach is likely to be via meters modified to measure this.

A further problem for advertisers is what value, if any, to put on such an advertising 'exposure'. To fastwind (or edit) accurately usually requires some attention to the commercials to know when to start and stop. For some advertisements a fastwound exposure may be incomprehensible and valueless. For well-known brands there is a reminder of the brand name, and for well-known commercials the amount of attention may be little different from a normal exposure. Some research is needed to evaluate the effect of advertisements which are fastwound. Uncertainty about this has led to a certain amount of controversy as to whether or not published media audiences for television commercials should include the video timeshift component. One view is that the video tape playback is an 'opportunity-to-see' like any other; the counterview requires the timeshift audiences to be separated to allow for fastwinding. This debate is so far unresolved.

Switching out during the commercial break

The use of remote controls enables the viewer to switch channels very quickly to see what is on another channel, even perhaps to monitor several channels. Surveys and observations in the UK and USA report that some viewers do this in commercial breaks ('Zipping'). Other devices are available to block out commercials by remote control ('Zapping'). This area of viewer control over advertising again presents a research challenge to establish the levels of this activity without bias. The best approach is probably by meters adjusted to register changes over very short time periods: such a project is under way in the UK.

Analysing viewing patterns

The use of continuous panels makes it possible to examine not only audiences to individual times, programmes and advertisements but the relationship between audiences at different times. This is of interest to both the programmer and the advertiser.

Ehrenberg and Goodhardt[56,57] extensively analysed the duplication of viewing between pairs of transmissions. Their findings include a duplication law which suggests that all pairs combine in the same way unless the transmissions are adjacent or nearly so. This implies that viewing is not very systematic and dependent upon strong personal preferences, but largely random. Having viewed one programme, a viewer is no more likely to view any one other programme more than another unless it is the next or next but one in time. This conclusion also holds good in the USA, and the work is carefully summarized in Goodhardt *et al.*[58]

This lack of selectivity probably arises because the viewer's own preferences are obscured by components of his viewing arising from other sources mentioned earlier. Certainly individuals have programme preferences and feel that they are exercising selectivity, as shown by Piepe *et al.*[59] in their work on class differences in relation to television. Non-selectivity does make coverage and frequency data relatively easy to predict in most cases. It is possible to estimate the data from formulae and tables, given information such as the number of spots in the schedule and the ratings they achieve. Studies in support of this finding are discussed by Ehrenberg and Twyman.[60,61] An internationally tested model was reported by Hulks and Thomas.[62] The performance of advertising schedules in terms of coverage and frequency is however most frequently assessed by direct computer analysis of panel data.

Measuring television advertising effectiveness

There are a number of areas of research which attempt to aid the advertiser in making decisions about television advertising. These can be broadly classified under the headings of content, volume and patterning.

Content is usually studied for individual commercials in the form of some pre- or post-testing of a specific advertisement. Most advertising research in the form of pre-testing examines responses to single advertisements. How much money an advertiser should spend is a question which cannot be answered directly by research. Ideally, a market model should be capable of showing the return in profits for money spent on advertising. In practice, budgets are fixed in a variety of ways as discussed by Broadbent.[63] A closely related problem is that of choosing between ways of using the medium in terms of the way spots are patterned in time.

The effects of alternative advertising strategy can be studied in a number of ways:

(a) *Econometric analysis.* This approach seeks to relate advertising activity to historical sales data and a summary of one approach is given by O'Herlihy.[64]

(b) *In-market experiments.* An advertiser can vary his advertising strategy either between different time periods in the same area or different areas in the same time period. The problems here are lack of controlled identical conditions in the two periods or areas, and uncertainty concerning over what period the effects should be measured. For these reasons, the results of such experiments are often inconclusive and advertisers seldom publish them. Examples of a model being used to assess in-market the difference in sales between alternative TV strategies, including advertising content, are given by Bloom and Twyman.[65]

(c) *Advertising laboratory experiments.* The best controlled design, reviewed by Haskins,[66] is what he called the 'controlled field experiment'. This is the situation where purchasing is measurable in as near to real-life conditions as possible for two matched populations identical in every way except in the advertising input they receive. In the USA this has been achieved for television by having alternative cables serving two panels in the same district, their input differing only in respect to the advertising experiments.

Experience with one surviving system in the USA was reviewed by Adler and Kuehn.[67] This approach has been made easier by the use of scanners in checkouts which easily record panel members' purchases. The potential role of an ADLAB in the UK has been reviewed by Corkindale.[68] Extremely advanced and sophisticated forms of ADLAB have developed in the USA, e.g. Behavior Scan.[69]

(d) *Tracking studies and campaign evaluation surveys.* There has been a considerable growth in the use of tracking studies in Europe over the last ten years. These studies use survey techniques to track various 'intermediate measures' of advertising effectiveness such as:

brand awareness and saliency;
brand image;
advertising awareness;
advertisement recognition;

Such studies relate the audience measurement OTSs or expenditure to levels of advertising awareness and the effects on attitudes to the brand. While this is a surrogate for evaluation in terms of sales it has value diagnostically by suggesting causes for success or failure in terms of attention, communication and persuasion. Some applications of this approach are given by Juchems and Twyman.[70] Tracking studies have proved particularly effective in relation to television where advertising awareness is generally easier to measure than for print. The way in which such studies are used is often criticized for concentrating too much on the attention-getting properties of advertisements.

Since tracking studies do try to go one stage beyond OTS to the actual representation of a message, they may prove to be a means of evaluating some of the new developments in TV advertising such as early morning transmissions, minority channels, pay-channels and even teletext.

Conclusions

Television *advertising* research starts from *media audience* measurement and has hitherto largely assumed a constant relationship between advertisement audiences and general levels of surrounding programme audiences. At the same time, the task of measuring general audience levels has been relatively easy, compared with other media measurement, because television viewing was readily identifiable in terms of place, time and memorable content. The heavy expenditure on television media research has occurred because of the immense detail which it has been possible to measure and which has therefore been demanded by advertisers. Media owners have readily accepted this because making television the most intensively researched medium itself attracts attention to, and involvement with, the medium.

The initial simple state of the medium upon which all this has been structured is, however, now changing rapidly. The range of choice is increasing as are the modes of accessing the medium.[71] This is leading to changes in the range of audience sizes and degree of selectivity and the nature of the total experience of watching television. The viewer has greater control over what he sees, when and where he sees it and, in the case of advertising, whether he sees it at all. As suggested above, the medium is changing from having a captive audience to being 'a captive medium'. Put another way, the medium is acquiring some of the characteristics of published media where there is more scope for the operation of selectivity of exposure and attention by the respondent. New media are emerging which fall neatly between broadcasting and publishing; for example the sale of video tapes containing advertising or carrying sponsorship.

These change create new challenges for electronic media research:

- audience measurement where time and place and mode of exposure are neither so memorable nor necessarily static enough to be meterable;
- faster changing modes of access to the medium making for greater difficulty in maintaining the representative structure of long-term panels;
- advertising exposure occurring under a wider variety of conditions creating a much less consistent relationship to surrounding programme audience size in terms of exposure, and a much greater range of viewing conditions and viewer control over them.

It seems likely therefore that the next decade will see more changes in requirements from television media research than have occurred over the last twenty years whose increasingly technically, sophisticated response to a largely constant set of requirements has been partly chronicled in this chapter.

Chapter 26

Radio, outdoor and cinema research

FRANK TEER

The attention of the media researcher is not unnaturally concentrated on the two main advertising media. Relatively little attention is given in the UK to the cinema, radio and posters as subjects for audience research, and the reasons are not hard to find. In UK advertising expenditure terms they are minor media. Together, in 1984 they accounted for just over 8% of £3119 milion spent on display advertising and 20% of the expenditure on television advertising alone. The 1984 figures were: posters and transport advertising £150m, cinema £16m and radio £86m. Whilst the relative importance of these media obviously varies from country to country, it is generally the case that television and print media are by far the most intensively researched.

As advertising media, they are very different in terms of the nature of the advertising presented and the quality of exposure offered. The creative opportunities of the cinema, with colour, sound, movement and a large screen, contrast with the limited message which can be transmitted in a poster advertisement. Radio, standing between the two, calls for special creative attention because of its total dependence on the aural sense. In terms of the quality of exposure delivered by each medium, the same contrast can be observed. The considerable absorption of the cinema audience is at one end of the attention spectrum, with posters at the other, the poster audience being almost totally 'casual'. Radio listening falls some way between the two. Often it does not claim the undivided attention of its audience, who may be working, driving, even reading, while listening. On the other hand, for some members of the audience there may be a very close and direct link between the presenter and the listener, offering very special opportunities to an advertiser.

Although so different in kind, these media have two very important characteristics in common as vehicles for advertising. First, they are used by national advertisers mainly as support media to press and/or television campaigns. This is true of all three for different reasons. *Cinema* offers an opportunity to reach population sub-groups who are relatively under-exposed to other forms of advertising: for example, young, unmarried people aged 16–24. *Radio* offers relatively low-cost repetition of an advertising message. *Posters* provide high coverage of the population and high repetition, both of which can be concentrated near the point of purchase. Second, all three media lend themselves to selective area campaigns. Blanket national or regional coverage is not obligatory. Advertisers with localized interest such as retailers, garages, etc, can make particularly effective use of the media, confining their expenditure purely to their areas of operation.

The role given to advertising in these media and the total sums expended on them affect the type and amount of research undertaken. The advertiser requires information about the audience before deciding to spend money on the medium, but the information he can expect must necessarily be restricted.

As with press and television, audience research should enable the advertiser to predict the size and nature of the audience to a series of advertisements. The advertiser wants to know how many people will see at least one advertisement in a campaign (its cover), and how many times on average each member of the audience is likely to see an advertisement (repetition). This information, ideally, should be available for target groups defined either in demographic or product usership terms, but at least he will require to know the nature of the audience as a whole in demographic terms.

Radio audience research

We are concerned only with research into the audiences of stations which carry advertising. Until the advent of Independent Local Radio in 1972, UK research into these radio audiences had been relatively spasmodic; before then the only commercial radio programmes received in the UK were those transmitted from abroad. A brief review of that research does, however, give an overview of the main research alternatives available to the audience researcher.

Early surveys, particularly for Radio Luxembourg, were based on large samples of individuals who were asked to recall their listening to radio in the previous 24 hours. The method has varied in detailed aspects from study to study but essentially was dependent on the memory of the respondent about particular stations listened to in specific time periods (sometimes as short as 15 minutes) over a 24-hour period (usually 'yesterday').

Surveys of this type, which measure listening over the preceding 24 hours (24-hour recall surveys), provide useful data for the advertiser. They measure the characteristics of the audience for any given time period and can be used to estimate the total audience for any given time spot, and thus, the cost per thousand members of the target audience reached by that spot.

Because the detailed listening data extend only over a 24-hour period, direct survey evidence of cumulative reach and frequency over a long time period cannot be directly adduced from the survey data. However, the cumulative audience and the amount of repetition delivered by a radio advertising campaign can be estimated from 24-hour data if these are combined with limited questions on listening frequency. American experience based on work carried out by Westinghouse Broadcasting indicates that these estimates can be refined to a considerable degree of accuracy. [1]

Because 24-hour recall surveys do not provide direct measurements of cumulative cover some users have favoured the diary as a method of collecting radio audience data. In November 1968 Radio Luxembourg used a seven-day diary to collect listening data. [2] In this technique, which is also extensively used in the United States and elsewhere, a sample of the general public are asked to keep a record of their radio listening (and sometimes also their television viewing and newspaper reading) over a seven-day time period. This record then gives the researcher direct evidence on the question of cumulative cover.

During the 'pirate' radio period in the mid-1960s, when unlicensed stations operated from off-shore bases (mainly on ships moored outside national waters), the radio research undertaken fell into two distinct types. In the first place the stations obtained, through 'omnibus' surveys, weekly audience figures based on questions such as 'Did you listen at all during the last seven days?' and 'When did you last listen?'. Weekly audience figures of this kind were little more than station popularity polls and were used to reinforce the stations' claims that they had a wide and interested audience. They were not particularly useful as media research. Consequently, the 'pirates' later undertook 24-hour recall surveys similar to the Luxembourg surveys and on one occasion used a seven-day diary.

Other methods of collecting radio audience data, in particular the telephone interview which has been extensively used in the USA, have not been favoured in the UK. Although there has been a considerable increase in the penetration of telephone ownership, there remains considerable doubt about the use of the telephone in radio audience research if information about long time periods is an essential requirement. At the same time it must be said that telephone research could be a very valuable tool for validation of methodology and for quick checks on changes in gross audience levels.

Effectively therefore there are two main alternative approaches: day-after recall, collecting information about 24-hours listening, and the weekly diary. There are many variants to these approaches and they each have their advantages and disadvantages.

Methodology

The objective of radio audience research is the same as any other media research – to estimate the opportunities to hear an advertisement or series of advertisements; this with a view to establishing the cost efficiency of the medium, a particular station or a specific schedule of advertisements. There are a number of measurement problems peculiar to radio which have to be considered in appraising the two main alternative approaches of 24-hour recall and personal diary.

Station identification

If a listener is to be asked to record or recall his listening behaviour there is a presumption that he is always aware of the name of the station to which he is listening. When there are a number of alternative stations with a similar format this presumption may not be completely valid. Some indication of the extent of this problem is shown by a small-scale pilot conducted by National Opinion Polls in the latter days of 'pirate' radio in 1966. This pilot consisted of a simple coincidental check in which interviewers called at homes and enquired if the radio was switched on and whether the respondent was listening to it. If the answer to both questions was 'yes', the interviewers went on to ask to which station the radio was tuned. Having recorded this, the interviewer then checked the set to determine whether it was, in fact, tuned to that station. This is a simple check of simultaneous recall. Out of 322 listeners interviewed, about 10% gave incorrect answers on the question of station. In the case of those who said they were listening to a commercial station, 18% incorrectly identified the station. Of those who said they were listening to a BBC broadcast, about 5% were incorrect.

This experiment was very limited in scope and neither investigated the causes of confusion nor the methods required to minimize it. It goes no further than to demonstrate that station identification is a problem and it was a significantly greater problem for commercial stations of the 'pop pirate' type than it was for BBC stations (as they were then).

This problem leads to the conclusion that the diary approach might be more helpful in ensuring attention is given to station identification when the listening event takes place.

The casualness of the event

There is a widespread view that much radio listening, especially to 'pop' stations, is casual in nature – that the radio does not demand the same degree of undivided attention as press or television. This seems to be borne out by the extent to which radio listening occurs while other activities are in progress. There is, therefore, some doubt whether this type of event can be recalled accurately 24 hours later or whenever the panel member fills in his or her diary. Memory cannot readily be jogged because programme lists consisting almost entirely of names of disc jockeys or programme presenters are unlikely to be adequate recall aids.

Twyman has commented on this particular feature and says:

All the advantages of radio as a medium, that it supplements people's ongoing lives rather than requiring everything else to come to a grinding halt, militate against accurate memory.

The audience to any transmission will comprise a mixture of people: those who are involved, those who have it as background, some who chose the programme, others who did not.

This casual integration with the rest of life is one reason why different research techniques yield different results. Research techniques vary according to:

- how far they reduce co-operation bias and sample the whole population
- their degree of reliance on unaided and unprompted memory
- the criterion of listening which they impose.[3]

It is possible that one of the advantages of the diary may lie in taking some of the casualness from this 'event'. Because panel members know that they have to record their listening, they will pay greater attention to it in terms of taking note of the station to which they are tuned and mentally noting the time.

The location of the event

Because of the portability of the transistor radio, listening can take place almost anywhere inside and outside the home. The radio audience is an extremely mobile one. In addition, because the radio is often used as background, it can be played at work or in a car. Although the majority of radio listening does in fact take place in the home, a substantial amount of it occurs outside the home.

In recent diary-based surveys carried out on behalf of the Association of Independent Radio Contractors, Research Surveys of Great Britain have found that of all listening to radio roughly one-quarter takes place outside the home. The proportion recorded in the surveys varies from area to area within the range of 19–35%. This is a substantial proportion of total listening and much of it is to radios not belonging to or tuned in by the listener, making further difficulties of recall and/or diary keeping.

These special difficulties serve to highlight some of the questions which need to be answered before opting conclusively for one measurement technique or the other. The problem is further confounded because the 24-hour recall method and the diary are subject to a considerable number of possible approaches – using quota or random samples, personal, postal or telephone interview, including or excluding measurements of other media, etc. That the chosen method should have validity seems to be accepted as a guiding principle but attempts at validation have proved inconclusive.

Validity requires that the chosen technique reliably reflects the 'real' audience. In using measures which depend on an individual's recall of an event, that measure may not reflect the true audience because of the frailty of memory. Listening occasions may be forgotton and the audience is consequently understated. If a diary method is used, individuals participating in the survey know that they have to record their listening and are likely to pay greater attention to it but diary-keeping could condition panel members into adopting a listening pattern (especially in the short term) which is not 'normal'. This could be either for prestige reasons or to make their own diary-keeping simpler. The act of completing a diary may make them more radio-conscious than previously and this might result in an overestimate of the actual audience.

As there are no independent audience data against which measurements of the above type can be checked, the only method of validating the information is the coincidental check. This technique requires that the methods being tested are put into operation simultaneously and an independent measure of the audience is taken by a method which is known to be valid. The coincidental check, which is a valid measure, requires that the radio listening of a large sample of individuals be checked at specific moments in time by observation. If a large enough sample of individuals is contacted at a precise point in time and a note taken of the station to which the individual is listening (if any) a reliable and valid estimate of the listening level at that time can be made. This was the method used by Television Audience Measurement Limited in the comparison surveys undertaken in the early days of commercial television in the UK.[4]

The need to validate measurement for all listening imposes considerable problems in designing suitable coincidental checking techniques. We have to cover listening in private households, in work places, in motor cars, as well as in public places. It is not impossible to devise a coincidental check to cover the audience at home and at work. The former would follow the television pattern and the latter would require sampling work places and determining whether any radios are being played, to which stations they are tuned, and what proportion of employees are listening to them at given moments in time. Listening out of doors is more difficult because the population of any outdoor location is constantly changing.

A number of radio audience validation surveys have been carried out in the United States and Canada:

(a) the ARB – RKO Radio Experiment;[5]
(b) ARMS – All Radio Methodology Study;[6]
(c) a report on the BBM Tests of Revised and Single-Media Diaries, February 1974;[7]
(d) Polyphase.[8]

The RKO survey concluded that multi-media diaries agreed with 'standard' and the radio-only diaries over-reported by a factor of two. ARMS concluded that radio-only diaries and personal interview recall came closest to 'standard'. The Canadian BBM Study showed television and radio diaries came closest to 'standard'. In all of these cases telephone coincidental checks were used as standard measurement (a measure which, of course, validates only 'in-home' listening). The Polyphase survey was an exploratory study rather than a validation exercise, but it did demonstrate that radio research was highly sensitive to bias through non-response and in particular that low response rates tended to produce inflated listening figures.

The inconclusiveness of this work is, perhaps, not surprising in view of the enormous variations in approach and the somewhat erratic quality of the sampling methods used for much radio research. One is tempted to conclude that either of the basic methods (diary or recall) will approach to standard if it is implemented with good sampling and interviewing and the appropriate memory and identification aids.

It is generally accepted that recall produces lower listening levels than diaries and that multi-media diaries produce lower listening levels than radio-only diaries.

In those parts of the world where radio research is undertaken with any degree of regularity the diary approach has generally found favour. The main reasons for the success of the diary have less to do with validity than economy. From the point of view of data yield the seven-day diary is a much more cost-efficient vehicle for data collection than a 24-hour recall study. Clearly if a sample of individuals completes a diary for a seven-day period the researcher collects seven times the amount of information compared with a 24-hour recall survey with the same sample size. Furthermore, the longer-term nature of the diary makes it simpler to produce evidence of the cumulative audience to more than one commercial.

UK research

The commencement of local commercial radio in the UK in 1972 led to considerable speculation about the type of research which would be undertaken. This speculation ran along two quite distinct and widely separated lines. On the one hand there was a belief that the local stations would not be able, or prepared, to finance expensive media research in their broadcasting areas. On the other hand, many advertisers and agencies were concerned that a formalized system for radio research should be implemented and that this system should be able to produce estimates of the cumulative audience and therefore include estimates of listening behaviour over a long time period, e.g. seven days.

Initially, the independent stations produced audience estimates by a variety of techniques ranging from popularity polls to diaries but during 1974 the Association of Independent Radio Contractors (AIRC) decided to establish a common method for audience research. They sought the guidance of advertisers and advertising agencies on survey methods and this led to the establishment of a Joint Industry Committee for Radio Audience Research (JICRAR). This committee recommended the adoption of diary research in the broadcasting area of each station.

AIRC issued a specification for this research which called for:

(a) the use of radio-only diaries covering a seven-day time-period;
(b) recording of listening to all radio – BBC and commercial;
(c) random samples of 1000 or 800 individuals in each area;
(d) personal placement and collection of diaries by interviewers;
(e) response rates of 65% or more;
(f) the collection of listening behaviour quarter-hour by quarter-hour (with the exception of the night hours of midnight to 6 a.m. when half-hourly information was thought to be acceptable);
(g) diaries to be placed with only one individual in each household;
(h) the collection by personal interview, at the diary placement stage, of information about exposure to other media and broad radio listening claims.

Subsequently, in October 1974, a contract for this research was placed by the Association of Independent Radio Contractors with Research Surveys of Great Britain, since when a series of surveys has been carried out in accordance with the above specification.[9]

Initially, these surveys were carried out in relatively discrete non-overlapping areas each measuring the audience of one local ILR station. However, as the number of commercial operators has increased to over 40, the number of individuals able to listen to more than one ILR station has increased considerably and the methodology has been changed to take this into account by ensuring that individuals who can hear more than one station are asked about all of these stations in the diary. Apart from this, the diary has remained relatively unchanged since the surveys commenced (see Fig. 26.1). It should be noted that several versions of the diaries are used in each area to vary the order of presentation of the stations in order to counter any biases resulting from 'order of appearance'.

As an aid to station identification the diary contains a description of the programme content of each station. In order to encourage co-operation from individuals who claim not to listen to the radio the diary contains a general information page which is not used in the analysis of results but requests information about radio listening and other activities on each day of the week.

Recent issues in UK research

Two questions have received major attention during the last ten years: the question of seasonal variations in audience levels and the accumulation of audiences over a time-period longer than one week.

DAYTIME 5.00 a.m.– 4.00p.m. Wednesday		STATION LISTENED TO							Where Listened	
		BRMB Radio	Radio Luxembourg	BBC Radio 1	BBC Radio 2	BBC Radio 3	BBC Radio 4	BBC Radio Birmingham	Listened at home	Listened elsewhere
		1	2	3	4	5	6	7	X	A
01	5.00– 5.30									
02	5.30– 6.00									
03	6.00– 6.15									
04	6.15– 6.30									
05	6.30– 6.45									
06	6.45– 7.00									
07	7.00– 7.15									
08	7.15– 7.30									
09	7.30– 7.45									
10	7.45– 8.00									
11	8.00– 8.15									
12	8.15– 8.30									
13	8.30– 8.45									
14	8.45– 9.00									
15	9.00– 9.15									
16	9.15– 9.30									
17	9.30– 9.45									
18	9.45–10.00									
19	10.00–10.15									
20	10.15–10.30									
21	10.30–10.45									
22	10.45–11.00									
23	11.00–11.15									
24	11.15–11.30									
25	11.30–11.45									
26	11.45–12.00									
27	12.00–12.15									
28	12.15–12.30									
29	12.30–12.45									
30	12.45– 1.00									
31	1.00– 1.15									
32	1.15– 1.30									
33	1.30– 1.45									
34	1.45– 2.00									
35	2.00– 2.15									
36	2.15– 2.30									
37	2.30– 2.45									
38	2.45– 3.00									
39	3.00– 3.15									
40	3.15– 3.30									
41	3.30– 3.45									
42	3.45– 4.00									

Have you recorded ALL your listening for today?

EVENING 4.00 p.m.–5.00a.m. Wednesday		STATION LISTENED TO							Where Listened	
		BRMB Radio	Radio Luxembourg	BBC Radio 1	BBC Radio 2	BBC Radio 3	BBC Radio 4	BBC Radio Birmingham	Listened at home	Listened elsewhere
		1	2	3	4	5	6	7	X	A
43	4.00– 4.15									
44	4.15– 4.30									
45	4.30– 4.45									
46	4.45– 5.00									
47	5.00– 5.15									
48	5.15– 5.30									
49	5.30– 5.45									
50	5.45– 6.00									
51	6.00– 6.15									
52	6.15– 6.30									
53	6.30– 6.45									
54	6.45– 7.00									
55	7.00– 7.15									
56	7.15– 7.30									
57	7.30– 7.45									
58	7.45– 8.00									
59	8.00– 8.15									
60	8.15– 8.30									
61	8.30– 8.45									
62	8.45– 9.00									
63	9.00– 9.15									
64	9.15– 9.30									
65	9.30– 9.45									
66	9.45–10.00									
67	10.00–10.15									
68	10.15–10.30									
69	10.30–10.45									
70	10.45–11.00									
71	11.00–11.15									
72	11.15–11.30									
73	11.30–11.45									
74	11.45–12.00									
75	12.00–12.30									
76	12.30– 1.00									
77	1.00– 1.30									
78	1.30– 2.00									
79	2.00– 2.30									
80	2.30– 3.00									
81	3.00– 3.30									
82	3.30– 4.00									
83	4.00– 4.30									
84	4.30– 5.00									

Please check ALL today's records for accuracy.

Fig. 26.1 Typical radio diary page.

Measurement of seasonality

Originally surveys were conducted as and when stations required them until in 1977 the first Network survey was carried out. This gave data for the first time for every station in the Network surveyed at the same time and also provided the first 'National' figures for Independent Local Radio (ILR).

A major industry survey has been conducted by AIRC every spring since 1977 and in the early days this was the subject of some criticism. It was felt by the advertising industry that the once-a-year spring survey might not be producing results which reflected the variations in audience across the year. To answer this criticism, major industry surveys were commissioned in the spring and autumn of 1980 and followed up by spring, summer and autumn surveys

in 1981. Some of the basic results emerging from these surveys are shown in
Table 26.1.

Table 26.1 UK. radio audience data

	Spring 1980	Autumn 1980	Spring 1981	Summer 1981	Autumn 1981
ILR weekly reach %	52	51	49	50	48
ILR peak 1/4 hour rating %	12	13	12	13	12
ILR average weekly hours of listening	13.5	13.8	13.7	13.9	13.9
Total radio average hours	23.4	22.6	23.2	22.9	23.3

The introduction of new stations means that successive surveys are not
completely comparable. Bearing this in mind, the audience estimates are very
stable. Of the two spring surveys, weekly reach for one is above and the
other below average, and peak rating to ILR varies by only one percentage
point. There are no appreciable differences for ILR on hours tuned and no
strong evidence to suggest that spring is different to the rest of the year. It was
therefore decided that as from 1982 the surveys would continue to be carried
out just once a year in the spring.

Cumulative audience to radio

In 1979 a sub-sample of diary completers across the whole ILR Network were
asked to fill in diaries for a further three weeks. A similar survey to this was
conducted in 1983 in four separate areas. From the results of these surveys, a
model has been generated which enables the audience to any station or the
ILR audience within regions to be predicted over four weeks.

The 1979 network subsample showed reach accumulating as follows:

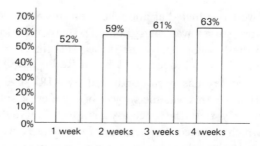

Fig. 26.2   ILR audience build-up.

As can be seen from this, most of the increase in reported listening takes place in the second week and overall there is an 11 % gain in reach over the four-week period. The increase is, however, by no means the same for different stations and depends on the reach achieved in Week 1. For example, a station with a 20 % weekly reach can expect to increase to around 31 % (an increase of more than 50 % in the *size* of its audience), whereas a station with a 70 % weekly reach will increase to about 78 % (an increase of not much more than 10 % in its numbers of listeners).

Further analyses of the 1983 four-week survey results have been carried out and used to generate a four-week prediction model. This enables potential advertisers to make forecasts of the cumulative weekly audience build-up provided by a radio advertising campaign in any area over a period of two, three or four weeks.

Analysis of results

The results of the JICRAR surveys are now reported in relatively standard forms.

Summary information is released in a published report showing the overall audience to each commercial radio station. Weekly totals and audiences by the time of day are shown. This is analysed by a set of standard demographic breakdowns.

In addition to the published report, radio station managements are supplied with a detailed analysis of the audience to each competitive service in their area including local and national BBC stations and Radio Luxembourg.

Access to the survey data is provided to any interested party through an on-line terminal analysis service. A wide range of easy-to-specify standard analyses have been developed for programme planners and in addition a schedule analysis facility is available. This allows any potential radio advertiser, at low cost, to examine the potential audience coverage and frequency of exposure provided by a radio campaign. These analyses can be carried out either at the station area level, across a region or across the whole Independent Radio Network.

Summary

During the first ten years of their existence, the surveys have on the whole produced results acceptable to advertisers and the stations and provide a valuable tool for selection of radio advertising campaigns. However, the specification set by JICRAR is onerous for the radio industry because the surveys are costly relative to the income of the stations. Bloom states that expenditure on audience surveys is 4 % of advertising revenue and claims that this is higher than for any other media.[10]

This burden is particularly heavy for the smaller stations and here the

JICRAR specification has been modified to allow them to use much smaller sample sizes. In fact, the minimum sample now required for publication is 300 adults. This is far too small for the purposes for which the measurement is intended and has clearly lead to considerable variation in audience levels from year to year. The sampling error associated with this sample size is unacceptable for an industry survey. It would be preferable to carry out less frequent surveys with a larger sample size than have year-on-year variations in weekly audience of as much as 6–7% which are probably not the result of programming changes or competitive activity but statistical volatility.

The sample sizes in JICRAR studies are generally much smaller than those used elsewhere, particularly in the USA and Australia. In the latter case sample sizes for each study are normally in excess of 2,000. The industry might therefore be advised to investigate other methods of cost-saving to finance sample size increases – for example, by changing the sampling approach and, in particular, dropping their requirement that only one individual in each household be interviewed. In Australia diaries are placed with all individuals aged 10 or over in each sampled household and whilst response rates are not as high as the UK they are acceptable at around 65–70%. The main reason for not using this method in the UK is because there is an alleged 'dependence' in radio listening, i.e., that people who live together tend to listen to the same radio stations. Whilst such 'dependence' no doubt exists in newspaper readership and TV viewing for obvious reasons, there is no evidence that it exists in radio listening. In fact, Australian evidence is to the contrary. Bearing in mind that there is on average well over one radio per home, opportunities to listen to different stations abound. Additionally, as already quoted, a high proportion of the audience listens to radio outside the home. A change in methodology to adopt this 'all members of the household approach' would undoubtedly save money and should be of high priority for methodological research.

Apart from these questions on sample size it is doubtful whether major enhancement of radio surveys is necessary. It is questionable whether the advertising industry in the UK is prepared to handle and use the considerable quantity of data already generated. With expenditure on the radio medium at a relatively low level, the amount of time and effort which can be devoted to media selection is also relatively small and detailed survey results can neither be absorbed nor used. On the other hand, the cost efficiency of radio schedules can only be appraised through analysis of reach (cover) and frequency (repetition) based on data of the type produced by JICRAR surveys. So called 'dipstick' surveys, which produce simple evidence of the weekly reach of a station, have little value in media research.

Questions are presently being asked about whether the existing methodology can stand the test of changes which are pending in the structure of broadcasting. It seems likely that the number of broadcasters will continue to increase in the UK, pirate stations are here again, local community radio stations may well develop, and some ILR stations will no doubt wish to take advantage of an opportunity to programme separately for VHF and medium wave. Furthermore, it is likely that there will be a new national commercial station at the end of the decade. Whilst these changes will increase the listener's choice, there seems little doubt that with minor modifications the existing methodology can cope. For example in Sydney, Australia, radio diaries completed on virtually the same basis as the UK diaries cover 16 pre-listed stations. It seems therefore likely that the established JICRAR system will remain the basis of UK radio audience research for some time to come.

Outdoor advertising research

The special feature of the poster which sets it apart from the other main advertising media is that its *sole* purpose in life is the transmission of an advertising message. While advertising may have an important economic role in the life of other media, their main role, so far as the public is concerned, is usually the dissemination of news or entertainment. The poster has *no* role other than advertising. An opportunity to see a poster advertisement cannot therefore be defined in terms of membership of the media audience, because the medium and advertisement are one and the same.

Because the poster is purely an advertising medium, the public do not seek to become members of the poster audience. This again contrasts with the other media, where it is necessary to get hold of a copy, turn on a set or buy a ticket to become a member of the audience. The events which qualify an individual as member of a cinema, TV, radio, newspaper or magazine audience may be memorable to a greater or lesser degree but insofar as they are memorable they are measurable. With posters, the event which qualifies an individual for membership of the audience is incidental, and in view of the number and variety of posters seen in the course of one day by each of us, each of these events is unlikely to be memorable. Clearly it would be impossible to differentiate these countless events into individual exposures. As a result the poster audience researcher has therefore generally approached the concept of 'opportunity to see' from the point of view of exposure to the environment of the advertisement.

A newspaper can be regarded as the environment of a press advertisement; exposure to the environment through readership creates an opportunity to see (OTS). In the same way, the environment of a poster site is a locality within which that site can be seen. Exposure to the environment and, therefore, an opportunity to see, arises when an individual moves into or through this locality. An opportunity to see thus defined seems less closely related to advertisement exposure than an opportunity to see advertisements in other media, because the 'event' is less directly related to the advertisement. However, so far as posters are concerned many researchers regarded it as the only feasible starting point for audience research. Conversely, a number of studies have been carried out in recent years, particularly in respect of transport advertising, where respondents have been asked to record in a diary where and when they saw particular advertisements, recognition being cued by photographs included in the diary. Using a restricted number of campaigns this technique appeared to generate a measure of OTS in line with the definition used for other media. However, it introduced a new series of problems especially regarding representativeness of the sample.

In any event the 'exposure to environment' measure of OTS has for the most part been used in the poster industry and, to an extent, accepted as a reasonable measurement, although acceptance has often been qualified by statements to the effect that factors should be applied to these measures to net down such gross values to a level that recognises the proportion of people who are actually likely to *look at* the poster site. Various schemes have been suggested for generating such factors but none have received universal acceptance by the industry so far. A noticeability factor scheme in the course of development by the OAA (the Outdoor Advertising Association) with guidance from the newly created Joint Industry Committee for Poster Audience Research (JICPAR) may resolve this particular problem.

For the most part, then, a member of the poster audience has traditionally been defined as a person who has an opportunity to see a poster, i.e. who 'passes by a place (on foot or in a vehicle) where a poster is or can be displayed'. It would clearly be an elaborate and expensive task to measure this in relation to all possible poster campaigns because the poster campaign is almost infinitely variable, consisting as it does of a selection of poster sites in a selection of towns.

The researcher therefore has attempted to measure the audience to the medium by reference to the opportunities to see a campaign consisting of a given number of average or representative sites distributed widely in a number of specific urban areas.

Audience measurement

Two approaches to poster audience measurement have been widely utilized. The first method has involved 'counting' passages past selected sites and the second has involved selecting individuals and determining which sites they then pass during a fixed time period. Both approaches have had their protagonists, and both have been fashionable at different times and in different countries. Whilst it may seem that there is some statistical equivalence between the two approaches, results based on the different approaches are unlikely to present similar results.

In principle, counting passages past sites could be done on the entire universe of sites. Indeed, if passages are vehicular passages it is tempting to believe that such information would be available from existing sources, such as

Transport Departments in Central and Local Government. As it happens neither vehicular or pedestrian passages are generally available in the kind of detail or on a sufficiently standard basis to make such data sufficiently accurate for wide scale use. However, the strength of the approach is well understood, in particular that counts can be restricted to 'relevant' passages, i.e. passages where there is a genuine opportunity to see, such counts being independent of any arbitrary residential restriction on the persons making these passages. On the other hand, count data cannot provide information on *frequency* of passages, and hence in campaign terms will not easily provide *coverage* information. Again, count data would appear to be site-specific, but this latter problem could and has been overcome through the development of models which link locational information on a site to its average audience level.

The *survey* approach is obviously more attractive to traditional market researchers. Its strengths are the opposite of the weaknesses of the 'count' approach: e.g. it is possible to obtain information on the frequency of passages. Its weaknesses include the necessity to identify respondents who can represent the relevant population for a group of sites, *a priori*. How do you define the populations relevant to a set of sites in central London, on major trunk roads or at a railway station? As we shall see later this problem has practical ramifications. Finally, it should be observed that just as for the count approach, so the survey approach requires some form of modelling if survey data are to provide a general solution.

The development of survey techniques for the measurement of poster audiences and, in consequence, a poster audience model, was largely due to Brian Copland whose work is standard reading for any student of outdoor research. The poster audience consists of people moving about in their environment and traditionally the measurement of that audience has been made by determining the journey patterns of the population of specific towns. This produced estimates of the number of passages past each poster site (opportunities to see, or OTS) made by each member of that population.

The major UK study was carried out on behalf of Mills and Allen in 1955 in nine Midland towns ranging in size from Dunstable to Nottingham.[11] This survey was extended to the Birmingham conurbation in 1964 (using a modified technique). In each town a random sample of respondents was questioned about their journeys during the week prior to the interview. The journeys were recorded in detail and related to poster location, each location being a group of more or less adjacent sites. From these data we can deduce for each town:

(a) the total number of opportunities to see posters at each location;
(b) the proportion of the population passing each location (i.e. coverage);
(c) how many times, on average, each member of the audience passed each location in, say, a week (i.e. repetition).

Having established the audience for each poster site in a specific town, it is then possible to establish the audience from that town for a campaign consisting of a number of sites in that town. This is done by selecting a sample of, say, 10 or 20 sites in the town and establishing by analysis the number of individuals who have passed at least one(cover) and the number of times each individual has passed any of the sites (repetition). By selecting a series of samples of this type from the poster locations in a specified town and averaging the results we can estimate the cover and repetition delivered by an 'average' campaign.

Copland carried out this procedure for each town and showed that certain patterns emerged:

(a) For each town the rate of increase in the percentage of population covered by campaigns of increasing size followed a simple exponential curve with a smaller rate of growth for larger towns (see Fig. 26.3).

(b) For each town the total OTS per head of population when plotted against the number of sites followed a straight line and the slope of this line increased as the size of the town fell (see Fig. 26.4). From this it can be seen that for any town the number of OTS per head of population was the product of the number of sites (S) and a constant (A) for that town.

(c) The repetition (or opportunities per head of audience – R) followed the same pattern as opportunities per head of population (A) but with the line shifted bodily upwards (see Fig. 26.5). (The extent of this displacement was similar in each town and averaged around 4.75.) Consequently, repetition can be written as $AS + 4.75$.

It has been noted that the value of A varies inversely with the size of town: the

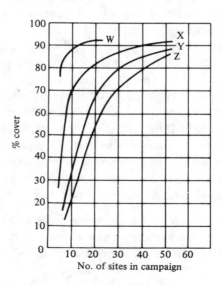

Fig. 26.3   Cover provided by campaigns of varying size in towns W, X, Y and Z.

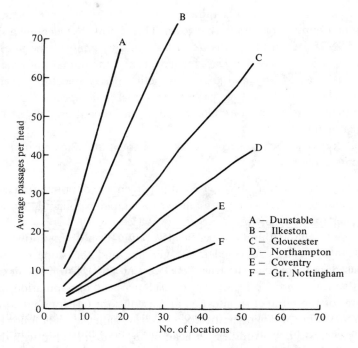

Fig. 26.6   Source: The Size and Nature of the Poster Audience, Study Two – May 1955.

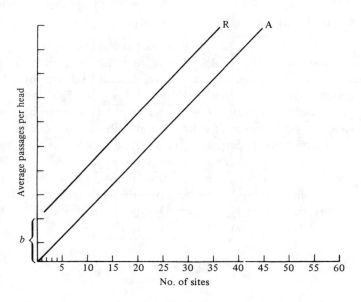

Fig. 26.5

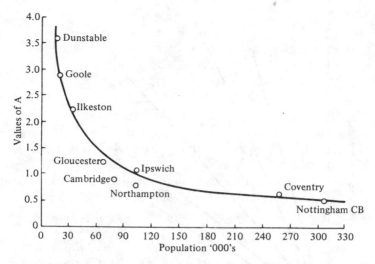

Fig. 26.6   Source: The Size and Nature of the Poster Audience, Study Two : May 1955.

smaller the town the higher the value of A. This, on reflection, is not surprising as the smaller the town the greater the chance that an individual will pass any one site.

Figure 26.6 shows how that A value varied in practice between Dunstable, where it was estimated at 3.5, and Nottingham, where the observed A value was estimated at 0.5. Generally it was found that the relationship could be approximated by the equation:

$$\log A = 0.73 \times \log \text{ population (000s)} + 1.41$$

although the values of the coefficients have varied from survey to survey. The formula or model, therefore, enables an A value and consequently OTS to be calculated for any town. Repetition and cover can also be computed for any town campaign, cover being calculated from $(AS/AS + 4.75) \times 100$.

The measurements on which this model was based were obtained by reference to journeys in a seven-day time period. Subsequent work established that cover and repetition for periods which are multiples of one week could be predicted by a simple multiplication of the A value.

One feature of the model is that it has been found to apply generally with minor modifications in a wide variety of countries. The only major observed difference is that the relationship between OTS per head of population and the OTS per head of audience can vary from country to country.

The coverage model has been generalized as

$$\text{Cover} = \frac{tAS}{tkAS + b}$$

where t = time in weeks
  A = a value for the urban area concerned
  S = number of sites in the campaign
  k = a constant for each country (GB = 1.0)
  b = a constant for each country (GB = 4.75)

It will be seen that in the generalized coverage model there is a one-to-one trade-off between the time required to achieve a predetermined level of coverage and the number of sites necessary to achieve it. This rather surprising result has attracted some criticism from researchers who argue that the increased coverage generated by doubling the number of sites in a campaign must be different in quality from the increased coverage gained by doubling the period of the campaign, but little work has been done on these qualitative differences.

The majority of the work undertaken of course relates to posters on static sites but the model has been, in principle, extended to advertising on mobile sites, e.g. advertising on the outside of public transport vehicles. The extension is complex and the work undertaken to date is limited. Again Copland is the main originator of this development and readers are referred to his work. [12-15] For a recent review of developments to the town poster model readers are recommended to read McDonald's 1981 Admap article. [16]

Data collection

The work to establish this model of the poster audience was undertaken in a number of countries and was spread over a long period of time. During the course of the work a number of modifications have been made to the data collection techniques.

The original approach was to collect by personal interview details of each individual's travel behaviour in the survey period. Details of each journey, including route and means of transport, had to be recorded and subsequently converted to passages past poster locations. There are two obvious disadvantages to this approach: it imposes a considerable strain on the memory of the respondent and the analysis of the data was very time consuming.

The difficulties have led to a change in approach, adopted in Britain and France, in which a random sample of sites are listed in the questionnaire and respondents are called upon to provide details of their journeys made past these 'key points' in a seven-day period. In Britain interview aids, known as location cards, were devised. These cards consist of a photograph and sketch map of each site location sampled, which serves to describe the precise location to the respondent and as a memory jogger.

Using a pack of such location cards, the interview proceeds on the following lines. 'Now, we just want to check the flow of traffic past various key points in the town. To make the inquiry easier we have prepared these pictures and diagrams of the places we want to ask about.'

NOW TAKE INFORMANT THROUGH THE LOCATION CARDS IN TURN ASKING ABOUT EACH ONE.
'Do you know where this is?'
IF 'NO' TRY TO EXPLAIN.
IF 'YES' ASK 'Have you ever been to this place?' (meaning the area marked by dotted lines on the location card map).
IF 'YES' ASK 'When were you last there, either *at* the exact spot or *passing through* it?' Probe: 'How long ago was that?', 'How were you travelling on that occasion?', 'How many times do you go there, or through there, in an average week these days?' IF LESS OFTEN THAN 'ONCE A WEEK' ASK 'How often do you go there?'

It was found when this technique was first applied that it produced slightly different results to the original approach. In particular, the levels of cover and repetition obtained using location cards was higher, either because memory is more effectively stimulated or as a result of overclaiming. (A more detailed discussion of this is to be found in the IPA Poster Audience Surveys 1964.) In 1974 the technique was further modified to permit the collection of 'passage' data over a wide area in the large conurbations. The earlier surveys had a limit of 60 poster locations: a limit imposed because of the burden which would have been placed on the interviewer in recording passages or in presenting location cards for a large number of sites. Research Services Ltd. in surveys for Gallaher [17] and British Posters [18] developed a much simpler technique for recording locations passed which made it possible to log passages by a very large number of sites – 1000 in the case of the London survey. The recording technique used relied on document reading facilities for registering the code number of each site in the area.

Demographic data

The poster audience model described gives basic data for the advertiser on the cover and repetition produced by campaigns of varying size and length but it does so only by reference to the adult population as a whole. It might be expected that cover and repetition would vary for different population subgroups and the evidence available suggests that this is so.

In a section of the Newport survey it was shown that much higher exposure levels were achieved among men, young people and members of socio-economic group C, with 147%, 131%, and 121% of average exposure. Housewives, on the other hand, achieved only 59% of average exposure. Results from the two 1974 surveys were less clear cut. Although the observed *A* values for men continued to be much higher than for women, the age and social class results seemed to be inconsistent from area to area. However, the 1974 surveys did represent a considerable step forward in providing coverage and repetition data for important population sub-groups.

The 1974 survey also represented a substantial step forward in terms of generally updating the data base for the poster audience model, thus rectifying a long-felt need. It is, however, somewhat surprising to note that the A values observed in these surveys were if anything lower than those estimated from the 1955 work. Because of an observed reduction in the value of b in these surveys there was little overall change in levels of cover and repetition. However, in view of the increase in traffic and mobility which had taken place in the last twenty years it would have been reasonable to expect a general increase in the value of A.

One might conclude that either the previous research tended to overstate the traffic parameter A or the 1974 surveys understated it. It is unfortunate that the latter surveys incorporated a change in technique with no attempt to calibrate the data to previous surveys. Certainly the nature of the task given to interviewers in the 1974 surveys may have led to fatigue and a consequential under-recording of journeys or passages.

The 1974 surveys also showed new values for b ranging from 4.52 in West Midlands to 3.43 in Crewe compared with the previously accepted figure of 4.75 based on the Newport work and 4 based on the original nine towns work. That there should be such variability in the value of b is perplexing. That its value in the more recent surveys should be generally below previous levels may be due to the exclusion from the sample of those aged 65 and over. The reader will recall that b represents the extent to which the line representing OTS per head of population is shifted upwards when presented as OTS per head of audience. This value must therefore represent an 'immobility element' indicating that there are members of the population who never become part of the audience because they do not move around. As immobility is related to age and infirmity it seems likely that the absence of the oldest age groups from the sample could lead to a reduction in the value of b.

Some other problems

The poster model relates to the levels of exposure generated by a random sample of sites. One question which needs to be answered is: how far do the sites selected for a typical campaign approximate to a random sample? To the extent that posters are bought on a package basis, i.e. where individual site selection is minimal, it might be expected that variations in the performance of individual sites would indeed cancel out and the package would approximate to a random sample of sites. However, this is not in fact the case because many sites are individually selected and many are allocated indefinitely to a number of major advertisers. To the extent that these specially selected sites are the 'better' sites, it should be expected that the remainder are of lower quality and consequently the delivery of a package of the latter would be below average.

Data from the OAA study, described below, has shown that the level of passages associated with individual sites is markedly skew, and can range from less than 3,000 passages per week through to rates in excess of a million. It will be seen that in a particular town the inclusion or exclusion of a few prime 'town centre' sites will effectively determine whether or not the campaign's delivery approximates to the theoretical A value.

The Copland model has also been attacked on the grounds that it relates poster audience solely to the town population. This has given rise to a number of specific practical problems, for example, how relevant is the resident population of a small market town where its hinterland is an area embracing a population many times larger than the town's? How relevant is the resident population of a seaside resort or a University town, or a town that is fed by a very large commuter population? However, the full extent of the population problem was raised by the 1974 Local Authority changes, which substantially increased the 'official' population of most towns and cities. The impact of these population changes on the corresponding A value for some towns and cities was equally significant, some towns showing increases in average passages per average site of nearly 50%.

In the Newport study the A values for four different categories of sites were examined showing that the variation between 'best' and 'worst' was as much as 50%. If the variation is as great as this, then the pre-empting of better sites by special selection must have considerable effect on the delivery of a package of sites. There seems to be little doubt that the advertiser would have been better served if the A values basic to the model could have been measured with reference to packages of sites available in practice for sale rather than a random sample of sites as a whole.

The OAA measurement scheme

Following the Congress on Outdoor Advertising in Nice, in April 1981, a Working Party was formed with the following brief:

> To define a practical method of site grading and classification for posters in the UK, which has consensus agreement from the interested parties....

After receiving evidence from interested bodies, a number of experiments were commissioned in Croydon, Ipswich and Northampton. The Working Party published its recommendations on the broad scheme for the classification and grading system at the end of 1981, and invited research agencies to submit tenders for the relevant fieldwork.

The final objective of the study was to produce a computer-based information system, containing data on every poster site in the UK and every advertising panel at each site. The data available for each panel was to cover:

(a) Classification information on the physical characteristics of the panel.

(b) Measurement of potential audience for each panel, both vehicular and pedestrian.
(c) A grading of the panel's audience potential based upon passages past the site qualified by the visibility of the panel to these people.

It was noted that pilot work showed that it should be possible to predict relative volume of pedestrian passages by measuring environmental factors such as:

population density;
number of bus routes;
type of location (shopping zone, commercial, residential etc) and similar factors.

The newly created Outdoor Advertising Association, a voluntary association of poster contractors who collectively controlled over 70% of all sites, took on the responsibility for the project. Two leading market research agencies were commissioned, respectively, to *classify* all OAA sites and secondly to develop poster audience *models* for both pedestrian and vehicular passage.

As input data to the OAA model it was necessary to take physical counts at a large sample of sites for both pedestrian and vehicular audiences, taking account of all relevant passage flows. In the event, separate models were developed for pedestrian and vehicular audiences and, within each type of audience, models were produced for average weekdays, Saturdays and Sundays. The models produced were far more complex than the Copland model and showed that poster audience was a function of a large number of factors including location distance from town centre, proximity to railway stations, the type of roads passing the site and so on. At the individual site level, these models performed well and used in the context of packages had prediction errors of very small order.

Having established a model for gross audiences, measured simply as passages past each site, the OAA then tackled the question of each panel's noticeability. Using the results of research previously carried out by individual specialist agencies and researchers elsewhere in Europe, a number of factors such as maximum distance of visibility, height above ground, angle of deflection to oncoming traffic, obstructions and illumination were determined as being critical to the effectiveness of an individual site. Each of these factors were then given scores which when added together could be applied to the individual flows passing each panel of a given size, which in turn were used to generate a net audience figure.

With the new OAA Poster Models many of the problems identified with the Copland model have been overcome. It remains however to adapt the latter to provide a coverage model based on the new estimates of passage data. Other challenges facing the industry include the development of methods for providing *audience classification* information and measuring poster *effectiveness*. In respect of the latter some published case histories exist, and recall methods have been used on a routine basis for evaluating individual campaigns. However there is, as yet, no accepted measure of effectiveness. Additionally, more work needs to be done to relate opportunities to see to actual sightings.

Cinema audience research

On the face of it, the cinema should be the simplest of all media for the researcher. The cinema audience is easy to define because qualification for membership depends on the purchase of a ticket and the total 'opportunities to see' delivered by the medium must equal sales of tickets. Although this tells us nothing about the composition of the audience, or the number of people represented by the total number of admissions, it is a reliable and accurate measure of 'opportunities' which can be used in conjunction with other research data. Admission figures are published monthly by the Department of Industry, but these figures in themselves are inadequate for campaign planning purposes, because the only breakdowns published are by cinema size and the Registrar General's standard regions. They do not tell us the total admission for a given period for a given selection of cinemas. Also, they are produced some 6 months after the month of report.

More up to date estimates are made by Marplan using admissions information for cinemas managed by the major circuits with an estimate based on returns from a sample of independents. Based on statistics of this type, estimates of admissions per seat per week can be made for each size category of cinema within region. Thus, although admissions to individual cinemas are not available, reasonable estimates of admissions to cinemas selected for a campaign can be provided by the screen advertising industry.

However, admissions themselves are only part of the story. We need to know the nature of the audience in demographic terms and the number of people attending the cinema at least once in the campaign period, i.e. the *cover* of the campaign. The calculation of repetition would then be a simple matter of dividing admissions by the cover. Preferably this information should be available for each demographic sub-group.

The major screen advertisers publish surveys concerning the cinema audience from time to time which have been useful in defining the audience in accurate terms, but the only continuous information available on the cinema audience is derived from the National Readership Survey (NRS). This survey contains three questions concerning cinema-going. These are:

(1) 'How often these days do you go to the cinema?'

Coded answers: Once a week or more often; two or three times a month;

once a month; once every two or three months; two or three times a year; less often; never go these days.

(2) 'How long ago was the last occasion you went to the cinema?'

Coded answers: Within last seven days; over seven days up to and including four weeks ago; over four weeks up to and including three months ago; over three months up to and including six months ago; over six months ago/can't remember when.

IF THE ANSWER TO QUESTION 2 IS 'within last four weeks'

(3) 'How many times have you been to the cinema in the last four weeks?'

Coded answers: once; twice; 3 times; 4 times; 5–6 times; 7–8 times; more than 8 times.

On the basis of these questions, it is possible to classify individuals into seven cinema-going frequency categories, based on their claimed frequency of visiting the cinema (Q.1). This frequency distribution has been used to make estimates of the coverage given by campaigns of varying lengths, and estimates can be made for any population sub-group classified in the NRS. The obvious method of calculating coverage is to assign probabilities of visiting the cinema in any given period based on an individual's claimed frequency. Thus, those who visit the cinema once or twice a week or more frequently have a probability of being covered by a one week campaign. Those who claim to go once in two weeks have a probability of a half, and so on. A probability estimate has to be made about the group who visit the cinema less often than once per month.

In a two-week campaign covering all cinemas, Table 26.2 illustrates how cover would be calculated, assuming for the sake of simplicity that all cinema-goers go at least once in every four weeks, and that data are available for four

Table 26.2 *Cinema campaign coverage*

Frequency category of visits	Percentage of population (say)	Probability of a visit in two weeks	Cover
1 per week	7%	1	7%
1 every 2 weeks	4%	1	4%
1 every 3 weeks	3%	2/3	2%
1 every 4 weeks	2%	1/2	1%
Total			14%

groups of people. Having calculated the cover of a campaign using all cinemas, the assumption then made is that a campaign covering half of all admissions would have half the 'national' cover, i.e. for the example in the Table 7%. Unfortunately, however, calculations of this kind are invalid because individuals tend to overestimate their cinema-going frequency. This can be evaluated by analysing their replies to the second question on the survey. This shows, for example, that only 96% of the group who claim to go twice a week or more often went to the cinema in the last four weeks preceding the interview.

As a result, work has been done [19] to calculate a cinema-going probability for each of the seven frequency-claim groups, and for each of a number of demographic sub-groups. Through this work, we can allocate to each individual in the survey a probability that he has visited the cinema in a four-week time period. For those who claim to visit the cinema once a month, for example, the probability that they have been in the last four weeks is 0.617. The probabilities derived from this analysis can then be substituted for probabilities based on claimed frequency.

It can be demonstrated that the cinema-going estimates obtained from this analysis are more accurate than estimates based on claimed frequencies. An analysis of Q.3 produced an estimate of 15.4 million admissions in a four-week period compared with the Department of Industry estimate of 16.5 million for a similar period.

The above technique can be used for much more sophisticated analysis. Cinema campaigns vary in length, but are generally considerably longer than four weeks. It is, therefore, important to be able to estimate cover for various campaign periods. By a simulation process in which cinema-going probabilities are derived for half-weekly periods, it is possible to expand the survey information to give coverage estimates for campaigns of any length. For each individual in the survey, the method adopted was to compute his probability of visiting the cinema in a half-week, and to allocate his visits in an 18 week period on a random basis. Thus, in the case of an individual who goes to the cinema weekly, and has a probability of visiting of 0.5 in a half-week, he should have made 18 visits in the chosen period. These visits would be randomly allocated to 18 half-weeks out of the total of 36. From a file of this kind, it is possible to estimate the cover and repetition given by campaigns of any length up to 18 weeks for any sub-group of the population. A complete frequency distribution of opportunities to see the campaign can also be derived.

Estimates of this kind, of course, assume that the campaign is using all cinemas. The method used to relate cover to campaigns using only a proportion of cinemas is a crude one. The assumption made is that if a campaign is using, say, 50% of the total cinema potential (measured in terms of cost) it would achieve 50% of the coverage of a similar campaign using all cinemas. It would, of course, be preferable to use admissions data for the cinemas in question compared with total admissions, but this is not always readily available.

Reach and frequency estimates are now published regularly by the Cinema Advertising Association. These reports show coverage and frequency achieved by campaigns for 1 to 52 weeks for a range of demographic, area, socio-economic and media usage groups.

A further problem in making this type of calculation is that it assumes that everyone visits only one cinema. The assumption built into the model is that a person's frequency of visiting a particular cinema is the same as his frequency of visiting *any* cinema. However, about one-quarter of those who go to the cinema in a four-weekly period visit more than one and as we move from a consideration of national coverage estimates to the coverage given by a *selection* of cinemas, we should take into account an individual's probability of visiting a particular cinema or selection of cinemas rather than any cinema. Coverage estimates made without taking this point into account are probably too low. The extent of that underestimate will depend on which cinemas are actually chosen for the campaign. A cinema in the centre of a large city will attract an audience from a wide area and many of the people visiting it will do so only infrequently. On the other hand, a suburban cinema or a cinema in a small town will tend to attract the same people week after week. It follows then that a city centre cinema will give a wider coverage than other establishments. In order to establish the effect of this on coverage estimates, we need to know *how many* cinemas have been visited by each individual during the campaign period, and we need more reliable admissions information.

In recent years more work has been undertaken on audience profiles for specific films or types of film. This work – Cinema & Video Industry Audience Research (CAVIAR) – was initiated by the Cinema Advertising Association and has been carried out by Carrick James Market Research.

The study provides comprehensive information on the size and shape of cinema (and video) film audiences. In particular, it covers:

(a) frequency of cinema attendance;
(b) recency of viewing;
(c) profile of audiences for specific types of films;
(d) profile of audiences for specific films;
(e) perceived cost of cinema visits;
(f) how far respondents live from nearest cinema.
    (plus other information on video film viewers).

A unique feature of the CAVIAR study is that it covers the 7–14 year olds, an otherwise unresearched sector of the population.

The information is collected by personal interview among a sample of 2,400 individuals, who are asked which films they have seen in a specific period and which of a predetermined list of films they have seen. From this audience profiles are derived for specific films and types of film. One analysis is by reference to the Film Censors' Certificate category. Clearly, this is useful information for the media planner in campaign selection.

To date, two surveys have been conducted – one from November 1983 to January 1984, and the second from September–October 1984. A third survey is commissioned for October–November 1985.

Apart from coverage and admissions estimates, there are one or two other aspects of cinema audience research which are worth a mention. First, the relationship between the total cinema audience and the *advertisement* audience has always been of interest to advertisers. In the cinema, the two must be very close in absolute terms. As any cinema-goer knows, it is almost impossible to avoid seeing the advertisements. Anyone in the auditorium when the advertisements are being shown must be exposed to them. It is, therefore, not unreasonable to assume a one-to-one relation between the audience of the medium and the audience of the advertisement, though this relationship might be more reliably estimated by determining the proportion of the audience which arrives before and arrives after the advertisements are screened. The screen advertising industry has also carried out work which demonstrates the high recall of cinema advertising which makes the medium such a potent one for its relatively small audience.

Second, although we have much information about the cinema audience in terms of its demographic characteristics, we do not know whether or how this varies according to the location and type of cinema. Is it possible to grade cinemas in terms of the composition of the audience they attract? Perhaps if we knew a little more about why people go to the cinema we could move closer to answering this type of question.

Third, what is the catchment area of a cinema? What determines its size and how do these areas overlap? These questions may be important for campaign planning, especially as the number of cinemas declines.

It seems doubtful, however, whether cinema audience research will be considerably extended. Since the first edition of this Handbook was published in 1971, annual cinema admissions have fallen from around 180 million to around 70 million in 1983 (an improvement over 1982). Interestingly, audiences improved in 1978, only to fall every year afterwards, until 1983 – no doubt to some extent this was influenced by the increasing penetration of video. This decline in audiences must inevitably influence the amount of research information which can be utilized in the campaign planning process for a dwindling medium.

Bibliography

Chapter 1

1. Tupper, E. and Wills, G. *Sources of UK Marketing Information*, Ernest Benn, 1975
2. Kingston, I. and Benjamin, W. *Directory of European Business Information Sources*, Ballinger, 1979
3. Hull, C. *Principal Sources of Marketing Information*, Times Newspapers, 1971
4. Anderson, P. *A Monograph on Desk Research*, ISBA
5. Foster, A. *Which Database*, Headland Press
6. Anderson, I. G. *Current British Directories*, C.B.D. Research
7. Prout, T. D. *Industrial Market Research Yearbook*, Gower Press, 1973
8. Daniels, L. M. *Business Information Sources*, University of California Press/Centre for Business Information, Paris

Chapter 2

1. Gellerman, S. W. *Motivation and Productivity*, American Management Association, 1963
2. Lunn, J. A. *Recent Developments in Market Segmentation*, ESOMAR Congress, 1969
3. Sampson, P. *An Examination of Exploratory Research Techniques*, ESOMAR Congress, 1969
4. Sampson, P. 'Research to Aid Personnel Selection for British Airways Cabin Staff: A Qualitative Research Approach', *Market Research Society Annual Conference, Proceedings*, March 1975
5. Sampson, P. 'Commonsense in Qualitative Research', *Commentary*, **9**, 1, 1967
6. Sheth, J. 'The Role of Motivation Research in Consumer Psychology', *ESOMAR Seminar on Developments in Consumer Psychology*, Maidenhead, Berks, 1973
7. Goldman, A. E. 'The Group Depth Interview', *Journal of Marketing*, **9**, 1, 1967
8. Gordon, W. J. J. *Synectics: the Development of Creative Capacity*, Harper and Row, New York, 1961
9. Getzels, J. W. and Jackson, P. W. *Creativity and Intelligence*, Wiley, New York, 1962
10. Hudson, L. *Contrary Imaginations*, Methuen, London, 1966
11. De Bono, E. *The Five-Day Course in Thinking*, Basic Books, New York, 1967
12. Sampson, P. 'Can Consumers Create New Products?' *Journal of the Market Research Society*, **12**, 1, 1970
13. Heylen, P. 'Towards an Implicit Psychoanalytic Model ('Libido Model') of Consumer Behaviour', *EMAS/ESOMAR Symposium on Methodological Advances in Marketing Research in Theory and Practice, Proceedings*, Copenhagen, 1984
14. Cooper, P. and Paule, J. *BPMRG Conference Proceedings*, 1982
15. Lunn, T., Cooper, P. and Murphy, O. 'The Fluctuating Fortunes of the UK Social Democratic Party', *European Research*, **12**, 1, 1984
16. Cowling, A. B. 'Use of Elicitation Technique for Producing Dimensions of Brand Choice', *Market Research Society Annual Conference, Proceedings*, March 1973
17. King, R. H. 'A Study of the Problem of Building a Model to Simulate the Cognitive

Processes of a Shopper in a Supermarket', in Haines, G. H. *Consumer Behaviour, Learning Models of Purchasing*, The Free Press, New York, 1969

18. Palmer, J. and Faivre, J. P. 'The Information Processing Theory of Consumer Behaviour', *European Research*, **1**, No. 6, November 1973

19. Kelly, G. A. *Psychology of Personal Constructs, Vols I and II*, Norton, New York, 1955

20. Bannister, D. 'Personal Construct Theory: a Summary and Experimental Paradigm', *Acta Psychologica*, **20**, 2, 1962.

21. Bannister, D. 'A New Theory of Personality', in Foss. B. M. (Ed.) *New Horizons in Psychology*, Penguin Books, London, 1966

22. Frost, W. A. K. and Braine, R. L. 'The Application of the Repertory Grid Technique to Problems in Market Research', *Commentary*, **9**, 3, 1967

23. Bannister, D. and Mair, J. M. M. *The Evaluation of Personal Constructs*, Academic Press, London, 1968

24. Riley, S. and Palmer, J. 'Of Attitudes and Latitudes: A Repertory Grid Study of Perceptions', *Journal of the Market Research Society*, **17**, 2, 1975

25. Sampson, P. 'Using the Repertory Grid Test', *Journal of Marketing Research*, **9**, 1972

26. Frost, W. A. K. 'The Development of a Technique for Television Programme Assessment'. *Journal of the Market Research Society*, **11**, 1, 1969

27. Clemens, N. J. S. and Thornton, C. 'Evaluating Non-existing Products', *Admap*, **4**, 5, 1968

28. Sampson, P. 'Methods of Obtaining Salient Beliefs', Burke Marketing Research (Interscan) *Technical Note No. 4*, 1974

29. Oppenheim, A. M. *Questionnaire Design and Attitude Measurement*, Heinemann, London, 1966

30. Chaplin, J. P. *Dictionary of Psychology*, Dell, New York, 1968

31. Murstein, B. I. (Ed.) *Handbook of Projective Techniques*, Basic Books, New York, 1965

32. Abelson, H. I. 'A Role Rehearsal Technique for Exploratory Research', *Public Opinion Quarterly*, **30**, 1966

33. Berent, P. H. 'The Depth Interview', *Journal of Advertising Research*, **6**, 2, 1962

34. Wilson, A. 'Industrial Marketing Research in Britain', *Journal of Marketing Research*, **6**, 1, 1969

35. Sampson, P. *A New Look at Qualitative Research*, Market Research Society Seminar on Psychological Methods in Market Research, 1967

36. Belson, W. 'Tape Recording: Its Effect on Accuracy of Response in Survey Interviews', *Journal of Marketing Research*, **4**, 1967

37. Berelson, B. 'Content Analysis', in Lindzey, G. (Ed.) *Handbook of Social Psychology*, Addison-Wesley, Cambridge, Mass., 1954

38. Holsti, O. R., Loomba, J. K. and North, R. C. 'Content Analysis', in Lindzey, G. and Aronson, E. (Eds.), *Handbook of Social Psychology*, Addison-Wesley, Cambridge, Mass., 1967

39. McDonald, C. D. P. and Blyth, W. G. 'How to Handle Soft Data – a Linguistic Approach', *Thomson Medals and Awards for Advertising Research*, 1971

40. McDonald, C. D. P. 'Linguistic Coding – a New Solution to an Old Problem', *Journal of the Market Research Society*, **15**, 3, 1973

41. Ring, E. 'Interpretation in Motivation Research', *ESOMAR Seminar on Developments in Consumer Psychology*, Maidenhead, Berks, 1973

42. Dyer, G. *Semiology/Structuralism*. Notes for Market Research Society Course, The Market Research Society, 1984

43. Berne, E. *Games People Play*, London, Deutsch, 1966

44. Berne, E. *What do you say after you say hello?* New York, Bantam Books, 1973

45. Blackstone, M. and Holmes, M. 'The Use of Transactional Analysis in the Development of a New Brand's Personality', *ESOMAR Seminar on New Product Development*, 1983

46. Klein, M. *Lives People live: A Textbook of Transactional Analysis*, Chichester, Wiley, 1980

47. Klein, M. *Discover Your Real Self*, London, Hutchinson, 1983

48. Schlackman, W. *A Discussion of the Use of Sensitivity Panels in Market Research*, Market Research Society Annual Conference Proceedings, 1984
49. Fuller, L. *Use of Panels for Qualitative Research*, Market Research Society Annual Conference Proceedings, 1984
50. Market Research Society Qualitative Research Study Group. *Qualitative Research – A Summary of the Concepts involved*, The Market Research Society, 1978
51. De Groot, G. 'Deep, Dangerous or Just Plain Dotty?', ESOMAR Seminar on Qualitative Methods of Research: A Matter of Interpretation, Amsterdam, 1986
52. Sampson, P. *Qualitative Research in Europe: the State of the Art and Art of the State*, ESOMAR Congress, 1985
53. Sampson, P. and Bhaduri, M. 'Getting the Basics Right. Qualitative Data; Interpretation or Misinterpretation?', ESOMAR Seminar on Qualitative Methods of Research: A Matter of Interpretation, Amsterdam, 1986

Chapter 3

1. Enis, B. M. and Cox, K. K. 'Ad Experiments for Management Decisions', *Journal of Advertising Research*, **15**, 2, 1975
2. Belson, W. A. *Studies in Readership*, published on behalf of the Institute of Practitioners in Advertising by Business Publications Ltd., 1962
3. Cox, D. R. *The Planning of Experiments*, Wiley, New York, 1958
4. Hoofnagle, W. S. 'Experimental Designs in Measuring the Effectiveness of Promotion', *Journal of Marketing Research*, May 1965
5. Greenhalgh, C. 'Some Techniques and Interesting Results in Discrimination Testing', *Journal of the Market Research Society*, January 1967
6. *The Effect of Alternative Wording on the Outcome of the EEC Referendum*, N.O.P. Market Research Ltd., February 1975
7. Woodside, A. G. and Waddle, G. C. 'Sales Effects of In-Store Advertising', *Journal of Advertising Research*, **15**, 3, 1975
8. Sheth, J. A. and Roscoe, A. M. 'Impact of Questionnaire Length, Follow-Up Methods and Geographical Location on Response Rate to a Mail Survey', *Journal of Applied Psychology*, **60**, 2, 1975
9. Ehrenberg, A. S. C. 'The Pattern of Consumer Purchases', *Applied Statistics*, **8**, 26–41, 1959
10. Goodhardt, G. J., Ehrenberg, A. S. C. and Chatfield, C. 'The Dirichlet: A Comprehensive Model of Buying Behaviour, *Journal of the Royal Statistical Society*, Series A, 1984
11. Colley, R. H. *Defining Advertising Goals for Measured Advertising Results*, Association of National Advertisers Inc., New York, 1961
12. Lynch, J. C. R. 'On the External Validity of Experiments in Consumer Research', *Journal of Consumer Research*, **9**, 3, December 1982
13. *Thomson Medals and Awards for Media Research*, Silver Medal papers, 1966
14. Broadbent, S. 'One way TV Advertisements work', *JMRS*, **21**, 3, 1979
15. Colman, S. and Brown, G. 'Advertising Tracking Studies and Sales Effects', *JMRS*, **25**, 2, 1983
16. Coombs, C. H. *A Theory of Data*, John Wiley and Sons, New York, 1964
17. Gilbert, G. N. *Modelling Society*, George Allen and Unwin, 1981
18. Blattberg, R. C. and Dolan, R. J. 'An Assessment of the Contribution of Log Linear Models to Marketing Research', *Journal of Marketing*, **45**, 2, Spring 1981
19. Rosenberg, M. J. and Abelson, R. P. 'An Analysis of Cognitive Balancing', in Hovland, C. I. and Rosenberg, M. J. (Eds.) *Attitude Organisation and Change*, Yale University Press, 1960
20. Hendrickson, A. E. *Choice Behaviour and Advertising*, ADMAP World Advertising Workshop, Southampton, October 1967
21. Cowling, A. B. and Nelson, E. H. *Predicting the Effects of Change*, Brighton Market Research Society Conference Paper, 1969

22. Westwood, D., Lunn, T. and Beazley, D. 'The Trade-off Model and its Extensions, *JMRS*, **16,** 3, 1974

23. Oppedijk van Veen, W. M. and Beazley, D. 'An Investigation of Alternative Methods of Applying the Trade-off Model', *JMRS*, **19,** 1, 1977

24. Ehrenberg, A. S. C. 'The Practical Meaning and Usefulness of the NBD/LSD Theory of Repeat Buying', *Applied Statistics*, **17,** 17–32, 1968

25. Parfitt, J. H. and Collins, B. J. K. 'The Use of Consumer Panels for Brandshare Prediction', *Journal of Marketing Research*, **5,** 2, 1968

26. Yankelovich, D., Skelly, F. and White, A. '*LTM Estimating Procedure*', in Wind, Y., Mahajan, V. and Cordozo, R. N. *New Product Forecasting*

27. Factor, S. and Sampson, P. 'Making Decisions about Launching New Products', *JMRS*, **25,** 2, 1983

28. Ehrenberg, A. S. C. and Goodhardt, G. J. 'Practical Applications of the Duplication of Viewing Law', *Journal of the Market Research Society*, January 1969

Chapter 4

1. Ehrenberg, A. S. C. *A Primer in Data Reduction*, Wiley, 1983

2. Hedges, B. 'Sampling', in Hoinville and Jowell (Eds.) *Survey Research Practice*, Heinemann, 1977

3. Kish, L. *Survey Sampling*, Wiley, 1965

4. *National Readership Survey* published by JICNARS

5. Harris, P. T. 'The Effect of Clustering on Costs and Sampling Errors of Random Samples', *Journal of the Market Research Society*, **19,** 3, 1977

6. Collins, M. and Butcher, B. 'Interviewer and Clustering Effects in an Attitude Survey', *Journal of the Market Research Society*, **25,** 1, 1983

7. Collins, M. and Goodhardt, G. 'Value for Money in Research Design', *Market Research Society Conference Papers*, 1978

8. Conway, S. 'The Weighting Game', *Market Research Society Conference Papers*, 1982

9. Moser, C. A. and Stuart, A. 'An Experimental Study of Quota Sampling', *Journal of the Royal Statistical Society*, Series **A,** 116, 1953

Chapter 5

1. Payne, S. L. *The Art of Asking Questions*, Princeton University Press, Princeton, New Jersey, 1951

2. Belson, W. A. *The Design and Understanding of Survey Questions*, Gower, 1981

3. Belson, W. A. *The Impact of Television*, London, Crosby Lockwood, 1967

4. Schumann, H. and Presser, S. *Questions and Answers in Attitude Surveys*, Academic Press Inc. (London) Ltd, 1981

5. Cannell, C. Miller, P. V. and Oksenberg, L., 'Research on Interviewing Techniques', in Leinhardt, S. (Ed.) *Sociological Methodology*, Jossey-Bass, 1981

6. Belson, W. A. *Studies in Readership*, London, Business Publications, on behalf of the IPA, 1962

7. Cannell, C. F., Oksenberg, L. and Converse, J. M., *Experiments in Interviewing Techniques*, Research Report Series, Institute for Social Research, University of Michigan, 1979

8. Cannell, C. F., Lawson, S. A. and Hausser, D. L. *A Technique for Evaluating Interviewer Performance*, Survey Research Centre, Institute for Social Research, University of Michigan, 1975

9. Morton-Williams, J. 'The Use of "Verbal Interaction Coding" for Evaluating a Questionnaire', *Quality and Quantity*, No. 13, 1979

10. Fishbein, M. (Ed.) *Readings in Attitude Theory and Measurement*, John Wiley and Sons, Inc., 1967

11. Fishbein, M. 'A Consideration of Beliefs and Their Role in Attitude Measurement', in Fishbein, M. (Ed.) *Readings in Attitude Theory and Measurement*, John Wiley and Sons, Inc. 1967

12. McKennell, A. C. *Aircraft Noise Annoyance around London (Heathrow) Airport*, Social Survey Report 337, Central Office of Information
13. Kalton, G., Roberts, J. and Holt, D. 'The Effects of Offering a Middle Response Option with Opinion Questions', *The Statistician*, **29**, 11–24, 1980
14. Belson, W. A. *A Study of the Effects of Reversing the Order of Presentation of Verbal Rating Scales*, Survey Research Centre Report, 1965
15. Morton-Williams, J. and Sykes, W. 'The Use of Interaction Coding & Follow-up Interviews to Investigate Comprehension of Survey Questions', *J. Market Research Society*, **26**, 2, 1984
16. Osgood, E. C., Suci, G. J. and Tannenbaum, P. H. *The Measurement of Meaning*, Urbana, University of Illinois Press, 1957
17. Joyce, T. *Techniques of Brand Image Measurement*, Market Research Society Annual Conference, 1963
18. Thurstone, L. L. 'Attitudes can be measured', *American Journal of Sociology*, **33**, 529–554, 1928. (Reprinted in *Readings in Attitude Theory and Measurement*, Fishbein, M. (Ed.), John Wiley and Sons, Inc. 1967)
19. Likert, R. 'The Method of Constructing an Attitude Scale', in Fishbein, M. (Ed.), *Readings in Attitude Theory and Measurement*, John Wiley and Sons, Inc., 1967
20. Stouffer, A. A., Guttmann, L., Suchman, E. A., Lazarsfeld, P. F., Star and Clausen, Studies in Social Psychology in World War II, *Measurement and Prediction*, Vol. 4, Princeton University Press, 1950
21. Morton-Williams, J. 'Research on the Market for National Savings', Case Study No. 3 in Adler, M. K. (Ed.), *Leading Case Histories in Market Research*, Business Books Ltd., 1971
22. McKennell, A. C. 'Surveying Attitude Structures: Discussion of Principles and Procedures', *Quality and Quantity*, **7**, 2, 1974
23. McKennell, A. C., 'Attitude Measurement: Use of Coefficient Alpha with Cluster or Factor Analysis', *Sociology*, **4**, 2, 1970
24. McQuitty, L. L., 'Hierarchical Linkage Analysis for the Isolation of Types', *Educ. and Psychol. Measurement* **20**, 1960
25. Hoinville, G. 'Multidimensional Trade Offs: An Appraisal of the Priority Evaluator Approach' (1975 Paper available from Social and Community Planning Research)
26. *The Classification of Occupation*, HMSO, 1980
27. *National Readership Survey*, JICNAS, 1983
28. Wolfe, A. (Ed.) *Standardised Questions*, Market Research Society, 1974

Further Reading on Questionnaire Design

Garden, R. L. *Interviewing: Strategy, Techniques and Tactics*, Dorsey Press, Homewood, Illinois, 1975
Hoinville, G., Jowell, R. M. *et al. Survey Research Practice*, Heinemann, 1978
Lemon, N. *Attitudes and Their Measurement*, Batsford, 1973
Oppenheim, A. N. *Questionnaire Design and Attitude Measurement*, Heinemann, London, 1966
Sudman, S. and Bradburn, N. M. *Asking Questions – A Practical Guide to Questionnaire Design*, Jossey-Bass Publishers, 1982

Chapter 6

Atkinson, J. A. *A Handbook For Interviewers*, The Government Social Survey, 1968
Atkinson, P. L. and Ogden, A. J. 'Sample Surveys at the Point-of-Sale: a Case History from the Petrol Market', *Journal of the Market Research Society*, **16**, 2, 1974
Belson, W. A. *Studies in Readership*, Business Publications Ltd., 1962
Belson, W. A. *Tape Recording: its Effect on Accuracy of Response in Survey Interviews*, The Survey Research Unit, The London School of Economics, 1963
Belson, W. A. *Respondent Understanding of Questions in the Survey Interview*, The Survey Research Unit, The London School of Economics, 1968

Berent, P. H. *Interview Recruitment and Training*, ESOMAR Congress, Evian, 1962

Brandsma, P. 'The Role and Influence of the Interviewer', *European Marketing Research Review*, **4,** 1, 1969

Drakeford, J. F. *A Critical Appraisal of Pilot Techniques in Qualitative Research*, ESOMAR Seminar on Attitude and Motivation Research, 1970

Ferber, R. and Wales, H. G. 'Detection and Correction of Interviewer Bias', *Public Opinion Quarterly*, **XVI,** 1, 1952

Hauck, M. and Steinkamp, S. *Survey Reliability and Interviewer Competence*, Studies in Consumer Savings No. 4, Bureau of Economics and Business Research, University of Illinois, Urbana, 1964

Hauck, M. 'Interviewer Compensation on Consumer Surveys', *Journal of the Market Research Society*, **14,** 1964

Horne, A., Morgan, J. and Page, J. 'Where do we go from here' (Gold Medal Winning Paper), *Journal of the Market Research Society*, **16,** 3, 1974

Hyman, H. *et al. Interviewing in Social Research*, Chicago, 1954

McCrossan, E. *A Handbook for Interviewers: a Manual of Social Survey Practice and Procedures on Structured Interviewing*, HMSO, London 1984

McFarlane-Smith, J. 'Selection and Training of Interviewers', *Journal of the Market Research Society*, **12,** 2, April 1970

McFarlane-Smith, J. *Interviewing in Market and Social Research*, Routledge and Kegan Paul, 1972

Market Research Society *First Report, Working Party on Interviewing Methods*

Mayer, C. S. 'Evaluating the Quality of Marketing Research Contractors', *Journal of the Market Research Society*, May 1967

Strothmann, K.-H. 'The Attitude to Interviews of Industrial Staff', *Journal of the Market Research Society (Commentary)* **VIII,** 1

Twigg, J. *What is Interviewer Bias?* ESOMAR Congress, 1969

Chapter 7

1. Melhuish, R. M. 'The Use and Operation of the Nielsen Indices', *Journal of the European Society for Opinion and Market Research*, **1,** 64–71, 1954
2. Norvik, H. *The Use of Retailer Panels for Test Marketing*, ESOMAR Conference, 1963
3. Yates, W. A. *Shop Audits in Marketing Evaluation, Now and in the Future*, Market Research Society Conference, 1967

Chapter 8

1. Parfitt, J. H. *'Tailor-Made' Panels–Combining the Advantages of Ad Hoc Survey and Consumer Panel Methods*, ESOMAR, Montreux Conference, 1975
2. Pymont, B. C. *The Development and Application of a New Micro-market Testing Technique*, ESOMAR Congress, 1970

   Pymont, B. C. *et al. Towards the Elimination of Risk from Investment in New Products*, ESOMAR Congress, 1976

   Parfitt, J. and Clay, R. *Panel Prediction Techniques – what we have learned and where we are going*, ESOMAR Congress, 1980
3. Parfitt, J. H. 'A Comparison of Purchase Recall with Diary Panel Records', *Journal of Advertising Research*, **7,** 3, September 1967.

   Also *How Accurately can Product Purchasing Behaviour be Measured by Recall at a Single Interview?*, Paper 26, ESOMAR, Vienna Congress, August 1967
4. Broadbent, S. and Mooney, P. *Can Informant Claims on Product Purchase made at an Interview be used for Media Planning?*, Paper 14, ESOMAR, Opatija Congress, September 1968

5. Collins, B. J. K. and Parfitt, J. H. 'The Use of Consumer Panels for Brand-share Prediction', *Journal of Marketing Research*, **V**, May 1968

 McGloughlin, I. and Parfitt, J. H. *The Use of Consumer Panels in the Evaluation of Promotional and Advertising Expenditure*, Paper 28 ESOMAR, Opatija Congress, September 1968

6. Ehrenberg, A. S. C. *Pack-Size Rates of Purchasing*, Paper 33, ESOMAR, Opatija Congress, September 1968

 Ehrenberg, A. S. C. 'The Practical Meaning and Usefulness of the NBD/LSD Theory of Repeat-Buying', *Applied Statistics*, **17**, 1968

 Ehrenberg, A. S. C. 'The Discovery and Use of Laws of Marketing', *Journal of Marketing*, **32**, 1968

Chapter 10

1. *Some books and papers on telephone surveys:*

 Blankenship, A. B. *Professional Telephone Surveys*, McGraw-Hill, 1977

 Dillman, D. *Mail and Telephone Surveys: The Total Design Method*, Wiley, New York, 1978

 Frey, J. S. *Survey Research by Telephone*, Sage, London, 1983

 Groves, R. and Kahn, R. L. *Surveys by Telephone*, Academic Press, London, 1979

 McDonald, C. *Telephone Surveys: A Review of Research Findings*, Market Research Society, London, 1981

 Panel on Telephone Interviews: five papers on the use of the telephone for international surveys. ICC/ESOMAR Symposium on International Marketing Research, Paris, 1984

 Report on a Feasibility Study of Telephone Interviewing in Social Research, Survey Methods Centre, Social and Community Planning Research, London, 1984

 Sykes, W. and Hoinville, G. *Methodological Research on Telephone Interviews*, Market Research Society Conference, 1984

2. *Plain Man's Guide to TGI*, BMRB, 1977

3. Erdos, P. L. *Professional Mail Survey*, McGraw-Hill, 1970

4. Scott, C. 'Research on Mail Surveys', *Royal Statistical Society Journal*, **124**, 2, 1961

5. Day, P. S. and Dunn, J. 'Estimating the Audience for Advertising on the Outside of Buses', *Applied Statistics*, **18**, 3, 1961

6. Konig, G. and Lovell, M. *The Measurement of Pupil Dilation as a Research Tool*, ESOMAR Conference Paper, 1965

7. Caffyn, J. A. and Brown, N. A. 'The Application of Psychological Ironmongery to Commercial Problems', *Commentary*, January 1965

8. Fletcher, R. *Reading Behaviour Reconsidered*, ESOMAR Conference Paper, 1969

9. Madge, C. and Huxley, J. *Mass-Observation*, 1937 (see also Harrisson, T., *Pub and the People*, Gollancz, 1943; *War Begins at Home*, Chatto and Windus, 1940)

10. Selltiz, J. Deutsch, L. and Cook, L. *Research Methods in Social Relations*, Methuen, 1960

11. Patrick, M. 'How to do the Washing Up in 41 Easy Stages', *Campaign* **20**, 4, 70

12. *Development of Method of Systematization of Observation of Driver Behaviour*, Road Research Laboratory, LR213, 1968

13. Malinowski, R. *A Nation-Wide Intelligence Service, First Year's Work*, Lindsay Drummond, 1938

Chapter 11

Collins, M. and Kalton, G. 'Coding Verbatim Answers to Open Questions', *Journal of the Market Research Society*, **22**, 4, October 1980

Collins, M. and O'Brien, J. 'How Reliable is the Coding Process?' *Market Research Society Conference*, March 1981

Kalton, G. and Stowell, R. 'A Study of Coder Variability', *Applied Statistics*, **28**, 3, 1979
Katz, I. M. 'Advances in Data Editing Techniques', *Market Research Society Conference*, March 1980
McDonald, C. 'Coding Open-ended Answers with the Help of a Computer', *Journal of the Market Research Society*, **24**, 1, January 1982
McDonald, C. 'Computer-aided Coding of Open Questions', *Market Research Society Conference*, March 1982

Chapter 12

1. Stuart, A. 'Standard Errors for Percentages', *Journal of the Royal Statistical Society*, Series C, Applied Statistics, **12**, No. 2, 87–101, 1963
2. Cochran, W. G. 'Some Methods for Strengthening the Common χ^2 tests', *Biometrics*, **10**, 417–451, 1964
3. David, H. A. *The Method of Paired Comparisons*, Charles Griffin
4. Scheffé, H. 'An Analysis of Variance for Paired Comparisons', *Journal of The American Statistical Association*, **47**, 381–400, 1952
5. Snedecor, G. W. and Cochran, W. G. *Statistical Methods (Sixth Edition)*, Iowa State University Press

Suggested Further Reading
Ferber, R. *Statistical Techniques in Market Research*, McGraw-Hill
Kendall, M. G. *Rank Correlation Methods*, Charles Griffin
Maxwell, A. E. *Analysing Qualitative Data*, Methuen
Mood, A. M. and Graybill, F. A. *Introduction to the Theory of Statistics*, McGraw-Hill
Quenouille, M. H. *Introductory Statistics*, Pergamon
Quenouille, M. H. *Rapid Statistical Calculations*, Charles Griffin
Siegel, S. *Non-Parametric Statistics for the Behavioural Sciences*, McGraw-Hill

Chapter 13

1. Collins, M. A. 'Three Approaches to a Multi-dimensional Problem', *Journal of the Market Research Society*, **11**, 3, 1969
2. Kendall, M. G. *A Course in Multivariate Analysis, Introduction*, Chas. Griffin, 1965
3. Ehrenberg, A. S. C. 'Some Queries to Factor Analysts', *The Statistician*, **13**, 4, 1963
4. Siegel, S. 'Measures of Correlation and their Tests of Significance', *Non-parametric Statistics for the Behavioural Sciences*, McGraw-Hill, New York, 1956
5. Hope, K. 'Principal Components', *Methods of Multivariate Analysis*, University of London Press, 1968
6. Christopher, M. A. *A Cluster Analysis of Towns in England and Wales according to their Suitability for Test Market Locations*, University of Bradford Research Project Series in Marketing, 1969
7. Moser, C. A. and Scott, W. *British Towns – A Statistical Study of their Social and Economic Differences*, Oliver and Boyd, 1961
8. Holmes, C. 'Construction and Stratification of a Sampling Frame of Primary Sampling Units', *The Statistician*, **19**, 1, 1969
9. Harman, H. H. 'Foundation of Factor Analysis', *Modern Factor Analysis, 2nd edition*, University of Chicago Press, 1967
10. Cooley, W. W. and Lohnes, P. R. 'Factor Analysis', *Multivariate Procedures for the Behavioural Sciences*, Wiley New York, 1962

11. Lawley, D. N. and Maxwell, A. E. *Factor Analysis as a Statistical Method*, Butterworth, 1963
12. Kaiser, H. F. *Comments in Communality and the Number of Factors*, Read at Conference, Washington University, St. Louis, 1960
13. Thurstone, L. L. *Multiple Factor Analysis*, University of Chicago Press, 1947
14. Hendrickson, A. E. and White, P. O. 'PROMAX' – A Quick Method for Rotation to Simple Structure', *British Journal of Statistical Psychology*, **17**, Part 1, 1964
15. Hill, P. B. 'Multivariate Analysis – What Payoff for the Marketing Man?', *Journal of the Market Research Society*, **12**, 3, 1970
16. Frost, W. A. K. 'The Development of a Technique for TV Programme Assessment', *Journal of the Market Research Society*, **11**, 1, 1969
17. Sokal, R. R. and Sneath, P. H. A. *Principles of Numerical Taxonomy*, W. H. Freeman, 1963
18. Joyce, T. and Channon, C. 'Classifying Market Survey Respondents', *Applied Statistics*, **XV**, 3, 1966
19. Inglis, J. and Johnson, D. 'Some Observations on the Developments in the Analysis of Multivariate Survey Data', *Journal of the Market Research Society*, **12**, 2, 1970
20. Emmett, B. P. 'The Exploration of Inter-relationships in Survey Data', *Journal of the Market Research Society*, **10**, 2, 1968
21. Punj, G. and Stewart, D. W. 'Cluster Analysis in Marketing Research: Review and Suggestions for Applications', *Journal of Marketing Research*, **20**, 2, May 1983
22. Van Ryzin, J. (Ed.) *Classification and Clustering*, Academic Press, 1977
23. Arabie, P., Carroll, J. D., DeSarbo, Wayne and Wind, J. 'Overlapping Clustering: A New Method for Product Positioning', *Journal of Marketing Research*, **18**, 3, Aug. 1981
24. Morgan, N. and Purnell, J. M. 'Isolating Openings for New Products in a Multi-Dimensional Space', *Journal of the Market Research Society*, **11**, 3, 1969
25. *Journal of the Market Research Society*, **11**, 1, 1969
26. Green, P. E., Carmone, F. J. and Fox, L. B. 'Television Programme Similarities: An Application of Subjective Clustering', *Journal of the Market Research Society*, **11**, 1, 1969
27. Ferber, R. 'Multiple Correlation Techniques', *Market Research*, McGraw-Hill, New York, 1949
28. Draper, N. R. and Smith, H. *Applied Regression Analysis*, Wiley, 1981
29. Frank, R. E. and Boyd, H. W. 'Are Private-Brand-Prone Grocery Customers Really Different?', *Journal of Advertising Research*, **5**, 4, 1965
30. Fornell, C. 'Three Approaches to Canonical Analysis', *Journal of Market Research Society*, **26**, 1, January 1984
31. Green, P. E. Halbert, M. H. and Robinson, P. J. 'Canonical Analysis: An Exposition and Illustrative Application', *Journal of Marketing Research*, **3**, February 1966
32. Sands, S. and Moore, P. 'Store Site Selection by Discriminant Analysis', *Journal of Market Research Society*, **23**, 1, January 1981
33. Belson, W. A. 'Principle of Biological Classification', *Applied Statistics*, **VIII**, 2, 1959
34. *Reader Categorisation Study: Indirect Measures of Exposure to Contents of Publications*
35. Sonquist, J. A. and Morgan, J. N. *The Detection of Interaction Effects*, Monograph 35, Survey Research Center, University of Michigan
36. Thompson, V. R. 'Sequential Dichotomisation: Two Techniques', *The Statistician*, **XXI**, 3, 1972
37. Willson, E. J. 'Computational Segmentation in the Context of Multivariate Statistics and Survey Analysis', *Journal of the Market Research Society*, **16**, 2, 1974
38. Sampson, P. 'The Selection of Cluster Defining Variables', *Journal of the Market Research Society*, **16**, 4, 1974
39. Assael, H. 'Segmenting Markets by Group Purchasing Behaviour: An Application of the A.I.D. Technique', *Journal of Marketing Research*, **VII**, May 1970
40. Harris. P. *Recent Developments in the Multivariate Analysis of Market Research Data*, Market Research Society Conference, March 1981

41. Doyle, P. and McGee 'Perceptions of the Preferences for Alternative Convenience Foods', *Journal of Market Research Society*, **15**, 1, 1973
42. Neidell, L. A. 'The Use of Non-metric Multi-dimensional Scaling in Marketing Analysis, *Journal of Marketing*, **33**, October 1969
43. Green, P. E. and Rao, V. R. 'Conjoint Measurement for Quantifying Judgemental Data', *Journal of Marketing Research*, **8**, August 1971
44. Van Veen, W. M. O. and Beazley, D. 'An Investigation of Alternative Methods of Applying the Trade-off Model', *Journal of Market Research Society*, **12**, 1, 1977
45. Guttman, L., Brown and Bignall. *The Relevance of the Non-metric Break-through of Marketing Research*, Market Research Society Conference, 1969
46. Sampson, P. *Some Experiences with Mapping*, Market Research Society Conference, 1977
47. Sheth, J. N. 'The Multivariate Revolution in Marketing Research', *Journal of Marketing*, **35**, 1971
48. Green, P. E. and Frank, R. F. *A Manager's Guide to Marketing Research*, Wiley New York, 1967

Chapter 14

1. Smith, W. 'Product Differentiation and Market Segmentation as Alternative Marketing Strategies', *Journal of Marketing*, July 1956
2. Frank, R. E. 'Market Segmentation Research: Findings and Implications', in Frank, Bass *et al.* (Eds.) *Applications of the Sciences in Marketing Management*, Wiley, New York, 1968
3. Head, M. 'What do Manufacturers want to know about People?, *Admap*, November 1981
4. Twedt, D. W. 'How Important to Marketing Strategy is the "Heavy Half" Theory?' *Journal of Marketing*, **28**, 1, 1964
5. Haley, R. I. 'Benefit Segmentation: a Decision-Oriented Research Tool', *Journal of Marketing*, **32**, July 1968
6. Frank, R. E. *But the Heavy Half is Already the Heavy Half*, Paper presented to the American Marketing Association's Conference in Philadelphia, June 17–19, 1968
7. Bass, F. M., Pessemeir, E. A. and Tigart, D. J. 'Complementary and Substitute Patterns of Purchasing and Use', *Journal of Advertising Research*, **9**, 2, 1969
8. Hansen, F. *Backward Segmentation using Hierarchical Clustering and Q-Factor Analysis*, *Proceedings of ESOMAR Seminar on Segmentation and Typology*, Brussels, 1972
9. Frank, R., Massy, W. and Wind, J. *Market Segmentations*, Prentice-Hall, 1972
10. Lunn, J. A. 'Exploratory Work on Social Class', *Commentary, The Journal of the Market Research Society*, **VII**, 3, July 1965
11. Jain, S. C. *Life Cycle Revisited: Applications in Consumer Research*, *Proceedings of the 5th Annual Conference of the Association for Consumer Research*, 1975
12. Cornish, P. 'Life Cycle and Income Segmentation: Sagacity', *Admap*, October 1981
13. Agostini, J. M. 'New Criteria for Classifying Informants in Market Research and Media Strategy', *Admap*, **3**, 9, 1967
14. Lunn, J. A. 'Psychological Classification', *The Journal of the Market Research Society*, **8**, 3, 161–173, July 1966
15. Massy, W. F., Frank, R. J. and Loudahl, T. M. *Purchasing Behaviour and Personal Attributes*, University of Pennsylvania Press, Philadelphia, 1968
16. Wells, W. D. 'Psychographics: A Critical Review', *Journal of Marketing Research*, **12**, 1975
17. Thomas, S. Bunting, C. and Nelson, E. H. *Social Change Analysis – A New Era for the Application of Research*, Market Research Society Annual Conference, 1982
18. Segnit, S. *Practical Applications of Life Style Research*, paper given at the Seminar on 'The Life Style Concept in Marketing' organized by the Market Research Society and the College for the Distributive Trades, London, 1975
19. Howard, J. A. and Sheth, J. N. *The Theory of Buyer Behaviour*, Wiley, New York, 1969

20. Lunn, J. A. *Classifying Consumers: Some Basic Principles and Recent Developments*, Proceedings of ESOMAR Seminar on *Classifying Consumers – A Need to Rethink*, Bruges 1982
21. Baldwin, E. S. and Lunn, J. A. *Researching the Changing Consumer*, *ESOMAR Annual Conference*, 1972
22. Beazley, D. and Lunn, J. A. *Shopping Styles and Strategies and their Relationships to In-Store Factors*, *ESOMAR Seminar on Management Information for Retail Organisations*, Lucerne; 1974
23. Seaman, D. K., Blamires, C. and Morgan, R. M. *Micro-Behavioural Modelling as an Aid to Retailer Strategies Planning*, Market Research Society Annual Conference, 1981
24. Webber, R. *Basic Principles of ACORN*, Seminar on 'ACORN in ACTION', CACI International, London, 1980
25. Winkler, A. 'Problems in Connection with the Use of Segmentation Methods with Examples from the Field of Consumer Goods', in Durand, J. (Ed.) *Market Segmentation*, papers from the conference organized by ADETEM, Paris, March 1969
26. Stefflre, V. 'Market Structure Studies: New Products for Old Markets', in Frank Bass *et al.* (Eds.) *Applications of the Sciences in Marketing Management*, Wiley, New York, 1968
27. Lunn, J. A. Cooper, P. and Murphy, O. M. 'The Fluctuating Fortunes of the UK Social Democratic Party', *European Research*, **12**, 1, 1984
28. Murphy, O. M. Lunn, J. A. and Cooper, P. *The Growing Pains of a New Political Party – The UK Social Democrats, An Application of Applied Creativity Research*, Annual Conference of the Dutch Market Research Society 1984
29. Sonquist, J. A. and Morgan, J. N. *The Detection of Interaction Effects*, Monograph No. 35, Survey Research Centre, University of Michigan, 1964
30. Kogan, M. and Wallace, J. C. 'A New Coefficient for Cluster Discrimination', *Australian Journal of Psychology*, **6**, 1969
31. Heller, H. E. 'Defining Target Markets by their Attitude Profiles', in Adler, L. and Crespi, I. (Eds.) *Attitude Research on the Rocks*, American Marketing Association, 1968
32. Grosse, W. and Lowe-Watson, D. *Changes in Market Segmentation Over Time*, ESOMAR Seminar on Segmentation and Typology, 1972
33. Lowe-Watson, D. *The Esso Cleveland Integration*, ESOMAR Annual Congress, 1972
34. Sherak, B. 'A Beer Segmentation and Brand Mapping Study', in Ɗurand, J. (Ed.) *Market Segmentation*, papers from the conference organized by ADETEM, Paris, March 1969
35. Lunn, J. A. and Morgan, R. M. 'Some Applications of the Trade-off Approach', in Bradley, U.B. *Applied Marketing and Social Research*, Van Nostrand Reinhold, London, 1982
36. Hendrickson, A. E. *Choice Behaviour and Advertising: A Theory and Two Models*, paper read at the Admap World Advertising Workshop, Southampton, October 18–22, 1967
37. Moss, M. *A Marketing Man's View of Research*, paper given at MRS Annual Conference, Brighton, 1967
38. Barnett, N. L. 'Beyond Market Segmentation', *Harvard Business Review*, January-February 1969
39. Beazley, D. 'Alternative Approaches to Brand Positioning Research: How Do We Choose?' in Green, P. E. and Christopher, M. (Eds.) *Brand Positioning*, Cranfield Institute of Technology, UK, 1973
40. Buckle, M. and Hughes-Hallett, A. *Getting the Best out of Brand Image Work*, *ESOMAR Annual Conference*, 1975
41. Green, P. E. and Tull, D. S. *Research for Marketing Decisions*, Prentice Hall, New Jersey, 1978
42. Lunn, J. A. 'Perspectives in Attitude Research', *Journal of the Market Research Society*, **II**, 3, 1969
43. Lunn, J. A. *Attitudes and Behaviour in Consumer Research: a Re-appraisal*, *ESOMAR Seminar on Attitude and Motivation Research*, 1970
44. Sheth, J. N. *Relevance of Segmentation for Market Planning*, *ESOMAR Seminar on Segmentation and Typology*, Brussels, 1972

45. Twigg, J. and Wolfe, A. 'Problems of Communicating the Results of Market Segmentation Studies', *Journal of the Market Research Society*, **10**, 4, October 1968
46. Hill, P. B. 'Multivariate Analysis – What Payoff for the Marketing Man?', *Journal of the Market Research Society*, **12**, 3, July 1970
47. Bowring, C. 'Different Strokes tor Different Folks: the Case for Developing Advertising Concepts from Consumer Typology', *Journal of the Market Research Society*, **27**, 4, 1985

Chapter 15

Comprehensive Descriptions of New Product Development Procedures (including further bibliography in most cases)

 1. Boyd, H. W., Westfall, R. and Stasch, 'Product Research', in *Marketing Research: Text and Cases*, Richard D. Irwin, 1980
 2. Esomar, *New Product Development*, ESOMAR Seminars 1979 and 1983
 3. Foxall, G. R. *Corporate Innovation: Marketing and Strategy*, Croom Helm, 1984
 4. Hisrich, R. D. and Peters, M. P. *Marketing a New Product*, Benjamin/Cummings Publishing Company Inc., 1978
 5. King, S. J. *Developing New Brands*, Pitman, 1973
 6. Kotler, P. *Marketing Management: Analysis, Planning and Control*, Prentice-Hall International, 1984
 7. Rothberg, R. B. *Corporate Strategy and Product Innovation*, Collier Macmillan, 1981
 8. Urban, G. L. and Hauser, J. R. *Design and Marketing of New Products*, Prentice-Hall, 1980

Particular Techniques mentioned in this Chapter

 9. White, R. *Consumer Product Development*, Longman, 1974
10. Goldsmith, R. 'Methodological Approaches to New Product Development', *Market Research Society Conference*, 1981
11. Greenhalgh, C. 'Generating New Product Ideas: A Review Paper', *ESOMAR Congress*, 1971
12. Verhage, B, Waalewijn, P. and Van Weele, A. J. 'New Product Development in Dutch Companies: The Idea Generation Stage', *European Journal of Marketing*, **15**, 5, 1981
13. Sands, S. 'Techniques for Creating New Product Ideas', *Management Decision*, **17**, 2, 1979
14. Vineall, M. G. and Origlia, C. 'Profitably Using Research to Identify, Develop and Launch a New Product', *ESOMAR Congress*, 1981
15. Twiss, B. 'Creativity and Problem Solving' in *Managing Technological Innovation*, Longman, 1974
16. Alford, C. L. and Mason, J. B. 'Generating New Product Ideas', *Journal of Advertising Research*, **15**, 6, 1975
17. Tauber, E. M. 'Heuristic Ideation Technique – A Systematic Procedure for New Product Search', *Journal of Marketing*, **36**, 1, 1972
18. Gordon, W. J. J. *Synectics*, Harper and Row, 1961
19. Von Hippel, E. 'Get New Product Ideas from Customers', *Harvard Business Review*, March/April 1982
20. Lanitis, T. 'How to Generate New Product Ideas', *Journal of Advertising Research*, **10**, 3, 1970
21. Tauber, E. M. 'Discovering New Product Opportunities with Problem Inventory Analysis', *Journal of Marketing*, **39**, 1, 1975
22. Fornell, C. and Marks, R. D. 'Problem Analysis: A Consumer-Based Methodology for the Discovery of New Product Ideas', *European Journal of Marketing*, **15**, 5, 1981
23. Kuehn, A. and Day, R. L. 'Strategy of Product Quality', *Harvard Business Review*, **40**, 6, 1962
24. Shocker, A. D. and Srinivasan, V. 'Multi-Attribute Approaches for Product Concept Evaluation and Generation: A Critical Review', *Journal of Marketing Research*, **16**, 2, 1979
25. Haefell, J. W. *Creativity and Invention*, Reinhold, 1962

26. Sampson, P. 'Can Consumers Create New Products?' *Journal of the Market Research Society*, **12**, 1, 1970

27. Holmes, C. and Keegan, S. 'Current and Developing Creative Research Methods in New Product Development', *Market Research Society Conference*, 1983

28. King, S. J. 'How Useful is Proposition Testing?', *Advertising Quarterly*, Winter 1965/66

29. Skelly, F. and Nelson, E. H. 'Market Segmentation and New Product Development', *Scientific Business*, **4**, 13, 1966

30. Iuso, W. 'Concept Testing: An Appropriate Approach', *Journal of Marketing Research*, **12**, 2, 1975

31. Midgley, D. F. *Innovation and New Product Marketing*, Croom Helm, 1977

32. Caffyn, J. M. and Loyd, A. 'Predicting the Effects of Brand Name and Consumer Proposition on Consumer Purchase Decisions: A Case History', *ESOMAR Congress*, 1968

33. Green, P. E. and Srinivasan, V. 'Conjoint Analysis in Consumer Research: Issues and Outlook', *Journal of Consumer Research*, **5**, 2, 1978

34. Johnson, R. M. 'Trade-off Analysis of Consumer Values', *Journal of Marketing Research*, **11**, 2, 1974

35. Westwood, R., Lunn, A. J. and Beazley, D. 'The Trade-Off Model and its Extensions', *Journal of the Market Research Society*, **16**, 3, 1974

36. Tauber, E. M. 'Reduce New Product Failures: Measure Needs as well as Product Interest', *Journal of Marketing*, **37**, 3, 1973

37. Tauber, E. M. 'Predictive Validity in Consumer Research', *Journal of Advertising Research*, **15**, 5, 1975

38. Twedt, D. W. 'How to Plan New Products, Improve Old Ones and Create Better Advertising', *Journal of Marketing*, **33**, 1, 1969

39. Thornton, C. 'Ranking New Product Openings in Multi-Dimensional Space', *Market Research Society Conference*, 1970

40. Batsell, R. R. and Wind, Y. 'Product Testing: Current Methods and Needed Developments', *Journal of the Market Research Society*, **22**, 2, 1980

41. Boyd, K. T. 'Product Testing', in Bradley U. (Ed.) *Applied Marketing and Social Research*, Van Nostrand Reinhold, 1982

42. Collins, M. 'Product Testing', in Aucamp, J. (Ed.) *The Effective Use of Market Research*, Staples Press, 1971

43. Day, R. L. 'Measuring Preferences' in Ferber, R. (Ed.) *Handbook of Marketing Research*, McGraw, 1974

44. Penny, J. C., Hunt, I. M. and Twyman, W. A. 'Product Testing Methodology in Relation to Marketing Problems: A Review', *Journal of the Market Research Society*, **14**, 1, 1972

45. Brown, G., Copeland, A. and Millward, M. 'Monadic Testing of New Products – An old Problem and Some New Solutions', *Journal of the Market Research Society*, **15**, 2, 1973

46. Rehorn, J. 'How should a Product score in a Blind Test to stand a Chance in the Market?' *ESOMAR Congress*, 1976

47. Brown, G. and Millward, M. 'New Product Evaluation – Art, Science or Wizardry', *Market Research Society Conference*, 1981

48. Bowles, T. 'From Product Testing to Marketing Decisions', *Market Research Society Conference*, 1981

49. Kondos, A. and Clunies-Ross, C. 'Sources of Bias in Sensory Evaluations as Applied to Food and Beverages', *ESOMAR Congress*, 1966

50. Green, P. E. and Srinivasan, V. 'Conjoint Analysis in Consumer Research: Status and Outlook', *Journal of Consumer Research*, **5**, 2, 1978

51. Westwood, R. A., Lunn, J. A. and Beazley, D. 'The Trade-Off Model and its Extensions', *Journal of the Market Research Society*, **16**, 3, 1974

52. Factor, S. and Sampson, P. 'Making Decisions about Launching New Products', *Journal of the Market Research Society*, **25**, 2, 1983

53. Wind, Y., Maharajan, V. and Cardozo, R. (Eds.) *New Product Forecasting*, Lexington Books, 1981

54. Godfrey, S. and Wilkinson, J. 'Predicting the Sales Potential of New Products: A Review of Current Methods and their Applicability to Different New Product Types', *ESOMAR Congress*, 1983

55. Godfrey, S. 'The Sensor Simulated Test Market System', Admap, October 1983

56. Clarke, K. and Roe, M. 'The Marketing Mix Test: Relating Expectations and Performance', *Market Research Society Conference*, 1977

57. Aspden, J. and Gurd, P. 'A Tool for the Eighties: Pricing Sensitivity Model', *Market Research Society Conference*, 1981

58. Frappa, J.-P. and Marbeau, Y. 'Pricing New Products at Better Value for Money: The Ultimate Challenge for Market Researchers', *ESOMAR Congress*, 1982

59. Gabor, A. and Granger, G. 'The Pricing of New Products' in Taylor, B. and Wills, G. (Eds) *Pricing Strategy*, Staples Press, 1969

60. Kraushar, P. M. and Sowter, A. P. 'Pricing Research', *Market Research Society Conference*, 1972

61. Blamires, C, 'Pricing Research Techniques: A Review and a New Approach', *Journal of the Market Research Society*, **23**, 3, 1981

62. Miln, D. A. and Topping, N. 'An Application of Market Research to Pricing and Price Elasticity', *Market Research Society Conference*, 1971

63. Lunn, J. A. and Morgan, R. P. 'Some Applications of the Trade-Off Approach', in Bradley, U. (Ed.) *Applied Marketing and Social Research*, Van Nostrand Reinhold, 1982

Chapter 16

1. Lovell, M. R. C. and Lannon, J. M. 'Difficulties with Recall', ESOMAR WAPOR Congress, August 1967

2. Axelrod, J. N. 'Attitude Measures that Predict Purchase', *Journal of Advertising Research*, March 1968

The divisions between 'Theoretical' and 'Practical' are arbitrary, and signify degree, rather than category.

Theoretical

Appel, V. and Blum, M. 'Ad Recognition and Respondent Set', *Journal of Advertising Research*, **1**, 4 June 1961

Dembar, W. N. *Psychology of Perception*, Holt, New York, 1965

Haskins, J. B. 'Factual Recall as a Measure of Advertising Effectiveness', *Journal of Advertising Research*, **4**, 1, March 1964

Hedges, A. *Testing to Destruction*, Institute of Practioners in Advertising, London, 1974

Hodock, C. L. 'Copy Testing and Strategic Positioning', *JAR* **20–1**, 1980

Joyce, T. 'What do we Know about the Way Advertising Works?', ESOMAR Seminar, 1967

King, S. 'How Useful is Proposition Testing?', *Advertising Quarterly*, Winter 1965/6

Krugmann, H. E. 'The Measurement of Advertising Involvement', *Public Opinion Quarterly*, Winter 1966–67

Leavitt, C. 'Classic Models of Communication Effects and Innovations in These Models', Annual Conference of American Association for Public Opinion Research, May 1970

Leigh, J. H. and Martin, C. R. Jr. 'Current Issues and Research in Advertising', Grad. School of Bus. Admin., Univ. of Michigan (Annually 1979–)

Lovell, M. R. C. and Lannon, J. M. 'Difficulties with Recall', ESOMAR WAPOR Congress, August 1967

Lucas, D. B. 'The ABC's of ARF's PARM', *Journal of Marketing*, July 1960

Morgensztern, A. 'How to Determine the Optimum Screening Frequency of a Movie Commercial', ESOMAR, 1967

Percy, L. and Woodside, A. G. *Advertising and Consumer Psychology*, Lexington Books, New York, 1983

Twyman, W. A. 'Designing Advertising Research for Marketing Decisions', *JMRS*, **15**, 2, April 1973

Wells, W. D., 'How Chronic Overclaimers distort Survey Findings', *Journal of Advertising Research*, **3**, 2, June 1963

Practical

Arnold, S. J. and Bird, R. J. 'Recall of Television Commercials', *PMRS Journal*, **1**, 1982

Axelrod, J. N. 'Attitude Measures that Predict Purchase', *Journal of Advertising Research*, March 1968

Buchanan, D. I. 'How Interest in the Product affects Recall: Print Ads vs. Commercials', *Journal of Advertising Research*, March 1964

Caffyn, J. M. and Brown, N. A., 'The Application of Psychological Iromongery to Commercial Problems', ESOMAR Congress, 1964

Clancy, K. J. and Ostlund, L. E. 'Commercial Effectiveness Measures', *JAR* **16**, 1, 1976

Colman, S. and Brown, G. 'Advertising Tracking Studies and Sales Effects', *JMRS*, **25**, 2, April 1983

Corkindale, D. 'Measuring the Sales Effectiveness of Advertising', *JMRS*, **26**, 1, 1984

Greenway, G. and De Groot, G. 'The Qualitative–Quantitative Dilemma: What's the Question?', *JMRS*, **25**, 2, 1983

Hess, E. 'Attitudes and Pupil Size', *Scientific American*, April 1965

King, S. 'Can Research Evaluate the Creative Content of Advertising?', *Admap*, June 1967

Konig, G. Lakaschus, C. and Lovell, M. R. C. 'The Measurement of Pupil Dilation as a Market Research Tool', ESOMAR WAPOR Congress, September 1965

Kubas, L. and Kastelic, T. 'Understanding Communications Effectiveness Measures', *PMRS Journal*, Toronto, **2**, Dec. 1983

Potter, J. 'Commercial Pre-testing', *Admap*, September 1971

Segnit, S. and Broadbent, S. R. 'Area Tests and Consumer Surveys to Measure Advertising Effectiveness', ESOMAR Congress, 1970

Starch, D. 'Measuring the Effect of Advertising on Sales', (5 articles) *Printers Ink*, March–May 1964

Winick, C. 'Three Measures of the Advertising Value of Media Context', *Journal of Advertising Research*, **2**, 2, June 1962

Wood, J. F., '*Pre-testing the Advertising*', *Admap*, September 1967

'Effective Advertising – Can Research Help?', (collected papers) ESOMAR, Jan. 1983

See also

Lovell, M. R. C. and Potter, J. *Assessing the Effectiveness of Advertising*, Business Books, London, 1975

Chapter 17

1. Pilditch, J. *The Silent Salesman*, Business Books, London, 1973
2. *How Housewives Really Shop*, Business Decisions Ltd., London, 1976
3. *The Shopping Expedition*, Business Decisions Ltd., London, 1977

4. Wells, W. D. and Lo Sciuto, L. A. 'Direct Observation of Purchasing Behaviour', *Journal of Marketing Research*, August 1966
5. Vineall, M. G. and Origlia, C. 'Profitably Using Research to Identify, Develop and Launch a New Product', Esomar Congress, Amsterdam, 1981
6. Schlaeppi, A. C. UK Market Research Society Seminar on 'Packaging Research', 1983
7. Dillon, P. J. 'The Tachistoscopic Fallacy', UK Market Research Society Annual Conference, 1969

Chapter 18

1. Parfitt, J. and McGloughlin, I. 'The Use of Consumer Panels in the Evaluation of Promotions', *Admap*, December 1968
2. Ehrenberg, A. S. C. and Goodhart, G. J. *Evaluating a Consumer Deal*, extracts from a case study for the J. Walter Thompson Co.
3. Simmons, M. 'Point-of-Sale Advertising', *Journal of the Market Research Society*, **10**, 2, April 1968

Further Reading

Adler, E. *The Neglect of Promotions Research during Economic Recession and Expansion*, Market Research Society Conference, April 1978
Altman, W. 'The Point of Point-of-Sale', *Marketing*, March 1969
'Buyers Attitudes to Below-the-Line', *The Grocer*, 1 June 1968
Christopher, M. 'The Whys and Wherefores of Below the Line', *The Financial Times*, 3 July 1969
Hearne, J. J. 'Does "Below the Line" Promotion Pay?' *The Financial Times*, 4 July 1968
Hoofnagle, W. S. 'Experimental Designs in Measuring the Effectiveness of Promotion', *Journal of Marketing Research*, **11,** May 1965
Kennedy, R. W. 'Merchandising and Point-of-Sale Evaluation', *Advertising Management*, April 1968
Quelch, J. A. and Cannon-Bonventre, K. 'Better Marketing at the Point of Purchase', *Harvard Business Review*, November-December 1983
'Retailer Attitudes to Promotions', *The Grocer*, 6 July 1968
Sampson, P. and Hooper, B. *Evaluating 'Below the Line' Expenditure*, The Thomson Medals and Awards for Advertising Research, 1969
Sunou, D. and Lin, L. Y. S. 'Sales Effects of Promotion and Advertising', *Journal of Marketing Research*, **18,** 5, October 1978
Weber, J. H. 'Can the Results of Sales Promotion be Predicted?', *Journal of Marketing*, January 1963
Willett, R. P. and Kollat, D. T. 'Customer Impulse Purchasing Behaviour: Some Research Notes and a Reply', *Journal of Marketing Research*, **V,** February 1967
Williams, J. *The Manual of Sales Promotion*, Innovation Limited, London, 1983
Wolfe, A. 'Planning and Pre-testing Sales Promotion Programmes', Seminar on 'Researching Below the Line', Market Research Society, London, 1983

Chapter 19

1. Christopher, M. *A Cluster Analysis of Towns in England and Wales According to their Suitability for Test Market Locations*, University of Bradford Management Centre, 1969
2. Schlaifer, R. *Probability and Statistics for Business Decisions*, McGraw-Hill, New York, 1959
3. Davis, E. J. *Experimental Marketing*, Nelson, 1970

Further Reading

Cox, K. R. and Enis, B. M. *Experimentation for Marketing Decisions*, Intertext Marketing Research Series, Aylesbury, England, 1973

Gold, J. A. 'Testing Test Market Predictions', *Journal of Marketing Research*, August 1964

Green, P. E. and Frank, R. E. 'Bayesian Statistics and Marketing Research', *Journal of the Royal Statistical Society*, Series C, **XV**, 3, November 1966

Katz, W. A. 'TV Viewer Fragmentation from Cable TV', *Journal of Advertising Research*, **22**, 6, 1983

Krugman, D. M. and Eckrich, D. 'Differences in Cable and Pay-Cable Audiences', *Journal of Advertising Research*, **22**, 4, 1982

Parfitt, J. H. and Collins, B. J. K. 'The Use of Consumer Panels for Brand-Share Prediction', *Journal of Marketing Research*, May 1968

Pymont, B. C. *The Development and Application of a New Micro Market Testing Technique*, ESOMAR Congress Papers, 1970

Sunoo, D. and Lin, L. Y. S. 'Sales Effects of Promotion and Advertising', *Journal of Advertising Research*, **18**, 5, 1978

Wills, G. 'Cost Benefit of a Test Market', *Management Decision*, Winter 1967

Zufryden, F. S. 'A Tested Model of Purchase Response to Advertising Exposures', *Journal of Advertising Research* **21**, 1, 1981

Zufryden, F. S. 'Predicted Trial, Repeat and Sales Response from Alternative Media Plans, Using Split-cable Data', *Journal of Advertising Research* **22**, 3, 1982

'Test Marketing Reduces Risks', *The Nielsen Researcher (Oxford edition)*, January–February 1973

Chapter 20

1. Kotler, P. and Lilien, G. *Marketing Decision Making: A Model Building Approach*, Harper and Row, New York, 1983
2. Massy, W. F., Montgomery, D. B. and Morrison, D. G. *Stochastic Models of Buying Behaviour*, MIT Press, Cambridge Mass., 1970
3. Sheth, J. N. (Ed.) *Models of Buyer Behaviour: Conceptual, Quantitative and Empirical*, Harper and Row, New York, 1974
4. Nicosia, F. M. and Wind, Y. (Eds) *The Uses of Theories and Models in Marketing: An Introduction*, Dryden Press, Illinois, 1977
5. Palmer, J. *A Survey of Market Modelling Practice*, ESOMAR Seminar on 'Market Modelling', 1975
6. Lunn, J. A. 'A Review of Consumer Decision Process Models', ESOMAR Conference, 1971 (reprinted in Sheth, J. N. (Ed.), Ref. 3).
7. Lunn, J. A. '*Applications of Behavioural Models to the Study of Individual Consumers*', in Nicosia, F. M. and Wind, Y. (Ref. 4)
8. Faivre, J. P. *Consumer Models as a Way to improve Management Decision Making*, ESOMAR Seminar on 'Developments in Consumer Psychology', 1973
9. Zaltman, G. '*The Structure and Purpose of Marketing Models*', in Nicosia, F. M. and Wind, Y. (Ref. 4)
10. Westwood, R. A., Lunn, J. A. and Beazley, D. 'The Trade-off Model and its Extensions', *Journal of the Market Research Society*, **16**, 3, 1974
11. Rothman, J. '*Experimental Designs and Models*', Chapter 3 of this Handbook
12. Howard, J. A. and Sheth, J. N. *The Theory of Buyer Behavior*, John Wiley, New York, 1969
13. Zaltman, G., Pinson, C. R. A. and Angelman, R. *Metatheory and Consumer Research*, Holt, Rinehart and Winston, New York, 1973
14. Sampson, P. *Consumer Behaviour Prediction and the Modelling Approach*, ESOMAR Annual Conference, 1974

15. Bettman, J. R. and Jones, J. M. 'Formal Models of Consumer Behaviour: A Conceptual Overview', *Journal of Business*, **45,** 4, 1900

16. Nicosia, F. M. '*Brand Choice: Toward Behaviour–Behaviouristic Models*', in Davis, H. L. (Ed.) *Behavioural and Management Science in Marketing*, Ronald Press, New York, 1976

17. Ehrenberg, A. S. C. 'Towards an Integrated Theory of Consumer Behaviour', *Journal of the Market Research Society*, **11,** 4, 1969

18. Wilkie, W. K. and Pessemier, G. A. 'Issues in Marketing's Use of Multi-Attribute Attitude Models', *Journal of Marketing Research*, **10,** 4, 1973

19. Fishbein, M. *Belief, Attitude, Intention and Behavior: An Introduction to Theory and Research Reading*, Addison-Wesley, New York, 1975

20. Engel, J. F., Kollat, D. T. and Blackwell, R. D. *Consumer Behavior*, Holt, Rinehart and Winston, New York, 1972

21. Nicosia, F. M. *Consumer Decision Processes*, Prentice Hall, New Jersey, 1966

22. Jacoby, J. 'Consumer Psychology as a Social Psychological Sphere of Action', *American Psychologist*, October 1975

23. Sheth, J. N. '*The Next Decade of Buyer Behaviour Theory and Research*', in Sheth, J. N. (Ed.) (Ref. 3)

24. McGuire, W. J. *The Guiding Theories Behind Attitude Change Research*, Third Annual Attitude Research Conference, American Marketing Association, 1970

25. Palmer, J. and Faivre, J. P. 'The Information Processing Theory of Consumer Behaviour', *European Research*, **1,** 6, 1973

26. Hughes, G. D. and Ray, M. (Eds) *Buyer/Consumer Information Processing*, University of North Carolina Press, Chapel Hill, 1974

27. Lunn, J. A. and Beazley, D. *The Role of the Threshold Model in the Assessment of Belief Importance and in Consumer Information Processing*, ESOMAR Seminar on 'Market Modelling', 1975

28. Beazley, D. and Westwood, R. A. *Modelling Choice Behaviour*, Market Research Society Conference, 1976

29. Van Raaij, W. F. *Evaluation Process Models: An Overview*, ESOMAR Seminar on 'Market Modelling', 1975

30. Westwood, P. A., Lunn, J. A. and Beazley, D. 'Models and Modelling: Part 1, New Approaches to Measuring Belief Importance', *European Research*, **2,** 3, 1974

31. Gunter, P. and Beazley, D. *An Application of Micro-Simulation Modelling to the Marketing of a Consumer Durable*, ESOMAR Conference, 1976

32. Faivre, J. P. and Sanchez, C. *The Validation of Marketing Models*, ESOMAR Conference on 'Market Modelling', 1975

33. Seaman, D., Blamires, C. and Morgan, R. *Micro Behavioural Modelling as an Aid to Retailer Strategic Planning*, Market Research Society Conference, 1981

34. Blamires, C. M. *Modelling: A Non-Technical Guide to its Role in Market Research*, Market Research Society Conference, 1985

35. Robinson, P. J. '*Comparison of pre-Test-Market New Product Forecasting Models*', in Wind, Y. *et al.* (ref. 36, chapter 7)

36. Wind, Y., Mahajan, V. and Cardozo, R. N. (Eds) *New Product Forecasting*, Lexington Books, 1982

37. Factor, S. and Sampson, P. *Making Decisions About Launching New Products*, Market Research Society Conference, 1983

38. Urban, G. L. and Katz, G. M. *Pre-Test-Market Models: Validation and Managerial Implications*, MIT Sloan School, Working Paper No. 1292-82 (April 1982)

39. Lin, L., Pioche, A. and Standen, P. *New Product Sales Forecasting: Recent Bases Experience in Europe and the United States*, ESOMAR Congress, 1982

40. Silk, A. J. and Urban, G. L. 'Pre-Test-Market Evaluation of New Packaged Goods: A Model and Measurement Methodology', *Journal of Marketing Research*, **15,** May 1978 (reprinted in Wind, Y. *et al.*, ref. 36, chapter 8)

41. Yankelovich, Skelly and Shite, '*LTM Estimating Procedures*', in Wind, Y. *et al.* (ref. 36, chapter 9)
42. Burger, P. C., Gundee, H. and Lavidge, R. 'COMP: A Comprehensive System for Evaluating New Products', in Wind, Y. *et al.* (ref. 36, chapter 10)
43. Godfrey, S. and Wilkinson, J. *Predicting the sales potential of new products – a review of current methods and their applicability to different new product types*, ESOMAR Congress, 1983
44. Blamires, C. 'Pricing Research Techniques: A Review and a New Approach', *Journal of the Market Research Society*, **23**, 3, 1981
45. Blamires, C. and Finer, P. *Micros and Modelling: Putting a New Slant on Established Techniques*, Market Research Society Conference 1982
46. Wheelwright, Y. and McGee, Y. *Forecasting – Methods and Applications*, Wiley Books, 1983

Further Reading

Aspden, J. and Gurd, P. *A Tool for the Eighties – Pricing Sensitivity Model*, Market Research Society Conference, 1981
Bolt, G. J. *Market and Sales Forecasting – A Total Approach*, Kogan Page Books, 2nd edition 1981
Lunn, J. A. and Morgan, R. '*Some Applications of the Trade-Off Approach*', in Bradley, U. (Ed.) *Applied Marketing and Social Research*, Van Nostrand Reinhold, 1982

Chapter 21

1. MacLeod, J. S. *The Marketing Power of Brand and Corporate Images*, Opinion Research Corporation, December 1961
2. Brien, A. 'Pleasure', *Punch*, 648, 22 October 1969
3. Lowe-Watson, D. *Advertising and the Buyer/Seller Relationship*, IPA Thesis Competition, 1967
4. Burnett, L. 'Advertising', *The New York Times*, 14 December 1969
5. Paterson, W. 'Try to Use the Same Language', *IAM* 12–14 June 1970
6. Shaw, J. F. *Trust Houses Forte: A Case Study in Corporate Advertising*, Thames Television Limited, 1974
7. Pilditch, J. *Communication by Design*, McGraw-Hill, 1970
8. Roberts, L. D. Letter to the Editor, *The Financial Times*, 19 March 1970

Further Reading

Bernstein, D. *Company Image and Reality – a Critique of Corporate Communications*, Holt Reinhart and Winston Ltd, 1984
Marquis, Harold H. *The Changing Corporate Image*, American Management Association, 1970
Martin Lipset, S. and Schneider, W. *The Confidence Gap: Business, Labor and Government in the Public Mind*, The Free Press, New York, 1983
Worcester, R. M. and Lewis, S. Mirror, Mirror, on the Wall, *Survey Magazine*, June, 1983
Worcester, R. M. 'Measuring the Impact of Corporate Advertising', *Admap*, September 1983

Chapter 22

1. *Consumer Finance Today*, Campbell Keegan Ltd., London, 1984
2. Swift, J. and English, J. *The Development of a Financial Panel and its Contribution to Financial Marketing*, Report of Annual Congress, ESOMAR, Amsterdam, 1983

Further Reading

The GEC Bid for AEI, J. Walter Thompson, London 1970

Kransdorff, A. 'How Spillers tried to win the war', *Financial Times*, 20 September 1982

Redwood, H. 'The Fisons Shareholder Survey', *Long-Range Planning*, April 1971

Worcester, R. M. and Hutton, P. F. 'Researching Shareholders Opinions', *Journal of General Management*, **8**, 2, Winter 1982/83

Chapter 23

1. Downham, J. S. 'Marketing Research in the Multi-National Corporations', *A.M.A. Conference*, USA, April 1972
2. Keegan, W. J. 'Five Strategies for Multi-National Marketing', *European Business*, January 1970
3. *International Marketing Research*, Report of ESOMAR Seminar, 1976
4. Aldridge, D. 'Highly Developed Research in Less Developed Countries', *ICC/ESOMAR Symposium on International Marketing Research*, Paris, 1984
5. Rohme, N. and Veldman, T. 'Harmonisation of Demographics', *Journal of the Market Research Society*, **25**, 1, January 1983 (previously an ESOMAR Congress paper)
6. Lovell, M. R. C. 'Examining the Multi-National Consumer', *ESOMAR Seminar on Developments in Consumer Psychology*, 1973
7. Berent, P. H. 'International Research is Different', *A.M.A. Conference*, USA, April 1975
8. Van der Reis, P. 'Problems in the Use of Rating Scales in Cross-cultural Research', *ICC/ESOMAR Symposium on International Marketing Research*, Paris, 1984
9. Hayes, P. J. 'The Cost Comparison of Market Research in Western Europe', *ICC/ESOMAR Symposium on International Marketing Research*, Paris, 1984
10. Sorensen, R. Z. and Wiechmann, U. E. 'How Multinationals View Marketing Standardisation', *Harvard Business Review*, May–June 1975
11. Hill, J. S. and Still, R. R. 'Adapting Products to LDC Tastes', *Harvard Business Review*, March–April 1984
12. Day, R. 'The Meaning of "Comparability" in Multi-Country Research and How to Achieve it', *ESOMAR Congress paper*, 1966
13. *International Marketing Research*, Supplement to the Market Research Society Newsletter, London, March 1976
14. Hibbert, E. P. 'Trade Intelligence Systems to Develop Exports', *International Marketing*, **1**, 3, 1982
15. Douglas, S. and Wind, Y. 'Environmental Factors and Marketing Practices', *European Journal of Marketing*, **7**, 3, 1973/4
16. Liander, B. (Ed.) *Comparative Analysis for International Marketing*, Marketing Science Institute, Boston, Allyn and Bacon, 1967
17. Whitley, E. W. 'Case History of a 16-Country Survey', *ESOMAR Seminar on Multi-Country Research*, 1971
18. *International Directory of Published Market Research*, British Overseas Trade Board, London, 1984
19. *Multi-Country Research*, Report of ESOMAR Seminar, 1971
20. Coleman, K. M. H. 'The Problem of International Pharmaceutical Marketing Research', *ESOMAR Seminar on Practice and Problems of International Pharmaceutical Research*, 1971
21. *International Marketing Research*, Report of ICC/ESOMAR Symposium, Paris, 1984
22. Mayer, C. S. 'Evaluating the Quality of Marketing Research Contractors', *Journal of Marketing Research*, May 1967
23. Marsh, C. *Guidelines for Commissioning an Interview Survey from a Research Company*, Survey Unit, Social Science Research Council, London, 1976

24. *Appraising Market Research Agencies*, Incorporated Society of British Advertisers, London, 1979

25. *The Market Research Society Yearbook* (contains a list of market research organizations and professional associations overseas, and also a guide to the commissioning of survey research), Market Research Society, London

26. *European Guide to Industrial Marketing Consultancy* (contains a section on the use and selection of consultants and a list of firms), Industrial Marketing Research Association, Lichfield, UK, 1983

27. *International Directory of Market Research Organisations*, Market Research Society and British Overseas Trade Board, London, 1985

28. *Marketing Research in Europe* (ESOMAR Yearbook). ESOMAR, Amsterdam

29. Douglas, S. P. and Craig, C. S. *International Marketing Research*, Prentice-Hall, New Jersey, 1983

30. *ICC/ESOMAR International Code of Marketing and Social Research Practice*, Paris and Amsterdam, 1986

31. De Jong, P. and Meyers, F. 'Some Reflections on the Measurement of Basic Attitudes in a Multi-Country Context', *ESOMAR Seminar on Multi-Country Research*, 1971

32. Barnard, P. 'Conducting and Co-ordinating Multi-country Quantitative Studies across Europe', *Journal of the Market Research Society*, **24**, 1, January 1982

33. ·*Guidelines: Reaching agreement on a marketing research project*, ICC/ESOMAR, Paris and Amsterdam, 1979

Further Reading

Downham, J. S. 'The European Market – how Common is Common?', *AMA Annual Marketing Conference*, USA, May 1982

Export Marketing Research Scheme (leaflet), British Overseas Trade Board, London, 1984

Linton, A. and Broadbent, S. 'International Life-Style Comparisons', *European Research*, March 1975

Loudon, D. L. 'The Influence of Environmental Variables on the Use of Marketing Research', *Management International Review* (Germany), **2/3**, 1975

Marketing Surveys Index. MSI and Institute of Marketing, London, 1984

Webster, L. 'Comparability in Multi-Country Surveys', *Esomar Congress*, 1965

Chapters 24–26: See Editor's Note on p. 801

Chapter 24

1. Ephron, E. H. 'Some Observations on Media Planning in the United States, *Admap*, **6**, 1, 1970

2. See, for example, 'National Savings Bank Investment Account "Save-by-post"', in Broadbent, Simon (Ed.) *Advertising Works*, Holt, Rinehart and Winston, London, 1983, vol. 2

3. Schyberger, Bo W:son. *Methods of Readership Research*, Department of Business Administration, University of Lund, Lund, 1964

4. Hess, Eva-Maria. *Leserschaftforschung in Deutschland. Ziele, Methoden, Techniken*, Burda, Offenburg, 1981

5. Landgrebe, Klaus *et al. Media Measurement and Media Choice: Ten Years of Progress... or Stagnation?* European Society for Opinion and Marketing Research, Amsterdam, 1980

6. (a) Henry, Harry (Ed.) *Readership Research: Theory and Practice*, Sigmatext, London, 1982
   (b) Henry, Harry (Ed.) *Readership Research: Montreal 1983*, Elsevier Science Publishers, Amsterdam, 1984
   (c) 3rd International Readership Research Symposium (Salzburg, 1985) – papers to be published during 1986

7. *Development Research for the 1968 National Readership Survey*, Joint Industry Committee for National Readership Surveys, London, 1968
8. Banik, Douglas. 'Magazine Audience Measurement in the United States – a Brief History and Review of Current Methods', in Henry, H. (Ed.) (ref. 6a)
9. 'Introduction, Comparisons with Other Data', in *Target Group Index*, British Market Research Bureau, London, 1969
10. De Hond, Maurice and Huzen, Walter, 'New Approach to Readership Surveys – the Media Scanner', in Henry, H. (Ed.) (ref. 6b)
11. Ryan, Michael, 'Telephone Interviewing can yield Better Readership Data than Personal Interviews', *Admap*, **17**, 1, 1981
12. Smith, H. A. 'The Use of Panels for the collection of Readership Data', in *The Thomson Medals and Awards for Media Research 1966*, The Thomson Organisation, London, 1967
    Agostini, J. M. The Possible Role of Readership Panels in Media Research and Media Planning', *ibid.*
    Joyce, T. and Bird, M. 'The Use of Panels for the Collection of Readership Data', *ibid.*
    Parfitt, J. H. 'The Use of Panels for the Collection of Readership and Other Data', *ibid.*
    Muller-Veeh, Dieter and Opfer, Gunda 'Study of the Reading Habits of Physicians: a Comparison between Diary and Interview', in *The challenge of the eighties*, Proceedings of the 32nd ESOMAR Congress, European Society for Opinion and Marketing Research, Amsterdam, 1979
    Ryan, Michael, 'Readership Panels: are they the Panacea for the Ills of the NRS, or will they just yield dry rot?', *Admap*, **18**, 3, 1982
    Buck, Stephan. 'Readership Panels: the Case for going ahead', *Admap*, **18**, 8, 1982
    Shepherd-Smith, Neil, 'Readership Panels: do the Practical Problems outweight the Theoretical Benefits?', *Admap*, **18**, 8, 1982
    Brown, Michael, 'Readership Panels: Roundabouts (and some Swings)', *Admap*, **18**, 8, 1982
    Parfitt, John 'Readership Panels: what work already done suggests', *Admap*, **18**, 8, 1982
    Ryan, Michael, A Medical Experiment with Readership Diaries', in Henry, H. (Ed.) (ref. 6a)
    Muller, Dieter, 'Media Quality Measurements in National Media Surveys', *ibid.*
    Buck, S. and Spackman, Nigel, 'The Potential Contribution of Readership Diary Panels', in Henry, H. (Ed.) (ref. 6b)
    Stocks, John, 'Comparison between Interview and Diary Data on Newspaper Readership', *ibid.*
13. De Koning, Coen C. J. 'Evidence from Panels in Readership', in Henry, H. (Ed.) (ref. 6a)
14. Langschmidt, Wally. *Reliability of Response in Readership Research*, SA Advertising Research Foundation, Johannesburg, 1978
    Denon, Liliana. 'The Effects of Changing the Filter', in Henry, H. (Ed.) (ref. 6a)
    Haukatsalo, Jean. 'Experiments with Filter Questions in Finland', *ibid.*
    Langhoff, Per. 'The effects of change of filters', in Henry, H. (Ed.) (ref. 6b)
15. Tennstädt, Friedrich and Noelle-Neumann, Elisabeth.'Experiments in the Measurement of Readership', *Journal of the Market Research Society* **21**, 4, 1979
    Tennstädt, Friedrich W. R. and Hansen, Jochen. 'Validating the Recency and Through-the-book Techniques', in Henry, H. (Ed.) (ref. 6a)
    Bennike Sigurd. 'The Danish Discs', *ibid.*
    Morgan, Roy 'How a Composite Method has overcome Telescoping, Prestige and Replication in Readership Research', in Henry, H. (Ed.) (ref. 6b)
    Tennstädt, Friedrich. 'Effects of Differing Methods on the Level of Magazine Readership Figures', *ibid.*
16. Tennstädt, Friedrich W. R. and Hansen, Jochen. *op. cit.*
    Withers, Hastings. 'Analysis of Readership Levels by Age of Issue', in Henry, H. (Ed.) (ref. 6b)
    Cornish, Pym and Brown, Michael. *Readership Measurement Reviewed. A Study of Development Options for the NRS*, Joint Industry Committee for National Readership Surveys, London, 1980

17. Tennstädt, Friedrich. *op. cit.*
18. Langschmidt, Wally. *Reliability of response in readership research, op. cit.*
    Aitchison, David. 'How Rotation Order affects Readership Figures', *Admap*, **17**, 1, 1981
    Tennstädt, Friedrich W. R. and Hansen, Jochen. *op. cit.*
    Whitley, Edward. 'Some Rotation Effects in the British Survey', in Henry, H. (Ed.) (ref. 6a)
    Ichac, Jean-Bernard. 'The Effect of Permutations in the Order of Presentations of Magazines', in Henry, H. (Ed.) (ref. 6b)
    Minter, Christopher. 'Rotation Effects in South East Asia', *ibid.*
19. Tennstädt, Friedrich and Noelle-Neumann, Elisabeth. *op. cit.*
20. Langschmidt, Wally. *Reliability of Response in Readership Research, op. cit.*
21. Hess, Eva-Maria and Scheler, Hans Erdmann. 'Multi-stage Experiments in Questionnaire Survey Methodology for Magazines in the AG. MA National Readership Survey: Findings and Consequences', in Henry, H. (Ed.) (ref. 6b)
22. Tennstädt, Friedrich W. R. and Hansen, Jochen. *op. cit.*
    Hess, Eva-Maria and Scheler, Hans Erdmann. *op. cit.*
    Tennstädt, Friedrich. *op. cit.*
23. Twyman, Tony and Worrall, Richard. 'Measurement of Average Issue Readership: JICMARS' Experimental Studies, *Admap*, **16**, 11, 1980
24. Appel, Valentine. 'Telescoping: the Skeleton in the Recent Reading Closet', in Henry, H. (Ed.) (ref. 6a)
25. Belson, W. A. *Studies in Readership*, Business Publications, London, 1962
    Belson, William, 'Measuring and then increasing the Accuracy of Britain's National Readership Survey: a Validation Project', in Henry, H. (Ed.) (ref. 6a)
26. Twyman, Tony and Worrall, Richard, *op. cit.*
    Twyman, W. A. 'A Comparison of Recency Average Issue Readership with Recognition Levels in the Medical Press', in Henry, H. (Ed.) (ref. 6a)
    Schiller, Clark, 'A Study of Overclaiming Readership using a Recent Reading Technique', *ibid.*
    Lysaker, Richard L. 'The ARF Certitude Tests', *ibid.*
    Joyce, Timothy, 'The Level of Magazine Reading', *ibid.*
    Stocks, John, 1984, *op. cit.*
27. Noelle-Neumann, E. Winning paper *The Roy Thomson Medals and Awards for Media Research*, The Thomson Organisation, London, 1962
28. Tennstädt, Friedrich W. R. and Hansen, Jochen. *op. cit.*
    Cornish, Pym. 'Replicated and parallel readership', in Henry, H. (Ed.) (ref. 6a)
    Shepherd-Smith, Neil. 'A Note on Replication and Recency', *ibid.*
    Morgan, Roy, *op. cit.*
29. *A New Measurement of Women's Magazines, Woman*, London, 1963
30. Joyce, Timothy. 'Readership Research: the Relationship between Recent Reading and Through-the-book (or, TTB = f(RR))', *Admap*, **18**, 2, 1982
    Tennstädt, Friedrich W. R. and Hansen, Jochen. *op. cit.*
    Clancy, Kevin J, Ostlund, Lyman E. and Wyner, Gordon A. 'False Reporting of Magazine Readership', *Journal of Advertising Research*, **19**, 5, 1979
    Marder, Eric. 'How Good is the Editorial Interest Method of Measuring Magazine Audiences?', *Journal of Advertising Research*, **7**, 1, 1967
    Lysaker, Richard L. *op. cit.*
    Joyce, Timothy. *op cit.*
31. Schreiber, Robert and Schiller, Clark. 'Electro-mechanical Devices for Recording Readership: a Report of a Development Project', in Henry, H. (Ed.) (ref. 6a)
32. Tennstädt, Friedrich W. R. *op. cit.*
    Douglas, Stephan and Lysaker, Richard. 'The Audience Levels produced by the "Claimed First Time Reading" Method', in Henry, H. (Ed.) (ref. 6b)

Eadie, Wayne and Lysaker, Richard. 'Developing a Magazine Readership Validating Technique', *ibid.*

De Hond, Maurice and Huzen, Walter, *op. cit.*

33. Smith, H. A. *et al.*, *op. cit.*

34. Greene, Jerome D. 'Reliability of Cumulative Magazine Audiences', *Journal of Advertising Research* **19**, 5, 1979

35. Tchaoussoglou, Costa J. and Van Vliet, Joop L. 'Frequency Scales and their Use', in Henry, H. (Ed.) (ref. 6a)

36. Meier, Erhard. *Summary of Current Readership Research. Survey Practices in 24 Countries*, Research Services, London, 1983

37. Corlett, T. *An Introduction to the Use and Interpretation of Reading Frequency Data*, Institute of Practitioners in Advertising, London, 1967

38. Müller-Veeh, Dieter and Opfer, Gunda. *op. cit.*

Tennstädt, W. R. and Hansen, Jochen, 1982, 'Frequency of Reading – Allensbach's Point of View', in Henry, H. (Ed.) (ref. 6a)

Denon, Liliana. 'A Comparison of Verbal and Numerical Frequency Scales', *ibid.*

Scheler, Hans-Erdmann, 'Frequency Scales in Germany', *ibid.*

Brown, Michael, 'Looking Back at UK Frequency Scale Development', *ibid.*

39. Mattison, Mark. 'Techniques for Developing Newspaper Audiences', *Journal of Advertising Research*, **22**, 2, 1982

Richard, Adam and Frankel, Martin. 'A Comparison of Reach and Frequency Estimates: Single Versus Dual Interview Approaches', in Henry, H. (Ed.) (ref. 6b)

40. Lucas, D. B. and Britt, S. H. 'Exposure of Advertisements', in *Measuring Advertising Effectiveness*, McGraw-Hill, New York, 1963

41. *Development Research for the 1968 National Readership Survey*, *op. cit.*

42. *Reader Categorisation Study: Indirect Measure of Exposures to Contents of Publications*, Joint Industry Committee for National Readership Surveys, London, 1972

43. Meier, Erhard. *op. cit.*

44. *Reading Intensity Scale: Interim Report on Calibration*, Joint Industry Committee for National Readership Surveys, London, 1970

45. Müller, Dieter. 'Media Quality Measurements in National Media Surveys' in Henry, H. (Ed.) (ref. 6a)

46. Quatresooz, Jean. 'Correlates of Advertising Impact in Newspapers and Magazines', *ibid.*

47. Noordhoff, J. D. *Ermittlung von Seitenkontakten – eine Dokumentation* (Arbeitsgemeinschaft Media-Analyse eV, Schriftenband 4) Media-Micro-Census, Frankfurt, 1976

48. *A Study of Printed Advertisement Rating Methods*, Advertising Research Foundation, New York, 1956

49. Fletcher, R. 'Reading Behaviour reconsidered', in *ESOMAR WAPOR Congress 1969*, European Society for Opinion and Marketing Research, Amsterdam 1969

50. Twyman, W. A. *The Measurement of Advertisement Page Exposure*, Agencies Research Consortium, London, 1972

51. Røhme, Nils *et al. Harmonisation of Demographics: an ESOMAR Committee report*, European Society for Opinion and Marketing Research, Amsterdam, 1984

52. *An Evaluation of Social Grade Validity*, Market Research Society, London, 1981

53. *Sagacity. A Special Analysis of 1981 NRS Data and MEAL Expenditure profiles*, Research Services, London, 1982

54. Bermingham, J., McDonald, C. and Baker, K. 'The Utility to Market Research of the Classification of Residential Neighbourhoods', in *Research for Action*, Proceedings of the 22nd Annual Conference, The Market Research Society, London, 1979

Baker, K. 'A Classification of Residential Neighbourhoods', *Admap*, **15**, 5, 1979

55. Cannon, Hugh M. and Linda, Gerald. 'Beyond Media Imperatives: Geodemographics Media Selection', *Journal of Advertising Research*, **22**, 3, 1982

56. Thomas, Judy. 'ACORN as an Alternative to Social Class in Identifying the *Observer* Reader', *Admap* **16,** 10, 1980

57. *The Target Group Index*, British Market Research Bureau, London, 1969

58. Hansen, Jochen. 'The Refinement of Multi-media Analyses – about Useful Criteria for Media Planning', in *Taking Stock: what have we learned and where are we going?*, Proceedings of the 33rd Congress, European Society for Opinion and Marketing Research, Amsterdam, 1980

Quatresooz, Jean. 'From Product Usage Data to a Description of the Readers in Lifestyle Terms', in Henry, H. (Ed.) (ref. 6a)

Jannacone, Constantino. 'Qualitative Data on Readership: Psychographics as a Marketing and Media Planning Tool', *ibid.*

Richard, Adam. 'VALS (Values and Lifestyle Segmentation), in Henry, H. (Ed.) (ref. 6b)

Munn, Mark. 'Life Styles of American Women and their Relationship to Magazine Reading', *ibid.*

59. *Markets and Media*, National Magazine Co., London, 1969

60. *A Qualitative Study of Regional Evening Newspapers*, Evening Newspaper Advertising Bureau, London, 1963

61. *'Qualitative Media Assessments'*, *TV Times*, London, 1967

62. Holland, Roger. 'Attitudes to Media', *Admap*, **14,** 11, 1978

63. *Publication Q*. Reader's Digest, London, 1972

64. Winick, C. 'Three Measures of the Advertising Value of Media Context', *Journal of Advertising Research*, **2,** 2, 1962

65. Broadbent, S. R. and Segnit, S. 'Beyond Cost per Thousand – an Examination of Media Weights', in *The Thomson Medals and Awards for Advertising Research 1968*, The Thomson Organisation, London, 1968

66. Joyce, Timothy. 'Attitude Research as a Measure of Media Values', *Admap*, **17,** 12, 1981

67. *'Page Traffic and Page Frequency of Three Leading Publications'*, *Radio Times*, London, 1965

68. *'Usage of Weekly Magazines'*, *TV Times*, London, 1974

69. Meier, Erhard, *op. cit.*

70. Assael, Henry and Cannon, Hugh, 'Do Demographics help in Media Selection?', *Journal of Advertising Research*, **19,** 6, 1979

71. Broadbent, S. R. 'Media Planning and Computers by 1970', in *The Thomson Medals and Awards for Media Research 1965*, The Thomson Organisation, London, 1966

Gensch, D. H. 'Computer Models in Advertising Media Selection', *Journal of Marketing Research*, **5,** 4, 1968

Brown, M. M. 'Media Selection Models Compared and Contrasted', *Admap*, **4**, 10, 1968

Media Research Group, 'Media Model Comparison', *Admap*, **5,** 3, 1969

Simon, Hermann and Thiel, Michael. 'Hits and Flops among German Media Models', *Journal of Advertising Research*, **20,** 6, 1980

Liebman, L., Makely, R. and Lee, E. 1982, 'A Multi-national Reach and Frequency Comparison', in Henry, H. (Ed.) (ref. 6a)

Thomas, Judy and Carpenter, Ron. 'A User View of Coverage Buildup, Ultimate Reach and Model Differences', *ibid.*

72. Broadbent, S. 'How to Approach the Computer', in *Spending Advertising Money*, Business Books, London, 1970

73. Jolson, Marvin A. 'How a Retailer compared Newspapers', *Journal of Advertising Research*, **19,** 6, 1979

Lynn, Jerry R. 'Newspaper Ad Impact in Nonmetropolitan Markets', *Journal of Advertising Research*, **21,** 4, 1981

74. Caffyn, J. 'Experimental Intermediate Studies', Market Research Society 12th Annual Conference, 1969

75. McDonald, C. D. P. 'Relationships between Advertising Exposure and Purchasing Behaviour', *ibid.*

76. 'A Major Advertiser Tests the Effectiveness of General Magazines and Television', *Admap*, **6,** 4, 1970
77. *A Study of the Effectiveness of Advertising Frequency in Magazines, Time Incorporated*, New York, 1982
78. See, for example, 'Advertising: Key to the Success of Kellogg's Super Noodles' (1983) in Broadbent, Simon (Ed.) *Advertising Works*, Holt, Rinehart and Winston, London, 1983, vol. 2
79. Wolfe, H. D., Brown, J. K., Clark Thompson, G. and Greenberg, H. *Evaluating Media* (Business policy Study No 121), National Industrial Conference Board, New York, 1966
80. Corkindale, David. 'A Manager's Guide to Measuring the Effects of Advertising', *Market Intelligence and Planning*, **1,** 2, 1983
81. Bird, Michael, 'Planning and Monitoring a Successful Magazine Launch', *European Research*, **8,** 3, 1980
82. Mooney, P. B. and Wicks, A. 'The Use of Market Research in the Launching of a New Evening Newspaper – a Case History', Market Research Society Annual Conference, 1966
    Bird, Michael, *op. cit.*
    Publishing a Better Product: Meeting the Needs of Readers and Advertisers, European Society for Opinion and Marketing Research, Amsterdam, 1983
83. Lighthart, Jan. 'Function Research within the Framework of Editorial Research for Regional Newspapers', *European Research*, **6,** 3, 1978
84. Constantine, Guy. 'Apples and Readership – for Publishers', in Henry, H. (Ed.) (ref. 6b)
85. Bush, C. F. (Ed.) *News Research for Better Newspapers*, Vols 1–4, American Newspaper Publisher Association Foundation, New York, 1966–69

Chapter 25

1. Ballington, G. (Ed.) 'The Computer comes to Media Buying', *Admap*, February 1975
2. IPA, *The Case for Integrating Media and Product Research*, Occasional Paper No. 19, 1967 and revision 1975
3. Agostini, J. M. 'The Marriage of Data from Various Surveys: An Expedient or a Unique Way to Make Progress?', *Admap*, October 1967
4. Buck, S. F. and Taylor, L. 'Consistency of Housewives ITV Viewing Intensity over Time', *Admap*, July/August 1970
5. Buck, S. F., Sherwood, R. and Twyman, W. A. *Panels and the Measurement of Change*, ESOMAR/WAPOR Congress, Montreux, 1975
6. Twyman, W. A. *Attention and the Measurement of Media Exposure for Press and Television*, ESOMAR Congress Proceedings, 1973
7. Twyman, W. A. *A Review of Research into Viewership of Television Advertising Breaks*, Institute of Practitioners in Advertising, London, 1971
8. ARF, *Electronic Test of In Home TV Viewing among those Families who Fail to Respond to the Doorbell*, Arrowhead Study No. 8, ARF 1968
9. TAM, *Comparison Survey of Audience Composition Techniques*, Television Audience Measurement, 1961
10. BMRB, *Television Presence Research*, Report to IPA/ISBA Presence Working Party, British Market Research Bureau, 1968 (see also earlier reports on Pilot Work)
11. Jictar/BMRB, *Television Audience Presence and Comparison with JICTAR Data*, JICTAR, London, March 1976
12. Contam, *How Good are Television Ratings?* (continued) CONTAM, 1969 (and ARF Conference, 1969)
13. London Press Exchange, *The Audience to Television Advertisements*, Research Services, 1961
14. TAM, *Two Studies in Housewife Attention During Commercial Breaks*, Television Audience Measurement, 1965

15. Twyman, W. A. *Techniques for Measuring Program vs Commercial Audiences*, ARF 15th Annual Conference, 1969 (see also IPA Forum No. 25, January 1969)
16. McCann-Erickson Ltd. *Television Audience Research: Presence and Attention Check*, London, September 1972
17. Ehrenberg, A. S. C. 'A Comparison of TV Audience Measures', *Journal of Advertising Research*, **4**, 4, 1964
18. Simmons, W. R. *Evaluating Television Measurement Systems*, ARF 14th Annual Conference, 1968
19. Consterdine, G. 'Amps TV Diaries', *Admap*, February 1968
20. London Weekend Television, *Viewing and Reading: Multi Media Audience Measurement Study*, London, March/November 1973
21. RKO General Broadcasting, *1967–8 Television Research Manual*, RKO, 1967
22. Mayer, M. *How Good are Television Ratings?* CONTAM, 1966
23. Ehrenberg, A. S. C. 'Surprise at Poly Channel', *Admap*, December 1966
24. Twyman, W. A. *Research into Methods of Measuring Television Audiences and Data Requirements for the British Television Advertising Industry*, ESOMAR 1969
25. JWT, *Television Viewing Diaries*, British Market Research Bureau, 1967 (see also Television Attention Research Reports, 1961–66)
26. Lintas, *Television in the Family Setting*, Research Bureau, 1962
27. Steiner, G. A. 'The People Look at Commercials', *Journal of Business*, **39**, 2, 1963 (and also *The People Look at Television*, Knopf, 1963)
28. Television Advertising Representatives, *Observiewing*, 1965
29. CBS, *Taking the Measure of Two Media*, CBS Television Network, 1962
30. Ted Bates Ltd, *The Ted Bates Viewing Study*, Ted Bates Ltd, London, Winter 1983/84
31. Collett, P. Video-recording the Viewers in their Natural Habitat, ESOMAR Seminar, 'New Developments in Media Research', Helsinki, April 1986
32. Stuart, A. *Reports to JICTAR* (unpublished) 1964
33. BBM Bureau of Measurement, *Quality Control Test*, BBM Toronto, April 1973
34. BBM Bureau of Measurement, *A Review of the 1974–5 Research Programme*, BBM Toronto, June 1975
35. BARB, *Proceedings of BARB '84 Seminar*, Broadcasters Audience Research Board, London 1984
36. Bermingham, J. and Liepelt, K. *Audience Composition Meters with Personal Push-Buttons – A Validation Study*, ESOMAR Seminar, 'Improving Media Research', Stockholm, April 1982
37. Teleskopie, *Summarising Reports and Analysis of Continuous Audience Research*, Allensbach/ Infas, December 1975
38. Pfifferling, J. *TV Audience Data Check-up – Research Instruments and Results in Comparison*, ESOMAR Seminar, 'Improving Media Research', Stockholm, April 1982
39. Cordell, W. N. and Rahmel, H. A. 'Are Nielsen Ratings Affected by Non-Co-operation, Conditioning or Response Error?', *Journal of Advertising Research*, **2**, 3, 1962
40. Joyce, T. 'Examples of Experimental Work with Media Panels', *Admap*, September 1967
41. Harvey, B. 'Non-Response in TV Meter Panels', *Journal of Advertising Research*, **8**, 1968
42. Stuart, A. *Sampling in Television Research*, ATV Technical Research Study, Associated Television, 1960
43. Silvey, R. and Emmett, B. 'What Makes Television Viewers Choose?', *New Society*, **24**, 14th March 1963
44. American Research Bureau, *Arbitron Replication: A Study of the Reliability of Broadcast Ratings*, ARB New York, 1974
45. Ehrenberg, A. S. C. and Goodhart, G. J. 'Attitudes to Episodes and Programmes', *Journal of the Market Research Society*, **23**, 189–208, 1982
46. Frost, W. A. K. 'The Development of a Technique for the Programme Assessment', *Journal of the Market Research Society*, **11**, 1, 1969
47. Kirsch, A. D. and Banks, S. 'Program Types Defined by Factor Analysis', *Journal of Advertising Research*, **2**, 3, 1962

48. Rothman, J. and Rauta, I. 'Towards a Typology of the Television Audience', *Journal of the Market Research Society*, **11,** 1, 1969
49. Institute of Practitioners in Advertising, *Attitudes Towards Advertising*, IPA, London, May 1975
50. Brown, M. M. 'Attitudes to Programmes and the Effect of Commercials', *Admap*, January 1967
51. Bogart, L. *Strategy in Advertising*, Harcourt Brace and World, 1967
52. Corlett, T. and Richardson, D. 'TV Attention – A Further Step', *Admap*, September 1970
53. Twyman, W. A. *Setting Television Advertising in Context*, ESOMAR Seminar, 'Beyond Vehicle Audiences', Budapest, March 1976
54. Krugman, H. E. *Processes Underlying Exposure to Advertising*, ARF 14th Annual Conference, 1968
55. Bunn, D. W. 'Audience Presence during Breaks in Television Programmes', *Journal of Advertising Research*, **22,** 5, October/November 1982
56. Ehrenberg, A. S. C. and Goodhart, G. J. 'Practical Applications of the Duplication of Viewing Law', *Journal of the Market Research Society*, **11,** 1, 1969
57. Goodhart, G. J. 'Constant in Duplicated Television Viewing', *Nature*, **212,** 1616, 1966
58. Goodhart, G. J., Ehrenberg, A. S. C. and Collins, M. A. *The Television Audience: Patterns of Viewing*, Saxon House, Lexington Books, Farnborough, England, 1975
59. Piepe, A., Emerson, M. and Cannon, J. *Television and the Working Class*, Saxon House, Lexington Books, Farnborough, England, 1975
60. Ehrenberg, A. S. C. and Twyman, W. A. 'On Measuring Television Audiences', *Journal of the Royal Statistical Society*, Series **A** (General), 130, 1967
61. Twyman, W. A. *The Prediction of Frequency Patterns*, An Experiment for JICTAR carried out by the Media Circle, 1967
62. Hulks, R. and Thomas, S. *An International Model for the Prediction of Television Coverage and Frequency Distributions – The Key to the Medium?* ESOMAR/WAPOR Congress, Budapest, 1973
63. Broadbent, S. *Spending Advertising Money*, 3rd Edition, Business Books, 1975
64. O'Herlihy, C. 'Current practice in media planning and how to improve', *Admap*, October 1983
65. Bloom, A. and Twyman, T. 'The Impact of Economic Change on the Evaluation of Advertising Campaigns', *Journal of the Market Research Society*, **20,** 2, 1978
66. Haskins, J. *How to Evaluate Mass Communications*, ARF Monograph, 1968
67. Adler, J. and Kuehn, A. A. *How Advertising works in Market Experiments*, ARF 15th Annual Conference, 1969
68. Corkindale, David R. 'Measuring the Sales Effectiveness of Advertising: The Role of an ADLAB in the UK', *Journal of the Market Research Society*, **26,** 1 29–50, 1984
69. Eskin, G. J. *The Behavior Scan System: an Application of New Techologies*, ESOMAR Congress, Rome, 1984
70. Juchems, A. and Twyman, W. A. *The Measurement of Advertising Awareness and its Applications*, 24th Market Research Society Conference, 1–18, 1981
71. Twyman, W. A. *Estimating Advertisement Exposure for Broadcast Media*, ESOMAR Seminar on 'Broadcasting and Research', Windsor, 1985

Chapter 26

Radio (with acknowledgement to A Higgs, RSGB)

1. Westinghouse Broadcasting Corporation, *Radio's New Math*
2. Radio Luxembourg Audience Panel, November 1968

3. Twyman, W. A. 'The State of Radio Research', *Admap*, August 1976
4. Television Audience Measurement Limited, *Comparison Surveys*, 1963
5. American Research Bureau/RKO General Broadcasting, *The Individual Diary Method of Radio Audience Measurement*, February 1965
6. ARMS, *All Radio Methodology Study*, 1967
7. BBM, *Tests of Revised and Single Media Diaries*, February 1974
8. Radio Advertising Representatives, *Polyphase: Radio Listening and the Problems of its Measurement*
9. JICRAR, *Radio Audience Surveys*, AIRC
10. Bloom, D. *Radio: Problems in Measuring an Invisible Medium*, Marker Research Society Conference, 1984

Posters (with acknowledgement to J. Jeffcott, McNair Anderson Associates Pty, Sydney)

11. Copland, B. D. *A Review of Poster Research*, Business Publications Ltd., 1963
12. Copland, B. D. *The Size and Nature of the Poster Audience Study II*, Mills & Rockley, 1955
13. Copland, B. D. *Transport Advertising Research*, Institute of Practitioners in Advertising, 1964
14. Copland, B. D. *London Travel Survey 1949*, London Transport Executive, 1950
15. Copland, B. D. *La Audience della Pubblicità Esterna Sui Meggi di Trasporto Pubblici*, Impressa Generale Pubblicità, 1968
16. McDonald, C. D. P. 'The Poster Model is Alive and Could be Better', *Admap*, March 1981
17. Research Services Ltd., *London and Leeds Poster Study for Gallaher Ltd and Advertising Agency Poster Bureau*, 1974
18. Research Services Ltd, *British Posters Traffic Study*, 1974

Cinema

19. Gray, S. *Simulation of Cinema Going Habits*, Computer Projects Ltd, 1969 (unpublished)
    See also:
    The Cinema Audience: Duplication of Media Survey, Screen Advertising Association, 1964
    The Cinema Audience: A National Survey, Screen Advertising Association, 1961

Editors' Note on Chapters 24–26

New developments, and the publication of fresh papers on the subject, are a constant and important feature of the media research field. These Chapters were fully up-to-date at the time of revision, but the reader is therefore strongly recommended to keep in touch with subsequent continuing developments reported (for print media research) at events such as the third International Readership Research Symposium – see ref. 6(c) of Chapter 24; and for television and radio research, new services and systems on offer as reported in the relevant professional journals and trade papers.

Biographies of contributors

PETER ARNOLD is currently Managing Director of Nova Research Limited, an *ad hoc* research arm of AIDCOM International plc. He started in market research with Mobil Oil UK before moving on to Research Surveys of Great Britain to become a supplier of research services. He subsequently joined MIL Research where his involvement in telephone research started in the late 1970s and has continued unabated through the last nine years of his market research career. He later became a Director of Business Decisions (another member of AIDCOM International) and in 1983 set up its subsidiary Telephone Research Ltd (of which company he is also a director).

CHRIS BLAMIRES is Managing Director of A.I.M. Market Research Ltd. and a partner in the Decision Modelling Consultancy, a specialist organization working solely in the field of Consumer Modelling. He entered research by joining the Co-operative Wholesale Society Market Research Department in 1973, after graduating from York University with a degree in economics and statistics. Following various posts in the research department, including responsibility for product testing, corporate and advertising research and various monitoring studies, he left in 1983 to set up A.I.M. Market Research Ltd. He is the author of several papers, including *Pricing Research Techniques* for which he was awarded the Market Research Society Silver Medal in 1982, and co-author of *Micro-Behavioural Modelling as an Aid to Retailer Strategic Planning*, a paper which won the award for Best MRS Conference Paper in 1981. He is currently Chairman of the Northern Branch of the Market Research Society, and a frequent speaker at MRS Conferences and seminars.

MICHAEL BROWN is the Technical Director of the South African Advertising Research Foundation. He obtained a BA degree from the University of Cambridge in natural sciences and economics. In 1954 he entered advertising, initially as an account executive, and then moved to the marketing and research side. He joined Lintas Ltd. in 1959 as Head of Media Research. In 1962 he moved to Research Bureau Ltd. (the Unilever market research company). In 1963/4 he was attached to the Research Department of Sullivan, Stauffer, Colwell and Bayles, New York, and then returned to RBL as Technical Manager, with responsibility for basic research in the advertising and product areas within an international programme. In 1968 he joined the Newspaper Publishers Association and was later appointed their Head of Marketing, before leaving to start his own business in 1971 as an independent marketing research consultant. He was first Technical Director and later Technical Consultant to the Joint Industry Committee for National Readership Surveys, between 1968, when JICNARS was founded, and his leaving the UK in 1983.

DAVID CHITTENDEN is Chairman and Managing Director of Hanover Marketing Services Limited, an independent consultancy set up in 1984 to undertake the design, control and interpretation of its clients' marketing research projects and programmes. After obtaining an honours degree in social anthropology at Cambridge, he became a research and marketing executive at Ogilvy and Mather, London, moving subsequently to research management positions at Ford of Europe, Attwood Statistics (Director, Surveys Division) and Marplan, London (Director). He was Managing Director of a UK research agency (Packaging and Perceptual Research Limited) from 1971 to 1976, when it merged with Business Decisions Limited, which in turn was acquired by AIDCOM International plc in 1980. He resigned from the Boards of Business Decisions Limited and AIDCOM Research Limited in May 1984 to set up his present company.

MARTIN COLLINS is Director of the Survey Methods Centre at Social and Community Planning Research and Visiting Professor of Market Research at the City University Business School. He also works as a consultant, mainly with Aske Research Ltd. He was formerly a director of that company and of Research Services Ltd. He was elected Chairman of the Market Research Society for 1985–6.

RICHARD DAVIES is Head of Market Research at Van den Bergh & Jurgens Ltd., the Edible Fats subsidiary of Unilever. After graduating from Southampton University with a degree in economics, he joined Nestlé, working as a Research Executive in their Market Research Department. As Nestlé conduct all their own market research, this provided a very broad based training in all aspects of market research, from fieldwork administration and control through to data interpretation and marketing implementation. In 1977 he joined Lever Brothers as Fabrics Market Research Manager, responsible for all market research on that company's washing powder brands. In 1982 he joined Van den Bergh as Head of Market Research, responsible for all aspects of market research within that company.

JOHN DAVIS is a member of the Senior Faculty at Henley: The Management College. Before joining the College in 1975 he had worked with Gillette, British Overseas Airways, the Attwood Group, the British Market Research Bureau and the J. Walter Thompson Company. He is a Fellow of the Marketing Society and of the Institute of Statisticians, and a Member of the Market Research Society. He is the author of *Experimental Marketing* and numerous papers, and was awarded the Gold Medal of the Market Research Society for his work on test marketing.

JOHN DOWNHAM is Head of Market Research, Marketing Division in Unilever where he is concerned with Unilever's development and application of market research facilities and methods worldwide. After graduating in philosophy, politics and economics at Oxford he joined the British Market Research Bureau as a research officer, becoming Managing Director in 1960. He joined Unilever at the end of 1963. He was a Council member of the UK Market Research Society from 1956 until 1962 and served as Chairman in 1959–60. A Council member of the European Society for Opinion and Marketing Research (ESOMAR) for six years, he is currently Chairman of its Committee on Professional Ethics and Standards. In this capacity he was a member of an ICC/ESOMAR Joint Working Party responsible for preparing a new revised International Code of Marketing and Social Research Practice in 1976–77, and for subsequently updating this. He is a former Vice-Chairman of the Institute of Statisticians, and currently a Council member and Chairman of the Membership Committee. He also belongs to the World Association for Public Opinion Research (WAPOR). In addition to papers at conferences and courses in a wide range of countries he has written many articles on market research and is author of *The Communication of Ideas*.

JOHN DRAKEFORD, after graduating in classics at Cambridge University, spent two years in accountancy before joining the Research Department of the leading advertising agency, Mather and Crowther Ltd. in 1957, where he was Research Manager from 1960–63. He then joined AGB Research, specializing in *ad hoc* surveys. He was a Director of Audits of Great Britain Ltd. and then of RSGB Ltd., responsible for a wide variety of *ad hoc* research projects, conducted on behalf of manufacturers, retailers, advertising agencies, media owners, central and local government and nationalized industries. He left the AGB group in 1974 to set up his own research company, Drakeford Survey Research Ltd., which is a member of the Association of British Market Research Companies (ABMRC). John Drakeford is a full member of the Market Research Society and has a particular interest in training courses for research. He has lectured widely on research topics both in the UK and in Europe, and also holds the Diploma of the Institute of Practitioners in Advertising.

LEONARD ENGLAND is now retired although a Research Associate at the London Business School. In 1969 he formed his own company, England Grosse and Associates Ltd., after being Managing Director of Mass-Observation Ltd. for twenty years. He began his market research career at this company where he was trained in many of the techniques described in his chapter. He has been Chairman of both the Market Research Society and of the Association of Market Survey Organisations. Among his main research interests are the need to maximize the use of market research techniques in fields such as social welfare, and to improve effective communication of results to management.

VALERIE FARBRIDGE first became involved with survey research when she joined Research Bureau Limited and worked as an interviewer on a wide range of surveys that took her to all parts of Great Britain. Since then she has had long and continuing roles in both the practice of questionnaire design and field management and the broader public-face issues of the industry. As practitioner, she is the Director of Fieldwork at NOP Market Research Limited, in which capacity she is responsible for one of the largest fieldforces in the UK. More broadly, she is currently a Vice-President of the Market Research Society of Great Britain, having been the Society's Chairman between 1981 and 1983 and served previously on the Society's Professional Standards and Public Relations Committees. In these offices she was largely responsible for the introduction of the Interviewer Card Scheme into the industry, and was a founder-member of the Field Managers' Study Group, whose objectives are the education of field staff and the raising and maintenance of fieldwork standards. In both her company and industry activities she has been a frequent speaker to specialist research audiences at home and abroad, and to the general public via the broadcast media.

COLIN GREENHALGH took a BA with honours in mathematics at Jesus College, Oxford, and started his market research career in 1955 with the British Market Research Bureau. He then moved to Tyne Tees Television where he was responsible for introducing the market research services supplied to advertisers who were test marketing in that region, and subsequently to the Research Bureau (Unilever) with a considerable product testing commitment. In 1963 he joined the Phillips Scott & Turner Company (now Sterling Health) as manager of their market research department. Later he became Management Services Controller of that company and had new product development responsibilities in Phillips Laboratories, its proprietary medicines division. He joined Taylor, Nelson & Associates as a Director in 1969, but in 1974 established his own company, Product Testing Research, to specialize in research of that type. He has frequently presented papers on product testing, new product development and other topics to market research courses and conferences in the UK and Europe. He is a former Council Member of the Market Research Society, and winner of the Society's Gold Medal both in 1968 and in 1973.

PAUL HARRIS is the Chief Statistician of NOP Market Research Ltd. He was formerly with the market research department of the Electricity Council and before that with the planning department of the Central Electricity Generating Board. He studied statistics at the Regent Street Polytechnic (now the Polytechnic of Central London) and is a fellow of the Institute of Statisticians. His interests include the application of multi-variate statistical methods to market research data, and the use of computers in statistical analysis, subjects on which he has given lectures for The Market Research Society. In 1978 he was awarded the Society's silver medal for a paper on the effects of clustering on random sample surveys.

CLIFF HOLMES is Managing Director of NOW Research, a member of the Gordon Simmons Research Group. After a period of five years in industry, he began his market research career with Marplan as a statistician. In 1967 he joined Research Services Ltd. as Head of Sampling and Statistics. He returned to Marplan in 1972 where he became Deputy Managing Director. He was with Business Decisions from 1981 to 1985 as Board Director and headed up a Research Division. Mr Holmes qualified with honours as a Member of the Institute of Statisticians and he has served on the Examining Board of the Institute. He has been a frequent lecturer for the Market Research Society, where he is a Member of Council, and convenor of the Society's residential course on Sampling and Statistics.

MARK LOVELL has been President of Groupe Innova Inc., of Montreal Canada, since it was founded. His research experience began in England when he joined the British Market Research Bureau in 1959. He occupied a number of senior board-level research posts in the UK, and from 1970 to 1975 was Research Director at Leo Burnett Ltd. In 1975 he moved to Canada to become Vice-President of the Creative Research Group Ltd. in Toronto, of which he is currently a Board Member, before setting up Groupe Innova. His background is psychology and he has published several books on children and child psychology and on parents. Among his recent books are *Saturday Parent* (under the pen name Peter Rowlands), now published in six languages, and *Love Me, Love My Kids* recently published in New York. Earlier he was joint author of *Assessing the Effectiveness of Advertising*, and the winner of three Thomson Awards for Advertising and Media Research (the Silver Medal in 1966 and Gold Medal in 1967 and 1968).

TONY LUNN is Executive Chairman of Advanced Behavioural Research (ABR) Limited, which he founded in 1985 along with four senior colleagues. His experience in marketing research includes 11 years as Executive Director of Research Bureau (Research International) Ltd, a Unilever subsidiary, and also six years as a Director of Cooper Research and Marketing Limited. His professional expertise includes market segmentation, attitude research (both qualitative and quantitative) and market modelling. He has published extensively in these areas, and has given papers on them in the UK, Europe and the USA. He is currently a Vice President of the Market Research Society and was Chairman of the Society during 1983–84. He won the MRS Coglan Award in 1979, the Society's Gold Medal in 1979 and the award for the best paper at the ESOMAR Annual Conference in 1984. He holds degrees in psychology at St John's College Oxford and Birkbeck College, London.

JEAN MORTON-WILLIAMS joined Social and Community Planning Research in 1970, an institute specializing in surveys for government departments, local government, universities and other bodies involved in social and policy research. After nine years as a research director concerned mainly with attitude and health research, she became Field Director and also Assistant Director of the SCPR Survey Methods Centre. She is a psychologist with a BA (Hons) from London University and a postgraduate diploma in occupational psychology. She came into survey research via the BBC Audience Research Department where she worked with Dr W. A. Belson on studies of the comprehensibility of programmes and of the effects of programmes on attitudes and knowledge. She joined McCann-Erickson Research Department under Harry Henry in 1957, became a Director of Marplan on its foundation in 1959 and, later, Assistant Managing Director. She moved to Market Investigations Ltd. in 1966 as Director in charge of psychological research where she was involved in several large-scale government attitude studies as well as commercial surveys. She has been a frequent speaker at Market Research Society weekend courses and winter and summer schools on motivation research and attitude measurement and has organized weekend courses on psychological methods, questionnaire design and qualitative research. She has also lectured extensively on various aspects of survey research.

NIGEL NEWSON-SMITH is Director of the Broadcasters' Audience Research Board. After taking a degree in theology and a post-graduate diploma in social science at Oxford, he began his research career with a spell as an interviewer with the Gallup Poll in 1958. He joined Nestlé in 1959 as a research assistant, later moving to Mather & Crowther (now O & M) as a research and marketing executive. His next job was as Market Research Manager at J. Lyons from where he moved to Imperial Group plc, first as Market Research Coordinator of Imperial Foods, then as Commercial Research Manager and finally as Group Planning Coordinator at the Group HQ. He is Past Chairman of AURA and of the ISBA Research Committee and Chairman of the Advertising Association's Research Committee, and has convened and lectured at MRS and IMRA courses. He is the author of several articles on market research and a member of the MRS.

JOHN PARFITT CBE graduated at LSE with a BSc (Econ) first class and entered Unilever as a Management Trainee in 1952, joining Market Research Division and later becoming Manager of the TV Research department. Subsequently Managing Director of Attwood Statistics in charge of the British and European Panel operations, and then Chairman/Managing Director of Mass Observation, he currently has his own research consultancy (John Parfitt and Associates) and is Managing Director of Market Potentials Ltd, a company specializing in short-term panel operations and share prediction (pre- and post-launch). He was Chairman of the Market Research Society in 1970. He has published a number of papers on panels both in America and Europe.

BRIAN PYMONT is a Director of Research Bureau (Research International) Ltd. He joined Unilever in 1957 as a management trainee and after experience in a marketing company joined RBL in 1963. After working on the general consumer research side he took responsibility in 1971 for all RBL's continuous research, which subsequently was formed into a separate subsidiary as RBL Forecast. Prominent among the RBL Forecast services is a range of regular distribution, prices and features checks, complemented by an *ad hoc* Retail Studies Unit providing detailed diagnostic information on a wide range of retailing issues. He has also made a speciality of test marketing research, involving the creation of a mini-test market technique aimed at the quantification of new product potential prior to actual launch into a test market. The technique employs a self-contained retail grocery operation, which adds another dimension to his experience of retailing.

JAMES ROTHMAN is an independent marketing and research consultant and holds a Cambridge MA degree in natural sciences (Part I) and economics (Part II). After starting his career in the electronics industry he entered market research as an executive with BMRB, where he was subsequently appointed a Group Head. He next became Chairman of Sales Research Services, and following the sale of that company to the Taylor Nelson Group he combined the functions of Joint Managing Director of Taylor Nelson Investment Services and Technical Director of Taylor Nelson & Associates. His main work interests now are media, social, economic and financial research and European comparative studies. He also acts as a consultant on survey re-analysis and the efficient design of complex research projects and provides a second opinion on research studies. He is the Director of JICNARS (the Joint Industry Committee responsible for the National Readership Survey) and a Visiting Research Fellow at Lancaster University. He has received the Coglan Award, the Thomson Gold Medal and Award for Media Research, and the Market Research Society Gold Medal. He is an external examiner at Surrey University and Joint Editor of the Journal of the Market Research Society.

GEOFFREY ROUGHTON is an Executive Director of AIDCOM International plc where he is responsible for their market research interests. He is a graduate of Trinity College, Cambridge, where he studied the unusual combination of engineering and English literature. His first job was as a trainee with the publishers, George Newnes Ltd. In 1956 he joined the Attwood Group of Companies as a Client Service Executive. He became a marketing consultant for a short time in 1958 before founding MAS Survey Research Ltd, of which he remained head until it was acquired by AIDCOM in 1982. He is a member of the Market Research Society and the Royal Statistical Society. He has been a Council member of the Association of Market Research Organisations. He has been active in British market research data processing for many years as well as speaking on courses and seminars on the subject.

PETER SAMPSON is Technical Director of The Burke Research Services Group, London and a member of the Euro-Burke Technical Development Committee, responsible for overseeing the technical standards of Burke Companies throughout Europe and implementing new research techniques. He graduated from the University of Exeter in 1959 with a degree in social science and entered market research straight away. He worked in the research departments of a number of leading advertising agencies and passed the professional examination of the Institute of Practitioners in Advertising with Distinction, before joining NOP in 1966 to establish a Research Division that included its Qualitative Research Unit. A founder director of Burke Marketing Research Limited in the UK, he has lectured on market research and psychology for the Market Research Society and for many years was a a part-time tutor in psychology for the University of London Extra-Mural Department. He has published over 60 papers on market research topics, covering consumer psychology from both qualitative and quantitative standpoints, and given papers at conferences throughout the world.

WILLIAM SCHLACKMAN received his education in psychology at Brooklyn College, the City College and New York University. Prior to his work in market research he was a clinical psychologist working in the area of personnel selection. This was followed by a period of freelance psychology in the area of motivational research. In 1956 he joined the Dichter organization. Between 1960 and 1962 he was Managing Director of Ernest Dichter Associates in London. He founded William Schlackman Ltd. in 1963.

DAVID SEAMAN is currently Planning and Research Manager Retail Planning Group, of the Cooperative Wholesale Society. He has worked for the Society for sixteen years in various research, marketing and information capacities. He has spoken and contributed to various Market Research Society conferences and courses, and was a co-author of *Micro Behavioural Modelling as an Aid to Retailer Strategic Planning*, awarded the title of the

Best Paper of the 1981 MRS Conference. Additionally he is a member of the MRS Diploma Examination Board and serves on the Northern MRS Organizing Committee. He holds a Diploma in Business Administration from the Manchester Business School.

MARTIN SIMMONS, co-founder of the Gordon Simmons Research Group in 1969, is Chairman of GSR's consumer and trade research companies. He has been involved with research agency management since the 1950s and is a leading authority within the industry, having frequently presented papers at Market Research Society and ESOMAR meetings. He has served on the Market Research Society's Council and is a Fellow of the Royal Statistical Society. He graduated from the London School of Economics with an honours degree in statistics.

ROGER STUBBS is Deputy Managing Director of MORI. A graduate in mathematics, economics and statistics from the University of Birmingham, he was head of the Statistics Section of the National Westminster Bank until 1972. Since then he has been with MORI, on the board since 1975, and is responsible for most of MORI's work in the financial relations field. A member of ESOMAR and a full member of the MRS, he is a frequent speaker and writer on financial and other research topics.

JOHN SWIFT is a graduate of the London School of Economics and has had a varied career on both the client and agency sides of the market research industry. Trained at Thomas Hedley (now Procter & Gamble) he subsequently worked in a research function in an advertising agency (London Press Exchange), a consumer goods manufacturer (Morphy Richards), an industrial and commercial consultancy (Metra Consulting Group) and a research agency (Market & Opinion Research International). He joined Lloyds Bank in 1972 to set up the research function in the Bank. This now highly developed activity he continues to lead.

FRANK TEER is a director of AGB Research plc in London. From 1977 until 1984 he was resident in Australia, and for most of that time was Joint Managing Director of McNair Anderson Associates, Australia's largest market research operation. From 1972 until 1977, he was Managing Director of Research Surveys of Great Britain Ltd, and previously, for 6 years, was Joint Managing Director of NOP Market Research. A graduate of the London School of Economics, he has lectured and broadcast on market research and opinion polling and is joint author with J. D. Spence of *Political Opinion Polls* and a contributor to *Political Opinion Polling* (edited by R. M. Worcester). He is a past Chairman of the Market Research Society, a fellow of the Royal Statistical Society, and a member of the European Society for Opinion and Marketing Research and the World Association for Public Opinion Research.

TONY TWYMAN is Joint Managing Director of RBL (Research International) Ltd. He was formerly a director of TAM and taught experimental psychology at Birkbeck College, London. Apart from his wide experience of *ad hoc* marketing and social research surveys he has for some years been responsible for a programme of basic methodological research. He has also been extensively involved with the problems of media research, internationally as well as in the UK, including acting as media research consultant to a number of bodies such as JICTAR (on television), the Association of Independent Radio Companies, and the Joint Industry Committee of Medical Advertisers for Readership Surveys. He has spoken and written internationally on many aspects of advertising and media research, as well as on other research topics.

GILL WELCH joined Research Bureau Ltd in 1973, after graduating from the University of Newcastle-upon-Tyne with honours in psychology. In 1975 she joined Unilever's Research Laboratory in Port Sunlight where she controlled a number of projects of basic consumer research in order to guide the Laboratory's main research and development work. Rejoining RBL in 1977 she has worked in a number of research areas. Since 1981 she has headed the Retail Studies Unit within RBL, conducting research both within and for a variety of trade sectors. She has been involved with a series of publications about grocery retailing, including the major study *Grocery Retailing – the next five years*, and has presented a number of papers at trade seminars and market research conferences.

ROBERT M. WORCESTER is Chairman and Managing Director of Market & Opinion Research International (MORI). Prior to his London appointment nearly two decades ago he was with Opinion Research Corporation, Princeton, New Jersey, USA. He was also Chairman of the Board of Market Insights, a Vice-President and Director of E.L. Reilly Co. Inc., and Director of Market Dynamics Inc., ORC subsidiaries. Prior to that he was a consultant with McKinsey & Company. He is Past President of the World Association for Public Opinion Research (WAPOR), and is a member of the European Society for Opinion and Marketing Research (ESOMAR), the Market Research Society of Great Britain and the British Institute of Management. A graduate of the University of Kansas, he has contributed papers to ESOMAR, WAPOR, and the Market Research Society Conferences and articles to a number of journals. He is co-Editor of *Consumer Market Research Handbook; Political Communications; Public Opinions, Private Polls; Strategic Research for Management Decision Making*; and is Editor of *Political Opinion Polling: An International Review*. He has lectured widely and in many countries on topics relating to opinion and attitude research. He writes a monthly column on 'Findings on Public Opinion Research' for *The Times* and serves as a consultant to *The Times, Sunday Times*, and *Economist Newspapers* and to the Leader of the Labour Party of Great Britain.

ICC/ESOMAR International Code of Marketing and Social Research Practice

International Chamber of Commerce and European Society for Opinion and Marketing Research

Market (and social) research has for more than 25 years been regulated by various voluntary Codes of Practice. These have been extended and elaborated over time as the techniques and practices of research have become more complex. Their primary objective is to help ensure that the rights of the public, particularly as respondents, are adequately protected, and also that the interests of both research agencies and their clients are mutually respected.

International Codes have existed since 1948, that prepared by the European Society for Opinion and Marketing Research being the first of its kind. In 1977 this and the Code of the International Chamber of Commerce were combined into a new joint International Code, a revised edition of which was published in 1986. This is reprinted here by permission of the two bodies involved. It is now the sole Code regulating research *internationally*, and has in addition been adopted by an increasing number of countries as their local national Code of Practice.

There are also certain Codes drawn up by national bodies, of which that prepared by the UK Market Research Society is the most extensive. The latter is in fact fully compatible with the International Code, although it covers a few additional aspects of research activities.

In carrying out research studies researchers must conform to the International Code, as well as (where relevant) any extra provisions of local Codes or national legislation. Good research is therefore not just a question of an intelligent approach to problem solving, and the creative application of sound techniques: it must also follow the high standards of professional and ethical practice exemplified by this Code.

FOREWORD

For many years the ICC and ESOMAR have promoted the application by all sectors concerned of rules reflecting a high level of ethics in marketing and opinion research.

The code of ethics set out in this publication drawn up jointly by the ICC and ESOMAR reflects the conviction common to both organizations that professional self-regulation can safeguard the legitimate interests of the community, while at the same time assuring the harmonious development of relations among the sectors directly involved. The Code is amended from time to time as necessary in order to reflect the changing environment in which research is carried out, and the changing technology of research itself.

The ESOMAR constitution requires the members of that organization to abide by this Code.

The ICC for its part recommends that all national and international professional associations representing the users and practitioners of market research adopt and apply these rules.

Both organizations wish to emphasize that the Code includes provisions for examining any alleged failure to observe its rules of conduct.

In addition to promoting this Code, the ICC and ESOMAR are continuously working together to foster the unification of commercial practice by issuing recommendations and guidelines intended to facilitate the establishment of contracts between users and practitioners of marketing research, and the efficient conduct of research projects.

Carl-Henrik Winqwist
Secretary General of the ICC

C.C.J. de Koning
President, ESOMAR

INTRODUCTION

Effective two-way communication between the suppliers and the consumers of goods and services of all kinds is vital to any modern society. Growing international links and interdependence reinforce this need. The supplier seeks to inform the consumer of what is available and where, using advertising and other forms of publicity to do so. In the other direction, the varied requirements of consumers must be made known to those who cater for their needs in both the private and public sectors of the economy, and this increasingly calls for the use of research.

Marketing research is concerned with analysing the markets for products and services of all kinds. In particular it involves the systematic study of behaviour, beliefs and opinions of both individuals and organizations. The measurement of public opinion on social, political and other issues has also long been linked with the field of marketing research; and in recent years similar approaches have been applied throughout very much wider fields of social research.

Although the subjects of study tend to differ, marketing research and social research have many interests, methods and problems in common. Both are involved with the analysis of available data, or the collection and analysis of new information, using sampling, questionnaire and other appropriate techniques. The issues dealt with in this Code therefore apply equally to both fields of research where they use similar methods of study.

It is against this background that Codes of Marketing Research Practice have been developed. The first, published in 1948 was that of the European Society for Opinion and Marketing Research (ESOMAR). This was followed by a number of Codes prepared by national marketing research organizations. In 1971 the International Chamber of Commerce (ICC), representing the international marketing community, set out to bring together and rationalize the major points contained in the existing Codes, publishing its own International Code after consultation with the marketing research and marketing bodies concerned.

Since 1971 the practice of marketing research has continued to evolve. New issues have arisen and additional safeguards have been incorporated into certain national Codes. In 1976 ESOMAR and the ICC both decided that it was necessary to revise their existing Codes to take account of these changes, and that it was at the same time highly desirable that there should be one International Code rather than two differing ones. A Joint Working Party representing both bodies was therefore set up to prepare a single revised Code, and this was adopted by the two organizations.

This International Code is designed to provide individuals and organizations concerned with a basic set of rules which are generally acceptable internationally. It applies to all international and national projects. In certain countries there are in addition national Codes, or requirements relating to the application of this International Code, which go further in dealing with specific points of practice. These national requirements (which in any case are compatible with those of the International Code) will in such cases also be followed. National and international practice must of course in all cases conform to the legislation and legal practice of the countries concerned.

Basic Principles

Marketing and social research depend upon public confidence: confidence that the research is conducted honestly, objectively, without unwelcome intrusion and without disadvantage to informants, and that it is based upon the willing cooperation of the public.

The general public and anyone else interested shall be entitled to complete assurance that every marketing research project is carried out strictly in accordance with this Code, and that their rights of privacy are respected. In particular, members of the general public must be assured absolutely that personal and/or confidential information supplied during the course of a marketing research study will not be made available without their agreement to any individual or organization, whether private or official, outside the researcher's own organization (as laid down in Section C), and that such information will not be used for any purposes other than marketing research.

Research should also be conducted according to accepted principles of fair competition, as generally understood and accepted, and to high technical standards. Marketing and social researchers should always be prepared to make available the necessary information whereby the quality of their work and the validity of their findings can be adequately assessed.

DEFINITIONS

In this Code:

(a) The term **marketing research** is defined as the systematic collection and objective recording, classification, analysis and presentation of data concerning the behaviour, needs, attitudes, opinions, motivations, etc. of individuals and organizations (commercial enterprises, public bodies, etc.) within the context of their economic, social, political and everyday activities. For the purposes of this Code, the term **marketing research** is taken to cover also **social research,** insofar as the latter uses similar approaches and techniques in its study of issues and problems not directly connected with the marketing of goods and services. Reference to the term **marketing research** shall throughout this Code therefore be held to include **social research** equally. The term also includes those forms of research commonly referred to as **industrial marketing research** and as **desk research,** especially where these are concerned with the acquisition of original data from the field and not simply the secondary analysis of already available data.

(b) The term **researcher** is defined as any individual, company, group, public or private institution, department, division, etc. which directly or indirectly conducts, or acts as a consultant in respect of, a **marketing research** project, survey, etc. or offers its services so to do. The term **researcher** also includes any department or division, etc. which may belong to or form part of the same organization as that of the **client**. The term **researcher** is further extended to cover responsibility for the procedures followed by any subcontractor from whom the **researcher** commissions any work (data collection or analysis, printing, professional consultancy, etc.) forming only part of the research project; in such cases the **researcher** is held responsible for ensuring that any such sub-contractor fully conforms to the provisions of this Code.

(c) The term **client** is defined as any individual, company, group, public or private institution, department, division, etc. (including any such department or division, etc. which may belong to, or form part of, the same organization as the **researcher**) which wholly or partly commissions, requests, authorises, or agrees to subscribe to a **marketing research** project or proposes so to do.

(d) The term **informant** is defined as any individual, group or organization from whom any information is sought by the **researcher** for the purposes of a **marketing research** project, survey, etc., regardless of the type of information sought or the method or technique used to obtain it. The term informant therefore covers not only cases where information is obtained by verbal techniques but also cases where non-verbal methods such as observation, postal surveys, mechanical, electrical or other recording equipment are used.

(e) The term **interview** is defined as any form of direct or indirect contact (including observation, electro-mechanical techniques, etc.) with **informants** the result of which is the acquisition of data or information which could be used in whole or in part for the purposes of a given **marketing research** project, survey, etc.

(f) The term **record(s)** is defined as any brief, proposal, questionnaire, check list, record sheet, audio or audio-visual recording or film, tabulation or computer print-out, EDP tape or other storage medium, formula, diagram, report, etc., in whatsoever form, in respect of any given **marketing research** project, survey, etc., whether in whole or in part. It includes **records** prepared by the **client** as well as by the **researcher.**

RULES

A. *Responsibilities towards informants*

Article 1

Any statement made to secure cooperation and all assurances given to an informant, whether oral or written, shall be factually correct and honoured.

Anonymity of Informants

Article 2

Subject only to the provisions of Article 3, the informant shall remain entirely anonymous. Special care must be taken to ensure that any record which contains a reference to the identity of an informant is securely and confidentially stored during any period before such reference is separated from that record and/or destroyed. No information which could be used to identify informants, either directly or indirectly, shall be revealed other than to research personnel within the researcher's own organization who require this knowledge for the administration and checking of interviews, data processing, etc. Such persons must explicitly agree to make no other use of such knowledge. All informants are entitled to be given full assurance on this point.

Article 3

The only exceptions to the above article 2 are as follows:

(a) If informants have been told of the identity of the client and the general purposes for which their names would be disclosed and have then consented in writing to this disclosure.
(b) Where disclosure of these names to a third party (e.g. a subcontractor) is essential for any purpose such as data processing or in order to conduct a further interview with the same informant (see also Article 4). In all such cases the researcher responsible for the original survey must ensure that any third parties so involved will themselves observe the provisions laid down in this Code.
(c) Where the informant is supplying information not in his role as a private individual but as an employee, officer or owner of an organization or firm, provided that the provisions of Article 5 are followed.

Article 4

Further interviews, after the first, shall only be sought with the same informants under one of the following conditions:

(a) in the course of carrying out normal quality control procedures, or
(b) if informants' permission has been obtained at a previous interview, or
(c) if it is pointed out to informants that this interview is consequent upon one they have previously given and they then give their permission before the collection of further data, or
(d) if it is essential to the research technique involved that informants do not realise that this interview is consequent upon one they have previously given, but they do give their permission before the collection of further data.

Article 5

If the informant is supplying information not in his role as a private individual but as an employee, officer or owner of an organization or firm, then it may be desirable to list his organization in the report. The report shall not however enable any particular piece of information to be related to any particular organization or person except with prior permission from the relevant informant, who shall be told of the extent to which it will be communicated.

Rights of the Informant

Article 6

All reasonable precautions shall be taken to ensure that the informant, and others closely associated with him, are in no way adversely affected or embarrassed as a result of any interview. This requirement covers the information to be obtained, the interviewing process itself, and the handling and testing of any products involved in the research. The purpose of the enquiry shall be revealed in cases where information given in ignorance of this knowledge could adversely affect the informant.

Article 7

The informant's right to withdraw, or to refuse to cooperate at any stage of the interview, shall be respected. Whatever the form of the interview, any or all of the information given by the informant must be destroyed without delay if the informant so requests. No procedure or technique which infringes this right shall be used.

Article 8

Informants shall be told in advance where observation or recording techniques are to be used. This requirement does not apply where the actions or statements of individuals are observed or recorded in public places in which they could reasonably expect to be observed and/or overheard by other people present, for example in a shop or in the street. In the latter case at least one of the following conditions shall be observed:

(a) all reasonable precautions are taken to ensure that the individual's anonymity is preserved; *and/or*

(b) the individual is told immediately after the event that his actions and/or statements have been observed or recorded or filmed, is given the opportunity to see or hear the relevant section of the record, and if he wishes, to have it destroyed or deleted.

Wherever questions are subsequently asked to the person observed, condition (b) above shall apply.

The observation or recording of normal activities in such places as distribution outlets accessible to ordinary customers – e.g. in carrying out distribution checks – need not involve the researcher in obtaining clearances or agreements for such work, but the researcher shall ensure that there is no substantial infringement of the privacy and anonymity of any individuals in such locations.

Article 9

As part of the research design a selling or simulated selling situation is sometimes incorporated in a survey (for example, in simulated test market techniques). In such cases it is especially important that the respondent or anyone else shall not be left with any impression, after the research has been concluded, that he has been participating in anything other than a genuine research project. After completion of the research the experimental nature of the selling situation should be explained, and wherever possible any money passed over by the respondent should be returned or otherwise reimbursed in some way acceptable to the respondent.

Article 10

Where observers other than the researcher are present at an interview, the researcher is responsible for ensuring that they are aware of the relevant provisions of this Code and have agreed to abide by these.

Article 11

The name and address of the researcher shall normally be made available to informants at the time of interview. Where an accommodation address is necessary for postal surveys, or where a 'cover name' is used for interviews, arrangements shall be made so that it is possible for informants subsequently to find without difficulty the name and address of the researcher.

Interviewing Children

Article 12

Special care shall be taken in interviewing children. Before they are interviewed, or asked to complete a questionnaire, the permission of a parent, guardian, or other person currently responsible for them (such as the responsible teacher) shall be obtained. In obtaining this permission, the interviewer shall describe the nature of the interview in sufficient detail to enable the responsible person to reach an informed decision. The responsible person shall also be specifically informed if it is intended to ask the children to test any products or samples.

B.   Relations with the general public and the business community

Article 13

No activity shall be deliberately or inadvertently misrepresented as marketing research. Specifically, the following activities shall in no way be associated, directly or by implication, with marketing research interviewing or activities:

(a) enquiries whose objectives are to obtain personal information about private individuals *per se*, whether for legal, political, supervisory (e.g. job performance), private or other purposes;

(b) the compilation of lists, registers or data banks for any purposes which are not marketing research;

(c) industrial, commercial or any other form of espionage;

(d) the acquisition of information for use by credit-rating or similar services;

(e) sales or promotional approaches to the informant;

(f) the collection of debts;

(g) direct or indirect attempts, including the framing of questions, to influence an informant's opinions or attitudes on any issue.

Article 14

Researchers shall not misrepresent themselves as having any qualifications, experience, skills or access to facilities which they do not in fact possess.

Article 15

Unjustified criticism and disparagement of competitors shall not be permitted.

Article 16

No one shall knowingly disseminate conclusions from a given research project or service that are inconsistent with or not warranted by the data.

C.   *The mutual responsibilities of clients and researchers*

Article 17

The relationship between a client and a researcher will generally be subject to a form of contract between them. This Code does not aim to limit the freedom of the parties to make whatever agreement they wish between themselves. However, any such agreement shall not depart from the requirements of this Code except in the case of certain specific articles, namely Articles 18–24 inclusive, 31 and 33. These are the only Articles which may be modified in this way by agreement between client and researcher.

Property of Marketing Research Records

Article 18

Marketing research proposals and quotations provided by a researcher at the request of a client and without an agreed payment remain the property of the researcher submitting them. In particular, prospective clients shall not communicate the proposals of one researcher to another researcher *except* where the latter is acting directly as a consultant to the client on the project concerned; nor shall the client use the proposals or quotations of one researcher to influence the proposals of another researcher. Similarly, the marketing research brief and specifications provided by a client remain the property of the client.

Article 19

The research findings and data from a marketing research project are the property of the client. Unless the prior written consent of the client has been obtained, no such findings or data shall be disclosed by the researcher to any third party.

Article 20

The research techniques and methods (including computer programs) used in a marketing research project do not become the property of the client, who has no exclusive right to their use.

Article 21

All records prepared by the researcher other than the report shall be the property of the researcher, who shall be entitled to destroy this material two years after completion of the study without reference to the client. The original questionnaires and similar basic field records may however be destroyed after a shorter period than this _provided that:_

(a) either all the research data they contain is preserved for further analysis (e.g. on tapes, punched cards or discs) for the full two-year period or
(b) the shorter period involved has been agreed with the client under Article 17.

Article 22

After the researcher has submitted his report upon the study to the agreed specification, the client shall be entitled to obtain from the researcher duplicate copies of completed questionnaires or other records, provided that the client shall bear the reasonable cost of preparing such duplicates, and that the request be made within the time limit set by Article 21. Article 22 shall not apply in the case of a project or service where it is clearly understood that the resulting reports are to be available for general purchase on a syndicated or subscription basis. Any duplicates provided shall not reveal the identity of informants.

Confidentiality

Article 23

Unless authorized to do so by the client, the researcher shall not reveal to informants, nor to any other person not directly concerned with the work of the study, the name of the client commissioning the study.

Article 24

All confidential information and material relating to the client shall not be divulged except to persons wholly or substantially engaged in the service of the researcher, including subcontractors, who need such information or material in order effectively to carry out the research work.

Client's Rights to Information about a Project

Article 25

The researcher shall clearly indicate to the client what parts of a project will be handled by subcontractors and, if the client requires, the identity of these.

Article 26

On request the client, or his mutually acceptable representative, may attend a limited number of interviews to observe the standards of the fieldwork. In certain types of research (e.g. panels) this may require the previous agreement of the informant to the presence of such an observer. The researcher is entitled to be recompensed if the client's desire to attent an interview interferes with, delays or increases the cost of the fieldwork. In the case of a multiclient study, the researcher may require that the observer in charge of checking the quality of the fieldwork is independent of any of the clients.

Article 27

When two or more projects are combined in one interview, or one project is carried out on behalf of more than one client, or a service is offered on the basis that it is also available on subscription to other potential clients, each client concerned shall be informed in advance that the project or service is not being offered on an exclusive basis. The identity of the other clients or potential clients need not however be disclosed.

Multiclient Studies

Article 28

The client shall not give any of the results of a multiclient study to any person outside his own organisation (the latter to be considered as including his consultants and advisers) unless he has first obtained the researcher's permission to do this.

Publishing of Results

Article 29

Reports and other records relevant to a marketing research project and provided by the researcher shall normally be for use solely by the client and his consultants or advisers. The contract between researcher and client should normally specify the copyright of the research findings and any arrangements with respect to the subsequent more general publication of these. In the absence of such a specific agreement, if the client intends any wider circulation of the results of a study either in whole or in part:

(a) the client shall agree in advance with the researcher the exact form and contents of publication or circulation: if agreement on this cannot be reached between client and researcher, the latter is entitled to refuse permission for his name to be quoted in connection with the study;

(b) where the results of a marketing research project are given any such wider circulation the client must at the same time make available the information listed under Article 34 about the published parts of the study. In default of this, the researcher himself is entitled to supply this information to anyone receiving the above-mentioned results.

(c) the client shall do his utmost to avoid the possibility of misinterpretation or the quotation of the results out of their proper context.

Article 30

Researchers shall not allow their names to be used as an assurance that a particular marketing research project has been carried out in conformity with this Code unless they are fully satisfied that the project has in every respect been controlled according to the Code's requirements.

Exclusivity

Article 31

In the absence of any contractual agreement to the contrary the client does not have the right to exclusive use of the researcher's services, whether in whole or in part.

D.   *Reporting standards*

Article 32

The researcher shall, when presenting the results of a marketing research project (whether such presentation is oral, in writing or in any other form), make a clear distinction between the results themselves and the researcher's interpretation of the data and his recommendations.

Article 33

Normally every report of a marketing research project shall contain an explanation of the points listed under Article 34, or a reference to a readily available separate document containing this explanation. The only exception to this article is in the case where it is agreed in advance between the client and the researcher that it is unnecessary to include all the listed information in the formal report or other document. Any such agreement shall in no way remove the entitlement of the client to receive any and all of the information freely upon request. Also this exception shall not apply in the case where any or all of the research report or findings are to be published or made available to recipients in addition to the original client.

Article 34

The following information shall be included in the report on a research project:

Background
(a) for whom and by whom the study was conducted;
(b) the purpose of the study;
(c) names of subcontractors and consultants performing any substantial part of the work.

Sample
(d) a description of the intended and actual universe covered;
(e) the size, nature and geographical distribution of the sample, both planned and achieved; and, where relevant, the extend to which any of the data collected were obtained from only a part of the total sample.
(f) details of the sampling method and of any weighting methods used;
(g) where technically relevant, a statement of response rate and a discussion of possible bias due to non-response.

Data collection
(h) a description of the method by which the information was collected (that is, whether by personal interview, postal or telephone interview, group discussion, mechanical recording device, observation or some other method);
(i) adequate description of field staff, briefing and field quality control methods used;
(j) the method of recruitment used for informants and the *general nature* of any incentives offered to them to secure their cooperation;
(k) the time at which the field work was done;
(l) in the case of 'desk research', a clear statement of the sources and their reliability.

Presentation of results
(m) the relevant factual findings obtained;
(n) bases of percentages, clearly indicating both weighted and unweighted bases;

(o) general indications of the probable statistical margins of error to be attached to the main findings, and of the levels of statistical significance of differences between key figures;

(p) questionnaires and other relevant documents used (or, in the case of a shared project that portion relating to the matter reported upon).

E.   *Implementation of the Code*

Article 35

Any person or organization involved in, or associated with, a marketing research project and/or proposal is responsible for actively applying the rules of this Code in the spirit as well as the letter.

Article 36

Any alleged infringements of the Code relating to a single country shall be reported without delay to the appropriate national body which has adopted this Code. Problems of interpretation and enforcement in such cases shall in the first place be the responsibility of the said national bodies which have adopted this Code and which are representative of all the interests directly concerned. Where such a suitable national body does not already exist it is urged that one be established speedily. The national body shall take such actions as it deems appropriate in relation to implementation of the Code, taking due account of any relevant national marketing research Codes and the laws of the country concerned. It is important that any decision taken under this Article should be notified to the secretariats of the ICC and ESOMAR, without revealing the names of the parties concerned.

Article 37

In cases where:

(a) an appropriate national body *does not exist;* or

(b) the national body concerned is for any reason *unable* to provide an interpretation of, or take action to enforce, the Code; or

(c) any of the parties involved *wishes to refer the problem to an international body* (either immediately or for a subsequent second opinion); or

(d) the problem involved *parties from different countries* (for example with an international marketing research project); the problem shall be referred to the secretariats of the ICC or of ESOMAR, who will consult one another on the issue. Where it proves impossible to resolve the problem informally, the secretariats will then convene a special body set up jointly by the ICC and ESOMAR for the purpose of dealing with this problem.

Index